NOTES ON GENESIS

SPURRELL

NOTES ON THE TEXT

OF THE

BOOK OF GENESIS

WITH AN APPENDIX

BY

G. J. SPURRELL, M.A.

FORMERLY HEBREW LECTURER AT WADHAM COLLEGE, OXFORD; EXAMINER IN THE UNIVERSITY OF LONDON—IN HEBREW AND NEW TESTAMENT GREEK, 1888–93 IN SEMITIC LANGUAGES, 1889, 1896, 1892, 1894, 1895; ASSISTANT MASTER AT THE MERCHANT TAYLORS' SCHOOL, LONDON

SECOND EDITION, REVISED AND CORRECTED

Wipf & Stock
PUBLISHERS
Eugene, Oregon

Wipf and Stock Publishers
199 W 8th Ave, Suite 3
Eugene, OR 97401

Notes on the Text of the Book of Genesis, Second Edition
By Spurrell, G. J.
ISBN: 1-59752-297-X
Publication date 7/1/2005
Previously published by Oxford at the Clarendon Press, 1896

PREFACE

TO THE FIRST EDITION.

THE present volume of notes was undertaken at the suggestion of Prof. Driver, and is mainly intended for students beginning the Hebrew language. The notes are taken chiefly from the best German commentaries, and do not aim at originality. The Versions have also been used, and references are given to various grammars, the writer's object being to adapt the book to the wants of students using different grammars. The Commentaries used are those by Tuch[1], Delitzsch[2], and Dillmann[3], to whom the writer is chiefly indebted; reference is also made to Mr. Wright's[4] Notes on Genesis, and (occasionally) to the commentary by the late Dr. Kalisch[5]. The Versions are quoted partly from the London Polyglot, and partly from separate editions.

---

1 The 2nd edition, by Arnold and Merx, Halle, 1871.

2 The 4th edition, Leipzig, 1872.

3 The references to Dillmann are to the 4th edition of his *Genesis*, in the *Kurzgefasstes Exeg. Handbuch zum alten Test.*, Leipzig, 1882. A 5th edition appeared in 1886, but as some of the sheets had already been printed off, the references to the 4th edition have been kept, and any changes in the 5th edition noted on the margin.

4 *The Book of Genesis in Hebrew*, by C. H. H. Wright, London, 1859.

5 *Historical and Critical Commentary on the Old Test.*, *Genesis*, London, 1858.

For the LXX, Lagarde's text has been used[1], reference being occasionally made to the text contained in the London Polyglot, and to Tischendorf's edition. The Targum of Onqelos, or Babylonian Targum, has been taken from the edition by Dr. Berliner[2], the text in the London Polyglot being compared, while the Targum of Pseudo-Jonathan and the Jerusalem Targum are quoted from the London Polyglot[3]. For the Peshiṭtā (Syriac) version the Polyglot and the edition by Lee[4], which is based on the text in the London Polyglot, have been used, while the Vulgate has been taken from a Paris edition[5] and the Polyglot. The other Greek versions (Aquila, Symmachus, and Theodotion) are usually cited second-hand, reference being also made to Field's edition of Origen's Hexapla[6]. The Arabic version of Saadiah has been quoted from the Polyglot: the Hebrew-Samaritan text and the Samaritan version are also cited from the same source[7]. The Grammars to which reference has been made are those of Gesenius, Davidson, Stade,

---

[1] *Genesis Graece*, edidit P. A. de Lagarde, Leipzig, 1868.

[2] In two parts, Berlin, 1884. The first part containing the text after the 'editio Sabioneta' of 1557, and the second part, the notes, introduction, and indices.

[3] The Targum of Pseudo-Jonathan and the Jerusalem Targum (which only exists in a fragmentary form) are really two recensions of one and the same Targum, the Jerusalem Targum; see Bleek's *Einleitung*, ed. Wellhausen, p. 606 f.; Eng. trans., ed. Venables, vol. ii. p. 439 f.

[4] London, 1823.

[5] Published by Garnier Brothers, without date.

[6] Oxford, 1875.

[7] The reader should consult the various 'Introductions' to the Old Testament on these versions (especially that of Wellhausen-Bleek, 1878 or 1886), or read the articles in Smith's *Dictionary of the Bible*.

Ewald, Olshausen, Böttcher (occasionally), Müller (for the Syntax only), and the treatise on the Tenses by Prof. Driver[1].

The text of Genesis that has been followed in compiling the notes is that of Baer (with a preface by Delitzsch), and the same text has been used in quoting passages from other books, the edition of Theile[2] being only cited in those portions of the Old Testament that have not yet been edited by Baer[3].

Two appendices have been added to the book: one on the structure of Genesis, as it was deemed necessary that the student should have some information about the modern views as to the criticism of the Pentateuch; and the other on the names of God, which could not be adequately discussed within the limits of a note.

The writer has to acknowledge the great obligations he is under to Prof. Driver for the valuable help he has rendered

---

[1] Gesenius' *Grammar*, translated by Davies, and edited by Mitchell, London, 1880 (since reprinted). Davidson's *Grammar*, Edinburgh, 8th edition, 1887. Stade, *Lehrbuch der hebräischen Grammatik*, Leipzig, 1879. Ewald, *Lehrbuch der hebräischen Sprache*, 8te Ausgabe, Göttingen, 1870: the Syntax (the third part of the Lehrbuch) has been translated by Kennedy, Edinburgh, 1879. Olshausen, *Lehrbuch der hebräisch. Sprache*, Braunschweig, 1861. Böttcher, *Lehrbuch der hebräisch. Sprache*, Leipzig, 1868. Aug. Müller, *Outlines of Hebrew Syntax*, translated by Robertson (being a translation of the third part of Müller's *Hebräische Schulgrammatik*, Halle, 1878), 1st edition, 1882; 2nd edition, 1887. Driver, *Hebrew Tenses*, 2nd edition, Oxford, 1881.

[2] 3rd edition, Leipzig, 1867.

[3] The following portions of the Bible have been published by Baer: *Genesis*, Leipzig, 1869; *Isaiah*, ib., 1872; *Job*, ib., 1875; *Minor Prophets*, ib., 1878; *The Psalms*, ib., 1880; *Proverbs*, ib., 1880; *Daniel, Ezra, Nehemiah*, ib., 1882; *Ezekiel*, ib., 1884; and *Canticles, Ruth, Lamentations, Ecclesiastes, Esther*, ib., 1886.

him in preparing these notes, and for kindly revising the proof-sheets. His thanks are also due to the Delegates of the Clarendon Press for their assistance in publishing the book, and to Mr. Pembrey, their Oriental reader, for the care which he has taken in passing the sheets through the press.

G. J. SPURRELL.

OXFORD, *July*, 1887.

PREFACE

TO THE SECOND EDITION.

In the present edition of the 'Notes on Genesis' a large amount of new matter has been incorporated into the book. An Introduction has been substituted for Appendix I, and the new edition has been enlarged by the addition of about forty new pages. Many of the notes have been recast and expanded, and many new notes have been added on different matters, generally points which were not commented on in the first edition, or inadequately treated. This will be seen in the fuller accounts of the different foreign nations mentioned in Genesis, cf. chaps. 10, 25. 36, 8, etc. More attention has also been given to the geography of Genesis. The sites of the different places mentioned and other matters appertaining to geography are generally quoted from Dillmann's *Genesis* [6], Smith's *Historical Geography*, and Bädeker's *Palestine*, 2nd English edition, 1894; so that the information on these points is as far as possible up to date.

The Grammars to which reference has been made are the same as in the former edition, with the addition of references to Davidson's *Hebrew Syntax*, and occasionally to König's

Lehrgebäude, I[1]. The 25th (German) edition of Gesenius-Kautzsch's Grammar has been used. As a translation of this work is in preparation, the references given in the notes will serve for the English edition[2]. The extracts from the different Versions are the same as in the first edition, with the exception of the LXX, which is now quoted from Swete's (Cambridge) edition.

The Introduction, which is a new feature in the book, has been compiled mainly from the writings of Dillmann, Wellhausen, Kuenen, Cornill, Driver, and more especially from the excellent *Einleitung in den Hexateuch*, by Dr. Holzinger[3].

The writer desires to acknowledge the valuable assistance he has received from his friend Mr. J. F. Stenning, Hebrew Lecturer at Wadham College, who kindly revised the proof-sheets and made several useful suggestions. He is also indebted to Mr. Pembrey, the Oriental reader at the University Press, for the skill and care with which he has prepared the sheets for press.

G. J. SPURRELL.

LONDON, *Dec.* 14, 1895.

---

[1] Part II of König's *Lehrgebäude* was not published in time to be used for the notes.

[2] This Grammar, which is very badly and clumsily arranged, is now superseded, as far as the Syntax is concerned, by Davidson's *Hebrew Syntax*.

[3] See the references in the notes appended to the Introduction.

CONTENTS.

ABBREVIATIONS USED[1].

A.V. = The Authorized Version, 1611.
Aq. = Aquila's Greek Version.
Aram. = Aramaic[2].
B. and D. = Baer and Delitzsch.
B. Jubil. = *The Book of Jubilees*, ed. R. Charles, Clarendon Press, 1894.
Bädeker, *Pal.* or *Palest.* = *Palestine and Syria*, 2nd (English edition), 1894.
Barth, *N. B.* = *Die Nominalbildung in den Semitischen Sprachen*, Leipzig, 1894.
Baumg. = Baumgarten.
Ber. Rab. = *Bereshith Rabba.*
Bernst. = Bernstein.
Boch. = Bochart.
Boh. = von Bohlen.
Bött. = Böttcher.
Böttcher, *Neue Aehr.* = *Neue Hebräische Aehrenlese* (in 3 vols.), Leipzig, 1849–65.
Budde, *Urgesch.* = *Die Biblische Urgeschichte*, Giessen, 1883.
C. I. S. = *Corpus Inscrip. Semiticarum*, Paris, 1881 et seq.
C. P. Ges. = *Hebrew and English Lexicon*, etc., Clarendon Press, 1892 et seq.
Dav. = Davidson, *Introductory Hebrew Grammar*, various years.
Dav., *S.* = *Hebrew Syntax*, 1894.
Del.[4] and Del.[5] = The 4th and 5th edd. of the Commentary on Genesis.
Del., *Par.* = *Wo lag das Paradies?* Leipzig, 1881.
Del., *Proleg.* = *Prolegomena*, Leipzig, 1886.
Di. = Dillmann.
Di., *N. D. J.* = Commentary on Num., Deut., and Josh.
Driver or Dr. = *Hebrew Tenses*, 3rd ed., 1892.
Driver, *Introd.* = *Introduction to the Lit. of the O. T.*, 5th ed., 1894.
Driver, *Sam.* = *Notes on the H. T. of the Books of Samuel*, 1890.
Ecclus. = Ecclesiasticus.
Ewald, *J. B.* = *Jahrbücher der biblischen Wissenschaft*, Göttingen, 1848 et seq.
Frankel, *Einfluss* or *Einfl.* = *Ueber den Einfluss der palästin. Exegese*

[1] Most of the abbreviations, with which the student will be familiar, are not given here.

[2] It should be pointed out that the languages usually called Chaldee, Syriac, and Samaritan are really three dialects of the Aramaic, and should be embraced under the term Aramaic.

auf die Alexandr. Hermeneutik, Leipzig, 1851.

Frankel, *Vorstudien* = *Vorstudien zu der Septuaginta*, Leipzig, 1841.

Ges. = Gesenius, *Hebr. Grammatik*, ed. Kautzsch, 25th ed., Leipzig, 1889.

Ges., *Th.* or *Thes.* = *Thesaurus*, Leipzig, 1829–58.

Glaser, *Skizze* = *Skizze der Geschichte und Geographie Arabiens*, 2 vols., 1890.

Gr. Ven. = *Versio Veneta*, see Bleek's *Introduction* (Eng. trans.), vol. ii. p. 430.

H. W. B. = Ges., *Handwörterbuch über das A. T.*, 12th ed., 1894.

Halévy, *Mél.* = *Mélanges*.

Halévy, *R.B.* = *Recherches Bibliques*.

Halévy, *R. E. J.* = *Revue des Études Juives*.

Hier. or Hieron. = Hieronymus, Jerome.

Hier., *Quaest.* = Hieronymus' *Quaestiones Hebraicae in libro Geneseos*, at the end of Lagarde's *Gen. Graece*, Leipzig, 1868.

Holz. or Holzinger = *Einleitung in den Hexateuch*, Freiburg i. B., and Leipzig, 1893.

J. A. = *Journal Asiatique*.

J. B. L. = *Journal of Biblical Literature and Exegesis*.

Jos. = Josephus.

Ke. = Keil.

Kn. = Knobel.

König, *Lehrg.* = *Histor. Krit. Lehrgebäude der Heb. Sprache*, 1 part, Leipzig, 1881.

Lagarde or Lag., *B. N.* = *Bildung der Nomina*.

Lagarde or Lag., *Symm.* = *Symmicta*.

Lenor. = Lenormant.

Levy, *Chald. W. B.* = *Chald. Wörterbuch*, Leipzig, 1881.

M. B. A. W. = *Monatsberichte der Berliner Akademie der Wissenschaften*, various years.

M. R. = *Outlines of Hebrew Syntax*, by A. Müller, translated by Robertson, 3rd ed., 1888.

Mid. Bem. = *Midrash Bemidbar*, on the book of Numbers.

Nöld. = Nöldeke.

Nöld., *Unters.* = *Untersuchungen zur Kritik des alten Test.*, Kiel, 1869.

Ols. = Olshausen.

Onom. = Onomasticon.

Onq. = Onqelos.

Pesh. = Peshiṭtā (Syriac) Version.

Proleg. or *Prol. Crit.* = *Prolegomena Critica in Vet. Test. Hebr.*, by H. L. Strack, Leipzig, 1873.

R. V. = Authorized Version revised, 1885.

Riehm, *H. W. B.* = *Handwörterbuch des Bibl. Alterthums*, 1875 and following years.

Rob., *Pal.* = *Palestine*, 1st ed., London, 1841.

S. B. A. W. = *Sitzungsberichte der Berliner Akademie der Wissenschaften.*

Saad. = Saadiah's Arabic Version.

Sam. = The Samaritan Version, and the Hebrew Text in Sam. characters, when both agree; the former is quoted as Sam. Ver., and the latter as Heb.-Sam.

Schrader (also Sch. and Schr.), *K.G.F.* = *Keilinschriften und Geschichtsforschung*.

Schrader, *C. O. T.* = *Die Keilinschriften und das alte Test.*, 2nd ed., 1883; translated into English by Whitehouse, 2 vols., London, 1885 and 1888.

Sh., *G.* = *The Historical Geography of the Holy Land*, by G. A. Smith, London, 1894.

Symm. = Symmachus' Greek Version.

Targ. Jer. = Jerusalem Targum.

Targ. Ps.-Jon. or Jon. = The Targum of Pseudo-Jonathan.

Targg. = Targums, when the three Targums agree.

Th. or Theod. = Theodotion's Greek Version.

Th. S. W. = *Theolog. Studien aus Würtemberg.*

Well., *Comp.* = Wellhausen, *Die Composition des Hexateuch's*, reprinted with an Appendix, 1889.

Well., *Sam.* = *Der Text der Bücher Samuelis untersucht*, 1872.

Winer, *R. W. B.* = *Biblisch. Real-Wörterbuch*, 1847–48, 3rd ed.

Wright, *Comp. Gram.* = *Lectures on the Comparative Grammar of the Semitic Languages*, 1890.

Z. A. = *Zeitschrift für Assyriologie.*

Z. A. S. A. = *Zeitschrift für aegyptische Sprache und Alterthümer.*

Z. A. T. W. = *Zeitschrift für die Alttest. Wissenschaft.*

Z. D. M. G. = *Zeitschrift der Deutschen Morgenländischen Gesellschaft.*

Z. D. P. V. = *Zeitschrift des Deutschen Palästina-Vereins.*

Z. K. S. F. = *Zeitschrift für Keilschriftforschung.*

וגו׳ = וְגוֹמֵר *et caetera.*

INTRODUCTION.

The book of Genesis, like the other books of the Hexateuch, was not the production of one author. A definite plan may be traced in the book, but the structure of the work forbids us to consider it as the production of one writer. This is clear, not only from the (apparently needless) repetitions that occur (e.g. 21, 1 a and 1 b; 4, 25 f., and 5, 1–6; 47, 29 ff., and 49, 29 ff.), but also from the different accounts of one and the same event which we meet with, not merely such as may be explained on the supposition that the author is really describing *different* events, or reproducing *different* traditions (e.g. the narratives contained in 12, 10 ff.; 20, 1 ff., and 26, 7 ff.; the story of Hagar and Ishmael, in 16, 1 ff., and 21, 12 ff.; the double covenant with Abram, chaps. 15 and 17; the double blessing of Jacob by Isaac, 27, 1 ff., and 28, 1 ff.; the double promise of a son to Sarah, 17, 17, and 18, 10 ff.; the three explanations of the name Isaac, 17, 17; 18, 12; 21, 6; the two explanations of the names, Edom in 25, 25. 30; of Issachar, Zebulun, and Joseph, in 30, 16–18. 20. 23 f.; of Maḥanaim, in 32, 3. 8; cf. also for Ishmael, 16, 11 f., and 21, 17; for Peniel, 32, 31, and the allusion in 33, 10), but such as mutually exclude one another, because the event narrated can only have happened once (e.g. the two accounts of the creation, in chaps. 1 and 2; the number of the animals that went into the ark and the time the flood continued on the earth, in chap. 6 f.; the dispersion of the nations, in chaps. 10 and 11, 1 ff., cf. 10, 25; the varying explanations of the names, Beersheba, in 21, 31. 26, 33; Israel, in 32, 29. 35, 10; Bethel and the pillar of Bethel, 28, 18 f. 35, 14 f.; the different accounts of the relations between Jacob and the Shechemites, in chaps. 34 and 48, 22; and the variations in the narrative in 37, 19–36,—the sale of Joseph by his brethren). Many other notices in Genesis also militate against the unity of authorship (e.g. that the limit of human life was reduced to 120 years, 6, 3 against 5, 11[1]; that Abraham begat many sons after the death of Sarah, 25, 1 ff. against 18, 11 f. 17, 17; that Esau had already settled in Seir when Jacob returned from Mesopotamia, 32, 4 ff. against 36, 6; that Rebekah's nurse came with Jacob from Mesopotamia, 35, 8 against 24, 59; that all Jacob's sons were born in Paddan Aram, 35, 26 against ver. 16 ff.; the different names of Esau's wives, 26, 34. 28, 9 against 36, 2 f.; the two accounts of Joseph's master, 37, 36 and 39, 1–40, 4; and the two narratives in 42, 27. 35 and 43, 21. Statements like 4, 14 f. 17 seem out of place in their present context; the differences in chronology, e.g. in the age of Sarah, in 17, 17, cf. 12, 4, and in 12, 11. 20, 2 ff.; in the case of Ishmael, 17, 24. 21, 5. 8 and 21, 15 f.; as to Isaac's approaching death, in 27, 1 f. 7. 10. 41 and in 35, 28 and 26, 34; in the account of Rachel's death in 35, 19, while in 37, 10 she is represented as still living); also 30, 25 f. does not agree with 31, 38. 41 (cf. Di., p. 345 f.); further, the ages of Jacob's sons which are given, or presupposed in chaps. 32–37 and chaps. 39–45, do not agree with 46, 8–27 (cf. Di., p. 380 f. and p. 478); even narratives are found in which some parts do not agree with the remainder of the

[1] Cf. the note, however, on 6, 3.

narrative (e.g. 31, 48–50, and 24, 62–67 and the beginning of the chapter)[1].

These discrepancies and difficulties in the book of Genesis, and similar ones in the other books of the Pentateuch, were not really discovered until the time of Ibn Ezra (twelfth century). The prevalent opinion among both Jews and Christians, was that Moses was the author of the Pentateuch. The same view was held by Philo, Josephus, and in the Talmud; and the only opposition it met with in the first centuries of our era, was from unimportant, heretical sects in the Church, especially the Gnostics.

Ibn Ezra—in criticising the views of Rabbi Isaac ben Salomo Israeli, of Kairoan in N. Africa 840–950[2], that Gen. 36, 31 could not have been written before the time of King Jehoshaphat—himself inclined to the opinion that portions of the Pentateuch could not have been written by Moses; cf. his *Comm.* on Gen. 12, 6. 22, 14. Deut. 1, 1. 3, 11. chap. 34. He did not deny the Mosaic authorship entirely. The views of other scholars up to the time of Astruc (1684–1766), the real founder of Pent. Criticism, must be omitted here[3].

Astruc, a Paris physician, published anonymously, in 1753, a work on the authorship and structure of the book of Genesis[4]. He first drew attention to the two different names of God, and inferred from this fact, the existence of two different documents, A Elohistic, and B Jehovistic. These proving insufficient, he assigned the narrative of the Flood, in which neither Jehovah nor Elohim occurred, to a third document C; and all the other passages, where neither name occurred, were apportioned to nine other documents of non-Hebrew origin. A and B

[1] Cf. Di., *Genesis*[6], p. ix f.; Holzinger, *Einleitung*, p. 15 f., and the authorities cited by him; and Driver, *Introd.*[5], p. 6 ff.

[2] Bleek-Well.[4], *Einleitung*, p. 16; cf. Holz., l.c., p. 28.

[3] They will be found in Bleek-Well., l.c., p. 18 ff.; Holz., l.c., p. 29 f.

[4] *Conjectures sur les memoires originaux dont il paroit que Moyse s'est servi pour composer le livre de la Genese*, Brussels, 1753.

alone were held to be real documents, the others fragments; and Moses was regarded as the author[1]. Eichorn arrived independently at practically the same conclusions as Astruc; but he examined the documents more thoroughly and completely, apportioning the different parts of Genesis and Exodus 1 and 2 to the Elohist and Jehovist. He also pointed out that the language of the two documents differed, and criticised the style and contents of the two sources. Ilgen made the next advance[2]. After he had examined the book of Genesis, he came to the conclusion that it was composed of seventeen documents to be referred to three authors; two Elohists and one Jehovist. These he called respectively 'The Sopher Eliel harischon,' 'the Sopher Eliel hascheni,' and the Jehovist. The three documents were independent, complete in themselves, and each exhibiting characteristic marks[3].

The next development was the hypothesis, that the Pentateuch was composed from fragments partly by different authors, and arranged by a collector or Redactor. This view was adopted, with various modifications, by several scholars; e. g. Vater, Hartmann, (and at first) De Wette, &c.[4]

The third stage in the history of the criticism of the Pentateuch was the theory that one of the documents was composed to complete and supplement the other. This opinion was accepted by Von Bohlen, Stähelin, Bleek, De Wette, Von Lengerke, and Delitzsch[4]. The question

---

[1] Cf. Holz., l. c., p. 40, and authorities cited by him. The view adopted by Astruc and his followers is called by German scholars *Die Urkundenhypothese*.

[2] *Die Urkunden des jerus. Tempelarchivs*, etc., Halle, 1798. Only vol. i, Genesis, was issued.

[3] Ilgen's division of the sources attracted little attention at first, but was revived in 1853, by Hupfeld.

[4] Full details in Holz., l. c., p. 43 f.; Cornill, *Einleitung*, p. 20 f. This hypothesis is called by German scholars *Die Fragmentenhypothese*, cf. Holz., l. c., p. 54 f.; Corn., l. c., p. 22 f.

was most thoroughly discussed by Tuch in his *Comm. über die Gen.*, 1838. He maintained that there were only two authors, one of whom supplemented or 'filled in' the work of the other; (i) the 'Grundschrift' or the Elohist, and (ii) the 'Supplementer' or Jehovist[1]. The first document was composed by a priest in the time of Saul, the second must be referred to the reign of Solomon. Stähelin extended the theory to the other books of the Pentateuch, to the books of Samuel and Kings, and to the other historical writings. He discovered in these two systems of legislation; the first or Elohim source, c. 1300 B.C., and the second or Jehovah source, in the time of Samuel. Stähelin's Jehovist contains the Jehovist, the Jehovistic Redactor, the Deuteronomist and the Deuteronomic Redactor, merged into one person. The other scholars, however, regarded the Jehovist as the author of Genesis, Numbers, and of Joshua in the original form, and believed that his work was again 'filled in' by the Deuteronomist.

The great objection to this hypothesis was the fact that it under-estimated the Jehovist. The Jehovist when carefully compared with the 'Grundschrift' was found to contain much that agreed with that document, and much that was in direct contradiction to it (e.g. the two accounts of the creation). And it became clear that the theory of a supplemental document was quite untenable. The two documents were therefore to be regarded as two distinct and independent works. Out of this change of view the present system of Pentateuch criticism was gradually evolved.

Among the scholars who were the first to adopt the new hypothesis were Gramberg[2] and Stähelin[3], who were both of

[1] The name adopted for this hypothesis by German scholars is the *Ergänzungshypothese*.

[2] *Liber Geneseos secundum fontes rite dignoscendos adumbratio nova*, 1828.

[3] *Krit. Untersuch. über die Genesis*, 1830.

opinion that Genesis was composed of two documents, the Elohist and Jehovist, and a compiler who is responsible for the present book of Genesis. Ewald held that the Pentateuch was composed of five documents, which were revised by the author of the fifth document. A sixth document (Deuteronomy) was added, and finally edited by a seventh hand who added Deut. 33[1].

The new hypothesis was further developed by Hupfeld[2]. He considers that three separate documents may be traced in Genesis—the 'Urschrift,' the first document, the younger Elohist, and the Jehovist. Each source is a coherent and complete narrative, and all three were composed independently. The three documents were worked up into the present text of Genesis by a later Redactor. Other scholars followed in Hupfeld's footsteps. Böhmer[3] differentiated the sources—printing them in different types—and drew attention to additions made by the Redactor. Knobel[4] divides the Pentateuch into the 'Grundschrift' = P (in the time of Saul), which was supplemented by the Jehovist, probably in the last years of Hezekiah, by extracts from the ספר הישר (cf. Josh. 10, 13. 2 Sam. 1, 8), which was edited in the Assyrian period, and partly corresponds to E, and from the ספר מלחמות יהוה (Num. 21, 14), which was composed in the time of Jehoshaphat, and partly corresponds to J. He also added many Jehovistic passages of his own. Finally, in the reign of Josiah, Deuteronomy was added, and Joshua, after revision, and thus the present Hexateuch was produced. Knobel's ספר הישר is really Hupfeld's second Elohist, while Hupfeld's Jehovist is divided by Knobel into the ספר

[1] For details, see Holz., l.c., p. 59 f.; Cornill, l.c., p. 24 f.

[2] *Die Quellen der Genesis und die Art ihrer Zusammensetzung*, 1853.

[3] *Liber Geneseos Pentateuchicus*, 1860; *Das erste Buch der Thora*, 1862.

[4] *Kurzgef. Handbuch*, Num., Deut., Josh., 1861.

מלחמות יי״, and the Jehovist. Knobel also considers that the prae-deuteronomic Redactor was the Jehovist. Kuenen's views (1861)[1]—(i) Book of Origins, (ii) Ihvhist, (iii) Younger Elohist—are similar. He does not admit a prae-deuteronomic Redactor, but considers that the whole Pentateuch was edited after the time of Deuteronomy, by one of the priests of Jerusalem, shortly before the beginning of the Babylonian captivity. Schrader's[2] three documents are (P) 'The Annalist,' who wrote when David was king of Judah; (E) 'The Theocratic Narrator,' a native of the northern kingdom, who flourished about 975–950, after the division of the kingdom. The 'Prophetic Narrator' (J), also belonging to the northern kingdom, in the time of Jeroboam, combined these two documents and augmented and expanded them with Jahvistic portions. The Deuteronomist in the time of Josiah, c. 622 B.C., wrote the greater part of Deuteronomy (chaps. 4, 44–28, 69), and later, after the destruction of Jerusalem, added Deut. 1–4, 43 and 29–31, 13, and combined the whole with the rest of the Pentateuch, and also revised the book of Joshua. Schrader agrees with Knobel that the Jehovist was the Redactor of the prae-deuteronomic Pentateuch.

Nöldeke[3] treats the 'Grundschrift' in a masterly manner. He emphasises the fact that the Redactor of the Pentateuch had the second Elohist and the Jehovist before him, not as two distinct sources, but already combined into one document.

The results obtained by the researches of these scholars were as follows:—The Pentateuch is composed of four documents, P or PC, The Priests' Code; E, the Second or Younger Elohist; J, the Jehovist; and D, Deuteronomy. E was usually regarded as earlier than J, and it was assumed that P, J, E were worked up into one whole, before D was added. Some (Knobel and Schrader) held that J was the

[1] *Onderzoek*[1]. [2] De Wette's *Einl.*[8], 1869.
[3] *Untersuchungen zur Kritik des A.T.*, 1869.

prae-deuteronomic Redactor, others thought that the Redactor was a different person. Some maintained that D was the Redactor of the Pentateuch, others that the Redactor was a distinct person. This view of the origin of the Pentateuch was, however, combated by Graf[1], who, following the opinion that had already been put forth by Reuss, George, and Vatke[2], independently of each other, propounded the view that the so-called 'Grundschrift' was not the oldest of the three documents, but the youngest. This was not, however, the original form of Graf's hypothesis. He first divided the 'Grundschrift' into two parts, and proceeded to show that the priestly or ritual laws, i.e. Ex. chaps. 25–31 and 35–40, all Leviticus, and the greater part of Numbers were post-deuteronomic; while the remainder of the 'Grundschrift' was prae-deuteronomic and antecedent to the Jehovist, i.e. the Jehovistic laws in Ex. chaps. 20–23. 13, 1–16. 34, 10–27, and the Jehovistic narratives, are prae-deuteronomic. Ezekiel is older than the ritual code and the laws in P. The order of the documents, according to Graf, was, the Grundschrift (the prae-deuteronomic portion), the Jehovist, and the Deuteronomist, the latter being the Redactor of the whole work. After the Babylonian exile the Pentateuch was completed by the addition of the post-deuteronomic portions by Ezra[3].

Graf apparently ignored Hupfeld's second Elohist. When, however, Riehm[4] and Nöldeke[5] had shown that this division of the 'Grundschrift' was, on philological grounds, impossible,

---

[1] *Die geschichtlichen Bücher des Alten Test.* (1866).

[2] Reuss, in a lecture in 1834, and afterwards in the article *Judenthum*, in Ersch and Gruber, *Encyc.*, 1850; Vatke, in *Die Religion des A. T. nach den Kanon. Büchern entwickelt*, i. 1835; and George, *Die älteren jüdischen Feste mit einer Kritik der Gesetzgebung des Pent.*, 1835.

[3] Cf. Holz., l. c., p. 65.

[4] *Studien und Krit.*, 1868, pp. 350–379.

[5] *Untersuchungen zur Kritik des A.T.*, Kiel, 1869.

Graf modified his view, and assigned the whole of the 'Grundschrift' to the post-exilic period[1]. The reasons alleged by Graf and his followers in support of this view are, that the history contained in the books of Judges, and Samuel, and to some extent in the books of Kings, is in contradiction to the laws usually regarded as Mosaic; and that these laws themselves were quite unknown at the period to which they are supposed to belong. Further, that the prophets of the eighth and seventh centuries are unacquainted with the Mosaic code.

Graf's views are accepted by Kuenen, Wellhausen, Budde, Cornill, and many other scholars[2]. Further researches and investigations have led to a practical agreement among most scholars that the Pentateuch consists of four documents, J, E, D, and P[3]. J is the earliest document and E slightly later. These two sources were united by a Jehovistic Redactor into JE[4]. This work contains mostly historical matter and a few laws (Ex. chaps. 20–23. 24). It is the opinion of many scholars that J and E, before they were combined into one whole, went through several editions, being revised and modified. These are distinguished as J^1, J^2, J^3, and E^1, E^2. D, at the time of Josiah, contained Deut. 12–26, it passed through several editions, and was finally combined with JE by the Deuteronomist, who also revised JE himself. This revision affected Genesis least; it is more evident in Exodus and Numbers, and most clearly seen in Joshua. Entirely distinct from this combination of JE and D, after Ezekiel,

---

[1] In Merx, *Archiv für Wissensch. Erforschung des A.T.*, i. 466–477.

[2] Cf. Holz., l.c., p. 66 f.

[3] The group of laws in Lev. chaps. 17–26 are usually designated 'the Law of Holiness' (H); cf. Dr., *Introd.*, p. 43 f., and the authorities cited there, and Holz., l.c., p. 406 f.

[4] The document J is called the Jahwist, and the document E, the Elohist. The work formed by the combination of the two is designated the Jehovist; cf. Holz., l.c., p. 71 f.; Dr., *Introd.*, p. 12.

during and after the exile, another work was composed, containing some historical matter, but chiefly legislation. This was the Priests' Code (P or P C), which seems to have been composed gradually (P^1, P^2, etc.) in the school of the priests. This was combined, probably by Ezra, with J, E, and D; and became, about 444 B.C., the recognised law book of the community[1].

Kuenen, in 1885[2], published the results of his investigation of the structure of the Hexateuch. J and E, according to Kuenen, were both written in the northern kingdom, J about the end of the ninth or beginning of the eighth century B.C.; E in the middle of the eighth century. J and E were subjected to several revisions, and in the process were considerably augmented and modified, and c. 600 B.C. (after Deuteronomy) were united into one document JE. In this work, Ex. chaps. 20–23 occupied the place now taken by Deuteronomy. The original Deuteronomy (D^1), i.e. Deut. chaps. 5–26. 28. 31, 9–13, was written in Josiah's reign, c. 622 B.C. and later, in the beginning of the Babylonian exile, Deut. 1–4, 40. chaps. 29 f. and 31, 1–8 (D^2) were added to D^1. During the exile, the Deuteronomist (D^3) worked up D^2 and JE into one document, and revised the whole work, especially Joshua. The priestly and ritual portions of the Pentateuch (P) were all composed after Deuteronomy. Firstly P^1, i.e. a collection of laws—a large portion of which is preserved in Lev. chaps. 17–26, and in numerous fragments in the rest of the Pentateuch[3]. This part of P was revised and arranged with reference to Ezekiel and shortly before the end of the Babylonian exile. All the other portions of the so-called 'Grundschrift,' from Gen. chap. 1—Josh. chap. 21, belong to P^2, which was gradually completed between 500–475 B.C. in Babylon. This P^2 had already been welded together with P^1, and in 444 B.C.

[1] Cf. Di., *N.D.J.*, p. 598. [2] *Onderzoek*[2] = *Hexateuch.*

[3] Kuenen's P^1 = H (Law of Holiness), see p. xxiii.

(in the assembly described in Neh. chaps. 8–10) was brought into use by Ezra as the recognised law book of the community. Later, this law book was augmented by all sorts of new laws, which were not known to Ezra (e.g. Ex. 29, 38–42. Lev. 6, 1–6. Num. 28, 1–6. Ex. 30, 11–16. Lev. 27, 32 f.), and c. 400 B.C. P^1+P^2 were welded together with JE+D. This composite work was probably subjected to a continuous criticism at the hands of the scribes until the third century B.C.

The Dates of the Codes.

The dates of the codes J and E are variously assigned by different scholars, and on this depends the question whether E is younger than J, or *vice versa.* Those who assign the priority to E are Schrader, E, 975–950 B.C., J, 825–800 B.C.; Reuss, J, 850–800 B.C., E, perhaps a little earlier; Dillmann, E, 900–850 B.C., so Kittel and Riehm; Dillmann, J, about 750 B.C., Kittel, 830–800 B.C., Riehm, c. 850 B.C.; Wellhausen, Kuenen, and Stade put J first, 850–800 B.C., and E about 750 B.C.[1]

The Three Documents J, E, and P.

The three codes J, E, and P are distinguished one from the other, not only by a difference, more or less distinctly marked, in their contents, but also by a peculiar usage of language. P, which has been largely employed in the composition of Genesis, can be more clearly separated from J and E, than these from one another, the points of demarcation between them being less clearly defined than in the case of P.

The Document J.

This document J—the supplemental document of the *Ergänzungshypothese* (cf. p. xix) — may be designated, as

[1] Cf. Holz., l.c., pp. 165 f. and 215 f.; Dr., *Introd.*, p. 116.

distinguished from P, the Prophetic Narrative. In the account of the family of Noah, the deluge, and in the table of nations, it is in substance closely akin to P, also in the portion of Genesis containing the history of Abraham it has several narratives in common with P (e.g. the separation of Lot and Abraham; the destruction of Sodom and Gomorrha; the story of Dinah; also cf. 47, 1–11. 29 ff. and 49, 29 ff.), but elsewhere in the history of the patriarchs, and in that of Joseph and Jacob, it is more closely connected with E, so much so, that from chap. 27 onwards, most of the narratives in J have their complete parallels in E.

In the sections in J which have their corresponding passages in E, the difference in style and contents is often clearly marked, e.g. in the two reports of the Abimelech story in chap. 20 and chap. 26, and of Hagar and Ishmael etc.; in other parallel passages the two narratives are practically alike, so that R could easily weld together the two accounts. On the other hand there is much that occurs in J with no corresponding account in E, e.g. the visit of the angels to Lot and Abraham; the origin of the nations of Moab and Ammon; the list of Nahor's descendants; Isaac in Philistia; the story of Dinah, of Judah and Tamar, etc. J and E are both independent documents, but the striking similarity between a great portion of their contents, would seem to indicate that J and E were closely connected with one another[1].

The main difference, however, between J and E, is that the narratives in J are marked by a peculiar literary style. E is full of details, often of no importance; J is distinguished by a fondness for picturesque description, by breadth and variety of ideas, and by the polished and artistic finish of his

[1] The question as to which document is dependent on the other, is discussed in Holz., l. c., p. 215 ff. Up to the time of Wellhausen, the general opinion was that E was the older document; so Schrader and Nöldeke. But Wellhausen and the followers of Graf regard J as older than E; cf. p. xxv.

narratives. Many passages of J, which we possess in their full form (chap. 2 f. 11, 1–9; cf. 18 f. 24. 43 f.), are masterpieces of narrative art, with which only a few out of E can be compared (chap. 22). 'His touch is singularly light, with a few strokes he paints a scene which, before he has finished, is impressed indelibly upon his reader's memory. In ease and grace his narratives are unsurpassed; everything is told with the precise amount of detail that is required; the narrative never lingers and the reader's interest is sustained to the end[1].' The dialogues, which are frequent in J, are another noticeable feature of the document (Gen. chaps. 18 f. 24. 43 f.).

The standpoint of J is prophetical. Many of his longer narratives abound in acute and instructive reflections, and in moral and religious truths. 'He deals with the problem of the origin of sin and evil in the world, and follows its growth (Gen. 2–4. 6, 1–8); he notices the evil condition of man's heart even after the Flood (8, 21); traces the development of heathen feeling and heathen manners (11, 1 ff. 9, 22 ff. 19, 1 ff. 31 ff.), and emphasises strongly the want of faith and disobedience visible even in the Israel of Moses' days (Ex. 16, 4–5. 25–30. 17, 2–7. 14, 11 f. chaps. 32–34. Num. 11. 14. 25, 1 ff. Deut. 31, 16–22). He shows, in opposition to this, how God works for the purpose of counteracting the ruin incident to man, partly by punishing, partly by choosing and educating, first Israel's forefathers to live as godlike men, and finally Israel itself to become the holy people of God. He represents Abraham's migration into Canaan as the result of a divine call and promise (Gen. 12, 1–3. 24, 7, contrast 20, 13 and Josh. 24, 3 in E); expresses clearly the aim and object of this call (18, 18 f.); exhibits in strong contrast to human sin the divine mercy, long-suffering and faithfulness (Gen. 6, 8. 8, 21 f. 18, 24 ff. Ex. 32–34); recognises the

[1] Driver, *Introd.*, p. 112.

universal significance of Israel in the midst of the nations of the world (Gen. 12, 2 f. 27, 29. Ex. 4, 22 f. 19, 5 f. Num. 24, 9); declares in classical words the final end of Israel's education (Num. 11, 29, cf. Ex. 19, 5 f.); and formulates under the term *belief* the spirit in which man should respond to the revealing work of God (Gen. 15, 6. Ex. 4, 1. 5. 8 f. 31. 14, 31. 19, 9, cf. Num. 14, 11. 20, 12, and Deut. 1, 32. 9, 23). And in order to illustrate the divine purposes of grace, as manifested in history, he introduces at points (fixed by tradition), prophetic glances into the future (Gen. 3, 15. 5, 29. 8, 21. 9, 25–27. 12, 2 f. 18, 18 f. 28, 14. Num. 24, 17 f.), as he also loves to point to the character of the nations or tribes as foreshadowed in their beginnings (Gen. 9, 22 ff. 16, 12. 19, 31 ff. 25, 25 ff. 34, 25 ff. 35, 22, cf. 49, 9 ff.)[1].'

Other characteristic features of J are, that he often in his narratives describes certain events as due to human and natural causes, whereas E assigns similar events to supernatural causes (e.g. Gen. 30, 14–16, contrast 30, 17 f.; 30, 28–43, contrast 31, 4 ff. Ex. 10, 13. 19. and 14, 21, etc.). J, too, in his representations of the Deity is more anthropomorphic than E; God appears in visible form to Abraham (Gen. chap. 18 f.), *meets* Moses (Ex. 4, 24, cf. Gen. 16, 7), *comes down* (Gen. 11, 5. 7. Ex. 3, 8. 19, 11, etc.), *is jealous of men* (Gen. 6, 3. 11, 6), *repents* (Gen. 6, 6), *grieves* (Gen. 6, 6), *swears* (Gen. 24, 7. Num. 11, 12, etc.), *is angry* (Ex. 4, 14. 32, 10. 12), *shuts the door of the Ark* (Gen. 7, 16), *smells the sweet savour* (Gen. 8, 21). Like E, J is fond of describing the consecration of the various sanctuaries in Palestine (Bethel, Gen. 12, 8. 28, 13–16; Shechem, 12, 6 f.; Beer-laḥai-roi, 16, 14; Beersheba, 21, 33. 26, 23. 28, 10; Mamre-Hebron, 13, 18. 18, 1, etc.)[2], but he expressly states

[1] Di., *N.D.J.*, p. 629 ff., as translated in Dr., *Introd.*, p. 113.

[2] J (like E) explains the origin of the names Beer-laḥai-roi, Beersheba, Bethel, Penuel, 32, 30; Succoth, 33, 17; and Abel-Mizraim, 50, 17.

that the patriarchs, when worshipping at the sanctuaries, '*called upon the name of Jehovah*' (Gen. 12, 7 f. 13, 18. 21, 33. 26, 5), to avoid any suspicion that the Holy places were used for the purposes of idolatry.

The Language of J.

Proper Names.

J uses יהוה as the name of God; אלהים is also used in special cases, e.g. when he reflects upon the contrast between the divine and human character (Gen. 32, 29. 31. 33, 10), also when a heathen is addressing an Israelite (Judg. 1, 7. Gen. 43, 29), or an Israelite a heathen (Gen. 20, 13. 40, 8. 41, 16. 25. 28. 32). The serpent in Gen. 3, 2 also uses אלהים, and Abimelech יהוה in Gen. 26, 28 f.

J has for Mesopotamia ארם נהרים; P has פדן ארם. ישׂראל is the name of the third Patriarch, after Gen. 32, 29 (generally). The Mount of 'the Law-giving' is סיני in J and P, חרב in E and D. In J the original inhabitants of Palestine are כנעני (Gen. 10, 18 b. 12, 6. 24, 3. 37, etc.), cf. J בנות כנעני (Gen. 24, 3. 37) = P בנות כנען (Gen. 28, 1. 6. 8).

Words and Phrases characteristic of J.

אבי פ״ connecting the different members of a genealogical table, Gen. 4, 20. 21. 10, 21. 11, 29.

אדמה '*surface of the earth*,' or as land suitable for cultivation. ארץ in its ordinary sense also occurs.

אחיו = the second son, after the first has been mentioned, in the formula שׁם אחיו, Gen. 4, 21. 10, 25; cf. 22, 21 (in appos.).

איש ואשתו, only in Gen. 7, 2. P has זָכָר וּנְקֵבָה.

אלה = *oath*, Gen. 24, 21. 26, 28. In other sources in a different sense.

ארח כנשׁים, Gen. 18, 11.

ארץ, in the phrase היה בארץ = '*to exist*,' Gen. 2, 5. 6, 4. So in J, Gen. 19, 31 איש אין בארץ, and Gen. 6, 6 עשׂה בארץ *to cause to exist.*

ארור, in curses, frequently.

לקח לו אשה, common in family tables, Gen. 4, 19. 6, 2.

בא אל־פ״, a constant euphemism in J.

באכה = '*up to a place*,' Gen. 10, 19. 30. 13, 10. 25, 18 (all).

בי אדני, common in J.

אבנה ממנה, Gen. 16, 2. 30, 3 b (all).

ברוך יהוה, Gen. 24, 31. 26, 29, and נברך בפ״ '*to bless oneself through any one*,' Gen. 12, 3. 28, 14.

דבר, in the phrase כדברים האלה, Gen. 24, 28. 39, 17. 19, etc., and דבר with suffixes, as in כדברך, Gen. 30, 34. 44, 10, etc.

היה '*to become something*,' which is expressed by a subs. or equivalent, Gen. 4, 2. 17. 20. 21. 10, 9.

זקונים with יָלַד, Gen. 21, 2 a; cf. 24, 36, and יֶלֶד Gen. 44, 20, of children born when the parents are old.

חִיָּה with the obj. זרע, Gen. 7, 3. 19, 32. 34 (all).

חן, in מצא חן, common in the phrase אם־נא מצאתי חן בעיניך (בעיניכם), Gen. 18, 3. 30, 27, etc., the expression מצא חן בעיני פ״ also occurs frequently in J, e.g. Gen. 6, 8. 19, 19. 32, 6, etc.

עשׂה חסד, frequently in the phrases עשׂה חסד עם or את, Gen. 19, 19. 24, 12. 14, etc.; עשׂה חסד ואמת עם, Gen. 24, 49. 32, 11. 47, 29, etc.

חָרֵב, in the story of the Flood, Gen. 8, 13 b, and חָרָבָה, Gen. 7, 22.

ידות = '*portions*,' Gen. 43, 34. 47, 24 (all).

ידע, euphemistic = '*to know*,' Gen. 4, 1. 19, 5. 24, 16. 38, 26, etc.

הבה, from יהב as interj., Gen. 11, 3. 4. 7. 38, 16. In E it also = '*to give*.'

ילד = '*to beget*,' Gen. 4, 18. 10, 8. 13. 22, 23.

יצג, the Hif'il הציג only occurs in Gen. in J, 30, 38. 33, 15. 43, 9. 47, 2.

יקום, Gen. 7, 4. 23. In Deut. 11, 6 the meaning is different.

ישב, in the phrase ישב בקרב פ׳, of foreigners dwelling in a land not their own, Gen. 24, 3. Josh. 6, 25, etc.

כָּבֵד, verb and adj. used in J = '*sore;*' (of famine) Gen. 43, 1. 47, 4; (of plagues) Ex. 9, 3. 18. 24 b; (of mourning) Gen. 50, 10. 11; = '*grievous*' (of sin) Gen. 18, 20; = *rich,*' Gen. 13, 2; = '*numerous,*' Gen. 50, 9. Ex. 8, 20; = '*to harden*' (the heart), Ex. 9, 7. 8, 11 a, etc.

כלה ל, frequently in J, Gen. 24, 15. 19. 45. 27, 30. 43, 2, etc., also occurs in D and P.

לב, in the different phrases אמר אל־לבו, Gen. 8, 21; אמר בלבו, Gen. 27, 41; דבר אל־לבי, Gen. 24, 45; התעצב אל לבו, Gen. 6, 6; and (?) שׂמח בלבו, Ex. 4, 14.

לין, frequently in J, Gen. 19, 2. 24, 23. 25. 54. 32, 14 a. Ex. 34, 25.

מלון is only found in J, Gen. 42, 27. 43, 21. Ex. 4, 24. Josh. 4, 3. 8.

התמהמה, only in J, Gen. 19, 16. 43, 10. J in 34, 19 has אֵחַר, E, 45, 9 עמד.

מולדת = *relatives* in J, Gen. 12, 1. 24, 4. 31, 3. 43, 7. In P = *posterity*, Gen. 48, 6.

מספוא, Gen. 24, 25. 32. 42, 2. 7. 43, 24 (all). E has מזון, Gen. 45, 23.

מקנה, in the phrases מקנה צאן, מ״ בקר, מ״ בהמה, Gen. 26, 14. 47, 17. 18.

כל־משפחות האדמה, Gen. 12, 3. 28, 14.

מנעורים, only in J, Gen. 8, 21. 46, 34.

נשמת חיים, only in J, Gen. 2, 7. 7, 22. In Gen. 6, 3 J uses רוח = *spirit* (of Jehovah). P uses רוח חיים, Gen. 6, 17. 7, 15.

ספה = '*sweep away,*' Gen. 18, 23 f. 19, 15. 17.

עבד with suffix = *I*, addressed to God, or a person of rank, common in J, Gen. 18, 3. 5. 19, 2. 19. 32, 11, etc.

עמד מן = '*to cease,*' Gen. 29, 35. 30, 9.

עָצַב in Nif'., Gen. 45, 5 a, and Hithpael, Gen. 6, 6. 34, 7, and עֶצֶב Gen. 3, 16, and עצבון Gen. 3, 16. 17. 5, 29.

עָתַר in Qal, Nif'., and Hif'., only in J. Qal in Gen. 25, 21. Ex. 8, 26. 10, 18, and Nif'. in Gen. 25, 21; Hif'. in Ex. 8, 4. 5. 9, 28.

הפלה = '*to separate, distinguish,*' Ex. 8, 18. 9, 4. 11, 7.

הפעם, Gen. 18, 32. 29, 34. 35, etc.; זאת הפעם, Gen. 2, 23; and also בפעם הזאת, Ex. 8, 28. D has בפעם ההוא, Ex. 9, 19. 10, 10.

פצר בפ״, only in J, Gen. 19, 3. 9. 33, 11 b.

נפל על־צוארי פ״, only in J, Gen. 33, 4. 45, 14. 46, 29, in the last two passages together with בכה ע״ צ״ פ״.

הצליח, seven times in J, Gen. 24, 21. 40. 42. 56. 39, 2. 3. 23.

צעיר and צעירה = *the younger of two brothers* or *sisters,* Gen. 19, 31. 34. 35. 38. 25, 23. 29, 26. 43, 33. 48, 14. '*The first-born*' is גדול, Gen. 27, 1. 15, or רב, Gen. 25, 23, or בכור, Gen. 38, 7. 43, 33. קטן = *youngest* also occurs in J, Gen. 43, 29. 44, 2. 23. 26.

צעקה = '*an evil report,*' Gen. 18, 21. 19, 13.

קרא, in the phrase על־כן קרא שם פ״ frequent in J, Gen. 11, 9. 16, 14. 19, 22. 25, 30, etc. The phrase קרא בשם יהוה only occurs in J, Gen. 4, 26. 12, 8. 13, 4. 21, 33. 26, 25.

קרה in Hif'., only in J, Gen. 24, 12. 27, 20. לקראת, in the phrase רוץ לקראת פ״, only found in J, Gen. 18, 2. 19, 1. 24, 17. 29, 13. 33, 4. לק״ alone is common in J, but is also found in the other sources.

שׂדה in J is generally regarded as '*pasture land,*' opposed to אֲדָמָה *arable land,* Gen. 25, 27. 30, 16. 34, 7.

עשׂב השׂדה, Gen. 2, 5. 3, 18. Ex. 9, 25 in J = עשׂב הארץ in E, Ex. 10, 12. 15.

שׂפה = '*language,*' only in J, Gen. 11, 1. 6. 7. 9. P uses לשׁון, Gen. 10, 5. 20. 31.

שׁפחה, J never uses אמה (E), Gen. 16, 1. 5. 6. 24, 35. 30, 7. 9. 10. 12, etc. P also uses שׁ״.

השׁקיף, found in J, Gen. 18, 16. 19, 28. 26, 8. Ex. 14, 24.

The Grammar of J.

There are no special peculiarities in the formation of words. The ending ון—which Di. cites—in the third and second pers. masc. pl. imperf. is found in E, and frequently in D.

J exhibits a preference for verbal suffixes, instead of using את with suffixes. So Gen. 24, verbal suffixes fourteen times; את with suffix three times; Judg. 1, verbal suffixes ten times; את with suffixes twice.

Peculiar constructions of verbs חִבֵּק and נָשַׁק, construed with an acc., while E uses ל with these verbs (in Pi'el); cf. Gen. 33, 4 with 29, 13. 31, 28. 32, 1. 45, 15. 48, 10. קָרָא = *to call any one, make him come*, is construed with ל not את in J, but this is also found in E, D, and P.

The genitive expressed by אשר ל is found in J, Gen. 29, 9. 40, 5. 47, 6 b; but also in E, Gen. 31, 19. In J מְעַט is used with the genitive following, so Gen. 18, 4. 24, 17. 43, 2. 11. 44, 25, while D puts the cstr. state before מְעַט, Deut. 26, 5. 28, 62. J is fond of using proper names of nations in the sing., so ישראל (but E בני ישראל) = *the Israelites*, מִצְרַיִם = *the Egyptians*, also the different tribes of Israel; cf. Judg. chap. 1. We find too אִישׁ יִשְׂרָאֵל, Josh. 9, 6, and in Josh. 17, 14 f. the tribes speak of themselves in the sing. Lastly may be noted, the use of sing. gentilic nouns, הַכְּנַעֲנִי, הַיְבוּסִי, etc., cf. Judg. 1, 1. 21. 27. 28. 29. 30. 32. 36.

In his syntax, J often employs periods with main and dependent clauses. He not only uses the ordinary means of connecting a verbal and nominal sentence, but is fond of employing the formulae וַיְהִי כִּי, Gen. 6, 1. 26, 8. 27, 1. 43, 21. 44, 24. Josh. 17, 13, and וַיְהִי כַּאֲשֶׁר, Gen. 12, 11. 24, 22. 52. 27, 30. 30, 35. 37, 23. 43, 2. Disjunctive interrogative sentences are frequent in J, Gen. 18, 21. 24, 21. Ex. 16, 4. 17, 7. J is fond of using זאת and זֶה, for emphasis, in מַה־זּאת,

Gen. 3, 13. 12, 18. 26, 10. 42, 28; מַה־זֶּה, Gen. 27, 20; לָמָּה זֶּה, Gen. 18, 13. 25, 22. 33, 15.

He also makes use of particles and conjunctions with great freedom, imparting to his style a certain vivacity, and expressing the various shades of meaning with more effect.

So אוּלַי in Gen. 16, 2. 18, 24. 28. 24, 5. 39. 43, 12.

אָכֵן, Gen. 28, 16.

בִּגְלַל, Gen. 12, 13. 30, 27. 39, 5.

בַּעֲבוּר, Gen. 3, 17. 8, 21. 12, 13. 16.

גַּם־גַּם, Gen. 24, 25. 43, 8. 44, 16. 46, 34. 47, 3. 50, 9.

כִּי־עַל־כֵּן, Gen. 18, 5. 19, 8. 38, 26. Num. 10, 31.

לְבִלְתִּי, Gen. 3, 11. 4, 15. 19, 21. 38, 9. Ex. 8, 18. 25. 9, 17.

לְנֹכַח, Gen. 25, 21. 30, 38 (P uses נֹכַח alone, Ex. 14, 2. 26, 35).

מֵאָז (infrequent), Gen. 39, 5. Ex. 9, 24 b.

J is also fond of using the precative נָא, instances in Gen. chaps. 19 and 24. J has נָא about forty times in Gen., E about six times. וְעַתָּה also occurs frequently in J, Gen. 3, 22. 4, 11. 11, 6. 12, 19. 24, 49. 30, 30, etc. J has וְעַתָּה seventeen times, E eight times, Gen. 20, 7. 21, 23. 31, 30. 44. 41, 33. 50, 17. 21. Ex. 33, 5. פֶּן is also frequently used, in J fourteen times, in E seven times, and fourteen times in D. J also employs טֶרֶם usually, Gen. 2, 5. 19, 4. 24, 15. 45. Ex. 9, 30. 10, 7. Josh. 2, 8. 3, 1, and once בְּטֶרֶם, Gen. 45, 28. Lastly the uses of prep. ל may be noted as particle of time = *about such and such a time*, Gen. 8, 11. 24, 11. 49, 27. Ex. 34, 2; also = *about such and such a time reckoned from to-day*, Gen. 7, 4; and = *after the lapse of a fixed period of time*, Gen. 7, 10, and the use of עוֹד with a suffix representing the subject, Gen. 18, 22. 43, 27. 28. 46, 30. Ex. 4, 18. 9, 2. 17. Num. 22, 30[1].

---

[1] Cf. Holz., l.c., p. 93 f., from whom the above examples and rules are mainly taken.

The following portions of Genesis are usually assigned to J: **2**, 4 b–**3**, 24. **4**, 1–26. **5**, 29. **6**, 1–4. 5–8. **7**, 1–5. 7–10 (mainly). 12. 16 b–17. 22. 23. **8**, 2 b–3 a. 6–12. 13 b. 20–22. **9**, 18–27. **10**, 8–19. 21. 24–30. **11**, 1–9. 28–30. **12**, 1–4 a. 6–20. **13**, 1–5. 7–11 a (to *East*). 12 b (from *and moved*)–18. **16**, 1 b–2. 4–14. **18**, 1–**19**, 28. 30–38. **21**, 1 a. 2 a. 33. **22**, 15–18. 20–24. chap. **24**. **25**, 1–6. 11 b. 18. 21–26 a. 27–34. **26**, 1–14. (15 R). 16–17. (18 R). 19–33. **27**, 1–45. **28**, 10. 13–16. 19. **29**, 2–14. 31–35. **30**, 3 b–5. 7. 9–16. 20 b (*now–sons*). 24–**31**, 1. 3. 46. 48–50. **32**, 3–13 a. 22. 24–32. **33**, 1–17. **34**, 2 b–3. 5. 7. 11–12. 19. 25 (partly). 26. 30–31. **35**, 14. 21–22 a. **37**, 12–21. 25–27. 28 b (to *silver*). 31–35. chap. **38**. chap. **39**. **42**, 38–**44**, 34[1]. **46**, 28–**47**, 4. 6 b (LXX). 13–26. 27 a (to *Goshen*). 29–31. **49**, 1 b–28 a (incorporated from an older document). **50**, 1–11. 14.

The Home of J.

The writer of J is commonly supposed to have been a native of the southern kingdom. This is the opinion of Ewald, Di., Well., Stade, Budde, Meyer, Kittel, and Cornill. The evidence they bring forward in favour of this view is as follows: Abraham and possibly Jacob are represented as living at Hebron, and not at Beersheba. In the history of Joseph, Judah appears as leader of the brethren, not Reuben. Aaron, the north Israelite, is not mentioned in J, and Joshua is not the prominent figure he is in E. It is also difficult to assume that Gen. 38, which contains traditions relating to the family history of Judah, could be of any particular interest to any one who was not a member of that tribe. Schrader, Reuss, and Kuenen hold that J as well as E belonged to the northern kingdom. The evidence in the case of J is not so convincing as in that of E. That the author of J was a native of the southern kingdom,

[1] With traces of E; cf. Holz., *Hex.*, Table I. p. 5.

is the opinion of a majority of scholars, and therefore may be provisionally accepted[1].

The Document E.

This document is called by Dillmann (*Gen.*[6], p. xi) the *Traditional History of Israel.* It is probably based on older written sources, cf. p. xlv, but in the main it derives its information from oral tradition, and preserves unchanged both the colouring and tone of tradition as current among the people[2]. 'The standpoint of E is the prophetical, though it is not brought so prominently forward as in J, and in general the narrative is more "objective," less consciously tinged by ethical and theological reflexion than that of J[3].' E, as compared with J and P, is fond of stating details and particulars. He has the best information on Egyptian matters. Proper names, such as Eliezer, Deborah, Potiphar, Phicol, Zaphenath-Paaneach, Asenath, Pithom, Raamses, etc., are only known to us from E. It has numerous chronological notices, e.g. the number of years Joseph and Joshua lived (Gen. 50, 22. 26. and Josh. 24, 29), and the time that Jacob sojourned with Laban, cf. also 40, 12–19. 42, 17. Ex. 3, 18. and 45, 6 with 41, 26. E supplies much important information as to the Aramaic origin of the Teraphim cultus, and the polytheism of Laban's family (31, 19f. 35, 2 ff.), and contains many peculiar notices and brief statements which bear the impress of the highest antiquity (15, 2? 20, 16. 31, 42. 21, 27 ff. Abraham's covenant with Abimelech). Angels are frequently mentioned by E: as guides and guardians of Israel (Ex. 14, 9. 33, 2), and as the channel of divine revelation between God and man, especially the patriarchs (21, 17. 22, 11. 28, 12). In

[1] Cf. Holz., p. 160 f.; Kuenen, *Hex.*, p. 230 f.; Driver, *Introd.*, p. 115 f.; Cornill, p. 51.

[2] Cf. the narratives 22, 1–14. chap. 31. 32, 24–32. Ex. chaps. 1–3, etc.

[3] Driver, *Introd.*, p. 111; cf. Di., *N. D. J.*, p. 619.

many of his narratives reference is made to the antiquities or localities in the Holy Land, and the local traditions attaching to them are recounted, so the altars on Moriah, 22, 9; at Bethel, 35, 1. 3. 7; at Shechem, 33, 19; the pillars at Bethel, 28, 18 f. and at Rachel's grave near Bethel, 35, 20; the pillar set up by Jacob and Laban in Gilead, 31, 45; and the Terebinth at Shechem, 35, 4; Jacob also sacrifices at Beersheba. E also mentions the burial-places of Deborah and Rachel, 35, 8. 19 f.; and Joshua and Eleazar, Josh. 24, 30. 33. E (like J) explains the origin of the names of places in Palestine, e.g. Beersheba, 21, 31; Maḥanaim, 32, 2; Jabboq, 32, 23; and Allon-Bachuth, 35, 8. Other points characteristic of E are: Abraham dwells chiefly in the Negeb (Gerar, Beersheba), chap. 20 f., not Hebron; Jacob is chiefly associated with Bethel, 28, 11 f., and Shechem, 33, 19 f.; Joseph is honoured above his brethren by a special blessing, 48, 8 ff., and in the history of Joseph Reuben is the leader of the brethren and intercedes for Joseph. E is fond of describing how God reveals Himself to man. He appears in a dream to Abimelech, Laban, Pharaoh, 20, 6. 31, 24. chap. 40 f.; to Abram 21, 12. 22, 1; and to Jacob and Joseph 28, 11 f. 37, 6 f. Abraham bears the title of 'Prophet,' 20, 7, with the power of effectual intercession, and Moses is expressly represented as a prophet (though he does not receive the title, as in Hos. 12, 14), 'entrusted by God with a prophet's mission (Ex. 3), and holding exceptionally intimate communion with Him (Ex. 33, 11. Num. 12, 6–8, cf. Deut. 34, 10)[1].' In the narrative of Joseph, which has been preserved by E in the most complete form, the whole tenor of the account is prophetic. It is clear from 50, 20 that the writer's object is to show how the divine plan of salvation, already communicated to Abraham and his descendants, would be gradually realized through human means, even though it be accomplished without the knowledge,

[1] Driver, *Introd.*, p. 112.

contrary to the wishes, and in spite of the errors of the human agents who actually carry into effect the divine purposes [1].

The Language of E.

Proper Names in E.

God is אלהים, אדני also occurs (Gen. 20, 4), and אל (Gen. 33, 20. 35, 7. 46, 3). In E the name יהוה is first revealed through Moses, but E continues to use אלהים, or האלהים freely, side by side with יהוה. אלהים is also used as an appellative noun in the formulae: אלהי אבי, א״ אביך, א״ אביו (Gen. 31, 5. 29. 42. 46, 1. 3. Ex. 18, 4). E uses אמרי as the name of the original inhabitants of Palestine (Gen. 48, 22. Num. 13, 29. 21, 21. 31, etc.). The Mount of Law-giving in E is חרב (Ex. 3, 1. 17, 6. 33, 6), it is also called הר יהוה in Num. 10, 33 a, and הר אלהים in Ex. 3, 1. 18, 5. 24, 13. E uses יעקב, not ישׂראל (generally) after Gen. 32. Moses' father-in-law is יִתְרוֹ or יֶתֶר (Ex. 3, 1. 4, 18. chap. 18). האיש משה is only found in E (Ex. 11, 3. Num. 12, 3); cf. זה משה האיש (Ex. 32, 1. 23).

Words and Phrases characteristic of E.

על אודות, frequently in E, Gen. 21, 11. 25. Ex. 18, 8. Num. 12, 1.

אמה, never שפחה (J), Gen. 20, 17. 21, 10. 12. 13. 30, 3. 31, 33, etc.; also found in D.

באשר with שם = *where*, Gen. 21, 17.

בזה, common in E, Gen. 48, 9 a. Ex. 24, 14. Num. 22, 19.

בטרם, Gen. 27, 4 b. 33 a. 41, 50. Ex. 1, 19. E never uses טרם.

בלעדי with suffix, Gen. 41, 16. 44 (all). In 41, 16 ב״ is used as in Gen. 14, 24; cf. 14, 24.

בעיר, only in E, Gen. 45, 17. Num. 20, 4. 8. 11; cf. Ex. 22, 4.

---

[1] Cf. Di., *N. D. J.*, p. 619 ff., from whom most of the above particulars are derived.

בעל, in all its meanings, is only found in the Hex. in E, Gen. 20, 3. 37, 19. Ex. 24, 14. Num. 21, 28, etc.; ב״ in E also = '*husband*,' Ex. 21, 3. 22, cf. Gen. 20, 3. In J (and P) the '*husband*' is אִישׁ, Gen. 3, 6. 16. 29, 34. 30, 15. 18. 20. J once has אדון = '*husband*,' Gen. 18, 22.

על־ברכי פ״, in the phrase '*to bear in the lap of another*,' Gen. 30, 3.

גדול and קטן = *elder* and *younger*, Gen. 29, 16. 18. 42, 13. 15. 20. 32. 34. In Gen. 41, 51 f. השני stands instead of הקטון.

דבר בפ״ '*to talk against any one*,' Num. 12, 1. 8. 21, 5. 7. דבר = *dispute* which is to be settled in a court of justice, Ex. 18, 16–19. 26. 22, 8. 24, 14; also in Deut. 17, 8.

דור דור, Ex. 3, 15. 17, 16. In Deut. 32, 7 דור ודור occurs.

דרך נשים, Gen. 31, 35; cf. p. xxix.

זוד, Ex. 18, 11, and הזיד, Ex. 21, 14 = *to act presumptuously*.

חִזֵּק לב = '*to harden the heart*,' Ex. 4, 21. 10, 20. 27; also התחזק, Gen. 48, 2. Num. 13, 20.

חלש, only in E, Ex. 17, 13. 32, 18; cf. גבורה = '*victory*,' and חלושה '*defeat*,' in Ex. 32, 18.

חרב, in the phrase בחרבך ובקשתך, Gen. 48, 22. Josh. 24, 12.

חרה בעיני פ״, Gen. 31, 35. 45, 5. E has also חרה ל without אף, Gen. 31, 36, and חרה אף פ״, Gen. 30, 2. Ex. 32, 19. Num. 11, 10. 33.

התודע, Gen. 45, 1.

הוכיח and נוכח, Hif'. = '*to call to account*,' Gen. 21, 25, and '*to decide a matter by arbitration*,' Gen. 31, 37. 42. Nif'. = '*justified*,' Gen. 20, 16. J has הוכיח twice = '*destine*,' or '*intend*,' Gen. 24, 14. 44.

יֶלֶד is common in E, Gen. 21, 8. 14. 15. 33, 5 b. 37, 30, etc. It also occurs in J, instead of the more usual word נער, Gen. 32, 23. 33, 1. 2. 6. 44, 20.

יפה־תאר ויפה מראה, and with fem. adj., Gen. 29, 17. 39, 6. 41, 18 (plural יפת). J uses טובת מ״, Gen. 24, 16. 26, 7.

נצב פתח אהל, only in E, Ex. 33, 8. Num. 16, 27.

כה in E is a local particle, Gen. 22, 5. 31, 37. Ex. 2, 12. In J כה is a temporal particle.

כלכל, only in E, Gen. 45, 11. 47, 12. 50, 21.

לבב, in E, Gen. 20, 5. 6. 31, 26. Ex. 14, 5. לב in J.

לחות האבן, characteristic of E, Ex. 24, 12. 31, 18 b. J and D have שני לחות אבנים, Ex. 34, 1. Deut. 4, 13. 5, 19. P uses לחות העדות, Ex. 31, 18 a. 32, 15 a. 34, 29.

מחנה, as a name of the camp which the Israelites moved from place to place as they journeyed, Ex. 32, 17. 19 a. 33, 7. 11. Num. 12, 14 f.; also occurs in D and P. J uses מחנה, in the sense '*company*,' Gen. 32, 8. 9. 11. 33, 8. 50, 9.

מצא '*to meet any one, to befall*,' Ex. 18, 8. Num. 20, 14. Deut. 31, 17. Josh. 2, 23.

משׂכרת, only in E, Gen. 29, 15. 31, 7. 41.

נכרי, Gen. 31, 15. Ex. 2, 22. 18, 3. 21, 8; also occurs in D.

נצל = '*to destroy*,' only occurs in E; Pi'el = '*plunder*,' Ex. 3, 22. 12, 36; Hif'. = '*to take away*,' Gen. 31, 9. 16; Hithpa'. = '*to strip off*' (ornaments), Ex. 33, 6.

נשׂא לפשע, only in E, Gen. 50, 17. Ex. 23, 21. Josh. 24, 19.

נתן = '*to permit*,' with acc. of pers. and inf. cstr. with ל, Gen. 20, 6. Ex. 3, 19. Num. 20, 21. 21, 23 (both inf. without ל). 22, 13.

התפלל '*to pray*,' with אל '*to*,' and בְּעַד '*for*,' Gen. 20, 7. 17. Num. 11, 2. 21, 7.

צדה, characteristic of E, Gen. 42, 25. 45, 21. Josh. 9, 11.

צעק אל, in the phrase צעק אל יהוה, very frequent in E, Gen. 41, 55. Ex. 5, 15. 14, 15 a. 17, 4. 22, 22. Num. 11, 2. 20, 16. Josh. 24, 7.

קוץ = '*to have a horror*' of anything, Ex. 1, 12. Num. 22, 3 b. J uses גור, Num. 22, 3 a; in P קוץ is used in a weaker sense, '*to feel disgust*,' Lev. 20, 23, so in E, Num. 21, 5.

קרה, Nif'. in E, Num. 23, 3. 4. 15. 16.

רגלים instead of פעמים, Num. 22, 28. 32. 33, and Ex. 23, 14.
מרגלים, Gen. 42, 9. 11. 14. 16. 31. 34, E.
רפא, used of God, Gen. 20, 17. Ex. 15, 26. Num. 12, 13.
שׂדה וכרם, Num. 16, 14. 20, 17. 21, 22; also שׂדה או כרם, Ex. 22, 4.
שׂים לגוי, Gen. 21, 13. 18. 46, 3. J uses עשׂה לגוי, Gen. 12, 2, and P נתן לגוי, Gen. 17, 20.
שׂר occurs frequently in E, Gen. 21, 22. 37, 36. chap. 40. 41, 9. 10. 12, etc. It is also found in the other documents.
שׂים חק ומשׁפט, Ex. 15, 25. Josh. 24, 25.
משׁרת משׁה, of Joshua, Ex. 24, 13. 33, 11.
התחת אלהים אני, Gen. 30, 2. 50, 19.
תלאה, only in E, Ex. 18, 8. Num. 20, 14, in the phrase '*the trouble which has befallen us*' (מצא).
תמול שׁלשׁם, frequent in E, Ex. 5, 8, without a prep. כת″ שׁ″ is also found in E, Gen. 31, 2. 5. Ex. 5, 7. 14. מת″ גם משׁ″ occurs once in E, Ex. 4, 10.

List of rare and archaic Words and Phrases in E.

אָבַק, in Nif'. = *to wrestle*, only in Gen. 32, 25 f.
אָמְנָה, Gen. 20, 12. Josh. 7, 20 (all).
גָּנַב לֵב, only in Gen. 31, 20. 26. 27.
דָּגָה = *to multiply*, only in Gen. 48, 16.
הָסָה, in Hif'. *to silence*, Num. 13, 30; only again in Pi'el, Neh. 8, 11.
זָבַד *to dower*, and זֶבֶד *dowry*, only Gen. 30, 20.
הִתְחַכֵּם, Ex. 1, 10; once again in Eccl. 7, 16.
חֵמֶת *skin for water*, Gen. 21, 14. 15. 19 (all).
טָחָה in מְטַחֲוֵי קֶשֶׁת, only Gen. 21, 16.
כֵּן *post* or *position*, Gen. 40, 13. 41, 13; also Dan. 11, 7 (LXX). 20. 21. 38 (all).
כֵּן, as adj. = *honest*, Gen. 42, 11. 19. 31–34.
מֶכֶר *price*, Num. 20, 19; again in Neh. 13, 16. Prov. 31, 10.
מֹנִים = *times*, only Gen. 31, 7. 41.

נִין וָנֶכֶד, Gen. 21, 23; only again, Is. 14, 22. Job 18, 19.

נַפְתּוּלִים *struggles*, once, Gen. 30, 8.

נִקָּיוֹן, Gen. 20, 5 f.; only again, Hos. 8, 5. Amos 4, 6. Pss. 26, 6. 73, 13.

מֵעוֹדִי עַד־הַיּוֹם הַזֶּה, only Gen. 48, 15. Num. 22, 30.

עָקַד *to bind*, Gen. 22, 9; and עָקֹד *striped*, Gen. 30, 35. 39. 40. 31, 8. 10. 12 (all).

פִּלֵּל = *to believe*, only Gen. 48, 11.

פָּתַר *to interpret dreams*, Gen. 40, 8 f. 41, 8 f.; and פִּתְרוֹן *interpretation*, Gen. 40, 5 f. 41, 11 (all).

נִצְמַד לְ *to attach oneself* (to Baal Peor), Num. 25, 3. 5 = Ps. 106, 28; cf. 2 Sam. 20, 8 (Pu'al), and Ps. 50, 19 (Hif'. with obj. מִרְמָה), (all).

צָנוּם *dry, unfruitful*, only Gen. 41, 23.

קְשִׂיטָה *a money weight*, Gen. 33, 19. Josh. 24, 32. Job 42, 11 (all).

רֹבֵה קֶשֶׁת (Mass. Text רֹבֶה קַשָּׁת), Gen. 21, 20.

Dillmann, *Gen.*[6], mentions, as characteristic of E:—

עַל־אוֹדוֹת, see above, p. xxxviii.

אָסוֹן '*harm* or *misfortune*,' Gen. 42, 4 b. 38. 44, 29. Ex. 21, 22 f.

פַּחַד יִצְחָק, as a name of God, Gen. 31, 42. 53.

The Grammar of E.

Special Forms characteristic of E.

Peculiar forms of the Infinitives. E writes, but not exclusively:—

הָלוֹךְ instead of לֶכֶת, Ex. 3, 19. Num. 22, 13. 14. 16.

דֵּעָה instead of דַּעַת, Ex. 2, 4.

רְדָה instead of רֶדֶת, Gen. 46, 3.

עֲשׂה, Gen. 50, 20; also עֲשׂוֹ, Gen. 31, 28.

רְאֹה, Gen. 48, 11.

עֲשֹׂהוּ, Ex. 18, 18.

In Num. 20, 21, נָתוֹן stands for תֵּת, but J also has this in Gen. 38, 9.

Unusual full forms of the Suffixes are attached to Nouns, so:—

קִרְבֶּנָה, Gen. 41, 21.
כֻּלָּנָה, 42, 36.
לְבַדְּנָה, 21, 29; also אַתֵּנָה, 31, 6.

E (contrast J) is fond of using the verbal suffixes with the acc. sign את, instead of attaching them to the verb. In Josh. chap. 24, E uses two verbal suffixes, and the suffix with את fourteen times; cf. also Gen. 40, 3 f. 6. 8. 11. 15. 17. 19. 48, 10–12. 15–17. 21.

Construction of Verbs:—

חִבֵּק and נִשֵּׁק take the obj. with לְ, Gen. 29, 13. 31, 28. 32, 1. 45, 15. 48, 10.

פָּגַע with בְּ, Gen. 28, 11. 32, 2; and with את or acc., Ex. 5, 3. 20. 23, 4.

שָׁמַע with בְּקוֹל occurs, Gen. 21, 12. 27, 13. 30, 6. Ex. 18, 19, and several times in D.

אָמַר with לְ or אֶל־ '*to say in reference to any one*,' Gen. 20, 2. 13.

The construction of אֱלֹהִים = '*God*' with a plural verb is found in E, Gen. 20, 13. 35, 7; cf. Josh. 24, 19. The use of the Ethic dat. (not connected with the Imper.) may also be noted, Gen. 21, 6. Ex. 18, 27 (all).

In E, the connection between the different portions of the sentence, or the different events in a narrative, is looser and more superficial than in J. The formulae וַיְהִי בָּעֵת הַהִיא, Gen. 21, 22, and especially וַיְהִי אַחַר (אַחֲרֵי) הַדְּבָרִים הָאֵלֶּה, Gen. 22, 1. 40, 1. 48, 1. Josh. 24, 29 are obviously used to bridge the gap between two narratives.

Characteristic of E is the unnecessary prolixity employed in addressing persons to whom an important communication has to be made: 'He called M. or N. (and the name of the person is frequently repeated by E), *and he answered, Here am I*, or *I hear*,' e.g. Gen. 22, 11. 46, 2. Ex. 3, 4; similarly, Gen. 22, 1. 7. 27, 1 b. 18. 31, 11. He commences his narrative of the dreams in Gen. 40, 9. 16. 41, 17. 22, with the superfluous formula בַּחֲלֹמִי וְהִנֵּה. These two artifices may have been borrowed from the colloquial language, which was actually used by the people [1].

The Code E in Genesis.

E is first found in the history of Abraham, chap. **15** or **20**. Chap. **15** (analysis uncertain [2]), vers. 6–11 and 17–18 are possibly J. **20**, 1–17 (18 R). **21**, 6–32 a (32 b R). (34 R). **22**, 1–14. 19. **28**, 11–12. 17–18. 20–22. **29**, 1. 15–23. 25–28. 30. **30**, 1–3 (to *knees*). 6. 8. 17–20 a. 20 c–23. **31**, 2. 4–18 a. 19–45. 47. 51–**32**, 2. 13 b–21. 23. **33**, 18 b–20. **35**, 1–8. 16–20. **37**, 2 b–11. 22–24. 28 a (to *pit*). 28 c–30. 36. chap. **40** (with traces of J) [3]. **41**, 1–45 (with traces of J) [3]. 47–57. **42**, 1–37. **45**, 1–**46**, 5 (with traces of J) [3]. 12. **48**, 1–2. 8–22 (in the main) [3]. **50**, 15–26.

The Home of E.

The generally accepted opinion of critics is, that the author of E was a native of the northern kingdom, an Ephraimite. The reason for this opinion is based on the following facts. The narrative bears a distinct Ephraimitic tinge. Joseph is the king among his brethren, and his father's favourite. Reuben, next to Joseph, is leader of his brethren, and not Judah. The sanctuaries of Bethel, Shechem, and Beersheba,

[1] For a full discussion of E, cf. Holz., l. c., p. 181 ff. See also Driver, *Introd.*, p. 111 f.

[2] Cf. Holz., l.c., Table I. p. 2, for the views of the different critics, Driver, *Introd.*, p. 14.

[3] Cf. Holz., l.c., Table I. pp. 4, 5; Driver, *Introd.*, p. 15 f.

as a place whither pilgrims journeyed, are especially prominent in E. Abraham also lives at Gerar and Beersheba, Jacob at Beersheba and Shechem. Ephraim is to receive the promises and privileges of Joseph. Joshua, the Ephraimite, is the servant and companion of Moses. The graves of Deborah, Rachel, Joseph, Joshua, Eliezer are mentioned by him as being in Ephraimite territory; Gen. 35, 8. 19 f. Josh. 24, 30. 32. 33[1].

Did J and E employ earlier sources in writing their narratives?

It is not impossible that J and E in composing their narratives made use of other sources. In E we find two of these quoted: the *Book of the Wars of Jehovah*, סֵפֶר מִלְחֲמֹת יי״, Num. 21, 14: and the *Book of Jashar*, סֵפֶר הַיָּשָׁר, Josh. 10, 12 f. 2 Sam. 1, 18 (David's lament over Saul's death), and an extract is quoted from each. The first of these two books was apparently a collection of songs, celebrating the victories of Israel over their enemies. The second was probably of a similar character: a collection of songs in praise of the noble deeds of the heroes of Israel[2]. At what date the collection was formed is quite uncertain[3]. We also

[1] Cf. Driver, *Introd.*, p. 115; Holz., l. c., p. 212 f.; Corn., l. c., p. 47 f.; Kuenen, *Hex.*, p. 228 f.

[2] What the name יָשָׁר means is uncertain. It has been variously rendered *Book of the Upright, Book of the Worshippers of Yahweh and their deeds.* Kuenen offers two interpretations, *The book of that which is right* (in Yahweh's sight), or *of him who is right* (in Yahweh's sight). Cf. *Hex.*, p. 35; Holz., l.c., p. 228.

[3] Reuss, Di., Kittel assign both books to the period of David or Solomon. Wellhausen thinks the ספר מלח״ contained an account of the Exodus, the Wandering in the Wilderness, and the Conquest of Canaan. Kuenen, Meyer, and Stade consider that both works were completed at a much later date; cf. Holz., l. c. Driver, *Introd.*, p. 114, calls attention to the fact that the Book of Jashar 'at least was not completed before the time of David' (cf. 1 Sam. 1, 18), 'though the nucleus of the collection may obviously have been formed earlier.'

have no information as to the contents or authors of the books. Other quotations in E are the poems or fragments: Ex. 15 (*The Song of Moses*), Num. 21, 17–18 (*The Song of the Well*), and vers. 27–30 (*The Song of triumph over the defeat of Sihon*). Possibly, these were contained in one of the two sources, and not improbably Judg. chap. 5 (*The Song of Deborah*). Other poetical passages are: (J) Gen. chap. 49[1]; Balaam's '*Parables*' in Num. 23, 7–10. 18–24. 24, 3–9. 15–24; *The Song of Moses*, Deut. 32, and *The Blessing of Moses*, Deut. 33. From what sources these extracts were derived it is impossible to ascertain[2]. It is also pointed out by Driver[3] that the command in Ex. 17, 14 'to write "in a book" the threat to extirpate Amalek, makes it probable that some written statement existed of the combat of Israel with Amalek, and of the oath sworn then by Jehovah to exterminate His people's foes.' The Ten Commandments in Ex. 20 must have existed in a written form before E incorporated them into his work, and the ordinances and precepts upon which the '*Greater Book of the Covenant*,' Ex. 20, 22–chap. 23 E, and the '*Little Book of the Covenant*,' Ex. 34, 11–26 J, are based[4], doubtless existed in a written shape before they were worked up into the narratives of E and J respectively. 'The existence of written laws c. 750 B.C. is implied by Hos. 8, 12[5].' Lastly, one other extract may be mentioned, Gen. chap. 14, a fragment usually assigned to R, of uncertain date, and of doubtful origin[6].

---

[1] For the analysis of Gen. chap. 49, cf. Holz., l.c., Table I. p. 5.

[2] Cf., for a full discussion, Holz., l.c., p. 230 f., and Cornill, l.c., p. 88 f.

[3] *Introd.*, p. 115.

[4] Cf. Holz., p. 242.

[5] Driver, *Introd.*, p. 115.

[6] Cf. Cornill, l.c., p. 72; Kuenen, *Hex.*, pp. 143, 324; Well., *Comp.*, pp. 26, 310.

The Document P.

P chiefly contains legislation, setting before us the various precepts and ordinances that were to be observed by Israel, and explaining their origin. The history contained in it is merely the framework in which to arrange the legislative matter. The thread of the narrative is very thin, and often only serves to carry on the chronology. Important events, however, are treated more in detail (e.g. the story of the creation, the deluge, the covenants with Noah and Abraham, the migration of the patriarchs into Egypt), especially such events as are narrated to explain the origin of various laws (e.g. 17, 23. 48, 3–8), in which case the narrative is generally full and detailed. Other events of less importance are only briefly described, partly in the form of genealogies (e.g. chap. 5. 11, 10 ff. 35, 22 ff.), and partly in the form of short summaries (e.g. chap. 10. 25, 12 ff. chap. 36). A strongly-marked characteristic of P is the careful and uniform attention he pays to chronology. In the whole period covered by his narrative the dates of the various events are stated in their proper chronological order (cf. the geneological tables, chaps. 5, 11, and 35), and even the month and day, in the case of important events, are duly stated (Gen. chaps. 7 f. and the History of Moses).

'The history advances along a well-defined line, marked by a gradually-diminishing length of human life, by the revelation of God under three distinct names, *Elohim*, *El Shaddai*, and *Jehovah*, by the blessing of Adam and its characteristic conditions, and by the subsequent covenants with Noah, Abraham, and Israel, each with its special "sign," the rainbow, the rite of circumcision, and the Sabbath (Gen. 9, 12 f. 17, 11. Ex. 31, 13)[1].' In the legal portions of P

[1] Driver, *Introd.*, p. 119; cf. Di., *N. D. J.*, p. 649.

a description is given of the development of the theocracy which is evidently intended to serve as a model. God is described as the Lord and Protector of Israel, whom they must serve and obey. A full and detailed account is given of the Tabernacle, and its services, of the Priests, and of the duties and obligations of the people towards God. The organisation of the people is minutely described, the division into Tribes, and these again divided into Families, each with the firstborn as Leader (Gen. 35, 23. 46, 8. 49, 28, etc.), and the welding together of these separate units into one organised community (עדה), which was the final court of appeal in all matters relating to the people (Num. 35, 24 f.).

The representations of the Deity in P are not so anthropomorphic as those in J and E. Angels and visions in dreams are nowhere mentioned. 'Certainly he speaks of God as "appearing" to men, and as "going up" from them (Gen. 17, 1. 22 f. 35, 9. 13. 48, 3. Ex. 6, 3), at important moments of history, but he gives no further description of His appearance: usually the revelation of God to men takes with him the form of simple *speaking* to them (Gen. 1, 29. 6, 13. 7, 1. 8, 15. 9, 1. Ex. 6, 2. 13 *al.*); only in the supreme revelation on Sinai (Ex. 24, 16 f., cf. 34, 29 b), and when he is in the Tent of Meeting (Ex. 40, 34 f.), does he describe Him as manifesting Himself in a form of light and fire (כבוד *glory*), and as speaking there with Moses (Num. 7, 89. Ex. 25, 22), as man to man, or in order that the people may recognise Him (Ex. 16, 10. Lev. 9, 6. 23 f. Num. 14, 10. 16, 19. 42. 20, 6). Wrath also proceeds from Him (Num. 16, 46), or destroying fire and death (Lev. 10, 2. Num. 14, 37. 16, 35. 45 f. 25, 8 f.). But anthropopathic expressions of God he avoids scrupulously; even anthropomorphic expressions are rare (Gen. 2, 2 f., cf. Ex. 31, 17 b), so that a purpose is here unmistakable. It may be that as a priest he was accustomed to think and speak of God more strictly and circumspectly than other writers, even those who were prophets. On the other hand, he nowhere touches on the deeper problems of theology. On such subjects as the justice of the Divine government of the world, the origin of sin and evil, the insufficiency of human righteousness (see, on the contrary, Gen. 5, 24. 6, 9), he does not pause to reflect; the free Divine choice, though not unknown to him (Num. 3, 12 f. 8, 16. 17, 5 ff. 18, 6), is at least not so designedly opposed to human claims as in J. His work contains no Messianic outlook into the future: his ideal lies in the theocracy as he conceives it realized by Moses and Joshua[1].

In his method of representation P is stereotyped, detailed, and circumstantial. He everywhere aims at strict accuracy, especially in all legal matters, and exhibits a marked fondness for recurrent formulae. His language is formal and precise; technical words and phrases, and certain turns of expression not found elsewhere, frequently recur. The manner in which the author handles his materials gives evidence of research and reflection, and a capacity for justly weighing and estimating the sources of information at his disposal (e.g. chaps. 1. 5. 10 f. 36. 46), while in describing the events of the past, and in accounts of foreign peoples, remarkable accuracy is displayed (e.g. 25, 16. 36, 15). Some of the peculiarities of the language of P may be noted.

The Language of P.

Proper Names in P.

P uses אלהים not יהוה, excepting in 17, 1. 21, 1 b, until Ex. 6, 2. God reveals Himself to the patriarchs Abraham, Isaac, and Jacob as אל שדי. He communicates the name יהוה first to Moses, and through him to the people, Ex. 6, 2 ff.,

[1] Di., *N. D. J.*, p. 653, as translated by Driver, *Introd.*, p. 121.

but in all the passages in P in Gen. when God appears to the patriarchs or they address Him, the name used is אל שׁדי, Gen. 17, 1. 28, 3. 35, 11. 48, 3. P speaks of God, before Ex. 6, 2 as אלהים, Gen. chap. 1, and in the story of the Flood, and uniformly throughout the book.

The people of Israel are always בני ישׂראל; Abraham, until 17, 5, is called אברם. P never used ישׂראל as a name for Jacob. The months are numbered, not named, Ex. 12, 2. 18. 40, 2. 17. Lev. 23, 5. Num. 9, 1. 5. 20, 1. Josh. 4, 19. The Hittites are always called in P בני חת, Gen. 23, 3. 5. 7. 10. 16. 25, 10. 27, 46 (בנות חת). 49, 32. J, E, and D use חתים, never בני חת, which only occurs in P. For the sing. P has חתי, Gen. 15, 20. 23, 10. 25, 9. 26, 34–36, 2. He also makes the Hittites into a Canaanitish tribe, when they were really settled in the district of Lebanon.

Special geographical names occur in P. ארץ is always prefixed to כנען, Gen. 11, 31. 12, 5. 16, 3. 23, 2, etc.; it is only omitted in the phrase בנות כנען, Gen. 28, 1. 36, 2; and in the same way ארץ מצרים, Ex. 16, 1. 3. 6. 19, 1. Num. 3, 13. 8, 17.

The following geographical names are characteristic of P:—

קרית ארבע for Hebron, Gen. 23, 2. 35, 27. Josh. 15, 13. 20, 7, etc.

מכפלה, Gen. 23, 9. 17. 19. 25, 9, etc.

פדן ארם, Gen. 25, 20. 28, 2. 5. 6. 7. 31, 18. 33, 18. 46, 15.

מדבר צן, Num. 13, 21. 20, 1a. 27, 14. Deut. 32, 51. Josh. 15, 1. In Num. 34, 4. Josh. 15, 3 צן alone.

ערבות מואב, Num. 22, 1. 26, 3. 63. 31, 12. 35, 1, etc.

The Mount of the Lawgiving is always סיני. Moses died on Mt. נבו, Num. 32, 38. Deut. 32, 49, Aaron on Mt. הור, Num. 20, 22 f.

Words and Phrases characteristic of P.

אזרח and א׳׳ הארץ, Ex. 12, 19. Lev. 16, 29. 17, 15. 18, 26, etc.

נאחז, Gen. 34, 10. 47, 27. Num. 32, 30. Josh. 22, 9. 19.

אחזה, Gen. 17, 8. 23, 4. 36, 43. 47, 11. 49, 30, etc.

לאכלה, Gen. 1, 29 f. 6, 21. Ex. 16, 15. Lev. 11, 39, etc.

אמות, as special name for an Arab tribe or family, Gen. 25, 16. Num. 25, 15 (all).

אני, 130 times in P; אנכי, once, Gen. 23, 4.

נאסף אל־עמיו, Gen. 25, 8. 17. 35, 29. 49, 29, Num. 20, 24, etc. In Num. 20, 26. 27, 13, without עמיו.

אשה, a technical term of the sacrificial lang., sixty times in P.

אתו and עמו, pleonastic in enumerations, Gen. 6, 18. 7, 7. 13. 8, 16. 18. 9, 8. 28, 4.

ב, in enumerations, Gen. 7, 21. 8, 17. 9, 10. 10, 5. Ex. 12, 19. Lev. 17, 15, etc.

בית אבות, Ex. 6, 14. 12, 3. Num. chaps. 1–4; also ראשי א׳׳ with בית omitted, Ex. 6, 25. Num. 31, 26. 32, 28, etc.

בן שנה, Gen. 5, 32. 7, 6, etc., and בן שנתו, Lev. 12, 6. 23, 12. Num. 6, 12. 14.

ברא '*to create*,' Gen. chap. 1 often, 2, 3. 4. 5, 2.

ברית, in the phrases הקים ברית and נתן ברית, Gen. 6, 18. 9, 9. 17, 2. Ex. 6, 4. Num. 25, 12.

כל־בשר, Gen. 6, 12 f. 7, 15 f. 8, 17. 9, 11. 15–17.

גוע, Gen. 6, 17. 7, 21. 25, 8. 35, 29. Num. 17, 27, etc.

גלגלת, in enumerations, Ex. 16, 16. Num. 1, 2. 18. 20. 3, 47.

דבה, Gen. 37, 2. Num. 13, 32. 14, 36.

דגל, Num. 1, 52. chap. 2. 10, 14. 18. 22. 25; also Cant. 2, 4.

די, Ex. 36, 5. 7. Lev. 5, 7. 12, 8, etc.

דמות, Gen. 1, 26. 5, 1. 3 (all).

דורות, Gen. 6, 9. 9, 12; in formulae לדורותם or לדורותיכם, Gen. 17, 7. 9. 12. Ex. 12, 14. 17. 16, 32 f. 27, 21. 30, 10.

זָכַר, of God remembering the covenant with the Patriarch, Gen. 8, 1. 19, 29. Ex. 2, 24. 6, 5.

זָכָר, Gen. 17, 10. 12. 23. 34, 15. 22. Ex. 12, 5. 48, and in זכר ונקבה, Gen. 1, 27. 5, 2. 6, 19. 7, 3, etc.

זרע, in phrases like אתה וזרעך אחריך, Gen. 9, 9. 17, 7. 35, 12. 48, 4, and וכל־זרעו אתו, 46, 6; ולזרעו אחריו, Ex. 28, 43. Num. 25, 13.

זרק, frequent in P, Ex. 9, 10. 29, 16. Lev. 1, 5. 11. 3, 2. 7, 2, etc.

חוץ, in the phrases מבית ומחוץ, Gen. 6, 14. Ex. 25, 11, and מחוץ ל, Lev. 10, 4. 24, 3, etc.

חיה, Gen. 7, 21. 8, 1. Lev. 5, 2, etc. = '*wild beasts*,' as opp. to בהמה '*tame beasts*,' also used in P in the ordinary sense '*beast*,' Gen. 1, 28. 8, 17. 9, 5. Lev. 11, 27, etc.; חית הארץ, Gen. 1, 24. 25. 30. 9, 2, only found in P in Genesis.

ביד פ״ with צוה, Ex. 35, 29. Lev. 8, 36; with פקד, Num. 4, 49; with דבר, Lev. 10, 11. Num. 17, 5; with נתן תורה, Lev. 26, 46, and in the formula על־פי יי״ ביד פ״, Num. 4, 37. 9, 23. 10, 13. Josh. 22, 9.

התודה, '*confess*,' Lev. 5, 5. 16, 21. 26, 40. Num. 5, 7.

הוליד = ילד, Gen. 5, 3–32 and often.

כבוד יהוה = generally in P, '*the presence of God manifest to the whole people*,' Ex. 16, 10. 24, 17. 29, 43. Lev. 9, 6, etc.

כבש '*to subdue*,' Gen. 1, 28. Num. 32, 22. 29. Josh. 18, 1 (all).

כהן = '*to perform the duties of a priest*,' only in P, occurs frequently; also כהנה = '*priesthood*' is only found in P, Ex. 29, 9. 40, 15. Num. 3, 10. 18, 1, etc.

כל, frequently in P, with ל, a generalizing formula, Gen. 9, 10 b. 23, 10 b. Ex. 14, 28. Lev. 5, 3. 11, 26. 16, 16. Num. 4, 27.

כסס, מכס, and מכסה, Ex. 12, 4. Lev. 27, 23. Num. 31, 28. 37–41 (all).

כפורים, only in P in O.T., Ex. 29, 36. 30, 10. 16. Lev. 23, 27. 28. 25, 9. Num. 5, 8. 29, 11 (all).

כרת, in the phrase (מישׂראל) נכרתה הנפש ההיא מעמיה, only in P, Gen. 17, 14. Ex. 12, 15. Lev. 7, 20. 21. 18, 29. Num. 9, 13, etc.; cf. ונכרת מעמיו, Ex. 30, 33. 38, ונכרת האיש ההוא מקרב עמו, Lev. 17, 4–9, and (=הנפשׁ) והכרתי אתה מקרב עמה, Lev. 17, 10. 20, 3. 5. 6.

לון = '*to murmur*,' only in P, Hif'., Ex. 16, 2. Num. 14, 27, etc.; in Nif'., Ex. 15, 24. Num. 14, 2, etc.

מאד מאד, and with ב, Gen. 7, 19. 17, 2. Ex. 1, 7. Num. 14, 7.

המגפה, with ותעצר, Num. 17, 13. 15. מגפה occurs elsewhere in P, Num. 14, 37. 17, 14. 25, 9. 19.

מגורים, only in P, Gen. 17, 8. 28, 4. 36, 7. 47, 9. Ex. 6, 4.

מגרשׁ, only in P, Lev. 25, 34. Num. 35, 2–5. 7.

מול, in the phrase המול לפ״ כל־זכר, Gen. 17, 10. 12. 34, 15. 22. Ex. 12, 48.

מושׁב, in the phrase בכל־מושׁבותיכם, Ex. 12, 20. 35, 3. Lev. 3, 17. Num. 35, 29; cf. Gen. 36, 43.

מטה (rarely שׁבט), Ex. 31, 2. 6. 35, 30. 34. Lev. 24, 11. Num. 1, 4. 21. 23, etc.

מין, frequent in Gen. chaps. 1. 6. 7. Lev. chap. 11.

מלאכה, in the phrase עשׂה מ״ '*to work*,' frequently with לא= '*to keep holiday*,' Ex. 12, 16. 31, 5. Lev. 7, 24. Num. 4, 3. 29, 7; and in מלאכת עבודה, Ex. 35, 24. 36, 1. Lev. 23, 7 f. Num. 28, 18, etc.

מָעַל '*to trespass*,' and מַעַל, Lev. 5, 15. 21. 26, 40. Num. 5, 6. 31, 16. Deut. 32, 51. Josh. 7, 1, etc.

ומעלה, with ages (20 years and upwards), Ex. 30, 14. 38, 26. Lev. 27, 7. Num. 1, 20, etc.

מקוה, Gen. 1, 10. Ex. 7, 19. Lev. 11, 36.

מקלט, Num. 35, 6. 11–15. 25–28. Josh. 20, 2. 21, 13. 32. 36.

מקנה, Gen. 17, 12 f. 23, 18. Lev. 25, 16, etc.; also מקנת כסף, Ex. 12, 44. Lev. 25, 51.

מקרא קדשׁ, Ex. 12, 16. Lev. 23, 2–4. Num. 28, 25, etc.; only in Hex. in P.

המשׁכן = '*the Tabernacle*,' and מ״ יי״ and similar additions, very common in Ex., Lev., and Num.

משמרת, with two meanings in P, (1) Ex. 12, 6. 16, 23. Num. 17, 25, etc. = '*to keep a thing*,' in the place of an inf.; (2) = '*what is to be observed*,' '*the commandment*,' with special reference to the service of the Levites, and often occurring in the phrase שמר מ״, Lev. 8, 35. Num. 1, 53, chap. 3. 4, 27, and often.

למשפחותיהם, and with other suffixes, Gen. 8, 19. 10, 5. 20. 31. Ex. 6, 17. 25, and elsewhere with extreme frequency.

נֶגֶף, Ex. 12, 13. 30, 12. Num. 8, 19. 17, 11 f., etc.

נחל without obj., very common in P, Num. 18, 20. 26, 55. 32, 19; the Hithpa'el, Lev. 25, 46. Num. 32, 18, etc.; and the Pi'el, Josh. 13, 32. 14, 1 are peculiar to P.

הניף, a technical term in the language of the sacrifice, Ex. 29, 24. 26. Lev. 7, 30. 8, 27. 29, etc.

נכח without ל (J E always לנכח), Ex. 14, 2. 26, 35. Josh. 15, 7; cf. אל נכח, Num. 19, 4 = motion towards.

בן־נכר, Gen. 17, 12. 27. Ex. 12, 43. Lev. 22, 25.

נפש = '*person*,' when the number of a family is stated, also = *slaves*, as opposed to other property, and in the phrases מכה נ״ and נכרתה הנ״ ההיא. All these uses of נפש are extremely common in P.

נקבה, alone, Lev. 4, 28. 32. 5, 6. Num. 31, 15. זכר ונ״, see זכר above.

נשיאים = זקני ישראל, in E, Gen. 17, 20. 25, 16. 34, 2. Ex. 16, 22. 34, 31. Num. 1, 16, etc. Synonyms are קריאי העדה and קראי מועד, Num. 1, 16. 16, 2.

השיג, in the phrase השיג יד פ״ '*to stretch out one's hand towards something*,' so '*to pay for anything*,' or '*be able to procure anything;*' without obj., Lev. 14, 21. 25, 26. 27, 8, etc.; with ל, Lev. 5, 11; with acc., 14, 22. 30–32, once again Ez. 46, 7.

נתן לגוי, Gen. 17, 20; cf. 48, 4.

סמים, in O.T., only in P, Ex. 25, 6. 30, 7. 31, 11. 35, 8. 39, 38, etc., and in Chronicles.

סמך יד, technical term of language of sacrifice, Ex. 29, 10. 15. 19. Lev. 1, 4, chaps. 3. 4. 8.

עדה, כל־העדה, כל־עדת ישׂראל, cf. עדת יהוה, Num. 27, 17, about 100 times in the Hex.

העדות = '*the tables of the law*,' P, Ex. 25, 16. 21. 27, 21. 30, 6, etc.; so ארון העדות, אהל העדות, מִשׁכּן הע״, all peculiar to P.

עדף, Ex. 16, 18. 23. 26, 12. Lev. 25, 27. Num. 3, 46–49.

עולם combined with ברית, Gen. 9, 16. 17, 7. Ex. 31, 16. Lev. 24, 8, etc.; with ברית מלח, Num. 18, 19; with חק, Ex. 29, 28. 30, 21. Lev. 6, 11. 7, 34, etc.; חקת, Ex. 12, 14. 17. 27, 21. Lev. 3, 17. 7, 36, etc.; אחזת, Gen. 17, 8. Lev. 25, 24; כהנת, Ex. 40, 15. Num. 25, 13; and with גאלת, Lev. 25, 32.

ערי הככר, Gen. 13, 12. 19, 29.

הערים וחצריהן, Josh. 13, 28. 15, 32. 18, 24. 19, 6.

על = '*in addition to*,' '*together with*,' frequent in sacrificial rules, Lev. 2, 16. 3, 4. 4, 9, etc.

עמי פ״ = '*kinsfolk*,' see on אסף and כרת, Gen. 17, 14. 25, 8. 17. 35, 29. Ex. 30, 33. Lev. 7, 20. 21, etc.

לעמת, Ex. 25, 27. 28, 27. 38, 18. Lev. 3, 9.

עִנָּה נפשׁ, Lev. 16, 29. 31. 23, 27. 32. Num. 29, 7. 30, 14.

עצם = the phrase עצם היום הזה, Gen. 7, 13. 17, 23. 26. Ex. 12, 17. Lev. 23, 14. 21. 28.

בין הערבים, Ex. 12, 6. 16, 12. 29, 39. 41. 30, 8. Lev. 23, 5. Num. 9, 3. 5. 11. 28, 4. 8 (all).

ערך = (1) '*preparation*,' '*setting in order*,' Ex. 40, 4. 23; = (2) '*estimation*,' '*value*,' Lev. 5, 15. 18. 25. 27, 2. 3–8, etc. Num. 18, 16.

עשׂרון, Ex. 29, 40. Lev. 14, 10. 21. 23, 13. 17. Num. 15, 4, etc.

לפי, frequent, Ex. 12, 4. 16, 16. Lev. 25, 16. 51, etc. כפי, only in P, Ex. 16, 21. Lev. 25, 52. Num. 6, 21. 35, 8; both = '*according to*,' על־פי in P = '*according to command of*,' Ex. 17, 1. Lev. 24, 12. Num. chaps. 3. 4. 9, etc.

פטר רחם occurs in the Decalogue in Ex. 34, 19. P has the longer formula בכל בכר פטר רחם, Ex. 13, 2. Num. 3, 12.

פלא, in the phrases פַּלֵּא נדר, Lev. 22, 21. Num. 15, 3. 8, and הפליא נ״, Lev. 27, 2. Num. 6, 2.

פרה ורבה, Gen. 12, 2. 28. 8, 17. 9, 1. 7. 17, 20, etc.

פרך, Ex. 1, 13 f. Lev. 25, 43. 46, 53, once in Ez. 34, 4 (all).

צבאות, of Israelites, not in a military sense, Ex. 6, 26. 7, 4. 12, 17. Num. 1, 3. 52. chaps. 33, 1. 2. and 10. 33, 1.

צרוע, for the usual מצרע, Lev. 13, 44 f. 14, 3. 22, 4. Num. 5, 2.

קדש הקדשים, technical term, = *the most holy place in the Tabernacle*, Ex. 26, 33 f. Num. 4, 4. 19; = *the incense altar*, Ex. 30, 10; = *the altar of burnt offering*, Ex. 29, 37. 40, 10; = *the utensils of the Tabernacle in general*, Ex. 30, 29; = *the Tabernacle as a whole*, Num. 18, 10; = *the definite portions of the sacrifices*, Lev. 21, 22. Occurs 25 times.

קנין, Gen. 31, 18. 34, 23. 36, 6. Lev. 22, 11. Josh. 14, 4.

קצף, Num. 1, 53. 17, 11. 18, 5. Josh. 9, 20. 22, 20.

קרבן, about 78 times in Hex., only in P.

רגם, Lev. 20, 2. 27. 24, 14. 16. 23. Num. 14, 10. 15, 35. 36. Josh. 7, 25. JE and D use סָקַל instead.

ריח ניחוח, once in J, Gen. 8, 21, elsewhere only in P. About 40 times, see Lev. chaps. 1. 2. 3.

רכוש, Gen. 12, 5. 13, 6. 31, 8. 36, 7, etc. רכש den. verb, Gen. 31, 18. 36, 6.

רֶמֶשׂ and רָמַשׂ, frequent in P, Gen. chaps. 1. 6. 7. 8. 9, etc.

שבתון, Ex. 16, 23. 31, 15. 35, 2. Lev. 16, 31, etc.

שגגה, Lev. 4, 2. 22. 27. 5, 15. 18. Num. 15, 24–29, etc.

שער, in the phrases כל-באי שער העיר and כל-יצאי ש״ הע״, Gen. 23, 10. 18. 34, 24 (all).

שפחה, Gen. 16, 1. 29. 24, 29. Lev. 19, 20.

שפטים, Ex. 6, 6. 7, 4. 12, 12. Num. 33, 4.

שָׁרַץ, Gen. 1, 20. 21. 7, 21. 8, 17. 9, 7. Ex. 1, 7, etc.

שֶׁרֶץ, Gen. 1, 20. 7, 21. Lev. 5, 2, and chap. 11.

תולדות, 27 times in P, and nowhere else in Hex. It occurs 9 times in formula אלה תו״, Gen. 2, 4 a. 5, 1, etc. In Num. chap. 1 it is found 12 times.

תור '*to spy*,' Num. chaps. 13 and 14. In JE and D תור '*to select* or *seek out*,' Num. 10, 33. Deut. 1, 33.

תושב, Gen. 23, 4. Ex. 12, 45. Lev. 22, 10. 25, 6. 23. 35. 40. 45. 47. Num. 35, 15.

תרומה, Ex. 25, 2. 29, 28. 30, 13, etc. About 40 times in Hex.

Instances of recurring Formulae.

When Divine commands are communicated to Moses or Joshua, it is narrated that '*God spake to Moses*' (or *to Moses and Aaron*, or *to Joshua*): דבר אל בני ישראל, or דבר אל־אהרן ואל־בניו, or דבר אל־פרעה מלך מצרים, and the like. Examples of the first formula occur in Ex. 14, 2. 15. 31, 13. Lev. 1, 2. 4, 2. 18, 2. Num. 5, 6. 12, etc., and the same formula with different persons, Ex. 6, 11. 29. 11, 2. Lev. 6, 18. 16, 2. Num. 6, 23, etc. The formula זה הדבר אשר צוה יהוה is frequently employed by Moses when he communicates to the people the Divine commands, see Ex. 16, 16. 32. 35, 4. Lev. 8, 5. 9, 6. 17, 2. Num. 30, 2. 36, 6.

P, in introducing the various Laws, uses two types of conditional sentence. When he states the law generally, without going into details, or without any reference to special cases, he uses a conditional sentence introduced by כי. This sentence is a compound nominal sentence, which always begins with איש (אשה) כי, or נפש כי, cf. Lev. 2, 1. 4, 2. 5, 1. 4. 15. 17. 21. Num. 5, 12. 9, 10. 27, 8. 30, 4, also נפש אשר, Lev. 5, 1 and איש אשר, Num. 5, 30. When he introduces any special cases of any law, or when he wishes to insert modifications of the law described, or to supplement it, he makes use of a conditional sentence which is a verbal sentence of the type, conjunction, verb, subject or sometimes conjunction, subject, verb. The conjunctions used are אם and ואם, cf. Lev. 4, 3. 13. 27. 5, 7. 11. 17. Num. 27, 9. 10. 11. 30, 6. 7. 9, etc.; אשׁר, Lev. 4, 22: כי and וכי, Lev. 2, 4. 13, 42. 14, 34. 15, 13. 25.

P, when stating that a Divine command has been performed by the person or persons concerned, frequently uses such formulae as ויעשׂ (ויעשׂו) ככל־אשׁר (כאשׁר) צוה אתו (אתם) יהוה כן עשׂה (עשׂו), Gen. 6, 22. Ex. 7, 6. 12, 28. 50. 25, 9. Lev. 4, 20. Num. 1, 54. 2, 34. 5, 4. 6, 21. 8, 20, etc.

The constantly recurring superscriptions and subscriptions beginning with אלה, זה, זאת are also characteristic of P:—

אלה תולדות, Gen. 2, 4a. 6, 9, etc.

אלה אלופי פ״, Gen. 36, 19. 43.

אלה (הם) בני פ״, Gen. 10, 20. 31. 25, 16. 36, 19. 20.

אלה המלכים, Gen. 36, 31.

אלה מסעי וגו״, Num. 33, 1.

אלה משׁפחת (בני) פ״, Gen. 10, 32. Ex. 6, 19.

אלה הנחלות, Josh. 19, 51.

אלה הפקדים, Num. 1, 44.

אלה פקדי משׁפחת פ״, Num. 4, 37. 41. 45.

אלה ראשׁי (בית) אבות פ״, Ex. 6, 14. 25b.

אלה שׁמות פ״, Gen. 25, 13. 16. 46, 8. Ex. 1, 1. 6, 16. Num. 1, 5, etc.

אלה שׁני חיי פ״, Gen. 25, 17; also

אלה אשׁר, Josh. 13, 32. 14, 1.

To these may be added:—

זה גבול, Josh. 15, 12.

זה קרבן פ״, Num. 7, 17. 23, etc.

זאת נחלת פ״, Josh. 13, 23. 28. 15, 20. 16, 8. 18, 20. 28, etc.

זאת עבדת משׁפחת בני וגו״, Num. 4, 28. 33.

The Grammar of P.

The Grammar is characterized by its simplicity and consistent adherence to rules. P, like D, occasionally uses fem. nouns for infinitives, cf. טהרה, Lev. 13, 7; קרבה, Lev. 16, 1; משמרת, Ex. 12, 6. 16, 23. 32. Num. 17, 25. 18, 8.

Syntax. P generally uses מאת instead of מאה. Even when מאה would be expected by rule, cf. Gen. 5, 3. 6. 18. 25. 28. 7, 24. 8, 3, and often. In compound numbers P rarely puts the smaller number after the larger, Gen. 17, 1. 24, as a rule the smaller number precedes, Gen. 5, 15. 17. 21.

Sometimes the substantive is without the article, while its qualifying adj. has it, so חיה הרמשׂת, Gen. 1, 28; יום הששי, 1, 31; יום השביעי, 2, 3.

P prefers the use of את with the suffixes to verbal suffixes. In Gen. chap. 1—Lev. chap. 6, את with suffix occurs 136 times, and the verbal suffix 73 times. In verbal constructions P exhibits no special peculiarities. In JE '*to walk before God*' is התהלך לפני יי" (J, Gen. 24, 40. 48, 15). P uses this construction in 17, 1, but elsewhere he has התהלך את־האלהים, Gen. 5, 22. 24. 6, 9. P uses אל and not ל or ב with שמע = '*to listen to any one*,' Gen. 23, 16. Ex. 7, 13. 22. 8, 15. 9, 12.

The Priests' Code in Genesis.

1, 1–**2**, 4 a. **5**, 1–28. 30–32. **6**, 9–22. **7**, 6. 7–9 (in parts). 11. 13–16a. 18–21. 24. **8**, 1–2 a. 3b–5. 13a. 14–19. **9**, 1–17. 28–29. **10**, 1–7. 20. 22–23. 31–32. **11**, 10–27. 31–32. **12**, 4b–5. **13**, 6. 11 b–12 a. **16**, 1 a. 3. 15–16. chap. **17**. **19**, 29. **21**, 1 b. 2 b–5. chap. **23**. **25**, 7–11 a. 12–17. 19–20. 26 b. **26**, 34–35. **27**, 46–**28**, 9. **29**, 24. 29. **31**, 18 b. **33**, 18 a. **34**[1], 1–2 a. 4. 6. 8–10. 13–18. 20–24. 25 (partly). 27–29.

[1] So Di. and Driver. Well., Kuenen, and Cornill assign none of chap. 34 to P; cf. Holz., *Hex.*, Table I. p. 4.

35, 9–13. 15. 22 b–29. chap. **36** (mainly)[1]. **37**, 1–2 a. **41**, 46. **46**, 6–27. **47**, 5–6 a (LXX). 7–11. 27 b–28. **48**, 3–6. 7 (if not P? R). **49**, 1 a. 28 b–33. **50**, 12–13[2].

How was Genesis compiled out of J, E, and P?

The following remarks may perhaps give a general idea of how Genesis arose out of the three documents, J, E, and P. It has been already remarked that a definite plan can be traced throughout the whole book. To put it as briefly as possible, the object of the book is to give an account of the history of Israel from the earliest times until the death of Joseph, to show how God created the world and mankind, preserved Noah from the deluge and made a covenant with him, chose Abram the descendant of Noah through Shem, and made a covenant with him, promising to him and his descendants the land of Canaan, and taking him under his especial protection, and imposing upon him the observance of several precepts. The history is carried on in the person of Isaac, to whom the promises made to Abraham are renewed; some account is given of Ishmael, who then disappears from the narrative, which employs itself with the fortunes of Jacob and Esau, the latter being dismissed after a short account of the relations between him and Jacob, and the course of the narrative confined to Jacob. We are next told of the birth of Jacob's sons and the sale of Joseph into Egypt, Joseph now becoming the prominent figure in the narrative. After some account of the journeys of Joseph's brethren into Egypt, and their meeting with Joseph who was regarded as dead, the history tells us of Jacob's migration

[1] Cf. Holz., l.c.

[2] Cf. Holz., l.c., p. 349 f. and pp. 332–475 for a full discussion of this document; see also Driver, *Introd.*, p. 118 f.

into Egypt, and finally relates Joseph's death, after he had removed his father's remains to Canaan and buried them in the Cave of Machpelah.

In compiling this history from the materials at his disposal the Redactor chose from his sources what was most suited to the plan of his work. Sometimes he merely makes small extracts from one document (e. g. 4, 17–24. 6, 1–4. 30, 32–42, merely small portions of fuller accounts), or notices individual points (e. g. 11, 29, Jiska mentioned; 20, 12, the relationship between Abram and Sarai, cf. 28, 22 (see 35, 7); 48, 22). At other times the portions taken from the documents are quoted in full, and for the most part are verbally transferred from the original (e. g. the narratives in P up to 11, 26), and sometimes again, whole passages from one document are omitted, possibly because they were at variance with the accounts given by the others (see in P the brief accounts in 11, 27–32; the omission of the introduction to the history of Abram, previous to chap. 12; of the Divine manifestation to Isaac, see 35, 12; of the sojourn of Jacob in Paddan Aram; of all the history of Joseph prior to Jacob's arrival in Egypt). Frequently extracts from J are given in an abridged form, in order that P may be reported more fully (cf. 2, 5 f. 4, 25 f., the Story of Creation, and the Table of Nations, J) and 16, 15 f. 21, 2 ff. 25, 7 ff. 32, 4. 35, 28 f. P. Elsewhere, however, in the story of the Patriarchs the extracts from J are abridged in favour of E. With the exception of the history of Joseph, E contains (from chap. 20 onwards) fewer passages which are verbally reported. Usually the portions in E are expanded by notices from J, or anything worth recording in E is incorporated into the narrative of J. When combining his sources the compiler, as far as possible, or as far as he deemed necessary, appears to have taken the narrative verbally from each and inserted both in his work (cf. chap. 2 f. side by side with chap. 1, chap. 27 side by side with 26, 34 f. and 28, 1–9; 48, 3–7 side by side with 48, 9–22). Elsewhere, as for example, where the event need only be quoted from one document (e.g. the birth or death of any person), he selects his account from one source, even though the same event be recorded in more than one document. In other cases the compiler found two accounts in the documents before him, agreeing in the main but differing in details, he would then weave one account into the other, omitting from each what could not be reconciled, and choosing from both what best suited the plan of his work (cf. chaps. 7 f. 10. 16. 25. 27–37. 39–50). It was not always possible, without further revision, to place side by side, or to weld together the individual extracts from two or three sources. So it was necessary to eliminate what was contradictory from one or other of the documents (e. g. 21, 17 ff. explanation of Ishmael's name, 32, 8 of Maḥanaim, 33, 10 of Peniel, cf. 31, 25), or to insert here and there small additions or remarks in order to fill up gaps and remove contradictions. So 4, 25. 10, 24. 21, 14. 26, 1 a. 15. 18. 35, 9, 37, 5b. 8b. 39, 1. 20. 43, 14. 46, 1. To the desire to produce a readable whole may be attributed the accommodation necessary to preserve consistency in the use of the names Abram and Sarai, in all passages previous to chap. 17, of the double name Yahweh Elohim in chaps. 2–3; also the change of Elohim into Yahweh in 17, 1. 21, 1. Another expedient was frequently employed with the same object in view, viz. transposing entire portions of the narrative (so 11, 1–9. 12, 10–20. 25, 5 f. 11 b. 25, 21 ff. 47, 12 ff.), or of brief notices (so 2, 4 a. 31, 45–50. 37, 26, etc.), consequently R was obliged to insert all kinds of small additions; cf. 1, 1. 9, 18. 13, 1. 3 f. 24, 62. In other passages the sources are loosely combined (e.g. 7, 7–9. 22. 15, 7 f. 31, 45 ff. chap. 36. 46, 8–27), the compiler now and then making additions of his own to bring the documents into harmony (e.g. 21, 34. 27, 46. 35, 5. 46, 12–20). Explanatory glosses are also found (e.g. 20, 18. 31, 47. 35, 6. and chap. 14 (where they are numerous), some of which may be due to a later corrector. All kinds of little additions occur, which are probably not derived from the sources themselves, but were inserted, either when the sources were welded together into one work, or some time after this. These insertions were added partly to explain the object of the narrative (15, 12–16. 22, 15–18. 26, 3 b–5); partly to make it harmonize with statements occurring elsewhere (25, 18 b. 35, 22 a, perhaps 4, 15 a), and partly to introduce new notices, or new phases of tradition which were not mentioned in the three chief documents (10, 9. 32, 33; perhaps 2, 10–14, and in 10, 14; 11, 28 b. 31 b. 15, 7. 22, 2, etc.). Sometimes possibly use was also made of materials taken from other sources than J, E, and P (e.g. perhaps in chap. 14)[1].

---

[1] Cf. Di.[6], p. xvi. For full details of the various works bearing on the criticism of the Pentateuch, see Driver, *Introd.*, p. 1 f., and cf. Di., *Gen.*[6], p. xx.

NOTES ON GENESIS.

1.

1. בראשית. '*In the beginning*,' as ἐν ἀρχῇ, in John 1, 1; not ἐν τῇ ἀρχῇ. בראשית is without the article, like בְּאָחוֹר, Prov. 29, 11; בְּיָד, Is. 28, 2; בְּקֶרִי, Lev. 26, 27.

The Vss. and most commentators render, '*In the beginning God created*,' etc.: the same rendering is perhaps indicated by the accents, בראשית being marked off by *Ṭifcha* from what follows[1]. If this rendering be adopted, בראשית must not be taken relatively, i.e. '*first of all*,' in opposition to a second or third, which might follow; for this is against the sense, as heaven and earth include all; and we should rather expect בָּרִאשֹׁנָה; but it must be taken absolutely, '*at first*' ('*uranfänglich*'): hence the choice of the expression בְּרֵאשִׁית, which does not occur elsewhere.

רֵאשִׁית = the beginning of a series, always relative to a genitive either expressed or (as here, Deut. 33, 21. Is. 46, 10) understood. As רֵאשִׁית everywhere else (except in these two passages) is followed by a genitive, Ewald, Bunsen, and others follow Rashi and Ibn Ezra, and render, '*At first, when*

[1] In 3, 1b and 5b. Deut. 28, 47b (מֵרֹב כֹּל׃). 61a (בְּסֵפֶר הַתּוֹרָה). Ex. 9, 24b (מֵאָז הָיְתָה לְגוֹי׃), we find *Ṭifcha*, the word so accented being closely connected in sense with the next following word. From these and similar passages it seems that the argument from the accents ought not to be pressed in this verse.

God created, etc. . . . (ver. 3) *then God said, Let there be light.*' A similar construction to Ex. 6, 28 בְּיוֹם דִּבֶּר יהוה, where יום in the construct state is followed by a sentence as its genitive; so in Gen. 39, 20a. Num. 3, 1. Deut. 4, 15. Hos. 1, 2. Ps. 90, 15, etc.; see Ewald, § 332 d; Dav., *S.*, § 25. ויאמר, in ver. 3, would then be the imperfect with waw conv. in answer to בראשית; cf. 19, 15 (כמו precedes). 27, 34 בִּשְׁמֹעַ עֵשָׂו . . . וַיִּצְעַק; Is. 6, 1 בִּשְׁנַת מוֹת הַמֶּלֶךְ . . . וָאֶרְאֶה; and see Ewald, § 344 b; Driver, § 127 β. (Boettcher (*Neue Aehr.* 1. 2–9) and others prefer to read בְּרֹא as in 5, 1, which would be the more common construction; but this is not necessary.) According to this interpretation verse 2 becomes a parenthesis, which is unnatural, as a long and heavy sentence at the beginning of the book would hardly be expected; cf. also Ryssel, *De Elohistae Pentateuchi sermone* (Lipsiae, 1878), p. 76. On the reading of the LXX, cf. Geiger, *Urschrift*, etc., pp. 344, 439, 444, who, following the tradition that this was one of the thirteen places that were altered for Ptolemy, considers that Rashi's construction was the traditional one, that of the LXX being an innovation.

ברא '*created*,' the common word in P in this connection, is restricted to the divine workmanship, and always implies the production of something new (in matter or form, as ver. 21), being used literally and metaphorically (e.g. Ps. 51, 12). It is never followed by an accusative of the material used, and thus implies the unconditioned operation (absolute causality) of the agent. Its original meaning is generally given as '*to cut*' (cf. the Pi'el in Josh. 17, 15. 18, and Ges. in *Thes.;* and C. P. Ges. *sub voce*), then '*to shape*,' '*form*,' and so '*create*,' but it does not in itself express the idea of creation out of nothing; cf. the Arabic خلق, prop. '*to smooth*,' '*polish*,' then '*to create*,' the word used by Saadiah here. In the Pi'el it is used of man, '*to cut with effort:*' contrast the intensive stem with Qal, the simple stem, used of the free-creating of God without any effort; cf. Ew., § 126 a. The Samaritan renders ברא by ࠀࠔࠋࠈ, which Del. explains as equivalent to ἐθεμελίωσε; see Heidenheim, *Bib. Sam.*, Heft i. p. 70, who mentions other explanations that have been suggested.

אֱלֹהִים, plural of אֱלוֹהַּ. The derivation of אלוה is disputed; see Appendix. אלהים *pluralis excellentiae*, with a singular verb; see Ges., § 124. 1 c; M. R., § 135. 2. So we find בְּעָלִים and אֲדֹנִים, used in a similar way, of human superiors; and in Is. 19, 4 אדנים קשה, singular and plural as here. אלהים is only joined with a plural verb in special cases; cf. the note on 20, 13, and Ewald, § 318 a; Dav., *S.*, § 116. R. 4.

את השמים. אֵת or אֶת־, the sign of the acc. when defined (Ges., § 117. 1; M. R., § 32; Dav., *S.*, § 72). It corresponds to the Phoenician אִיַת, which was probably the original form of את (a noun substantive from אוה; cf. Schröder, *Phoen. Gram.*, § 123); cf. the Arabic إِيَّا, Aramaic יָת, Syriac ܝܳܬ (found twelve times in the Pesh. O.T.). It is usually explained as = '*essence*,' or '*existence*,' but according to usage has so little emphasis, that it is merely inserted to mark the definite object; cf. Ges., *Thes.*, p. 169 a, where its etymology is discussed, Ges., l. c. 1, foot-note 3, and Ols., *Gramm.*, p. 432.

שמים, only occurs in the plural in Hebrew. The singular form would probably be שְׁמַי, cf. מַי, the assumed sing. of מַיִם, a trace of which perhaps survives in the pr. n. אֲחוּמַי, 1 Chr. 4, 2, and see Wright, *Comp. Gram.*, p. 150.

2. **תהו ובהו**. תֹּהוּ = '*wasteness*,' or '*bareness*.' Sometimes the word is used metaphorically, e. g. of idols, as vain, unrewarding, 1 Sam. 12, 21. Is. 44, 9. In Hebrew the root תהה is not found.

בֹּהוּ = '*emptiness*,' '*desolation*.' This word is always found in immediate or parallel connection with תֹּהוּ; it only occurs twice again, viz. Jer. 4, 23. Is. 34, 11 (possibly borrowed from this passage). A root בהה is not found in Hebrew. In Arabic we find بَهِيَ = '*vacua et inanis fuit*' domus.

תֹּהוּ = תָּהְוָ and בֹּהוּ = בָּהְוָ, like קֹדֶשׁ from קָדְשְׁ, are both segholates, from verbs ל״ה, properly ל״ו. On the segholates (so called from the helping vowel seghol, which replaces the shewa under the second consonant), see Ges., § 93; on תהו and בהו in particular, § 84 a, 1 b, and 93. Rem. 6; Stade, § 198 a; also Dav., §§ 29 and 45.

The ו before בהו has a pretonic qameç, joining together the two nouns, which are closely connected, so 2, 9. 8, 22 יום וָלילה; see Ges., § 104. 2. Rem. e; Dav., § 15 d; cf. especially Rem. with Ges., l. c.

רוח אלהים. '*The Spirit of God*,' the life-giving and life-preserving power (Pss. 33, 6. 104, 29), not a '*wind sent by God*,' as apparently Onqelos, וְרוּחָא מִן קֳדָם יְיָ, and others (e. g. Ephrem and Saadiah), for מרחפת does not suit this rendering, and the dividing of the waters in ver. 7, which separated the earth from the water, forbids us to think of a wind sent by God to dry up the earth.

מרחפת. The usual fem. form with the participle, cf. Ges., § 94. 1 and 2. Observe that this fem. form is accented, like the segholates, on the penult. The word occurs again in Deut. 32, 11, of an eagle brooding over its young. The original meaning of the root is '*to be loose*' or '*slack*,' and so '*to hover with loose wing*,' the figure here being that of a bird hovering over its young. The root is more widely used in Syriac, the Pa'el ܪܰܚܶܦ being equivalent to the Heb. root in Deut. l. c., which the Pesh. renders as here with ܡܪܰܚܦܳܐ; cf.

Bernstein, *Syr. Chrest.*, p. 173. 4, and *Lex.*, p. 480, the Syriac word having also the notion of fructifying and fertilizing. The Talmud, *Tract. Chag.*, c. 2, fol. 15, refers thus to this passage, כיונה מרחפת על בניה ואינה נוגעת '*as a dove hovering over its young without touching them;*' cf. also Matt. 3, 16, and the paraphrase of Milton, *Par. Lost*, Bk. 7, 235:—

> '*His brooding wings the Spirit of God outspread,*
> *And vital virtue infused, and vital warmth*
> *Throughout the fluid mass.*'

3. יְהִי, imperf. apoc. from יִהְיֶה, for יִהְיְ weakened from יַהְיְ (like פְּרִי from פְּרְיְ, weakened from פַּרְיְ, Ges., § 24, 1 b; so דְּמְכֶם thinned from דַּמְכֶם, see Ges., § 27. 3. Rem. 3 b), cf. Ges., § 75. Rem. 3 e and § 93. Rem. 6; Dav., § 45. On the thinning of ַ into ִ, see Wright, *Arab. Gram.*, i. § 90. Rem. ad fin.

וַֽיְהִי. The Grave Metheg (see Ges., § 16. 2. 2; Stade, § 54 c; cf. also Dav., § 10, foot-note) is not found with pathach followed by ְ except in וַֽיְחִי and וַֽיְהִי, *when they stand before Maqqeph, or with the accent Pashta.*

4. וַיַּרְא. Imperf. with waw conv. On the apocopated form יַרְא out of יִרְאֶה, see Ges., § 75. Rem. 3 c; Dav., § 45. The so-called waw conversive or consecutive is confined to the language of the ancient Hebrews and their neighbours the Moabites, whose language, as we now know, was so closely allied to their own. Besides the O. T. it occurs on the Siloam inscription, first deciphered by Prof. Sayce, and is frequent on the inscription of Mesha, commonly called the Moabite stone: it is also found in later Hebrew writings composed in imitation of Biblical Hebrew. If we remember that the tenses in Hebrew do not indicate the *date*, but the *state* of an action, i.e. whether it be *complete* or *incomplete*, the explanation of this peculiar Hebrew construction will

not be far to seek. The imperf. denotes an action as entering on completion. When we have a series of events, each single event need not necessarily be regarded as completed and independent, but each may be regarded as related to the preceding one, one event stepping into its place after the other, the date at which each successive event comes in being determined by the ו, which connects the new event with a point previously marked in the narrative. Thus here ברא, ver. 1, is the starting-point in the narrative, to which ויאמר first and then ויהי are related: and the narrative developes itself, each fresh event stepping into the place prepared for it by its predecessor. This construction begins to fall into disuse in later Hebrew. It should be remembered that an imperf. with waw conv. never refers to the future unless its preceding perfect to which it is related is the so-called prophetic perfect, which describes future events which are certain to take place as already accomplished, and so regarded as past, e.g. Is. 9, 5. See further, Driver, *Heb. Tenses*, c. vi, 3rd ed.; also Ges., §§ 49, 111; M. R., § 16 f.; Dav., *S.*, § 47 f. Ewald aptly terms this construction the *relatively-progressive imperfect.*

וירא . . . כי טוב. Hebrew says, '*And He saw the light, that it was good:*' English more tersely, '*He saw that the light was good;*' so 6, 2. 12, 14. 49, 15. See Ewald, § 336 a, 2; and cf. Ges., § 117. 1. Rem. 6; Dav., *S.*, § 146.

בין . . . בין, in ver. 6 בין . . . ל: the former scheme (בין . . . בין) is by far the most common, the latter (בין . . . ל) only occurs twice again in the Pentateuch, viz. Lev. 20, 25. 27, 33, being rare, and generally confined to late writers; cf. however 2 Sam. 19, 36 בין טוב לרע.

5. קָרא לילה, the tone is here thrown back to avoid the concurrence of two tone syllables; so 3, 19 תֹּאכַל לֶחֶם,

4, 17 בֹּנֶה עִיר, and often; see Ges., § 29. 3 b, and the note on 4, 17.

יום אחד. '*One day*,' so R. V., not as the A. V., '*the first day*.' אחד has not, strictly speaking, a corresponding ordinal, though it is possible to use ראשון as such. Here אחד may stand, as at the head of a series the ordinal is not needed; see Ewald, § 269 a. So 2, 11. 4, 19. 2 Sam. 4, 2.

6. וִיהִי for וְיִהְיֶה, by Ges., § 24. 1 a; Dav., § 15 d. Rem. Cf. also Ges., § 104. 2 d.

ויהי מבדיל. Render, '*and let it be* (permanently) *dividing*.' When any special stress is laid upon the continuance of the action, the participle with היה is used by the best writers, but is more frequently affected by later writers (e. g. 2 Kings 17 it occurs nine times), and is exceedingly common in the Mishna. As Driver, p. 170, points out, two cases of this use of היה are to be distinguished. Here and in Deut. 9, 7. 28, 29. Is. 30, 20, etc., the state described by the particip. and היה stands upon an independent footing. In the instances quoted in the note on 4, 17, the state thus described is regarded as implicitly related to another event. Cf. also Ges., § 116. 5. Rem. 2; M. R., § 14. 2 a; Dav., *S.*, § 100. R. 2; Ryssel, *De Elohistae Pentateuchi sermone*, p. 58. For the Mishna usage, see *Lehrb. der Neuhebräisch. Sprache*, § 96 b, by Strack and Siegfried.

בין מים לָמים. ל with pretonic qameç; so לָתֵת, לָשֶׁבֶת, לָבוֹא, etc.; cf. Ges., § 102. 2 c; Dav., § 14. 1 d.

רקיע from רקע, Qal = '*to strike*,' '*stamp*,' '*make firm*;' Pi'el, '*to spread out by striking*:' according to LXX, Aq., Symm., Theod. στερέωμα, Vulg. '*firmamentum*.'

7. וַיַּעַשׂ. The form is (1) יַעֲשֶׂה, then (2) by apocopation יַעַשׂ like a segholate, e. g. נַעַר, then (3) with a helping vowel

(here pathach on account of the guttural ע) יַעַשׂ (like נַעַר), the ע preserving the original pathach with the prefix י, as in the Arabic; cf. يَقْتُلُ (the regular form = the Heb. יִקְטֹל), see Wright, *Arab. Gram.*, i. p. 62: cf. further, Ges., § 75. Rem. 3 d; Dav., § 45; Driver, p. 52, foot-note 1.

7^b^. At the end of ver. 6 the LXX read καὶ ἐγένετο οὕτως instead of at the end of ver. 7, which suits ver. 6^b^ better than ver. 7^b^; as elsewhere, e. g. vers. 9. 11. 15. 24. 30, ויהי כן immediately follows what God says. Possibly it has been misplaced in the Mass. text, and the LXX preserve it in the original position.

8^a^. שׁמים. After this word the LXX have in their text καὶ ἴδεν ὁ Θεὸς ὅτι καλόν, which is wanting in the Mass. text, but would be expected here (as in vers. 3. 10) at the end of the second day's work. In the account of the third day's work it occurs twice, in LXX and Mass. text, ver. 10 and ver. 12. Possibly the addition in the LXX text is, as Frankel, *Einfluss*, p. 60, points out, due to a reviser who wished to make 8^a^ parallel with 3. 10. 12. The Mass. text again may have omitted the formula of divine approval here, as the complete division of the waters was not made until the third day.

9. ותראה, jussive, although the shortened form is not used; cf. 41, 34. Ruth 1, 8 Ktb. Job 3, 9. In the regular verb, with the exception of the Hif'il stem, the ordinary imperfect must serve as jussive, there being only one form for both tenses; see Ges., § 48, especially 2 and 4; Dav., § 23. On the syntax of the jussive, see Driver, c. iv; Ges., § 109; M. R., § 8; Dav., *S.*, § 61 f.

11. דשׁא = '*grass*' or '*grasslike plants*,' the first verdure that covered the earth young and fresh, appearing after rain,

2 Sam. 23, 4. Job 38, 27, or after the old grass had gone, Prov. 27, 25.

עֵשֶׂב. A wider term including herbs useful for men, Ps. 104, 14. Gen. 3, 18.

תַּֽדְשֵׁא (the metheg under תַּ is inserted to secure the proper pronunciation of ד before שׁ) is Hif'il denominative from דֶּשֶׁא = '*to make* or *produce*' דשא; so מָטָר '*rain*,' הִמְטִיר '*to make rain*,' שֹׁרֶשׁ '*a root*,' הִשְׁרִישׁ '*to send out roots*.' Hif'il the causative stem, expressing with denominatives the idea of producing or putting forth that of which the original noun is the name, Ges., § 53. 2. So מזריע זרע.

The construction of a verb with a cognate accusative is common in Hebrew, so in 27, 34 ויצעק צעקה, Zech. 1, 14 קנאתי . . . קנאה, and often; see Ges., § 117. 2, and Rem. a and b; M. R., § 36; Dav., *S.*, § 67 b and R. 2; the same construction occurs again in ver. 20.

Render, '*Let the earth bring forth young grass, herbs yielding seed*,' with the accents, עֵשֶׂב being in apposition to דשא; see Ges., § 131. 2 a; M. R., § 71. 2; Dav., *S.*, § 29 b; not as the LXX, βοτάνην χόρτου (also Aq. and Th.), Vulg. '*herbam virentem*,' connecting דשא in the cstr. state with עֵשֶׂב. But דשא is never used thus in the O. T., it may be preceded by יֶרֶק '*greenness*,' '*viror*,' 2 Kings 19, 26. Ps. 37, 2. Is. 37, 27, but cannot be followed by עֵשֶׂב as genitive.

עֵץ פְּרִי '*fruit trees*,' עֵץ being used collectively, lit. '*trees of fruit*.' The use of words in the singular to denote collective ideas is especially frequent in Hebrew; cf. אדם, coll. '*mankind*' (without a plural), אויב = '*enemies*,' נפשׁ '*living beings*.' Often the fem. ending is employed to express a collective idea, so עננה '*clouds*,' ארחה '*caravan*,' גוֹלה '*exiles;*' see Ges., § 123 b; M. R., § 61; Dav., *S.*, § 17.

למינו '*after its kind.*' Emphasis is laid on the fact that each was adapted for continuance; the עשׂב flowered and so produced its seed; the עץ bore fruit containing seed or stones necessary for reproduction. מין is a common word in P.

אשר זרעו בו '*in which* (fruit) *is its seed,*' i. e. for propagation (Di.).

12. ותוצא. Hif'il, imperf. apoc. with waw conv. from יצא, a verb פ״י, properly פ״ו. The form is יוֹצִיא = יַוְצִיא, cf. יַקְטִיל.

לְמִינֵהוּ for לְמִינוֹ. The suffix ֵ-הוּ for וֹ—except in words that are derived from verbs ל״ה, such as שָׂדֶה, מַעֲשֶׂה, מִקְנֶה, etc.—outside this word (where it is found fourteen times), only occurs in אוֹרֵהוּ for אורו, Job 25, 3; פִּילַגְשֵׁהוּ for פִּילַגְשׁוֹ, Judg. 19, 24; מוֹטֵהוּ for מוטו, Nah. 1, 13; see Ges., § 91. 1. Rem. b; Ewald, § 247 d; Stade, § 345 c, who remarks that the *ê* of these forms is to be explained as an extension of a short *e*,—which has arisen out of short *a* (cf. § 84. 4),—which is still preserved before the suffix of the second pers. masc. sing. in pause, e. g. שְׁמֶךָ, נַפְשֶׁךָ.

14. יהי מארות. On the construction here, see Ges., § 145. 7 a; M. R., § 133; Dav., *S.*, § 113 b.

מאור. Nouns formed by prefixing מ denote often instruments or places, e. g. מַפְתֵּחַ '*a key,*' מַזְלֵג '*a fork,*' מִרְעֶה '*a pasture,*' מַאֲרָב '*a lurking-place;*' see further, Ges., § 85, 48; Ewald, § 160 b; and Stade, § 268 ff. Render, '*luminaries.*'

והיו. The perf. with waw conv. in continuation of the voluntative יהי, so in 28, 3 יברך אתך... והיית, 31, 44 נכרתה ברית... והיה, Ex. 5, 7; cf. Ges., § 112. 3, c, β; M. R., § 24. 1 a; Driver, § 113. 2 a; Dav., *S.*, § 55 a.

לאותות וגו״ may be rendered in three different ways: I. As a ἓν διὰ δυοῖν, '*for signs of seasons, and for days and for years;'* see Ges., *Lehrgeb.*, p. 854, and cf. 3, 16. II. '*For signs and for set times, and for days and years.*' III. '*For signs, as well for times, as also for days and years*' (Tuch). Against III. Del.[4] remarks that the correlatives '*as well,*' '*as also*' are not sufficiently clearly expressed by ו . . . ו, as, for example, in Ps. 76, 7; nor is this rendering suitable to the simplicity of the narrative. On I. it may be remarked that though the hendiadys may be possible in 3, 16, it is by no means necessary there, and Job 10, 17. 2 Chron. 16, 14 (cited by Ges. l. c.) are not parallel. II. is the simplest and best rendering, and is adopted by the Vss., Kn., Del., Di., and others.

אותות. 'The luminaries were to be אותות, i. e. signs, partly in an ordinary way as marks of the different regions of heaven, of the weather, and partly in an extraordinary way, e.g. through eclipses of the sun and moon, the appearances of comets, etc., which were regarded by the ancients as foreshadowing extraordinary events (Joel 3, 3 f. Jer. 10, 2. Matt. 24, 29).' Knobel in Di.

מועדים. מועד from יעד (ועד), '*to fix,*' denotes any '*stated place,*' as in the phrase אהל מועד '*tent of meeting,*' or as here, '*any fixed, stated time;*' cf. 17, 21. The מועדים here mean set times or seasons, in particular, stated annual feasts, also periods in animal (cf. Jer. 8, 7, of the stork) and vegetable life, and the seasons suitable to the various occupations and employments of man.

ולימים ושנים. On the pointing וְ, cf. Ges., § 104. 2 c; Dav., § 15. 1 c. '*For days and for years,*' i. e. for distinguishing and counting the days, some being short, others long, according to the season of the year: the years also being long and short, according as they are reckoned by the sun or moon. The מאורות had a threefold aim: (1) to divide the day and night; (2) to fix the calendar; (3) to give light on the earth.

16. The lights more exactly defined. שְׁנֵי; on the various ways in which the numerals may be connected with substantives, see Ges., § 134; M. R., § 96 ff.; Dav., *S.*, § 35 ff. On the article with גדולים, see Ges., § 126. 5; M. R., § 85; Dav., *S.*, § 30.

את המאור הגדול. On this method of expressing the comparative, cf. Ges., § 133. 2; M. R., § 86.

ואת המאור . . . הכוכבים. '*And the lesser light with the stars to govern the night.*' ואת הכוכבים is closely attached to את המאור הקטן; see 2, 9. 12, 17. 43, 18; Dr., *Sam.*, p. 292.

18. וְלַהבדיל, the ל is pointed with ֲ by Ges., § 10. 2. Rem.; see also Stade, § 105; and König, *Lehrg.*, p. 73.

20. נפש חיה '*living beings*,' an explanatory apposition to שֶׁרֶץ; so the Pesh.: not as the LXX, Vulg., etc., as a genitive after שֶׁרֶץ; see on ver. 11 דשא עשב. שָׁרַץ and שֶׁרֶץ are frequently found in P.

יעופף. Pilel from עוּף, a denom. from עוֹף; on this form of the intensive stem, cf. Ges., § 72. 7; Dav., § 40. 6. Pilel, because a great number of birds is meant; at the same time expressing the idea of 'up and down,' 'to and fro;' cf. Di. in loc.

על פני רקיע '*in front of*,' on the side turned towards the earth, i. e. in the air, for which Hebrew has no special expression (Del., Di.).

21. תנינים. LXX, κήτη; Pesh. ܬܢܝܢܐ; Vulg. '*cete*.' From תנן '*to stretch out*,' and used Ex. 7, 9. Deut. 32, 33, for a serpent, but more frequently for the crocodile, see Is. 27, 1. 51, 9; and also for other marine animals, Job. 7, 12. Ps. 148, 7. Render, '*sea monsters*.'

ואת כל נפש החיה. חיה is an adj., not a substantive (its use as a substantive is only poetical, being then equivalent to the prose חיים). נפש is practically limited and determined by כל, hence the adj. has the article, though it is absent with the noun: cf. 9, 10; Dav., *S.*, §§ 32, R. 2. 99, R. 1. This usage is rare, but is met with occasionally at all periods of the language; see Ges., §§ 117. 1. R. 2, and 126. 5. R. 1 a; M. R., § 85. R. c; Driver, § 209. 1; and *Journal of Phil.*, xi. 229 (where nearly all the examples are collected). Ewald, § 335 a, explains נפש הח״ as = '*the soul that lives*,' regarding the adj. with the article as virtually = to a participle and article as in ver. 28.

אשר שרצו המים '*wherewith the waters swarm.*' אשר is the acc. after שרץ. Verbs of *abounding in*, and *wanting*, govern the acc.; see Ges., § 117. 4. Rem. 4 b; M. R., § 35; Dav., *S.*, § 73 c; and 9, 2.

לְמִינֵהֶם *scriptio defectiva*, for לְמִינֵיהֶם; cf. 4, 4 חֶלְבֵהֶן.

עוף כנף '*birds* (coll.) *of wing*.' On the construction of a subs., where in English an adj. is used, see Ges., § 128. 2 i; M. R., § 79; Dav., *S.*, § 24.

למינהו. See on ver. 12.

22. ויברך. On the position of the tone, cf. Ges., § 64. 3. Rem. 2.

24. וחיתו. חיתו with the old, so-called case ending ו. Probably the ending ו was that of the nominative; compare the Arabic nominative ending *u*, but in Hebrew its distinctive use as a mark of the nom. was lost. These terminations ו or י, also the ending י., have no meaning in Hebrew, and are retained as mere binding vowels in particular phrases (י. especially in participles before a preposition) as archaisms, or in imitation of archaisms; see Ges., § 90. 3 b; Dav., § 17;

Stade, § 344; Driver, p. 237 f.; and cf. בְּנוֹ בְעֹר in Num. 24, 3. 15, and מַעְיְנוֹ מָיִם in Ps. 114, 8.

חית הארץ is one of the characteristic expressions of P.

26. נעשׂה '*let us make.*' Verbs ל״ה hardly ever take the ־ָה of the cohortative, and verbs ל״א only very rarely; cf. Ges., §§ 75. 6 and 108, foot-note; M. R., § 9; Dav., *S.*, § 62; and Driver, c. iv, esp. § 47.

We have the plural again in 11, 7 and Is. 6, 8, and it has been explained in various ways.

I. The Fathers here see a reference to the Trinity, and many moderns have followed them; but as Del. (*Comm.*, 4th ed., p. 101) and Oehl. (*Theol. of O. T.*, § 36) remark, the *mysterium Trinitatis* is not sufficiently manifest in the O. T. to warrant this interpretation. II. Tuch and others account for the plural on the ground that in a case of reflection or self-consultation, the subject stands as the object, in antithesis to itself, the speaker conceiving himself as addressing himself; cf. Hitzig and Del. on Is. 6, 8; Tuch, *Comm.*, 2nd ed., p. 23. But as Del. and Di. point out, there is no proof of the existence of such a plural. III. Kn. and others explain the plural from the custom which monarchs have of using the first person plural in decrees, etc.; but though this occurs continually in the Qoran, and is found in the Bible, Ezr. 4, 18. 1 Macc. 10, 19. 11, 31. 15, 9 (of Persian and Greek rulers), it was never used in this way by the Hebrews. IV. Di., *Comm.*, p. 31, proposes a new explanation; his words are, 'We should rather remember that the Hebrew who speaks of God as אלהים in the plural, regarded Him as the living, personal conception of a fullness of power and might; God could thus, differently from men, speak of Himself in the plural.' A plausible explanation, but perhaps hardly so natural as the one Del. adopts. V. Del. and others may possibly be right when they refer the plural, as in Is. 6, 8, to the angels. God announces to them His resolve to create man, without however allowing them to participate in His creation: cf. Del. here, and for the idea 1 Kings 22, 19–22. Dan. 4, 14. 7, 10, Job 1. Luke 2, 9. This is an old interpretation, and is the one adopted by Philo (διαλέγεται ὁ τῶν ὅλων πατὴρ ταῖς ἑαυτοῦ δυνάμεσιν, quoted by Del.[5], p. 64), Targ. Jon., which has וַאֲמַר יְיָ לְמַלְאֲכַיָּא דִּמְשַׁמְּשִׁין קוֹמוֹי וגו׳ ('*Y. spake to His angels who minister before Him*,' etc.), Rashi, Ibn Ezra. Is. 40, 13. 14 and 44, 24 are cited against this view, but are not conclusive: for as Del.[4] (substantially repeated in 5th ed.) remarks on this passage, 'A co-ordinate sharing in the act of *creation* He does not grant them, any more than in Is. 6, 8 in the act of *sending*: but He invites their participation or interest in what He is doing, as the creating of a being, who although of the earth, yet stands in a close relation to them and to Him, is the point now in question.'

אדם '*mankind*,' collective, as the pl. ירדו shows.

אדם. The word is found in Hebrew and Phoenician, and is preserved in Sabaean (*C. I. S.*, iv. 1. lin. 4); but in Syriac and Arabic it only occurs as a proper name. In the Hebrew text here, the name אדם is clearly connected with אדמה '*earth*,' as though = '*the earth-born*,' γηγενής, γήϊνος. This, however, cannot be, as a derivation, philologically defended. Another derivation is from אָדֹם '*to be red*;' cf. Joseph., *Ant.*, i. 1. 2 (Ἄδαμος σημαίνει πυρρὸς ἐπειδήπερ ἀπὸ τῆς πυρρᾶς γῆς φυραθείσης ἐγεγόνει); so many moderns, e. g. Ges., Tuch. אדמה would then = '*the* (*red*) *earth*,' possibly alluding to the colour of the soil in Palestine! But as Di. points out, the two words cannot be regarded as limited to Palestine only, nor is the term 'red' characteristic of all men. Another explanation is based on the meaning of the root preserved in Arabic, '*to attach oneself to*,' so אדם = '*animal sociabile*.' This, however, is not very probable. The comparison with the Assyr. *admu*, '*young*' (of a bird), Del., *Proleg.*, 103 f. and *Assyr. Wörterbuch*, is also doubtful. Any certain etymology for אדם has not as yet been found, see further Di., p. 53, and Del.[5] on 2, 6.

בצלמנו וגו״. צלם = '*figure*,' '*image*,' εἰκών. דמות is more abstract = '*likeness*,' ὁμοίωσις. 'The Greek and Latin Fathers make a distinction between צלם and דמות, referring צלם to the physical or inborn, דמות to the ethical or receptive side of the Divine image (Ebenbild),' Di. But the absence of ו between the two words (only the LXX have καί), and a comparison of ver. 27 and 9, 6, where only the one, with 5, 1, where only the other occurs, do not favour this view. The two words are almost synonymous, the second being added to emphasize the first (Di.).

דגת, collective, '*fishes*' = דגי הים, 9, 2. Ps. 8, 9.

27. ברא אתו '*made He him*,' i.e. mankind. אדם conceived as collective, mankind in general being spoken of.

זכר ונקבה ברא אתם '*male and female made He them*,' the two sexes are mentioned, hence the plural אֹתָם.

28. פרו ורבו. פרה joined with רבה is characteristic of P.

הרמשׂת. The art. supplies the place of the relative in English; see Dav. *S.*, § 99 and R. 1; M. R., § 92. Rem. a; Ewald, § 335 a, and cf. Ges., § 138. 3. Rem. b. On the article with רמשׂת, after a subs. defined by כל, see Driver, § 209. 2; and cf. 7, 21. Lev. 11. 46.

29. נָתַתִּי for נָתַנְתִּי; see Ges., § 66. 2. Rem. 3. '*I give*,' the prophetic perf., 'the event being regarded as so certain, it is already conceived of as actually come to pass;' cf. Ges.,

§ 106. 3; M.R. 3. 1; Dav., *S.*, § 41; more fully, Driver, §§ 13, 14. See 9, 13. 15, 18. 17, 20. 23, 11. 13. 41, 41.

אשר בו, lit. '*which is in it*,' i.e. '*wherein*,' see Ges., § 138. 1. and Rem. 2; Dav., *S.*, § 9 c, and R. 1.

30. את כל ירק וגו״. The verb נתתי here seems to have dropped out. To make the acc. dependent on the נתתי in ver. 29 is difficult, as לכם יהיה לאכלה intervenes, and these words can hardly be, as Di. suggests, a parenthesis. The Vulg. paraphrases '*ut habeant ad vescendum*.' The Arab. adds جَعَلْتُهُ '*I have appointed it*' or '*set it*.'

כל ירק עשב = '*all verdure of herbs*;' cf. Ex. 10, 15 ולא נותר כל ירק בעץ.

עשב = '*herb*,' in its widest sense, the green of it being emphasized as that which animals commonly live on.

31. יום הששי. Common words like יום are sometimes treated as definite in themselves, and may then dispense with the article; cf. 2, 3 יום השביעי (also Ex. 20, 10). 1 Kings 7, 12 חצר הגדולה, also ver. 8 חצר האחרת, Ez. 40, 28. 31. 2 Chron. 23, 20 שער העליון, Neh. 3, 6 שער הישנה, also *Journ. Phil.*, xi. 229 f.; Ges., § 126. 5. R. 1 a; Ew., § 293 a; Dav., *S.*, § 32. R. 2; and Dr., § 209. 1. On the relation in which the Cosmogony of Genesis stands to modern science, cf. Driver in the *Expositor*, Jan. 1886, pp. 23–45.

2.

1. צבאם, applied zeugmatically to השמים והארץ. The phrase '*host of heaven*' is common in the O.T., e.g. 1 Kings 22, 19 (='*the angel hosts*'). Josh. 5, 14 f. (='*army* or *host of God*'). Ps. 103, 21 (of the elements). The phrase '*host of the earth*,' here due to the צבא השמים, is not common elsewhere, we find instead מלא הארץ, Is. 34, 1.

2. ויכל. *'And God ended,'* not as a pluperfect as some render. It is very doubtful whether an imperf. with waw conv. can stand for a pluperfect, if no perfect in a pluperfect sense precedes, and it is scarcely consistent with the meaning of the idiom; cf. on 1, 4. When a writer wishes to mark that a pluperfect sense is necessary, he usually separates the ו from the verb, which then naturally passes over into the perfect (ואלהים כלה). For a full discussion of the question and an examination of the instances in which waw conv. with the imperfect has been supposed to be equivalent to a pluperfect, see Driver, § 76. Obs.

כלה = here *'to bring to an end,' 'to leave off;'* cf. Ex. 34, 33. 1 Sam. 10, 13. Ez. 43, 23 (where כלה occurs with מן). This *'leaving off* or *resting'* fills up the seventh day, just as the work of creation the six preceding days. 'God did not create anything on the seventh day,' Kn. The Sam., LXX, Pesh., Ber. Rab. read ששי for שביעי; an intentional alteration to avoid the idea that God created anything on the seventh day.

מְלַאכְתּוֹ from מְלָאכָה, which has arisen out of מַלְאָכָה, the weak letter א surrendering its vowel to the preceding vowelless consonant, and the pathach under the prefix מ disappearing and its place being taken by shewa vocal; cf. Stade, § 110 c and § 112 b; Ges., § 23. 2 and § 95. 3. In the form with the suffix וֹ, the pathach under the ל is due to the syllable being short and unaccented.

3. ויברך. If the penult. is an open syllable waw conv. frequently draws back the tone on to it, leaving the last syllable a short unaccented syllable; see Dav., § 23. 3 b; Driver, § 69; Ges., § 49. 2 b. Cf. 1, 11. 22, and often.

את יום השביעי. Cf. on 1, 31.

אשר ברא אלהים לעשות. Two renderings are possible, (I) '*which God had created in respect of making,*' *quae creaverat Deus faciendo.* The inf. cstr. being used to define a preceding verb, as in Judg. 9, 56 אשר עשה . . . . להרג; 2 Kings 19, 11 עשו . . . . להחרימם; Ps. 103, 20 עשי דברו לשמע; cf. Ges., § 45. 2; Ewald, § 280 d; M. R., § 113 ad fin. But as ברא in this construction would be followed by אשר (=מלאכה), which is against the usage of the language, and for which עשה מלאכה would stand, Di. (II) prefers rendering with Ewald, § 285 a, '*in making which he had created,*' i. e. '*which he had made creatively*' (cf. Del.[5] *die er schöpferisch ausgeführt hatte*), אשר being acc. after לעשות, and the latter word being defined by ברא; cf. הרבה להתפלל, הפליא להעזר, הגדיל לעשות. The LXX have ὧν ἤρξατο ὁ Θεὸς ποιῆσαι, a paraphrase. The Pesh. ܕܒܪܐ ܐܠܗܐ ܠܡܥܒܕ, as the Hebrew, so Onq. דִּבְרָא יְיָ לְמֶעְבַּד. Vulg. '*quod creavit Deus ut faceret.*'

4. אלה תולדות. '*These are the generations of the heavens and the earth when they were created.*' תולדות,—which only occurs in the pl. cstr. state,—when it stands before a proper name signifies '*generations,*' not as a *nom. act.*, but in the sense '*those who are brought forth,*' so=*family*, '*the details about those who spring from any one;*' hence in the title of a book or chapter, '*the history of the families springing from any one.*' LXX, γένεσις; in this passage βίβλος γενέσεως. Here תולדות=the '*creatures,*' i. e. '*the things brought into existence when heaven and earth were created.*' Elsewhere תולדות always refers to what follows, e. g. 5, 1. 6, 9. 10, 1, but in this chap. no history of the heavens and the earth follows, so Schrader and others suppose that this half verse properly ought to precede 1, 1, its present position being perhaps due to the compiler of the book, who inserted it here in order to form a transition to 2, 4 b, ff. The אלה (as it stands now)

points backwards, and may be rendered, '*Such then are the generations:*' so Job 18, 21. Ps. 73, 12. Gen. 10, 20. 31. 32. Cf. further, Del., *Comm.*[5], p. 72 f.; Di., p. 38 f.; Tuch, p. 49; Driver, *Introd.*, p. 5. The heading אלה תולדות is peculiar to P: so 5, 1. 6, 9. 10, 1, etc.; and as the remainder of chap. 2 is not taken from this document, the formula as it now stands must be regarded as a 'subscription' to chap. 1. In all the other cases, however, where these words occur in P., they are always the 'superscription' to the following narrative.

יהוה אלהים, the combined name '*Yahweh Elohim*,' is only found once again in the Pent. (viz. Ex. 9, 30) outside Genesis, but occurs in Joshua. On the Tetragrammaton, יהוה, cf. Appendix. P uses אלהים till Ex. 6, 3.

ארץ ושמים. Only once again, in Ps. 148, 13.

בהבראם. Inf. Nif'. with ב prefixed, and the suff. of the third pers. pl. masc., from ברא. The ה is written smaller than the other letters, and is marked by the Massoretes ה״ זְעֵירָא, i. e. *He small.* Tuch remarks on this: 'The ה minusc. in בהבראם (cf. 5, 2) has a critical significance, and points to a variant reading, Qal (viz. בְּבָרְאָם), not Hof'., as Rosenmüller thinks. Similarly Lev. 1, 1.' Cf. Di., p. 39, who apparently endorses this view. Other instances of letters written smaller or larger than the other letters will be found in Strack, *Prolegomena critica*, p. 92, e. g. *litterae majusculae* in Lev. 11, 42, גָּחוֹן, with waw larger than the other three letters; in Num. 14, 17, י in יִגְדַּל; in Deut. 34, 12, ל in יִשְׂרָאֵל; and *litterae minusculae* in Deut. 32, 18, י in תֶּשִׁי; Esth. 9, 9, ש in פַּרְמַשְׁתָּא: see also Bleek (*Introduction*, § 357 f.) [Eng. transl.], or Keil (*Introduction*, § 205) [Eng. transl.]. A list of the '*litterae majusculae et minusculae*' will be found in *Ochla we Ochla* (ed.

Frensdorff), Nos. 82–84; Buxtorf, *Tiberias* (1665 ed.). They are not expressly mentioned in the Talmud, and probably in the course of time became more numerous. Buxtorf, l. c., enumerates thirty-one instances of the *lit. majusc.*, and thirty-two of the *lit. minusc.* The Jews give fanciful explanations. The two following—viz. on this passage, and 23, 2—are cited from the *Tiberias*, p. 147 ff. '"ה in voce בהבראם "*quando creata fuerant illa*," nempe, coelum et terra, Gen. 2, 4. Ad indicandum, fore ut omnia creata minuantur et intereant: et ut littera ה constat ex lineis dissolutis et ab invicem separatis, sic creata cuncta dissolventur, sicut scriptum est: "*Coeli velut fumus evanescent, et terra ut pannus veterascet, et habitatores ejus similiter morientur*," Is. 51, 6. Hebraei litterarum mysteria sectantes, notant innui transpositionem hujus litterae, ut ex בהבראם fiat באברהם "*propter Abraham*," i. e. propter fideles creatum esse mundum: illi enim soli Deum propter admiranda creationis opera laudant.' And on the small כ in 23, 2 (p. 152): 'ad indicandum, planctum et luctum propter mortuos, viris minuendum esse, ne modum excedat, quod et Abrahamum fecisse, externo litterae signo indicatum fuit.' See another Jewish explanation of Gen. 2, 4, from the Talmud, *Tract. Menachoth*, fol. 29, col. 2, in Hershon, *The Pentateuch according to the Talmud*, p. 92 (Eng. transl.).

Render, '*When they were created*,' lit. '*in their being created;*' a common use of the inf. cstr., like the Greek construction ἐν τῷ, with the inf.; see Ges., § 114. 2, 3; M. R., § 111 b.

4^b. The narrative begins here. '*In the day of God's making*,' i. e. '*when God made*,' etc. On the construction, see Ges., § 115. 2, 3; M. R., § 111 a, § 118; Dav., *S.*, §§ 90 b, 91 a.

ביום,=lit. '*in the day of*,' is freely used for '*at the time of;*' so 3, 5 ביום אכלכם; Is. 11, 16 ביום עלותו; Jer. 11, 7 ביום העלת. עֲשׂוֹת J.=בְּרֹא in P.

The apodosis to 4^b, ביום עשות, may be either ver. 7 or ver. 5. If we take ver. 7 as the apodosis, then vers. 5, 6 will be a parenthesis descriptive of the earth's condition before God created mankind, and we should have to render it as follows:—'*When Yahweh Elohim made earth and heaven* (*now no shrub of the field was yet on the earth, and no herb of the field had yet sprung up; for Yahweh Elohim had not sent rain upon the earth, and there was no man to till the ground; and a mist used to go up and water all the surface of the ground*), *then Yahweh Elohim formed*,' etc. So Bunsen, Di., and Schrader.

If we make ver. 5 the apodosis, then the rendering would be, '*When Yahweh Elohim made earth and heaven, then there was no shrub of the field*,' etc. So Tuch and Kn.

Against the first rendering it may be urged that the construction is too involved, and seems to identify a *period* (ver. 6), with a *point* (ver. 7) of time. To make וכל שיח the apodosis to 4^b is against the division of the verses and the syntax (Del.); cf., however, on the latter point, Driver, §§ 123 and 124, who cites Lev. 7, 16^b. Josh. 3, 3, and other instances of the imperf. separated from ו, after a time determination, and this passage may possibly be explained in the same way. The argument, too, from the division of the verses is hardly conclusive. Del. takes apparently 4^b and 4^a, after the analogy of 5, 1, as belonging together, and regards vers. 5 and 6 as independent sentences introductory to ver. 7, which beginning with ויצר ('*so he formed*') expresses the main point, viz. the creation of man.

5. On the imperf. after טֶרֶם, cf. Ges., § 107. 1. Rem. 1; M. R., § 6. 1; Ewald, § 337 c; Driver, § 27 b; Dav., *S.*, § 45. Ewald, l. c., remarks that טרם for the most part stands in circumstantial clauses, preceded by the subject.

כל indefinite, and with the negative = '*none*,' Germ. *kein*: cf. Ges., § 152. 1 a; M. R., § 142; Ewald, § 323 b; Dav., *S.*, § 11. R. 1 b. On אין, see Ges., l. c. 1 c; Ewald, § 321 a; M. R., § 140; Dav., *S.*, § 127 b.

On the position of אין in the sentence, cf. Num. 20, 5 ומים אין, M. R., § 79. 6 b. Rem. a; Dav., *S.*, l. c.

6. יעלה. The imperf. used in a frequentative sense, and followed by a perfect with waw conv. והשקה. The companion construction to the imperf. with waw conv. is that of the perfect with waw conv. According to Ewald, § 234 a, b, this construction was originally due to the opposite construction of the perfect, followed by an imperfect with waw conv.; just as the two tenses are in many aspects opposite one to the other, so the peculiar idiomatic use of the one, generated a corresponding idiomatic use of the other as its counterpart. Ols., cited by Driver, remarks that this use of the perfect rests originally on a 'play of the imagination,' in virtue of which an action when brought into relation with a preceding occurrence as its *consequence*, from the character of inevitability it then assumes, is contemplated as actually completed. In this construction 'the nascent action (i. e. the action of the imperf.) is conceived of as advancing to completion (the action of the perfect with waw conv.), as no longer remaining in suspension, but as being (so to say) precipitated.' Driver, *Tenses*, p. 117. Compare c. viii, where a full discussion of this idiom will be found, and the rules concerning the shifting of the tone one place forward with the waw conv. are noted. When the waw and the verb are separated, the imperf. reappears. Cf. also Ewald, §§ 136 c, 342 b, 1; M. R., §§ 23, 25; Ges., § 112. 3 a. Other instances of the imperf. as a frequentative, followed by a perf. with waw conv.,

are 6, 4. 29, 2. 3 ישקו . . . ונאספו . . . וגללו . . . והשקו . . . והשיבו; 1 Kings 14, 28 ישאום . . . והשיבום; 2 Kings 3, 25 . . . ישליכו ומלאוה, etc. See also Dav., *S.*, §§ 44 b, 54 b.

אד only occurs in this passage and Job 36, 27. The LXX render here by πηγή, and in Job, l. c., by νεφέλη, which is also Onqelos' rendering here (עֲנָנָא). Pesh. and Vulg. have respectively ܡܒܘܥܐ and '*fons.*' Saadiah agrees with the ordinary rendering '*mist,*' '*vapour,*' بُخَار. The word אֵד appears to be confined to Hebrew. Ges. in the *Thesaurus*, p. 35, is in error when he says that the word אֵד is used in the Targ., Job 3, 5. Prov. 23, 33. He has accidentally written 'Targum' for '*the Commentary of Rabbi Levi ben Gerson*' (of Provence, died 1370), cited by Buxtorf, *Lexicon. Chald. Talm. et Rabb.*, p. 69.

7. וייצר. On the form of this פ״י verb, see Ges., § 70. 1; Dav., § 39. 2.

האדם. On the derivation of אדם, compare the note on 1, 26. The author connects אדם with אדמה, as though he would imply that man bore in his name a mark of his earthly origin. On the article with אדם, cf. Ges., § 126. 2 d; Ewald, 277 c; M. R., § 66. Rem. a; Dav., *S.*, § 21 c.

עפר is a second accusative, specifying or defining the material used in the operation; see Ges., § 117. 5 b. δ; Ewald, § 284 a. 1; M. R., § 45. 5; Driver, § 195. 1 (Tertiary predicate); Dav., *S.*, § 76. Cf. Ex. 20, 25.

חיים. The masc. plural used to form an abstract noun. 'The plural may serve to collect together the scattered items into a higher idea, so as to form the signification of an abstract,' Ewald, § 179, who gives as other instances נדדים '*flittings,*' Job 7, 4; עועים '*perverseness;*' סנורים '*blindness;*' cf. also Stade, § 324 b, who remarks 'that חיים is the only word of this sort in general use, the other instances that occur being archaisms, and belonging to the conventional language of the Law, or of Poets or Prophets.' See also Ges., § 124. 1 b; Dav., *S.*, § 16.

ויהי . . . לנפש. In the sense of '*become*,' היה ל, cf. 17, 4. 18, 18, etc., is more frequent than היה, followed by the simple subst., as in 4, 20. 21. 19, 26.

נֶפֶשׁ in Heb. = the breath of life that is in every individual being. Man derives this breath of life from God immediately (Job 27, 3. Is. 42, 5), animals from the earth (1, 20. 24), and so only mediately from God, yet participating in God's spirit (Job 34, 14 f. Ps. 104, 30). In this direct inspiration lies man's pre-eminence over the animal world, stress being laid on the manner in which man 'became a living soul.' He comes into existence as a personal being in a personal relation with God. Cf. Oehl., § 70. Onq. renders נפש חיה by רוּחַ מְמַלְּלָא '*a talking spirit.*'

8. גן בעדן. '*A garden in Eden.*' עֵדֶן as an appellative means '*loveliness*,' '*delight*,' but is here clearly the name of the place where the garden was situated. The LXX render here παράδεισον ἐν Ἐδέμ; ver. 15 (incorrectly) παραδείσῳ τῆς τρυφῆς, so 3, 24, and Vulg. '*Paradisum voluptatis.*' Pesh. has ܦܪܕܝܣܐ ܒܥܕܢ, Saadiah جِنَانًا في عَدْنٍ. Schr., *C. O. T.*, p. 26 f., says 'Eden, Heb. עֵדֶן, has originally nothing to do with עֵדֶן, pl. עֲדָנִים "*loveliness*," but is a word that came over to the Hebrews from the Babylonians, meaning properly "*field*," "*plain*;" in Assyrian *i-di-nu*.' עֵדֶן, pointed with ֶ ֶ, to distinguish it perhaps from עֵדֶן with ֵ ֶ, is a pr. n., the name of a district in Mesopotamia, or Assyria, which, according to 2 Kings 19, 12. Is. 37, 12, came under the rule of Assyria. עֵדֶן has not yet been identified; cf. further, Di., pp. 55 and 61 ff.; Del.[5], p. 79.

מקדם is local, not temporal (for ויטע is against this), = '*eastwards*,' '*on the east of*' (a further definition of the position of Eden; cf. 3, 24. 11, 2. 13, 11), i.e. from the standpoint of the narrator in Palestine.

9. ויצמח. The shortened form of the Hif'. imperf.; see Ges., § 65. 1 c. Rem. 3; Dav., § 37. 1, 2.

ועץ הדעת טוב ורע = '*and the tree of knowledge of* (lit. *of the knowing*) *good and evil*;' i.e. the tree, the partaking of the fruit of which would cause persons to know good and evil.

טוב ורע cannot be genitive after דעת, as a word defined by being in the construct state does not take the article, but must be regarded as the accusative; cf. Jer. 22, 16 הלא היא הדעת אתי '*was not that the knowing me?*' see Ewald, § 236 a; M. R., § 110. Rem.; Ges., § 115. 1. Rem. 3; Dav., *S.*, § 19. The article prefixed to an inf. cstr. is very rare.

טוב וָרע. On the pointing of ו with ָ, see on 1, 2.

10. '*And a river was going out of Eden, to water the garden; and from thence it separated itself, and became four branches.*'

יוצא. The part. denoting continuous, unintermittent action; see Ges., § 107. 1. Rem. 2; Driver, § 21; M. R., § 14. 2 a; cf. Dav., *S.*, § 97. R.

יפרד. On the imperf. as a freq. in past time, see Driver, § 30 a; M. R., § 6. 2 a; Dav., *S.*, § 44 b.

והיה; cf. on והשקה, ver. 6.

11. פִּישׁוֹן =, according to Gesenius, '*streaming*,' or '*stream*,' from a root פושׁ '*to burst forth.*' It is not found again in the Canonical books of the Old Testament, but is

mentioned in Ecclesiasticus 24, 25, together with the Tigris. The Arabic of Saadiah has اَلنّيل '*the Nile.*' The other versions follow the Heb. text. Its position is more closely defined by the mention of the land (חוילה) round which it flows. Joseph. (*Ant.*, i. 1. 3), the Fathers (Euseb., Aug., Hier.), and others identify it with the Ganges; Reland and others consider it is the Phasis; Del. and the moderns, the Indus. החוילה occurs only here with the art.; in 10, 7. 29, it is mentioned partly among the Cushites, and partly among the sons of Joqtan, together with Ophir. It also occurs in the phrase (25, 18) מחוילה עד שור; cf. 1 Sam. 15, 7, and Dr., *Sam.*, p. 94.

Ḥavila in 25, 18 and 1 Sam. 15, 7 seems to have been the eastern frontier of the Ishmaelites and Amalekites on the Persian gulf. The moderns identify the Ḥavila of this verse with India; according to their view פישון is the Indus. That one of the rivers here mentioned was an Indian one, was the view prevalent among the ancients; and the identification of חוילה with India, and פישון with the Indus, is strengthened by the fact that the products of the land of חוילה, viz. זהב, בדלח, שהם, are mentioned by ancient writers as being found in India; the gold of the Indus district being celebrated among classical writers, as that of Ophir was among biblical: cf. Her., iii. 106; Diod. Sic., ii. 36; Curt., viii. 9. 18. Cf. 1 Kings 10, 11. Ps. 45, 10. Job 22, 24: see further, Del.[5], p. 82; Di., p. 60[1]. חוילה has the article by Ewald, § 277 c; cf. ver. 7. It seems to indicate, as Di. remarks, that the Hebrews had not then forgotten the original meaning of the word, '*the sand land' par excellence.* The חוילה mentioned in 10, 7 (cf. 1 Chron. 1, 9) among the sons of Cush seems to denote a place distinct

[1] The name may possibly = '*Sandland,*' or '*Land of golden sand,* connected with חול '*sand.*'

from those intended here, and in 25, 18. 1 Sam. 15, 7. It is perhaps to be identified with the modern Zeila on the Abyssinian coast, south of Bab-el-Mandeb. Cf. the note on 10, 7.

הוּא הַסֹּבֵב = '*that is the one encompassing the whole land of Ḥavila.*' The article with the predicate, cf. Driver, § 135. 7; see also Ges., §§ 116. 5. Rem. 1, 126. 2 i. Rem.; Dav., *S.*, § 19. R. 3. סֹבֵב without the article would = '*is encompassing.*' The word סבב does not of necessity imply a complete surrounding; cf. Num. 21, 4. Judg. 11, 18. Ps. 26, 6.

On the relative construction אשר שם, cf. Ges., § 138. 1. and R. 2; M. R., § 156 d; Dav., *S.*, § 9. R. 1.

12. וזהב. The ו is pointed וּ by Ges., § 104. 2 c. On the ֲ under the ז, to emphasize the sibilant, see Ges., § 10. 2. Rem. A; Stade, § 105. Cf. 3, 17 (תֹּאכֲלֶנָּה). 25, 22. 27, 26. 29, 3. 8 (וְגָֽלֲלוּ). וּ is marked with metheg, as in Judg. 5, 12, וּֽשֲׁבֵה: see Ges., § 16. 2, 1 a; Stade, § 52 d.

הוא in the Pent., with the exception of eleven places, is of common gender. The punctuators, however, by pointing it הִוא, indicate that they meant it to be read as הִיא, the usual form of the fem.: cf. Ewald, § 184 c; Ges., § 32. iii. 6; Stade, § 171 c. 2. This has usually been explained as an archaism, but Nöld., *Z. D. M. G.*, xx. (1866), p. 458, has pointed out that this cannot be philologically sustained, if we compare the other Semitic languages, all of which exhibit distinct forms for the masc. and fem. He, shewing that the double form must have existed *before* the different branches of the Semitic race had parted from their common home, rejects the supposition that the fem. הִיא was at an early date lost, and again introduced into the language at a later period from the Aramaic, but admits that he has no plausible solution of the anomaly to offer. Only he is convinced 'that it cannot be explained as an archaism (dass es mit dem Archaismus nichts ist); at the most it might be an artificial archaism.' Stade, l.c., regards it as 'a mistake of tradition,' and adds, 'probably the use of הוא for both genders arose from a MS., which both for הוא and היא wrote defectively הא, as it is found on the Moabite stone and Phoenician inscriptions. This הא was thoughtlessly always miswritten הוא.' Del., in the '*Zeitschrift für Kirchliche Wissenschaft und Kirchliches Leben*,' i. p. 393 ff., has accepted Nöldeke's statement that it cannot be an archaism, and accounts for the fem. as follows: 'Though through all Hebrew, even in the post-biblical literature (cf. p. 395 of his article), the distinction of gender was not sharply defined; yet at the time of the revision of the text, the use of הוא for the fem. was regarded as a mistake (for outside the Pentateuch it is unheard of, and not found in the Hebrew-Samaritan Pentateuch). In the recension of the text however it was presupposed that in the language at the time of Moses, although it possessed for the fem. the form היא, the use of הוא as of double gender prevailed, and the distinction of gender was at the lowest stage of its development.'

Stade's view (cf. Ges., *Gram.*, l. c. 6 b. end), that היא and הוא were both originally written הא, and that the last redactors of the text have almost everywhere written this הוא without regard to gender, is borne out by the הא on the Moabite stone, line 6, וַיֹּאמֶר גַּם־הוּא=ויאמר גם הא, and line 27 בת בֵּית בָּמוֹת כִּי הָרוּס הוּא=במת כי הרס הא (cf. Mic. 5, 1, בית לחם, masculine); and in Phoenician; see *C. I. S.*, vol. i. p. 4 (Inscription of Yehawmelek, king of Gebal), line 9, מלך צדק הא; line 13, מלאכת הא: p. 14 (Inscription of Eṣmunazar, king of Sidon), line 10, אדם הא; line 11, ממלכת הא. Cf. line 22, הממלכת הא. This is probably the best explanation of the anomaly[1]. See also C. P. Ges., p. 214 b. The art. is pointed according to Ges., § 35. 2 A; Dav., § 11 b. הוא is here defined by the art. by Ges., § 126. 5; M. R., § 85; Dav., § 13. Rule 1; *S.*, § 6.

הבדלח. '*Bdellium*,' a transparent kind of gum, with a pleasant smell, and of wax-like appearance; found, according to Pliny, in India, Arabia, Media, and Babylonia: so Jos., Aq., Symm., Theod., and Vulg. In Greek the by-forms *βδέλλα*, *μάδελκον* occur. The LXX have *ἄνθραξ* here, but in Num. 11, 7 (the only other passage where the word occurs) *κρύσταλλος*, regarding בדלח as a stone, but this would have required אֶבֶן before it. The Pesh. has ܒܘܪܘܟܣܐ (reading ר for ד), which apparently can be used of pearls or crystals. Saad. and others render *pearls* (so also Ges. in *Th.*), which meaning would be suitable here—between זהב and שהם but hardly in Num. 11, 7 (Del.), and according to Tuch was first derived from this passage in order that some object of equal value with זהב and שהם might be mentioned; but cf. 1 Kings 10, 2. 10. The etymology is doubtful.

השהם. Probably the *Prasius* or *Beryl.* The art. as in הזהב, according to Ges., § 126. 3 b; M. R., § 68; Dav., *S.*, § 22 d. The LXX here give *ὁ λίθος ὁ πράσινος*, perhaps meaning the beryl, Vulg. '*lapis onychinus*,' Pesh. ܒܘܪܠܐ, Onq. בּוּרְלָא. Elsewhere variously rendered, onyx, sardonyx, sardius, which all belong to the same species (chalcedony), or beryl (more correctly chrysopras): cf. *H. W. B.*, 11th ed., Di. in loco. The etymology is doubtful.

[1] It is not certain that הוא=היא is confined to the Pentateuch. It seems to be found in the *Codex Petropolitanus* (916 A.D.), edited by Dr. Strack, 1876. Delitzsch denies this (see p. 394 of his article), but admits that the distinction between ו and י is slight. Cf. also on this point, Baer, *Ezech.*, p. 108 f.

13. גִּיחוֹן. A similar formation to פִּישׁוֹן. From גִּיחַ '*to burst forth*.' This river flowed round the land of כּוּשׁ, and is quite distinct from the גיחון mentioned in 1 Kings 1, 33. 38. 45. 2 Chron. 32, 30. 33, 14. The LXX have here Γηών, Vulg. '*Gehon*,' so the other Vss. The LXX in Jer. 2, 18 translate the Heb. שִׁיחוֹר, Nile, by Γηών; cf. Ecclesiasticus 24, 27. Josephus and the Fathers also consider the Nile the river here meant, so many moderns. כּוּשׁ is Ethiopia. Thus if גִּיחוֹן is the Nile, we have a river taking its source in Asia, flowing round the African כּוּשׁ! Others consider כּוּשׁ as representing only the Asiatic Cushites, and identify גיחון with either the Ganges or Oxus. Reland identifies it with the Araxes. Del. and Di. (provisionally) decide for the Nile, explaining the anomaly above noted, as having arisen through the ignorance of the ancients of geography; see their commentaries in loco.

14. חִדֶּקֶל,='*the Tigris*,' occurs again Dan. 10, 4. The Heb. name agrees with the Sumerian *Idigna*, and the Bab.-Assyr. *Idiglat* (Schr., *C. O. T.*, 32 f.; Del., *Par.*, 170). In Aramaic the name is דִּיגְלַת (so Onq. here); the Pesh. has ܕܶܩܠܰܬ, Arab. دِجْلَة. 'The Aryan name (Old Persian *Tigra*, Pahlawi דגרת, Greek Τίγρης, Τίγρις), according to the express tradition of the ancients (Strabo, xi. 14, 8; Pliny, vi. 31; Curt., iv. 9), designates the river as "*the arrow-swift*," Old Baktrian *tighra*="*pointed*," *tighri*="*arrow*."' Dillmann.

קִדְמַת. Render, '*in front of Assyria*,' i.e. from the standpoint of the narrator; so LXX κατέναντι, Pesh. ܠܩܘܒܠ. Others (the Targg., Aq., Tuch) render '*east of*,' thus including Mesopotamia in the term אַשּׁוּר; but then the narrator could not have spoken of the Tigris as being east of Assyria, for he must have known that Assyria extended far east of the Tigris. Mesopotamia, too, is called ארם נהרים in 24, 10; for this meaning of קדמת, cf. 4, 16. 1 Sam. 13, 5. Ez. 39, 11 (all). Cf. Di., p. 59.

פרת. '*The Euphrates*,' not further defined, as being familiar to every Hebrew reader. It is often mentioned in O.T. as '*the great river*,' or '*the river*' κατ' ἐξοχήν. Together with the Heb.-Aramaic name, we have now the Old Persian '*Ufrâtu*,' and the Babylonian-Assyrian '*Burattuv*,' '*Purâtu*.' A Semitic etymology is still unknown; see Di. in loc., and M. and V. in *H. W. B.*, 11th ed., p. 702 a.

15. וינחהו. The Hif'. imperf. with waw conv. from נוח: see Ges., § 72. Rem. 9; Dav., § 40, esp. Rem. c. N.B. הֵנִיחַ='*to cause to rest*,' הִנִּיחַ '*to place*,' '*set*,' '*lay down*.'

לעבדה ולשמרה. The inf. cstr. with suffixes follows the analogy of the segholate nouns: see Ges., § 61. 1; Dav., § 31. 4. Possibly the suffixes should be pointed הּ, as גַּן is generally masc., cf. note on 9, 21.

16. ויצו על '*laid a command on him*.' More usually צוה,= '*to command*,' is followed by an acc., or the prep. ל, or אל (cf. 28, 6. Is. 5, 6. Amos 2, 12), the words of the command being introduced by לאמר.

אכל תאכל. '*Thou mayest indeed eat*.' The inf. abs. being prefixed to the verb. 'The inf. abs. expresses the idea of the verb simply, without conditions of person, mood, etc.; hence, when it precedes the finite verb, there is first the idea bare, and then the idea modified; and the effect of the whole is to express with some variety of emphasis the *fact* (not the *quality*) of the action as now predicated in the finite verb.' Dav., § 27, rule at end. See also Ewald, § 312 a; Ges., § 113. 3 a; Dav., *S.*, §§ 85, 86; M.R., § 37.

On the potential use of the imperf., see Driver, § 38 a; Ges., § 107. 4 b; M. R., § 7. 2 a; Dav., *S.*, § 43 b.

אכל is one of the five verbs that form their imperf. with ḥolem in the first syllable: see Ges., § 68. 1; Dav., § 35.

17. '*But from the tree of knowledge of good and evil, thou shalt not eat of it.*' On the preposition with the suffix, repeating the substantive (a use allied to that of the *casus pendens*), see Ges., § 135. 1. Rem. 2, foot-note 1; Driver, § 197. Obs. 1; Ewald, § 309 a, ad fin.; Dav., *S.*, § 106 b.

אכלך is an instance of an inf. cstr. with the suffix departing from the analogy of segholate nouns: cf. ver. 15, and see Ges., § 61. 1. Rem. 2.

18. לא טוב היות. The inf. cstr. as the subject of a sentence: cf. Ges., § 114. 1 a; M. R., § 112 b; Dav., *S.*, § 90.

אעשׂה לו. The ל of לו has a *dag. forte conjunctivum* or *euphonicum:* see Ges., § 20. 2; Dav., § 7. 4, foot-note; cf. ver. 28. The LXX and Vulg. here have read the plural, to bring the text into conformity with 1, 26.

עזר כנגדו, lit. '*a help as before him*,' i.e. '*a help corresponding to him*,' '*meet for him*,' A.V. LXX have here κατ' αὐτόν, in ver. 20 ὅμοιος αὐτῷ; so the Pesh. and Vulg. In Rabbinic, כנגד='*corresponding to:*' see Ges., *Thes.*, p. 847. עזר is used concretely, as in Ps. 70, 6: cf. Nah. 3, 9.

19. ויצר is written defectively for וייצר, which occurs in ver. 7. The verb must not be rendered as a pluperfect. It appears that the narrator conceived the formation of animals as posterior to that of man. For the question of the use of the imperf. with waw conv. as a pluperfect, cf. the note on ver. 2.

כל חית השׂדה J, P כל חית הארץ (1, 25. 30; cf. 9, 10).

מה. On the punctuation of מה, see Ges., § 37. 1; Dav., § 13. 'The punctuation is quite like that of the article.'

מה יקרא '*what he would call them;*' cf. Driver, § 39 β; Dav., *S.*, § 43 b.

וכל אשר יקרא. The imperf. according to Driver, § 38 β; Dav., *S.*, § 44 b; '*all whatever he called them.*'

נפש חיה. These words may perhaps be considered a gloss on לו (cf. Ges., § 131. 2. Rem. c, foot-note 3). Such a redundancy as we find in the text here is common in Aramaic, which would say לָהּ לְנַפְשָׁא חַיְתָא; and there are genuine examples of it in the O.T., e.g. Ex. 2, 6. 1 Sam. 21, 14 (see Ges., l. c. Rem. 4 b; M. R., § 72. 3. Rem. a; Dav., *S.*, § 29. R. 7), but none so harsh as this (note especially the masc. לו). In late Hebrew this redundancy might be an Aramaism, but that can hardly be the case in this passage. נפש חיה='*living creatures,*' נפש being collective. חיה is a fem. adj. (חיה='*life*' is only poetical; see on 1, 21). As the text stands we have לו masc. followed by נפש חיה fem., which is difficult. Del. supposes that נפש חיה (cf. נפש in 46, 27. Num. 31, 28) was construed *ad sensum* as a masc.; but these passages are scarcely parallel.

20. וּלְאָדָם, pointing the ל with ־ָ. The word is not used as a proper name until 4, 25. In these three chapters (1–3) it is, with the exception of this verse and 3, 17. 21, always pointed with the article. But cf. M. R., § 66. Rem. a.

לא מצא. I. Impersonally, '*One did not find for mankind.*' II. '*For himself* (לנפשו=לאדם) *he* (*man*) *did not find.*' III. '*For mankind* (*God*) *did not find.*' III. is not probable, as we have האדם already as subj. at the beginning of the verse. If I. be adopted, מצא would be impers. by Ges., § 144. 3; M. R., § 123. 2, cf. on 11, 9, and לאדם could stand without the art., as in 1, 26. Tuch adopts II. Del. and Di. propose a rendering that differs slightly from any of these:

'*He* (*man*) *did not find for man*,' i.e. '*for a human being, like himself*,' etc.; almost the same as II, though they do not take לאדם as directly equivalent to לנפשו. Ols. reads וְהָאָדָם, which would remove the difficulty as to the subject of לא מצא.

21. תחתנה '*in its place*;' the suffix is a verbal one, cf. Ges., § 103. 1. Rem. 3; Stade, § 378 a. 1: with the nominal suffix it would be תַּחְתֶּיהָ.

23. '*This now is . . . this shall be called woman*.' The connection of אשה with איש is preserved by the Vulg., which renders them by '*virago*' and '*vir*,' respectively, probably following Symm., who has ἀνδρίς and ἀνήρ; so Luther, *Männin*. The two words, however, in Hebrew come from different roots. Cf. C. P. Ges., *sub voce*.

לקֳחה. The form is made more distinct by the fuller shewa; see Ges., § 10. 2 B, and § 52. 1. Rem. 2. The dag. in the ק has fallen away in accordance with the rule, that any doubled letter pointed with shewa, may drop its doubling; hence the Raphe, see Dav., § 7. 4, foot-note a; Ges., § 20. 3 b, where the letters that commonly admit of this loss of the dag. are mentioned. The aspirates, however, very rarely omit the dag.; cf. note on 18, 5.

24. '*Therefore doth a man leave his father and his mother and cleave unto his wife, and they become one flesh*.' The imperf. as freq. followed by the perf. with waw conv., in present time, as before (ver. 6) in past time; so Ps. 17, 14. 49, 11. 73, 10–11; Ges., § 112. 3 b; Dr., § 113. 4 a; Dav., *S.*, §§ 44 a, 54 a. These words are the narrator's comment, as in 26, 33. 32, 33, as they would be unnatural if assigned to the man, who had no knowledge of a father or mother.

The LXX, Pesh., Vulg., and Sam. insert שְׁנֵיהֶם '*and they two become*;' and the text is quoted thus in the N. T., Matt.

19, 5. Mark 10, 7; cf. 1 Cor. 6, 16. Eph. 5, 31. It may have fallen out of the Heb. text through the שְׁנֵיהֶם of ver. 25.

25. עֲרוּמִּים marked by the Massoretes, מ׳ בדגש '*mem with dagesh.*' On the apparent anomaly of a long vowel in a toneless syllable, see Dav., § 3. 2; Stade, § 327 a. This word occurs again, with the same points, in Job 22, 6.

יִתְבֹּשָׁשׁוּ. Hithpolel of בּוֹשׁ, only occurs in this passage; see Ges., § 72. 7; Dav., § 26. 3 c. Render, '*were not ashamed before one another,*' i. e. '*not in the habit of being ashamed,*' etc. The Hithp. is reciprocal, cf. התראה in 42, 1. The imperf. according to Driver, § 30 a; Ewald, § 136 c.

3.

1. והנחש היה ערום מכל חית וגו״. '*Now the serpent was more cunning than all the beasts of the field,*' etc. On the use of מִן in expressing the comparative, see Ges., § 133. 1; M. R., § 49. 2; Dav., *S.*, § 33.

אַף כִּי, lit.='*and that . . . !*' is placed first in the sentence to denote astonishment, which may be expressed by a note of interrogation. Render, '*And* (*is it really the case*) *that?*' cf. Ewald, § 354 c; M. R., § 143 b. There is no necessity to suppose that the ה interrog. has fallen out.

לא . . . כל='*not any;*' see Ges., § 152. 1 a; M. R., § 142; cf. 2, 5 and Dav., *S.*, § 127 a.

3. תְמֻתוּן. This form of the plural of the imperfect in וּן, which always in Hebrew has the tone, is the common ending in the pl. imperf. 3rd pers. masc. and 2nd masc. in classical Arabic (the abbreviated form being reserved for the subj. and jussive moods), and in Aramaic, but is not found in Ethiopic in the written language. It is tolerably common

in Hebrew, and is probably not to be regarded as a mark of antiquity, but as a weightier form, being especially frequent in the elevated prose style and in poetry. 'I. It is found in various cases of pause, as here, and Ex. 1, 22 תחיון. II. As an emphatic form, e. g. in Deut. 1, 29 לא תערצון ולא תיראון; Josh. 4, 6 כי ישאלון: especially after particles or nouns, which expect a verb after them, e. g. כה, כל אשר, הדבר אשר, למה, לא, למען, פן. III. As a rhythmical form to ensure a fuller sound for the word, Hab. 3, 7 ירגזון; Ps. 4, 3 תאהבון. IV. As an audible connecting link, similar to the -εν, -σιν before ἀ, ἁ in Greek: so 32, 20 תדברון before אל עשו. Judg. 6, 31 תושיעון before אתו: most commonly before א, but also before ע, ה, ו, and מ. Many common verbs, as אמר, דבר, ידע, שוב, etc., have preserved the ון; while others, as ירד, ישב, נתן, etc., do not receive it any longer. It is found in all classes of verbs, with the single exception of verbs ע״ע, and is very frequent in verbs ל״ה and ע״ו. Qal, as a light form, has it more frequently than the heavier reflexive forms. It occurs more commonly in the 3rd pers. than the 2nd pers. pl., as this form is far more frequent, but is by no means uncommon in the 2nd pers. pl. in certain verbs, e. g. דבר, שמע, עשה, אמר, שמר. It is found in the oldest prose, e. g. in Gen. (twelve times), Ex. (twenty-eight times), Num. (seven times), Josh. (nine times), Judg. (eight times), 1 Sam. (eight times); being especially frequent in Exodus, which contains many old pieces; also in old poetry, e. g. Ex. 15. 2 Sam. 22 (once), and some Psalms and old prophets, e. g. Is., Mic., Joel, Hos., Amos. In Job, Deut., Is. 24–27, 40 ff., Pss. 58, 89, 104, etc., it is more artificial (a revived archaism). In the gnomic poetry (Prov.) it is rare, and does not occur in the erotic and purely elegiac (Song of Songs, Lam.). Leviticus has it very rarely, Ezekiel never. More modern prose writings (Ruth, Kings) have it only in colloquial passages. The books of Chronicles have preserved it in some passages from more ancient sources, while they reject it in others. In Ezra, Neh., Esther, Dan. (Heb.), Eccles. there are no examples of וּן.' See further, Böttcher, *Lehrbuch*, ii. § 930 (from whom the above paragraph slightly abbreviated is borrowed), where a full list of the passages, where the ending וּן occurs, is given; and cf. Wright, *Arab. Gram.*, i. p. 63; Stade, § 521 a, *a*; Ges., § 72. 7. Rem. 4, and § 47. 3. Rem. 4; Dav., § 21. Rem. a. It may be observed that some of Böttcher's distinctions seem doubtful and arbitrary.

4. לֹא מוֹת תְּמֻתוּן. The negative should stand between the inf. and the verb; see Ges., § 113. 3. Rem. 3; Ewald, § 312 b. 1; who cite Amos 9, 8. Ps. 49, 8 as parallel to this passage. Its unusual position here is probably due to a desire to keep the formula מוֹת תָּמוּת from 2, 17 unchanged. Cf. Dav., *S.*, § 86 b. Render, '*Ye shall by no means die.*'

5. ידֵעַ. The participle as a true present (the subject does not precede, as a slight emphasis is laid on the verb, so 18, 17 הַמְכַסֶּה אֲנִי; 19, 13 כִּי מַשְׁחִיתִים אֲנַחְנוּ; cf. Dr., § 135. 4; Dav., *S.*, § 100 b), Dr., § 135. 2 and Obs.; cf. Ges., § 116. 5 a.

בְּיוֹם אֲכָלְכֶם . . . וְנִפְקְחוּ. '*In the day ye eat . . . your eyes shall be opened.*' The perf. with waw conv. after a time determination; see Ges., § 112. 5 c; Dr., § 123 β; M.R., §§ 26, 132 b; Dav., *S.*, § 56. Waw in this usage is to be noticed. It assumes a stronger demonstrative force than it has in the ordinary cases of the perf. with waw conv. (cf. Driver, § 122), when used to introduce the predicate or the apodosis; so in Ex. 16, 6 עֶרֶב וִידַעְתֶּם '*at evening, (then) ye shall know.*' 1 Kings 13, 31 בְּמוֹתִי וּקְבַרְתֶּם אֹתִי '*when I die, (then) ye shall bury me.*' Ez. 24, 24 b בְּבֹאָהּ וִידַעְתֶּם '*when it comes, (then) ye shall know.*'

כאלהים *'as gods.'* Targ. Onq. כְּרַבְרְבִין *'as princes,'* perhaps intentionally to avoid an anthropomorphic idea. Targ. Jon. כְּמַלְאָכִין רַבְרְבִין דְּחַכְמִין *'as mighty princes who know,'* connecting יודעי with אלהים, which is grammatically possible. The Samaritan has ࠊࠌࠋࠀࠊࠉࠄ *'like angels.'* יֹדְעֵי is perhaps best taken (so the accents) as second predicate to והייתם.

6. ולהשׂכיל. The LXX, Pesh., Vulg., and some moderns render, *'to look at,'* or *'regard,'* a meaning which השׂכיל never has. Render, *'to become wise,'* lit. *'to gain insight,'* Di. *'um Einsicht zu gewinnen.'* Rashi's note here is כמו שׁאמר לה יודעי טוב ורע *'compare his saying to her, "knowing good and evil."'*

וַיֹּאכַל. Pausal form of יֹאכַל; cf. Ges., § 29. 4 c, note, with § 68. 1. The LXX and Sam. read ויאכלו (plural), the waw might have arisen out of the following waw in ותפקחנה. The plural is not necessary.

7. כי עירומם הם. The pronoun stands here by M. R., § 125; cf. ver. 11; and Ges., § 141. 4.

עלה תאנה, lit. *'leaf of a fig,'* i.e. *'fig-leaf,'* here collective, *'fig-leaves.'*

ויעשׂו להם *'and they made themselves.'* The personal pronoun is used for the reflexive, as often with this verb; cf. Ges., § 135. 3; M. R., § 89 a; Dav., *S.*, § 11 b.

8. קול, not *'the voice,'* but *'the sound,'* as in 2 Sam. 5, 24. 1 Kings 14, 6. Render, *'The sound of Y. (while) walking* (acc.) *in the garden,'* and cf. Driver, p. 204; Dav., *S.*, § 70.

לרוח היום. *'About the cool of the day,'* so 8, 11 לעת ערב *'about eventide;'* 17, 21 למועד הזה *'about this date;'* also Is. 7, 15 לדעתו *'about (the time of) his knowing;'* cf. Ges., § 119. 3 c;

M. R., § 51. 2. In the East, towards evening a cool breeze springs up (cf. Song of Songs 2, 17. 4, 6) and the Oriental goes out; so 24, 63 לפנות הערב. The LXX render well τὸ δειλινόν. In 18, 1 the noontide is called חם היום '*the heat of the day*' (LXX, excellently, μεσημβρίας); Abraham being described as sitting in the door of his tent.

9. אַיֶּכָּה. The suffix (as it is pointed) is a verbal one; cf. Ges., § 100. 5; M. R., § 39; אַיֶּכָּה standing for אַיֶנְכָּה; cf. Prov. 2, 11 תִּנְצְרֶכָּה, and with the nun, Jer. 22, 24 אֶתְּקֶנְךָּ[1]; see Ges., § 58. 4; Dav., § 31. 5. Stade, § 355 b. 3, remarks that 'It is due to false analogy if the Pausal suffix ֶךָּ is transferred from the verb to a noun,' and cites with this passage, Prov. 25, 16 דַּיֶּךָּ, and other instances. It is possible, however, that the vowel points in these cases are not to be trusted as they stand in our texts.

The ה at the end of איכה is merely a *scriptio plena* (found both in obj. and subj. suffixes),—as Prov. 2, 11 תנצרכה; cf. ver. 12 נתתה. Ex. 15, 11 כמכה (twice). 1 Sam. 1, 26 עמכה,—and in no way affects the sense.

10. אָנֹכִי. The Mass. note here is מלעל, i.e. the word is, contrary to rule, accented on the penult.; cf. Ges., § 29. 4 c; Dav., § 10. 5 b. As a rule the vowel in pause is lengthened, this cannot take place here as the vowel is already long. The accents :ֽ, ֔, and (sometimes) ֒ usually effect this lengthening, when it is possible, in pause. Here the minor distinctive accent ֖ (*Ṭifcha*) exercises a pausal influence,

[1] On the forms of the Imperf. with the suffix and so-called *nun demonstrative* or *energetic*, the reader may consult Wright, *Comp. Gram.* p. 193 f. It should be remembered that the *nun* belongs not to the suffix, but to the energetic form of the Imperf., which is still preserved in Arabic.

there being a sufficient break in the sense for the voice naturally to rest; cf. Driver, § 103, and 15, 14 יַעֲבֹ֫דוּ (the tone drawn back and the vowel lengthened), which the Massoretes have not noticed. אתה and עתה, like אנכי, transfer the accent to the penult. in pause.

11. כי עירם אתה is really the object to מי הגיד, see M. R., § 161 b, where it is designated 'an object sentence;' cf. 1, 4 and Dav., *S.*, § 146.

לבלתי. בלתי is used regularly to negative the inf. cstr. after ל; cf. Ges., § 114. 3. R. 2; M. R., § 140. R. a; Dav., *S.*, § 95.

המן. On the pointing of ה interrog., see Ges., § 100. 4, s.p.; Dav., § 49. 2. Here ה introduces a simple interrogative sentence (cf. Ges., § 150. 2; M. R., § 143; Dav., *S.*, § 122), the answer being uncertain (affirmative or negative). הלא = Latin *nonne,* the answer expected being in the affirmative.

12. האשה . . . עמדי, a *casus pendens.* '*The woman which etc. . . . she gave me.*' הוא is resumptive and is inserted for emphasis; see Ges., § 135. 1. Rem. 2; Driver, §§ 123. Obs. 199; cf. 15, 4 כי אם אשר יצא ממעיך הוא יירשך; 24, 7 . . . יהוה הוא ישלח. The *casus pendens* is often used to relieve a long and unwieldy sentence. See also Dav., *S.*, § 106.

ואֹכֵל. The pausal form of the 1st person. In ver. 6 we have ותאכַל and ויאכַל as the pausal forms of the 3rd pers. fem. sing. and 3rd pers. masc. sing. respectively; see Ges., § 68. 1.

13. מה זאת עשית: cf. 12, 18. With the verb עשׂה, מה זאת is generally employed, with other verbs מה זה, e.g. 27, 20. זה and זאת are used, after the manner of an adverb, to emphasize interrog. words, see Ges., § 136. R. 2; Dav., *S.*, § 7 c; M. R., § 93. Rem. c. Render, '*What then hast thou done?*'

The A. V. and Pesh. render it as a relative sentence, '*What is this thou hast done?*' Del. adopts the former rendering, remarking (in edit. 4) that the corresponding question in Arabic, whether the demonstrative belongs to the interrogative, or whether it should be rendered as our Eng. Ver. does, was a subject of dispute among the Arabic grammarians. He points out that the Massoretic punctuation favours the first rendering. LXX render slightly differently, τί τοῦτο ἐποίησας; so Vulg. *quare hoc fecisti?* On the dag. in the ז of זּאת, see on 2, 18.

14. ארור אתה מכל וגו׳. LXX, ἐπικατάρατος σὺ ἀπὸ πάντων κ.τ.λ. Vulg. *maledictus es inter omnia*, etc. Render as the Vulg. '*Cursed art thou among all beasts*,' i.e. '*marked out by a curse from*,' etc. מִן as in Ex. 19, 5. Deut. 14, 2. Judg. 5, 24. Amos 3, 2; cf. Ges., § 119. 3 d. The other renderings, '*cursed by all beasts*,' i. e. '*these shall hate and abhor the serpent*,' or '*more cursed than*,' as apparently A. V., are untenable: for, as Knobel points out, the curse comes from God, not from the beasts, who had no reason to curse, and is aimed at the serpent only, not at the other beasts, as there is no ground assigned for cursing these.

כל ימי חייך, acc. of time; cf. Ges., § 118. 3b; M. R., § 42.

15. הוא ישופך ראש וגו׳. ראש and עקב are accusatives of nearer definition; cf. Ges., § 117. 5 d; M. R., § 44 and Rem. a; Ewald, § 281 c; Dav., *S.*, § 71; so 37, 21 לא נכנו נפש; Deut. 33, 11 מחץ מתנים קמיו; Jer. 2, 16. Ps. 3, 8. Hebrew in this respect is analogous to Greek; cf. τυφλὸς τά τ' ὦτα τόν τε νοῦν τά τ' ὄμματ' εἶ, '*blind both in ears and mind and eyes art thou;*' βλέπω κολοιὸν τὤμματ' ἐκκεκομμένον, '*I see a jackdaw pecked out as to his eyes.*' שׁוּף occurs again Job 9, 17. Ps. 139, 11. The only meaning which can be philologically defended

is '*crush.*' This meaning suits Job 9, 17, but not Ps. 139, 11. The alternative rendering is, '*lie in wait for,*' a kindred form with שׁאף '*to pant after,*' cf. Amos 8, 4; it suits Ps. 139, 11 (cf. Del. in loc.) better than '*crush,*' but a word = '*cover*' is required there: hence some read there יְשׁוּכֵּנִי, so Ew., Ges. in *Th.* שׁוּף = '*to crush*' is justified by the Aramaic usage of שׁוּף and ܫܦ or ܫܳܦ, e.g. in Onq., Deut. 9, 21 וְשָׁפִית יָתֵיהּ '*and I crushed it,*' i.e. the calf; Targ. on Job 14, 19 אַבְנַיָּא שָׁיְפָא מַיָּא '*the water crushes the stones.*' And in Ex. 32, 20 (Pesh.) ܘܫܳܦܶܗ ܒܫܽܘܦܺܝܢܳܐ (= Heb. ויטחן) '*and crushed* (better *scraped*) *it with a file.*' [It should be remarked that in Syriac the roots ܫܘܦ and ܫܦܦ are confounded one with the other, as Bernstein points out l. c.] Cf. Levy, *Chald. Wörterb.*; Bernst., *Lex. Syr. sub voce.* Di. admits that the meaning '*crush*' suits the first part of the clause, i. e. the man's crushing the serpent's head, but denies its application to the serpent, and adopts the rendering '*lie in wait for,*' which he attempts to justify by appealing to שׁאף; but this meaning is not so certain as the meaning '*crush,*' and the double acc. after the rendering '*lie in wait for*' is difficult. שׁוּף is applied to the serpent in the second half of the verse by a kind of zeugma, the same verb being used to express the mutual nature of the enmity (Kal.); compare Del.[5], and Tuch, 2nd ed., who compares '*feriri a serpente,*' Pliny, xxix. 4. 22. The Vss. render variously. In the LXX the reading varies, both τηρήσει . . . τηρήσεις (Swete) and τειρήσει . . . τειρήσεις occurring. The Vulg. has '*ipsa conteret caput tuum, et tu insidiaberis calcaneo ejus;*' but שׁוּף cannot have a different meaning in each half of the sentence. Pesh. has ܗܽܘ ܢܶܫܽܘܦ ܪܺܫܳܟ ܘܰܐܢ̱ܬ ܬܶܡܚܽܘܢܳܝܗܝ ܒܥܶܩܒܶܗ, using different words in the two parts of the clause, but giving שׁוּף a similar sense in each half. Onq. paraphrases הוּא יְהֵא דְכִיר [לָךְ] מָה דַעֲבַדְתְּ לֵיהּ מִלְּקַדְמִין וְאַתְּ תְּהֵי

נְטַר לֵיהּ לְסוֹפָא׃ '*he will remember against thee what thou hast done to him from the beginning, and thou wilt guard against him to the end.*' Targg. Jon. and Jer. paraphrase widely, but seem to have rendered שׁוּף '*crush.*'

16. הרבה ארבה '*with a multiplying, I will multiply,*' i.e. '*I will greatly multiply;*' cf. the rule on 2, 16. רבה has two forms for the inf. abs. Hif'il: (1) הַרְבֵּה (which would be the regular form) used as an adverb; (2) הַרְבָּה, see Ges., § 75. iv. Rem. 15: only here and 16, 10. 22, 17.

עצבונך והרונך. Not a hendiadys, '*the pain of thy conception,*' but '*thy pain and (especially) thy conception:*' waw attaching the *particular* הרונך to the *general* עצבנך; cf. Ps. 18, 1. Is. 2, 1; and see Ges., § 154, foot-note b. הרון is an abnormal formation, which occurs nowhere else in the O. T. The abs. state is הֵרָיוֹן (Hos. 9, 11. Ruth 4, 13), cstr. הֶרְיוֹן; with suffix הֶרְיוֹנֵךְ and shortened הֵרֹנֵךְ; see Stade, § 296. 2.

תשוקתך. The LXX here, and 4, 7, render with ἀποστροφή, possibly reading תשובתך; cf. their rendering in 1 Sam. 7, 17. Frankel, *Einfluss*, p. 10, suggests that the LXX rendering is a free euphemistic translation of the Heb. word. The word תשוקה is only found once again outside the book of Genesis, viz. in the Song of Songs 7, 11 אני לדודי ועלי תשוקתו; LXX, ἐγὼ τῷ ἀδελφιδῷ μου, καὶ ἐπ' ἐμὲ ἡ ἐπιστροφὴ αὐτοῦ.

17. ולאדם. On the pointing וְלָאָדָם, adopted by some, see the note on 2, 20.

בעבורך. The LXX (ἐν τοῖς ἔργοις σου) and Vulg. ('*in opere tuo*') seem to have read עבודך, which they apparently took as עֲבוֹדָתְךָ. Tuch considers the variant as perhaps due to the parallel passage 4, 12. Cf. also Geiger, *Urschrift*, p. 456.

18. קוץ ודרדר. Cf. Hos. 10, 8. Only in Isaiah do we

find the phrase שָׁמִיר וָשַׁיִת, e.g. Is. 5, 6. דרדר occurs but once again in Hos. l. c.

ואכלת. Notice the place of the tone, which has been thrown forward one place by waw conv. with the perfect; see for details, Driver, §§ 106, 110: cf. also Ges., § 49. 3; M. R., § 23; and Dav., § 23. 3.

19. תאכל לחם. For position of tone, see note on 4, 17.

עד שׁובך אל האדמה. On the construction, see Ges., § 114. 2. 3; M. R., § 111 b; Dav., *S.*, §§ 91, 92; cf. on 2, 4. Render, '*until thou return;*' שׁובך (as Arabic shews; see Wright, *Arab. Gram.*, i. p. 311) is to be regarded as a subst. in the genitive case after עד. Cf. Ges., l. c. 1 b.

כי ממנה. Some render, '*from which thou wast taken,*' lit. '*which from it thou wast taken;*' כִּי being regarded as equivalent to the relative אשׁר; so in 4, 25; for constr. cf. Ges., § 138. 1; M. R., § 156: so all the Vss. here and in 4, 25, except the Sam., which has [Samaritan] here and [Samaritan] in 4, 25. But as the passages cited in defence of this are not conclusive, it is better to render '*for*' here and in 4, 25. '*Until thou returnest unto the ground; for thou wast taken from it*' (pause, this half of the verse being marked off from the second half by *Athnach* [֑], the second strongest prose accent): '*for dust thou art,*' etc.

20. חוה = '*Life*' or '*Living,*' not '*Life-giver.*' חַיָּה = חַוָּה, the form used here is antiquated in Heb., but חוא = חיה *vixit*, is preserved in Phoenician (Di.). LXX here Ζωή, in the other passage where it occurs (4, 1) Εὔα. Ζωή is probably intentionally used by the LXX, being occasioned by the explanatory addition כי הוא היתה וגו׳. Cf. also C. P. Ges., *sub voc.*

22. *'And Yahweh Elohim said, Behold the man hath become as one of us, so as to know . . . and now that he may not stretch forth his hand and take,'* etc.

כאחד ממנו. On the construct state before the preposition, see Ges., § 130. 1; M. R., § 73. Rem. a; Dav., *S.*, § 35. R. 2. It is especially frequent with אחד and מן, Lev. 13, 2. Num. 16, 15. 1 Sam. 9, 3. 1 Kings 19, 2, etc.

לדעת וגו׳=*'so as to know:'* cf. 1 Sam. 12, 17 לשאל לכם מלך; Prov. 26, 2 כצפור לנוד כדרור לעוף. On this gerundial usage of the inf. with ל, see Driver, § 205; Dav., *S.*, § 93.

פן is used here independently, as in Ex. 13, 17; cf. Ewald, § 337 b; M. R., § 164 b; 'without indicating that the sentence which it introduces is dependent on another.' See also Ges., § 152, 1 i. The formula, *'For he said . . . lest,'* occurs frequently, and always implies that some precaution is taken by the speaker to prevent what he fears happening; e.g. Ps. 38, 17 (compare Del., *Die Psalmen*[5], ad loc.); Gen. 38, 11. 42, 4. Ex. 13, 17, etc. Cf. Dav., *S.*, § 127 c.

ולקח. The perfect with waw conv. after the imperfect with פן; so 19, 19 פן תדבקני . . . ומתי; Ex. 1, 10 פן ירבה והיה. Three times (Ps. 2, 12. Jer. 51, 46. Prov. 31, 5) we find the imperf. repeated after פן, instead of a perf. with waw conv.; see Driver, § 115 end, § 116; Ges., § 112. 3 c. *a*; Dav., *S.*, § 53 c.

וָחַי. Perf. with waw conv. pointed with pretonic qameç; so 19, 19 וָמַתִּי (notice the tone; cf. the note there); 44, 22 וָמֵת: see on 1, 2.

חי is perf. from חָיַי: see Ges., § 76. 2 g; Dav., § 42.

24. את הכרובים *'the cherubim.'* These appear in the Old Testament always in connection with God's manifesting himself to the world. In the tabernacle they hovered over

the ark (Ex. 25, 18 ff.). In Solomon's temple they are represented as stationed on the floor of the Holy of Holies, spreading out their wings from one side to the other (1 Kings 6, 23. 1 Chron. 28, 18). In Ez. 1 and 10 they form God's living chariot, in which he appears to the prophet; and in Ps. 18, 11. 2 Sam. 22, 11 God is represented as riding on a cherub to judgment: cf. Ps. 80, 2. 1 Sam. 4, 4. 2 Sam. 6, 2, where God is described as יוֹשֵׁב הכ״. From 1 Kings, l.c., we find that the cherub had an upright form, partly human, with one face (Ex. 25, 20), two wings (1 Kings 6, 24), and possibly hands. In Ez. 1 and 10 a somewhat fuller and different description of the cherubim is given: 'with the similitude of a man, four wings' (Ez. 1, 11. 23), two of which served to cover their bodies, and with two of which they flew; and under their wings human hands (Ez. 1, 8. 10, 7. 8. 21), with four faces (Ez. 1, 10. 10, 14), one human, one that of a lion, one that of an ox, and one that of an eagle, and the soles of their feet like those of a calf (Ez. 1, 7). Lastly (Ez. 1, 18. 10, 12; cf. Rev. 4, 6), their whole body was studded with eyes. It is uncertain whence the Hebrews derived their idea of the cherubim; possibly the winged forms on the Assyrio-Babylonian and Egyptian monuments exercised some influence on their conception of the cherub, but it is doubtful whether they borrowed the idea from either the Egyptians or Assyrians (cf. the authorities cited below).

The etymology of the word is uncertain. (i) Some connect it with the Aramaic ܟܪܒ, כְּרַב *aravit;* so כְּרוּב=*arator, bos:* cf. Ez. 10, 14 with 1, 10. (ii) Another view is that כְּרוּב is transposed for רְכוּב=*'chariot,'* i.e. *'the divine chariot:'* cf. 1 Chron. 28, 18, where the כרובים are explained by תבנית המרכבה; so Rödig. in Ges., *Thes.;* M. and V., *H.W.B.*, 11th ed. (iii) Hyde (quoted by Ges., *Thes.*, p. 710) considers that

כרוב=קרוב, i.e. '*he who is near God,*' '*his servant.*' (iv) Maurer on Is. 6, 2 explains כרוב as from כרב=כרם, Arab. كَرُمَ '*nobilis fuit.*' (v) Another view is that כרוב is to be connected with the Arab. كرب '*adstringere,*' so כרוב '*a strong being*' (Rosenmüller); cf. viii. (vi) Ges. in the *Thes.* proposes a derivation from כרב=חרם, Arab. حرم '*prohibuit a communi usu.*' כרוב= '*custos,*' '*satelles,*' i.e. Dei, 'qui profanos arcet.' All these are most precarious and improbable. (vii) Vatke, see Ges., *Thes.*, 711, assigned a Persian origin to the word, regarding it as the same as the Greek γρύψ, γρυπός, 'quod a Pers. گرفتن (greifen) *prehendere, tenere,* derivabat Chr. Th. Tychsen (Heeren's *Ideen,* i. p. 386), vel idem esse volunt atque γρυπός *naso adunco nostrove praeditus.*' (viii) Del., *Par.*, 154, connects it with an Assyrian root '*karâbu*' (from which an adj. '*karûbu*' is derived)='*to be great, powerful;*' cf. Schr., *C. O. T.*, p. 39. The word reads like a foreign one, but it seems that nothing can be affirmed as to its meaning with certainty. See further, Di. in *Schenkel's Bibel Lex.*, 1. 509 ff.; Keil., *Bib. Arch.*, 2nd ed., i. 92 ff.; Winer[3], *R. W. B.*; Riehm, *H. W. B.*, art. *Cherubim;* Del. *Comm.*[5] and Di. *Comm.* on this passage; also Cheyne, art. *Cherub,* in *Ency. Brit.*

ואת להט החרב וגו' '*and the blade of the waving sword.*'

הַחֶרֶב. The article (pointed according to Ges., § 35. 2 A; Dav., § 11 b) is placed before the genitive, and *not* before the cstr. state, cf. Ges., § 125. 1; M. R., § 76. II. a; Dav., *S.*, § 20.

המתהפכת, lit.='*the one turning itself about:*' cf. on 2, 11; also M. R., § 92. Rem. a. The form is a participle fem. sing. Hithpa'el of הפך, being formed as a segholate noun, and so accented on the penult.: see Ges., § 95. Rem. 2. 3; Dav., add. notes to 3rd Dec.

את דרך עץ החיים *'the way to the tree of life:'* so 16, 7 דרך שׁור *'the way to Shur;'* 38, 14 דרך תמנתה *'the way to Timnah;'* 48, 7 בדרך אפרת *'on the way to Ephrath.'* Cf. Ges., § 128. 2 b; Dav., *S.*, § 23. Hebrew uses the cstr. state (implying belonging to) to denote ideas which are made clearer in English by the use of a preposition.

4.

1. ידע *'to get to know,' 'make the acquaintance of,'* so euphemistically=*'concubuit cum ea;'* used again in this sense vers. 17. 25. 24, 16, and often. This meaning has passed over into Hellenistic Greek; cf. *γιγνώσκειν*, often used by the LXX for the Hebrew ידע, e.g. here. Cf. also in the New Testament, Luke 1, 34 *ἐπεὶ ἄνδρα οὐ γιγνώσκω.* The Pesh. has ܚܟܡ, which is again used in the same sense in their version of Matt. 1, 25 *οὐκ ἐγίνωσκεν αὐτήν*=ܘܠܐ ܚܟܡܗ̇.

קין *'Kain,'* elsewhere a nom. app.=*'spear,'* 2 Sam. 21, 16, or a nom. prop. of a people, Num. 24, 22. Judg. 4, 11. The text here seems to connect קין with the root קנה *'to gain,' 'acquire;'* but this explanation must not be regarded as an etymology. The name was given, not because it was derived from קנה, but as recalling to mind this word: compare such proper names as נח, שׁמואל, משׁה (not *derived from,* but *recalling to mind* מֹשׁה). Gesenius derives קין here from קין= *'to forge,'* Arab. قَانَ, قَيْن, *'a smith,'* Syr. ܩܝܢܳܝܐ; and supposes that קַיִן in this passage means *'spear,'* as in 2 Sam. 21, 16.

את יהוה. LXX, *διὰ τοῦ Θεοῦ.* Pesh. ܠܡܪܝܐ *'for the Lord.'* Onq. מִן קֳדָם יְיָ *'from before Yahweh.'* Vulg. *'per Deum.'* The Targ. of Ps.-Jon. has קְנֵיתִי לְגַבְרָא יַת־מַלְאֲכָא דַיְיָ *'I have gotten as man the angel of the Lord,'* possibly meaning the Messiah. The את has been variously explained. I. Di. and others render '*with Yahweh*,' i. e. through his assistance, with his help; so LXX, though it is uncertain whether διά is a free rendering, or whether they had מֵאֵת for אֵת in their text, and similarly the Vulg. and Onqelos. Elsewhere, to be sure, we find עם used in this sense, and not את; cf., for example, 1 Sam. 14, 45 כי עם אלהים עשׂה; still את may be regarded as synonymous with עם, as may be inferred from its alternative usage with עם in the phrase '*to be with one*,' i. e. help him; cf. 26, 3 עמך with 21, 20 את הנער. 28, 15. 31, 3 עם, but 26, 24. 39, 2 את. II. *a.* Others (Luther, etc.) render '*I have gained a man, the Lord;*' את יהוה being a second acc. of nearer definition, so 6, 10 שׁלשׁה בנים את שׁם; 26, 34; Judg. 3, 15; Eve supposing she had given birth to the Messiah; see Ps.-Jon., above. *b.* Or as Umbreit, '*I possess as a man, Yahweh*,' אישׁ acc. of the predicate. But against *a* it may be urged that there is nothing in the text to justify the idea that Eve thought she had given birth to the Messiah (cf. also 3, 15); and against *b* that it gives no explanation of the name of the child.

2. ותסף ללדת '*and she bare again;*' cf. ver. 12. The finite verb in Hebrew corresponds to the adverb in our idiom. We find other verbs used in Hebrew to express adverbs, e. g. מהר '*to hasten;*' cf. Ges., § 120. 1 f. (cf. also § 114. 2. Rem. 3); M. R., § 114 a; Dav., *S.*, § 82.

ויהי הבל רעה צאן וקין. וקין is placed before the verb to which it belongs in order to slightly emphasize the contrast between the occupations of Kain and Abel. M. R., § 131. 1 b. Rem. c, compares μέν . . . δέ in Greek. הבל has been explained as meaning '*a breath*,' '*nothing*,' possibly with reference to his short life; but it is doubtful if the name can be brought into connection with this meaning. It has also been suggested that הבל might be a variation of יבל ver. 20. See Ew., *J. B.* vi. 7 ff. Others connect the word with the Assyr. *ablu*=son; cf. *C. O. T.* Gloss, *s. v.* הבל.

רֹעֵה is a participle in the cstr. state, '*a shepherd of;*' רֹעֶה would be the abs. state, and צֹאן would then be in the acc. case. Both constructions are possible, cf. 22, 12 יְרֵא אֱלֹהִים with Ex. 9, 20 הַיָּרֵא אֶת־דְּבַר יְהוָֹה; see other examples in Ges., § 116. 3; M. R., § 121; Dav., *S.*, § 98.

3. מפרי. The prep. מִן must be taken here in a partitive sense, '*some of,*' cf. 8, 20 ויקח מכל־הבהמה; 27, 28 ויתן לך אלהים מטל; Ex. 12, 7. Ges., § 119. 3 d. foot-note 1; Dav., *S.*, § 101. R. c.

מנחה. 1. '*a gift,*' 2. '*an offering* (to God),' but not to be taken in this passage in its more restricted sense '*the meal offering,*' as opposed to זבח, '*the meat offering.*' The LXX render it here by *θυσίαν*.

4. '*And Abel too brought.*' גם with the pronoun repeated is emphatic; cf. ver. 26 ולשת גם הוא.

ומחלבהן, *scriptio defectiva*, for ומחלביהן. The sing. form of the word would be חלבהן. Other instances of *scriptio defectiva* are, 1, 21 למינהם. Job 42, 10 רֵעֵהוּ for רֵעֵיהוּ. Ex. 33, 13 דרכֶך for דרכֶיך; see Ges., § 91. 2. Rem. 1. 'The singular would be permissible here (Lev. 8, 16. 25), but would not express the plurality of animals so distinctly' (Di.). The plural here, as in Lev. 6, 5, = '*fat pieces.*' In the Levitical service the offering of the first-born of the flock and their fat portions is enjoined; cf. Num. 18, 17. Render, '*and* (*indeed*) *of their fat pieces.*' The waw is *waw explicativum*, see Ges., § 154. foot-note b, and cf. Judg. 7, 22. 1 Sam. 17, 40. Is. 57, 11; Dav., *S.*, § 136. R. c.

וַיִּשַׁע. Impf. Qal from שָׁעָה, apocopated from יִשְׁעֶה,

יִשַׁע=יִשְׁעְ; cf. Ges., § 75. Rem. 1. 3 a, b, c; so יִחַר from יִחְרֶה in ver. 5. The verb שׁעה is rare in prose.

5. ויחר לקין. So 18, 30. 32. 31, 36, and often. I. Either אף may be understood, '*it* (*anger*) *was hot for Kain,*' or II. חרה may be taken impersonally, '*it was hot to Kain.*' On this impersonal use of the 3rd perf. sing., cf. Ges., § 144. 2; M. R., § 124; Dav., *S.*, § 109.

7. Render, '*Is there not, if thou doest well, lifting up? and if thou doest not well, at the door sin croucheth; and towards thee is its desire, but thou oughtest to rule over it.*' שְׂאֵת (for שְׂאֵת inf. cstr. of נשׂא, cf. Ges., § 76. 2 a) must be explained from the phrase נשׂא פנים='*to lift up* (*one's own*) *face,*' the opposite of נפלו פנים in verse 6; so Tuch, Ke., Del., and Di.: cf. also the usage of language in Job 10, 15. 11, 15. 22, 26. Lifting up of the face='*cheerfulness, joy;*' falling of the face, '*sadness* or *moroseness.*' The Vss. render variously. LXX has οὐκ ἐὰν ὀρθῶς προσενέγκῃς, ὀρθῶς δὲ μὴ διέλῃς, ἥμαρτες; ἡσύχασον, possibly connecting שְׂאֵת with מַשְׂאֵת 43, 34, and reading לְנַתֵּחַ instead of לַפֶּתַח, and perhaps חָטָאתָ רְבַץ instead of חַטָּאת רֹבֵץ; cf. their rendering of רבץ in Job 11, 19. Pesh. has, ܗܐ ܐܢ ܬܛܝܒ ܡܩܒܠ ܐܢܬ ܘܐܢ ܠܐ ܬܛܝܒ ܥܠ ܬܪܥܐ ܚܛܝܬܐ ܪܒܝܥܐ '*Behold if thou doest well thou receivest; and if thou doest not well, at the door sin croucheth,*' taking שׂאת in the sense of receiving; so Vulg. '*Nonne si bene egeris recipies, sin autem male, statim in foribus peccatum aderit,*' but this is not in keeping with the context. Onq. has, הֲלָא אִם־תּוֹטֵיב עוֹבָדָךְ יִשְׁתְּבֵיק לָךְ וְאִם לָא תוֹטֵיב עוֹבָדָךְ לְיוֹם דִּינָא חֶטְאָה נְטִיר עָתִיד לְאִיתְפְּרָעָא מִינָּךְ אִם־לָא־תְתוּב וְאִם־תְּתוּב יִשְׁתְּבֵק לָךְ '*If thou doest thy work well thou wilt be pardoned; but if thou doest not thy work well, for the day of judgment the sin is laid up, ready to take vengeance upon thee, if thou dost not repent; but if thou*

'*repentest thou shalt be forgiven,*' paraphrasing, but taking שׂאת in the sense '*forgive:*' this rendering of Onqelos' is also out of harmony with the context.

לפתח חטאת רבץ. '*Sin is at the door* (cf. Prov. 9, 14) *a lurker.*' Sin is compared to a ravenous beast lying in wait for its prey; perhaps a lion is here intended (cf. the Arabic name for the lion الرابض '*the lier in wait*'); cf. 1 Pet. 5, 8. As חטאת is fem., רבץ must be taken as a substantive, on the construction cf. M. R., § 135. 4 a; Ewald, § 318 a; Kalisch, *Heb. Gram.*, I. § 77. 13; and Ges., § 145. 7 b. Rem. 3. This is the ordinary explanation of the verse. It is possible, however, that the text is corrupt. The mention of the '*house door*' is strange, and the lion can hardly be described as lurking outside the door of a dwelling-place, nor are the words תשוקה and תמשל בו very suitable expressions in this connection. Di. suggests as an emendation רֹבֶצֶת or תִּרְבַּץ and תְּשׁוּקָתָהּ and בָּהּ. 'Sin' would then be figuratively depicted as a woman who tempts or leads astray. On the trans. of the LXX here, see Del.[5] ad loc.

8. ויאמר קין וגו׳. LXX, Itala, Pesh., Vulg., Sam., Targ. Jer. have given in their translations נלכה השׂדה, which does not stand in the Mass. text; and it is not improbable that these Versions have preserved the original text. Frankel, *Einfl.*, p. 55, certainly objects to נלכה on the ground that a Hebrew would say נֵצֵא, not נֵלְכָה, and regards the addition in the LXX as a gloss; but though this is the more usual phrase, yet we have 27, 5 וילך עשׂו השׂדה; Ruth 2, 2 אלכה נא השׂדה, cf. also Lagarde, *Symm.* i. 57. Some MSS. note a lacuna here [פסקא]; two expressly note no lacuna (בלא פסקא, Wright); and according to Del.[4] it is doubtful whether the פסקא is found in the best authorities. Del.[5] renders,

'*And Kain said it to his brother,*' etc., explaining (on the analogy of 2 Chron. 1, 2 f. and 32, 24) that what Kain said may be easily perceived from what follows. But in 2 Chron. 1, 2 f. אמר=צִוָּה, and the explanation is hardly so natural as to suppose an omission of '*let us go into the field.*' Some (Bött., Kn.) read וישמר, cf. 2 Sam. 11, 16 '*he laid in wait for.*' Tuch, comparing Ex. 19, 25, where he takes ויאמר אליהם (as אמר is always followed by what is said) in the sense '*Moses spake to the people what God had said to him,*' ver. 7 (cf. Ewald, § 303 b, 2), renders, '*And Kain said it,*' viz. what God had said to him. This is, according to Di., improbable. He also points out that ויאמר is not=וַיְדַבֵּר, and that in Ex., l. c., an extract from one document (J) abruptly terminates (leaving אמר without an object), in order that the compiler may make use of another of his sources (E); cf. Driver, *Introd.*, p. 29.

בהיותם וגו״, lit. '*In their being in the field,*' i.e. '*when they were in the field.*' LXX, ἐν τῷ εἶναι αὐτοὺς κ.τ.λ., cf. 2, 4 בהבראם and the note there, and see Dav., *S.*, § 92.

10. מה עשית. מה pointed with ֶ before the guttural with ָ, according to Ges., § 37. 1; Dav., § 13, 'מה assumes a pointing quite like the article.'

קול דמי. I. '*Hark, thy brother's blood crying!*' קול is used as an interjection, as in Is. 13, 4. Jer. 10, 22; cf. Ewald, § 317 c. Ges., § 146. 1. Rem. 1: צעקים being in apposition to דמים. II. M. R., § 135. 3 c, takes it apparently as an instance of the predicate agreeing with the genitive instead of the cstr. state, as is always the case, for example, with כל; M. R. renders, '*The voice of thy brother's blood-drops cry.*' The Sam. reads צעק. דמים=blood violently shed.

11. ארור אתה מן האדמה. Cf. 3, 14. I. '*Cursed art*

thou away from the ground,' or II. '*Cursed art thou from,*' etc., i.e. the curse shall strike thee from the ground, cf. ver. 12. I. is adopted by Tuch and Del., II. by Ibn Ezra, Kn., Keil. The rendering '*Cursed art thou by*' is untenable, as curses are represented in the Old Testament as coming from God or man, never from the ground. The rendering '*More cursed art thou than*'—though 3, 17. 8, 21 may be cited in its favour—does not suit the context here; cf. ver. 14, which favours I, more stress being laid in the narrative on Kain's banishment than on the unfruitfulness of the soil, or on the difference in the curses laid on Kain and the ground.

אשר פצתה את פיה. Cf. Is. 5, 14 לכן הרחיבה שׁאל נפשׁה ופערה פיה לבלי חק.

12. לא תסף תת. The jussive with לא is rare, cf. 24, 8. Joel 2, 2. Ez. 48, 14; Driver, § 50 a. Obs.; Ges., § 109. 1. Rem. 1; Dav., *S.*, § 63. R. 3.

כחה. Cf. Job 31, 39 אם כחה אכלתי.

נע ונד. The LXX paraphrased to reproduce the paronomasia, στένων καὶ τρέμων; Hier., '*vagus et profugus.*'

13. גדול עוני מנשׂא, lit. '*Greater is my punishment than bearing,*' i.e. '*my punishment is too great to bear.*' מִן before the inf. cstr., as in Ps. 40, 6 עצמו מספר. 1 Kings 8, 64 קטון מהכיל. Cf. Ges., § 133. 1. Rem. 2; Dav., *S.*, § 34. R. 2.

עון = '*sin,*' including its consequence, punishment, which is represented as a burden heavy to bear; cf. Is. 24, 20. Ps. 38, 5.

נְשֹׂא, inf. cstr. with the נ retained, Ges., § 76. 2 a; cf. Num. 20, 21 נְתֹן and Gen. 38, 9 נְתָן־, by the side of the more usual form תֵּת. The Vss. mostly render, '*My transgression is greater than forgiving,*' i.e. '*too great to be forgiven,*' which is grammatically possible, but not so suitable here, as in ver. 14, Kain speaks of his punishment, not with a view to its removal through the forgiveness of his offence, but with a desire that it should be mitigated.

14. כל מצאי=*'every one that findeth me,'* lit. *'my finder.'* The participle may either govern its case like the verb, or may stand as a substantive in the cstr. state followed (as here) by a suffix or a genitive; cf. Ges., § 116. 3; M. R., § 121; cf. also § 80. 2 a and Gen. 32, 12 יְרֵא אֹתוֹ *'timens eum,'* 23, 10. 18 באי שער עירו; Ex. 1, 4 יצאי ירך יעקב. Comp. note on ver. 2.

15. כל הרג קין, *casus absolutus, 'Every one that slayeth Kain, he (Kain) shall be avenged'* (cf. ver. 24); or impersonally *'vengeance shall be taken,'* cf. the Nif. in Ex. 21, 20, and the Hof. in ver. 21: and this is perhaps preferable, the change of subject involved in the first way being a little harsh, though perhaps supported by ver. 24. כל הרג קין=*'every one,* or *any one, that killeth,'* is virtually a hypothetical sentence, *'if any one kills Kain;'* cf. ver. 14. 9, 6, and Driver, p. 147, foot-note 2; Ges., 116. 5. Rem. 5; Ewald, § 341 e; Dav., *S.*, § 132. R. 2.

שבעתים=*'sevenfold,'* so ארבעתים, 2 Sam. 12, 6, *'fourfold;'* see Ges., § 97. Rem. 1. It may be interpreted, with Tuch, as meaning, Kain's murder shall be avenged with a vengeance seven times greater than the vengeance taken on Abel's; sevenfold meaning, as in Prov. 24, 16, *'manifold,' 'many times.'* Cf. also Dav., *S.*, § 38. R. 5.

יקם does not mean *'shall be punished, shall suffer punishment,'* so perhaps LXX, ἑπτὰ ἐκδικούμενα παραλύσει, but *'shall be avenged.'*

וישם יהוה לקין אות. The אות was given to Kain for

his protection, and not as a token of the truth of what God had said, for Kain did not express any doubt as to the truth of what he had been told, and stress is rather laid in the narrative on Kain's immunity from death in the event of any one attacking him.

וישם . . . לקין. '*And Y. gave Kain a sign.*' לקין='*for Kain's protection,*' rather than '*on Kain,*' which would require על or ב, cf. Ex. 10, 2. Is. 66, 19. What this אות was, cannot be determined; some have conjectured that Kain had a mark set on his forehead, perhaps a horn; others (Haitsma quoted by Di., p. 98) an inscription set somewhere on his person, commencing with כל, and ending with יקם; but there is nothing in the narrative to throw any light on the nature of the אות given to Kain. The LXX have καὶ ἔθετο Κύριος ὁ Θεὸς σημεῖον τῷ Κάιν; Pesh. ܣܡ ܐܠܗܐ ܠܩܐܝܢ; Onq. וְשַׁוִּי יְיָ לְקַיִן אָתָא וגו׳.

לבלתי הכות אתו, not לבלתי הכותו, because that might mean '*that he might not smite;*' cf. Ges., § 117. 1. Rem. 3. The usual order is here departed from, and the object coming after the infinitive precedes the subject; cf. Ges., § 115. 3 Rem.; Ewald, § 307 b: see also Is. 20, 1 בשלח אתו סרגון. Prov. 25, 8 בהכלים אתך רעך. לבלתי . . . כל='*that no one,*' just as לא כל='*no one;*' cf. 3, 1 לא תאכל מכל עץ '*thou shalt eat of no tree,*' and see also Dav., *S.*, §§ 95, 148.

16. **נוד** must be the name of a place, as we may infer from וישב, and its position after ארץ and before קדמת; not an apposition to the subject, as Hieron., *Quaest.* p. 9 σαλευόμενος, i.e. *instabilis et fluctuans* . . . , the Vulg. '*profugus in terra,*' connecting נוד with נד '*to wander,*' and Onq., who render גָּלֵי וּמְטַלְטַל. The position of נוד is as uncertain as that of the garden of Eden. The narrative regards it as lying

towards the east, perhaps (cf. קדמת עדן) on the east of Eden. J, however, always uses מִקֶּדֶם לְ='*east of*,' cf. 2, 8. 3, 24. 11, 2. 13, 11, so possibly קדמת עדן here, is an addition by the author of 2, 10–14; cf. Di., p. 98. נוד='*banishment*.'

17. חנוך='*dedication*,' from חנך '*to dedicate*,' prob. a denom. from the root of חך '*a gum*' (for חֵנֶךְ), prop. '*to rub the gums*;' so in Arabic; it being customary to rub the gums of new-born children with date syrup, which was regarded as an act of dedication or initiation into life; cf. Del.[5], p. 125, Prov. 22, 6.

ויהי בנה עיר '*and he was building a city*,' i.e. at the time when חנוך was born, the city was not completed, otherwise the narrator would have written בָּנָה (pf.) or וַיִּבֶן (impf. with waw conver.). Other instances where the subst. verb היה is added to the participle to mark more prominently the duration of the action (i.e. that it is incomplete) are to be found in 37, 2 היה רעה '*was shepherding*;' 39, 22 היה עשׂה; see on 1, 6. Ryssel, however, *De Elohist. Pent. sermone*, p. 59, takes this passage differently, his words are 'Prorsus aliter res se habet Gen. 4, 17, ubi participium loco nominis ponitur ["*Städtebauer*"];' so Del.[5], Di. The former rendering seems simpler. For conjectures as to the city חנוך, see Di., p. 99.

בֹּנה עיר. The retrogression of the tone in בנה is due to the following tone-syllable in עיר. Two tone-syllables usually do not come together, either the first word is accented on the penult., or deprived of all accent by being connected with the second by Maqqef; cf. Ges., § 29. 3 b; Driver, § 100: so 1, 5 קֹרא לילה. 3, 19 תֹּאכל לחם. 21, 5 בהֹולד לו. 39, 14 לֹצחק בנו.

18. ויולד . . . עירד. The passive verb is followed by the acc. case, as in 17, 5. 21, 5. 27, 42. 40, 20, etc.; cf. Ges., § 121. 1; Ewald, § 295b; M. R., § 47; Dav., *S.*, §§ 79, 81. R. 3.

The meanings of some of the *nomina propria* which follow are very obscure; cf. Di. ad loc. and Budde, *Urgesch.*, p. 124 f.

עירד may mean '*he who flees*,' or '*the one who flees*,' from ערד, Arab. عرد '*to flee*.' LXX give it by Γαιδάδ, which is interesting as throwing light on their pronunciation of the Heb. ע; cf. עמורה, Γόμορρα; עזה, Γάζα; עתליה, Γοθολία; רעואל, 'Ραγουήλ; עתניאל, Γοθονιήλ; רעמה, 'Ρεγμά; see Wright, *Comp. Gram.*, p. 42 f.

מחויאל, of which מחייאל is another form, perhaps means '*blotted out by God*,' or '*stricken of God*,' = מְחוּי אֵל. LXX, Μαλελεήλ. מתושאל Ges., *Thes.* '*man that is of God*,' being composed of מְתוּ, i.e. מת with the old case ending ו, which is found again in מתושלח and פנואל; cf. Ges., § 90. 3 b; Stade, § 344 b, and esp. Driver, p. 238: of שׁ, the relative pronoun, in Assyrian *sha*, and of אל '*God*.' מת is preserved in Ethiopic, where it often has the meaning '*husband*,' as Is. 54, 1. Luke 2, 36. Gen. 2, 23, in the Ethiopic version; see Di., *Ethiop. Lex.*, p. 183. The relative שׁ is not found in the Pentateuch, unless we adopt the view of some interpreters who consider בשגם in 6, 3 to consist of ב, שׁ, and גם; and שלה in 49, 10 to be equivalent to שֶׁלֹּה, i.e. אֲשֶׁר לוֹ. It is found in Judg. 5, 7. 6, 17, where it may be due to a north Palestinian dialect, and in the Song of Songs; also in later writings, e.g. Eccles., Lam., late Pss.; while in Phoenician (see Schröder, *Phön. Gram.*, pp. 162–166, and the inscriptions cited by him, note 2, p. 162) אש is the common form, the form אשר being never used. This explanation of the name מתושאל is corroborated by the Assyrian; cf. Hommel, *Z.D.M.G.*, xxxii. 714, and Lenor., *Les Origines de l'Histoire*[2], p. 262 f. It is, however, against the analogy of compound proper names like פְּנוּאֵל, שְׁמוּאֵל etc., which have no שׁ. If 'מ = '*man of God*,' we should expect the form מְתוּאֵל, rather than מְתוּשָׁאֵל. A less probable explanation is '*Man of Entreaty*' from שָׁאַל and מֵת. The LXX have Μαθουσάλα.

ועירד ילד. ילד is generally used of the mother, and the Hif'. הוליד of the father; cf. 10, 8 ff. 22, 23.

לֶמֶךְ cannot be explained from the Hebrew. In Arabic يَلْمَكٌ = '*a strong young man;*' possibly למך is to be connected with this.

19. Lamech was the first to introduce polygamy, in opposition to the divine injunction in 2, 24.

The names of the wives are given here because it is necessary for the understanding of the song.

עָדָה = '*adornment;*' צִלָּה '*shade:*' but these two meanings are not quite certain.

שְׁתֵּי constr. of שְׁתַּיִם. According to Ges., § 97. 1. footnote 1, the dag. lene after a vocal shewa is due to the fact that the full form of word was אֶשְׁתַּיִם. According to Stade, p. 216, 'שְׁתַּיִם is formed after the analogy of שְׁנַיִם from שְׁתַּיִם.'

20. The names in this verse are very obscure; cf. Di. for explanations that have been attempted.

יושב אהל ומקנה. Jabal was the father of those who dwelt (the sing. taken collectively) in tents, and had cattle, i.e. the first to introduce nomad life. יושב is connected by zeugma with מקנה; cf. Hos. 2, 20. Is. 42, 5. Josh. 4, 10. ישב with the acc. or gen. of the place that is dwelt in, so Ps. 22, 4 יושב תהלות ישראל; cf. Is. 33, 14, where יגור is construed with an acc. of the place dwelt in.

מקנה '*possession,*' then '*possession of cattle,*' a wider idea than צאן; it comprehends also (e.g. 26, 14. 47, 17) larger cattle, sometimes camels and asses; cf. Ex. 9, 3. Job 1, 3.

21. אבי כל תפש כנור וגו״. '*The father of all those who*

handle harp and pipe.' LXX somewhat freely, ὁ καταδείξας ψαλτήριον καὶ κιθάραν. כִּנּוֹר, according to Ewald (*Lehrbuch*, § 79 d, § 118 a), who seeks to connect it with κιθάρα, is abbreviated from כִּנְתָּר or כִּנְתּוֹר. According to *H. W. B.*, 11th ed., it is a modified form of כִּנָּר; cf. כִּנֶּרֶת, Arab. كِنَّارَةٌ, Aramaic כִּנָּרָא, כִּנּוֹרָא, ܟܢܳܪܳܐ; from כנר an assumed onomatopoetic root[1]. Josephus, *Arch.*, vii. 12. 3, describes it as being ten-stringed, and says that it was touched with the plectrum, but cf. 1 Sam. 16, 23. 18, 10. 19, 9. where David is said to touch it with his hand.

עוגב occurs only four times in the Old Testament; here, Job 21, 12. 30, 31 (see Baer in loco, p. 50). Ps. 150, 4; and is taken by the LXX (κιθάραν) and Pesh. (ܟܢܳܪܳܐ) as a string-instrument; it is better to take it with Targ. Jer., LXX in Ps. 150, and Rabb. as='*pipe*,' perhaps '*a shepherd's pipe.*' In the Hebrew translation of the Aramaic parts of Daniel it is used in 3, 5. 10. 15 for סומפוניה.

22. לטשׁ כל חרשׁ. '*A sharpener* (or *hammerer*) *of every kind of instrument of brass and iron.*' The A.V. takes לטשׁ in a metaphorical sense '*a sharpener*,' i. e. '*instructor of every worker in brass*,' etc.; R.V. '*forger*;' Marg. '*an instructor.*' חרשׁ='*an instrument*' does not occur again in the O. T.; the passage (1 Kings 7, 14) cited in *H. W. B.*, 11th ed., being an instance of its ordinary meaning, '*workman.*'

The rendering above given is that of Tuch, Del., and most moderns. Dillmann, however, in his note on the passage remarks: 'This explanation, which since Tuch is the one usually adopted, is hardly the meaning of the Massoretes, who—judging from the accent on לטשׁ and the pronunciation חֹרֵשׁ (where one would rather expect חָרָשׁ)—

[1] Barth., *N. B.*, p. 65, is of opinion that כִּנּוֹר = Arab. كِرَانٌ.

perhaps supplied (cf. Targ.?) אֲבִי from ver. 21, before כל, '*a hammerer*, (*father*) *of every brass and iron smith*.' The falling out of אבי must have been very old, as the Vss. do not give it. The LXX have καὶ ἦν σφυροκόπος χαλκεὺς χαλκοῦ καὶ σιδήρου, taking חרש as a masculine, omitting כל, and apparently reading ויהי for קין, unless we suppose that καὶ ἦν is a corruption of καίν. Similarly Vulg. '*malleator et faber in cuncta opera aeris et ferri*,' supporting to some extent Dillmann's view. Onq. paraphrases רַבְּהוֹן דְּכָל יָדְעֵי עִיבִידַת נְחָשָׁא וּבַרְזְלָא, but apparently did not view חרש as='*an instrument*.' Ps.-Jon. has much the same as Onq., רַב לְכָל־אוּמָן דְּיָדַע בַּעֲבִידַת '*the master of every workman who understands the working in*' etc.; also taking חרש as a participle. If חרש be taken as a subst. it is a participle neuter; cf. יוֹתֵר '*that which remains over*,' '*that which is gained*,' so '*an advantage, benefit, gain*,' נבל; in Isa. 28, 4 ציצת נבל; cf. Num. 24, 20, Ps. 73, 10. Prov. 6, 24; and Ges., § 128. 2. Rem. 3. Budde, *Urgeschichte*, p. 137 f., doubts the correctness of the text and emends as follows. He omits the words קין . . . ברזל, ver. 22, and adds at the end of the ver. וַיְהִי לֶמֶךְ חֹרֵשׁ נְחֹשֶׁת וּבַרְזֶל וַיֹּאמֶר לֶמֶךְ וגו׳ (23). Such a violent reconstruction of the text, however, can scarcely be regarded as legitimate criticism. נעמה='*die Liebliche, the amiable, lovely one*.'

23, 24. Lamech's Song. It consists of three verses, each containing two lines. It may be rendered thus:

23 (α). '*Ada and Zillah hear my voice;*'
(β). '*Ye wives of Lamech, give ear unto my speech:*'
(α). '*Surely a man have I slain for wounding me,*'
(β). '*And a young man for bruising me:*'
24 (α). '*If Kain shall be avenged sevenfold,*'
(β). '*Then Lamech seven and seventyfold.*'

With ver. 23, cf. Isa. 28, 23. 32, 9.

23. שְׁמַעַן for שְׁמַעְנָה; cf. קְרֶאֶן, Ex. 2, 20, and Ges., § 46. Rem. 3; Stade, § 612 a. Possibly the text should in each case be emended, שְׁמַעַן being punctuated שְׁמַעְןָ, and קְרֶאֶן, קְרֶאןָ; cf. Ruth 1, 20.

כי not '*for*,' nor = the ὅτι *recitativum*, of the N. T., introducing the words of the speaker (as e.g. 21, 30); but = '*certainly*, *surely*;' cf. Ex. 4, 25.

לפצעי...לחברתי. The suffixes are *objective;* cf. Ges., § 135. 4; M. R., § 78; Dav., *S.*, § 23. Cf. LXX, εἰς τραῦμα ἐμοὶ . . . εἰς μώλωπα ἐμοί. So Vulg.

ל = '*on account of;*' cf. M. R., § 51. 4; Ges., § 119. 3 c; see Num. 16, 34 לקולם.

The perfects may best be taken, with the Vss., as real perfects, and not as perfects of certainty. Lamech has killed men and will not, should necessity occasion it, hesitate to kill others. Jewish fancy narrates that Lamech killed Kain (אִישׁ) and Tubal Kain (יֶלֶד). But only one act is intended, the repetition being due to the parallelism common in Hebrew poetry.

The song is probably a triumphal song on the invention of war weapons. Lamech boasts that if Kain would be avenged sevenfold, surely he, with his instruments, would be able to take a far greater vengeance (seventy-sevenfold). For a mere wound inflicted on him, he has punished the inflicter with death; and in the possession of his weapons he feels himself superior to his ancestors, and able to dispense with divine protection. The poetical words האזין and אמרה and the parallelism which is observed throughout the three verses are noticeable.

25. שֵׁת = *Satz*, *Setzling*, and then *Ersatz*, '*substitute*.'

כִּי שָׁת־לִי. Qameç remains, notwithstanding the Maqqef,

and is on this account marked with firm Metheg; see Ges., § 16. 2 b; cf. § 9. 12. Rem. 1 d. כי הרגו קין; cf. on 3, 19.

26. ולשת גם הוא. The pronoun is repeated separately, to emphasize the noun; cf. Ges., § 135. 2 c; Ewald, § 311 a and § 314 a; M. R., § 72. 1. R. a; Dav., *S.*, § 1, cf. 10, 21.

אנוש = '*man*,' from אנשׁ '*to be weak*;' or from אנשׂ = the Arabic أَنِسَ '*to attach oneself to*,' so *animal sociabile*. Cf. C. P. Ges., p. 60.

אז הוחל. The indeterminate 3rd pers. sing.; see Ges., § 144. 3 e, and the note on ver. 5: cf. Lam. 5, 5 לא הונח לנו. The LXX have οὗτος ἤλπισεν, perhaps reading הֵחֵל and זֶה; cf. Frankel, *Einfluss*, p. 41, on their reading. Onq. has בְּכֵין בְּיוֹמוֹהִי חֲלוּ בְּנֵי אֱנָשָׁא מִלְּצַלָּאָה בִּשְׁמָא דַיְיָ '*thus in his days the children of men ceased praying in the name of the Lord*;' so Ps.-Jon., taking הוחל as = '*profanari*,' and paraphrasing to avoid the idea of profaning Y.'s name, so that the commencement of idolatry is here mentioned. This, however, is not probable. Aq. has correctly τότε ἤρχθη, also Symmachus ἀρχὴ ἐγένετο. Di. remarks on this verse: 'It is, moreover, quite possible that the original reading was הֵחֵל (=זֶה) ז, i. e. "*This one began*" (so LXX, Vulg., B. Jubil.), and אז הוחל (so, read as a passive, already in Aquila and Symmachus, but with the meaning ἀρχή) stood in connection with the view taken by the Targum.'

לקרא בשם. Not merely '*to call with Yahweh's name*,' '*to mention Him*;' but '*to worship Him*.'

5.

A short notice of the generations from Adam to Noah, connecting the history of the creation, the first chief event, with that of the flood, the second important event in the narrative. The number of generations from Adam to Noah is ten. In the accounts of the first nine generations, the name of the first-born is always given, the age of the father at the time of his birth, the number of years which the father lived after the birth of his first-born, and the total length of his life. In the case of each, mention is made that he begat sons and daughters (ויולד בנים ובנות). In the notice of Noah however, no mention is made of the number of years he lived after the birth of his three sons, nor of the total number of his years when he died, this being narrated, chaps. 7, 11. 9, 28. On the deviations in the chronology followed by the Hebrew text, the LXX, and the Samaritan, cf. Di., p. 110, and the authorities cited by him, p. 112; Del.[5], *Comm.*, p. 136, and more especially for the LXX chronology; Frankel, *Einfluss*, p. 70. The following table, taken from Di., p. 110, gives the variations in the chronology of the Hebrew, LXX, and Samaritan texts.

	Heb. Text.			Sam. Ver.			Septuagint.		
Adam	130	800	930	130	800	930	230	700	930
Seth	105	807	912	105	807	912	205	707	912
Enosh	90	815	905	90	815	905	190	715	905
Kenan	70	840	910	70	840	910	170	740	910
Mahalalel ...	65	830	895	65	830	895	165	730	895
Jared	162	800	962	62	785	847	162	800	962
Enoch	65	300	365	65	300	365	165	200	365
Methuselah ...	187	782	969	67	653	720	167	802	969
Lamech	182	595	777	53	600	653	188	565	753
Noah	500	...	...	500	...	...	500	...	...
Up to the flood .	100	...	(950)	100	...	(950)	100	...	(950)

In each of the three tables marked Heb. Text, Sam. Ver., Septuagint, the first column gives the years each patriarch lived until he begat children; the second, the number of years in each life after the birth of the first child; and the third, the total number of years each individual lived.

1. ספר תולדות only here: elsewhere in P תולדות alone; cf. 2, 4. 6, 9. Num. 3, 1.

3. ויחי אדם שלשים וגו׳. מאה שנה is equally common with מאת שנה; cf. Ges., § 134. 1. Rem.; M. R., § 98. The acc. is acc. of time, in answer to the question '*how long?*' cf. M. R., § 42 a; Ges., § 118. 3 b; Dav., *S.*, § 68.

ויולד, viz. a son or child. Olshausen proposes to insert בֵּן here, but unnecessarily, the object being contained in the verb, as in 6, 4 וילדו להם; 16, 1 לא ילדה לו.

5. כל ימי אדם וגו׳. The predicate usually, after כל, agrees with the genitive, and not with the noun in the cstr. state: cf. Ges., § 146. 1. R. 2; M. R., § 135. 3 a; Dav., *S.*, § 116. R. 2.

תשע מאת שנה ושלשים שנה. The noun שנה repeated with the ten; cf. Ges., § 134. 3; M. R., § 97. Rem. c. Dav., *S.*, § 37. R. 3. חַי is perf. from חיי, as in 3, 22.

6. חמש שנים ומאת שנה. The noun repeated with the lesser number (from 3–9 inclusive) in the pl., and with the greater in the singular. See reference to Grammars in preceding note.

22. ויתהלך חנוך את; so Noah, 6, 9, walked with God; cf. a similar use of the Qal in Mic. 6, 8. Mal. 2, 6. התהלך את is used of confidential intercourse with God, a closer relationship to God than is implied in '*walking before God*' (17, 1), or, '*walking after God*' (Deut. 13. 5); cf. 1 Sam. 25, 15 of the intercourse between David's followers and Nabal's servants. The LXX have here Εὐηρέστησεν δὲ Ἐνὼχ τῷ Θεῷ, perhaps to avoid an anthropomorphic idea; cf. Ecclus. 44,

16. 49, 14, and Heb. 11, 5 *πίστει Ἐνώχ*. Onq. paraphrases וְהַלֵּיךְ חֲנוֹךְ בְּדַחַלְתָּא דַיְיָ *'Enoch walked in the fear of Yahweh.'* The Pesh. renders as the LXX, ܘܫܦܪ ܚܢܘܟ ܠܐܠܗܐ *'Enoch pleased God.'*

24. ואיננו כי לקח אתו. *'And he was not, for Elohim took him;'* cf. the usage of אֵין in Is. 17, 14. Ps. 103, 16. 1 Kings 20, 40, of sudden disappearance. On its use in the narrative style, cf. Ewald, § 321 a; M. R., § 128, 2 a. כי לקח אתו א״, that is, without dying, otherwise we should expect וימת; cf. 2 Kings 2 (Elijah's removal from earth to heaven, without tasting death). The reason for כי לקח אתו is to be found in the first half of the verse, viz. his piety; cf. Heb. 11, 5, and Onq.; not, as some suppose, the danger of his relapsing into sin: so Ber. Rabb. c. 24. Frankel, *Einfluss*, p. 43, cites this passage as one of the places where the LXX translators had the Haggada in view. LXX have *καὶ οὐχ ηὑρίσκετο διότι μετέθηκεν αὐτὸν ὁ Θεός*. So Vulg. Onq. וְלֵיתוֹהִי אֲרֵי (לָא) אֲמִית יָתֵיהּ יְיָ (cf. Frankel, p. 44, note d, who omits לא, so Berliner in his edition of Onqelos [ed. 1884, Berlin], p. 5; cf. part 2, p. 3) = *'And he was not, for Yahweh did (not) slay him.'* The Pesh. follows the Heb. text. In Ecclus. 44, 16 Enoch is called *ὑπόδειγμα μετανοίας ταῖς γενεαῖς*, and in the book of Enoch (translated by R. H. Charles[1]) and the N. T. book of Jude, 14 et seq., he is described as a seer and prophet, who announced the coming of God, to punish the world for its sin.

29. ויקרא את שמו נח. נח generally derived from נוח *'to rest,'* = *'rest,'* but doubtfully as the word is always written נֹחַ in the O. T.—as if from a root נָח,—not נוֹחַ. Ewald connects this root נָח with נָא = *'to be fresh,'* or *'new,'* and Halévy (*R. E. J.*, xxii. p. 611) regards it as the verb from which

[1] See *Jewish Quarterly Review*, Oct., 1893, et seq.

נִיחֹחַ comes, assigning to it the meaning '*to be pleasant*,' and seeing in the p. n. נֹחַ (*agrément de sacrifice*) an allusion to 8, 21. Cf. further, Di., p. 116. The explanation given in the text, זה ינחמנו, is not strictly an etymology at all, as נח cannot be connected with נחם, which is an entirely different stem; but the similarity in sound led the narrator to connect in thought נח with נחם, just as משׁה is a reminiscence of משׁה '*to draw out*,' yet cannot be etymologically connected with that word. The LXX render ינחמנו as though they read it יְנִיחֵנוּ (not יַנִּיחֵנוּ, which would rather mean '*to set, place*'). Rashi perceiving the etymological difficulty, fancifully explains ינחמנו as though it were=יניח ממנו '*make to rest from us*.' His words are ינח ממנו את עצבון ידינו עד שׁלא בא נוח לא היה להם כלי מחרישׁה והוא הכין להם והיתה הארץ מוציאה קוצים ודרדרים כשׁזרעים חטים מקללתו שׁל אדם הראשׁון ובימי נוח נחה וזהו ינחמנו '*He will make the toil of our hands cease from us: before Noah came they had no instruments to plough with, but he made them some, and the earth used to bring forth thorns and thistles when they sowed wheat, on account of the curse of the first man, but in the days of Noah* (*the earth*) *had rest, and this is the meaning of* ינחמנו.'

ממעשׂנו ומעצבון וגו׳. '*From our work and labour* (*arising*) *from the ground*;' better than מן־האדמה '*because of the ground*,' as A.V.; for the curse comes to man from the ground, which brought forth קוץ ודרדר when it was tilled (3, 18).

6.

1. לרב is inf. cstr. of רבב '*to be many*,' '*gross sein*;' רבה= '*to become many*,' '*gross werden*.' The apodosis of the sentence begins with ver. 2 ויראו.

2. טבות is used in a physical sense here='*comely*;' cf. 24, 16. Ex. 2, 2.

מכל אשר בחרו. מִן is used to particularise the idea as in 7, 22. 9, 10; cf. Ewald, § 278 c; Dav., *S.*, § 101. R. c.

בני האלהים. This phrase, elsewhere in the O. T., always means '*the angels*,' with reference to their nature as beings of a higher, diviner type (being called מלאכים, with regard to their office as messengers executing the divine commands); so Job 1, 6. 2, 1. 38, 7. Dan. 3, 25 ('*a son of the gods*'), but never בני יהוה. The same meaning is usually assigned to it here by ancient interpreters, e. g. Philo, *Book of Enoch*, etc.; cf. Jude 6. 2 Peter 2, 4; the moderns also mostly explain it in the same way; so Tuch, Knobel, Schrader, Del., Di., etc. As, however, the idea of a carnal connection between the angels and daughters of men was very repugnant to a refined mode of thought, and especially objectionable to the Christian mind (cf. Matt. 22, 30), many attempts were made to explain these words in a way that would not cause offence. Thus, Targg., Onq. and Ps.-Jon. both render בְּנֵי רַבְרְבַיָּא '*sons of nobles*,' from the use of אלהים in Ex. 21, 6; 22, 7 (which, however, are very different passages from this). Rashi has בני השׂרים והשׁפטים '*the sons of princes and judges*;' others explain בני האלהים similarly as the sons of those of higher rank, opposed to בנות האדם the daughters of those of lower rank. In favour of this interpretation, Pss. 82, 6. 49, 3 are quoted. But in the first of these passages the expression is not the same, and the application evidently different; in the second, the opposite to אדם is אישׁ, not אלהים; further האדם, in vers. 1 and 4 (='*the human race*'), is against this view. Another explanation is that adopted by the Fathers, e. g. Ephrem Syrus, Theodoret (cf. Del.[5], p. 146), who interpret the sons of God in a spiritual sense as the pious ones, those who lead the lives of angels; viewing these as the descendants of Seth, and regarding the בנות האדם as the daughters of the wicked, the offspring of the line of Kain. But there is nothing in either chap. 4 or 5 to bear out this view, and the expression '*sons of God*' as a name for pious men is not usual in the O. T.; and it is scarcely conceivable that האדם in ver. 2^{b} is to be taken in a different sense from the האדם in ver. 1^{a}, which would be required if this view were adopted. The Vss. render variously. The reading of the LXX is uncertain, *υἱοὶ τοῦ Θεοῦ* is found, and also *ἄγγελοι τοῦ Θεοῦ* (Swete); cf. Lagarde, *Genesis Graece*, p. 20. The Pesh. has here ܒܢܝ̈ ܐܠܗܝܡ merely transliterating the Heb. words; so in Job 1, 6. 2, 1; Aquila, *υἱοὶ τῶν Θεῶν*, on which Hieron., *Quaest.* ed. Lagarde, p. 11, says, '*Deos intelligens sanctos sive angelos;*' Symm., *οἱ υἱοὶ τῶν δυναστευόντων* (agreeing with the old Jewish view); Itala (from LXX), '*angeli Dei;*' Vulgate, '*filii Dei.*'

3. לא ידון רוחי. רוחי is rather the breath of life which Yahweh Elohim (2, 7) breathed into man's nostrils when he created him ('the principle of physical and spiritual life,' Di.), than the Holy Spirit (as the Targg. of Ps.-Jon., Jer.; Symm., etc.) working in man, and judging him; for the determination on Yahweh's part to deprive man of His spirit, as the latter half of the verse shows, really means depriving him of life.

יָדוֹן is not jussive, but (as in יָבוֹא from בוֹא not בּוֹא) has the intransitive punctuation of the imperf.; cf. Ew., § 138 b; Stade, § 490 c; Ges. § 72. Rem. 1. 2. The Vss. (LXX, Pesh., Onq., Vulg.) either read יָדוּר, or according to others יָלוּן or יִכּוֹן (Halévy, *Rev. Crit.*, 1883, p. 273), or guessed at the meaning of the word, rendering it '*abide*' or '*remain.*' It is now generally rendered either '*be abased,*' so Ges., *Th.*,

Ew., from the Arabic دَانَ; or '*rule*,' Del., Knobel, Budde; דון being=דִּין, Job 19, 29 Qri (?) and Zech. 3, 7 וגם־אתה תדין את־ביתי. Del. also compares אָדוֹן, which he takes to be an elative form for *adwan* from דון, but cf. C. P. Ges., *s. v.* אָדוֹן. The rendering '*rule in*,' although uncertain, is perhaps preferable to '*be abased*,' as the latter trans. ascribes to the word a signification which it has ceased to have in Hebrew. The rendering offered by the Vss. '*abide in*' best suits the context, but it does not seem possible to get it out of the present text. Cf. C. P. Ges., *sub voce*. The Targg. (Ps.-Jon., Jer.) and others take it as synonymous with דין, and render '*judge*,' but this does not suit the context so well as '*be abased*,' or '*rule*.' The A. V. renders '*my spirit shall not strive*,' so Joseph Kimchi and Rashi, regarding דון as equivalent to דין, and giving it the meaning of the Nif'al נדון (cf. נשפט), a meaning which in Nif'al depends on the reciprocal signification of the conjugation, and so cannot be assigned to Qal.

בשגם הוא בשר. The best attested reading is that adopted by Baer and Del. in their edit. of *Genesis*, Leipz., 1869, בְּשַׁגַּם with pathach. The reading in the ordinary editions is בְּשַׁגָּם with qameç. The meaning of these words is disputed. There are two general explanations. That adopted by Delitzsch, '*For that he too is flesh*,' or '*For that he indeed is flesh*,' בְּשַׁגַּם being treated as compounded of בְּ the prep., the relative ־שֶׁ[1] (cf. on 4, 18), and the particle

[1] It is now generally recognised (Wright, however, *Comp. Gram.*, p. 119, still adheres to the old view) that the fragment שׁ has nothing to do with the rel. אשׁר, but that ־שַׁ, ־שֶׁ, originally ثَ, is only another form of the Aramaic relative conjunction ܕ, דִּ. It has been supposed that the rel. שׁ is characteristic of the dialect spoken in Northern Israel, cf. Dr., *Introd.*, pp. 422, 563. Whether the Inscription רבע של רבע נצג,

גַּם *also;* cf. באשר, 39, 9. But against this it may be urged that (*a*) the relative שׁ never occurs in the Pentateuch, though defended by some by an appeal to the pr. n. מתושאל, 4, 18; מישאל, Ex. 6, 22. Lev. 10, 4; which are not, however, of any weight for prose usage, and both of which may be explained otherwise: and that (*b*) גם is here superfluous. The second explanation is that adopted by Ges., Tuch, Ew., Budde, who read בְּשַׁגָּם, and take it as inf. cstr. from שׁגג=שׁגה, with the affix of the third pers. m. pl. (cf. Ges., § 67, Rem. 3; Ewald, § 238 b), and renders, '*On account of their error* or *transgression he* (*mankind*) *is flesh.*' Against this it may be urged (*a*) that הוא is masc. sing., while שׁגם has the third pl. m. affix; cf., however, Ewald, § 319 a, where other instances of a similar *Enallage numeri* are to be found, or the suffix in בְּשַׁגָּם may refer to 'the sons of God;' cf. Budde, *Urgesch.*, p. 23 f.: (*b*) that שׁגג is scarcely the word that would be expected in this connection, and it is here hardly general enough: (*c*) that the reading with qameç is not so well attested as that with pathach; cf. Del.[4], p. 195. The text is probably corrupt: but the emendations that have been proposed are not satisfactory: e.g. באשר גם, or נפשם,

---

'the *fourth of* a *fourth of* a?,' preserved on a weight discovered on the site of Samaria and prob. dating from the eighth cent. B.C., confirms this view or not is very doubtful. The real text of the Inscription has not yet been accurately deciphered, and the reading שׁל may be incorrect: see authorities in Driver, l.c., and cf. Robertson Smith in *Academy*, Nov. 18, 1893. See also *Z. D. M. G.* xxxii. 711 ff., and a note in the American Journal, *Hebraica*, April, 1885, p. 249, where a third view of the relation between שׁ and אשׁר is mentioned, which makes שׁ the original relative, and derives אשׁר from it by prefixing an independent pronominal stem *a*, and affixing lă (which appears also in the Arabic relative allaḍi (اَلَّذِى), ל being then hardened to ר; cf. Sperling, *Die nota relationis im Hebräischen*, Jena, 1876. See also C. P. Ges., *sub voce* אֲשֶׁר, and Wright, l. c., p. 118 f.

לבשׁ גם. The Vss. give—LXX, *διὰ τὸ εἶναι αὐτοὺς σάρκας*; Pesh. ܡܛܠ ܕܒܣܪܐ ܐܢܘܢ; Onq. בְּדִיל דְּאִינּוּן בִּסְרָא; Vulg. '*quia caro est*,' all expressing the sense '*For that*.'

והיו ימיו מאה וגו'. '*So his days shall be*,' or '*so let his days be*,' etc., i.e. he shall have a respite of a hundred and twenty years. This seems better than the other explanation, that human life should be limited to a hundred and twenty years; for many post-diluvian Patriarchs reached a far higher age, e.g. Abraham, 25, 7; and it cannot be regarded as a general statement to which there might be exceptions, as the exceptions are too numerous (all the post-diluvian Fathers, from Shem to Terach, reach a higher age than the limit here assigned; cf. 11, 10 et seq.)[1].

4. הנפילים. According to the ancients (LXX, Pesh., Onq., Sam., Saad.), a name for giants; cf. Num. 13, 33 ושם ראינו הנפילים בני ענק. No clear etymology can be found in Hebrew; perhaps the word was derived from a Canaanitish dialect. It has been connected with the root נפל '*to fall*:' thus many of the Fathers consider these נפילים to have been fallen angels; but there is nothing in the narrative to justify this, and the narrator appears to distinguish the נפילים from the בני האלהים. Others render '*Robbers, Tyrants*,' lit. those who fall upon others; so Aq. *οἱ ἐπιπίπτοντες*; Symm. *οἱ βίαιοι*; but נפל only means '*to fall upon*,' '*attack*' in certain connections; cf. Josh. 11, 7. Job 1, 15. Gen. 43, 18. Others (Tuch, Knobel) connect the word with a root נפל, supposed to possess the sense of פלא, and consider it to allude to their

[1] Di., however, denies the force of this objection, pointing out that the writer here (J) has composed his narrative without regard to P, the document in which the ages of the Patriarchs down to Moses exceed 120 years. Cf. his *Comm.*, p. 123, but see Del.[5], p. 151.

extraordinary size, but this is precarious. Other conjectures will be found in Lenormant, *Les Origines de l'histoire*[2], etc. i. p. 344.

הָהֵם is always pointed with ָ, although ֵ would be expected here; cf. ver. 19 הָחַי; and Ges., § 35. 2 A.

אשר יבאו . . . וילדו. Render, '*When the sons of God went in . . . and they bare.*' אשר, connecting the new sentence with a preceding particle of time (אחרי כן)[1], may be rendered '*when*;' cf. 45, 6. 1 Sam. 20, 31. 2 Sam. 19, 25 after יום; Deut. 4, 10. Ps. 95, 9[a] and [b]. The imperf. as a frequentative past, followed by the perf. with waw consec.; cf. Driver, § 113. 4 β: cf. 2, 6. 29, 2 f. Ex. 33, 7–11. The subject to וילדו is the בנות האדם: cf. for the change of subject, 9, 27. 15, 13.

המה refers to the נפילים in the first half of the verse, not to an object to וילדו, which has been left out, as this would be very forced.

אנשי השם is co-ordinate with אשר מעולם. '*The men of repute*;' cf. Num. 16, 2 אנשי שם. A word in the construct state cannot take the article, so it is defined by the article being attached to the following genitive, Ges., § 127 b.; M. R., § 76. N. B. Whether such a combination as אנשי השם means I. '*The men of repute*,' or II. '*Men of the repute*,' or III. '*The men of the repute*,' can only be decided by the context. Hebrew has only one way of defining the first, or the second, or both parts of a construct state, and following genitive combination. Cf. also Dav., *S.*, § 20. R. 2.

---

[1] Well. (*Comp.*, p. 308) and Budde (*Urgesch.*, p. 34) regard וגם אחרי כן as a later addition due to one who had Num. 13, 33 before him.

5. רַבָּה is accented *milra'*, and so is an adj., and not the perfect fem., from רבב, which would be *mil'el.*

כל יצר מחשבות לבו. '*Every form of the thoughts of his heart,*' יצר, I. '*form, shape,*' physically; II. tropically applied to what is fashioned in the mind, imagination; cf. 8, 21. Is. 26, 3. The LXX paraphrase πᾶς τις διανοεῖται ἐν τῇ καρδίᾳ, on which cf. Frankel, *Einfluss*, p. 10.

רק רע '*only evil,*' i.e. '*utterly, hopelessly, nothing but evil:*' cf. a similar use of רק in Deut. 28, 33 רק עשׁוק ורצוץ; Is. 28, 19 והיה רק זועה.

6. ויתעצב אל לבו. '*And was pained in his heart.*' LXX, καὶ διενοήθη. Onq. וַאֲמַר [בְּמֵימְרֵהּ] לְמִיתְבַּר תּוּקְפְּהוֹן כִּרְעוּתֵיהּ '*And spake by his Word, to break their strength according to his will.*' Ps.-Jon. וְאִידְיַין עֲלֵיהוֹן בְּמֵימְרֵהּ '*And disputed with his Word concerning them;*' so Sam. and Targ. Jer. All intentional, in order to avoid an anthropomorphic idea.

7. בהמה = usually '*tame,*' '*domestic animals;*' here used of '*tame* and *wild animals,*' as in ver. 20; 7, 23. 8, 17.

9. אלה תולדות. Cf. on 2, 4.

נח איש צדיק תמים. Render, '*Noah was an upright man, perfect among his contemporaries;*' according to the accents and the order of the words.

10. שלשה בנים. Masc. nouns take the numeral in the fem. form, and vice versa; see Ges., § 97; Dav., § 48. The number 2 *agrees* in gender with the word which it enumerates, and is an exception to this rule. The numerals from 2–10 are substantive, אחד, fem. אחת, *one* is an adj., and agrees with its noun.

11. ותמלא הארץ חמס. Cf. ver. 13 מלאה הארץ חמס and see note on 1, 21.

13. קץ כל בשר בא לפני. *'The end* (i.e. *the destruction*) *of all flesh* (*man and beast*) *has come before me.'* Not *'The end of all flesh has come to my knowledge,'* which would rather be בא אלי (cf. 18, 21. Ex. 3, 9), but *'has come before my mind, is determined on by me'* (cf. Job 10, 13. 23, 14), Kn.; or (Ez. 7, 6) *'has come before me'* (ver. 11), i.e. according to my decision and resolve, Di.

כָּל־בָּשָׂר is characteristic of P.

מפניהם *'from before them,'* i.e. *'because of them, through their influence;'* cf. Ex. 8, 20 תשחת הארץ מפני הערב. The pl. suffix is used because בשר must be taken collectively.

את הארץ *'with the earth.'* So LXX, Onq., Vulg. Pesh. has ܥܠ ܐܪܥܐ *'on the earth;'* Sam. ࠌࠍ ࠄࠀࠓࠑ *'from the earth,'* perhaps reading (wrongly) מאת by repeating the final ם of משחיתם.

14. תבת עצי גפר. תבה only occurs in Gen., chaps. 6–9, and Ex. 2, 3. 5; it is thought by some to be an Egyptian word; see Gesenius, *Th. sub voce*, and M. V., *H. W. B.*, p. 893. Others (cf. Halévy, *J. A.*, viii. 12, p. 516 f. Jensen, *Z. A.*, iv. 273) regard it as a loan word from the Assyrio-Babylonian. The Semitic etymologies given by Del.[5], *Comm.*, p. 169 (from תּוּב, a secondary formation of אוּב *'to be hollow'*), and Dietrich, *Abhandl. zur Semit. Wortforschung*, p. 33 (who regards the word as Semitic, and as standing 'in lebendigem zusammenhange' (in actual connection) with אֵבֶה *'a reed;'* comparing the derivation of תבה from אֵבֶה with those of תֵּבֵל, ܬܒܠ, from אבל; תּוֹם, from תאם; in all of which the א is suppressed), are untenable. The LXX here have κιβωτόν; in Exodus θίβιν; the Vulg. has *'arcam'* here, and in Exodus *'fiscellam;'* Targg. תֵּיבוּתָא, Pesh. ܩܒܘܬܐ, which is the Greek κιβωτός.

עצי גפר only occurs here. עצים = '*wood*' when cut down, '*logs*,' as opposed to עץ, '*trees*' growing; so חִטָּה, and חִטִּים, sing. '*wheat*' growing, and pl. '*wheat*' when cut down, '*grain*;' כסף '*silver*' in general, כְּסָפִים '*pieces of silver*,' Ges., § 124. 1. R. 1 a; Stade, § 333; Dav., *S.*, § 17. R. 1.

גפר is probably a resinous coniferous tree (Nadelbaum), perhaps the old name for the cypress, which was used by the Phoenicians for shipbuilding, and is elsewhere called ברוש. גפר only occurs here, and is a word of doubtful derivation. Ges. in *Thes.* cfs. כֹּפֶר, Lagarde (*Semitica*, i. 64, *Symm.*, ii. 93; *B. N.*, 217 ff.) regards the word as inferred from גָּפְרִית, or as a corruption for גָּפְרִית, cf. Di., p. 140. The LXX, Itala, and Vulg. did not understand the meaning of the word, and resorted to conjecture. The LXX have ξύλων τετραγώνων; the Itala, '*ligna quadrata*;' the Vulg. '*ligna laevigata*.' Onq. and Ps.-Jon. render '*cedar trees*;' the Pesh. has ܩܝܣܐ ܕܟܘܫܐ, which Walton renders '*de ligno viminis*;' but this is doubtful. Possibly it should be rendered '*juniper wood*;' see Löw, *Aram. Pflanzennamen*, *s. v.*

קנים. '*In cells shalt thou make the ark*;' קנים being acc. of manner or product, after a verb of making; cf. Ex. 38, 3 כל כליו עשה נחשת '*all its vessels he made brass*,' i. e. so that they consisted of brass; 27, 9. 1 Kings 18, 32. Is. 3, 7; cf. Ewald, § 284. a. 1; Ges., § 117. 5 c; M. R., § 45. 5; Dav., *S.*, § 76. Possibly the text originally ran קנים קנים, so Lag., Budde, etc.

עשה . . . וכפרת. The perf. with waw conv. in continuation of an imper.; cf. Dr., § 112; Dav., *S.*, § 55; Ges., § 112. 3 c. γ; M. R., § 24. 1 a; cf. 8, 17. 27, 43 f. Lev. 24, 14 הוצא את המקלל . . . וסמכו. 2 Sam. 11, 15. וכפרת has the tone thrown forward on to the last syllable, after the waw conv.; cf. the note on 3, 18. כפר is a denominative from כֹּפֶר. See Ges., § 43. Rem. 2.

בכפר = '*with bitumen*' or '*asphalt.*' The word is found in Aram. and Arabic, and also occurs in the Babylonian story of the flood. The article is used here with a material which was well known; cf. Ges., § 126. 3. Rem. b; M. R., § 68; Dav., *S.*, § 22 d; and 11, 3. 13, 2.

15. וזה אשר תעשה, lit. '*this is what thou shalt make it;*' i. e. '*this is how thou shalt make it.*'

16. צהר, only here in the sing., prop. = '*light,*' and then '*an inlet for light,*' so '*window.*' So all Vss. except the LXX, and most moderns. צהר is regarded as a feminine, so חַלּוֹן, Ez. 41, 16. 26; cf. Ges., § 122. 3 b and d; Ewald, § 174 c (γ), who classes צהר, as fem., among the nouns denoting places in which man is wont to move, or things which man uses, comparing חצר '*a court,*' Ez. 10, 4. 5; מחנה '*camp,*' in Gen. 32, 9; רחוב '*a street,*' Dan. 9, 25. In 8, 6 (J), the ark has a single window חַלּוֹן, i. e. 'a lattice-work window,' which could be opened and shut at will. צֹהַר (P) = merely 'an opening for light.' It is possible to render צהר collectively (? Pesh.) = '*windows,*' so Ges., *Thes.*, *s. v.*

ואל אמה תכלנה מלמעלה. Render, '*And up to a cubit shalt thou complete it from above.*' Tuch supposed that a single window, a cubit square, was meant, and that it was probably intended for Noah's cell while the animals were left in darkness. But there is nothing in the text to warrant either of these opinions. Equally improbable is the view adopted by Keil, Knobel, and Del.[4], viz. '*up to a cubit from above,*' i. e. the covering or roof of the ark, so that there would be the space of a cubit between the roof and the צהר. According to this view the size of the window would be left undefined, and we would rather expect מִלְמַעְלָה to stand after אַמָּה. Di. and Del.[5] consider the opening to have been a cubit high, and to have run round the four sides of the ark, a little below the roof, being interrupted merely by the beams supporting the roof; there would then be really a continuous row of windows. Di. appeals to the Pesh. in favour of his view, and claims כַּלָּה as suiting this meaning, and one would naturally assume that the ark would require more than one window; whether the Hebrew text, however, can bear the meaning Di. puts upon it, is questionable.

17. ואני הנני מביא. The participle as future (*futurum instans*), which it represents as already 'beginning;' frequently with הנה preceding it; cf. Ges., § 116. 5 c; M. R., § 14. Rem. a; Driver, § 135. 3; Dav., *S.*, § 100. R. 1.

את המבול מים. Not '*the flood of waters*,' but in app. '*the flood* [*even*] *waters*.' So Ps. 60, 5 יין תרעלה, lit '*wine, reeling*.'

מים. On the subst. in apposition, cf. M. R., § 76. Rem. b; Ewald, § 287 h; Driver, § 188. 1. The emendation מִיָּם is unnecessary and unsuitable. More probable is the suggestion that מים here (and 7, 6) is a gloss on מַבּוּל; see Ges., § 131. 2 e. Rem. 4 foot-note. Di., however, p. 141, denies this, regarding the words מים על־הארץ as an explanation, by the author, of the archaic word מַבּוּל; cf. Dav., *S.*, § 29 b. In Is 54, 9 the flood is called מֵי נֹחַ.

גוע in the Pent. and Josh. is peculiar to P.

18. והקימתי. הקים ברית and נתן ברית, 9, 12 are marks of P.

19. הָחַי only punctuated so in this passage; cf. Is. 17, 8 and the note on ver. 4.

זכר ונקבה, characteristic of P.

20. למינהו. See on 1, 12. רֶמֶשׂ and רָמַשׂ belong to the language of P.

21. קח לך . . . ואספת; cf. on ver. 14. אכלה is another characteristic of P.

22. כן עשׂה is rare outside P.

7.

1. וכל ביתך. Cf. the fuller description of Noah's family in P, 6, 18. 7, 13. 8, 16. 18.

2. שׁבעה שׁבעה. '*Seven by seven,*' i. e. '*by sevens;*' see Ges., § 134. 5; M.R., § 72. 2; Ewald, § 313 a; Dav., *S.*, § 29. R. 8; cf. Zech. 4, 2. Num. 3, 47. 17, 17 מטה מטה '*rod, rod,*' '*a rod each;*' 2 Kings 17, 29 גוי גוי '*nation, nation,*' i. e. '*every single nation:*' cf. also Mark 6, 39 *συμπόσια συμπόσια*; 40 *πρασιαὶ πρασιαί*. The repetition of a noun indicates that the action expressed in the sentence is performed on different individuals of the class denoted by the noun; thus the repetition serves to express the *distributive* relation. Some think that seven individuals of each kind were to be selected, the seventh possibly being intended for sacrifice (Del.). But the addition of איש ואשתו seems to indicate that '*seven pairs*' were intended. In the case of the unclean animals we have שׁנים once, i. e. '*one pair,*' and we may reasonably presume that had the narrator intended seven individual animals here, we should have had שׁבעה once. This also suits ver. 9 better (the animals went in שׁנים שׁנים by twos). שׁבעה שׁבעה in the next verse is to be taken in the same way.

אֲשֶׁר לֹא . . . הִוא; cf. 17, 12. 1 Kings 9, 20 etc. On

the pers. pronoun after אשר לא, see Driver, § 198. Obs. 1; Ges., § 138. 1; Dav., *S.*, § 9. R. 2.

4. כי לימים עוד שבעה. *'For after yet seven days.'* For this use of the preposition ל, cf. 2 Sam. 13, 23 ויהי לשנתים ימים; Ex. 8, 19 למחר יהיה האות הזה; M. R., § 51. 2.

ארבעים יום. Certain nouns are used after the numerals in the sing.; cf. Ges., § 134. 2 and R. 1; M. R., § 97; Dav., *S.*, § 37. R. 1.

ומחיתי. P uses שִׁחֵת or הִשְׁחִית; cf. 6, 13. 17.

כל היקום. היקום, which always has the י without a dagesh, is a subst. formed from the analogy of the imperfect. See, however, Barth., *N. B.*, p. 181, who denies this, and explains יקום from an original קִיּוּם by transposition. Render, *'Every existing thing.'*

6. בן שש מאות שנה. The adj. is expressed by joining to a subst., denoting a reference or relationship, a genitive expressing the attribute or thing; cf. Ges., § 128. 2. Rem. 2 c; M. R., § 79. 6 d; Dav., *S.*, § 24. R. 3.

והמבול היה מים. *'When the flood was, waters,'* etc. מים, as the text stands, is an explanatory apposition to המבול; cf. however, the note on 6, 17. היה = *'accidit,' 'came;'* LXX, ἐγένετο, but Swete reads ἦν. The second half of the verse is a circ. clause; see Ewald, § 341 d; Driver, § 169: cf. 19, 4. 24, 45 and Ges., § 164. 1 a. The R. V. keeps the old rendering, *'the flood of waters,'* which is a paraphrase adopted for the sake of English idiom.

7. ויבא נח ובניו. *'And Noah came in and his sons,'* etc. When the predicate *precedes* a compound subj., it frequently stands in the sing.; Ges., § 146. 2 b; M. R., § 138; Dav., *S.*, § 114 b.

11. בשנת שש מאות... לחיי וגו׳, lit. '*in the year of six hundred years to the life of N.*,' i. e. '*in the six hundredth year of N.'s life.*' The cardinals, for numbers beyond ten, are used for the ordinals; cf. Ges., § 134. 4; M. R., § 100 a; Ewald, § 287 k; Dav., *S.*, § 38 b.

לחיי נח. The genitive is often expressed thus by ל, when a writer wishes to avoid a string of construct states, or—as here—when any word intervenes between the construct state and the genitive. Cf. Ges., § 129. 1 d; M. R., § 83; Dav., *S.*, § 28. R. 5.

וארבות=lit. '*the latticed windows*,' from ארב '*to intertwine.*' The LXX have οἱ καταράκται, Vulg. '*cataractae*,' Aq. and Symm. αἱ θυρίδες: cf. ארבת ממרום, Is. 24, 18; also Job 38, 16. Prov. 8, 28 on the whole verse.

13. בעצם היום הזה. '*On this very day*;' see Ges., § 139. 3; M. R., § 90; Ewald, § 286 f; and cf. 17, 23; Ex. 24, 10 כעצם השמים '*as the very heavens*;' Josh. 10, 27 עד עצם היום הזה '*until this very day.*' Cf. Dav., *S.*, § 11 c.

בא. It is not necessary to take this in a pluperfect sense, the rendering '*came*' is quite suitable.

שלשת. Here the numeral very exceptionally *agrees* in gender with its substantive; cf. Ges., § 97. 1, note; Ewald, § 267 c: other instances are Ez. 7, 2 Ktb.; Zech. 3, 9. 4, 2. Job 1, 4. Cf. Dav., *S.*, § 36. R. 3.

14. כל צפור כל כנף. The same phrase occurs in Ez. 17, 23; cf. also 39, 4. Ps. 148, 10. Lit. '*every bird of every wing*,' i.e. '*all sorts of birds*,' '*every species of birds.*' צפור is properly '*a small bird*,' so called from its twittering or chirping. Di. and Del., however, regard the two phrases as in apposition, and render '*every bird, every winged thing*,' כנף including insects.

16. הבאים = '*those that came*,' lit. '*the ones coming*:' see Ewald, § 335; Dav., *S.*, § 99. The article is equivalent to the rel. pronoun: cf. Neh. 4, 12 הבונים '*those that built*;' Ex. 1, 1 הבאים מצרימה '*those who came to Egypt*;' 10, 8 הַהֹלְכִים.

19. מאד מאד (cf. 17, 2. 6. 20) is repeated to imply intensity; cf. Ges., § 133. 3. Rem. 3; M. R., § 72. 1. מאד מאד is peculiar to P; so 17 l.c., Num. 14, 7.

20. חמש עשרה אמה. אמה is acc. of measure, answering to the question '*how far?*' Ges., § 118. 2 c; M. R., § 41 c; Dav., *S.*, § 69 c.

21. בעוף ובבהמה. ב is used to specify the whole according to its contents (a construction characteristic of P); cf. M. R., § 52. 1; cf. 8, 17. 9, 10. 17, 23. Ex. 12, 19. Render, '*And all flesh died . . . consisting of fowl*,' etc.

22. חָרָבָה, with firm ָ under ח, the noun being of the form יַבָּשָׁה.

23. וימח. The better-attested reading has no dag. in the מ; so the form would be apoc. impf. Qal from מחה (see Ges., § 75. Rem. 3 a), and would mean '*He* (*God*), or *it* (*the flood*) *blotted out*,' the first rendering being the best. The reading with dag. in the מ would be imperf. apoc. Nifᶜ., for which we should rather expect וַיִּמָּח with ָ, but cf. Ewald, § 224 c, and Ps. 109, 13. 14: the acc. might stand after a passive, as in 4, 18; but a passive would hardly be expected with וַיִּמָּחוּ following in the same verse. The accent on the penult. points to the imperf. Qal: in the imperf. Nifᶜ. it could not be drawn back, as the penult. would be a closed syllable.

ואשר אתו. אשר = '*ii qui*,' contains in itself the demons. pronoun, Ges., § 138. 2; cf. M. R., § 158; Dav., *S.*, § 10.

8.

3. וישובו המים . . . הלוך ושוב. The inf. abs. הלוך is added to שׁוב to emphasize the continuance of the abating of the waters, just as in vers. 5. 7; 12, 9: cf. Ges., § 113. 3. R. 2; Ewald, § 280 b; M. R., § 37 b; Dav., *S.*, § 86. c and R. 4.

4. ותנח is impf. Qal with waw conv. from נוּחַ, like וַיָּסַר from סור, וַיָּזַר from זור, וַיָּנַע from נוע: cf. Ges., § 72. Rem. 4; Stade, § 484 d.

על הרי אררט = '*on (one of) the mountains of A.*' The plural as in Judg. 12, 7: see Ges., § 124. 1. R. 2; Dav., *S.*, § 17. R. 3. אררט is in the O. T., 2 Kings 19, 37=Is. 37, 38 and Jer. 51, 27 (together with מני and אשכנז), the name of a land. In Isaiah l.c. the LXX translate אררט by Ἀρμενία, and acc. to Schrader, *C. O. T.*, p. 53, and Glossary (cf. Lagarde, *Armen. Studien*, § 100); Armenia is called in Assyrian *Urarṭu.* Hieron., on Is. 37, 38, describes Ararat more closely as the fruitful plain lying at the foot of mount Taurus, through which the Araxes flows; and Moses of Chorene calls this part of Armenia *Ajrarat.* Kiepert (*M. B. A. W.*, 1869, 228 A; *Geogr.* 75) connects the Ἀλαρόδιοι of Herodotus, iii. 94, vii. 79, with this name (Di.). Since the first cent. A. D. the common opinion among Jews (cf. the Targums) and Christians (Eph. Syr., Pesh. on Gen. 8, 4) in the East identified Ararat with the land of Qardu, i. e. the old Karduchia on the left bank of the Upper Tigris; and the mountain where the ark landed with mount Gûdi, SW. of the Van lake. This identification, however, is not supported by the usage of language in the Bible. From the time of Josephus (*Ant.*, i. 3, 5) it has been usual to consider Mount Massis, the loftiest of the hills, in the land of Ararat, which rises to a considerable height, on the right bank of the Araxes, and is always covered with snow, as the spot where the ark landed. This mountain is situated twelve hours SW. of the town of Eriwan. See Di. and Del.[5] ad loc.

5. היו הלוך וחסור. The more usual cstr. with היה to emphasize the continuance of the action would be the participle: cf. on 1, 6; see Ewald, § 280 b.

באחד לחדש. יום is omitted by Ges., § 134. 4. Rem.; M. R., § 100 a. Rem. a; Dav., *S.*, § 38 c.

7. הערב. The article is generic. The individual as representative of its species is distinguished from the animals belonging to other species; cf. Ges., § 126. 4; Ewald, § 277 a; M. R., § 68; Dav., *S.*, § 22 c; 1 Sam. 17, 34 ובא הארי; 1 Kings 20, 36. Others explain the article on the ground that Noah had only one raven with him in the ark, which is somewhat difficult to prove, or had merely a male raven; but ערב is used of both the male and female bird, and does not admit of a distinction of gender: cf. יונה used of both sexes; so דבורה '*bee;*' cf. Ewald, § 175 b; Ges., § 122. 2 c.

יבשׁת is inf. cstr. with the fem. ending, like יכלת, Num. 14, 16. This ending is usual only with verbs פ״י and פ״ן; cf. Ges., §§ 69. 2. R. 1, 83. 1; Stade, §§ 199 c. 2, 208 c, 619 g; Ewald, § 239. a (who classes these instances as abstract formations with an inf. force).

8. הקלו. On the pointing of ה interrog., see Ges., § 100. 4; Dav., § 49. 2. The indirect question is here identical in form with the direct; cf. Ges., § 150. 2. Rem. 2 c; M. R., § 146; Ewald, § 324 c (a); Dav., *S.*, § 125.

9. מנוח '*a resting-place.*' Cf. the note on 1, 14.

10. ויחל is, according to form, Qal or Hif'. imperf. (of

חוּל or חִיל); according to usage, Hif'. Only one other instance is cited in Ges., *H. W. B.*, 11th ed. (where the Hif'il means '*to wait*'), viz. Judg. 3, 25. Di. wishes to emend after Ols. to וייחל; cf. ver. 12, as the meaning '*wait*' elsewhere is expressed by the Pi'el or Hif'il of יחל, or (ver. 12) by the Nif'.; but he apparently overlooks Judg. 3, 25.

ויוסף שַׁלַּח. In the combination of a verb and inf. construct, two constructions are possible: (*a*) The verb governs the inf. cstr. as an acc., as here and ver. 12; (*β*) ל the prep. is prefixed to the inf. cstr., as in 11, 8 ויחדלו לבנות; cf. M. R., §§ 112 a, 114; Ges., § 120. 1; Dav., *S.*, §§ 82, 83.

11. עלה זית טרף '*a fresh olive leaf.*' טרף, prop.= '*a plucked* (*leaf*),' from טרף '*carpere*;' cf. طَرُفَ '*to be fresh, new*,' prop. '*to be freshly plucked.*'

'That the olive tree is found in Armenia, Strabo shows, xi. 14. 4: and that it also thrives under water is attested by Theophr., *Hist. pl.* iv. 8; Plin., *N. H.*, xiii. 50,' Tuch in Di.

12. וייחל is impf. Nif'. from יחל. In Ez. 19, 5 (the only other example of a Nif'al form of this verb) we have נוֹחֲלָה, if the text be correct. Ges., § 69. Rem. 5, explains it as an instance of the Nif'al of a verb פ״י (orig. פ״ו), written with י instead of ו; cf. יִיָּרֶה, Ex. 19, 13. 1 Sam. 13, 8 וייחל Ktb.; so Ewald, § 140 b. Stade is doubtless right in emending to וַיְיַחֵל; see §§ 115 note, and 504 a.

13. בראשון. See on ver. 5 (באחד); cf. Ges., § 134. 4 and the note on 7, 11.

16. Render, '*Go thou forth from the ark with thy wife*,' etc. Notice the difference between the English and Hebrew idiom. English says, '*Go forth with*,' Heb. '*Go forth, thou and thy wife.*'

17. בעוף. Cf. the note on 7, 21.

הוצא . . . וישרצו. Cf. the note on 6, 14. The Ktb. הוֹצֵא (cf. 19, 12) is the regular imper. Hif'. from יצא, הוֹצֵא arising out of הַוְצֵא; see Ges., § 24. 2 b; Dav., § 9. Rem. b. One fails to see why the Massoretes should prefer the irregular Kri הַיְצֵא to the regular Ktb. Other instances of the Hif'il of verbs פ״י retaining their י as a consonant when we should expect ֵי or וֹ, are Hos. 7, 12 אַיְסִרֵם; Prov. 4, 25 יַיְשִׁרוּ; 1 Chr. 12, 2 מַיְמִינִים; cf. Ges., § 70, 2; König, *Lehrg.* p. 641. Stade, § 120, considers all the instances cited (except 1 Chr. 12, 2) suspicious. Cf. Ps. 5, 9 where, as here, for the Ktb. הושר the Kri הַיְשַׁר is substituted.

21. וירח יי״ את ריח הניחח. וירח is impf. Hif'. from רוּחַ, shortened from יָרִיחַ, after the waw conv.; cf. Ges., § 72. Rem. 7; Stade, § 499 f.

ריח הניחח. '*The odour of satisfaction.*' נִיחֹחַ is a similar formation to נִיצוֹץ, the only other instance of this formation of nouns; Stade, § 233. Ewald, § 156. 2 b, forms ניחח from the verbal stem נוֹחֵחַ, and cites as a third instance of the same formation כִּידוֹר, Job 15, 24, which Stade has apparently overlooked (see § 216, however). The ריח ניחח is the pleasant odour which rose up from the sacrifice. In the technical language of the sacrifice (Opfersprache) it is the common expression used for the favourable acceptance of an offering, or rather of the sentiments and wishes to which the sacrifice gives expression (Di.).

אל לבו = '*to Himself,*' thus a paraphrase for the reflexive pronoun: for other methods of supplying the reflexive pr. in Heb., see Ges., § 139. 2; M. R., § 89 b. The LXX paraphrase here with διανοηθείς, Symm. has εἶπε Κύριος πρὸς ἑαυτόν, Onq. has וַאֲמַר יְיָ בְּמֵימְרֵיהּ, '*Y. spake by his Word,*' so Ps.-Jon.

The Pesh. follows the Heb. text with ܟܠܗܘܢ. The same idiom recurs 24, 45. 27, 41; cf. Dav., *S.*, § 11 c.

22. The composite subject when *followed* by its predicate, takes the latter in the plural; so in 18, 11. 2 Sam. 16, 15; cf. Ges. § 146. 2 a; Dav., *S.*, § 114; M. R., § 138.

זרע וקציר are '*the seed time and harvest,*' dividing the year into two halves, which are described as '*seed time and harvest,*' also '*cold and heat,*' which roughly correspond to the זרע and קציר respectively. '*The summer and winter*' again correspond to the חם and קר. The season or half-year, which is called זרע, חרף, and קר, began possibly with the fifteenth of Tisri, and ended on the fifteenth of Nisan; while the other half of the year, called קציר, קיץ, and חם, extended from the fifteenth of Nisan to the fifteenth of Tisri. The Jewish expositors, following Rashi, consider the seasons mentioned here as six, each of two months' duration. The punctuation is noticeable: קר וָחם, קיץ וָחרף, יום וָלילה, in pairs, the second member of each pair being connected by ו with pretonic qameç.

9.

2. ומוראכם וחתכם. Render, '*And the fear of you, and the dread of you.*' The suffixes are objective. The genitive in Heb. may be either subjective or objective, the latter embracing many different shades of meaning, often being represented in English by a preposition, e.g. 3, 24 דרך עץ החיים, see the notes there and on 4, 23, and cf. 16, 5. 18, 20. 27, 13. 41. 29, 13. 42, 19. 44, 2. 50, 4; Ewald, § 286 b. Previous to the flood, the beasts lived at peace with man, and without fear, now they must fear and dread him (Di.). בכל אשר וגו״='*with all wherewith the ground swarms, and with*

all the fishes of the sea, into your hand they are given.' The ב of 'concomitance,' as in Ex. 10, 9. 15, 19. 1 Kings 10, 2. Jer. 11, 19, and often.

אשׁר (acc., see on 1, 21), as in Lev. 20, 25 ובכל אשׁר תרמשׂ האדמה.

בידכם. יֶדְכֶם out of יַדְכֶם; cf. Ewald, § 255 c; Stade, § 81 b; Ges., § 27. Rem. 2 a. *'Into your power they are given,'* a power even over their lives; cf. Lev. 26, 25. Deut. 1, 27, etc. [misquoted 1, 57, Kn. in Di.].

3. אשׁר הוא חי, lit. *'which, it is alive.'* הוא does not take the place of the copula *'is,'* but resumes the relative אשׁר. Compare ver. 18 חם הוא אבי; 2, 14. 19. Cf. Driver, § 199. Obs., with Ges., § 138. 1; M. R., § 156 a. אשׁר may be described as the link connecting the two sentences, *'every creeping thing'* and *'it is alive;'* so Num. 9, 13. 14, 8. 27. 35, 31. 1 Sam. 10, 19. See also Dav., *S.*, § 9 a and R. 2.

לְאָכְלָה. אכלה always occurs in this particular phrase, and always with another dative (except Jer. 12, 9). אכלה (as distinguished from אֹכֶל, מַאֲכָל, and אֲכִילָה)=לאכל generalized; a thing that is given on a particular occasion לֶאֱכֹל, is given for a continuance לְאָכְלָה; see Driver, *Journ. of Phil.*, No. 22, p. 217.

4. בנפשׁו דמו. ב=*'with,'* as in 32, 11 בְּמַקְלִי *'with my staff;'* Ps. 42, 11 ברצח בעצמותי *'with crushing in my bones.'* דמו is an explanatory app. to נפשׁו, defining it more closely, Ges. § 131. 2. Rem. 4; M. R., § 71. 2 a. The LXX with their πλὴν κρέας ἐν αἵματι ψυχῆς seem to have transposed the words, and read בְּדַם נֶפֶשׁ. Frankel, *Einfluss*, p. 53 note, explains it by the Halacha, which refers the command forbidding the *'Blutgenuss'* chiefly to the blood that flows out

and causes death (*Kerithoth*, 20 b דם שהנפש יוצאה בו '*the blood wherein the life goes out*'). The blood is not actually the life itself, but through the blood the life becomes apparent to the senses, and the fact that it exists perceptible; cf. Lev. 17, 11. 14. Deut. 12, 23.

5. את דמכם לנפשתיכם. '*But the blood of your lives* (i.e. *belonging to*) *will I require; from the hand of every living creature will I require it: and from the hand of man, from the hand of each one's brother will I require the life of man.*' Tuch and others render, '*your blood for your lives,*' i.e. '*for their protection;*' לנפשתיכם being *dat. commodi;* so Deut. 4, 15 ונשמרתם מאד לנפשתיכם, and Josh. 23, 11; but this is not suitable to the context: in 4 the דם and נפש are practically identical. Better לנפשתיכם = '*belonging to your souls;*' so the LXX, τὸ ὑμέτερον αἷμα τῶν ψυχῶν ὑμῶν, Vulg. '*sanguinem enim animarum vestrarum,*' Pesh. ܒܪܡ ܕܡܟܘܢ ܕܢܦܫܬܟܘܢ; cf. Ges., § 129. 1. 2. Other renderings, which are not so good, are '*according to your souls,*' or '*whoever's soul it is, to whom it belongs;*' cf. ver. 10, defining distributively the whole to which the part belongs, Del.; and '*your blood as your souls,*' or '*your blood,*' (that is to say) '*your souls,*' according to vers. 4. 5[b], ל as in Job 39, 16 (*as though not her own*); Ewald, § 217 d and § 310 a. דִּמְכֶם is thinned from דַּמְכֶם, Ges., § 93. 2. Rem. 3.

מיד כל חיה. '*From the hand of every beast.*' According to Ex. 21, 28 f., the ox that gored any one, so that he or she died, was to be stoned to death (סקול יסקל).

מיד איש אחיו = '*from the hand of each one's brother.*' According to the ordinary explanation מִיַּד אִישׁ אָחִיו stands instead of מִיַּד אֲחִי אִישׁ, אִישׁ, the noun which ought to be in the genitive, after אֲחִי, being prefixed for emphasis, and referred back to by the pronominal suffix in אָחִיו; so Di. comparing Ewald, § 278 b. Kautzsch, however, offers two other explanations of the phrase, (1) אָחִיו is to be regarded as in apposition to אִישׁ, cf. 15, 10 and probably Num. 17, 17, so Del.[5], who also compares 41, 12 and 42, 35; or (2) אִישׁ is prefixed as a sort of *casus pendens*, and is more closely defined by the suffix in אָחִיו, so 42, 25. Ex. 28, 21. Cf. further Ges., § 139, 1; M. R., § 94. Rem. a, and esp. Budde, *Urgesch.*, p. 283 ff., who explains the phrase on the analogy of Zech. 7, 10 as inverted for the more usual אִישׁ מִיַּד אָחִיו; cf. ܚܕ̈ܕܐ in Aramaic, and ἀλλήλων in Greek, and see Ewald, § 301 b; Dav., *S.*, § 11 d. Pesh., Vulg., Sam. apparently read אִישׁ וְאָחִיו. מיד איש אחיו is coordinate with מיד אדם.

6. באדם. The LXX ἀντὶ τοῦ αἵματος αὐτοῦ, either reading בְּדָם or confusing in sound באדם and בדם; compare their rendering of לכן as though it were=לא כן, viz. 4, 15. 30, 15.

באדם. The ב must be regarded as ב of instrument; cf. Hos. 1, 7. 1 Sam. 28, 6. Ps. 18, 30, but this is not usual; passives in Heb. are generally construed with מן of the agent, as in ver. 11 יכרת . . . ממי, or ל, as in 14, 19 ברוך לאל עליון; cf. Ges., § 121. 3; M. R., §§ 49. 4, 51. 3. R. a; Dav., *S.*, § 81.

צלם אלהים is an expression characteristic of P.

9. ואני הנני מקים. When the pronoun precedes הנה, אני is the form used: when it follows, אנכי is preferred; see *Journ. of Phil.*, No. 22, p. 226.

הקים ברית. ברית, when used with הקים, always has a suffix; the phrase הקים ברית denotes the perpetuation of a covenant already, at least in idea, existing, rather than the formation of one altogether new, which is expressed by כרת ברית; see *Journ. of Phil.*, l.c.

אתכם ואת זרעכם '*with you and with your seed,*' a phrase characteristic of P.

10. את כל נפש החיה. The adj. alone defined, the noun being regarded as sufficiently definite through the preceding כל; cf. on 1, 21.

מכל יוצאי '*all whatever;*' מן denoting the *genus ex quo*, the general to which the particular partitively belongs, as in 6, 2. 7, 22; Ges., § 119. 3. R. d. foot-note. ל, as in 23, 10 לכל באי='*with respect to,*' etc.; cf. Lev. 11, 42. 16, 21; Ewald, § 310 a (ל with a generalizing and particularizing force).

13. נתתי. '*I set,*' as in 1, 29 הנה נתתי; cf. Driver, § 14 a; Ewald, § 135 c.

14. בענני. ענן. Inf. Pi'el with the prep. ב, and suffix of the 1st pers. sing. נ is pointed with ־ֵ, as the doubling of the letter has fallen away; cf. Ges., § 10. 2. Rem. A; the more regular form of the inf. Pi'el would be בְּעַנְּנִי.

עַנֵּן is a denom. of ענן. Render, '*when I cloud my clouds;*' the apodosis begins with ver. 15, ונראתה being a continuation of the inf.; see Ges., § 114. 3. Rem. 1; Dr., § 118; Dav., *S.*, § 50 a.

18. היצאים. Here the participle must be rendered as past, '*those who went out,*' equivalent to אשר יצאו, but neater; cf. Ges., § 116. 2 and 5 b; M.R., § 14; so 27, 33 הַצָּד, 35, 3 הָעֹנֶה, 43, 18 הַשָּׁב, etc.

19. ומאלה נפצה כל הארץ. '*And out of these was the whole earth overspread.*' נפצה is a lightened form of the 3rd pers. fem. perf., Nif'. sing. of פצץ=פוץ; cf. 1 Sam. 13, 11. Is. 33, 3 (נפצו); Ewald, § 193 c (who compares נָסַבָּה from סבב; נָקַטָּה from קטט; נָבַקָּה from בקק); Ges., § 67, note 11.

20. ויחל נח . . . ויטע. Render, '*And Noah the husbandman began and planted.*' So most moderns; cf. Ges., § 120. 2 a

and 26, 18 (וַיָּשָׁב . . . וַיַּחְפֹּר). Some, however (Tuch, Kn.), appealing to Ewald, § 298 b (cf. M. R., § 43 a) and 1 Sam. 3, 2 החלו כהות—which is scarcely parallel—render, '*And Noah began to be a husbandman, and planted;*' but this would require איש אדמה instead of איש האדמה; cf. 25, 27 איש שׂדה (for M. R.'s explanation, § 76 b. Rem. a, is hardly satisfactory), and what is noticeable in the narrative is, not that Noah began to be a husbandman, but that he began the cultivation of the vine. A slightly different expl. in Dav., *S.*, § 83. R. 2.

21. וישת. The imperf. apoc. Qal of שׁתה without a helping vowel; see Ges., § 75. Rem. 3 c and § 28. 4; Stade, §§ 70 a. 2. 2, 101 c, 489 b.

אָהֳלֹה for אָהֳלוֹ. ה for ו is the older and original form of the suffix. The *ô* arose by contraction from *ahu*, *au*, but the ה was retained in writing. The ה is also preserved in Arabic, and on the Moabite stone, e.g. l. 5 בארצה=בְּאַרְצוֹ; l. 7 בה ובבתה=בּוֹ וּבְבֵיתוֹ; other examples in lines 9. 10. 19. 25. אהלה always has a Kri, אהלו; cf. Ges., § 91. 1. Rem. 2; Stade, §§ 28 a, 345 b. ה‍ֹ for ו‍ֹ occurs, however, elsewhere in the O. T., and is by no means confined to the oldest books.

22. חם may be called the father of Canaan here with reference to ver. 25.

ויגד, sc. '*it;*' see Ges., § 117. 1. Rem. 4; cf. note on 27, 14.

23. השׂמלה. '*The upper garment,*' also used (e.g. by the poor) as a covering by night; cf. Ex. 22, 26. Deut. 24, 13.

24. מיינו '*from his wine,*' i.e. his intoxication which the wine had caused, as in 1 Sam. 1, 14. 25, 37.

בנו הקטן, i.e. '*his youngest son,*' cf. 1 Sam. 16, 11. 17, 14. If two were compared one with the other, הקטן might= '*younger*' or '*youngest,*' when more than two are compared, it='*youngest*,' cf. Del.[5], ad loc. This rendering, however, does not agree with 5, 32. 6, 10. 7, 13. 10, 1 (all P) and 9, 18 (J), in which verses the order of the sons is Shem, Ham, Japhet. In 9, 18 R may have corrected J from P, but failed to do so in this verse; Di., p. 160; cf. Budde, *Urgesch.*, p. 299 ff.

25. עבד עבדים='*servant of servants*,' i.e. '*meanest servant*;' cf. שיר השירים '*song of songs*,' '*choicest song*;' see Ges., § 133. 3. R. 2; M. R., § 81 a; Dav., *S.*, § 34. R. 4. Canaan is made Shem and Japhet's servant. As Noah's son Ham sinned against him, so shall he (Ham) be punished through his own son Canaan, by the curse laid upon him by Noah. The settlements of Canaan on the islands and coasts of Asia Minor were at an early date overcome by the Japhetic races. Cf. Di., ad loc.

26. למו is poetical for לָהֶם, as often; cf. Stade, § 345 c, note 1; Ges., § 103. 2, foot-note 2. Shem is not blessed directly, but the God of Shem (Deut. 33, 20), i. e. Shem is blessed through his God, the highest possible form of blessing. If God is to be blessed for His goodness, which is implied in blessing Him, how great must be the happiness of those who are under His protection and enjoy His favour.

27. '*May God spread out Japhet far, and may he dwell in the tents of Shem.*' Onq., Baumg., etc. take God as the subject to וישכן; but God cannot be spoken of as dwelling in a tent, and we should in this case rather expect והוא ישכן. Some again (Ges., Schr.) take שֵׁם as meaning '*repute*;' cf. 6, 4 אנשי שם; but this is not suitable to the context, and Japhet could not at that date have had any opportunity of acquiring fame. Dwelling in the tents of Shem does not mean conquest, but points to the friendly relations that should exist

between the Semitic and Japhetic races; the latter participating in the honour paid the former, and sharing the religious privileges enjoyed by them.

10.

In chapter 5 we had a list of the descendants of Adam, containing ten generations, and ending with Noah. In chapter 10 we have a continuation of the list found in chapter 5, viz. a genealogical table of the sons of Noah, and the various peoples that sprang from them. In the first verse we find the sons of Noah given in the same order as in 5, 32; but in verse 2—in accordance with the custom observed in the book of Genesis, to first notice the side branches of the family tree, in order to prepare the way for mentioning the chief line—we have the order, Japhet, Ham, Shem; Ham standing next to Shem, being, through Canaan, Mizraim, and Cush, more closely allied to him than Japhet was. It should be observed in these תולדות that the list of nations is by no means complete. We find no mention made of nations of a more modern origin, such as Moabites, Edomites, Ishmaelites, Keturaeans, nor of some nations, such as the Rephaim and Amalekites, who were of very ancient descent; also we find no allusion to the Chinese and the other Mongolian races of Eastern Asia, to the Indians or Eranians, probably because they were entirely unknown in Palestine at the time of the narrator. 'In general the notice embraces the peoples who were grouped round the basin of the Mediterranean and its vicinity, the peoples of the so-called Caucasian race' (Di.). The nations mentioned in this table are regarded as the individuals of a large family, as sons, grandsons, and great-grandsons, of a common father, e.g. just as Shem, Ham, and Japhet are Noah's sons, so the Chittim and Dodanim in ver. 4 are the grandsons of Japhet; cf. ver. 6, Mizraim as the son of Ham; ver. 13, Ludim as the son of Mizraim; and (ver. 16) the similar use of the patronymics (the Amorite and Jebusite being spoken of as the children of Canaan; compare vers. 17. 18).

The table falls into three chief divisions, viz. I. 2–5. The Descendants of Japhet, the Northern Races. II. 6–20. The Descendants of Ham, the Southern Races. III. 21–31. The Descendants of Shem, the Central Races. The list is repeated with some variations in 1 Chr. 1, 4–23. For a list of works bearing on this chapter, see Dillmann's *Commentary*, p. 170. In the following notes—which are not intended to form a complete commentary on the chapter—Dillmann has been chiefly followed, and for fuller information his notes and the works there cited should be consulted.

1. תולדות. Cf. the note on 2, 4.

ויפת. ו with pretonic qameç, see on 1, 2.

2–5. The Descendants of Japhet.

2. גמר. LXX, Γαμέρ, mentioned again in Ez. 38, 6 (LXX, Γομέρ), as an ally of Gog of Magog. Josephus, *Ant.*, i. 6. 1, considers that גמר = the Γαλάται, who were formerly called Γομαρεῖς, in Northern Phrygia. Bochart also decides for Phrygia. 'Usually, since the time of Calmet, supposed to be the *Cimmerii* (Κιμμέριοι, Hom. *Od.*, xi. 14), who dwelt north of the Pontus Euxinus and Lake Maeotis (Her. iv. 11 f.; Strabo, iii. 2, 12 etc.), were driven out in the eighth century by the Scythians, journeyed through Thrace, and reinforced by the Τήρης and other tribes, at the beginning of the seventh century crossed the Bosphorus and entered Asia Minor,' Di. Others (Kiepert, Lagarde, etc.) consider that גמר is

Cappadocia, called by the Armenians *Gamir* (Pl.). Saadiah explains גמר by الترك '*the Turks*.' The name is found in the Assyrian inscriptions, '*Gimirrai=those who belong to the people* (Ass. *land*) *of Gimir*;' i.e. the inhabitants of the district between the north-western provinces of the Assyrians, in the east, and of the Lydians in the west, i.e. of Cappadocia. They are first mentioned in the time of Esarhaddon and Assurbanipal. Whether the land was called after the *Gimirrai*, earlier than this time, is uncertain. Cf. Schrader, *C.O.T.*, i. p. 62, ii. p. 123; Del., *Par.*, 245, etc.

מגוג. 'The second son of Japhet must be sought for between Gomer and Media. In Ez. 38, 2. 6. 15. 39, 6 Magog appears as a remote and warlike people in the far north, having Tubal and Meschek under them, and to whom Gomer and the House of Togarma have attached themselves.' Josephus l. c. and Hieron., *Quaest.* ed. Lagarde, p. 14, explain מגוג as '*the Scythians*,' the people of lake Maeotis and the Caucasus, and this view is the one commonly adopted since the time of Bochart. See further Di., ad loc., who mentions some explanations of the name that have been suggested.

מדי. '*The Medes*,' elsewhere mentioned in the O. T., viz. 2 Kings 17, 6. 18, 11. Jer. 25, 25. 51, 11. 28. Is. 13, 17f. 21, 2. The name is found on the Assyrian inscriptions, '*Madai*' ('*Ma-da-ai*'); see Schrader, *C.O.T.*, p. 62.

יון. '*The Ionians*' (Ἰάονες, Ἰάϝονες), in the whole of the East, up to India, the name for the Greeks; also found on the Assyrian inscriptions of Sargon II '*Javnai*' ('*Ja-av-naai*'), Schrader, *C.O.T.*, p. 63; and according to Sayce in the Tel-el-Amarna Tablet, xlii. a. 16; see *Academy*, 1891, p. 341. They are frequently mentioned in the O. T., e. g. Joel 4, 6. Ez. 27, 13. Is. 66, 19. Dan. 8, 21. 10, 20. 11, 2.

תובל ומשך. 'Always (except Is. 66, 19, Mass. text, and Ps. 120, 5) joined together. In Ez. 32, 26 they are mentioned as having suffered severe reverses, in Ez. 27, 13 (together with Javan, possibly from Gen. 10, 2) as connected by trade with the Tyrians, whom they supplied with slaves and vessels of brass. In Ez. 38, 2 f. 39, 1 they are spoken of as forming the flower of the army of the Scythian king Gog, in Is. 66, 19, LXX, as distant peoples. They are usually identified with the *Tibareni* and *Moschi*, who inhabited the hill country on the south-east of the Black Sea, the *Moschi* between the sources of the Phasis and Cyrus, the *Tibareni* east of the Thermodon, in Pontus. In the Assyrian inscriptions (see Schrader, *C. O. T.*, p. 64 ff.) their territory extended further south, the "*Tabali*" ("*Tibareni*") up to Cilicia and the "*Muski*" ("*Moschi*") north-eastwards of the *Tabali*. Josephus, *Ant.*, i. 6. 1, explains תובל as the *Iberians* in the Caucasus land, and משך as Μάζακα in Cappadocia (being deceived by the similarity in sound).'

תירס is mentioned nowhere else, but must, according to its position, be looked for either east of משך, or in the west, and more towards the south than משך. Since Josephus תירס has been usually identified with the *Thracians*, but Di. questions the suitability of this identification, as תירס = the *Thracians* would be already included in the Gomer group. Other conjectures are Τύρης, Τύρας, i.e. the Dniester with the people dwelling on it, the Τυρῖται (Her. iv. 51); the Τυρσηνοί (Tuch, Nöld., Di.), who belonged to the *Pelasgi*, and who made themselves by their acts of piracy a terror to the islands and coasts of the Aegean Sea between Greece and Asia Minor (Her. i. 57. 94; Thuc. iv. 109); see Tuch, p. 171; Di., p. 175.

3. The sons of Gomer.

אשכנז, 'the first son of Gomer, is mentioned in Jer. 51, 27 together with Ararat and Minni, i.e. with North-eastern and South-eastern Armenia.' Josephus explains by Ῥηγῖνες, who are otherwise unknown. The Ber. Rabba gives Asia; and the Jews of the Middle Ages, Germany. 'אשכנז—whether the ending *az* was the original ending of patronymics or not (see Lagarde, *Gesammel. Abhand.*, 255, but cf. *Armen. Stud.*, § 143; *Mittheil*, i. 225)—appears to be the old name of a people who were spread over Mysia and Phrygia. For Ascanios occurs in Homer (*Il.* ii. 862 ff., xiii. 793, etc.) as the name of a Mysian and Phrygian prince, and the same name at a later date was still attached to the lake of Kelaenae in Phrygia, and to one near Nicaea in Bithynia, and also to a river, a district and other localities (Strab., 12, 4. 5 ff., 14, 5. 29; Pliny, 4, § 71. 5, § 121, etc.; Steph. Byz. see Ἀσκανία),' Di. In Jeremiah the Western Armenians are intended, i.e. the *Ascanians*, who had emigrated from Phrygia into Western Armenia, and Tuch, Ges., and Schr. consider this to be the case in the present passage.

ריפת, in 1 Chr. 1, 6 דיפת. Josephus explains by *Ripheans*, i.e. *Paphlagonians*. Bochart and Lagarde the river Ῥῆβας, a river of Bithynia which falls into the Black Sea, and the district Ῥηβαντία on the Thracian Bosphorus. Di., however, thinks that ריפת cannot be placed so far west. Most expositors, however, prefer the view that ריפת = the fabulous ὄρη Ῥιπαῖα, which were regarded by the ancients as the boundary of the northern side of the earth. Saadiah and the modern Jews apply ריפת fancifully to France. The LXX have Ῥιφάθ here and in 1 Chr. l. c.

תגרמה, mentioned in Ez. 38, 6 together with Gomer,

in the army of Gog; and in Ez. 27, 14 after Javan, Tubal, and Meshek, as supplying horses and mules for the Tyrian traders: both times called in Ez. בית תגרמה. Josephus understood תגרמה to mean the *Phrygians*. But as the *Phrygians* are already included in אשכנז, the view that ת׳= *the Armenians*, is to be preferred; 'according to the oldest sense of the word, Western Armenia,' Di. With this identification, Phrygia, Paphlagonia, and Western Armenia naturally follow one another in the direction from west to east. The LXX have the name slightly altered, Θοργαμά; Codex A, Θεργαμά (so Swete); cf. Lagarde, *Gen. Graece*, p. 34. Whether the town *Tilgarimmu*, in Melitene, mentioned in the Cuneiform inscriptions (see Del., *Par.*, p. 296, etc.) is to be connected with תגרמה, is uncertain.

4. The sons of Javan.

אלישה, mentioned in Ez. 27, 7, '*the coastlands of Elishah*,' whence purple was obtained. Josephus thinks that אלישה means the *Aeolians*; so Del.[5] The Targ. of Jonathan here takes it to=*Hellas*. Others, *Elis* (Boch.). But Di. objects, firstly, that שה—for the Greek nom. ending *s*—is inconceivable, and secondly that Greece and the Greeks are already included in Javan. He suggests *Italy* and *Sicily*, citing the Targ. to Ez. l.c. מְדִינַת אִיטַלְיָא. This would not be unsuitable here, and would fit in with the statement in Ez. l.c. (איי אל׳). Cf. Sh., *G.*, p. 136. What, however, the name itself (? Ἰλλυρ-ια) means, remains to be explained. Stade considers that אלישה is Carthage, but it seems doubtful whether Carthage was ever called Elissa, and the phrase איי אלישה hardly suits this identification.

תרשיש is frequently mentioned in the O.T. Josephus thinks *Tarsus* in Cilicia is intended, but the more generally accepted view is that *Tartessus* in Spain is meant, which was celebrated in the east for its abundance of silver, and carried on an extensive trade with Tyre (cf. Her. i. 163, iv. 152; Is. 23). 'Not the town as a Phoenician colony (Stade), but the land and people is intended,' Di. *Tartessus* embraced the coastland from Gibraltar to the mouth of the Baetis or Guadalquiver. The Tarshish navy, mentioned in the book of Kings (1 Kings 10, 22. 22, 49), was not a navy that was intended to traffic with Tarshish, but is a term for large vessels, just as we speak of East or West-Indiamen; cf. Ges., *Thes.*, p. 1315.

כתים. *Cyprus* and its inhabitants, where was an old town Κίττιον (cf. *C. I. S.*, i. 137), the modern Larnaka (Schrader), which Josephus mentions in his explanation of the name. The Assyrian name of the island was '*Jatnâna*' or '*Atnâna*;' see Schrader, *C. O. T.*, p. 68 f. The name seems at a later date to have included other islands and coastlands; cf. Jer. 2, 10. Ez. 27, 6 איי כתים. Dan. 11, 30.

דדנים. So the Targg., Pesh., and Vulg.; but the LXX and Sam. give רדנים, as 1 Chr. 1, 7. The reading רדנים is generally accepted as the correct one, as דדנים cannot be suitably explained. Conjectural explanations that have been offered are *Dodona*, the seat of the famous oracle in Epirus, which would be unsuitable here; or דדנים=the Δάρδανοι; Targ. Jon. דְּרְדַּנְיָא, Jer. Targ. דּוֹדַנְיָא, i.e. the *Trojans*. With the other reading רדנים Bochart explains the word as meaning the *Rhone*, and the people dwelling near it: more probable, however, is the explanation by which רדנים= *Rhodes*, or in a more general sense the *Rhodian Islands*, i.e. the islands of the Aegean Sea. In Ez. 27, 15 the LXX give the correct reading, Ῥόδιοι for בְּנֵי דְדָן. Cf. Sh., *G.*, p. 135.

5. 'In ver. 20 and ver. 31 we find at the conclusion of the list אלה בני חם and אלה בני שם respectively; and we should expect here אלה בני יפת. As מאלה cannot refer to בני יפת in ver. 2, but to בני יון ver. 4 (since Magog, Media, etc. cannot be spoken of as populating the sea coasts), and as, moreover, בארצתם does not agree with איי הגוים, these three words (אלה בני יפת) must be inserted before בארצתם, without its being, on account of this, necessary to strike out מאלה . . . הגוים as a gloss,' Di. This emendation, proposed by Ilgen, is adopted also by Ewald, and Del.

Render, '*From these have the sea-lands of the peoples separated themselves. (These are the sons of Japhet) in their lands, each according to his language, according to their families, by their peoples.*' איים denotes regularly '*the islands and coastlands*' of the Mediterranean.

On ב = '*by, according to*,' cf. vers. 20 and 31 and see on 7, 21.

6–20. The Descendants of Ham.

6. כוש, 'called by ancient Egyptians "*Kaṣ, Keṣ*," and used as the name of a people of a reddish-brown colour, between Egypt and Abyssinia, viz. in the East between the Nile and the sea.' In the O. T. Cush seems to have had a wider and narrower signification. In 2, 13 and here it has a wider meaning, and is used to denote the southern limit of the known world, including the inhabitants of the coastland of Southern Arabia. From Isaiah's time and onwards it was used with a more limited signification, as the special name of the state Napata situated at the foot of mount *Barkal*, viz. *Ethiopia*. כוש is found on the Assyrian inscriptions ('*Kusi*') as the name of Ethiopia; see Schrader, *C. O. T.*, p. 68. 'It is

not very probable that the *Kaṣṣi* of the Inscriptions (Fried. Del., *Die Sprache der Kossäer*, 1884), i.e. the Κίσσιοι in Susiania, and the Κοσσαῖοι in the neighbourhood of Mt. Zagros, are connected with the biblical *Kuṣ*,' Di.

מִצְרַיִם. *Egypt.* Assyr. '*Muṣur*, *Muṣru*, *Miṣir*,' Schrader, *C.O.T.*, p. 71. The dual form of the word in Hebrew probably is used with reference to the two parts of Egypt, upper and lower, which are always mentioned on the oldest Egyptian monuments when the whole of Egypt is spoken of. The dual form is used in the Mass. text when only Lower Egypt is meant, Upper Egypt being expressly excluded, e.g. Is. 11, 11. Jer. 44, 1. 15. Various etymologies have been suggested for the name. Bochart thinks that מֵצֶר = '*walling in*,' and Egypt would then = the land *that is shut off* or *walled in*; but this opinion of Bochart's merely rests on the use of the name in Is. 19, 6. 37, 25. Another derivation (Ges. in the *Thes.*, p. 815) is from מצר which occurs in Aram., Assyr., and Arab. = '*a limit, province*,' so מצרים = '*the two lands*.'

פוט. This name occurs frequently in the O.T. In Nah. 3, 9 פוט is mentioned with Cush, Mizraim, and Lubim; in Jer. 46, 9 in the Egyptian army, together with Cush and Ludim; cf. Ez. 30, 5. In Ez. 27, 10 the soldiers of פוט are found among the Tyrian mercenaries, together with those of Persia and Lud; and again in Ez. 38, 5 פוט occurs with Persia and Cush in Gog's army. In the LXX, Is. 66, 19 (Mass. text פול), it is spoken of as a distant nation of the west. The LXX in Jer. and Ez. translate it by Λίβυες, so Josephus: and this is the view generally adopted. Knobel (*Völkertafel*, p. 296) points out that the Coptic name for Libya was *Phaiat*. Ptol. iv. 1. 3, Pliny v. 1 mention a river Φθούθ or *Fut* in Libya.

כנען (usually derived from כנע '*to be low, depressed*')='*the low land*,' cf. Num. 13, 29 as opposed to the high lands of Aramea. This, however, Di. disputes, and regards כנען as the original name of the low land by the sea and the Jordan, which was afterwards extended to all the country west of the Jordan; cf. Sh., *G.*, p. 4 f. Canaan embraced all this district, exclusive of Philistia, but inclusive of Phoenicia. It is remarkable that כנען—though the language of the land was Semitic—should be found among the sons of Ham. Perhaps this was due to a sense of their different origin; it being more or less certain that they were emigrants from the south, from the neighbourhood of the Persian Gulf (see Di., p. 180, and the authorities he cites in favour of the view of the southern origin of the Canaanites, viz. Her. i. 1, vii. 89; Justin. xviii. 3; Strabo i. 2. 35, xvi. 3. 4; Dion. per. 906; compare *The Book of Jubilees*, c. 10; see also Schröder, *Phön. Gram.*, p. 4). On the Assyrian name for Canaan '*mât Aḥarri*,' '*the Westland*,' see Schrader, *C.O.T.*, p. 72. In the Tel-el-Amarna letters (cir. 1400 B.C.) frequent mention is made of the land *Kinaḫḫi* or land of the *Kunaḫa*, that is, Canaanites, see Di. l.c., and authorities cited by him.

7. The sons of Cush.

סבא is mentioned in Ps. 72, 10 together with שׁבא, as a distant land in the south. In Is. 43, 3. 45, 14 it is spoken of together with Egypt and Cush; and in 45, 14 the סבאים are described as being very tall. Since Josephus (*Ant.*, ii. 10. 2), סבא has usually been identified with *Meroë*; and possibly this identification is supported by a comparison of Is. 45, 14 with 18, 2. 7 (Her. iii. 20. 114). Di., however, prefers to identify סבא with a branch of the Cushites, dwelling on the Arabian sea, more to the east of Napata; and he conjectures that remains of this proper name are to be found in *Asta-soba* and *Soba*, the capital of the Christian kingdom of *Senaâr* in the Middle Ages. His reason for objecting to the identification given by Josephus is that the kingdom of Cush, even when it reached from Napata to the southern island of Meroë, was never called by the Egyptians סבא, and that its name in the O. T. is always Cush.

חוילה. Cf. on 2, 11. Di. supposes that a trace of this people is to be found in the name Κόλπος Αὐαλίτης or 'Αβαλίτης, and the people 'Αβαλῖται, on the African coast near the Straits of Bab-el-Mandeb. This would suit the order of the enumeration. In ver. 29 חוילה is mentioned among the sons of Joqtan on the Persian Gulf; and we must either suppose that there was more than one חוילה, or that a great Cushite people were scattered over the east and south coast of Arabia, who also had penetrated to the west coast of north-eastern Africa, and there left traces of their name. Possibly, as Tuch suggests, the difference is due to two different accounts.

סבתה. Josephus, *Ant.*, i. 6. 2, explains by 'Ασταβάροι, i.e. the inhabitants of *Astaboras*, now *Atbara*, in Abyssinia, which Gesenius in the *Thes.* approves. More general is the view held by Tuch and Del., that סבתה is to be connected with the old Arabian town Σάββαθα or *Sabota*, the capital of the *Chatramotitae*, which had sixty temples, and was a great emporium of the frankincense trade. Its name was written in Sabaean שבות.

רעמה, LXX, 'Ρεγμά, cf. on 4, 18, is mentioned in Ez. 27, 22 in connection with שׁבא, as a trading people, who supplied the Tyrians with spices, precious stones, and gold. Tuch and others identify רעמה with 'Ρῆγμα or 'Ρέγμα, mentioned by Ptolemy and Steph. Byz., a town with a harbour on the Arabian side of the Persian Gulf. Di. prefers to identify it with the רעמה of the Sabaean inscriptions, in the neighbourhood of מען *Me'in*, north of *Marib*. He also compares the Ῥαμμανῖται, mentioned by Strabo, xvi. 4. 24, in connection with this identification, who dwelt between the Μιναῖοι and the Χατραμωτῖται.

סבתכא is unknown. Those who consider that רעמה is situated on the Persian Gulf compare Σαμυδάκη, a seaport town and river in Carmania; so Bochart. The Targ. of Jon. here, and the Targ. to Chron., give זִנְגָאֵי, i.e. *Zingis*, on the east coast of Africa.

The sons of Ra'ma.

שׁבא. '*The Sabaeans*,' often mentioned in the O. T. as a distant land and people, whose great wealth in gold, precious stones, frankincense, and cassia, was brought, partly by themselves, and partly by others, to the north. They dwelt in south-western Arabia, the capital of their empire being *Mariaba* or *Saba*, three days' journey from *Ṣan'â*. Their language was Semitic. See, further, Di., p. 182 f.

דדן, mentioned in 25, 3 among the descendants of Keturah. Possibly there were two different accounts of their origin, both of which have been employed by the narrator. In Ez. 38, 13 דדן is mentioned together with שׁבא, as a most important trading nation, and in Ex. 27, 20 as supplying Tyre with costly coverlets. In Is. 21, 13 the caravans of Dedan are mentioned, and in Jer. 25, 23. 49, 8 it is spoken of together with the Edomites and other desert tribes of Arabia. In Ez. 25, 13 דדן is the nation on the frontier of Edom. The Cushite Dedan, since Boch., has usually been placed on the Persian Gulf, and a trace of the name is supposed to have been found in *Daden* (دادن, Aram. ܕܝܕܢ; see Ges., *Thes.*), one of the Bahrein Islands. Di., however, points out that it is unnecessary to assume the existence of a Cushite Dedan, as distinct from the Dedan mentioned in 25, 3. The Dedanites (according to all the other places where the name occurs) are to be found in north-western Arabia in the neighbourhood of Khaibar, el-'Ulâ, el-Ḥiǵr, where the trade-routes from south, east, and central Arabia meet. A trace of them is probably to be found in the ruins of Daidân, west of Têmâ, south-east of Aila. We may assume that they also had stations on the southern, eastern, and northern trade-routes. It is, moreover, possible that they were originally to be found settled still further south. דדן occurs in the Sabaean inscriptions, Di. After the exile the Dedanites disappeared, their place being taken by the Gerrheans (on the west of the Persian Gulf). On this word and שׁבא in the Assyrian inscriptions, see Schrader, *C.O.T.*, pp. 74, 131 ff.

8. ילד. P would use הוליד; so in 6, 10.

נמרד. LXX, Νεβρώδ. Found once again in Micah 5, 5. Its derivation is uncertain; some derive it from מרד '*to revolt;*' so נמרד '*rebeller,*' cf. *H. W. B.*, 11th ed. The name has not yet been discovered in the Assyrian inscriptions. The Assyriologists identify the Nimrod of the Bible with the Babylonian hero *Iṣtubar;* see Schrader, *C. O. T.*, p. 75; and Haupt quoted by Schrader, l.c., believes that the name can mean, as an old Babylonian gentilic, '*he who is of Marad,*' *Marad* (also *Amarad*) being a town of central Babylonia. See, further, Di., p. 184.

גבור = '*a mighty man,*' cf. Ps. 52, 3; a powerful ruler, who, by his courage, activity, and the terror he inspired, reduced all around him, either voluntarily or involuntarily, to submission, Del.[4]; cf. ver. 10.

9. Nimrod was also distinguished as a mighty huntsman. גבור ציד=‘*a hero in* (lit. *of*) *the chase.*’

לפני יהוה (cf. Jon. 3, 3 לאלהים; τῷ Θεῷ, Acts 7, 20). The expression is doubtless taken from the mouth of the people, and denotes that he was exceptionally mighty, a person whom God himself must regard as *sui generis;* cf. Pss. 36, 7. 104, 16. Onq. has גִּבַּר תַּקִּיף=‘*a mighty hero;*’ LXX, γίγας κυνηγὸς ἐναντίον Κυρίου τοῦ Θεοῦ.

על כן יאמר. This formula is also used elsewhere in citing what was well known as a proverb, e. g. Num. 21, 14; cf. 1 Sam. 10, 12. 19, 24, also Gen. 22, 14, and (for Impf.) cf. Dr., § 33 a; Dav., *S.*, § 44 a; Ges., § 107. 2 b; M. R., § 6. 3.

10. בבל. Cf. 11, 9.

ארך. LXX, Ὀρέχ. The Targg. of Jon. and Jer., also Ephrem Syrus and Jerome, take this to be *Edessa* (ܐܘܪܗܝ), but incorrectly, as Edessa is a Mesopotamian, not a Babylonian town. Bochart and others identify it with *Arecca*, on the lower Tigris, on the frontier of Susiania. More probably it is Ὀρχοή, mentioned by Ptol. v. 20. 7; the modern *Warka*, on the left bank of the lower Euphrates, south-east of Babylon. Its name on the inscriptions is ‘*Arku*’ or ‘*Urku*,’ interpreted by Oppert as meaning ‘*Moon-town;*’ but see Schrader, *C. O. T.*, p. 76 f.

אכד. LXX, Ἀρχάδ. The position of אכד was, until recently, unknown. Knobel explains it by Ἀκκήτη, a district north of Babylon. In the Assyr. inscriptions not only do we find the land of *Akkad* mentioned, but also the ancient royal title ‘*King of the Sumiri and Akkadi*,’ which was assumed by the later

Assyrian and Babylonian monarchs. Akkad may be regarded as the name for North, or Upper Babylonia. A town Akkad has now been discovered on an inscription, of the reign of Nebuchadnezzar I, unearthed by Rassam at Abu-Habba, but its position has not yet been definitely ascertained. Cf. Di. and see Schrader, *C. O. T.*, p. 78.

כלנה. LXX, Χαλαννή. In Amos 6, 2 it has the form כַּלְנֵה, and in Is. 10, 9 כַּלְנוֹ; but it is uncertain whether כלנה in this verse is identical with these. It has not yet been found in the Assyrian inscriptions. The Targ. Ps.-Jon. and Targ. Jer., also Ephrem, Jerome, etc., identify it with *Ctesiphon Seleucia*, on the Tigris. G. Rawlinson (*Anc. Mon.*, i. p. 20), cited by Di., thinks it is *Nippur* (Niffer), following the Talmud.

בארץ שנער. *Shin'ar* is Babylonia proper, exclusive of Mesopotamia, the Bab. *Irâq* of the Arabs. Shin'ar is commonly understood to be a dialectic variation of the Bab. Assyrian '*Šumer;*' '*Šumer*' being the name of the southern portion of Babylonia, the northern part being *Akkad.* The Hebrews would then have applied the original name of south Babylonia to all Babylonia; see Schrader, *C. O. T.*, p. 103 f. Di., however, now thinks that the comparison of שנער with *Šumer* is improbable, and mentions Halévy's proposal to read שְׁנֵי עָר, '*the two cities;*' he also points out that in one of the Tel-el-Amarna letters, from the King of Alašija in Mesopotamia to Amenophis III, Babylonia is named *Šanḫar* = שִׁנְעָר. Cf. Halévy, *J. A.*, viii. 12, p. 507 f. Onq. has בְּאַרְעָא דְבָבֶל '*in the land of Babel.*' The word occurs besides in Josh. 7, 21. Is. 11, 11. Dan. 1, 2. Zech. 5, 11.

11. Render, '*From that land he went forth to Asshur,*' etc. This translation is not only demanded by ver. 22, where

Asshur is enumerated among the sons of Shem, but by ver. 10, אשּׁוּר here, being opposed to Shinar in that verse. The versions, however, except Targ. Jon., take אשּׁוּר as subject, as though it were the name of a person, which is never the case in the O. T. אשּׁוּר is here taken in its geographical sense, and denotes the district on the east bank of the Tigris, as the site of the cities assigned to it shews; cf. 2, 14.

אשּׁוּר is the acc. of motion towards, without the ending ָה; cf. 35, 1. 3. 43, 15. Ex. 4, 19, and constantly; see Ges., § 118. 2; M. R., § 41 a; Dav., *S.*, § 69 b.

נינוה. LXX, Νινευή, Assyrian '*Ninua*,' also '*Ninâ*,' on the east bank of the Tigris, opposite the modern Mosul, now Kujundschik. Cf. Schrader, *C. O. T.*, p. 82.

רחבת עיר = lit. '*streets of a city*,' or '*wide places of a city;*' unless it be preferred to regard the two words as in apposition. The LXX have τὴν 'Ροωβὼς πόλιν. Probably רחבת עיר is distinct from רחבות הנהר in 36, 37, though it has been conjectured that the two are identical, and that it is *Rahaba* on the Euphrates; see Tuch, p. 189. Di. supposes that, according to its name, it formed a sort of suburb of Nineveh, the position of which is now unknown; so Del. in his *Paradies*, p. 261, comparing '*Ri(rê)-bit ir Ni-na-a*' in the inscription of Asarhaddon (i. 53), etc.; see Schrader, *C. O. T.*, p. 84.

כלח was formerly identified with Καλαχηνή of Strabo, perhaps חֲלַח, whither (according to 2 Kings 17, 6. 18, 11) a portion of the ten tribes was carried away captive by Shalmaneser. More probably it is the same as *Kalḥu* of the inscriptions, built about 1300 by Shalmaneser I, and re-founded by Asurnâṣirhabal (883–859), and raised to the position of a royal residence (see Schrader, *C.O.T.*, p. 81). *Kalḥu* occupied the site of the present village and hill of *Nimrud*, in the most southern angle of the triangle formed by the Tigris and Zâb; see Di., p. 87. It is distinct from חלח mentioned above.

12. רסן, LXX, Δάσεμ, cf. Lag., *Gen. Graece*, p. 36, is only mentioned here, and is not found on the inscriptions; but as it lies between Nineveh and Kelach, it is to be sought for between *Kujundschik* and *Nimrud*. Prof. Sayce identifies it with *Rêṣ-eni*, i.e. ראש עין; see *Academy*, May 1, 1880, and Schrader, *C.O.T.*, p. 83 f.

הוא העיר הגדולה cannot refer to רסן alone, as nothing further is known of the large city of Resen; and from its position between Nineveh and Kelach, it must be regarded as insignificant. We must therefore refer it either to the four cities, or to Nineveh, together with the other three; Nineveh being regarded as forming with the other three a great city; cf. Jon. 1, 2. 3, 2. 4, 11.

13. The sons of Mizraim.

לודים, 1 Chron. 1, 11 לודיים Ktb. We find the לודים (in Jer. 46, 9. Ez. 27, 10. 30, 5) mentioned as bow men in the army of the Egyptians, or Tyrians; in Jer. and Ez. 30, 5, with Cush and Phut; in Ez. 27, 10, with Persia and Phut; and in Is. 66, 19, among the most distant people. In Is. l.c. and the two passages in Ez., the sing. form לוד is used. They are identified by Hitzig with the *Libyans;* by Movers (*Phoen.*, ii. 1. 377 ff.) with the Berber tribe of *Lewâta* dwelling on the Syrtes; by Knobel with the Egyptised portion of the Semitic לוד (cf. ver. 22), who had settled in north-eastern Egypt. All these identifications are precarious. A people of western lower Egypt, or on its borders, seems to be required to explain לודים. לוד in ver. 22 is different from the לודים here mentioned; cf. further, Di. and Tuch on this verse.

ענמים. LXX, Αἰνεμετιείμ, uncertain. Pesh. has ܡܟܒܬܡ, which Tuch emends to ܟܒܥܢܡ. Kn. and Bunsen connect it with '*emhit*,' i.e. '*north*,' and explain it as North Egypt. Ebers explains ענמים as = '*an-amu*,' the wandering Amu or Asiatic herdsmen who had settled on the Bucolic arm of the Nile, where there was pasture for their cattle.

להבים. LXX, Λαβιείμ—probably identical with the לובים in Nah. 3, 9. 2 Chron. 12, 3. 16, 8. Dan. 11, 43—are the *Libyans*, old Egyptian '*Tehennu*' ('*Thihenu*'), also '*Lebu*' or '*Rebu*.' Wright compares for the interchange of ה and ו, לודים, Sam. להדים; בוש, Syr. ܒܗܬ; רוץ, Syr. ܪܗܛ. 'The name here is to be understood of the Libyans on the borders of Egypt,' Di.

נפתחים. LXX, Lag. reads Νεφθαλείμ, and Swete gives Νεφθαλιείμ, both editions place the word after Λουδιείμ, and not as in Heb. text at the end of the verse. Pesh. has ܡܦܬܘܚܝܡ, with ܡ for ܢ. Bochart identifies נפתחים with Νέφθυς, in Plut. *de Isid.*, p. 96, the most northern portion of Egypt on the sea-shore. More probable is the identification proposed by Ebers, '*na-ptah*,' = οἱ τοῦ Φθᾶ, i.e. *those belonging to Ptah* or *Hephaestus*, the Memphitic Egyptians. Erman (quoted by Di., p. 189) reads פתמחים, i.e. *Northern Land*, as opposed to פתרס = *Southern Land*.

14. פתרסים, derived from פתרס, which (see Is. 11, 11. Jer. 44, 1. 15. Ez. 29, 14. 30, 14) signifies Upper Egypt (Thebais).

כסלחים. LXX, Χασμωνιείμ; cf. Lag., *Gen. Graece*, p. 36.

Since Bochart's time, usually identified with the *Colchians* on the Black Sea, because these (according to Herodotus, Strabo, and others) were descendants of the Egyptians. Knobel and others identify כסל״ with the dry and salty strip of land stretching from the eastern mouth of the Nile along the sea up to the southern frontier of Palestine, with lake Sirbonis and mount Casius or the Κασιῶτις, which, according to Ptolemy, belonged to Egypt. The name, in this case, may be = the Coptic *kas-lôkh*, '*hot mountain*.' But this identification is doubtful; see Di. here.

אשר יצאו משם פלשתים. If כסלחים are the *Colchians*, this notice is senseless, and then we must assume that here and in 1 Chron. 1, 12 the words are out of place, and should come after כפתרים. Kn. and Del. keep the present order of the text, and distinguish between earlier Philistines who came from the כסלחים, and later Philistines who came from כפתר; but in Deut. 2, 23. Amos 9, 7. Jer. 47, 4, the Philistines are spoken of as coming from כפתור, and no mention is made of any such double origin. Di. prefers to assume that the first immigration of the Philistines was not made directly from Crete, but came by the way of the Egyptian sea coast, near to the כסלחים. The versions follow the order of the Mass. text. פלשתים = probably '*emigrants*' or '*strangers*,' from פלש, Eth. *falasa*, '*to wander*.' פלשת, *Philistia*, is called Παλαιστίνη by Josephus, and this name afterwards was used as the name of the whole land of Canaan. In Assyrian it is '*Palaštav*' or '*Pilišta*;' see Schrader, *C.O.T.*, p. 86. For the Philistines, cf. Sh., *G.*, p. 169 f.; Bäd., *Pal.*, p. 154 f.

כפתרים. Not the *Cappadocians*, as LXX in Deut. 2, 23. Amos 9, 7; Vulg. (everywhere else, but here '*Caphtorim*'), Targg. Onq., Ps.-Jon., and Jer., and Pesh.; but more probably *Crete;* not only because such an important island would scarcely be omitted in this table of nations, but also because *Kaftor* in Jer. 47, 4 is expressly mentioned as an אִי, and the Philistines in 1 Sam. 30. 14. Ez. 25, 16. Zeph. 2, 5, etc. are called כְּרֵתִים: cf. Tac., *Hist.*, v. 2, who indirectly testifies to the origin of the Philistines from Crete; see Del.[5], p. 217 f.; and Sh., *G.*, pp. 135, 170†, 198.

15. The descendants of Canaan.

צידון the first-born, perhaps '*the fisher-town*' (from צַיִד), the oldest settlement of the Canaanites, and the only one of all the Phoenician towns known to Homer. In Josh. 11, 8. 19, 28 it is called צידון רבה. Even when Tyre had gained a reputation, the Phoenicians were still called Sidonians; Deut. 3, 9. Josh. 13, 6. 1 Kings 11, 5. 16, 31. The absence of any mention of Tyre in the table is noticeable; cf. Di., p. 190 f.

חת. 'The form חת (without ִי—, although חתים, instead of בְּנֵי חֵת, is commonly found in P) points to the name of a people of wide range,' Di. חת=the '*Cheta*' of the Egyptian Monuments, who in the period from the 18th to the 20th dynasty were the ruling nation in Syria, between the Orontes and Euphrates, up to Asia Minor. Brought under the rule of Egypt by Thutmosis II, they soon penetrated further south and became, as we learn from the Tel-el-Amarna Letters, in the time of Amenophis III and IV, dangerous foes of the Phoenician coast towns, up to that time under the sway of Egypt. Palestine was again brought entirely under Egyptian control by the campaigns of Seti I and Ramses II, but in N. Syria the '*Cheta*' maintained their supremacy. In the Assyrian inscriptions, the '*Hatti*,' in this sense, are often mentioned from 1100 onwards, but from the end of the eighth century, when these territories were absorbed by the Assyrian Empire, the name is applied, in a more limited sense, to the Hittites in Palestine (cf. Schrader, *K.G.F.*, p. 225 ff.; *C.O.T.*, p. 91 ff.); and the author of Gen. x seems to refer mainly, if not exclusively, to the חת in Canaan. Their chief city was Kadesh on the Orontes. In 1 Kings 10, 29. 2 Kings 7, 6 Hittite kings are mentioned in Syria; and the Hittites in the O. T. may very possibly be offshoots of these Syrian Hittites, see further, Di.; Sayce in the *Trans. of the Soc. of Bib. Arch.*, vii. 2. 248 ff.; Cheyne, *Enc. Brit. s. v.;* Wright, *Empire of the Hittites.*

16. היבוסי. '*The Jebusites*,' who dwelt in and around Jebus, afterwards called Jerusalem.

האמרי. '*The Amorites*,' who dwelt in the hill country of Ephraim and Judah, and spread out far into the south; the most powerful and warlike of all the Canaanitish tribes. In E and D האמרי is the general name for the original inhabitants of Palestine, before the coming of the Israelites, while J uses the title כנעני. Cf. *Amar*, the name of Palestine in the Egyptian Monuments, and *Amurra*, in the Tel-el-Amarna Letters. Deut. 3, 9 is a specimen of the Amorite language, Di. אמרי = prob. '*those who dwell on high ground*' (cf. Num. 13, 29), from אֱמֹר = אָמִיר, Is. 17, 9, '*top*,' '*height*.'

גרגשי. '*The Girgashites*,' cf. 15, 21. Deut. 7, 1, their position is uncertain: possibly they must be sought for in the west Jordan land; cf. Josh. 24, 11.

17. החוי. '*The Hivites*.' חוי possibly = '*those who live in town-communities* (*Stadtgemeinden*), חַוֹּת,' Di.; cf. 34, 2. Josh. 9. Later they are found in the Lebanon and Hermon districts, perhaps driven thither by the Israelites; Josh. 11, 3. Judg. 3, 3. 2 Sam. 24, 7. Cf. Ewald, *His.*, i. p. 237 (Eng. Trans.).

The פרזי, i. e. '*Perizzites*,' '*those who dwell in open villages*,' פרזות, who are mentioned in 13, 7. 15, 20, are not found in this table; see Di., p. 192.

הערקי are the Phoenicians of Ἄρκη (Aram. ארקא דלבנון), at the foot of mount Lebanon, about five hours north of Tripolis, the birth-place of the emperor Alexander Severus. Ἄρκη has been rediscovered in the modern *Tell Arqa* and village *Arqa*. LXX, Ἀρουκαῖος. In Assyrian '*Arḳa*;' see Schrader, *C.O.T.*, p. 87.

הסיני. 'The Phoenicians of Sin.' Hieron., *Quaest.* ed. Lag., p. 17, mentions a town *Sin*, not far from *Arqa*. Breydenbach (see Di., p. 192) in 1483 found a village *Syn*, half a mile from the river *Arqa*.

18. הארודי. LXX, τὸν Ἀράδιον. '*The Aradians*,' mentioned in Ez. 27, 8. 11 as the sailors and warriors of the Tyrians, are the inhabitants of Ἄραδος, a Phoenician city built on a rocky island north of Tripolis, according to Strabo, by exiles from Sidon. But this does not prove that there were no Aradians at an earlier date; see Di., p. 192. Arvad is frequently found on the Assyrian inscriptions '*Ar-va-da*, *Aruada*;' see Schrader, *C.O.T.*, p. 87 f. Cf. Bäd., *Pal.*, p. 382.

הצמרי. 'The Phoenicians of Simyra,' south of Aradus, north of Tripolis, mentioned by Strabo. In Assyrian '*Ṣi-mir-ra*;' see Schrader, *C. O. T.*, p. 89, and in the Tel-el-Amarna Letters *Ṣumura* and *Ṣumur*. The name is still preserved in *Sumra*, a small village, cf. Bäd., *Pal.*, p. 379.

החמתי. '*The inhabitants of Hamath*[1],' the modern

[1] Arab. حَمَاة, Ass. *Amattu*, Del., *Par.*, p. 275 f., *Proleg.*, p. 174.

Ḥamâ, about thirty-eight hours N. of Damascus, on the Orontes (cf. Bäd., *Pal.*, p. 396 f.), often mentioned in the O. T., and Assyrian inscriptions up to Sargon's time, '*mat Hamatti;*' see Schrader, *C. O. T.*, p. 90.

נָפֹצוּ is Nif'. of פוץ; there is no necessity to take it with Ewald from פצץ.

הכנעני, used here and ver. 19 in its narrower sense, excluding the Phoenicians and Syrians.

20. באכה *scriptio plena*, for בֹּאֲךָ; באכה here, ver. 30, 13, 10. 25, 18, is to be taken as an adv. acc. for the fuller עד באך, 19, 22, lit. '*as thou comest;*' cf. on 13, 10.

גררה. '*Gerar*,' in Philistia, it was more towards the south than Gaza. On the ה of motion towards, see Ges., § 90. 2; Dav., § 17. 3.

עזה. '*Gaza*,' the southernmost frontier stronghold in Philistia; see Sh., *G.*, p. 181 f.; Bäd., *Pal.*, p. 154 f.

סדמה ועמרה ואדמה וצבים, the four cities of the plain, mentioned with Bela in 14, 2. They probably occupied the ground now covered by the southern portion of the Dead Sea; see Di., p. 237.

לשע. Hieron. and Targ. Jer. identify it with *Callirrhoe*, on the east side of the Dead Sea, in the *Wady Zerka Ma'in*, celebrated afterwards for its hot springs. But Di. objects to this identification, as Callirrhoe lies too far north; and points out, that according to the analogy of the preceding verse, a town on this side of the Dead Sea or of the Ghor is required.

21–31. THE DESCENDANTS OF SHEM.

21. ולשם . . . גם הוא; see the note on 4, 26.

עבר; see the note on 14, 13.

אחי יפת הגדול. Render, '*The elder brother of Japhet.*' The rendering '*Brother of Japhet, the elder,*' adopted by the LXX, Symm., Massoretes, Rashi, and others, is refuted by the fact that the limitation of גדול to the age would only then be sufficiently indicated if the text ran בן נח הגדול (9, 24. 27, 1. 15. 42). הגדול without בן or אח cannot = '*natu major.*' On הגדול, as comparative (or superlative), see on 9, 24; and cf. Dav., *S.*, §§ 27, 34; Ges., § 133. 2. 3.

22. עילם = '*Elam*' and '*the Elamites,*' the land and people on the east of the lower Tigris, south of Assyria and Media, north of the Persian Gulf; nearly corresponding to the more modern *Susiana* and *Elymais*. 'עילם neither here nor elsewhere in the O. T. included Persia or all the land up to India,' Di. In Assyrian '*'Ilam*' or '*'Ilamti*;' see Schrader, *C.O.T.*, p. 96.

אשור. '*Assyria and the Assyrians,*' 'for the most part on the eastern side of the central Tigris, between Armenia, Susiana, and Media; its extent cannot be accurately defined; so called after its old capital and deity *Ašur*;' see Schrader, *C.O.T.*, p. 97, also p. 35. The Assyrians (as their inscriptions testify) spoke a Semitic language.

ארפכשד, since Bochart's time usually explained by Ἀρραπαχῖτις (Ptol. vi. 1. 2), the hill country of the upper Zab (east of Carduchia or Gordyene). The name occurs frequently in the Assyrian inscriptions as *Arbaḫa*, or *Arabḫa*, but its meaning is not clear. Ges., Kn., and others explain it as = '*boundary of the Chaldeans*' from ארף = Arab. أُرْفَةٌ '*boundary,*' and כשד = *Chaldean*; cf. Josephus' statement that the Chaldeans were descended from Ἀρφαξάδης. Schrader and others object to the identification of אר״ with Arrapachitis, as the Assyrian inscriptions never mention Chaldeans as settled in those districts. Di. thinks, that following the geographical notices in the inscriptions, the '*land of the Chaldeans*' must be sought in the south, but not in Accadia (Neuville) or Babylonia (Fried. Del. and Schr.), as this land was well known to the Hebrews under other names. He regards ארפכשד as being the territory of the Chaldeans from the Persian Gulf towards the North. He draws attention to the fact that *Karduniaš*, the Assyrian name at a later date for Babylonia in general, was originally the title of the Babylonian coast lands, and that it signifies '*land of the Chaldeans*.' Cf. his *Comm.*, p. 195 f.

לוד. Apparently '*the Lydians*' and '*Lydia*.' It is not, however, clear why Lydians should be placed among the Semites. Their language was not Semitic, and they do not appear to have formed a portion of any Semitic kingdom. See Di., p. 196, and Del.[5] ad loc. There is no reason to assume that the narrator here wishes to limit the title to the Lydians of Asia Minor. In the other passages in the O. T. where לוד occurs, the African Lydians are probably meant, though Stade and Fried. Del. question the existence of African לודים: cf. also Schrader, *C. O. T.*, p. 98 f.

ארם. 'Rather the name of a people than a land, and with a wider meaning than Syria, so that when it is more accurately spoken of, some addition is made to the name, as ארם נהרים, ארם דמשק. ארם = the peoples of Syria and Mesopotamia, up to the upper plains of the Tigris and the valley-land within the Taurus, which was at a later date considered as belonging to Armenia. The explanation of the name as '*Highland*' is very doubtful. In Assyrian '*Aramu*,' '*Arumu*,' and '*Arimu*;' see Schrader, *C. O. T.*, p. 100.

23. The sons of Aram[1].

עוץ is mentioned in 22, 21 as the first son of Nahor; in 36, 28 as a son of Dishan (דישן); in Job 1, 1 as a people north-east of Edom. In Jer. 25, 20 kings of the land of Uz are spoken of, and in Lam. 4, 21 Edomites are mentioned as dwelling in the land of Uz. According to Josephus, *Ant.*, i. 6. 4, Uz founded Trachonitis and Damascus. 'All this points to a people who were widely scattered in southern Syria and the Wilderness, viz. in the neighbourhood of Hauran and Damascus,' Di. Cf. also Robertson Smith, *Kinship*, p. 261, and Glaser, *Skizzen der Gesch. und Geograph. Arabiens*, ii. p. 411 f.

חול is uncertain. Josephus, *Ant.*, i. 6. 4, gives חול as the founder of Armenia. Bochart refers it to Χολοβοτήνη in Armenia. It is usually identified (see Di., p. 197) with Ḥule (الحولة), a name that still attaches itself to lake Merom in Galilee and the marshy land around it, but also to a district between Emesa and Tripolis. A district '*Ḥuli(j)a*' near mount Masius is mentioned in the Assyrian inscriptions; see Del., *Par.*, p. 259.

גתר is unknown. Josephus l. c. mentions גתר as the founder of the Bactrians. Jerome supposes גתר to be *the Carians*. Clericus takes it to be '*Karthara*' on the Tigris; see Tuch, p. 204.

מש. Heb.-Sam. משא; LXX, Μοσόχ, 1 Chron. 1, 17 מֶשֶׁךְ; cf. Ps. 120, 5. Josephus l. c. explains by Μησαναῖοι, at the mouths of the Euphrates and Tigris (Syr. ܡܫܡܫ). More probable is Bochart's identification with Mons Masius, north of Nisibis.

---

[1] These words are wanting in 1 Chron. 1, 17.

24. The descendants of Arpachshad.

שלח and עבר the son of שלח, also found in 11, 12. 14.

25. ילד. On the passive, see 4, 18.

פלג, the same individual is mentioned in 11, 18.

נפלגה הארץ. '*The earth was divided,*' i. e. the population of the earth; possibly to be referred to 11, 1–9; cf. Ps. 55, 10; or it may refer to some partition of the soil amongst distinct nations, in which case we should expect to find חלק. פלג may have been used here on account of the proper name פלג.

יקטן. '*Joqtan.*' 'Joqtan, from the notices in the Bible, was regarded by the Arab genealogists under the name "*Qaḥṭân,*" as the ancestor of the genuine Arabs in Arabia proper, from whom the old prehistoric inhabitants, as '*Ad, Thamûd, Gadîs*, etc. on the one hand, and the Ishmaelites of the north (Gen. 25, 12 ff.) on the other, were distinguished,' Di. The name '*Qaḥṭân*' is still preserved as the name of a district and a tribe in northern Yemen.

26. אלמודד. The אל in this word is usually explained as the Arabic article, and this is the view evidently adopted by the punctuators. Other alleged instances of the Arabic article in Hebrew words, are אֶלְגָּבִישׁ, אַלְגּוּמִים, אַלְקוּם, and the p. n. אֶלְתּוֹלָד, cf. C. P. Ges., p. 38, and *H. W. B.*, 11th ed. *sub voce.* It is more probable, however, that אל, as in many other Sabaean names, should be read אֵל '*God,*' and that מודד comes from the root ידד, so that the word = אל + מודד '*God (is) a loving one,*' or = אלם + ודד '*Il loves*' (ם is then the mimation). Cf. D. H. Müller, *Z. D. M. G.*, xxxviii. 18, and Glaser, *Skizzen*, ii. p. 280. The identification of this name is uncertain. Bochart connects it with the 'Αλλου-

μαιῶται of Ptolemy in the midst of Yemen. Tuch corrects it into אלמורד, i. e. مُرَاد, grandson of Sabas, who, with his tribe, inhabited the hill country of Yemen, near زبيد.

שלף is uncertain. 'Bochart compares the Σαλαπηνοί of Ptolemy, vi. 7. 23; Knobel, a district *Salfie* (سلفية in Niebuhr, *Arab.*, p. 247), south-westward of *Ṣan'â*; Osiander, *Sulaf* or *Salif*, the name of a tribe in Yemen,' Di., p. 198 f.

חצרמות, rediscovered on the Sabaean inscriptions as חצרמות, i. e. Ḥaḍramaut (حَضْرَمَوْت), is the name of a district east of Yemen on the sea coast, which is probably identical with the land of the Χατραμωτῖται, one of the four chief tribes dwelling in southern Arabia (Strabo, xvi. 4. 2). Their capital was Σάβατα, cf. ver. 7. The name is preserved at the present day.

ירח is uncertain. 'As the word means "*moon*" in Heb., Sab., and Geez, Bochart conjectured the بني هلال "*sons of the new moon*" or *Alilaei* in northern Yemen; Michaelis, the *moon-coast* and *moon-mountain*, غبّ القمر or جبل in eastern Ḥaḍramaut,' Di.

27. הדורם, Heb.-Sam. אדורם, is unknown. The Ἀδραμῖται of Ptolemy, or the *Atramitae* of Pliny, have been suggested, but they probably belong to חצרמות.

אוזל, Heb.-Sam. איזל, LXX, Αἰζήλ (Lagarde, Αἰβήλ, so Tisch.'s text), according to Arab tradition, was the old name of the capital of Yemen, called, since the Ethiopic occupation in the fifth century A. D., *Ṣan'â* (صنعاء). See further, Di., p. 199.

דקלה is unknown. Perhaps = '*a palm-bearing district*' (Arab. دَقَل '*a palm tree*'). Bochart identified it with the *Minaei* of Pliny and Strabo.

28. עובל, 1 Chron. 1, 22 עיבל, so Heb.-Sam., Vulg. '*Ebal*,' LXX, Γεβάλ and Εὐάλ, is unknown. Swete's edition of the LXX omits the word.

אבימאל is unknown. Cf. the Sabaean אבמעתתר = '*a father is 'Attar*,' Hal., *Melanges*, p. 86. D. H. Müller, *Z.D.M.G.*, xxxvii. 18.

שבא, see ver. 7. '*The Sabaeans*,' here as the descendants of Joqtan, among the Arabs; in 25, 3, among the descendants of Abraham and Keturah. There is no reason to assume that there were three distinct Sabaean peoples as Kn. does. Cf. Schrader, *C.O.T.*, p. 103.

29. אופר is mentioned, from Solomon's time onwards, as the land whence the fleet of Hiram and Solomon, after a three years' voyage, brought gold, precious stones, sandalwood, silver, ivory, apes, and peacocks (1 Kings 9, 28. 10, 11. 22. 2 Chron. 8, 18. 9, 10), and whose gold became proverbial as fine gold (Ps. 45, 10. Job 22, 24. 28, 16. Is. 13, 12. 1 Chron. 29, 4). Its position has been disputed, but as it is mentioned among the sons of Joqtan it must perhaps be sought for in Arabia (cf. ver. 30), probably on the southern or south-eastern coast. On the Arabian coast, however, no suitable place with which Ophir can be identified is at present known. Ophir has also been identified with *Supara* on the coast of Malabar (Ptol. vii. 1. 6); with *Sofala* on the east coast of Africa, opposite Madagascar, in the neighbourhood of which the ruins of Zimbabye have been recently discovered; and with *Abhira* on the coast of the Indus Delta. It has also been supposed that Ophir must be located somewhere on the west coast of Arabia, between Ḥiǵâz and Yemen, where much gold and silver were found in former times; so Sprenger and Riehm. See further, Di., p. 200.

חוילה. Cf. ver. 7, and 2, 11. 'Assuming that there was a חוילה in north-west Arabia, on the Persian Gulf (cf. 25, 18. 1 Sam. 15, 7 [1], and Gen. 2, 11), the Χαυλοταῖοι of Strabo (xvi. 4. 2) and *Ḥuwaila* in Bahrein on the coast may be compared (Niebuhr, *Arab.*, p. 342),' Di. Glaser, *Skizzen*, ii. pp. 267, 325 f., 339 f., thinks that חוילה here = the district of Yemâma; cf. Di., p. 200.

יובב is unknown. Bochart compares the Ἰωβαρῖται of Ptol. vi. 7. 24 (which he emends to Ἰωβαβῖται) on the coast of the Indian Ocean; Halévy and Glaser the tribe יהיבב mentioned in Sabaean inscriptions.

30. מֵשָׁא is uncertain. Bochart, Μοῦζα, a seaport town within the Bab-el-Mandeb; Knobel, *Bischa*, in northern Yemen; Tuch and others, *Mesene*, a district at the head of the Persian Gulf. The LXX read מַשָּׂא (Μασσηέ), cf. 25, 14. This is possibly the correct reading here, as משׂא in northern Arabia would more probably be known to the Hebrews than Mesene; cf. Hal., *Mél.*, p. 91 f.

ספרה הר הקדם. Render, '*Towards Sephar, towards the mountain of the east.*' הר הקדם cannot be predicate of the sentence on account of its position, nor in apposition to ספרה, because nothing is known of a mountain bearing this name. סְפָר is usually regarded as ظفار, either the Himyaritic royal city *Ẓaphar* near *Yerîm*, in Yemen, or the coast town *Ẓaphar*, situated in eastern Ḥaḍramaut (Mahra), near *Mirbâṭ*, called at the present time *Isfor*. It is not clear which Ẓaphar is intended here. Di. thinks that the identification of סְפָר is still uncertain, but points out that it should probably be sought for in southern Arabia, and must have been more or less known to the Hebrews. Cf. his *Comm.*, p. 201.

[1] The reading in 1 Sam. 15, 7 is doubtful. Wel. reads טֵילָם, cf. *Sam.*, p. 97; Driver, *Sam.*, ad loc.

הר הקדם. Hardly the Arabian hill country (*Neǵd*), as this would only be suitable if הר הק״ could be subject to ויהי מושבם. If it is dependant on באכה (Kn., Del., etc.), it must be the name of a mountain range in the south, possibly the so-called '*Incense-mountains*' (הר הלבנה, Ibn-Ezra on Gen. 1, 11), between Ḥaḍramaut and Mahra.

11.

1. ויהי. The imperf. with waw conv. commencing the narrative, the chapter being loosely connected with the preceding one; cf. Ges., § 111. 2; Dav., *S.*, § 51.

כל הארץ שפה וגו״. '*The whole earth was one tongue.*' The predicate in Hebrew, as in Arabic, is often a substantive, where in our idiom an adj. is used, or some such phrase as '*consists of*,' '*contains.*' This construction is commonly used in designating the material out of which an object is made, and in specifying weights or measures, etc.; but an extension of this usage is also often found in Hebrew, 'when terms other than material attributes are treated similarly;' Dr., § 189. 2; Ewald, § 296 b; Ges., § 141. 1. R. 1; Dav., *S.*, § 29 e; M. R., § 125. R. a; cf. 2 Sam. 17, 3 כל העם יהיה שלום; Job 3, 4 היום ההוא יהי חשך; Is. 27, 10, and often.

שפה = lit. '*lip*,' then '*language;*' so in Is. 19, 18 שפת כנען; 33, 19 עמקי שפה; cf. Ez. 3, 5. P uses לשון in this sense, 10, 5. 20. 31; cf. Deut. 28, 49.

דברים אחדים = lit. '*single words*,' i. e. '*the same*' or '*similar words.*' The use of אחדים in the phrase ימים אחדים 27, 44. 29, 20. Dan. 11, 20, meaning '*single*,' i. e. '*a few days*,' is different from its use here.

2. נסע does not only mean '*to break up the camp*,' but '*to strike the tents and move onward on the journey.*'

מקדם. Not *'from the east,'* but as 13, 11 *'eastwards'* (cf. M. R., § 49. Rem. d. 12, 8), i. e. 'from the standpoint of the author, in Palestine (29, 1),' Di.

בקעה, prop. *'a split'* or *'cleft,'* but according to the usage of the language, *'a plain lying in a broad valley,' 'a valley plain;'* cf. the Syriac ܦܩܥܬܐ *'campus patens.'* The distinction between geographical synonyms should be noted; see Stanley, *Sinai and Palestine*, App., § 5, where the בקעות mentioned in the O. T. are enumerated, and Sh., *G.*, pp. 384, 654.

בארץ שׁנער. Cf. on 10, 10.

3. איש אל רעהו. *'One to the other.'* On this mode of expressing the reciprocal relation, see Ges., § 139. 1 c; M. R., § 72. 3. Rem. a; cf. § 94 c. Rem. a; Dav., *S.*, § 11. R. c.

הבה is properly imper. with ה cohort. (Ges., § 48. 5; Stade, § 592 c) from the root יהב *'to give,'* which, though common in Aramaic and Arabic (وهب), is confined in Heb. to the imper. sing. and plural. הבה sing. sometimes has the force of an interjection, so here, *'up,' 'come on;'* A. V. *'go to,'* so vers. 4. 7. Ex. 1, 10. For the form, cf. Ges., § 69. 2. Rem. 2. Other verbal forms used as interjections are ראה *'see!'* לכה *'come!'* cf. Stade, § 380.

נלבנה. *'Let us bake;'* the imperf. with ה cohort., to express the intention with greater energy; cf. Ges., §§ 48. 3, 108. 1 a; Dav., *S.*, § 61 f.; M. R., § 9; Driver, § 49 β. The verb לבן is a denominative from לְבֵנָה.

לבנים *'bricks,'* perhaps so called as being baked white by the heat of the sun. The word occurs in Assyr. under the form *libittu*, cstr. state *libnat*, Schrader, *C. O. T.*, p. 106.

לשׂרפה. Dat. of the product; cf. 2, 22. Amos 5, 8, lit. *'into what is burnt,'* i. e. *'bricks.'* Render, *'And let us burn them into bricks.'* The bricks here mentioned were different from those made of a mixture of straw and clay, Ex. 1, 14. 5, 7.

4. וראשו בשמים. Render, '*With its top in the heavens.*' The clause is a simple circumstantial one; cf. 24, 10. 25, 26; Dr., § 159; Ewald, § 341 a; Dav., *S.*, § 138 a; so Is. 6, 6 ובידו רצפה; Zech. 2, 5 ובידו חבל מדה. In Deut. 1, 28 we have the word ערים qualified by בצורות בשמים '*fortified in the heavens,*' i.e. '*with high and lofty fortifications;*' cf. Dan. 4, 8. 17.

נעשה לנו שם, lit. '*let us make us a name,*' i.e. '*let us gain an honourable name;*' so Is. 63, 12. Jer. 32, 20. פן נפוץ refers to both halves of the first part of the verse. They had a double object in view, to found a city, and gain for themselves an honourable name; the city being a common place of assembly for all, and so a means of keeping them together and preventing their being scattered over the earth. Others connect פן נפוץ closely with שם, and take that word in the sense of '*monument*' = Arab. سِمَةٌ, as in 2 Sam. 8, 13. This however is doubtful, and here unsuitable.

פן נפוץ. LXX, πρὸ τοῦ διασπαρῆναι ἡμᾶς, and Vulg. '*antequam dividamur,*' apparently taking פן as though it were לפני.

6. '*Behold one people (are they), and one language have they all.*' The A.V. '*The people is one,*' is scarcely correct, as that would be rather אחד העם. The R.V. renders, '*Behold they are one people,*' etc.

החלם is inf. cstr. Hif'il of חלל, with the ה pointed with pathach instead of a composite sheva, on account of the following guttural ח; cf. Stade, § 80. 2 b; Ges., § 67. Rem. 6; Ewald, § 199 a. So Esth. 6, 13 הַחִלּוֹתָ; Is. 9, 3 הַחִתֹּתָ.

וזה החלם וגו״=lit. '*and this is their beginning to do,*' i.e. 'merely the commencement of their plan.'

יבצר=lit. '*will be cut off,*' i.e. '*they will not be debarred from it;*' so once besides, Job 42, 2 לא יבצר ממך מזמה.

יָזְמוּ is a lightened form of יָזֹמּוּ from זמם; so נָבְלָה, ver. 7, for נָבֹלָּה; cf. 9, 19, and Ges., § 67. Rem. 11; Stade, § 521 a, β, who explains the form in question as formed after the analogy of the third pers. pl. perf., instead of יָזֹמּוּ or יָזֵמּוּ; cf. Ewald, § 193 c.

7. נבלה. See note on ver. 6; and on the first pers. pl., see on 1, 26. The word was probably chosen with reference to the name בָּבֶל.

אשׁר, expressing the result rather than the aim, ='*so that,*' not '*that;*' cf. Ex. 20, 26. Deut. 4, 10. 40. In Gen. 3, 22, we have פן introducing the negative final clause; see Ges., § 165. 2; M. R., § 164 b; Ewald, § 337 b. 2; Dav., *S.*, § 149.

איש שׂפת רעהו. Cf. on ver. 3. שׁמע=not merely '*to hear,*' but '*to understand,*' as in Deut. 28, 49. Is. 33, 19.

8. ויחדלו לבנת. After verbs of '*ceasing,*' '*hastening,*' etc., two constructions are usually possible; either the inf. cstr. with ל as here, or the inf. cstr. alone; cf. Ges., § 120. 1; Ewald, § 285. 1; Dav., *S.*, § 82 †. With חדל, מִן may be used, see Ex. 23, 5. 1 Kings 15, 21.

9. על כן קרא. '*Therefore they called its name Babel,*' i.e. '*they, people called.*' On the so-called impersonal use of the third pers. perf. masc. sing. (=קָרָא הַקֹּרֵא), cf. Ges., § 144. 3 a; M. R., § 123. 2; Dav., *S.*, § 108 and R. 1.

בָּבֶל, according to the etymology given in the text, is from בלל. בבל must then be regarded as contracted from בַּלְבֵּל;

cf. קִיקָלוֹן from קִלְקָלוֹן; עֲזָאזֵל for עֲזַלְזֵל; see Ewald, § 158 c; Stade, § 124 a; cf. also the Syriac ܒܠܒܠܐ *'confusion of speech;'* Arab. تَبَلْبَلَ This is the Hebrew explanation of the name. For the Babylonian it had another meaning, which is probably the correct one. Some (Eich., Winer) derive it from *Bâb Bel,* باب بل *'gate,'* i.e. *'court of Bel;'* following the ancients, see Steph. of Byzant.; compare the Aramaic and Talmudic ܒܒܐ, בבא = *'gate,'* also the names of the Talmud Tracts בבא קמא *'the front gate;'* בבא בתרא *'the back gate;'* בבא מציעא *'the middle gate;'* others, from בית בל = בבל, so Tuch, comparing for the contraction בְּעֶשְׁתְּרָה, Josh. 21, 27 = בית עשׁתרה *'Temple of Ashtoreth,'* and the Phoen. בת עתר = בעתר *'Temple of 'Athor;' Inscr. Melitensis,* 5, l. 4; Schröder, *Phoen. Gramm.*, p. 235; cf. p. 108 (see, however, *C. I. S.*, i. p. 163); and the Syriac ܒܝܬ ܢܘܢ = ܒܠܢܘܢ; see further, Tuch, p. 221. The name as given on the Assyrian inscriptions is *Bâb-Il* = *'Gate of God,'* or (later) *Bâb-Ilâni* = *'Gate of the Gods,'* which is certainly the most probable meaning; cf. Schrader, *C. O. T.*, p. 112 ff.; Del., *Par.*, p. 212 ff.; so most moderns.

In the following verses, 10–32, we have a genealogical table carrying on the history of the patriarchs from Shem to Abram—the founder of the house of Israel—and his two brothers Nahor and Haran. This table is in many respects very similar to the one found in chap. 5. In both ten generations are given, Abram closing the list here, and Noah in chap. 5. In both lists the ages of the persons mentioned are considerably higher than those usually reached. Here, as well as chap. 5, we find the length of each person's life reckoned, both from his own birth to the birth of his first son, and from that event to his death. The LXX and the Samaritan deviate in their methods of reckoning the years here, as well as in the earlier chapter, as may be seen from the following table taken from Dillmann, p. 209.

	Hebrew Text.			LXX Text.			Samaritan Tex		
	The years before the birth of the first son.	The remaining years of the life.	Total years of life.	The years before the birth of the first son.	The remaining years of the life.	Total years of life.	The years before the birth of the first son.	The remaining years of the life.	Total years
Shem ...	100	500	600	100	500	600	100	500	60
Arpachshad	35	403	438	135	400 (430)	535 (565)	135	303	43
Kainan ...	...	...	...	130	330	460	...	...	..
Shelach ...	30	403	433	130	330	460	130	303	43
Eber ...	34	430	464	134	270 (370)	404 (504)	134	270	40
Peleg ...	30	209	239	130	209	339	130	109	23
Reu ...	32	207	239	132	207	339	132	107	23
Serug ...	30	200	230	130	200	330	130	100	23
Nahor ...	29	119	148	179 (79)	125 (129)	304 (208)	79	69	14
Terach ...	70	(135)	(205)	70	(135)	(205)	70	(75)	(14

In both chapters the Hebrew text has most probably preserved the more correct lists, though the Samaritan is perhaps the most consistent of the three tables. The Samaritan list never allows the son to live to a greater age than the father; so the numbers, e.g. in the cases of Terach and Eber, have to be lowered in order to carry out this rule. With the single exception of Terach, the Sam. text increases the number of years before the birth of the first son, and in all cases, except that of Shem, decreases the number of years which each person lived after the birth of the first son.

The Sam. text in the third column agrees with the Hebrew, with the exception of the cases of Eber and Terach. The LXX text, having a large number of variants, is more or less uncertain. Like the Sam. text, seventy years seem to have been the limit before which no children were begotten, and with the exception of Shem,—where all three texts are the same, and Nahor, where one hundred and fifty years are added, with a variant, seventy-nine,—the LXX add one hundred years to the number each person lived before the birth of the first son. In the second column the readings are uncertain, but sometimes the numbers are lower than the corresponding numbers in the Heb. text. In the third column, the LXX have always higher numbers than the Hebrew, except in the cases of Shem, of Eber (reading doubtful, variant 504) and Terach; the LXX in the latter case agreeing with the Heb. text. The years of Kainan's life are only given in the LXX text.

The object of this table, as of that in chap. 5, was probably twofold, to give some account of the period from the flood to Abram's birth, a period treated as uneventful, and to draw attention to the gradual decline in the number of years reached by each patriarch.

12. On the proper names in this chap., cf. Di. and Del.[5]

28. על פני תרח. '*Coram eo*,' i.e. so that he witnessed it, '*during his life-time;*' compare Num. 3, 4. Deut. 21, 16 (Kn.).

אור כשׂדים occurs again ver. 31. 15, 7. Neh. 9, 7, but not elsewhere. It is not quite clear whether אור is to be regarded as a proper name or as an appellative = '*district*.' The LXX have χώρα τῶν Χαλδαίων (Acts 7, 4 ἐκ γῆς Χαλδαίων), χώρα possibly having arisen from a reading חור (but the article is against this), unless we suppose that the reading χώρα has arisen out of χωρ, and was then supplied with the article, and so ἐν τῇ χώρᾳ. Kn. takes אור as = הור '*mountain*,' but this is very doubtful. J. D. Michaelis, and others, have identified אור with the castle of Ur, lying within the Persian frontier, and six days' journey north of Hatra, mentioned by Amm. Marc. xxv. 8. But the Ur mentioned by Marcellinus was first founded by the Persians or Parthians (Del.[5]), and being in an unfruitful and barren district would hardly be a suitable place for Abram, the shepherd-prince. Besides, כשדים points rather to the land about the lower Euphrates than to Mesopotamia, and most of the ancients (cf. Di.) hold the view that Ur was in Babylonia (Chaldea or Shinar). Another identification is that proposed by Sir Henry and Prof. George Rawlinson, Ur being אֶרֶךְ (which occurs only in 10, 10), i.e. the present Warka, on the left bank of the lower Euphrates; the name being explained by them as meaning '*the moon city*,' after the Arab. قمر. This view has been adopted by Loftus, *Trav.*, p. 126. The opinion most current among modern expositors is that אור is Mugheir (*El-Muqayyar*), a little south of Warka, on the right bank of the Euphrates, where ruins are still to be found. The name אור is found on the inscriptions in the form *Uru* (seat of the moon-god worship: cf. Eupolemos in Euseb., *Praep. Evang.*, ix. 17 πόλις τῆς Βαβυλωνίας Καμαρίνη, ἥν τινες λέγουσι πόλιν Οὐρίην), one of the oldest of the Babylonian royal towns in Sumer; see Schrader, *C. O. T.*, p. 114 ff.; Del., *Par.*, pp. 200, 226, and F. Brown, *J. B. L.*, Dec. 1887, p. 46 ff. כשדים would then be an addition due to the Jews, and not part of the native name; cf. Di., p. 214. Kittel (*Th. St. W.*, vii. p. 215 ff.: cf. his *Gesch.*, i. p. 163 ff.) considers that Ur Casdim must be sought for in Armenia or in northern Mesopotamia. He oes not dispute the existence of an Assyrian *Ur*, but holds ıat the Ur in this passage must be distinct from Ur in outh Babylonia.

The Casdim were the inhabitants of south Babylonia and abylon; they are not mentioned in the Bible or on the ıonuments before the time of Isaiah (see 23, 13). The ame in a wider sense might possibly have included Meso-otamia. The origin of the Casdim is obscure, but they eem to have been a tribe which from small beginnings radually acquired supremacy over south Babylonia and the apital; cf. Sayce, *Ency. Brit.*, art. *Babylonia.* The Talmud, *aba Bathra*, 91, places Ur Casdim in the neighbourhood f Babylon. Ur Casdim has also been identified,—but with-ut any great probability,—with Edessa (in Syr. ܐܘܪܗܝ), by litzig. The Syrian Christians boast of Edessa as being ıe Ur Casdim of Abraham. The old interpretation current mong the Jews (also found in the Qoran, Sur. 21) takes אור as meaning fire, and narrates that Abraham confessed ıe true God, and denied the gods of Nimrod, so he was ıst into the fire, but saved in a miraculous manner by God. lier. probably had this in view when he translated Neh. 9, 7, '*duxisti eum de igne Chaldaeorum*,' see Del.[5], p. 242, and eer, *Das Leben Abraham's nach Auffassung der jüdischen age*, 1859.

30. וָלָד, only here and as Ktib in 2 Sam. 6, 23 for יֶלֶד; ıe original ו of the root, which still exists in Arabic وَلَدٌ, وَلَدَ, ıd reappears in the Hif'. and Nif'. of the verb in Hebrew, here preserved.

31. וַיֵּצְאוּ אִתָּם. '*They went out with them.*' The mean-g of the text is not clear. אִתָּם may not be rendered '*with e another*,' as the suffix cannot be taken as reciprocal. To

regard Abraham and Terach as the subj. of ויצאו, and t
refer אִתָּם to Lot and Sarai or *vice versa,* is quite arbitrary an
not justified by the Hebrew. Nor can אתם be taken as=th
retinue who accompanied Abraham and Terach, as these hav
not been mentioned previously. The text seems to be cor
rupt. Either read with the LXX וַיּוֹצֵא אֹתָם ἐξήγαγεν αὐτούς
so Sam., Vulg., Del.[5]; or with the Pesh. וַיֵּצֵא אִתָּם, ܘܢܦܩ
ܥܡܗܘܢ, so Ilg. Ols. Terach would be the subject wit
either rendering.

חָרָן, Assyr. *Ḥarran*, Syr. ܚܪܢ, Arab. حَرّان, Gk. Καρραι
Lat. *Carrae*, was situated in north-west Mesopotamia, nin
hours SSE. of Edessa, on the little river Gullâb.

12.

1. וַיֹּאמֶר. A. V. wrongly, '*Now the Lord had said,*' mor
correctly R. V., '*Now the Lord said,*' the passage being lik
Judg. 17, 1. 1 Sam. 9, 1; a new narrative is commenced
amplifying the preceding one which is regarded as a whole
the association of the two being in *thought*, not in *time*
cf. Driver, § 76 γ. Whether the imperf. with waw conv. ca
denote a pluperfect is very doubtful; see note on 1, 2. Driver
l. c. Obs., fully discusses the question, and arrives at th
conclusion that there is not sufficient evidence to justify th
adoption of a pluperfect rendering in the place of the simpl
past.

לֶךְ לְךָ (once again in Pent., Gen. 22, 2) '*get thee,*' th
dat. adds an element of feeling to the bald לֵךְ, implyin
a reference to, or a regard for, the person addressed. Th
dative is often found similarly after verbs of motion, e. g
Deut. 1, 7. 40. 5, 27, etc.; see Ges., § 119. 3 c. 2; Ewald
§ 315 a; Dav., *S.*, § 101. R. b; M. R., § 51. 3. R. a. 3.

מארצך, probably Harran; cf. ver. 4 with 24, 4. 7. 38. In Acts 7, 2 מארצך is taken as Ur Casdim; so Hupfeld.

אַרְאֶךָּ for אַרְאֶנְךָּ. Impf. Hif‘. of ראה with the so-called נ demons.; the verb ראה and other verbs ל״ה frequently use the suffix with נ; cf. Stade, §§ 576 c, 127 b; Ges., § 58. 4; Dav., § 31. 5; and see foot-note on 3, 9.

2. ואעשך וגו׳ '*And I will make thee into a great nation, and I will bless thee and make thy name great, and be thou* (i. e. *that thou mayest be*) *a blessing*.' The imperfects in this and the following verse are to be taken as cohortatives, expressing with greater energy the intention of the speaker, see Driver, § 49 a; Ges., § 108. 1 a; M. R., § 9; Dav., *S.*, § 62. This rendering is simpler than to translate ואעשך and the other imperfs. '*that I may*' etc., regarding them as dependent on לך לך in ver. 1.

וֶהְיֵה, pointed according to Ges., § 63. Rem. 5; Stade, § 592 d. Here the imperative with waw is used where a voluntative with weak waw would be expected, to express the intention or purpose with greater energy; cf. 20, 7 וחיה; 2 Sam. 21, 3 וברכו; Driver, § 65; Ges., § 110. 2 b; M. R., § 10; Ewald, § 347 a; Dav., *S.*, § 65 d.

ברכה. '*And be a blessing*,' LXX, καὶ ἔσῃ εὐλογημένος (Swete prefers εὐλογητός), cf. Ps. 21, 7. Is. 19, 24; God will bless him, and men will bless him, in that they will use his name as a formula of blessing, cf. ver. 3, Zech. 8, 13; he himself too will be a source of blessing to others; cf. ver. 3 a.

3. ומקללך. LXX, Pesh., Vulg., Sam. read the pl. וּמְקַלְלֶיךָ. The Mass. reading is the better one, 'God does not expect that *many* will so far forget themselves as to curse him' (Di.).

ונברכו. LXX, εὐλογηθήσονται ἐν σοί; Ecclus. 44, 21. Acts 3, 25. Gal. 3, 8; so Onq. and Vulg., rendering as a passive, '*shall be blessed:*' it is interpreted in the N. T. as meaning that in Christ all the nations should be blessed. The Nif'. would then be passive, as in 18, 18. 28, 14. But in 22, 18. 26, 4, we find the reflex. Hithp'. והתברכו, which can scarcely be taken as passive, but must = '*all peoples shall bless themselves with thy seed,*' i. e. wish that they may be as blessed as Israel; cf. 48, 20. Jer. 29, 22. Is. 65, 16; the Nif'al is also taken as a reflexive here by Del., Di., and most moderns, after Rashi. Di. remarks that it would not be unreasonable to expect the Pu'al in these passages if the passive sense were intended. Tuch slightly alters the meaning, and renders both Hithp'. and Nif'. '*to call oneself happy,*' i. e. '*to regard oneself as blessed*' (ב = *through* any one), which is perhaps not impossible, but at least for the Hithp'. improbable.

5. רכוש = '*moveable property.*' LXX, τὰ ὑπάρχοντα.

הנפש אשר עשו. '*The souls which they had gotten in H.*' הנפש is used collectively. The meaning of these words is not the persons whom they had begotten (Luth.), but the slaves they had acquired during their sojourn in Harran. עשו occurs again in this sense in 31, 1. Deut. 8, 17. 18. נפש as in נפשות ביתו, 36, 6; נפש אדם, Ez. 27, 13, etc.; cf. a similar use of ψυχή, 1 Macc. 10, 33. Rev. 18, 13. רכש and רכוש are characteristic of P, נפש in this sense is also common in P, so 17, 14. 36, 6. 46, 15. 18. 22. 25, and often. Onq. renders, וְאַף נַפְשָׁתָא דְּשַׁעְבִּידוּ לְאוֹרַיְתָא בְּחָרָן. '*And also the souls which they had subjected to the law in Harran,*' possibly, as Tuch suggests, to avoid the suspicion that strangers accompanied Abram to Canaan.

6. מקום שכם. '*To the district of Shechem.*' מקום as in

Ex. 3, 8 אל מקום הכנעני. Di., however, renders '*to the sanctuary* (*Kultstätte*) *at Shechem*,' comparing 22, 3 f. 28, 11, etc. Shechem (cf. 33, 18) is the modern Nablous (نابلس), one of the best known towns of Mid-Canaan, in the hill country of Ephraim, situated between Mount Ephraim and Mount Gerizim. Its Roman name was Flavia Neapolis.

עד אלון מורה. '*To the terebinth of Moreh.*' Del., and others, regarding מ״ as a proper name. Di. renders '*The terebinth of the teacher.*' אלון מרה is probably to be explained, according to Deut. 11, 30 אלוני מרה, as a terebinth grove, where in ancient times the priests who were seers or prophets had their dwelling, and gave instruction and information to those who resorted to them. The fact that Jacob (35, 4) buried the idols and amulets at Shechem, and that Joshua—after the address to the tribes at Shechem, previous to his death, wherein the covenant between them and God was renewed—raised a stone there as a testimony (Josh. 24, 26), is not without significance, as pointing to the religious character belonging to the locality. Perhaps, as Di. suggests, this grove at Shechem is the same as the terebinth of the Wizards, Judg. 9, 37. On the question of sacred trees, cf. Rob. Smith, *Relig. of Semites*, p. 185.

אֵלוֹן, to which אֵילָה and אַיִל belong, was probably '*the terebinth*,' while אַלּוֹן, and prob. also אַלָּה (Josh. 24, 26), was '*the oak.*' The terebinth, being less common than the oak, was more suitable for marking out any spot (Di.). The LXX translate אֵלוֹן, and (sometimes) אַלּוֹן, by δρῦς, and the Massoretic pointing varies, e. g. cf. Josh. 19, 33 and Judg. 4, 11. In Aramaic ܐܝܠܢܐ means a tree in general (cf. δρῦς and *tree*), and it is possible that איל and אלון might be used of other great trees (Ges., *Th.*, 51 a). The Targg. of Onq. and

Ps.-Jon. render אלון by מֵישְׁרֵי *'plain,'* which the Vulg. *'convallis illustris'* and A. V. follow (R. V. has *'oak,'* marg. *terebinth*). From this, perhaps, we may infer that they were acquainted with the idolatrous sense of אלון, for they often render בעל in the same way. Pesh. has ܒܒܠܘܛܐ ܕܡܡܪܐ *'at the oak of Mamre,'* so also Saadiah.

מורה. LXX render by ὑψηλός, Vulg. *'illustris,'* prob. taking מוֹרֶה as though it were מַרְאֶה (a confusion between the sound of the two words).

הכנעני אז בארץ. אָז points to a time when the Canaanites should not be in the land as rulers of the same, this notice was perhaps inserted with reference to the promise made in ver. 7.

הכנעני has the article, 'a generic word being used collectively to denote all the individuals belonging to it,' Ges., § 125. 2; Ewald, § 277 c; Dav., *S.*, § 22 a.

8. ויט אהלה. אהלה, ה for ו; cf. the note on 9, 21.

מים *'on the west,'* the Mediterranean sea forming the western boundary of Palestine. This use of ים (cf. נגב in ver. 9) as marking a point of the compass is purely Palestinian.

ביתאל . . . מקדם is a simple circ. clause, without any connecting particle; cf. 32, 12. 31. 1 Sam. 26, 13; Ges., § 156. 2; Driver, § 161. 1; Dav., *S.*, § 140; M. R., § 153.

העי. *'Ai,'* lit. *'the stone heap,' par excellence;* cf. for the article thus used with a pr. name, Ges., § 125. 2; M. R., § 66. Rem. a; Dav., *S.*, § 20. R. 1.

9. הלוך ונסוע, cf. on 8, 3.

הנגבה. Cf. ver. 8. *'Towards the south.'* LXX, ἐν τῇ ἐρήμῳ; Aq. better, νότονδε; Symm. εἰς νότον. נֶגֶב = *'dryness, dry land,'* with the art., is the name of the southern portion of the territory of the Hebrews, to the north of which were the Shephelah (low country), the mountains, and the wilderness of Judah. The district is partly, land capable of cultivation, and partly a waste. South of it lies the wilderness proper, stretching across to Mount Sinai. Cf. Josh. 15, 21 ff.; and Sh., *G.*, pp. 49 f., 278 f. The use of this word=*south*, is purely Palestinian, cf. on ים, ver. 8.

10. וירד. ירד is the usual word in the O.T. for a journey from the high land of Canaan into the valley of the Nile, e.g. Is. 31, 1; עלה for the journey from Egypt to Palestine; cf. 13, 1. 44, 23. 24. 46, 4.

11. הקריב לבוא, lit. '*draw near to come,*' i.e. '*came near;*' cf. on 11, 8, and see Ges., § 114, 2. R. 3; Dav., *S.*, § 82.

יפת מראה. The adj. in the cstr. state is defined by a following genitive; cf. נקי כפים '*with clean hands,*' lit. '*clean of hands;*' אגמי נפש '*sorrowful in spirit;*' ערל שׂפתים '*uncircumcised of lips,*' Ges., § 128. 3; M. R., § 80. 2 b; Ewald, § 288 c. 3; Dav., *S.*, § 24 d. Render, '*That thou art fair to look at.*'

12. ואתך יחיו. אתך, by being placed first, varies the two clauses, and is more emphatic.

13. אמרי נא אחתי את. כִּי is omitted in the *oratio indirecta*, as in 41, 15. Is. 48, 8. Hos. 7, 2; Ges., § 157 a; Ewald, § 338 a; M. R., § 162; Dav., *S.*, § 146. R. 1.

למען ייטב . . . וחיתה. The perfect with waw conv., after an imperf. with למען; cf. 18, 19 למען אשר יצוה . . . ושמרו, Is. 28, 13 למען ילכו וכשלו; cf. Ges., § 112. 3 c. *a*; Driver, § 115 (p. 134); M. R., § 24. 2 a; Dav., *S.*, § 53 c.

15. ויהַלְּלו is pointed with a comp. shewa, the dagesh in the first ל being omitted, by Ges., § 10. 2. Rem. A; Stade, § 136. 2 (who cites ל as one of the consonants that frequently

give up their doubling when pointed with shewa). The shewa is here composite instead of simple, by Stade, § 105, Ges. l.c., i.e. ḥâṭêph-pathach is used instead of a simple shewa after a vowel with Metheg, when two similar sounds follow one another, so צֹורֲרִים Ps. 8, 3, גּוֹזֲזֶיהָ Is. 53, 7, הֲרֲרֵי Ps. 87, 1.

בית פרעה is acc. of place, in answer to the question '*whither?*' see Ges., § 118. 2; M. R., § 41 a; Ewald, § 281 d; Dav., *S.*, § 69 b; cf. 24, 16. 27, 3. 31, 4. 39, 1. 42, 38. 43, 17. 45, 25.

פרעה, Josephus, *Ant.*, viii. 6. 2, explains the name as= '*the king*,' so Ges., in *Thes.*, p. 1129. Stern gives as the hieroglyphic form of the name *p-ur-ā*, i.e. '*the great prince*,' '*the greatest of all*,' a title given, since king Šišaq, to all the Pharaohs, and which has passed over into Coptic, where ⲡ-ⲟⲩⲣⲟ, ⲡ-ⲉⲣⲣⲟ='*the king*' (Peyron, *Lex.*, 150). Di., p. 227, Lauth, de Rougé, Brugsch, Ebers, and Erman prefer to explain פרעה (from a notice in Horapollo, i. 62 οἶκος μέγας) as=*per'o* (*per-aa*, *per-ao*), '*the great house*,' a title given to the reigning monarch, similar to the modern '*Sublime Porte*.' It remained the usual title of the Egyptian kings up to the time of the Persian conquest. The title פרעה is often found on the oldest monuments, Ebers, *Egypt. und die B.M.*, p. 264.

16. The presents Abram received from Pharaoh are elsewhere mentioned as forming the riches of a nomad prince; cf. 24, 35. 32, 15. Job 1, 3. 42, 12.

ויהי לו, lit. '*and there was to him*,' i.e. *he had;* for the singular, cf. (note on) 1, 14. 13, 5. 30, 43. 32, 6. Num. 9, 6. 1 Kings 11, 3.

17. וינגע . . . פרעה נגעים. נגע, Qal='*to touch*,' Pi'el, intens. '*to touch heavily*,' '*smite*.' A verb in Hebrew is frequently followed by a noun, derived from it, in the acc.; cf.

note on 1, 11, and add examples 30, 8. 40, 8. 50, 10. Deut. 7, 23. 2 Sam. 4, 5. נֶגַע and נָגַע are often used in this connection, e.g. 2 Kings 15, 5. 1 Sam. 6, 9. Job 19, 21 (both with יד). Ex. 11, 1.

18. למה. On the pointing here and ver. 19, cf. Ges., § 102. 2 d; Stade, § 372 b.

19. Render, '*Why didst thou say, She is my sister, so that I took her to be my wife* (i.e. *and so lead me to take her*)?' The second idea being really a consequence of the first, the waw conv. may be rendered, '*so that* or *and so*;' see Driver, § 74 a, and p. 136; Ges., § 111. 3 b. Rem.; and cf. 20, 12. 23, 20. 31, 27.

20. ויצו עליו '*commanded concerning him*;' cf. Num. 8, 22. 2 Sam. 14, 8.

וישלחו '*and they brought him on his way* or *escorted him*;' cf. the N.T. προπέμπειν, Acts 15, 3. 21, 5.

13.

2. במקנה בכסף ובזהב. The article is generic, being used with different materials which are generally known; cf. note on 2, 11. So in 6, 14. 11, 3. 1 Kings 10, 27. 2 Chron. 2, 13. 14. Di. suggests that the Massoretes possibly had the particular wealth acquired by Abram in Egypt in their mind, and so inserted the article.

3. למסעיו '*by his stations*' (stationenweise), implying that he proceeded gradually, adapting his speed to the requirements of the flocks and herds he had with him; cf. Ex. 17, 1, where LXX render κατὰ παρεμβολὰς αὐτῶν, Ex. 40, 36. Num. 33, 2. The מסעים are the مَرَاحِل '*day-journeys*,' by which they still reckon at the present time in the east (Tuch). The LXX (καὶ ἐπορεύθη ὅθεν ἦλθεν) and Vulg. (*re-*

versus est per iter, quo venerat) take the מסעים as the places Abram had halted at on his journey down to Egypt, but this is not so suitable. ל with the pl. is used distributively here, as in Ps. 73, 14 לבקרים '*morning-wise;*' Job 7, 18; see Ewald, § 217 d, a; M. R., § 51. 5, who explains the usage somewhat differently from Ewald; Dav., *S.*, § 101, R. b.

ועד ביתאל. When the two prepositions '*from . . . to*' are both expressed, a ו '*and*' is generally inserted before the second. '*From the south to Bethel,*' lit. '*from the south and* (*then further*) *to Bethel;*' cf. M. R., § 49. 1 b; Ges., § 154. foot-note b; Dav., *S.*, § 101. R. b.

5. אֹהָלִים for אֳהָלִים, explained incorrectly by Ges., § 23. 3, 2; § 93. 1. Rem. 3, as a Syriasm. Stade, § 109, cf. § 327 b. 3, rightly points out that the lengthening of the ḥâṭêph qameç into ḥolem before the guttural ה is due to the influence of the counter-tone, marked by metheg: other instances are פֹּעֳלוֹ instead of פָּעֳלוֹ; אֹהָלִי. The change is less frequent with ḥâṭêph qameç than qameç ḥâṭûph.

6. ולא נשׂא אתם. Cf. 36, 7 לא יכלה ארץ מגוריהם לשׂאת אתם. נשׂא, the verb comes first, and is put in the nearer gender, the masc., though the subj. הארץ is fem.; cf. Ewald, § 339 c. 1; and note on 1, 14.

לשׁבת. ישׁב in this connection is characteristic of P, so ver. 12. 36, 7. 37, 1, also נשׂא.

7. יֹשֵׁב. Render, '*was dwelling.*' On the participle used of past time, see Driver, § 135, 1; cf. 19, 1. 37, 7. 41, 1–3. 42, 23, etc.; and Ges., § 116. 5 b; Dav., *S.*, § 100. R. 1. The plural is more usual when the predicate follows a compound subject; cf. on 8, 22 and Prov. 27, 9. 2 Sam. 20, 10. Neh. 6, 12; Ewald, § 339 c. 2; Ges., § 146. 2 a; M. R., § 138; Dav., *S.*, § 114. The second noun holds a more

subordinate position than the first, the waw being almost '*with*' (waw of association), '*The Canaanite with the P.*' On פרזי, cf. 10, 17.

8. אנשים אחים, in apposition; see Ges., § 131. 2 a; Dav., *S.*, § 29 b, and cf. 21, 20. Num. 32, 14. Deut. 22, 28. אחים = '*relatives*,' not to be taken strictly in the sense '*brothers*;' cf. 14, 16. 29, 12.

9. '*Is not all the land before thee? pray separate thyself from me, if towards the left, then I will go to the right, and if towards the right, then I will go to the left.*' The hyp. sentence is similar in form to ואם מעט ואוסיפה לך, 2 Sam. 12, 8. The simple waw introducing the apod. is very rare; cf. Driver, § 136 β*; Dav., *S.*, § 130. R. 2; M. R., § 165. השמאל and הימין are acc. of place; cf. on 12, 15; תִּפָּרֵד being understood with each.

הימין and השמאיל are denominatives from ימין and שמאל respectively; on the quad. form of the latter, see Ges., § 56; Stade, § 627. Onq. renders שמאל by לְצִיפּוּנָא '*to the north*,' and יָמִין by לְדָרוֹמָא '*to the south*.' In Arabic أَشْأَمَ, IV conj., = '*to go to Syria*' (اَلشَّأْم), and أَيْمَنَ, IV conj., = '*to go to Yemen*' (اَلْيَمَن), lit. '*to go to the left and right*,' respectively; see other similar instances in Wright, *Arab. Gram.*, i. p. 36.

מעלי '*from my presence*,' 25, 6. Ex. 10, 28.

10. ככר הירדן recurs 1 Kings 7, 46. Cf. in the N. T. Matt. 3, 5. Luke 3, 3 ἡ περίχωρος τοῦ Ἰορδάνου; more frequently we find merely הככר, 19, 17. 25. 28. Deut. 34, 3. 2 Sam. 18, 23. The district (prop. circle) of the Jordan is the land on both sides of the Jordan, from lake Tiberias to the Dead Sea, called by Josephus τὸ μέγα πεδίον, *Bell. Jud.*, iv. 8. 2. Elsewhere in the O. T. it was also called הערבה (at

the present time *El-Ghôr*); cf. Sh., *G.*, pp. 47, 482 f., 505; Bäd., *Pal.*, p. xlvii. The valley of Siddim, 14, 3, also belonged to the ככר.

משקה = '*well watered,*' lit. '*a well-watered place;*' it occurs again Ez. 45, 15 משקה ישׂראל; cf. Is. 58, 11 כגן רוה.

כגן יהוה, probably referring to the garden of Eden, 2, 8. LXX, *ὡς ὁ παράδεισος τοῦ Θεοῦ*; Pesh. ܐܝܟ ܦܪܕܝܣܐ ܕܐܠܗܐ. Del.[4] and Schumann, however, regard יהוה as used in a superlative sense, and render, '*as a beautiful garden;*' cf. 10, 9 and the note there. This rendering, however, is not so natural as the other. In Is. 51, 3 we have גן יהוה, and in Ez. 36, 35 גן עדן, used in comparisons.

כארץ מצרים is added to tone down the previous גן עדן, the comparison with the garden of Eden being a somewhat too lofty conception.

באכה. '*On the way to,*' lit. '*as thou comest;*' for the second pers. sing. used impersonally, cf. Ges., § 144. 3 c; Dav., *S.*, § 108. R. 3; M. R., § 123. 4. The second pers. thus used occurs chiefly in this phrase; again 10, 19. 30. The form of the suff. ־כה is merely an orthographic variation for the more usual ־ךָ, e.g. 19, 22.

צער. LXX, *Ζόγορα*, also called בֶּלַע, 14, 2. A small town, generally regarded as situated on the south-east end of the Dead Sea. See on 19, 22. Pesh. reads צען (ܕܡܛܝܬ ܠܡܕܝܢܬܐ ܕܨܥܢ), which Ebers, *Egypt.*, p. 272, accepts as the real reading. With this reading, which however is not necessary, באכה צער would refer to ארץ מצרים alone, and not to the whole sentence. Trumbull (quoted by Del.[5]) supposes that צער is a name of the eastern border land of Lower Egypt, but cf. 10, 19.

12. ויאהל. This verb is a denom. from אהל '*a tent,*' =

'*to tent,*' i.e. '*to wander about nomad fashion,*' hence, perhaps, the pl. בערי. Render, '*Moved with his tents towards Sodom.*'

13. חַטָּאִים '*sinners,*' i.e. '*habitual sinners,*' different from חֹטְאִים '*people sinning,*' not necessarily as a habit; cf. Ges., § 84. 17; Barth, *N.B.*, p. 49 f., and Ryssel, *De Eloh. Pent. sermone*, p. 40.

ליהוה '*towards,*' i.e. '*against Yahweh.*' Cf. 20, 6. 39, 9. Or, '*to Yahweh,*' i.e. in his sight, ל=לפני 7, 1. So possibly the Mass. Text.

14b. Cf. 28, 14 ימה וקדמה וצפנה ונגבה.

15. אתננה is impf. Qal of נָתַן, with the suffix strengthened by the so-called נ *demonstrativum*; see note on 12, 1 אַרְאֶךָּ. Notice the *casus pendens*, here marked as the acc. by את, כי את כל הארץ '*For all the land . . . I will give it;*' cf. Driver, § 197. 6; Dav., *S.*, § 106 c; and 21, 13.

16. אשר אם יוכל, either I. '*so that, if any one could number,*' etc.; cf. 11, 7. 22, 14. 24, 3, so Pesh. ܕܐܢ, Driver, p. 183; Ges., § 166. 2; or II. Tuch, '*quem [pulverem] si quis,*' אשר referring to עפר in the first half of the verse, and עפר being repeated in the second half, where we would rather expect אתו. Tuch compares 50, 13 (=49, 30), where, however, אֵת rather means '*with;*' and Ewald, § 331 c. 3, cites Num. 26, 64. Jer. 31, 31, which are apparently quite regular. The LXX have simply εἰ δύναταί τις, not translating אשר. Perhaps, however, it is simplest to regard אשר as in Deut. 3, 24. 1 Kings 3, 12. 13, as a link which cannot be literally translated.

14.

1. בימי אמרפל וגו׳. The four kings' names are all genitives after the construct state בימי. Hebrew prefers, as a rule, to repeat the construct state before each genitive;

cf. Ges., § 128. 1; Dav., *S.*, § 28. R. 4; M. R., § 75 c; Ryssel, *De Eloh. Pent. sermone*, p. 61. The four kings, the subject to עשׂו in ver. 2, are not given again, as they can easily be inferred from ver. 1; cf. Ewald, § 303 b. 1; 9, 6 כי בצלם אלהים עשׂה '*For in God's image, He* (*God*),' etc., Esth. 2, 21. The renderings of the LXX, ἐν τῇ βασιλείᾳ τῇ Ἀμαρφὰλ βασιλέως Σεννaάρ, and Vulg. '*factum est in illo tempore ut*,' are probably merely intended to explain the meaning of the verse, and do not of necessity presuppose any variant. Clericus' emendation, inserting אברם before אמרפל, adopted by Ewald in his *Komp. der Gen.*, p. 221, is not necessary.

The meanings of the names in this verse are obscure. אמרפל, LXX Ἀμαρφάλ (assuming it is a corruption out of אמרפי), is identified by Schr. (*S. B. A. W.*, 1887, p. 603), Hal. (*R. B.*, x. 254) with the great Babylonian king *Ḥammurabi*, cir. 2100, who reigned about fifty-five years, overcame Elam, and finally succeeded in uniting the various Babylonian principalities into one state, with the capital Babylon. Cf. Di., p. 236. אריוך is perhaps *Êri-aku* or *Riv-aku*, '*Servant of the moon-god*' (*aku*), vassal king of Larsam, under his father *Kudur-mabug*, king of Elam, see further Schr., *C. O. T.*, ii. p. 297 f.; Del.[5], p. 263; Del., *Par.*, p. 224; cf. Judith 1, 6 Ἀριὼχ ὁ βασιλεὺς Ἐλυμαίων; Dan. 2, 14 אַרְיוֹךְ רַב טַבָּחַיָּא '*A. chief of the executioners.*' אלסר is identified with תְּלַשָּׂר, Is. 37, 12, by Targ. Ps.-Jon.; with Pontus, by Symm. and Vulg.; with Artemita, in south Assyria, by Kn.; with Kal'ah Sirgat, by Sayce. More recently (e.g. by Rawl., Del., Sch.) with the old Babylonian town Larsam or Larsav, the modern Senkereh, to the south-east of Uruk, cf. Loftus, *Chaldaea and Susiana*, p. 240 f. כדרלעמר, LXX Χοδολλογομόρ (notice the γ = ע, and cf. on 4, 18). On the Assyr. inscriptions several kings of Elam have names compounded with *Kudur*.

In the inscriptions the name of a deity *Lagamar* has been found. The name would perhaps=*Crown of Lagamar;* cf. Schr., *C. O. T.*, p. 121 ff. תדעל, LXX Θαργάλ, uncertain. Lenor. makes it=Akk. *tar-gal*, '*great Son.*' גוים, not a nom. appel. as A.V., '*King of nations*,' so Onq., for this rendering is too indefinite, and gives no suitable sense without some further name to define it; but a proper name, compared variously with the '*circuit* ("*Galil*") *of the nations*' (Is. 8, 23), Pamphylia (Symm.), and איי הגוים 10, 5 (Ges., Nöld.). Others, as H. Rawl., connect it with the *Gutî*, *Ḳutî* that are frequently found in the inscriptions; cf. Schr., *K. G. F.*, 258, 271, 294, 451, 473; a powerful tribe, dwelling between the Zab and Dijâla (Gyndes), Di., p. 237. R. V. has '*Goiim*,' marg. '*nations*.'

2. The proper names in this verse are even more uncertain than those in ver. 1, the readings being possibly corrupt; cf. the LXX text with the Hebrew. These five towns were, with the exception of Zoar, according to the narrative in chap. 19, destroyed.

3. חברו אל. A pregnant construction; cf. ver. 15. Render, '*Came allied to the valley of Siddim;*' cf. Josh. 10, 6 כי נקבצו אלינו '*for they have gathered together* [*and come*] *unto us.*' Other instances of preg. cstr. are to be found in Ewald, § 282 c; Ges., § 119. 4; Dav., *S.*, § 101.

עמק השׂדים. '*Valley of Siddim*,' i.e. '*Valley of the level fields*,' so Onq. מֵישַׁר חַקְלַיָא; Aq., Symm., Theod. κοιλὰς τῶν ἀλσῶν, so Vulg. The Pesh. takes השׂדים, as='*the inhabitants of Sodom*,' and renders ܒܥܘܡܩܐ ܕܣܕܘܡܝܐ. Others connect it with the Arabic شدّ '*stony ground.*' LXX have here φάραγξ ἡ ἁλυκή, and in ver. 9 κοιλὰς ἡ ἁλυκή. Cf. Sh., *G.*, p. 503. On עמק, see Stanley, *Sinai and Palestine*, App., § 1.

ים המלח. יָם with qameç is the construct state. יַם with pathach and maqqeph occurs as cstr. state twenty-three times, and always of the Red Sea (יַם־סוּף). יָם with qameç occurs as construct state twenty-four times, seventeen times *without* maqqeph, and seven times with maqqeph, but never of the Red Sea. Cf. Del. on Is. 11, 15.

4. שְׁתֵּים עֶשְׂרֵה שָׁנָה, acc. of time, in answer to the question '*how long?*'

וּשְׁלֹשׁ עֶשְׂרֵה, acc. of time, in answer to the question '*when?*' cf. Ges., § 118. 3 a and b; M. R., § 42 a and b; Ewald, § 300 a; Dav., *S.*, § 68. When a *particular* point of time is mentioned, the preps. ב, ל, or כ are used; so Ols. and Nöld. prefer the reading of the Sam. here, viz. ובשלש—cf. M. R., § 42 b—as being more correct; see the next verse.

5. הרפאים. '*The Refa'im,*' or '*sons of the Rafa,*' i. e. '*Giants,*' so LXX and Pesh. here. Partly the ordinary name of the giant aborigines of Canaan, in the western and eastern Jordan-land, whose territory was promised Abram's descendants, 15, 20; partly a special name of the giants in Bashan, as here and Deut. 3, 11. Josh. 13, 12. The last traces of them in the O.T. are in 2 Sam. 21, 15 ff. ילידי הרפה, where they are spoken of among the Philistines at the time of David.

עַשְׁתְּרֹת קַרְנַיִם[1], also simply עַשְׁתָּרֹת, Deut. 1, 4, and בית עשתרת = בעשתרה, Josh. 21, 27, was one of the principal towns of Bashan, identified with the present Tel 'Aštere, two and a half hours from Nawâ, nearly between Nawâ and M'zârîb; it is situated on a hill in a rich meadow-land, well watered, and many ruins are still to be found (Ritter in Di.,

[1] The LXX, Codex Vat. reads Ἀσταρὼθ καὶ Καρναΐν, and Kuenen thinks it possible that this is the true reading, cf. Rob. Smith, *Religion of the Semites*, p. 310.

p. 238); cf. Bäd., *Pal.*, p. 198. Wetzstein, however, prefers to identify it with Bosra, one hour and three quarters from Edrei, where ruins have been found. The name means '*The two-horned Ashtoreth*,' who, as the goddess of the moon, was represented with two horns. The name עשׁתרת occurs frequently in Phoenician inscriptions, e. g. Eṣmunazar's inscription, line 18, בת לבעל צדן ובת לעשׁתרת (cf. *C. I. S.*, vol. i. p. 14; and Dr., *Sam.*, p. 49), '*a temple for the Baal of Sidon, and a temple for Astarte.*' קרנים by itself is not found in the O. T. It probably was near עשׁתרת, and the two may have been regarded as one town, or עשׁתרת ק״ may be taken as meaning Ashtoreth near Ḳarnaim. The town was probably so called as being devoted to the worship of Ashtoreth.

ואת הזוזים בהם, possibly identical, as Ges. supposed, with the זמזמים, Deut. 2, 20, the name given by the Ammonites to the רפאים who formerly dwelt in their land. LXX have here, ἔθνη ἰσχυρὰ ἅμα αὐτοῖς, reading בָּהֶם and (?) עִזּוּזִים: so Pesh. Onq. has תַּקִּיפַיָּא, and gives for בָּהֶם, דִּבְהַמְתָּא '*who were in Hamta* (?).' It is quite uncertain where הם was. Tuch conjectures that Ham was perhaps the old name of the capital Rabbath Ammon.

האימים, perhaps '*the terrible ones.*' The giant aborigines of the land of Moab; cf. Deut. 2, 10. 11, where they are expressly mentioned as the original inhabitants of Moab.

בשׁוה קריתים = '*in the plain (of) Kiryathaim.*' שׁוה is found only once again, in ver. 17, both vowels being unchangeable; cf. Driver, § 190. Obs. end; Lag., *B.N.*, p. 43. In Num. 32, 37. Josh. 13, 19 the town Kiryathaim is mentioned as belonging to the Reubenites; in Jer. 48, 23. Ezek. 25, 9 to the Moabites; it was situated, according to the Onomas., four hours south-west of Mêdebâ. The ruins are called at the present day Ḳarêyât (east of Makaur (Machaerus) and south of mount 'Attârûs). קריתים = '*double town* (?).'

6. ואת החרי. The original inhabitants of Edom, Deut. 2, 12. 22; the hill country between the Dead Sea and the Ælanitic gulf.

בהררם '*on their mountain*,' for בְּהָרָם. LXX, ἐν τοῖς ὄρεσιν; so Sam. reading בהררי, cstr. pl. On the pointing, compare on 12, 15 (and add to the instances there, צְלָלָיו and גְּלָלָיו); הַרְרֵי and the other forms of הר, which resolve the doubled letter, and write it instead twice, are found in poetry and higher prose, as Deut. 8, 9: other instances of a doubled letter being written twice, instead of having a dagesh, are חֲנַנְכֶם, inf. cstr. of חנן, Is. 30, 18; מדדו for מדו, from מדד, Ez. 43, 10; עֲמָמִים = עַמִּים, Neh. 9, 22. 24 [cf. the regular emph. pl. in Aramaic עַמְמַיָּא]; and in poetry, Judg. 5, 14. See also Ges., § 93. 1. Rem. 7.

עד איל פארן = '*to the terebinth of P.*;' cf. on 12, 6. איל פארן is possibly identical with the well-known port Elath, on the Ælanitic gulf, variously called אילת, אילה, or אילות, in the O. T., which were perhaps abbreviated names of more modern origin, for the full name איל פארן.

7. עין משפט. '*Well of judgment*,' i.e. a place where decisions were given to disputants, perhaps the seat of a temple or oracle; cf. the other name קדש. The position of *Qadesh*, so often mentioned in the Pentateuch, is still uncertain. Three identifications are given by Di., p. 239: I. that it is to be sought for in '*Ain el Weibeh*, near the Arabah, 30° 42′ lat. (Robinson). A view now generally abandoned. II. Identical with *Qâdûs*, about eleven kilometers north of mount Mâdara, in the neighbourhood of the Wady-el-Yemen, one day's journey from Hebron (Wetzstein,

in Del., *Gen.*[4], p. 574; cf. Del.[5], p. 266). 'But this situation is too far north, and neither suits Gen. 16, 14 nor the history of Moses,' Di. More probable is III. Prof. E. H. Palmer and others identify it with *Ain Qudês*, on the western slope of the 'Azâzimeh (Machra) Plateau, south of Elusa, four and a half hours east-south-east of the Well of Hagar. See also Trumbull (*Kadesh Barnea*, 1884, p. 241 and *passim*).

חצצן תמר. Cf. 2 Chron. 20, 2, where it is explained by היא עין גדי '*En-gedi*,' on the west side of the Dead Sea, noted for its palm trees. Knobel prefers to identify it with עיר התמרים, Judg. 1, 16, or תָּמָר, Ez. 47, 19. 48, 28 (as Engedi lay too far north), on the south-east border of the Holy Land, the modern Kurnub (Di.). Cf. Sh., *G.*, pp. 269 f., 507; Bäd., *Pal.*, p. 140. The name perhaps means '*Palm rows*,' or '*cutting of Palms*,' but this is not certain.

10. בארת בארת חמר, lit. '*pits, pits of asphalt*,' i.e. '*full of asphalt pits.*' On the repetition of the noun to express plurality, cf. Ges., § 123 d. 3; Ewald, § 313 a; M. R., § 72. 2; Dav., *S.*, § 29. R. 8. בארת בארת חמר; the first two nouns are both construct states to the genitive חמר, the first of the two being an instance of the so-called *suspended construct state*, cf. Ps. 78, 9 נוֹשְׁקֵי רוֹמֵי קָשֶׁת, the second noun explaining the first, which is in the construct state, its proper genitive being קָשֶׁת; so נַהֲרֵי נַחֲלֵי דְּבַשׁ, Job 20, 17, נחלי explaining נהרי, the נהרי being really cstr. state before the genitive דבש; cf. Ewald, § 289 c; M. R., § 73, note a. 4; Ges., § 130. 5; Dav., *S.*, § 28. R. 6.

ועמק השדים בארת וגו׳. Note the form of the predicate in Hebrew. In English we say, '*The valley of Siddim was full of slime pits*,' i.e. we have to use some term such as, *consist of*, *contains*, or the like, to express the relation between the subject and the predicate. In Hebrew the predicate is expressed by the simple noun. '*The valley of Siddim was slime pits.*' Cf. Ex. 9, 31 השׂערה אביב והפשתה גבעול; Ps. 23, 5 כוסי רויה; so 13, 10. Is. 5, 12. Ps. 45, 9. Ezr. 10, 13; cf. note on 11, 1, and Driver, § 188.

חמר is '*asphalt*' or '*bitumen*,' found in the neighbourhood of the Dead Sea and of Babylon. The Babylonians used it as mortar; cf. 11, 3. See Sh., *G.*, p. 500f.; Bäd., *Pal.*, p. 170.

מלך סדם ועמרה. LXX, βασιλεὺς Σοδόμων καὶ βασιλεὺς Γομόρρας, so Pesh. and Sam., reading מלך סדם ומלך עמרה, which would be the more correct expression; cf. on ver. 1. The second מלך might have slipped out by homoioteleuton.

ויפלו שמה. Rather the followers of the kings, for the king of Sodom (ver. 17) at least escaped.

הֶרָה. הַר, with the acc. ending ה, implying motion towards, '*mountainwards*.' The form is pointed with ֶ instead of ַ, because the short a (pathach) before a guttural with long a (qameç) is changed into é (seghol); cf. הֶחָכָם for הַחָכָם, Ewald, §§ 70 a, 71. הֶרָה, however, seems to be the only instance of this with ר. Delitzsch compares סֶלָה for סַלָּה, the doubling being resolved, and the ַ changed into ֶ; also פַּדֶּנָה 28, 2 and כַּרְמֶלָה 1 Sam. 25, 5 for פַּדֶּנָּה and כַּרְמִלָּה respectively, cf. his *Comm. on the Psalms*, 5th ed., p. 78 (on Ps. 3).

11. רכשׁ. LXX, τὴν ἵππον, reading the word as though it were רֶכֶשׁ.

13. ויבא הפליט. '*And the fugitive came*,' i. e. 'the fugitive or escaped one, who in such cases is wont to come,' see esp. Ez. 24, 26. 33, 21. 22. Or it may be taken as a collective. On the article with פליט, see Ewald, § 277 a; Ges., § 126. 4; Dav., *S.*, § 22 b; M. R., § 68; cf. המגיד, 2 Sam. 15, 13.

העברי. '*The Hebrew.*' עברי means '*one who has come* מעבר *from the other side of a river.*' If this name was given to the Israelites by the Canaanites (Reuss, Stade, etc.), the name being Hebrew, the people who gave it them must have spoken the same language as they did. It is only used in O. T. to or by foreigners, or when the Hebrews are mentioned in opposition to other nations. The name Israelite was, on the other hand, a patronymic, and the national name used by the people themselves (cf., however, Robertson-Smith, *Ency. Brit.*, 9th edit., art. *Hebrew Lang. and Lit.*). The river from beyond which the Hebrews came is, according to some, the Euphrates, cf. Josh. 24, 2 ff. 14 f.; so most commentators. Reuss and Stade prefer the Jordan, on the ground that the Hebrews on their return from Egypt spent some time in the land east of Jordan, leaving the Canaanites in possession of that on the west, which, however, does not seem very conclusive against the general view. LXX render it here τῷ περάτῃ, Vulg. '*Transeuphratensis.*' Another explanation is that עברי is a patronymic from עבר, mentioned as an ancestor of Abram, 10, 24. 11, 14. 15. Num. 24, 24. See Di., p. 211[1].

באלני ממרא. Cf. on 12, 6. The terebinth grove being named after the Amorite Mamre, who possibly owned or planted it.

והם בעלי ברית אברם. '*They being confederates of Abram,*' notice the circ. clause. The text literally translated is, '*And they* (*were*) *owners of a covenant with A.;*' בעל being

[1] Robertson-Smith, l. c., mentions a modified form of the usual etymology of '*eber*, the word being taken in the Arabic sense = *a river bank.* The Hebrews would then be 'dwellers in a land of rivers.' This would suit Peleg (the water-course) as in Arabic we have the district Falag so called 'because it is furrowed by waters.'

used to form an adjective here, as in 37, 19 בעל החלמות= '*dreamer;*' 49, 23 בעלי חצים='*bow-men* (lit. *arrow-men*);' בעל שֵׂעָר='*hairy,*' 2 Kings 1, 8; בעל כנף='*winged,*' Prov. 1, 17, etc. Cf. Ges., § 129. 2. Rem. 2 b; Dav., *S.*, § 24. R. 3; M. R., § 79. 6 d. We have a similar expression to בעלי ברית in Neh. 6, 18, viz. בַּעֲלֵי שְׁבוּעָה. The phrase בעל ברית occurs nowhere else. In Judg. 8, 33. 9, 4 it is a proper name.

14. וירק is the imperf. apoc. Hif'. of רוק='*to empty out,*' e.g. arrows from a quiver, or a sword from the sheath, Ex. 15, 9. Lev. 26, 33. Ps. 35, 3; but only in this passage and Ps. 18, 43 with a personal object. Render, '*Let loose.*' LXX have ἠρίθμησεν, '*mustered,*' reading וירק as though it were וַיָּדֶק, which the Heb.-Sam. has, and which seems to have been the reading of the Sam. text, which has [Samaritan] '*recensuit,*' and the Vulg. '*numeravit.*'

חניכיו ילידי ביתו. חניכיו='*his tried ones*' (חניך is a ἅπαξ. λεγ.); cf. the Arab. حَنِيك='*experienced;*' LXX, τοὺς ἰδίους; who were ילידי ביתו '*home-born slaves,*' as opposed to מקנת כסף, 17, 12. 23, who were purchased slaves (or גֵּר, Ex. 23, 12); cf. the similar phrases, בן־בית, 15, 3; בן־אמה, Ex. 23, 12.

דן, i.e. Laish, on the N. frontier of Canaan, which in the time of the Judges received the name of Dan, Josh. 19, 47. Judg. 18, 29; the modern *Tell el-Ḳâḍi*, cf. Bäd., *Pal.*, p. 264, but Sh., *G.*, p. 480, takes it as = Bâniâs.

15. ויחלק עליהם, lit. '*he divided himself against them,*' i.e. '*he divided his forces and fell upon them;*' cf. Job 1, 17. 1 Sam. 11, 11, for a similar manœuvre. For the *cstr. praegnans* cf. on ver. 3.

חובה is on the left, i.e. north of Damascus, identified by Wetzstein with Ḥoba, twenty hours north of Damascus, in the neighbourhood of Ḥimṣ and Tadmor; cf. Del., *Gen.*[4], p. 561.

17. עמק שוה הוא עמק וגו׳—mentioned again 2 Sam. 18, 18, as the place where Absalom set up his monument—is hardly identical with שוה קריתים ver. 5, as it is now mentioned as though it were not previously known, and its position not far from Salem is against this identification, cf. ver. 18. It is usually—following Josephus' notice, *Ant.*, vii. 10. 3, that Absalom's pillar was two stadia distant from Jerusalem—supposed to be in the neighbourhood of Jerusalem. Cf. Neubauer, *Géog. du Talmud*, p. 50 f.

18. שלם. Generally taken as Jerusalem, so Del., Kn., Targg., Hieron. (*Quaest.*), Joseph., etc. Others, Roed. in Ges., *Thes.*, and Tuch, identify it with the Σαλείμ of John 3, 23, cf. Judith 4, 4, which, according to Eusebius and Hieron., was eight Roman miles south of Scythopolis (see, however, Riehm, *H.W.B.*, p. 32 f.; Del.[5], p. 269). In Ps. 76, 3 Salem is certainly Jerusalem. The objections to its being Jerusalem are: I. That this city lay too far south. II. That its old name was Jebus; cf. Judg. 19, 10. III. That Ps. 76, 3 is late, and the שלם there is a late poetical abbreviation of ירושלם. But as Del.[5], p. 269, shews, Jerusalem would not necessarily be too far out of the way—whether Abram returned down the Jordan valley to Sodom, or took his way home through Samaria to Hebron—for the king of Sodom to come and meet him from the south-east, and Melchizedek out of Jerusalem. Further, the facts (I) that in Josh. 10, 1 there is a king of Jerusalem bearing the name אדני צדק, which is very similar to מלכיצדק[1], and (II) that the comparison of

[1] But Well. and Budde (*Richter und Samuel*, p. 63) assert that אדני צדק is a later alteration of אֲדֹנִי־בֶזֶק, which is the reading of the LXX in Josh. 10, 1; cf. Judg. 1, 5. Kittel, however, disputes this, see his *Gesch.* i. p. 277 f. It may be remarked that the name *Urusalim* is found in the Tel-el-Amarna Letters, i.e. in the year 1400 B.C. Cf. Di., p. 243.

David, Ps. 110, 4 (cf. Heb. c. 7 Melchizedek a type of Christ), with Melchizedek would be far more suitable if he were king of Jerusalem, favour the identification with Jerusalem. The other two objections are not conclusive; it is quite uncertain that שׁלם is a poetical abbreviation of ירוּשׁלם, and that the old name of Jerusalem was Jebus is not of necessity fatal, as the name שׁלם might have been intentionally chosen with some hidden significance, just like מוריה 22, 2. The name מלכי צדק may=*my king is Ṣidiq*, Ṣidiq being the name of a deity, see Baudissin, *Studien zur Sem. Religionsgesch.*, i. 15, and cf. E. Nestle, *Israelit. Eigennamen*, p. 175 ff.

כהן לאל עליון=not '*the priest*,' as A.V., but '*a priest of God most high*,' so R.V.; see Ges., § 129. 1 a; Dav., *S.*, § 28, R. 5. אל ע״ as a proper name (cf. אל שׁדי) has no article; so כהן might mean '*the priest*,' or '*a priest*;' but to avoid this ambiguity of meaning, the construction with the prep. לְ, instead of the construct state, is chosen; cf. M.R., § 76 b; Ewald, § 292 a. 2. עליון in the O.T. when joined with יהוה, or אל, never has the article.

19. ברוך . . . לאל עליון '*blessed by God*,' לְ after the passive denotes the agent: cf. 25, 21. 31, 15. Ex. 12, 16; Ges., § 121. 3; Dav., *S.*, § 81; Ewald, § 295 c; M. R., § 51. 3. Rem. a.

קֹנֵה combines the double idea of *creating* and *possessing*. קנה is cstr. state, followed by two genitives; cf. note on ver. 1. Possibly the two words, heaven and earth, were conceived of as really forming one idea='*the world*,' and so construed as though one word stood; cf. on ver. 1.

The phrase קנה שׁמים וארץ is only found in this chapter.

19^b to 20^a are poetical in form. Notice קֹנֵה for בֹּרֵא or

עֹשֵׂה, צָרֶיךָ for אֹיְבֶיךָ, and מִגֵּן, which occurs twice again, Hos. 11, 8. Prov. 4, 9; all poetical words, though צרים is also found in prose writings; also the poetical sounding אל עליון.

22. הרמתי ידי. *'I lift up my hand,'* i.e. 'I have, just at the moment of speaking, lifted up;' the perfect is used for the immediate past; cf. Driver, § 10; Ges., § 106. 2b; Dav., *S.*, § 40b; M.R., § 2.1; the meaning being, I swear by Yahweh, etc.; cf. Ex. 6, 8. Num. 14, 30. Deut. 32, 40 כי אשא אל שמים ידי (of God, always נשא יד, Del.); Dan. 12, 7 וירם ימינו ושמאלו אל השמים; see also Ex. 17, 16.

23. אם. The negative particle אִם is often used in the oath-formulae. The oath-formula would run in full somewhat as follows: *'I swear, if I do so and so, may God,'* etc.; then the second portion being omitted, the first part came to have a negative force, so אם=*I will not*, and אם לא=*I will* (Num. 14, 28). Render, *'I lift up my hand . . . that I will not take from a thread even to a shoe latchet, of all which is thine,'* i. e. 'I will not even take the most trifling thing for myself.' On this use of אם, see Ges., § 149 a; Dav., *S.*, § 120; Ewald, § 356 a; M. R., § 168 b.

24. Render, *'Nought for me, only that which the young men have eaten, and the portion of the men who went with me: 'Aner, 'Eschol, and Mamre, let them take their portion.'* Note the *casus pendens* רק אשר . . . ענר אשכל וממרא: cf. 3, 12.

15.

1. שכרך הרבה מאד=*'Thy reward shall be very great.'* שכרך וגו״ can scarcely be taken as a second predicate to אנכי, as this would rather require ו, and God cannot be regarded as Himself the reward.

הַרְבֵּה, inf. abs. Hif'. of רבה, see on 3, 16. This inf. (properly a subst.), which is generally used as an adverb, is here regarded as an adj., and used as a predicate; cf. מְעַט, used quite similarly in 47, 9 מעט ורעים היו ימי שני חיי; and תְּמוֹל in Job 8, 9 כי תמול אנחנו; Ewald, § 296 d; cf. also Ges., § 141. 1 e; Dav., *S.*, § 29 e. The Sam. has a correction אַרְבֶּה, which is easier.

2. ואנכי הולך עריריר. Circ. clause; cf. note on 20, 3. Render, '*Seeing that I am going to die childless.*' הלך '*e vita decedere;*' cf. 25, 32. Ps. 39, 14. 2 Chron. 21, 20. עֲרִירִי is acc. of condition; see Dav., *S.*, § 70; Ges., § 118. 5 a; M.R., § 43 a, and cf. 25, 8. 37, 35. 38, 11. 44, 33. ערירי, lit.= '*bare, naked,*' but restricted by usage to one who has no children; cf. Jer. 22, 30. Lev. 20, 20. 21 (all).

ובן משק ביתי='*and the son of the possession of my household,*'=*my heir.* משק from משק,=משך='*to draw, to hold, grasp*' (the form being perhaps chosen on account of its similarity in sound to דמשק)='*possession;*' cf. מִמְשָׁק, Zeph. 2, 9.

בן משק=יורש in ver. 3, the construction being the same as in בעל ברית 14, 13, which compare. Theod., Vulg. render בן משק '*son of the manager,*' i.e. '*of the steward,*' משק being from שקק, with the meaning, '*to go about busily,*' cf. מֶמֶר from מרר; which is possible, but forced and unsuitable. The other VSS. vary. The LXX have ὁ δὲ υἱὸς Μασὲκ τῆς οἰκογενοῦς μου (their rendering of בן ביתי in the next verse is ὁ δὲ οἰκογενής μου), τῆς οἰκογενοῦς being either a mistake for οἰκίας, or υἱὸς is a gloss, and the word should be οἰκογενής; see Frankel, *Einf.*, p. 17. Onq. has וּבַר פַּרְנָסָא הָדֵין דִּבְבֵיתִי הוּא דַמַּסְקָאָה אֱלִיעֶזֶר '*this nourisher who is in my house, he is the Damascene, Eliezer.*'

The Pesh. has ܘܐܠܝܥܙܪ ܕܪܡܣܘܩܝܐ ܒܪ ܒܝܬܝ ܗܘ ܝܪܬ ܠܝ '*Eliezer the Damascene, the son of my house, he will be my heir.*' Aq. has ὁ υἱὸς τοῦ ποτίζοντος οἰκιάν μου, connecting מֶשֶׁק with מַשְׁקֶה '*a cup-bearer.*'

הוא דמשק אליעזר cannot be rendered with the Pesh. ܘܐܠܝܥܙܪ ܕܪܡܣܘܩܝܐ '*Eliezer the Damascene*' (so A. V., but R. V. '*Dammesek Eliezer*'), for this would either be אליעזר הדמשקי, or אליעזר איש דמשק, or אליעזר בן דמשק. Hos. 12, 8, which Gesenius cites in favour of this rendering, is not conclusive, the more correct rendering there being '*Canaan! in his hand are deceitful balances;*' see Cheyne's *Hosea*, Cambridge, 1884, p. 115. Besides, בן ביתי in the next verse is not compatible with this explanation, see on 14, 14. The LXX and Vulg. translate the two words as one proper name, '*Dammesek Eliezer,*' which is contrary to usage, men never having double names. Del. considers אליעזר as in apposition to דמשק, but one would hardly explain the name of a town by that of a person. Hitzig and Tuch reject הוא דמשק as a gloss; but this weakens the sentence, and, as Di. remarks, leaves the choice of the rare word משק unexplained. Ewald, § 286 c, renders דמשק אליעזר '*Damascus of Eliezer,*' i. e. the city of Damascus, regarded as a community with which Eliezer was associated; cf. גבעת שאול; and Di., adopting Ewald's construction, explains as follows: 'These words could be well explained if Eliezer not only had a prominent position in Abram's household, but also was closely connected with Damascus; then we might expect, failing other heirs, that Abram's property would in time fall to him, and return with him to Damascus when he went back thither. We certainly do not read of any such relationship between Damascus and Eliezer, but then this is the only passage where Eliezer is mentioned, and the Damascenes still in Greek times boasted of their connection with Abram' (cf. Del.[5], ad loc.). This is perhaps the best explanation of this passage. The only objection to it is that one would rather expect Eliezer to be mentioned as בֶּן־מֶשֶׁק, not the city Damascus.

3. הן לי לא נתתה. Observe the emphatic position of לִי.

4. הוא is inserted for emphasis, as in 3, 12 הוא נתנה לי, which compare.

6. והאמן ביהוה. The perf. with waw conv. would here be quite out of place. It could hardly be frequentative, as believing in a person cannot be conceived of as a frequentative act. Kautzsch, however, in Ges., § 112. 6 β, describes it as a kind of frequentative, comparing 34, 5. Num. 21, 20. Cf. also Dav., *S.*, § 58. R. 1. Like the other instances in 21, 25. 28, 6. 38, 5—cf. Driver, § 133—this is probably not a perfect with waw conv., but a case of the perfect with simple waw, where an imperf. with waw conversive would be expected.

ויחשבה לו וגו'. Verbs of *considering* are either construed as here, with two accusatives, or with one acc. and the prep. ל; see Ges., § 117. 5 c; Dav., *S.*, § 76; M. R., § 45. 5 with § 51. 1 end; cf. 38, 15. 50, 20. In Ps. 106, 31 we have ותחשב לו לצדקה; and the LXX of this passage, *καὶ ἐλογίσθη αὐτῷ εἰς δικαιοσύνην* (as though they read ל here), is quoted three times in the N. T., Rom. 4, 3. Gal. 3, 6. James 2, 23.

8. בַּמָּה. The pathach is not the article, but the preps. ב, כ, ל before many short pronouns are pointed with long *a* (cf. Ewald, § 243 b; Ges., § 102. 2 c and d), but with מה the

union is still closer, the vowel being doubled and the long *a* shortened into short *a;* see also Stade, § 134 f.; cf. כַּמָּה.

9. מְשֻׁלֶּשׁ, not '*threefold*,' i.e. '*three of each kind*,' as Onq. and Rashi, but '*three years old*.' This is the only passage where it occurs in this sense, but doubtless the LXX are right in reading it in 1 Sam. 1, 24 (בפר משלש for בפרים שלשה).

10. איש בתרו לקראת רעהו = '*each piece over against the other;*' cf. on 9, 5 איש אחיו, and the use of אשה of inanimate things in Ex. 26, 3. 5. Ez. 1, 9. 3, 13.

ואת הצפר לא בתר. '*But the birds he did not divide.*' צפור is collective, as in Ps. 8, 9.

בָּתָר, a rare word; cf. Jer. 34, 18 f., possibly an allusion to this passage.

11. העיט. The generic use of the article, as in 8, 7, which compare.

הפגרים '*the carcases*,' always used of dead bodies in Hebrew. In Syriac ܦܓܪܐ is used of a body, whether living or dead; cf. Bernstein, *Lex. Syr.*, p. 390 b. So פגר in Aramaic; cf. Levy, *Chald. W. B.*, p. 254 b *sub voce.*

וישב אתם. Hif'. of נשב. '*And he scared them away*,' lit. '*blew them away*.' The LXX read the consonants as וַיֵּשֶׁב אִתָּם συνεκάθισεν αὐτοῖς.

12. ויהי השמש לבוא. Render, '*And it came to pass, when the sun was about to set*.' The ויהי does not here, combined with לבא, form the predicate to השמש, but stands alone. השמש לבא is a complete sentence in itself; לבא, the inf. cstr. with ל, being used as a periphrastic future; cf. Hos. 9, 13 ואפרים להוציא להורג '*and Ephraim is for bringing forth*,' etc., Is. 10, 32 בנוב לעמד '*in Nob is he for tarrying;*' Josh. 2, 5 ויהי השער לסגור '*and it came to pass, the gate being*

about to be shut;' cf. Driver, § 204 [cf. also § 165], where numerous instances are cited, Ewald, § 217 d. b; and Dav., *S.*, § 94. Ges., § 114. 2. Rem. 2, and M. R., § 113, combine the היה with the inf. cstr., which, here at any rate, is quite unnecessary.

תרדמה *'a deep sleep.'* LXX here, and 2, 21 ἔκστασις, *'a trance.'*

והנה אימה חשכה גדלה. Render, *'And a very terrible darkness,'* lit. *'a terror, great darkness.'* חשכה גדלה being an explanatory apposition to אימה.

נפלת. The participle is more graphic than the perfect נפלה would be. Render, *'was falling.'*

13. בארץ לא להם. *'In a land not theirs;'* cf. Hab. 1, 6 לרשת משכנות לא לו; Prov. 26, 17 על ריב לא לו. The relative, which here would stand in the nominative, being omitted, the antecedent being indefinite; M. R., § 159 a; Ges., § 155. 2 a; Ewald, § 332 a. 1; Dav., *S.*, § 143 a; see also Wright, *Arab. Gram.*, ii. p. 343, the construction in Arabic being the same as in Hebrew.

ועבדום. *'And they (the Hebrews) shall serve them (the strangers = the Egyptians).'* LXX, καὶ δουλώσουσιν αὐτούς, cited Acts 7, 7, *'and they shall enslave them,'* which would require ועבדו בם; cf. Ex. 1, 14. Jer. 22, 13. עבד with the acc. is δουλεύω; in Hif'., or Qal with ב, δουλόω.

14. *'The nation which they shall serve am I judging,'* Driver, § 135. 3. The participle as *futurum instans;* cf. on 6, 17.

16. ודור רביעי. *'In the fourth generation.'* LXX freely, τετάρτῃ δὲ γενεᾷ. The construction strictly is (Ewald, § 279 d), *'And as a fourth generation, they shall return;'* as in Deut. 4,

27. Zech. 2, 8. Jer. 31, 7; acc. of the complement, or condition, cf. Ges., § 118. 5 c; Dav., *S.*, § 71. R. 1.

17. '*And it came to pass, the sun having gone down.*' השמש באה, being a circ. clause, by Driver, § 165; Dav., *S.*, § 141, ויהי does not belong to באה, which is accented on the penult., and is thus *perfect* (see Driver, foot-note, p. 18), and so incapable of being combined with ויהי as predicate. Ryssel, *De Eloh. Pent. sermone*, p. 59, is surely in error when he speaks of באה as participle ('ubi in participio באה nihil nisi notio diuturnitatis inest'). The ordinary editions and that of Baer have the accent on the penult.

ועלטה היה. The subject in the feminine is followed by the predicate in the masculine. Perhaps, as Müller suggests (M. R., § 39. Rem. a), עלטה was regarded as acc. after היה, '*and there became darkness* (i. e. *it turned to a darkness*);' see also Ges., § 145. 7. Rem. 3; Dav., *S.*, § 113 a.

18. כרת . . . ברית, lit. '*to cut a covenant*'=ὅρκια τέμνειν, *foedera icere;* on the difference between כרת ברית and הקים ברית, see on 9, 9. Cf. also Rob. Smith, *Religion of the Semites*, p. 480.

נתתי '*I give*,' lit. '*I have given;*' the act is regarded as so certain of its fulfilment that it is looked upon as already accomplished; hence the use of the perfect in promises, contracts, etc.; see M. R., § 3. 1 a; Ges., § 106. 3 a; Dav., *S.*, § 41 a; Driver, § 13; cf. 23, 11. Ruth 4, 3.

מנהר מצרים. The southern boundary of the promised land is elsewhere (Num. 34, 5. Josh. 15, 4. Is. 27, 12) the נחל מצרים, the modern Wady el-'Arîš, and this has led Knobel to identify the נהר מצרים of this verse with the נחל מצרים. But even if נהר can be used of smaller rivers and canals (2 Kings 5, 12. Job 14, 11. 28, 11. Ez. 1, 3. 3, 15), it seems more natural to identify the נהר מצרים here with the Nile or eastern arm of the Nile. In the time of David and Solomon (1 Kings 5, 1. 8, 65) the kingdom under their rule reached from the Euphrates to the Egyptian frontier.

עד . . . נהר פרת. Cf. Ex. 23, 31. Deut. 1, 7. Josh. 1, 4. Is. 27, 12. Notice the difference of idiom. In English we say '*the river Euphrates*,' while in Hebrew we find '*the river of Euphrates*;' cf. Ges., § 128. 2 d; Dav., *S.*, § 24 a; M. R., § 79. 1; Ewald, § 287 e. b, who compares the German '*Rheinfluss*.'

16.

1. הגר probably a Semitic name='*flight*' (Arabic هجر '*to flee*,' هِجْرَة '*flight*'), and scarcely, as she was an Egyptian, her real name. Perhaps, as Del. suggests, she was given to Sarai by Pharaoh, cf. 12, 16; and according to this the Midrash explains the name fancifully, as = הא איגרא '*behold, a reward*.' The Arab nomad tribe הגרים, Ps. 83, 7, derive their name from הגר.

2. מלדת lit. '*away from bearing*,' i. e. '*so that I cannot bring forth*;' cf. 18, 25 מעשׂת; 23, 6 מקבר מתך; 27, 1 מראת, etc.; and see Ges., § 119. 3 d. 1; Dav., *S.*, § 101. R. c; M. R., § 49. 1. R. c.

אבנה as in 30, 3; cf. Ruth 4, 11. Ex. 1, 21. Deut. 25, 9, etc. The form is not a Nif'al denominative from בֵּן '*a son*,' but the ordinary imperf. Nif'al of בָּנָה '*to build*,' used in a figurative sense.

3. עשׂר שׁנים לשבת. ל in the place of the genitive, as in 7, 11 (and regularly in dates, Ex. 16, 1. 19, 1, etc.) שׁשׁ מאות שׁנה לחיי נח; cf. the note there.

4. ותקל, cf. 1 Sam. 1, 6 f., is the imperf. Qal (intrans.) of

verb ע״ע with ־ָ; cf. יֵמַר, יֵרַךְ, etc.; Ges., § 67. Rem. 3; Stade, § 510 g. The two forms of the imperf. are, I. יָסֹב, with the ב doubled when it ceases to be final. II. יִסֹּב trans. (intrans. יִסַּב), with the ס doubled. In תֵּקַל the doubling has been given up, and compensation made by lengthening the ־ִ into ־ֵ, as is usual with gutturals; cf. תֵּרַע, יֵחַת, יֵחַם.

5. חמסי. '*The wrong done to me.*' Obj. genitive; cf. on 9, 2. Misunderstood by LXX, ἀδικοῦμαι ἐκ σοῦ; and Vulg. '*inique agis contra me;*' for חמסי עליך is an interjectional clause, '*the wrong done me, be upon thee!*'

וביניך. The point over the second yod (Mass. note, נקוד על י״ בתרא *point on the last yod*) probably marks it as superfluous, because the form elsewhere is בֵּינְךָ, in pause בֵּינֶךָ; cf. 17, 2. 7. The other passages where points are found over words in Genesis are, 18, 9. 19, 33. 33, 4. 37, 12.

7. וַיִּמְצָאָהּ (cf. 1 Chron. 20, 2) is the companion form of וַיִּמְצָאֶהָ, which, however, does not occur in this verb; cf. וַיַּכִּירָהּ, 37, 33; וַתִּתְּנֶהָ, 2 Chron. 20, 7; the imperf. taking the affix of the third pers. fem. sing. either in the form ־ָהּ or ־ֶהָ.

על עין המים, probably the well-known fountain on the way to שׁוּר; hence the article.

בדרך שׁור. '*On the way to Shur;*' cf. 3, 24 דרך עץ החיים.

שׁור must have been somewhere on the N. E. frontier between Palestine and Egypt. Josephus, *Ant.*, vi. 7, 3, erroneously supposed that שׁוּר was Pelusium, which is סִין. Saadiah holds that שׁור was Ǵifâr, جفار. 'The Arab. geographers understand by the wilderness of Ǵifâr (as distinct from the wilderness of the children of Israel, or Paran), the desert strip of land—which required five or six days' journey to traverse—bounded on the east by the desert of Paran, between Rafia in Philistia, up to lake Tennis (Menzaleh), and from thence to Qulzum or Suez; in a word, the western declivity of the desert of Paran towards Egypt' (Dillmann). The name probably means '*wall.*'

8. אי מזה באת, more frequently the imperfect was used in questions after למה, מאין, etc., as being less outspoken and more courteous than the perfect. The perfect would = '*Whence hast thou come?*' the imperf. '*Whence art thou coming?*' or '*Whence mayest thou be coming?*' See Driver § 39 γ; 42. 7 (all). Cf. Dav., *S.*, § 45. R. 1.

אי מזה. Cf. Ewald, § 326 a. מאין = simply '*whence*', with a verb or substantive, see Gen. 42, 7. Num. 11, 13 אי מזה is used similarly, but admits of being joined with a substantive, as 2 Sam. 15, 2 אי מזה עיר אתה; Jon. 1, 8 ואי מזה עם אתה; but this is not frequent. אי זה = '*where*', but is used rather of things (e.g. with בית, דרך, מקום) than persons; for which איפה is the common word, as in 37, 16.

11. הרה is a fem. part.; cf. 2 Sam. 11, 5 הרה אנכי; the masc. would be הָרֶה, like יָפֶה, כָּלֶה (fem. pl. כָּלוֹת, Deut 28, 32).

יֹלַדְתְּ. The participle fem. We have here the ground form of יֹלֶדֶת, which has remained unchanged, and not passed over into the segholate form יֹלֶדֶת. This ground form reappears before the suffixes, e.g. יֹולַדְתִּי, יֹולַדְתֵּךְ, etc.; cf. Dav., § 29; Ges., § 94. 2, and see § 80, 2 b. Ewald, § 188 b and König, *Lehrg.*, i. 404 f., suppose that as this form is only found when the second pers. is spoken about, the word was so pointed on account of its similarity with the second pers. fem. sing. It occurs again Judg. 13, 5. 7, but in Is. 7, 14, with the third pers., the pointing is יֹלֶדֶת.

וקראת. Here (J) the mother names the child, as in 4, 1. 25. 19, 37 f., etc.; in P the father, so 5, 3. 16, 15. 17, 19, etc. וקראת is pointed in Baer and Del. edition וְקָרָאתְ, in the common editions וְקָרָאת. The second pers. sing. fem. is, in verbs ל״א, usually pointed *without* the shewa; cf. Ewald, § 195 b, who mentions the two ways of pointing, and cites הָיִיתְ as well.

12. פרא אדם. '*A wild ass of a man*,' i.e. a man like the wild ass, who lives in the desert, wanders about at will, and cannot be tamed; cf. Job 39, 5. פֶּרֶא is the onager, Arab. فَرَأ, *asinus ferus;* Assyr. *purivu*. The construction is the same as in Prov. 21, 20 כסיל אדם; Is. 29, 19 אביוני אדם; and probably Is. 9, 5 פלא יועץ, 'the subordinated noun describing merely the relation of the individual [part] to the whole [genus]: the figurative to the actual,' Ewald, § 287 g; cf. M. R., § 79. 2. Rem. a; Ges., § 128. 2 e; Dav., *S.*, § 24 a.

על פני. Tuch renders '*east of*,' referring to Ishmael's geographical position; cf. 23, 19. 25, 18, but this is unnatural and forced. The text apparently means, Ishmael shall live close to his brethren, before their face, but shall not be on friendly terms with them. This meaning seems to suit ידו בכל ויד כל בו better.

13. אתה אל ראי='*thou art the God of seeing*,' i.e. '*the all-seeing God*.' Tuch explains, 'the God who appears, manifests himself;' but this does not suit the explanation which follows in the second half of the verse.

כי אמרה וגו״. '*For she said, Have I even here looked after Him that seeth me?*' i.e. Have I even here in the wilderness, where I should not expect to see God, seen Him? *He* saw her, but *she* did not see Him; but after He had gone, she perceived that He had been there.

רֳאִי is a substantive; out of pause pointed רְאִי, in pause רֹאִי; cf. Job 33, 21 מֵרֹאִי; Nah. 3, 6 כְּרֹאִי (both Baer and Del.); 1 Sam. 16, 12 רֹאִי = '*vision*,' '*seeing*.' Cf. צֹרִי, pausal form of צְרִי, Ez. 27, 17; חֹלִי, pausal form of חֳלִי, Deut. 7, 15. ראי at the end of the verse, pointed רֹאִי, and Job 7, 8 רֹאִי (both Baer and Del.; ordinary editions have רֳאִי; cf. Del., *Gen.*[4], p. 321), is the participle act. of ראה, with the suffix of the *noun* = *my seer*, just as דְּבָרִי = *my word*, differing from רֹאֵנִי, where the suffix is a verbal one and would = '*he who* or *one who sees me*.' The LXX erroneously take אֵל־רֳאִי as אֵל רֹאִי, and render ὁ Θεὸς ὁ ἐπιδών με, and paraphrase the second half of the verse with καὶ γὰρ ἐνώπιον ἴδον ὀφθέντα μοι. Pesh. has, ܐܢܬ ܗܘ ܐܠܗܐ ܚܙܘܐ ܡܛܠ ܕܐܡܪܐ ܗܘܬ ܕܗܐ ܐܦ ܚܙܘܐ ܚܙܝܬ ܒܬܪ ܕܚܙܢܝ = '*thou art God in a vision, for she said, Lo, indeed a vision I have seen, after that He hath seen me;*' taking ראי in *a* as a substantive, and paraphrasing *b*. Onq. has a paraphrase אַתְּ הוּא אֱלָהָא חָזֵי כוֹלָּא אֲרֵי אֲמַרַת אַף אֲנָא שָׁרֵיתִי חָזְיָא בָּתַר דְּאִתְגְּלִי לִי '*thou art God, seeing everything; for she said, Here indeed I begin seeing* (= *living*, so some moderns, Tuch, etc., a sense ראה does not bear), *after He revealed Himself to me*.' The Vulg., with '*Profecto hic vidi posteriora videntis me*,' takes אחרי, like אֲחֹרַי in Ex. 33, 23; cf. 2 Sam. 2, 23 באחרי החנית.

14. '*Therefore they called the well, well of the Living one, who sees me*' (lit. *my seer*, see above). קרא is the so-called impersonal 3 per. perf., cf. 11, 9 = '*Man nannte den Brunnen*.' The rend. '*Well of the seeing alive* (*lebendig-sehen*),' Tuch., Hengstenb., and others (רֹאִי as pausal form of רְאִי see

above), i.e. 'where one sees God and remains alive,' is most improbable, and presupposes a compound (Wortcomposition), which is impossible in Hebrew (Di.). Wellhausen, *Hist. of Israel*, Eng. transl., p. 326, proposes to emend the text thus, הגם [אלהם] ראיתי [ואחי] אחרי ראי '*have I seen* [*God and remained alive*] *after* [*my*] *vision?*' cf. for the popular belief that one who saw God died, 19, 17. Ex. 3, 6. 19, 21. Mich. emends בְּאֵר לְחִי רָאִי '*well of the jawbone* (i.e. *rock?* Judg. 15, 19) *of vision.*' With the naming of the well, cf. 22, 14. 28, 19. 32, 31.

The position of the Hagar-well is uncertain, see some identifications that have been proposed in Del., *Gen.*[5], p. 287. Del. follows Rowlands and Trumbull in regarding the Hagar-well as identical with Muweilih, south of Beersheba, a station on the caravan route from Beersheba, along the Gebel-es-Sûr, which stretches from north to south. Cf. Sh., *G.*, p. 283.

בֶּרֶד, position unknown. Cf. Di., p. 256; *Z.D.P.V.*, xiv. p. 82; Well., *Sam.*, p. 213.

17.

1. אל שדי. אֵל. The oldest and most general name of God, and restricted as a rule to Yahweh, but occasionally used of other gods. The word is most common in poetry, elsewhere always with some qualifying word, such as עֶלְיוֹן (14, 18), עוֹלָם (21, 33), קַנָּא, אֱמֶת, זָר, or as here שַׁדַּי: it only takes the suffix of the first person sing. אֵלִי. On אל, see Appendix.

שַׁדַּי, according to P the name of God revealed to the Patriarchs (see Di., *Exodus*, p. 54), 28, 3. 35, 11 (cf. 43, 14). 48, 3 (cf. 49, 25). Ex. 6, 3 (in all these passages, except 49, 25, with אֵל). In poetry and the poetical style (Ruth 1, 21) we find שדי alone, it is very often found in Job. It is explained by the Rabbins as = ·שֶׁ (·שֶׁ) and דַּי *'he who is sufficient,' 'the all-sufficient,'* but such compounded names are not found in Hebrew; so Aq., Symm., and Theod. Possibly the same explanation underlies the pointing adopted by the Massoretes. Nöld. interprets the name as = שֵׁדַי or שֵׁדַי, *'my Lord'* (שֵׁד = Arab. سَيِّد; cf., however, on שֵׁד, Assyr. *Šîdu*, Schrader, *C.O.T.*, p. 148). But Gen. 17, 1 and 35, 11 (God himself speaks) are against this explanation, also the fact that שדי is never used when God is addressed. Fried. Del. (*Proleg.*, p. 96) takes the word as = *'The high* or *lofty one,'* from Ass. *Šadû*. But as Di. points out, this assigns to the root שדה a meaning it certainly has not in Heb., and only doubtfully in Ass. Di. connects the name with the root שדד (Joel 1, 15) *'he that exercises authority,' 'the all-powerful,'* שדד = *'to exercise power,' 'to rule'* (cf. LXX and Vulg.). The ending ◌ִי (or ◌ַי if Mass. text be followed) would then be either an adj. ending (Ewald, § 164), or used to form an abstract noun = *'Omnipotence'* (Stade, § 301). Ewald, § 155, proposed a similar explanation, assuming a root שדד = שדה, the form would then be an intensive adj. like דַּיָּן, חַלָּשׁ; שדי would probably, in this case, have to be pointed שַׁדָּי. (See above on Mass. points.) The LXX render it always in Genesis by a pronoun, here ὁ Θεός σου; cf. 49, 25 and Ex. 6, 3 (αὐτῶν), but elsewhere (often in Job) they have sometimes παντοκράτωρ, sometimes ἱκανός. The Vulg. has *'omnipotens'* here. See further, Di., p. 259 f.

לפני = *'before me,'* i.e. under my eyes, in consciousness of my presence, 24, 40. Is. 38, 3; different from התהלך את, 5, 22. 6, 9.

2. במאד מאד. Cf. on 7, 19; and see Dav., *S.*, § 34.

4. *'As for me, behold my covenant is with thee, and thou*

shalt become a father of a multitude of nations.' אֲנִי is prefixed, as in 6, 17. 9, 9, for emphasis: it is opposed to וְאַתָּה, in ver. 9.

והיית לאב. והיית, perf. with waw conv., though no imperfect precedes; compare the companion construction of waw conv. with the imperf. when no perfect precedes. So 26, 22 ופרינו; Ex. 6, 6 והוצאתי; Driver, § 119 a.

אב, cstr. state for אֲבִי, is chosen on account of the name Abraham. This form is also found in proper names, e.g. אבשלום, אבנר, but not so frequently as the longer form אבי.

המון גוים. המון is used here instead of the more usual קהל, 28, 3. 35, 11, on account of the etymology of אברהם, suggested by the writer in ver. 5.

5. **ולא יקרא . . . את שמך.** The acc. after the passive verb as in 4, 18, which compare.

אברהם, אַבְרָם = '*exalted father;*' unless we assume that it is equivalent to אבירם, when it might = (Di) '*Father of Ram,*' or '(*the*) *Exalted One is* (*my*) *Father;*' cf. the Assyr. male p. n. *Abu-ra-mu*, Schrader, *C.O.T.*, p. 190, and see Bäthgen, *Beitr. zur Semit. Religionsg.*, p. 155 ff. The etymology of the second name אברהם given in the text is really no etymology, but merely a play on the words; cf. the etymologies given for נח, קין; the name being changed into Abraham, because thus pronounced, an assonance was produced between the הם of המון and אברהם. אברהם does not = *Father of a multitude.* The etymology is quite unknown. It is also impossible to decide whether אברהם is the original form, and אברם a contraction of this (Ewald, Stade), or *vice versa* אברהם an expansion of an original אברם. As there is no proof that a רהם = רום exists in Hebrew, the former conjecture is perhaps more probable than the latter. A word רהם, = '*multitude*,' does not exist. That the author could have had in view the Arab. رُهَام, mentioned in the Qamus, is not conceivable.

אב המון . . . נתתיך. נתן, with two accusatives, in the sense '*to make any one anything*,' Ges., § 117. 5 c; Dav., *S.*, § 76; M. R., § 45, 5; so 1 Kings 14, 7. 16, 2. Jer. 1, 5. The other construction with ל in place of the second acc. is equally common; cf. ver. 6. 48, 4. Is. 49, 6, etc.

7. לדרתם = '*throughout their generations*' (successively); the plural suffix is used, זרע being taken collectively. למשפחותם would be '*throughout their families*' (contemporaneously). Formulae of this kind are common in P; so 8, 19. 10, 5. 20. 31. 32. 25, 16. 36, 40.

להיות לך . . . אחריך, i.e. Abraham's descendants will stand in a close relationship to God as His servants, and be under His protection. He will protect and specially favour them, they will serve and worship Him as their God, Ex. 6, 7. Deut. 26, 17.

8. אחזה, מגורים, and ארץ כנען are all marks of P. Also the phrase, '*Thou and thy seed after thee*,' vers. 7–10.

10. המול לכם כל זכר. הִמּוֹל is inf. abs. Nif'. of מלל or מול; cf. Ges., § 67. Rem. 5. The infinitive abs. is here emphatically prefixed to indicate a command; cf. Ewald, § 328 c; Dav., *S.*, § 88 b. c. and R. 5; M. R., § 106. 1 c; cf. Ex. 20, 8. Render, '*Every male to be circumcised*,' i.e. '*let every male be circumcised*.' See also Ges., § 113. 4 b. Rem.

11. וּנְמַלְתֶּם is Nif'. of מלל for נְמַלּוֹתֶם; a root נמל does not exist; cf. תַּמְנוּ, Num. 17, 28, for תַּמּוֹנוּ; הֲתִלֹּתָ, where one would expect הֲתִילּוֹתָ, Ewald, § 234 e; Ges., § 67. Rem. 11;

cf. on 11, 6. The perf. with waw consec. is in continuation of the imperative, which is implied in the last verse in the inf. abs. הִמּוֹל, cf. Ges., § 112. 4 b; Dav., *S.*, § 55 a; Driver, § 113. 1.

בשׂר is acc. of respect or specification, as in 3, 15, which compare. See also 1 Kings 15, 23 חלה את רגליו.

12. יִמּוֹל is imperf. Nif'. of מלל (for יִמַּל, the regular form, Job 14, 2); cf. תִּדֹּמִּי, Jer. 48, 2, as though they were from verbs ע״ו; cf. Ges., § 67. Rem. 5; Stade, § 504 e, who apparently regards יִמּוֹל as from a verb מול.

ובן שׁמנת ימים וגו״. '*Every male, when eight days old, shall be circumcised for you throughout your generations.*' בן שׁמנת ימים is a secondary predicate; cf. Is. 65, 20 כי הנער בן מאה שׁנה ימות; Job 15, 7 הראישׁון אדם תולד; cf. Driver, § 161. 3; Dav., *S.*, § 71. R. 1.

בן נכר, a mark of P; so ver. 27. Ex. 12, 43. Lev. 22, 25. מקנה and כל זכר are also characteristic of P.

13. The repetition after ver. 12 is in the legal style of this writer (P); cf. 26 f.

14. '*The uncircumcised male who shall not be circumcised as to the flesh of his foreskin—that soul shall be cut off from his people, my covenant he has violated.*' The subject is placed first for emphasis, as a *casus pendens*, and taken up by הנפשׁ ההוא, instead of by a pronoun; cf. M. R., § 132 a; Driver, § 197. Obs. 2; Ex. 12, 15 and Deut. 17, 12.

עמים = '*fellow-tribesmen.*' A peculiar use, found chiefly in one or two stereotyped phrases.

ונכרתה. Being cut off from one's fellow-tribesmen is probably to be explained of sudden removal by God, rather than death inflicted by man; cf. Di., p. 262 et sq.; Del.[5], p. 294. Tuch explains it as = מות יומת, but if this were here intended, it would probably have been added; cf. Ex. 31, 14.

ונכרתה is perf. with waw consec., after a *casus pendens;* cf. Ex. 12, 15 כי כל אכל . . . ונכרתה; Deut. 17, 12 והאיש אשר יעשׂה . . . ומת האיש ההוא; see Driver, § 123 a; Ges., § 112. 5 a. ζ; Dav., *S.*, § 56. ונכרתה הנפש ההיא is a phrase characteristic of P; so Ex. 12, 15. 19. Lev. 7, 20 ff. Num. 9, 13.

הֵפַר. Pausal form for הֵפֵר, so הֵתַז, Is. 18, 5; Ewald, § 93 a. 2; Stade, § 393 b. β; Ges., § 29. 4, c. note.

15. שׂרי. The name שׂרה, = '*princess*,' being the feminine form of שׂר. The meaning of שָׂרַי is not so clear; the LXX have Σάρα; so סִינַי Σινᾶ. Possibly the name שׂרי was an older form of the name שׂרה (with ىَ fem. = הָ), (Di.); cf. Lag., *B.N.*, p. 92 f. The ending ־ַי is hardly an adjectival ending, as we should rather expect a fem. form. Another explanation is that שָׂרַי is from שָׂרָה, 32, 29; and so = '*the contentious, disputing one;*' cf. שָׂרַי = שָׂרָה, which is quite possible, but cannot be regarded as certain. (So perhaps LXX.) Other explanations are that שׂרי = '*the merry one,*' שׂרה '*one that makes merry, delights (erfreuende)*,' from سرّ, which Di. says violates both the laws of sound and form; or from the Arabic سَرُوَ سَرِيَ سَرَا '*generosus fuit,*' so '*the liberal, generous one.*'

17. הלבן. ה interrog. pointed with dag., acc. to Ges., § 100. 4; Dav., § 49. 2.

ואם שׂרה הבת. The repetition of the interrog. ה of the first member, after the ואם of the second member of a double interrogative clause, is uncommon [this seems to be the only instance]; cf. Ges., § 150. 2. Rem. 2 b; Dav., *S.*, § 126. R. 2; M. R., § 145; Ewald, § 324 c.

18. לו ישמעאל יחיה וגו״ = '*if Ishmael may live before thee*,' and as no apodosis follows, '*would that Ishmael might live*;' cf. Driver, § 142; M. R., § 147; Ewald, § 329 b; Ges., § 151. 2; Dav., *S.*, § 134. לו is also followed (exceptionally) by the imperative, 23, 13, or jussive, 30, 34.

19. ילדת . . . וקראת. The participle used as future, followed by the perf. with waw consec.; so 6, 17. 48, 4 (cf. note); Driver, § 113. 1. The accent on וקרׄאת is not thrown forward on to the last syllable by the waw conv., in accordance with the rule, that in the perfect Qal of verbs ל״א and ל״ה the waw conv. does not cause the accent to move forward, Driver, § 110. 4; cf. והׄיית, ver. 4.

20. ולישמעאל. '*And with regard to I.*;' cf. 19, 21 גם לדבר הזה '*also with regard to this matter*;' 42, 9 אשר חלם להם '*which he dreamt about them*;' cf. M. R., § 51. 5. Rem. b; Ges., § 119. 3 c. 4; Dav., *S.*, § 101. R. b.

ברכתי . . . והפריתי, the perfect with waw conv., after a prophetic perfect; so Deut. 15, 6 ברכך . . . והעבטת; Num. 24, 17 דרך כוכב . . . וקם, Is. 2, 11. 43, 14; cf. Driver, § 113. 1 ad fin.; Ges., § 112. 3 c. δ; Dav., *S.*, § 41. R. 1; M. R., § 24. 2 b. Rem. b; Ewald, § 342 b. 2.

נשיאם. נשׂיא is almost confined to P in the Pent. and Josh.

ונתתיו לגוי גדול; cf. 48, 4 ונתתיך לקהל עמים, both in P.

23. וימל is imperf. Qal of מלל or מול, the form with waw conv. and retrogression of the tone being the same in both verbs.

בעצם היום הזה. Cf. on 7, 13.

24. בהמלו is either reflexive, '*in his circumcising himself*,' i.e. '*when he circumcised himself*,' or better passive (see ver. 25, where Ishmael could hardly circumcise himself), '*in his being circumcised*,' i.e. '*when he was circumcised*.'

26. נִמּוֹל 'is the Nif'. of מול, formed from the form מלל, Ewald, § 140,' Di. See also Ges., § 72. Rem. 9; Stade, § 397 b. γ; cf. נִחַת from חתת, נִחַר from חרר. Stade and Ges. both regard it, however, as the Nif'al proper of מול, comparing נֵעוֹר from עור. So, apparently, Wright, *Comp. Gram.*, p. 255, who takes נִמּוֹל for *namâl* (*namwal*).

18.

1. והוא ישב פתח וגו". Circ. clause, '*While he was sitting at the door of the tent*.' LXX excellently, καθημένου αὐτοῦ; cf. note on 20, 3. פתח וגו". is acc. of place, in answer to the question '*where?*' Ges., § 118. 2 b; M. R., § 41 b; Dav., *S.*, § 69 a; and especially Driver, § 191. Obs. 2.

כחם היום, LXX μεσημβρίας; cf. 1 Sam. 11, 9 בחם השמש; Neh. 7, 3 עד חם השמש; see also on 3, 8 לרוח היום='*at even*.' חם היום='*the heat of the day*,' i.e. noon.

2. וַיִּשְׁתַּחוּ, in pause וַיִּשְׁתָּחוּ, is the apocopated imperf. of הִשְׁתַּחֲוָה, a rare Hithpalel form, from שחה '*to bow*,' formed by a repetition of the third radical; cf. מטחוים in 21, 16, and Wright, *Comp. Gram.*, p. 219. יִשְׁתַּחוּ is for יִשְׁתַּחְוְ, analogous to the segholate form שְׁחוּ for שְׁחְוְ; cf. Ges., § 75. Rem. 18; Stade, § 502 a.

ארצה='*to the ground*,' lit. '*earthwards*,' ה (as the position of the tone shews) being the ה of motion.

3. אֲדֹנָי is marked by the Massoretes קדש '*holy*,' i.e. that God is here intended; cf. the Mass. note on 19, 2, and Ges.,

§ 135. 5. R. 3; Stade, § 359 e. The Sam. read the word אֲדֹנַי 'my lords,' as is clear from the use of the plural suffixes in בעיניכם for בעיניך, and עבדכם for עבדך, and the plural תעברו for תעבר. Dathe and Tiele correct the text into אֲדֹנִי; so Di., who points out that in this verse Abraham addresses one of the three men whom he, possibly, recognised as the leader of the party (contrast ver. 4, where all are addressed). Di. further considers that Abraham first discovers the divine character of his guests in the course of the conversation (ver. 13), for if he had perceived it at once, the honour he paid them would really be no honour, and the offering of food and drink without meaning; further, it would have been no trial of Abraham's faith, had he known that it was Yahweh who conversed with him. Tuch, Knobel, and Del. follow the Massoretic punctuation.

אם נא מצאתי. נא is added to shew the precative nature of the entire sentence; cf. 30, 27. 33, 10. So Ges. in *Th.*, p. 834 b, 'si—quod opto magis quam sumere audeo—gratiam inveni.'

4. '*Let there be taken a little water, and wash your feet, and rest yourself under the tree.*' The feet were washed before every meal; cf. 19, 2. 24, 32. Luke 7, 44.

תחת העץ '*under the tree.*' It is not necessary to take העץ collectively, as three people could very well sit down under one tree.

5. ואקחה. ק without dagesh, and pointed with Raphe, see note on 2, 23; and cf. Stade, § 41. Raphe is only found in accurate texts. The letters ב, ג, ד, כ, פ (?), ת, pointed with shewa, sometimes (though rarely) omit the *dagesh forte*, cf. Ges., § 20. 3 b; Stade, § 41. Render, '*And let me take a morsel of bread.*' פת לחם '*a morsel of bread;*' cf. Judg.

19, 5; a modest way of describing the rich meal he will set before them (Di.).

כי על כן=‘*quandoquidem*,’ Ewald, § 353 a; ‘*for as much as*,’ the reason being adduced the second time by the demonstrative ‘*therefore*’ after the relative [conjunction]; cf. Ges., § 158, foot-note 2.

6. האהלה is accented on the penult., as the locative ה does not take the accent, and אהל is a seg. noun: cf. Ges., § 90. 2 a[1]; Dav., § 17, 3. In the ordinary editions of the text and in B. and D. there is a misprint here (see *Jesaias*, p. v, note): read הָאֹהֱלָה. So חֹרְשָׁה, נֶגְבָּה (13, 14).

מהרי שלש וגו׳. ‘*Bring quickly three measures of meal;*’ מהרי, lit. ‘*hasten*.’ Or, as מהר with the acc. is rare (cf. 1 Kings 22, 9. Is. 5, 19), it may be rendered ‘*Be quick! three measures of meal!*’

קמח is the acc., ‘*three measures in meal*,’ or ‘*as to meal*,’ the acc. perhaps being an acc. of specification, cf. Driver, § 194; Ges., § 131. 2 c. M.R., § 71. 4, and Dav., *S.*, § 29 d, regard קמח as in apposition, so apparently Ewald, § 287 i; cf. Ex. 9, 8 מלא חפניכם פיח; Ruth 2, 17 איפה שעורים.

סלת is in apposition to קמח, defining it more closely, ‘*meal, fine flour*.’ Three seahs of meal made an ephah, something over an English bushel. The large quantity was probably intended as a mark of distinction; cf. 43, 34. 1 Sam. 9, 22 f.

עגות. ג without dagesh; cf. B. and D., *Gen.*, p. 77. The cakes were small round cakes, baked in the hot ashes, so called from their round form. Greek ἐγκρυφίαι, which word the LXX use here.

---

[1] The statement in Ges. l. c. that ה ָ is accented, is incorrect.

9. אֵלָיו, the points above the word probably indicate a various reading לו; cf. on 16, 5.

10. כעת חיה = '*next spring*;' explained, ver. 14, by למועד; in 2 Kings 4, 16. 17 we have the fuller phrase למועד הזה כעת חיה. LXX have κατὰ τὸν καιρὸν τοῦτον (from ver. 14) εἰς ὥρας, i. e. '*about this time next year*.' The phrase literally translated = '*about the time* (*when it is*) *reviving*,' i. e. '*when this time lives again*;' cf. Ges. in *Th.*, p. 470; and *Gram.*, § 118. 6 b. חיה does not qualify עת, which has the article, but is predicate; cf. Ex. 9, 18 כָּעֵת מָחָר '*about the time when it is to-morrow*.' The full expression would be כִּהְיוֹת העת מחר, and כִּהְיוֹת העת חיה. In 17, 21 we have the time stated more clearly, למעד הזה בשנה האחרת; cf. 1 Sam. 1, 20 לתקופות הימים.

והוא אחריו. '*It* (*the door*) *being behind him* (*the speaker*);' so the Massoretic text. The LXX, οὖσα ὄπισθεν αὐτοῦ, took הוא here as הִיא, cf. on 2, 12, and referred it to Sarah.

11. באים בימים = '*well on in days*.' So 24, 1; Josh. 13, 1, etc.; cf. προβεβηκότες ἐν ταῖς ἡμέραις in Luke 1, 7.

חדל, as ver. 11 is a circumstantial sentence, explanatory of what takes place in ver. 12, חדל must be translated '*there had ceased*.'

12. '*And Sarah laughed within herself, saying, After I have grown old, shall I have pleasure, my lord being old?*' LXX, ἐγέλασεν δὲ Σάρρα ἐν ἑαυτῇ, λέγουσα, Οὔπω μέν μοι γέγονεν ἕως τοῦ νῦν. ὁ δὲ κύριός μου πρεσβύτερος; leaving אחרי untranslated, and apparently taking בְּלֹתִי = בִּלְתִּי, and עֶדְנָה = עֲדֶנָּה = עַד־הֵנָּה.

Contrast the explanation of P in 17, 17.

14. היפלא מיהוה דבר. '*Is anything too hard* (lit. *wonderful, extraordinary*) *for Yahweh?*' cf. Jer. 32, 17

לא יפלא ממך כל דבר, and ver. 27 הממני יפלא כל דבר; Deut. 17, 8 כי יפלא ממך דבר. Cf. Ges., § 133. 1. Rem. 2; Dav., *S.*, § 34. R. 2.

מְיְהוָֹה. י pointed with shewa: so B. and D. Ordinary texts have מֵיהוָֹה, without shewa. The shewa is inserted according to the Massoretic note, quoted by Del.[5], p. 298, משה מפיק וכלב מכנים, i. e. '*Moses leads* (*Israel*) *out, and Caleb leads them in*,' which is the Massoretic way of saying that the letters ה, שׁ, מ make the א of אדני—the vowels of which are always in the text placed under יהוה—heard; while after the letters ב, ל, כ, the א is not sounded as a consonant, e. g. בַּיהוָֹה=בַּאדוֹנָי for בַּאֲדֹנָי; the latter part of the rule holds good for ו. So וַיהוָֹה=וַאדוֹנָי for וַאֲדוֹנָי; cf. Ges., § 23. 2; Stade, § 112 b. note, who gives instances, e. g. Mic. 4, 13. Neh. 8, 10. Gen. 40, 1 (cf. B. and D.'s editions here), where ֲ does not become ַ.

15. לא כי צחקת '*nay,* (*for* i. e. *but*) *thou didst laugh*,' לא כי, as in 19, 2. 42, 12. כי in antithesis after לא, cf. Dav., *S.*, § 118; Ges., § 163. 1.

16. ואברהם הלך עמם לשלחם '*while Abraham went with them to escort them*,' circ. clause, as in vers. 12. 18. 19, 1. 24, 10. 15. 56. 25, 26. 28, 12. 44, 26; cf. Driver, § 159; M. R., § 152; Dav., *S.*, § 138 c; Ges., § 141. 2. R. 2.

לשלחם. Cf. on 12, 20.

17–19. '*And Yahweh said* (i. e. *to Himself*), *Shall I hide from Abraham what I am going to do,* (18) *seeing that Abraham will surely become a great and powerful nation, and all the nations of the earth will bless themselves in him?* (19) *For I have chosen him, to the end that he may charge his sons, and his house after him, and that they may observe Yahweh's way, by doing righteousness and right; so that Yahweh may bring upon Abraham that which He hath promised concerning him.'*

17. המכסה, the participle preceding the subject, as in Num. 11, 29. Ez. 9, 8; see Ges., § 141. 4; Dav., *S.*, § 104 c; cf. note on 3, 5.

18. היו יהיה. הָיוֹ is for הָיֹה, the Ḥolem quiescing in a Waw, instead of a He; cf. 26, 28 רָאוֹ; Is. 22, 13 שָׁתוֹ; see Ges., § 75. Rem. 2; Stade, § 623 a.

ונברכו. Cf. on 12, 3.

19. ידעתיו. Cf. Amos 3, 2. Hos. 13, 5, ידע here, and in the two passages cited, = '*to know a person thoroughly*,' and so, after becoming well acquainted with him, '*to choose* or *select him*,' almost = בחר; cf. a similar use of προγινώσκειν, Rom. 8, 29.

למען אשר, stronger than כִּי, = '*eo consilio ut*,' '*with the intention of*,' '*to the end that*,' R.V., always introduces the intention; so Lev. 17, 5. Josh. 3, 4. Jer. 42, 6; Ewald, § 337 b; Ges., § 165. 2; Dav., *S.*, § 149. A.V. is incorrect, למען always = *ut*.

למען אשר יצוה . . . ושמרו. Cf. on 12, 13. The LXX have ᾔδειν γὰρ ὅτι συντάξει, misunderstanding the text; so Pesh. and Vulg.

20. '*And Yahweh said, The cry concerning Sodom and Gomorrah, it is indeed great; and their sin, it is indeed very heavy.*'

זעקת is *gen. object.*, as in 9, 2. 16, 5, which compare.

זעקת and חטאתם are *casus abs.* רַ֫בָּה has the accent on the penult., and so is third pers. perf. from רבב. Wellhausen renders, '*It is a report about Sodom and Gomorrah, that their sin is great, that it is very heavy;*' ו before חטאתם being struck out; which Di. rejects on the grounds that זעקה does not mean '*a report*,' and that God would not listen to a report.

כי = '*indeed*' or '*it is the case that*,' as in Is. 7, 9. Ps. 118, 10; cf. Ges., § 148. Rem. 2; Dav., *S.*, § 118; Ewald, § 330 b; unless it is assumed, with Lagarde and Olshausen, that שׁמעתי has fallen out at the beginning of the sentence. The LXX omit כי.

21. '*I will indeed go down, that I may see whether they have altogether done according to the cry concerning them, that has come up to me.*'

הבּ֫אה is pointed by the Massoretes as perfect, with the article, which has apparently the force of the relative; cf. Ewald, § 331 b. As this usage is rare outside the later books of the Bible, Ewald, l. c., and Di. reject it here, and point as a participle. Cf. Ges., § 138. 3 b; Dav., *S.*, § 22. R. 4. M. R., § 92. Rem. a, points out (citing cases, e. g. 1 Kings 11, 9 and Gen. 12, 7) that the Massora itself varies on this point. The participle here is more natural, and only involves a change in the position of the accent, from the penult. to the last syllable; so 46, 27. For the various cases where the art. seems to possess a relative force, the reader may refer to Driver, *Sam.*, p. 57 f.

עשׂו כלה, separated by the accents, so to be taken alone, כלה='*omnino*,' as in Ex. 11, 1 כשׁלחו כלה גרשׁ יגרשׁ אתכם. In other passages עשׂה כלה means '*to utterly destroy*;' cf. Nah. 1, 8. Zeph. 1, 18.

22. ואברהם עודנו עמד לפני יהוה. According to a tradition found as early as the Mechilta (on Ex. 15, 7) and often repeated, this verse originally ran ויהוה עודנו עמד לפני אברהם, but was altered as too anthropomorphic; עמד לפני

having the notion of serving. But 19, 27 is against this, and all the versions follow the text as we now have it, and read לפני יהוה. This and similar corrections, called *Tiqqune Sopherim*, are not to be regarded as real various readings, but merely as changes proposed by the Massoretes, to avoid expressing anything in the text that was repugnant to them; cf. Strack, *Proleg. Crit.*, p. 87. Geiger, *Urschrift*, p. 331, considers that יהוה עודנו עמד לפני אברהם is the real reading, citing the Talmud and Midrash in support of his view. There are eighteen such passages in the O. T., but only this one in Genesis. Cf. further, Strack, l. c., who cites authorities; also Bleek's *Introduction*, 4th ed. [Wellhausen], p. 624. The eighteen instances are given in Levy's *Chald. W. B. über die Targ.*, ii. p. 553 b; the larger Massora, on Num. 1, 1; and in the *Dikduke Ha-ṭ'amim*, edit. Baer and Strack, Leipzig, 1879, § 57.

24. ולא תשא למקום. נשׂא ל, sc. עון or פשע = '*to take away the sin for any one*,' so '*to forgive*.'

25. '*Far be it from Thee to do according to this thing, to slay the righteous with the wicked, and that the righteous should be as the wicked, far be it from Thee; shall the Judge of all the earth not execute judgment?*'

להמית . . . והיה, the cstr. inf. breaking off into a perfect with waw conv.: the perfect is used here, as a possible case is stated, and not a fact; in which case we should find the imperf. with waw conv., as in 39, 18 כהרימי . . . ואקרא; cf. Driver, § 118 (see the preceding section); Ges., § 112. 3 c. η; Dav., *S.*, § 96; so 27, 45 עד שׁוב . . . ושׁכח, Ex. 1, 16 בילדכן . . . וראיתן, 2 Sam. 13, 28 כטוב . . . ואמרתי.

חללה = '*profanum* (lit. *in profanum*), *nefas tibi sit*.' Del. compares the Targ.-Talmud חלין הוא לך '*it is unholy for thee*.'

The ה is not the feminine ending, as the word is accented on the penult.; cf. 44, 7 חלילה לעבדיך. See also Barth, *N.B.*, p. 136.

מעשׂת, מן as in 16, 2, which compare.

27. עפר ואפר. Notice the alliteration, and cf. תהו ובהו, 1, 2. נע ונד, 4, 14. הוד והדר, Ps. 21, 6.

28. יחסרון. See on 3, 3.

חסר being one of the verbs of *abounding* and *wanting*, takes the acc.; cf. note on 1, 21.

30. אל נא יחר לאדני וגו״. '*O let not my Lord be angry, and let me speak.*' יִחַר is apoc. from יֶחֱרֶה. The jussive here expresses an entreaty or request; cf. 9, 27. 31, 49; Driver, § 50 γ; Ges., § 109. 1 a and b; M. R., § 8. 2; Dav., *S.*, § 63 c. ואדברה, the cohortative here and in ver. 32, may be explained by Driver, § 49 β (used in asking permission), as in 33, 14. 50, 5. Jer. 18, 18, or by Ges., § 108. 2 a ('*that I may speak*'); Dav., *S.*, § 65. R. 1.

19.

1. שני המלאכים = not as A.V. '*two angels,*' but '*two of the angels,*' i.e. two of the three mentioned in 18, 2. On the construction, cf. Ges., § 134. 1 a; M. R., § 96 b; Dav., *S.*, § 36 b.

ולוט ישב. Circ. clause, as in 18, 1; cf. also on 13, 7. Render, '*While Lot was sitting in the gate.*' The city gate in the east was usually a vaulted entrance, with large recesses on either side; here business matters were settled, and the affairs of the town and all public matters discussed and arranged; cf. 23, 10. 18. 34, 20. Deut. 21, 19.

2. הִנֶּה נָּא, with short *e* (Seghol) (only here; cf. Ewald, § 91 d) and *dagesh forte conj.*, is unique; see also Ges., § 20. 2 a. Rem. 1.

אֲדֹנַי is marked by the Massoretes נ״ בפתח וחול (i.e. ' נ *pointed with pathach and profane*,' i.e. '*not used of God*').

סורו נא וגו״. It was regarded as a neglect of the duties of hospitality to allow strangers to spend the night in the street; cf. Judg. 19, 15, and contrast with this inhospitality, 24, 25. Ex. 2, 20. Judg. 13, 15. 'The modern Arabs consider it a privilege to lodge strangers who may come to them, and often disputes arise as to who shall have this honour.' Kn. cited by Di.

והשׁכמתם. השׁכים prop.='*to shoulder* or *place on the shoulders*,' i.e. to put one's baggage on the beasts of burden, which was done early in the morning, so '*to rise early*, *to resume the journey*.' The verb is a denom. from שְׁכֶם '*a shoulder*,' or rather '*the portion of the back between the shoulders*,' where any burden would be carried.

לֹּא, with emphatic or euphonic dagesh; an unusual use of dagesh, generally considered to be for the purpose of securing a clear and distinct pronunciation of the consonant: cf. Stade, § 40 c; Ges., § 20. 2 a. 2. Rem.; so קוּמוּ צְּאוּ, ver. 14; ויאמרו לֹּא, 1 Sam. 8, 19; cf. Ex. 12, 31. Deut. 2, 24. It is only found in accurate editions and MSS. See also Del., *Commentary on Ps.* 94, 12, 5th ed.; Baer, *Liber Prov.*, Pref., p. xiv; König, *Lehrg.*, p. 59.

3. מִשְׁתֶּה, prop. '*a drinking feast*,' then generally '*a meal* or *banquet*;' cf. 21, 8. 26, 30.

מצות='*sweet* or *unsoured*,' i.e. '*unleavened cakes*' (from מצץ '*to lap, suck*'), and so more quickly prepared.

4. טרם וגו״; cf. on 2, 5. Render, '*They had not yet gone to sleep, when the men of the city, the men of Sodom, surrounded the house, both young and old, all the people in a body.*'

נָסַבּוּ is third perf. pl. Nif'. of סבב=נִסְבְּבוּ. Nif'al being originally Naf'al; the pathach being thinned down into ḥireq; cf. Dav., § 25. Rem. a; Ges., § 51. 1; and compare the Arabic vii form إِنْقَتَلَ (in-qatala) and such Heb. forms as נוֹשַׁב=נִוְשַׁב, נַעֲשָׂה (Dav., § 9. 1. Rem. b; Ges., § 24. 2 b); Wright, *Gram. Arab.*, i. p. 42. נִסְבַּב becomes נָסַב, and the pathach under the nun, standing in an open syllable before the tone, becomes tone-long qameç: cf. Stade, § 86. 3; Dav., § 6. 2 b; see also Ges., § 27. 2 a.

מקצה=lit. '*from the end,*' i. e. including the whole, so in Jer. 51, 31. Cf. Judg. 18, 2. 1 Kings 12, 31 (not '*of the lowest,*' but '*of the whole body of the people*'). The full expression would be מִקָּצֶה . . . וְעַד־קָצֶה, 47, 21. Jer. 12, 12. etc.

5. הלילה='*to-night,*' '*this night,*' the article, as in היום, השנה, has a demonstrative force: Ges., § 126. 1 a; Dav., *S.*, § 21. R. 1; Ewald, § 277 a. 3. So in 30, 15.

6. פתח . . . דלת. דלת='*the door of the house,*' פתח= '*the entrance (gate).*'

7. אחי='*my friends;*' cf. 29, 4. Judg. 19, 23.

8. אל for אלה is found eight times in the Pentateuch and once besides (1 Chron. 20, 8), and always (except Chron. l.c.) with the article; see Ges., § 34. 1. Rem.; Dav., § 13. Rem. a; Stade, § 171 b. It is commonly explained as an archaism, but this is very doubtful. Robertson-Smith (in Wright, *Comp. Gram.*, p. 108[1]) regards it as merely a '*scriptio defectiva.*'

(הָאֵל) as in Phoenician; cf. *C. I. S.*, I. 3. lin. 22; 14. lin. 5; 93. lin. 3. He considers הָאֵל in any case as younger than הָאֵלֶּה.

9. גֶּשׁ־הָלְאָה. So in correct editions; the ordinary editions have הָֽלְאָה, with metheg, which is wrongly placed, as the tone is on the penult. LXX, Ἀπόστα ἐκεῖ. Vulg. '*recede illuc*;' cf. Is. 49, 20 גְּשָׁה־לִּי '*stand away*.' Render, '*Stand back*.'

האחד . . . שׁפוט. '*This one came in to sojourn and goes on playing the judge*;' cf. 31, 15 ויאכל גם אכל את כספנו '*and goes on to eat up our silver*;' Job 10, 8 ותבלעני '*and yet thou goest on to swallow me up*;' cf. Driver, § 79, 'The action or its results continuing into the writer's present;' also Ewald, §§ 231 b, 342 a. 1 a.

שׁפוט. When the inf. abs. *follows* the finite verb, it generally denotes a continued or lasting action; cf. Ges., § 113. 3 b; Ewald, § 280 b; and Dav., *S.*, § 86. R. 1.

הָאֶחָד. The הָ is the article, *not* the ה interrogative.

11. בסנורים '*with blindness*;' not absolute blindness, but temporary loss of sight; the word only occurs once again, 2 Kings 6, 18. עִוָּרוֹן, Zech. 12, 4. Deut. 28, 28 is different = *blindness*, not merely a temporary affliction. סנורים is from סַנְוֵר [Safel of נור (نَوَّرَ)] = '*to make blind*,' which occurs in Aramaic; cited by Levy, *Chald. W. B. sub voce*, as occurring in Num. 16, 14 Targ. Ps.-Jon. (תסנוור). On the causative conjunction of the verb in Semitic, that has שׁ or ס as initial letter, cf. Wright, *Comp. Gram.*, p. 205; see also Delitzsch, *Assyr. Gram.*, p. 231. The article is according to Ges., § 126. 3. Rem. c; Dav., *S.*, § 22. R. 1;

LXX, *ἀορασία*; Onq. שַׁבְרְרַיָּא *'fatuitas;'* Syr. ܫܘܪܒܠܐ *'illusiones.'*

מקטן ועד גדול. Cf. 1 Sam. 5, 9. 30, 2; lit. = *'from a little one even unto a great one,'* i.e. *'all,'* every one being regarded as either small or great, so the two extremes would embrace all persons.

מן . . . ועד as in 13, 3. 14, 23, and often.

12. עד מי לך פה = *'Who hast thou still here?'* i.e. 'hast thou any more belonging to thee in Sodom besides those in thy house?'

חָתָן, perhaps collective = *'sons-in-law;'* but the singular without the suffix is strange, as one would expect חֲתָנֶיךָ, which the Pesh. has, ܚܬܢܝܟ. Di. conjectures that ובנ was inserted between יך and חתנ, as no mention is made elsewhere of sons which Lot had before the destruction.

13. כי משחתים אנחנו. The participle is used of future time (with the subject following, cf. 3, 5). See note on 6, 17, and cf. 15, 14. 17, 19. 18, 17. 41, 25. 28. Ex. 9, 3.

צעקתם = *'the cry concerning them;'* cf. on 18, 20.

את פני יהוה as in ver. 27. 33, 18. Ex. 34, 23. 1 Sam. 1, 22. Ps. 16, 11.

14. לקחי *'who were to take,'* *'the takers of his daughters;'* so Ewald, § 335 b; Ges., § 116. 2; better than (LXX, Targ. Ps.-Jon., Kimchi, Del.) *'who had taken,'* which would be more naturally expressed by אשר and the perf.; and Lot would scarcely leave his married daughters in Sodom without calling them away.

קומו צאוּ. צ with emphatic dag. (see on ver. 2), to

ensure the clear pronunciation of the צ between the two u-sounds.

היה כ . . . = '*to appear as*,' for which there is no proper word in Hebrew; cf. 27, 12. 40, 10.

15. Render, '*And when the morning dawned, the angels urged Lot, saying, Take thy wife and thy two daughters that are with thee, lest thou be swept away in the punishment of the city.*'

וכמו השחר עלה. כמו = כאשר is rare and poetical, Is. 26, 18. Ps. 58, 8; cf. M. R., § 60; Ewald, § 337 c; Dav., *S.*, § 145 a.

ויאיצו is imperf. Hif'. of אוץ. The waw conv. is used after a time determination: so 22, 4 ביום השלישי וישא אברהם, 1 Sam. 21, 6 בצאתי ויהיו, Josh. 22, 7 כי שלחם . . . ויברכם; cf. Driver, § 127 b; Ges., § 111. 1. Rem. 1; M. R., § 132 b; Dav., *S.*, § 50 b.

הנמצאת, lit. '*who are found*,' i.e. who are with thee in thy house; cf. 1 Sam. 13, 15. 21, 4. The participle may often be rendered by the present, as in 4, 10. 16, 8. 37, 16, etc. הנמצאת probably refers to את אשתך as well as to ואת שתי בנותיך.

פן תספה. ספה = '*to be snatched off, carried away*;' so 1 Sam. 12, 25. Num. 16, 26.

עון = '*punishment*;' cf. 4, 13.

16. ויתמהמה, imperf. Hithpalpal of מהה; cf. יתמרמר from מרר, Dan. 8, 7; Ges., § 55. 4; Stade, § 503.

בחמלת יהוה = '*through Yahweh's sparing him*,' i.e. '*because Yahweh spared him*,' the subject of the inf. construct following in the genitive; cf. M. R., § 117; Ges., § 115. 2.

Rem. 1; Dav., *S.*, § 91 a: also Ps. 133, 1 שׁבת אחים, Is. 47, 9 בעצמת חבריך. The inf. cstr. חמלת has the fem. cstr. ending; here intentionally, as בחמלה יהוה could not be taken as construct state with a following genitive. The inf. with fem. ending ה is common, especially in particular words, viz. אַהֲבָה, יִרְאָה, שִׂנְאָה, occasionally we find קִרְבָה, דַּאֲבָה, חֶזְקָה, דָּבְקָה; cf. Stade, p. 339; Ges., § 45. 1. Rem. b.

17. אל תביט. The jussive form תַּבֵּט would rather be expected after אַל, but cf. 9, 25. Ps. 121, 3 אַל־יָנוּם, 1 Sam. 25, 25 אַל . . . יָשִׂים; see Driver, § 47; Ges., § 107. 4 a. 2. Rem.

18. אדֹנָי, noted by the Massoretes קדש; אֲלֵהֶם does not of necessity imply that Lot did not recognise that Yahweh was speaking with him, and that אֲדֹנָי = '*my lords*,' pausal form of אֲדֹנַי; as in ver. 19 we find singular suffixes. The Pesh. and Saadiah regard אדני as חול, but the LXX, Onq., Vulg., and Sam. as קדש; so Del.

19. פֶּן־תִּדְבָּקַנִי. Imperf. with the so-called union vowel pathach instead of tsere; cf. 29, 32 יֶאֱהָבַנִי; see Ges., § 60. Rem. 2; Stade, § 636 b, who cites 1 Kings 2, 24 Kri וַיּוֹשִׁיבַנִי, Is. 56, 3 יַבְדִּילַנִי, Job 9, 18 יַשְׂבִּיעַנִי.

וָמֵתִּי. ו with pretonic qameç, the tone is not thrown forward, because the word is in pause; see Driver, § 110, 2. מַתְתִּי = מַתִּי. The perf. with waw conv., as in 3, 22, which compare.

22. צוער, probably one hour south-east of the Dead Sea, in that portion of the Arabah which is now called Ghor eṣ Ṣâfia, the modern Chirbet eṣ Ṣâfia. In 14, 2. 8 its older name is given, בלע; cf. Wetz. in Del., *Gen.*[4], p. 564, and Di., p. 273, who remarks that the name was still in existence at the time of the Crusades (Segor; cf. LXX Σηγώρ); the

Arab geographers call it Soghar or Zoghar, and the Dead Sea, the Sea of Zoghar. Robinson, Winer, Tuch, and others think that צוער was situated in the beautiful oasis El-Mezra'a, on the neck of land or peninsula which stretched from the east into the Dead Sea. Cf. Bädeker, *Palest.*, p. 145; the *Z.D.P.V.*, ii. p. 212 f.; and Sh., *G.*, p. 505 f.

23. השמש . . . צערה[1]. '*The sun had risen over the earth when Lot came to Zoar;*' cf. 29, 9. 44, 3. 4 . . . הם יצאו העיר ויוסף אמר, Judg. 3, 24 והוא יצא ועבדיו באו; also 38, 25. Judg. 18, 3. Time or place determinations are generally subordinated to the main clause in a sentence; here and in the other instances cited, the time determination is co-ordinate, and placed first for emphasis; cf. Driver, § 169. Cf. also, Ges., § 164 b; Dav., *S.*, § 141 and R. 2; M. R., § 154.

24. מאת יהוה מן השמים, the fire and brimstone are described as proceeding both *from Yahweh* and *out of heaven*, מן השמים and מאת יהוה; cf. 2 Kings 1, 12. Job 1, 16. Di. comparing Mic. 5, 6 supposes that מאת יהוה, like the Greek ἐκ Διός, was an archaïc expression, similar in meaning to מן השמים, by which it is explained; cf. Ewald, *Hist. of Israel* (Eng. trans.), ii. p. 157.

מאת = παρά with the genitive. מן = ἐκ.

25. ויהפך. מהפכה is a technical word, always used of the destruction of Sodom and Gomorrah (to which there is at least an allusion even in Is. 1, 7), just as מַבּוּל is always used of the great Deluge.

26. מאחריו '*from behind him,*' i.e. Lot; she was

[1] Baer and Delitzsch's reading צֹ֫עֲרָה should be corrected into צֹ֫עֲרָה: see *Jesaias*, p. v, note.

following Lot, and out of curiosity turned her face away from him.

28. עלה is pluperfect, 'The smoke had begun to ascend before Abraham looked.' Driver, § 16; Dav., *S.*, § 39 c.

כקיטר הכבשן. Cf. Ex. 19, 18: '*Like the smoke of a smelting furnace.*' כבשן = '*a smelting oven.*' תנור '*a baking oven.*'

29. בהפך את הערים. The subject is omitted as it is clear from the context: cf. on 24, 30. The inf. cstr. always puts its object in the same case as the verb does from which it is derived; cf. M. R., § 116; Ges., § 115. 1; Dav., § 91 b.

30. במערה. '*In the cave;*' either the generic article, as in 14, 13. 15, 11, or possibly a particular cave was meant, which the narrator could speak of as '*the cave;*' cf. 16, 7.

33. תַּשְׁקֶיןָ. *Scriptio defectiva* for תַּשְׁקֶינָה; cf. Ges., § 47. Rem. 3. This defective form is found occasionally, but by no means uniformly, in the Pent. It occurs also elsewhere, e. g. in Ezekiel תִּהְיֶיןָ four times, with the full form also four times.

בלילה הוא. הוא without the article—which would be expected, as לילה is defined—as being in itself definite; cf. 30, 16. 32, 23. 1 Sam. 19, 10 (all): see Ges., § 126. 5. Rem. 1 b; M. R., § 85. Rem. c; Dav., *S.*, §§ 6, 32. R. 3. This is a very rare variation for the more usual בלילה ההוא, but we find on the Moabite Stone, l. 3, הבמת זאת.

וּבְקוּמָהּ with a point on the ו; cf. ver. 35 בְּקֻמָהּ. Possibly the point refers to a various reading בְּקֻמָהּ, as in ver. 35. Hieron., *Quaest.*, ed. Lag., p. 30 (Appendix to the *Genesis*

Graece), says: 'Denique Hebraei quod sequitur *et nesciuit cum dormisset cum ea et cum surrexisset ab eo* adpungunt desuper quasi incredibile et quod rerum natura non capiat coire quempiam nescientem;' cf. Strack, p. 88.

34. ממחרת. The ending ָת in this word is quite unique, and apparently without analogy; cf. Stade, § 308 d. Ges., § 80. Rem. 2 b, classes it among nouns with the rarer fem. ending ָת, e.g. Canaanitish names of towns, cf. אפרת, בעלת, חמת, and other names such as תִּמְנָת, prob. abbreviated for תִּמְנָתָה, also נַחֲלָת, prob. for נַחֲלָתִי; cf. Stade, l.c. Olshausen, *Grammar*, § 38 c, explains the form by contraction out of מְאָחֳרַת. Another explanation (cf. Levy, *Chald. W. B.*, i. p. 330) is that it is contracted out of יום אחר; cf. the Aramaic word יוֹם חֲרָא=יוֹמְחְרָא.

36. מאביהן. מן is used intentionally instead of ל (38, 18 b), on account of the etymology in ver. 37; cf. vers. 32. 34.

37. מואב. LXX add the explanation, λέγουσα, Ἐκ τοῦ πατρός μου, i.e. מֵאָב '*from the father*' (like קין, נח, not a strict etymology): another explanation is that the word is compounded of מי for מֵי '*water*,'=מוי in Aramaic (cf. Is. 25, 10, and the prop. name מהדבא, Moab. Stone, l. 8 = Biblical מי דבא, see Schlottmann, *Siegessäule Mesa's*, Halle, 1870, p. 41; and מוֹפַעַת, Ktb., Jer. 48, 21; Kri, מֵיפַעַת (cf. 1 Chron. 6, 64), a town of the Levites, in the territory of Reuben, which afterwards belonged to Moab), and אָב, the meaning being then '*semen patris*.'

38. בן־עמי='*son of my people*,' after which the LXX insert, λέγουσα, Υἱὸς γένους μου. עַמּוֹן='*belonging to the people*' (abs. then concrete) bears the same relation to עם as אַגְמוֹן to אֲגַם (Del.).

20.

1. ארצה הנגב. '*To the land of the south.*' ה locative and the construct state; cf. Ges., § 90. 2 a; Stade, § 342 d; Dav., *S.*, § 27: so Ex. 4, 20 ארצה מצרים; Gen. 43, 17 ביתה יוסף; Deut. 4, 41 מזרחה שמש; other instances in Genesis are (?) 24, 67. 28, 2. 46, 1. On the Negeb, cf. note on 12, 9.

גרר is identified by Rowlands, Robinson, Kiepert, and Bädeker, *Palest.*, p. 157, etc., with the modern Umm el-Ǵerâr, three hours SSE. of Gaza, on a broad and deep torrent flowing from the SE., the Ǵurf el-Ǵerâr, the upper portion of the Wady Gazzeh, which forms a junction with the Wady eš-Šeriʿa, a little above Ǵerâr. Thomson, Trumbull (*Kadesh Barnea*, p. 61 ff.), and Guthe (*Z.D.P.V.*, viii. p. 215) prefer to place it in or near the Wady Ǵerûr, a branch of the Wady eš-Šeraif, which enters the Wady el-ʿArîš, to the SW. of Kadesh; cf. Di., p. 279 f., who points out that objections may be urged against both identifications.

2. אל־שׂרה = '*concerning Sarah:*' so ver. 13 אמרי לי; 32, 30 לשמי; cf. Ob. 1. Ps. 3, 3; see Ewald, § 217 c; Ges., § 119. 3 c. 4; Dav., *S.*, § 101. R. b.

3. והוא בעלת בעל '*she being married;*' so Deut. 22, 22 אשה בעלת בעל; cf. Is. 62, 5. On the circumstantial clause here, cf. Driver, § 160; Ges., § 141. 2. R. 2; Dav., *S.*, §§ 105, 138 a; M. R., § 152; so in 15, 2. 18, 1. 8. 10. 13. 27. 24, 31. 62. 37, 2. 44, 14.

4. הגוי גם צדיק. גם (emphasizing the following צדיק) = ὅμως; cf. Ewald, § 354 a; Ges., § 154. foot-note c: so ver. 5 והיא גם הוא, ver. 6 ואחשך גם אנכי; cf. Dav., *S.*, § 107.

6. מחטו for מֵחֲטֹא, written according to the sound. Cf. 2 Kings 13, 6 הֶחֱטִי; Jer. 32, 35 החטי. The Kri gives the ordinary form מחטא. Cf. Stade, §§ 29 and 143e. 2, who regards it as a mistake, like רָאוֹ for רָאֹה, יָצָתִי for יָצָאתִי, both written according to their pronunciation. Ges., § 75. Rem. 21 c, takes חטו as an instance of a verb ל״א following the form of a verb ל״ה.

לא נתתיך לנגע = '*I did not allow thee,*' etc. '*To let,*' or '*allow,*' is always expressed thus in Heb.; so 31, 7 ולא נתנו אלהים להרע; Judg. 1, 34 כי לא נתנו לרדת; see Ges., § 114. 2. Rem. 3; Dav., *S.*, § 82 b.

7. נביא, as under God's protection; cf. Ps. 105, 15. נָבִיא possibly comes from a root נבא = '*to express,*' '*announce*' (so quite commonly in Assyrian). The original meaning of נביא is *active*, not *passive*, '*the announcer, speaker,*' i. e. of God, or of divine mysteries: the form being an intensive form of the part. act.; cf. the Arabic نَبِئٌ or نَبِيٌّ, a noun of the form فَعِيل, with an active meaning like the Heb. חסיל. Cf. Wright, *Arab. Gram.*, i. p. 151, and Fleischer in Del., *Gen.*[4], p. 551; see also Barth, *N. B.*, p. 184. Bleek (*Einleitung*[4], p. 306) thinks that נבא may be connected with נבע = '*ebullire,*' and so '*to pour forth words,*' '*to speak,*' נביא = '*speaker.*' This however is doubtful, as נבא does not actually occur with the meaning '*gush up.*' See a good note on נביא in Robertson-Smith, *Prophets*, p. 389 f.

וחיה. Cf. 45, 18, and see note on 12, 2.

ואם אינך משיב. '*And if thou art not going to restore;*' the affirmative form would be אם ישך משיב; cf. 43, 5 ואם אינך משלח, neg.; and ver. 4 אם ישך משלח, affirmative. אין and יש are often used thus in hypothetical sentences. Cf. note on 24, 42.

כי מות תמות אתה וכל וגו״. When the compound subject is a pronoun and noun (or its equivalent), the pronoun must be expressed whether the verb be sing. or plural. Cf. 7, 1. 14, 15. 24, 54. 31, 21; Judg. 7, 10. 11, 38; and see Dav., *S.*, § 114 c.

9. מעשים אשר לא יעשו=‘*deeds which ought not to be done;*’ cf. 4, 7 ואתה תמשל בו ‘*thou shouldest rule over him;*’ 34, 7 וכן לא יעשה ‘*so it should not be done;*’ Ex. 10, 26 מה נעבד ‘*how we ought to serve;*’ see Driver, § 39 *a*; M. R., 7. 2 b; Ges., § 107. 2 b; Dav., *S.*, § 44 a.

10. מה ראית=‘*what hadst thou in view?*’ so ראה in Ps. 66, 18 און אם ראיתי.

11. כי אמרתי, supply עשיתי from עשית in ver. 10 ‘(*I did it*) *because I thought;*’ cf. 27, 20. 31, 31. Ex. 1, 19.

רק. Knobel and Del. render (I) ‘*surely;*’ cf. Num. 20, 19 רק אין דבר; Ps. 32, 6 רק לשטף מים רבים. (II) Di. prefers to translate ‘*only,*’ ‘*at least,*’ not considering the two passages above cited decisive.

אין יראת . . . והרגוני. ‘*There is no fear of God in this place, and they will kill me;*’ cf. 2 Sam. 14, 7 וכבו ‘*and they will quench;*’ Gen. 34, 30 ואני מתי מספר ונאספו עלי. Cf. Dr., § 119 a; Dav., *S.*, § 57. R. 1; Ges., § 112. 4 a; M. R., § 24. 2 b.

12. ‘*And she is also really my sister, the daughter of my father, only not the daughter of my mother, so she became my wife;*’ cf. on 12, 19. Such marriages, though prevalent among other nations, e.g. in Canaan, Assyria, Persia, Egypt, Arabia, were forbidden in the Levitical law, Lev. 18, 9. 11. 20, 17. Deut. 27, 22. From this passage it would seem that

they were customary also among the Hebrews in pre-Mosaïc times.

13. התעו . . . אלהים, marked by the Massoretes קדש, to shew that the true God is meant, although the verb is plural; possibly the plural here is used because Abraham was conversing with a heathen. Cf. 35, 7, where probably the angels are included under אלהים; see Ewald, § 318 a; Ges., § 145. 3. Rem.; Dav., *S.*, § 116. R. 4; M. R., § 135. 2. The Heb.-Samaritan text here, and 35, 7, read the singular. The later books of the Bible also avoid the plural; cf. Neh. 9, 18 with Ex. 32, 4.

16. אלף כסף=*'a thousand shekels of silver.'* שקל omitted (cf. 8, 5) by Ges., § 134. 3. Rem. 3; Dav., *S.*, § 37. R. 4; M. R., § 71. 4.

The thousand shekels of silver could hardly be the value of the presents given to Abraham, ver. 14, for such a valuation of these gifts is here quite out of place; besides the present here mentioned is given to Abraham for Sarah, and on account of the insult she had suffered; whilst the one in ver. 14 was for Abraham himself.

הוא refers to the gift, not to Abraham; as in the latter case, no reason would be assigned for giving the thousand shekels.

לכל אשר אתך. Render, *'It is for thee a covering of the eyes for all those who are with thee;'* i. e. it is intended for Sarah, and given for her sake, and will blind the eyes of all those that are with her, so that they will be oblivious of what has happened, and regard the insult, to which she has been subjected, as though it had never occurred; cf. 32, 21. Job 9, 24. So Di., who regards לכל as introducing those whose eyes are to be covered, and לך as a *dat. comm.* Tuch and Kn. render לכל אשר וגו׳ as=*'with regard to all that which has befallen thee,'* a meaning the words will hardly bear. Del.[4] renders as though the text were וּלְכָל־, which reading the LXX (*καὶ πάσαις*) and the Sam. follow. In Ed.[5] he renders, *'Let this be for thee a covering of the eyes for all those who are with thee,'* or *'with reference to all, etc.'* Then לך=the person whose eyes are to be covered, and the ל in לכל must be the dat. of reference. This rendering does not seem to be so natural as that adopted by Di.

ואת כל is separated from אתך by the accents, and connected with ונכחת. Render, *'And among all* (or *"in the judgment of all,"* cf. Is. 59, 12) *so art thou justified.'* ואת כל is taken by Tuch in close connection with אתך *'for all which has happened* (*with*) *unto thee and* (*with*) *unto all.'* But ואת כל can hardly mean this, and nothing had happened את כל *'with all.'*

ונכחת probably ought to be pointed וְנֹכַחַתְּ (in pause וְנֹכָחַתְּ), so Di.; cf. König, *Lehrg.*, i. p. 423, which is the usual form of the second pers. fem. perf. in a ל guttural verb, as the ו is difficult before anything but a second perf. To take the form נֹכָחַת as second perf., comparing לָקַחַת, 30, 15, is unsafe, as לקחת there is probably infinitive. Del.[5] takes נכחת as participle fem. standing for ונכחת את, and renders, *'and with all justified,'* viz. *'thou standest justified.'* The Mass. points seem to intend ונכחת as perf. third pers. fem., which is pointed without shewa under the ת, to distinguish it from the second pers. fem. perf., which has shewa. The rendering would then be, *'And with regard to all—so it is settled;'* but then the feminine would not be necessary.

נכחת may here be either pass. of הוכיח, with an acc. of the thing, Job 13, 15. 19, 5 = '*to represent as right;*' or passive of הוכיח ל, Is. 11, 4. Job 16, 21 '*to procure right for.*' Ges. renders ונכחת '*and she stood reproved,*' which is possible, but unsuitable, as Abimelech is not reproaching Sarah. It is not improbable that the sentence is corrupt.

כסות עינים; cf. כפר פנים in 32, 21. Job 9, 24 פני שׁפטיה יכסה, and כסה, Ps. 85, 3, of covering sin; כפר, Jer. 18, 23, of atoning, lit. covering, guilt; cf. also 1 Sam. 12, 3 ואעלים עיני בו (if the Mass. text is correct here, but see LXX, and Driver in loc.). The rendering of כסות by '*veil*' is unsuitable, and not supported by 12, 14. 24, 16. 29, 16. 17, compared with 24, 65; as it is not certain from these passages that women wore veils first when they were engaged (Tuch). Besides, a thousand shekels would be rather a high price to give for a veil, about £100. LXX have *ταῦτα ἔσται σοι εἰς τιμὴν τοῦ προσώπου σου, καὶ πάσαις ταῖς μετὰ σοῦ, καὶ πάντα ἀλήθευσον*: *πάντα ἀλήθευσον* being, perhaps, a guess on the part of the translator, who misunderstood the original. Onq. has: הָא הוּא לִיךְ כְּסוּת דִּיקַר חֲלָף דִּשְׁלַחִית דְּבַרְתִּיךְ וַחֲזֵית יָתִיךְ וְיַת כָּל דְּעִימִּיךְ וְעַל כָּל מָא דְּאָמַרְתְּ אִיתּוֹכַחַת '*Behold, it is unto thee for a covering of glory, because I sent (and) took thee, and saw thee, and all that is with thee, and concerning all that thou hast spoken, thou hast proved thyself right.*' The Pesh. has: ܗܐ ܝܗܒܬ ܐܠܦ ܕܟܣܦ ܠܐܚܘܟܝ ܘܗܐ ܐܦ ܗܘ ܝܗܝܒ ܠܟܝ ܡܛܠ ܕܟܣܝܬܝ ܥܝܢܐ ܕܟܠ ܕܥܡܝ ܘܥܠ ܟܠܡܕܡ ܐܬܟܣܣܬܝܢܝ '*Behold, I give a thousand of silver to thy brother, and behold it is also given to thee, because thou hast covered the eyes of all those who are with me, and concerning everything, thou hast reproved me.*' Vulg. '*Ecce mille argenteos dedi fratri tuo; hoc erit tibi in velamen oculorum ad omnes qui tecum sunt, et quocumque perrexeris: mementoque te deprehensam.*'

17. ואמהתיו possibly = '*concubines;*' אמה (for שפחה) occurs frequently in E. שפחה has sometimes a more servile sense than אמה; cf. 1 Sam. 25, 41.

וילדו = '*they bare,*' masc. for fem.; cf. 30, 39; see Ges., § 145. 7. R. 1; Dav., *S.*, § 113 b; or as ילד is also used of the male, e.g. Zech. 13, 3. Hos. 9, 16 '*they begat,*' Abimelech being included in the subject.

21.

1. פקד. P uses זכר, not פקד; so 8, 1. 19, 29.

2. זקניו = '*his old age.*' So—always in the plural—חיים '*life;*' נעורים '*youth*' (all nouns denoting space of time); cf. שמים, צוארים, nouns denoting extension of space; see note on 2, 7, and cf. Ewald, § 178 a, b.

3. הַנּוֹלַד־לוֹ. Participle Nif'. of ילד, with the qameç shortened into pathach, on account of the following maqqef. Others take it as perf. Nif'. with the article הַנּוֹלַד=אֲשֶׁר נוֹלַד; cf. on 18, 21.

יצחק. Other nouns (mostly proper names) formed after the analogy of the imperfect Qal are יַעֲקֹב, יִדְלָף, 22, 22, יִדְבָּשׁ, יִבְשָׂם, יַהְוֶה = יְהוָֹה, according to the pointing usually adopted by modern scholars (see App.). יְשִׁימָה (in בית הישימות) is possibly an abstract noun of this form; cf. also יוֹנָה = '*a dove,*' יַחְמוּר '*a stag;*' see Stade, § 259 a; and cf. Barth, *N. B.*, p. 227.

5. בְּהִוָּלֶד לוֹ. On the construction, cf. on 4, 18. בְּהִוָּלֶד is accented on the penult. to avoid the concurrence of two tone-syllables, this shortens the tsere in the last syllable into seghol; cf. on 4, 17. Two tone-syllables may however

come together, if the first word is separated from the second, by a distinctive accent.

6. '*And Sarah said, Laughter hath God prepared for me, every one who hears will laugh at me.*'

יצחק לי. צחק with ל='*to laugh at*' (as is clearly shown by Job 5, 22. 39, 7. 18. 22. Ps. 59, 9), here rather in astonishment than in derision. A.V. '*will laugh with me;*' so VSS., but incorrectly.

יְצַחֶק, with shewa resolved into ḥateph pathach; so even where no guttural follows, cf. 2, 12. 23. Jer. 22, 15 הֲתִמְלֹךְ.

7. מי מלל וגו״. Render, '*Who could have said to Abraham?*' 'The perfect is used in questions to express astonishment at what appears to the speaker in the highest degree improbable,' Driver, § 19; cf. 18, 12 היתה לי עדנה; 1 Sam. 26, 9 מי שלח . . . ונקה; Num. 23, 10 מי מנה עפר; see also Ges., § 106. 4; Dav., *S.*, § 41. R. 2; M. R., § 3. 2. note a. LXX have ἀναγγελεῖ, '*who shall say.*' Tuch renders, '*who says,*' which would rather be יַגִּיד or יְמַלֵּל, admitting, however, that the perfect in interrogative sentences usually refers to a past act.

מלל is only found in Hebrew three times again, viz. in Ps. 106, 2. Job 8, 2 and 33, 3. It is a common word in Aramaic for the Heb. דִּבֵּר.

היניקה בנים. '*Sarah will suckle children:*' היניקה is prophetic perfect; cf. Num. 24, 17 דרך כוכב; Is. 5, 13 לכן גלה עמי; Jer. 2, 26 כן הוביש בית ישראל; and often, and see note on 1, 29.

בנים is generic plural, as in Ex. 21, 22 . . . כי ינצו אנשים

ויצאו ילדיה; Is. 37, 3 כי באו בנים וגו׳; Dav., *S.*, § 17. R. 3; Ges., § 124. 1. R. 2.

8. ויגמל, pausal form, Ges., § 51. Rem. 2; Stade, § 504 b, who gives other instances, viz. וַיֵּחָנַק, וַיִּנָּפַשׁ, וַיֵּאָמַר, וַיֵּאָנַשׁ.

9. מְצַחֵק. So Baer and Delitzsch, who compare Ex. 32, 6 לְצַחֵק, Deut. 32, 11 יְרַחֵף, where the ordinary editions point (as they do here) with tsere; see Ges., § 52. 2. R. 2; Stade, § 88. 3 a. מצחק (LXX παίζοντα, with the gloss μετὰ Ἰσαὰκ τοῦ υἱοῦ ἑαυτῆς; so Vulg. '*ludentem cum Isaac filio suo*')='*playing, sporting;*' cf. Ex. 32, 6. Judg. 16, 25: צחק in Pi'el, without a preposition, being always used in a good sense. A.V. here and 39, 14 render צחק by '*to mock;*' so Kimchi and some moderns, e.g. Baumgarten, Keil. Cf. Gal. 4, 29, where the apostle speaks of Isaac and Ishmael, ὁ κατὰ σάρκα γεννηθεὶς ἐδίωκε τὸν κατὰ πνεῦμα.

11. על אודת = lit. '*on account of the circumstances,*' then simply, '*on account of;*' an uncommon expression, found again in ver. 25. Ex. 18, 8. Num. 12, 1. 13, 24, etc.

12. יקרא לך; cf. 48, 16 ויקרא בהם שמי. Render, '*In* (or *through*) *Isaac will a seed be called for thee,*' i.e. 'in the line of Isaac will those descendants from thee come, who shall bear thy name, and as such be heirs of the divine promise, viz. the Israelites, who were the offspring of Abraham, chosen by God,' Kn. in Di.; cf. Rom. 9, 7. Heb. 11, 18; see also 17, 19. 21.

13. Construction as in 47, 21. 13, 15; cf. note on 13, 15, also Ges., § 143. Rem. 1; M. R., § 132 a.

14. וחמת מים. חֵמֶת, cstr. state of חֵמֶת, a word which

only occurs in this chapter, perhaps so pointed (Tuch) to distinguish it from חֲמַת *'anger.'*

שֹׂם is perfect, *'he placed it,'* i. e. the skin of water. The clause is a circumstantial clause, appended without any connecting particle; cf. 44, 12 החל; 48, 14 שִׂכֵּל; Judg. 6, 19 שׂם; Driver, § 163; Ewald, § 346 a; M. R., § 153; Dav., *S.*, § 41. R. 3; Ges., § 156. 3 a.

ואת הילד is acc. after ויתן, not שׂם, which at any rate would not suit the present narrative. LXX seem to have read וישׂם על שׁכמה את הילד, *καὶ ἐπέθηκεν ἐπὶ τὸν ὦμον αὐτῆς τὸ παιδίον*, but badly, as Ishmael, cf. 17, 25, would be about fourteen years old. Vulg. better, *'tollens panem et utrem aquae, imposuit scapulae ejus, tradiditque puerum.'*

וַתֵּתַע is imperf. Qal apoc. from תעה. יִתְעֶה=יִתְע, then with a helping vowel יִתַע, and lengthening hireq into tsere, יֵתַע; cf. Ges., § 75. Rem. 3; Driver, p. 52. foot-note 1 (where the analogy between the apocopated forms of verbs ל״ה and the segholate nouns is noticed); Stade, § 545 d; cf. § 489 b.

במדבר באר שׁבע, i.e. the southern frontier of Canaan.

16. לה is ethic dative; common with verbs of motion, esp. in the imperative; cf. לך לך, 12, 1,—and note on that passage,—22, 2; לכו לכם, Josh. 22, 4; see M. R., § 51. 3. R. a. 3.

הרחק וגו״=*'about a bow-shot off,'* lit. *'distant like the shooters with the bow.'* הרחק is inf. abs.=*'making far;'* cf. Ex. 33, 7. Josh. 3, 16; see Ewald, § 280 a; used here as an adverb (cf. Ges., § 113. 2; Dav., *S.*, § 87)=*'at a distance.'*

מטחוי is participle plural, cstr. state, Pilel from טחה; cf. Ges., § 75. Rem. 18; Stade, § 155 b; also § 279, the word only occurs here.

אראה במות. ראה with ב, as in 44, 34; see Ges., § 119. 3 b. 2.

17. **באשר הוא**=במקום אשר. Cf. Ges., § 138. 2 Rem.; Dav., *S.*, § 10. Rem. 3, and 2 Sam. 15, 21. Jer. 22, 12, and often.

18. **החזיקי את ידך בו**, lit.=*'make fast thy hand on him,'* i.e. 'take hold of him,' which is more commonly expressed without יד, החזיק ב.

19. **באר מים** *'a spring of water.'* באר=*'a spring,'* בור *'a cistern for rain-water.'*

וַתַּשְׁקְ is apoc. imperf. Hif'. of שקה, without a helping vowel; cf. on ver. 15: so ותבך, ver. 16, apoc. imperf. Qal of בכה.

20. **ויהי רבה קשת**. Two renderings may be noticed: (I) *'And he became, as he grew up, an archer;'* cf. Job 39, 4 יחלמו בניהם ירבו בבר; Zech. 10, 8 ורבו כמו רבו. So the Mass. and Hieron., but רֹבֶה=*'growing up'* is superfluous after וַיִּגְדָּל. (II) Del.[5] renders, *'And he became a shooter*, (viz.) *a bow-man,'* קַשָּׁת being a closer definition of רבה, and רבה=רבב (cf. 49, 23) and רמה (cf. Jer. 4, 29. Ps. 78, 9); cf. 13, 8. 1 Kings 1, 1; see note on 13, 8. LXX render *ἐγένετο δὲ τοξότης*, but whether they read the text רֹבֶה קֶשֶׁת or קַשָּׁת passing over רֹבֶה, is quite uncertain. The Vulg. takes רבה= *'juvenis,' 'factusque est juvenis sagittarius.'* Onq. has וַהֲוָה רָבְיָא קַשָּׁתָא, which probably ought to be rendered, *'And the youth became an archer'* (רָבְיָא being Onqelos' translation of הנער or הילד in vers. 8. 14. 15. 16. 17); cf. Levy, *Chald. W. B.*, ii. pp. 395, 400. Di. adopts the reading of Kn.

רֹבֵה קֶשֶׁת *'a shooter of the bow,' 'a bow-man;'* taking רבה, as Del. does=רבב and רמה; cf. the rendering of the LXX. A passage somewhat similar to this is 1 Kings 5, 29 נֹשֵׂא סַבָּל. The Itureans and Kedarenes, both descendants of Ishmael, cf. 25, 13. 15, were celebrated as bow-men; cf. Is. 21, 17.

21. במדבר פארן. The desert-plateau, bounded on the S. by the Gebel-et-Tih, E. by the Arabah, and the N. end of the Ælanitic Gulf; W. by the Wilderness of Shur (16, 7). Northwards it extends to the Negeb and the Wilderness of Judah; i. e. up to the Wilderness of Zin (Num. 13, 21. 20, 1) or Kadesh (Ps. 29, 8). The Wady-el-'Arîš flows through it; cf. with this ver. (E) 14, 6. Num. 13, 3. 26 (P). Dt. 33, 2. Hab. 3, 3, and Di. on Num. 10, 12.

22–24.

22. LXX have here and ver. 32, *καὶ 'Οχοζὰθ ὁ νυμφαγωγὸς αὐτοῦ*, probably a gloss which has crept in from 26, 26.

23. *'And now swear unto me by God here, that thou wilt not lie unto me or my offspring or offshoot.'*

הנה is not '*these things,*' but '*here;*' cf. 15, 16: properly '*hither*' (German, *hier, hierher*).

ולניני ולנכדי, only Job 18, 19. Is. 14, 22: notice the alliteration, and cf. on 18, 27. The two words always stand together='*proles et soboles.*'

25. והוכח. Di. (cf. Dav., *S.*, § 58 b) explains this on the ground that the conversation took place before the actual swearing, but one does not quite see why the writer should have used a perfect with waw (apparently weak waw, as waw consecutive seems quite out of place here) to express this, and not the perfect separated from the waw by some intervening word; Driver, § 76. Obs. The perfect here

seems to be the same as והאמין in 15, 6; cf. the note there. The text, however, may be corrupt; cf. Ges., § 112. 6 γ.

באר המים, on the article, cf. on 16, 7.

26. וגם . . . לא . . . וגם . . . לא = '*neither . . . nor*;' cf. Num. 23, 25 גם קב לא תקבנו גם ברך לא תברכנו.

29. מה הנה שבע כבשת האלה. כבשות has no article, it may perhaps be regarded as defined by the numeral שֶׁבַע. See Ges., § 126. 5. Rem. 1 a; Dav., *S.*, § 32. R. 2; and cf. 41, 26.

הנה, not '*here*,' but '*what are they*, *these seven lambs*;' cf. Zech. 1, 9. 4, 5; and see Driver, § 201, 2; Ewald, § 325 a. Compare also Ges., § 141. 3.

לְבַדְּנָה (for the form לְבַדְּהֶן=לְבַדְּהֶנָּה; cf. the rare forms (nearly all of which occur in pause) כֻּלָּנָה, 42, 36; Prov. 31, 29, and כֻּלְּהֶנָּה, 1 Kings 7, 37, etc.; הנה, which as a separate pronoun is pointed הֵנָּה, being affixed; cf. Ges. § 91. 1. Rem. 2; Stade, § 352 b; Wright, *Comp. Gram.*, p. 156 f.

30. כי את שבע. כי, like the ὅτι *recitantis* in Greek, introduces the words of the speaker.

תהיה לי לעדה. תהיה does not refer to כבשת, but to the whole transaction, '*it shall be for a witness*;' cf. Job 4, 5. Mic. 1, 9.

The number seven had for the ancients a special significance as the sacred number; cf. Ex. 37, 23. Lev. 4, 6; so solemn oaths were attested, either by the presence of seven witnesses (Her. iii. 8) or by the slaughter of seven animals, as here; cf. the word נִשְׁבַּע '*to swear*,' probably a denom. from שֶׁבַע '*seven*' = '*to use* or *call seven*,' so the name באר שבע may mean '*well of seven*,' or '*well of an oath*,' שבע=שבועה; cf. the proper names אלישבע, יהושבע.

31. באר שבע is the modern Bîr es-Seba' (بير السبع), twelve hours south of Hebron. Ruins are still to be seen there, in the neighbourhood of which are two cisterns of excellent water; cf. Sh., *G.*, p. 284 f.

33. אשל='*tamarisk*,' Arab. أَثْل; cf. Löw, *Aram. Pflanzenn.*, 65. The renderings of the VSS., LXX ἄρουρα, Aq. δενδρών, Sym. φυτεία, Onq. נִיצְבָא, were perhaps intentionally adopted for the same reason as מֵישְׁרָא in 12, 6 for אלון, i.e. to avoid any reference to the sacred tree; see the note there, ad fin.; and on tree worship, Rob. Smith, *Relig. of the Semites*, p. 185 ff.

22.

1. Di. and Del. render, '*And it came to pass after these things, when God proved Abraham, that he said*,' etc., regarding ויאמר as the apod., and ואלהים נסה as a circ. clause. The ordinary translation which takes ואלהים נ״ as apodosis is to be preferred, as being simpler. Cf. Driver, § 78; Ges., § 111. 2; Dav., *S.*, § 51. R. 1.

2. את יחידך '*thine only one*.' LXX τὸν ἀγαπητόν; cf. Prov. 4, 3, LXX. According to Frankel, *Einfluss*, p. 7, the rendering of the LXX was intentional, as Abraham had another son Ishmael. Isaac is called a בן יחיד, as the son of Abraham by his own wife Sarah, not as the only remaining son after Ishmael was sent away; all through the narrative Isaac and Ishmael are regarded by the writer as standing in a different relation to Abraham; cf. chap. 21 with chap. 16.

ארץ המריה. '*To the district of Moriah*;' cf. Num. 32, 1. Josh. 8, 1. 10, 41, where ארץ occurs again in the sense of '*district*.' מריה with the article (cf. העי '*Ai*,' הירדן '*Jordan*,' הלבנן '*Lebanon*') is the name of the hill on which in later times the temple stood, 2 Chron. 3, 1. Jos., *Ant.*, i. 13. 1 f.

This is the view usually adopted by modern expositors, as Del., Di., but is not without difficulties. Moriah does not appear to have been commonly used as a name for the Temple hill, which was generally called Sion. The district around Moriah could hardly be spoken of as ארץ מוריה, and Moriah itself then described as one of the mountains in this district. Well. (*Comp.*, p. 20) supposes that the Chronicler, following Gen. 22, invented the name Moriah, and that in the Genesis text some other name originally stood; cf. Kuenen, *Hexateuch*, p. 254, and Di., ad loc. Tuch prefers the view that מריה here=the מורה in 12, 6, near Shechem, called Judg. 7, 1 גבעת המורה, on the ground of the LXX reading εἰς τὴν γῆν τὴν ὑψηλήν, and in 12, 6 τὴν δρῦν τὴν ὑψηλήν. But this Moreh was a place of no significance in the history of Israel, and too far from Beersheba to be reached in three days. Further, no great stress can be laid on the reading of the LXX either here or in 12, 6, their translation being probably a mere guess, as it can hardly be a rendering of the Hebrew text. The VSS. render variously, and throw no light on the question. Vulg. has '*terram visionis*.' Onq. לְאַרַע פּוּלְחָנָא '*land of worship*.' Pesh. ܠܐܪܥܐ ܕܐܡܘܪܝܐ=ארץ האמורי, cf. their rendering of 2 Chron. 3, 1, '*land of the Amorites*;' also Geiger, *Urschrift*, p. 278. Di., p. 292, seems inclined to think that the Pesh. may have preserved the original reading.

המריה. The derivation is unknown, but seems to have been connected by a *play* with ראה; cf. vers. 8 and 14. For derivations of the word that have been suggested, cf. Ges., *Thes.*, p. 819; C. P. Ges., *sub voce*; also a note by Cheyne in the American Journal *Hebraica*, April, 1885, p. 252. It cannot mean '*shown of Jah*,' which would be מָרְאִיָּה (cf. מַעֲשֵׂיָה).

4. ביום השלישי is connected by the LXX with וילך in ver. 3, but incorrectly.

וישא is the imperf. with waw consec. after a time determination; cf. on 19, 15.

5. נלכה. Cohortative, expressing the intention more strongly than the simple imperf.; cf. Driver, § 49 a.

כה has here a local force, as Gen. 31, 37 (rare).

7. הִנֶּנִּי, also pointed הִנְנִי, and in pause הִנֶּנִי; cf. Dav., § 49; Ges., § 100. 5; Stade, § 380. The suffix is a verbal suffix here with the nun demonstrative; cf. Stade, § 359 b. 4.

8. אלהים יראה לו = '*God will provide him*' etc.; cf. 41, 33 ועתה ירא פרעה; 1 Sam. 16, 1 כי ראיתי בבניו לי, 17 ראו נא לי איש.

12. '*And He said, Stretch not forth thine hand to the boy, and do not do anything to him; for now I know that thou art a fearer of God* (cf. note on 4, 14); *for thou hast not withheld thy son, thine only one, from me.*'

ולא חשׂכת is almost = כי לא חשׂכת, which would be more emphatic: וְ here expresses a consequence; see M. R., § 148 c; Ges., § 158; cf. its use in the waw conv. in 20, 12, '*and so she became my wife;*' 23, 20; Driver, § 74.

מאומה from מאום '*a spot,*' '*a dot,*' then '*anything;*' cf. the French *point.*

13. אַחַר. Sam., LXX, Targ.-Ps. Jon., Pesh., forty-two Codices (Tuch and Wright) read אחד, i. e. '*a single ram,*' rams in ordinary cases going about in flocks (Tuch), which is preferred by some, e.g. Ewald, but which is not so probable, for אחד looks like an emendation of אחר, and אחר explains

how it was that Abraham did not see the ram before. Geiger, *Urschrift*, p. 244, reads אֶחָד, regarding Isaac as the one lamb (das Opferlamm), and the ram caught in the thicket as '*the other*:' and thinks, that as this view was objectionable, the reading was corrected into אחד, which was again changed into אַחַר. This however is improbable. אחר is not *temporal*, but *local* = '*behind*;' cf. Ps. 68, 26; so תחת, as an adv., 49, 25, and a prep.: על, as an adv., 2 Sam. 23, 1, and a prep.

נֶאֱחַז. Perf., so Baer and Del., '*it was caught*;' another reading is נֶאֱחָז, participle, '*caught*;' so Theile.

בַּסְּבַךְ. So Baer and Del.; cf. וּזֲהַב, 2, 12. Ordinary editions point בַּסְּבָךְ. Render, '*In a thicket*.'

14. יהוה יראה = '*Yahweh sees*,' i.e. '*provides*;' cf. ver. 8; so LXX, Κύριος ἴδεν.

אשר וגו׳. '*So that it is said* (i.e. "*people are in the habit of saying*"), *In the mountain of the Lord provision shall be made*' (cf. 10, 9).

יראה = '*provision shall be made*,' suits the context, but is a doubtful rendering, as the Nif'al does not occur elsewhere in this sense. Some render (apparently the Massor.), '*On the mountain of Yahweh He* (*Yahweh*) *appears*;' but this is very awkward, and the point to be explained is not so much Yahweh's appearance (there was no real vision, only a voice from heaven) as the providing of a substitute, ver. 8. Di. renders according to Ewald (§ 332 d), '*On the mountain where Yahweh is seen*,' lit. '*On the mountain of Yahweh's appearing*;' cf. Hos. 1, 2. Ps. 4, 8, which however gives no suitable sense; as one cannot regard it as a proverb to say, '*On the mountain where Yahweh appeared*,' we should rather expect הר יי׳ יראה '*the mountain where Yahweh appeared*:' in either case the sentence is very incomplete. The rendering '*provision shall be made*' may perhaps be accepted in lieu of a better translation; the Qal clearly means '*to provide*,' the Nif'al may be regarded as its passive, though no other instance of this use can be cited. The LXX, ἐν τῷ ὄρει Κύριος ὤφθη, would require בָּהָר יהוה יֵרָאֶה. The text would be easier of explanation if יֵרָאֶה at the end of the verse were pointed יִרְאֶה; so Vulgate.

16. כי introduces the contents of the oath; cf. 2 Sam. 3, 35. Jer. 22, 24.

17. ויירש. The imperf. with simple waw used as a jussive, '*And may thy seed possess the gate of thy enemies*;' cf. 9, 27. 17, 2. 27, 29; Driver, § 134: the ordinary construction would be the perfect with waw consec. וְיָרַשׁ; cf. ver. 18. Here possibly the imperf. with simple waw was chosen intentionally. וְיָרַשׁ would = '*and thy seed shall*,' in continuation of ארבה.

18. עקב אשר שמעת בקלי = '*Because thou hast listened to my voice*,' lit. '*as a reward for listening to*,' etc. עקב אשר recurs in 26, 5. 2 Sam. 12, 6 (all). עֵקֶב without אשר is used similarly, e.g. Deut. 8, 20 ('*as a punishment for*').

20–24. A short notice of the family of Abraham's brother Nahor. It is probably inserted here, as Ribqah, Isaac's wife, was the daughter of Bethuel, Nahor's son, cf. ver. 23[1]. The families here mentioned can only be partially identified.

21. עוץ. Cf. 10, 23, probably to be taken in a more limited sense here (Di.).

בוז is mentioned in Jer. 25, 23, together with Dedân and Têmâ, and so must be sought for in the neighbourhood of

[1] Di., however, thinks that 23 a ובתואל ילד את רבקה is an insertion by R. instead of an original ואת לבן ואת רבקה, to harmonize with 25, 20 (P), cf. 28, 2. 7 (P). In 29, 5 (J), Laban is the son of Nahor; cf. notes on 24, 15. 24. 47. 50.

Edom. Elihu, Job's fourth adversary, was a Buzite, Job 32, 2. Del., *Par.*, p. 307, compares the land *Bâzu* mentioned in Asarhaddon's inscriptions.

קמואל אבי ארם. קמואל is otherwise unknown. In 10, 22 ארם is the son of Shem. Perhaps ארם here, as Di. suggests, was the name of a single people, ארם in 10, 22 (P) being the name of a nation in a wider sense.

22. כֶּשֶׂד. It is uncertain whether כשׂד is to be considered as the ancestor of the whole family of the כשׂדים, or of one tribe of the same.

חזו is very uncertain; the Arab geographers (cf. Di., p. 295) mention a حَزَّة in Mesopotamia, between Nisibis and Râs 'Ain. An Assyrian *Chazu* is found on Asarhaddon's inscriptions (cf. Del., *Par.*, p. 306 f.), possibly this is the same as the חזו in this verse.

פלדש is unknown; ידלף is also unknown; בתואל is unknown as the name of a place; in 25, 20. 28, 5 it is the proper name of a person.

24. ופילגשׁו, *casus pendens*, the narrative being resumed by waw conv., '*And his concubine, whose name was R'uma, she bare;*' cf. 30, 30. Ex. 9, 21. 1 Sam. 14, 19. 1 Kings 11, 26; Ewald, § 344 b; Driver, § 127 a; M. R., § 132 c; Ges., § 111. 2. Rem. 2; Dav., *S.*, § 50 b.

פילגשׁו. פִּילֶגֶשׁ, also פִּלֶגֶשׁ. The derivation of the word is doubtful. It may be of foreign origin; cf. Ew., § 106. c 3. Cf. the Gk. πάλλαξ and Lat. *pellex*, and see C. P. Ges. *sub voce.*

טבח, גחם, and תחשׁ are all uncertain; מעכה, also ארם מעכה, 1 Ch. 19, 6, a district and kingdom at the foot of Mount Hermon, not far from Geshur; cf. Deut. 3, 14. Josh. 12, 5. 13, 11. 2 Sam. 10, 6. 8.

23.

1. שְׁנֵי חַיֵּי שָׂרָה. The phrase שני חיי פ״ is only found (in the Pent.) in P; so 25, 7. 47, 9. 28.

2. קִרְיַת אַרְבַּע. '*Arba' city*,' so called perhaps from Arba', one of the giants who formed the original inhabitants of the land; cf. Josh. 14, 15. 15, 13. 21, 11. Others (Ewald, etc.) explain it as = '*Four town*,' i.e. '*town of the four quarters*,' a possible explanation of the name, perhaps favoured by 35, 27 where ארבע has the art. Here and in 35, 27. Josh. 20, 7. 21, 11 (P). 15, 13. (? D[2]) קרית ארבע is also called Hebron—cf. Num. 13, 22—which seems to have been the more modern name of the town; cf. Josh. 14, 15. Judg. 1, 10. In ver. 19 Mamre is identified with Hebron, and in 35, 27 the town is thrice named, Mamre, Kiryath Arba', and Hebron; so that Mamre was either another name of Hebron, or must have formed a portion of it, or have belonged to it. The LXX have an addition in their text, ἥ ἐστιν ἐν τῷ κοιλώματι, perhaps a marginal gloss, occasioned by 37, 14 מעמק חברון. The Sam. also insert אל עמק between ארבע and הוא. Hebron, the modern *El-Ḫalîl* is about eight hours south of Jerusalem, almost mid-way between that city and Beersheba. It lies in a narrow, deep valley which declines from the NW. to the SE., the town being built on both sides of the valley. The mosque, which is erected at the S.E. end of the town, encloses the cave of Machpelah. Cf. Di., p. 299; Bäd., *Pal.*, p. 137 f.; Sh., *G.*, p. 317 f.

לִבְכֹּתָהּ, with כף זעירא, '*small Caph:*' there seems to be no reason for כ being written smaller than the other letters here, see another instance 2, 4, and the note there; cf. Strack, *Proleg.*, p. 92, who does not, however, mention this passage or 2, 4.

3. מֵתוֹ '*his dead:*' of common gender here, as in Lev. 21, 11. Num. 6, 6; contrast Zech. 11, 9 הַמֵּתָה '*the dying one.*' The distinction of gender in the case of a dead person being less regarded than in that of a living person (Del.); cf. Ges., § 122. 2. Rem. 1; M. R., § 62.

אל בני חת. בני חת is only found in P: in 14, 13 they are called Amorites, and in Judg. 1, 10 Canaanites.

4. Family graves were not uncommon among the people of high rank; cf. Judg. 8, 32. 2 Sam. 2, 32. 1 Kings 13, 30, and Is. 22, 16, where Shebna the scribe hews out of the rock a sepulchre for himself.

תושב is characteristic of P.

6. As לאמר לו (ver. 5) is a very unusual phrase (לאמר אליהם is found once, Lev. 11, 1), Hitzig's conjecture לוּ שְׁמָעֵנוּ—which is adopted by most commentators, and brings the text here in accordance with ver. 13—seems preferable. So in ver. 15 we must read לוּ אֲדוֹנִי. לוּ then, here and vers. 13. 15, will be followed by the imperative (cf. 17, 18 with the imperf.; 30, 34 with the jussive); see Ges., § 110. 1. Rem. 2; Dav., *S.*, § 134, '*Pray hear us.*' 'In accordance with the politeness which both parties endeavour to shew (Di.).' LXX and Sam. understand לו as = לא; then the text ought to be inverted לא אדני שמענו, as in ver. 11.

נשיא אלהים = '*a prince of God,*' i.e. belonging to God, under God's protection, and blessed by Him, and so a mighty and distinguished prince; cf. Pss. 36, 7. 80, 11.

במבחר קברינו, lit. = '*in the choice of our sepulchres,*' i.e.

'*in our choicest sepulchre,*' cf. Is. 22, 7 מבחר עמקיך. The usual order of the words is here abandoned, the noun expressing the quality preceding, instead of following, the noun which it qualifies; cf. Ges., § 128. 2. Rem. 1; and see also Dav., *S.*, § 34. R. 5.

יִכְלֶה = יִכְלָא, a verb ל״א following the conjugation of a verb ל״ה; cf. Ges., § 75. Rem. 21 c; Stade, § 143 e, note 1 *a*.

מקבר מתך; cf. on 16, 2 מלדת.

8. אם יש את נפשכם, lit. = '*if it is with your soul,*' i.e. '*if it be your intention;*' cf. 2 Kings 9, 15 אם־יש נפשכם; Ges., § 159. 3. 5.

9. המכפלה. LXX, τὸ σπήλαιον τὸ διπλοῦν, Vulg. '*speluncam duplicem,*' i.e. a cave with two entrances or two compartments, from the root כפל; but—as may be seen from vers. 17. 19, and 49, 30—המכפלה is a proper name.

בכסף מלא = '*for full money,*' i.e. for its full value in money; cf. 1 Chron. 21, 22 תנה לי מקום הגרן . . . בכסף מלא, 24 לא כי קנה אקנה בכסף מלא.

10. לכל באי שער וגו׳. Cf. on 9, 10 and Ewald, § 310 a. באי וגו׳ is the shorter form for באים ויוצאים. Render as R.V., '*Even of all those entering the gate of his city,*' i.e. his fellow-citizens. ל = the German *nämlich*, '*I mean*' or '*that is to say.*'

11. לא אדני שמעני. '*Nay, my lord, hear me.*' Hitzig and Maurer read לא as לו = לוּא; cf. vers. 13. 15, and see 1 Sam. 14, 30. 2 Sam. 18, 12, which is unnecessary, as לא suits the context better, Ephron refusing at first to receive anything for the field till Abraham presses it upon him.

The same politeness and apparent unwillingness to sell anything, but rather to give it, still prevails in the east; cf. Del.[4], p. 553, and [5], p. 334.

נתתי is perfect of certitude, often used in contracts or promises; cf. Ruth 4, 3 מכרה נעמי '*No'omi is selling*,' 1 Kings 3, 13 גם אשר לא שאלת נתתי לך; Is. 43, 20 כי נתתי במדבר מים; cf. Driver, § 13; M. R., § 3. 1 a; Dav., *S.*, § 41 a; Ges., § 106. 3 a.

13. '*And he spake unto Ephron in the ears of the people of the land, saying, If only thou—pray hear me—I give the money for the field, take it from me, that I may bury my dead there.*' The optative sentence beginning with אם is broken off, and continued with לו and the imperative. Olshausen supposes that some words have dropped out of the text after אתה. Hitzig ingeniously renders אִם אָתָה, as perfect Qal of אות '*if thou art willing*,' which is quite suitable; but the Qal of אות occurs nowhere else, the verb being only found in the Nif'al; cf. 34, 15. LXX have ἐπειδὴ πρὸς ἐμοῦ εἶ; πρὸς ἐμοῦ = '*on my side*,' cf. LXX, 29, 34 and 31, 5, and Dr., p. 182.

15. Cf. on ver. 6. The LXX and Sam. have also read לא here.

16. עבר לסחר. '*Current with the merchants*;' the art. is according to Ges., § 126. 3 a; M. R., § 68; Dav., *S.*, § 22 b; cf. the shorter phrase in 2 Kings 12, 5 כסף עבר '*current money*,' i. e. such as the merchants would accept. 'People had at that time no coins issued by the State, but only bits of metal—which came into use through the requirements of trade—of fixed weights, and possibly with the weight marked on them; these pieces were weighed to avoid any fraud,' Knobel, cited by Di., p. 298.

17. ויקם. '*So the field .... was ensured to Abraham*;'

cf. Driver, § 74 a; M. R., § 18. Rem. a; Ges., § 111. 3 a. קום in this sense occurs again in Lev. 25, 30. 27, 14. 17. 19. This use of קום is peculiar to P.

לפני ממרא=‘*before*,’ i. e. ‘*east of*;’ so על פני in ver. 19; cf. 16, 12.

18. בכל באי וגו״. ב corresponds to ל in ver. 10; it is distributive here, as in 7, 21, which compare.

19. שׂדה המכפלה. מכפלה is only found in P; so again 25, 9. 49, 30. 50, 13.

ממרא הוא חברון. Observe that P never mentions the אלוני ממרא (13, 18. 14, 13. 18, 1), but calls the place ממרא; so 25, 9. 35, 27. 49, 30. 50, 13.

24.

2. זקן ביתו=‘*the old one of his house*,’ i. e. ‘*the oldest*;’ so 42, 13 הקטן ‘*the young one*,’ i. e. ‘*the youngest one*;’ 2 Chron. 21, 17 קטן בניו ‘*his youngest son*;’ cf. M. R., § 81 b, and note on 10, 21. Probably Eliezer is the servant here intended. The Targ. Ps.-Jon. mentions him here expressly by name. Each large household had a servant of this sort; cf. Joseph in 39, 4. 22 (Ps. 105, 21), also 43, 16. 44, 1 אשׁר על ביתו. At a later period the office was one of the important posts at court; cf. 1 Kings 4, 6. Is. 22, 15.

שׂים נא ידך תחת ירכי=‘*place thy hand under my thigh*,’ i. e. swear to me; cf. 47, 29, which is the only other passage where this mode of swearing is mentioned. Some (Tuch, Del.) see a reference to circumcision in these words. Others (Di.) explain—from 46, 26. Ex. 1, 5. Judg. 8, 30—the words symbolically, as invoking his descendants to maintain the oath and avenge any infraction of it; cf. Di., p. 301, who cites an instance of a similar form of oath among the Bedouins in Egypt; also the following extract from the *Journals of Expeditions in North-west and West Australia*, by George Grey, vol. ii, p. 342, London, 1841: 'Genesis, chap. 24, ver. 9,' after quoting the verse from the A.V. the writer continues, 'this is exactly the form that is observed in south-western Australia, when the natives swear amity to one another, or pledge themselves to aid one another in avenging a death. One native remains seated on the ground with his heels tucked under him in the eastern manner; the one who is about to narrate a death to him approaches slowly and with averted face, and seats himself cross-legged upon the thighs of the other; they are thus placed thigh to thigh, and squeezing their bodies together they place breast to breast—both then avert their faces, their eyes frequently fill with tears—no single word is spoken, and the one who is seated uppermost *places his hands under the thighs of his friend;* having remained thus seated for a minute or two, he rises up and withdraws to a little distance without speaking, but an inviolate pledge to avenge the death has by this ceremony passed between the two[1].' Ibn Ezra in his commentary on the passage has the following: שׂים נא ידך תחת ירכי. יש אמר רמז למילה ואילו היה כן היה נשבע בברית המילה לא בשם והקרוב אלי שהיה משפט בימים ההם לשום אדם ידו תחת ירך מי שהוא ברשותו והטעם אם אתה ברשותי שים נא ידך תחת ירכי והאדון יושב והירך על היד כטעם הנה ידי תחת רשותך לעשות רצונך וזה המשפט עדיין הוא בארץ הודו. '*Some say this refers to circumcision; but if this were so, he would have sworn by the*

[1] For this reference I am indebted to Prof. Driver, who kindly sent me a note he had received on this verse from Dr. Tylor, the Reader (now Prof.) in Anthropology at Oxford.

covenant of circumcision, and not by Jehovah. What appears most probable to me is, that it was a custom in those days for a man to place his hand under the thigh of him in whose service he was: the meaning would then be, "if thou art in my service, place thy hand, I pray, under my thigh;" the master would thus be sitting with his thigh on the (servant's) hand; the meaning being, "behold, my hand is under thy authority to do thy will;" and this custom still exists in India.'

4. כי = '*but*,' after the negative; cf. 45, 8. 1 Kings 21, 15; see Ewald, § 354 a (who compares the German *sondern* (not *aber*) after *nicht*); Ges., § 163. 1; Dav., *S.*, § 155. Fifteen MSS. and the Heb.-Sam. Codex read כִּי־אִם.

לבני ליצחק. When the pr. name follows the subs., the preposition must be repeated; cf. 4, 2. 21, 10. 48, 13 (an exception in ver. 12); when it precedes, it only stands with the pr. name; cf. 11, 31. 12, 5. 14, 16. 16, 3. 20, 14. 22, 20; see M. R., § 71. 1. Rem. a; Dav., *S.*, § 29 a.

5. הֶהָשֵׁב. ה pointed with seghol before the guttural with qameç, Ges., § 100. 4; Dav., § 49. 2 d.

7. '*The God of the heavens who took me . . . may He* (emphatic) *send His angel before thee, and mayest thou*,' etc.

ישלח . . . ולקחת. The perfect with waw conv. after the imperfect as a jussive; cf. 1, 14 (note), 28, 3. 43, 14. 47, 29 f., and often; see Driver, § 113. 2 a, cf. § 111.

8. ואם לא תאבה . . . ונקית. '*But if she does not consent, then thou art free*.' נִקִּיתָ for נִקֵּיתָ, Ges., § 75. Rem. 7: the tone does not advance with ו conv. as the verb is a ל״ה verb; cf. Stade, § 470 b. note.

משבעתי זאת. זאת without the article as regularly after

a word with a pronom. affix; see Ewald, § 293 a; Driver, § 209. Obs.; Ges., § 126. 5. R. 1 b; Dav., *S.*, § 32 and R. 3.

לא תשב. Cf. the note on 4, 12.

9. אדניו is *pluralis excellentiae*, referring to Abraham; see Ewald, § 178 b; Ges., § 124. 1 c; Dav., *S.*, § 16 c; cf. Stade, § 324 a; so 40, 1 לאדוניהם למלך, of Pharaoh; 42, 30 אדוני הארץ, of Joseph.

10. כל טוב אדניו. LXX. ἀπὸ πάντων τῶν ἀγαθῶν; so 45, 18 את טוב ארץ מצרים; 2 Kings 8, 9 וכל טוב דמשק.

ארם נהרים. '*Aram of the two rivers*,' i.e. Mesopotamia, Deut. 23, 5. Judg. 3, 8. The two rivers are usually identified with the Euphrates and Tigris, so Del.[5] Halévy, cited by Di., p. 302, takes them to be the Euphrates and Chrysorrhoas. Di. himself, with greater probability, thinks that the Euphrates and Chaboras (חָבוֹר) are the two rivers intended.

11. אל באר המים, i.e. the fountain that is usually to be found near a town; cf. Ex. 2, 15; see Ewald, § 277 a.

12. הַקְרֵה נא. '*Pray cause it to meet me;*' cf. 9, 22 for the omission of the acc., and the note there; see also 27, 20 כי הקרה יהוה אלהיך לפני.

14. '*May it be that the damsel to whom I shall say, Pray let down thy pitcher that I may drink, and she answer, Drink, and I will also water thy camels;* (*may it be that*) *her thou hast adjudged to thy servant Isaac, and thereby I shall know that thou hast shewn my master kindness.*'

וְהָיָה is the perf. with waw conv., where no imperf. precedes, used as a precative or mild imperative; cf. 47, 23 וזרעתם את האדמה; Deut. 7, 9 וידעת; Driver, § 119 d; Ges., § 112. 4 b. R.

אשר אמר . . . ואמרה. ואמרה is perf. with waw conv. after an imperf. with אשר; cf. ver. 43, where the relative is avoided; so Lev. 21, 10 אשר יוצק . . . ומלא; Is. 56, 4 אשר ישמרו . . . ובחרו; Judg. 1, 12. 1 Sam. 17, 26; see Driver, p. 131.

הנער . . . אשקה is a *casus pendens*, resumed in אֹתָהּ, which stands before its verb for emphasis; cf. 26, 15. 28, 13; Driver, § 197. 1; Dav., *S.*, § 106 c; Ges., § 143 b. The text is to be pointed הַנַּעֲר, this word being of common gender in the Pentateuch, also in Ruth 2, 21; cf. Ges., § 122. 2. Rem. 2 and § 2. 5. Rem.; Dav., *S.*, § 12 c; Ewald, § 175 b; Stade, § 309 d, who regards נער as 'a remnant of an older period of the language, when the feminine ending did not exist.' The Kri directs the ordinary form to be read.

בָּהּ is not '*through her,*' Ribqah, but '*thereby;*' cf. 15, 6. 8. 42, 36. 47, 26. Ex. 10, 11. Num. 14, 41; Dav., *S.*, § 1. R. 2; Ges., § 135. 5. R. 2; M. R., § 63.

15. '*And it came to pass before he had done speaking, that, behold, R. was coming out,*' etc. טרם כלה, the perf. after טרם is very rare (Driver, p. 32. foot-note 1), contrast ver. 45 טרם אכלה. The perfect after טרם is found again, 1 Sam. 3, 7 טרם ידע את יי" (if the punctuation is right), but immediately afterwards וטרם יגלה; cf. בטרם, Ps. 90, 2 בטרם . . . ילדו; Prov. 8, 25 בטרם הרים הטבעו; see Ewald, § 337. 3 c; Ges., § 107. 1. Rem. 1.

אשר ילדה לבתואל וגו". Possibly לבתואל בן is a later addition to the text, which originally may have run אֲשֶׁר יָלְדָה מִלְכָּה. Cf. Di. ad loc., who points out that the passive is strange and, that to describe Bethuel as '*the son of Milkah,*' here and ver. 24 is unusual, men generally being named after the father. Laban too, in 29, 5 is described as the '*son of Nahor,*' cf. 24, 48, not of Bethuel. In ver. 24 Di.

proposes to read instead of בתואל אנכי בן מלכה,—מלכה אנכי, cf. 34. 1.

וכדה על שכמה. '*With her pitcher on her shoulder,*' circ. clause; Dav., *S.*, § 138; cf. note on 18, 16.

16. **טבת מראה.** Cf. 12, 11 יפת מראה, and the note there, and add 26, 7. 29, 17. 39, 6. 41, 2–6.

בתולה = '*a virgin,*' from בתל '*secludere,*' Arab. بَتَلَ '*secuit, separavit,*' the maiden who lives in seclusion in her parents' home. עלמה from עלם, Arab. غَلِمَ '*to be strong,*' '*fully ripe,*' = the maiden who had reached a marriageable age, *puella nubilis.* In עלמה stress is laid on the fact that the maiden is of a marriageable age, in בתולה that she is a virgin; so here we have the addition ואיש לא ידעה.

19. **עד אם כלו לשתת.** '*Until they shall have finished drinking,*' כלו being a future perfect; so עד אם דברתי, ver. 33. Is. 30, 17 עד אם נותרתם כתרן; and with the fuller phrase, עד אשר אם, Gen. 28, 15 עד אשר אם עשיתי; Num. 32, 17 עד אשר אם הביאנם; see Driver, § 17; M. R., § 3. 2; Ges., § 106. 3 c; Dav., *S.*, § 41 c.

21. **והאיש משתאה לה מחריש.** '*And the man was watching her in silence.*'

משתאה is the construct state before the preposition לה; cf. הוסי בו, Ps. 2, 12; יושבי בארץ, Is. 9, 1; משחרי לטרף, Job 24, 5; see Ewald, § 289 b; Ges., § 130. 1; Dav., *S.*, § 28. R. 1; M. R., § 73. R. a.

מחריש defines משתאה more clearly; cf. Num. 16, 27 יצאו נצבים; Judg. 1, 7 בהנות ידיהם ורגליהם מקצצים היו מלקטים; Jer. 41, 6 ויצא . . . הלך . . . ובכה; cf. Ewald, § 341 b. 3; Dr., § 161. 2; Dav., *S.*, § 70; Ges., §§ 118. 5; 120. 1 a; M. R., § 43.

22. נזם is '*a nose ring;*' cf. ver. 47, where על אפה is added; here the Sam. have וישׂם על אפה after מִשקלו, which Di. considers the original reading.

בקע is '*a half-shekel,*' it occurs once again, Ex. 38, 26.

עשׂרה. שקל must be understood here, as in 20, 16.

23. בית אביך is acc. of place, as in 18, 1, which compare.

27. אנכי בדרך נחני וגו״. '*As for me, in the way hath Y. guided me.*' אנכי, *casus pendens;* cf. 17, 4. 48, 7. 49, 8; see Driver, § 197. 4; M. R., § 129; and cf. note on ver. 14.

בדרך, i.e. without any mistakes, straight to the house of his master's kinsmen (or kinsman if the reading of the LXX אֲחִי be followed; cf. ver. 48 and Di.'s proposed emendation in ver. 15); cf. ver. 48 בדרך אמת.

28. לבית אמה, i.e. to the female members of the family. Ribqah, as a בתולה, would live apart from the men, among the females of the family.

29b. וירץ לבן . . . אל העין. Di. regards this half-verse as out of place here [er greift in unerträglicher (durch ver. 10 nicht zu rechtfertigender) Weise dem ver. 30 vor], having been placed here, instead of after ver. 30a (before ויבא), by a copyist's mistake. Knobel regards it as a doublet, or in ver. 30, ויבא may be explained by Driver, § 76 γ, as giving a more detailed account of Laban's running.

30. כראת את הנזם. On the inf. cstr. without a subject, cf. M. R., §§ 111 b, 117; Dav., *S.*, § 91. R. 1; Ewald, § 304 a; 19, 29. 25, 26 בלדת אתם; 1 Sam. 18, 19 בעת תת את מרב; 2 Sam. 17, 9 כנפל בהם בתחלה; Ps. 42, 4 באמר אלי כל היום. The Sam. read the more correct form כראתו '*when he saw.*'

In Ges., § 115. 2. foot-note 1, it is suggested that the text originally was כִּרְאוֹת לָבָן.

הִנֵּה עֹמֵד. הנה, placed before the participle, as in 38, 24 וגם הנה הרה; Is. 29, 8 והנה אֹכל, to arrest the attention and give more liveliness to the narrative; cf. Ewald, § 306 d; Driver, § 135. 3. Obs. 1. The subject to the participle is omitted as in 37, 15. 41, 1 etc. See on 32, 7.

31. '*And he said, Come in, blessed of the Lord, why dost thou stand without, seeing I have prepared my house, and a place for the camels?*' cf. ver. 56; Josh. 17, 14 ואני עם רב '*seeing I am a great people;*' Judg. 3, 26 והוא עבר '*he having passed;*' see note on 20, 3, and cf. Ges., § 142. R. 1.

32. Laban is probably the subject to ויפתח and ויתן, as one can hardly suppose that Abraham's servant would be so inhospitably treated that he had to unsaddle his own camels. It would be easier if the text ran וַיָּבֵא (instead of וַיָּבֹא), which Dathe and Olsh. prefer, but this again would require את האיש instead of האיש.

33. The Ktb. is וַיִּישֶׂם '*he (Laban) set,*' imperf. Qal of ישׂם = שׂוּם; cf. 50, 26 ויישם without Kri. But as the root ישׂם does not exist, it is better to follow the Kri here וַיּוּשַׂם '*and there was placed,*' impf. Hof'al of שׂוּם, with pathach not qameç; cf. König, *Lehrg.*, i. p. 435 f., and see Baer and Del., *Genesis*, p. 77. Stade, § 500 γ, reads here וַיָּשֶׂם, the ordinary imperf. Qal of שׂוּם. Ewald, § 131 d, considers that the û of the passive here, 50, 26 and Ex. 30, 32 (ייסך from סוך), has been sharpened into î.

38. אִם לֹא, prop. = '*if not,*' after a negative '*but;*' cf. (possibly) Ez. 3, 6 אם לא אליהם שלחתיך; see Ges., § 149. Rem. a.

אם לא . . . תלך . . . ולקחת. The imperf. with waw conv. after אִם in an oath. So Ez. 20, 33 f. . . . אם לא אמלך . . . והוצאתי . . . וקבצתי; see Driver, § 115.

42–43. אם ישך . . . מצליח . . . והיה; cf. Lev. 3, 7 אם כשׂב הוא מקריב . . . והקריב; Judg. 6, 36 f. . . . אם ישך מושיע וידעתי; hypothetical sentences with a participle, with or without יֵשׁ or אין in the protasis, and the perfect with waw conv. in the apodosis; see Driver, § 137 a; Ewald, § 355 b. 1; M. R., § 166. 2; Ges., § 159. 3. 5; Dav., *S.*, § 130 a; cf. 20, 7, and ver. 49, where imperatives take the place of the perfect with waw conv. in the apodosis; and 43, 4, where the cohortative stands in the apodosis.

46. וָאֵשְׁתְּ. The short form of the first pers. sing. imperf. in ל״ה verbs is not quite so frequent as the long. Böttcher, cited by Driver (*Tenses*, p. 74. note 4), mentions forty-nine instances of the short form, and fifty-three of the long. In the other persons, on the contrary, the full form is very exceptional.

47. בתואל בן may be a gloss, cf. on ver. 15.

וָאָשִׂם In the first pers. sing. imperf. with waw conv., the tone is not drawn back. Cf. Driver, p. 74. foot-note 2.

48. ואשתחוה here, and וָאֲצַוֶּה, Deut. 1, 16. 18, are the only instances of the first pers. with ה ֶ in the Pentateuch. Cf. Ges., § 75. Rem. 3 e.

בדרך אמת '*in the right way;*' cf. ver. 27.

49. '*And now, if ye are going to deal kindly and straightforwardly with my master, tell me; and if not, tell me; that I may turn to the right hand, or to the left;*' cf. ver. 42 f. and the authorities there cited.

50. As Bethuel is not mentioned in vers. 53. 55 ff. the word may, as Di. suggests, be an insertion here; cf. ver. 15.

55. יָמִים אוֹ עָשׂוֹר, lit.=*'days or ten,'* i.e. *'a week or ten days;'* cf. 4, 3 ויהי מקץ ימים; LXX, *ἡμέρας ὡσεὶ δέκα.* The Pesh. has ܝܪܚܐ ܒܝܘܡܬܐ *'a month in days,'* Sam. ימים או חדש; possibly, as Ols. suggests, חדש has fallen out before ימים; cf. 29, 14. עָשׂוֹר=*decas, 'a space of ten days.'*

56. ויהוה הצליח דרכי. *'Seeing Yahweh hath prospered my way;'* cf. 18, 16.

57. ונשאלה את פיה. *'And let us ask her, herself,'* lit. *'ask her mouth,'* i.e. let her speak for herself; cf. Josh. 9, 14 ואת פי יהוה לא שאלו; Is. 30, 2 ופי לא שאלו.

62. *'Now Isaac had come;'* בא is pluperf., accounting for Isaac's presence when Ribqah arrived; cf. Driver, p. 84.

בא מבוא באר usually would mean, *'had come from coming to the well,'* etc., i.e. had returned from a journey thither. But לֶכֶת is the more suitable word for a journey. Del.[5] takes מבוא as=מִלְּבוֹא, 1 Kings 8, 65,—cf. לָבוֹא 35, 16 and לְבֹא Num. 13, 21,—and explains the sentence as = not that he was just returning from a visit to the Hagar well, but from an evening walk in the direction of this his favourite place, a place hallowed by a manifestation of God. Houbigant reads מֵעַם for מבוא, Lagarde מִבְּאֵר. But against Del., and against the proposed emendations, it may be urged that one does not see why the place where he came from should be noted. One would rather expect to be told where he had come to, or where he was. Ewald, § 136 h, renders, *'er war eben gekommen nach'* (*he had just come to*), but how this can be got out of the Heb. text is not quite clear. Di. offers two solutions of the question; either (1) to strike out מבוא, or

(II) to read מדבר from במדבר, which the Samaritan and LXX have instead of מְבוֹא. '*Isaac had come to the wilderness of Beer-laḥayroi, for he lived in the south*' (circ. clause; cf. note on 20, 3 and see Dr., p. 199). Beer-Laḥayroi would then be the place where Isaac met his bride.

63. לשׂוח variously rendered: I. '*To meditate*,' either over his approaching marriage (Del.), or on matters connected with his flocks (Tuch); so LXX, ἀδολεσχῆσαι, Vulg. '*ad meditandum in agro*;' לָשׂוּחַ = לָשִׂיחַ in Ps. 119, 148; cf. Ps. 77, 4. 7. II. The Targg., Sam., etc. render, '*to pray*;' cf. Ps. 102, 1 שִׂיחוֹ, with תפלה in the parallel member of the verse. III. Aq. ὁμιλῆσαι and Sym. λαλῆσαι take לשׂוח as = '*to talk*.' IV. Knobel and Ewald render, '*to wail* or *lament*,' comparing שִׂיחַ in Pss. 55, 3. 18. 142, 3. Job 7, 11, etc. (see ver. 67). V. Bött., *Neue Heb. Aehr.*, renders, '*to fetch brushwood*:' the verb being a denom. from שִׂיחַ, but this denom. cannot be proved to exist from other passages; cf. Ibn Ezra, ללכת בין השׂיחים '*to walk between the shrubs*.' VI. Ges. reads לָשׂוּט; cf. the Pesh., which has ܠܡܬܚܠܟܘ '*to walk*,' and ver. 65 ההלך בשׂדה. It is not improbable that the Pesh. has preserved the original text. If the reading be not altered to לָשׂוּט, perhaps rendering IV. '*to lament*' should be adopted, as this suits the context (ver. 67) better than I. '*to meditate*.'

לפנות ערב, i.e. when the Oriental used to go out; cf. 3, 8 לרוח היום.

64. ותפל מעל הגמל; so 2 Kings 5, 21 ויפל מעל המרכבה. In Judg. 1, 14 (= Josh. 15, 18) we find צנח '*to spring quickly from the ass*.' LXX here κατεπήδησεν.

65. מי האיש הלזה. '*Who is yonder man?*' cf. Ges.,

§ 34. 2. R. 2; Dav., § 13; Stade, § 172 b. הלזה (only here and 37, 19), cf. the Arabic ٱلَّذِى = *who, which;* and Wright, *Comp. Gram.*, p. 117.

הצעיף only occurs again in 38, 14. 19. It comes from the root צעף = Arabic ضعف, conj. III = *duplicavit*, '*to lay* or *fold together;*' cf. Del.[5], p. 345, and Dr., p. 223, who points out that Lagarde, *Semitica*, p. 24, holds that צעיף is properly some *square* garment.

67. האהלה שרה. אהל with the article and ה of motion. The presence of the article before the noun, which is (apparently) in the construct state, is explained by Ewald, § 290 d, as a loose co-ordination of the two words, instead of the second being subordinate to the first; cf. 1 Kings 14, 24. Di. rightly regards שרה אמו as inexplicable, and considers that the words are a gloss to bring about a closer connection with chap. 23. See also, Ges., § 127. Rem. 4 a; Dav., *S.*, § 20. R. 4.

25.

1. אשה, not in the sense Sarah was, but a concubine; cf. ver. 6, where she is called a פלגש, and 1 Chron. 1, 32.

קטורה, pr. name = '*incense.*'

2. Many of the following tribes cannot be identified with certainty, as they have either disappeared at an early date, or become merged into other tribes. The genealogy occurs again in 1 Chron. 1, 32 ff. in an abbreviated form.

Keturah bare Abraham six sons (five if we regard מדן and מדין as one and the same).

זמרן, perhaps from זֶמֶר, a species of '*antelope.*' Knobel compares זמרן with Ζαβράμ, the royal town of the Κιναιδοκολπῖται, to the west of Mecca, on the Red Sea, mentioned in

Ptol. vi. 7, 5, but whether they are identical is uncertain. Grotius and Del.[4] consider the Zamareni of Pliny vi. 32 as more probable.

יקשן is identified by Tuch with יָקְטָן (10, 26); by Ewald with כּוּשָׁן, Hab. 3, 7; by Knobel with the Κασσανῖται of Ptol. vi. 7, 6, south of the Kinaedokolpites, on the Red Sea, but these are the Gassanides (cf. Del.[5] here and Di.).

מדין and מדן, the best known of the sons of Keturah. מדינים and מדנים occur again in 37, 28. 36 as names of the same people, so that probably מדן and מדין are but different forms of the same name. The Midianites are often mentioned in the O.T.; in 37, 28. 36 (E) they are spoken of as carrying on trade with Egypt. In Ex. 2 and 18 we find them dwelling in the Sinaitic peninsula, and in Num. 22, 4. 7. 25, 6. 17 f. 31, 1 ff. they are mentioned among Israel's enemies in the land east of the Jordan. In the time of the Judges (cf. Judg. 6 ff.) hordes of Midianites overran Palestine. They are also mentioned in Is. 60, 6 as a trading people. Their territory on the east of the Ælanitic Gulf stretched from the neighbourhood of Sinai northwards to the territory of the Moabites; see further, Di., p. 309, who suggests that the two tribes mentioned here may have been neighbours.

ישבק is unknown. Fried. Del. thinks that it is Jasbuq, mentioned in the Cuneiform inscriptions; cf. *Z. K. S. F.*, ii. 92.

שוח is mentioned in Job 2, 11 as a tribe in the neighbourhood of the land of עוץ, but otherwise unknown. Del., *Par.*, p. 297 f. (see also Schrader, *K. G. F.*, pp. 142 f., 222), compares the Assyrian *Suchu*, on the right bank of the Euphrates, between the estuary of the Beliḫ and that of the

Chaboras; apparently accepted by Di., who also mentions another identification with the Σαύη of Ptol. v. 19, 5; cf. Di., l. c.

3. On שׁבא and דדן, see 10, 7. Probably the northern branches of these two great Arab tribes are here meant, the genealogy in these verses being more limited in range than that in chap. 10 (Di.). Of the sons of Dedan nothing further is known; see conjectures in Di., p. 309; Del.[5], p. 347.

4. עיפה occurs again in Is. 60, 6, mentioned with Midian as rich in camels, and as bringing gold and incense from Sheba. Del., *Par.*, p. 304, compares the *Ḥajapâ* of the inscriptions, a North Arabian people between Mecca and Medina. The other names do not occur elsewhere; see Di., p. 310, for conjectures about them.

8. ושׂבע. Sam., LXX, ושׂבע ימים as in 35, 29.

ויאסף אל עמיו. '*And was gathered to his people;*' cf. the synonymous expressions, בוא אל אבותיך, 15, 15; נאסף אל אבותיו, Judg. 2, 10; and שׁכב עם אבותיך, Deut. 31, 16. The phrase נאסף אל עמיו is peculiar to P; so in 35, 29. 49, 33, etc.

10. השׂדה is in apposition to שׂדה עפרן in ver. 9.

שׁמה = not '*thither*,' but, in a weaker sense, '*there;*' so Jer. 18, 2 ושׁמה אשׁמיעך את דברי; 2 Kings 23, 8 אשׁר קטרו שׁמה הכהנים; see Ges., § 90. 2 b.

13. בשׁמתם לתולדתם. '*With their names, according to their genealogies.*' The two words are to be taken closely together.

נבית the best known and most important of the descendants of Ishmael, '*the Nabatheans.*' The Nabatheans dwelt in Arabia Petrea. In Is. 60, 7 they are mentioned with Kedar; the two names also being found together on the Assyrian inscriptions of Assurbanipal (Schr., *C. O. T.*, p. 133). Probably they are identical with the Nabataei and Cedrei, mentioned together by Pliny, v. 12. The only other notices about נביות in the O. T. are that Esau (28, 9. 36, 3) married Maḥalath (called, 36, 3, Basemath), the sister of Nebayoth, and Is. l.c., that they were rich in cattle. In the history of Israel, up to the Persian period, the Nabatheans are nowhere mentioned, but probably their name is found in the Assyrian inscriptions (Schr., *K. G. F.*, p. 102) *Nabaitai*. After the breaking asunder and division of the Macedonian kingdom, the Nabatheans appear, as an important Arabian people, occupying the territory of the Idumeans in S. Canaan, their capital being Petra. After the fall of the Selucidaean kingdom they gained the supremacy in the land on the east of the Jordan, and in the Syrian Desert (1 Macc. 5, 25. 9, 35), as far as the Haurân and Damascus (Jos., *Ant.*, xiii. 15. 2), and penetrated south, not only to Elath, but for some distance into Arabia proper (Diod., 3. 43. Steph. Byz.), so that at that time they were regarded as the Arabians, on the frontier of the Syrians (Strabo, xvi. 4. 18. 21; Pliny, xii. § 73), and the whole land from the Euphrates to the Red Sea was called Nabatene (Jos., *Ant.*, i. 12. 4). They had their own kings, and were of great repute both as warriors and as successful traders. Their kingdom was destroyed by Trajan, and fresh hordes of Arabs entered the extensive territories over which they had previously ruled. Whether these later Nabatheans are to be connected with the Nebayoth is uncertain. Cf. Di., p. 313 (from whom the above paragraph is adapted); Del.[5], p. 350 f.; see further, Di., p. 312; Sh., *G.*, p. 547, cf. p. 620 f.; Bäd., *Pal.*, p. lvi.

קדר. '*The Kedarenes.*' A nomad tribe in the Syro-Arabian desert; they are frequently mentioned in the O. T. in the time of the kings. In Is. 21, 16 f. they are described as skilled bow-men; Song of Songs 1, 5, as dwelling in black tents, but Is. 42, 11. Jer. 49, 31, in open villages. In Is. 60, 7. Jer. 49, 32 they are spoken of as rich in camels and flocks; and in Ez. 27, 21 as trading with Tyre. The Rabbis use the name קדר for Arabia in general, לשון קדר being the Arabic language.

אדבאל and מבשׂם are unknown names.

14. משׁמע is uncertain; cf. Di., p. 313 f.

דומה is probably different from the Duma of Is. 21, 11. and Josh. 15, 52. Wetzstein identifies דומה here with the Duma in East Haurân. Di. and Del. consider it to be the Δούμαθα of Steph. Byz., Domata of Pliny, vi. 32, the modern دومة الجندل = '*the rocky Duma,*' in the lowest-lying district of the Syrian Nufûd land; the so-called Gôf (Del.), on the borders of Syria and Arabia.

משׂא, usually connected with the Μασανοί of Ptol. v. 19. 2, north-east of Duma. In Assurbanipal's inscriptions, *Mas'u* is found together with *Nabaitai* and *Ḳidri*, Schr., *K. G. F.*, p. 102; *C. O. T.*, p. 135.

15. חדד is unknown. Baer and Del. read חדד, Theile חדר, with the marg. note, בספרים אחרים חדד, i.e. '*in other copies* חדד;' so 1 Chron. 1, 30, Sam., Josephus. The Massora mentions the reading here as being חדד, not חדר; cf. Baer and Del., *Gen.*, p. 77 f.

תימא is identified by Wetzstein with Taimâ, three-quarters of an hour from Duma, in the Haurân; by Knobel with Θαιμοί, Ptol. vi. 7. 17, on the Persian Gulf, or the Banu Taim (بنو تيم) also on the Persian Gulf; by Di. and Del. with תימא, a tribe mentioned in Jer. 25, 23. Job 6, 19, as traders (cf. Is. 21, 14)=تَيْمَآءُ, on the western border of the Neǵd, S. E. of the northern end of the Ælanitic Gulf; also found on the inscriptions, together with the *Mas'ai* (Schr., *C. O. T.*, p. 135 f.). On the inscriptions discovered at Têmâ by Huber and Euting, see *S. B. A. W.*, 1884, p. 813 f.

יטור and נפיש are mentioned (1 Chron. 5, 18 ff.) as neighbours of the tribes east of the Jordan, who made war against them and partially subdued them; נפיש is otherwise unknown. יטור, '*the Itureans*,' are frequently mentioned from 105 B.C. as a wild and rapacious people dwelling in mountains which were difficult of access and full of caves. In the Roman period they seem to have been located in the hill country of Lebanon and Anti-Lebanon, but may, at an earlier date, have possessed territories further south. They were famous bow-men; cf. Di., p. 314; Sh., *G.*, p. 544 f.

קדמה, not mentioned elsewhere.

16. בחצריהם ובטירתם. '*In their villages and in their encampments*,' i.e. who dwelt partly in unwalled villages (Lev. 25, 31. Is. 42, 11) and partly in moveable camps (Num. 31, 10. Ez. 25, 4). 'טירה is from טור, and means "*a camp*," the tents being pitched in the form of a circle; cf. the modern دُوَار; see Burckh., *Bed.* 26,' Kn. in Di., p. 315. LXX, ἐν ταῖς σκηναῖς αὐτῶν, καὶ ἐν ταῖς ἐπαύλεσιν αὐτῶν.

לאמתם. '*According to their tribes.*' אמה only occurs here and in Num. 25, 15 (both P), and is used of an Arab tribe: the word is more an Arabic than a Hebrew word, and its use here and Num. 25, 15 is perhaps, as Di. suggests, intentional. Ryssel, *De Eloh. Pent. sermone*, p. 71, says of אמה, 'quae vox ad sermonem populi Midianitici spectat (eodem sensu dictum atque apud Scotos *clan* apud Arabes *gum* = قَوْم).'

18. חוילה. See 10, 29[1]. It is not the Indian Ḥavila, but the land of the Χαυλοταῖοι (cf. حويلة in Niebuhr, *Beschreibung von Arabien*, p. 342) of Strabo, xvi. 4. 2, between the Nabatheans and the Agroeans. Thus the Ishmaelites spread themselves over the country between the Persian Gulf to the wilderness of Shur, on the confines of Egypt.

שׁור . . . על פני מצרים. See on 16, 7.

באכה אשׁורה. '*In the direction of Ashur.*' באכה, cf. on 13, 10. אשׁורה is explained by Del.[5] as meaning 'up to the lands under the Assyrian rule (bis nach den Ländern assyrischer Herrschaft).' He admits, however, that a comparison with 1 Sam. 27, 8 arouses a suspicion that these words are a gloss, erroneously explaining שׁור, although the statement itself that the Ishmaelites' territories extended right up to the Euphrates, is quite correct; cf. Jos., *Ant.*, i. 12, 4. Nöldeke (*Unters.*, p. 26) considers that אשׁורה is the name of an Egyptian place, which has been corrupted in the Heb. text. According to Hupfeld it has arisen out of באכה שׁורה (1 Sam. 15, 7) by corruption. Well. (*Comp.*, p. 22) and Del. (*Par.*, p. 131) think that it is an instance of dittography for עד שׁור.

על פני = '*east of;*' cf. 16, 12.

נפל = '*settled;*' in 16, 12 שׁכן is used of Ishmael; cf. Judg. 7, 12 וכל בני קדם נפלים בעמק.

19–34.

20. פדן ארם = שׂדה ארם in Hos. 12, 13, '*Mesopotamia.*' 'פדן in Aramaic = "*a yoke,*" and in Arabic (where it is a

[1] Del., *Par.*, pp. 12 ff., 57 ff., identifies חוילה in all passages with N.E. part of Syrian desert; so E. Meyer, *Gesch. Alterth.*, i. 224; Glases, *Skizzen*, ii. 323 ff., with Central and N.E. Arabia.

Nabathean foreign word, *Ǵawâlîqi*, 112. 2) = "*ploughing oxen*," and then their "*plough*," so a fixed measure of land, like *jugum, jugerum* (Lane, p. 2353; *Z. D. P. V.*, ix. 54), and is regarded by Lagarde (*Proph. Chald.*, p. xliii) as Persian. But II. Raw., 62. 33, *padanu* (which as *padânu* means elsewhere, according to Schrader, *C. O. T.*, ii. p. 295, "*way, path*") is equivalent to *ginû* (*garden*) and *iḳlu* (*field*), (compare Del., *Par.*, p. 135), and so it might have meant "*field*" or "*plain*" in Assyrian (cf. فَدّان "*depression, plain*," Ges., *Thes.*, p. 1092). It is most probable that שׂדה ארם in Hos. l. c. is the Hebrew translation of the word. In 24, 10 (J) we have ארם נהרים for פדן ארם (P). The LXX and Vulg. render it *Mesopotamia Syriae* or *Mesopotamia;* cf. the *campos Mesopotamiae* in Curt. iii. 2. 3; v. 1. 15. From this it by no means follows that the two ideas are completely identical, still less that Paddan Aram was the district round Ḥarran. "Still it is worth noticing that the name פדן (cf. 48, 7) attaches to a place *Faddân*, and a *Tell Faddân*, in the neighbourhood of Ḥarran (see authorities in Di., p. 318). That the neighbourhood of Edessa and Ḥarran is a plain surrounded by mountains is evident from Edrisi p. Jaub. ii. 153; Wilh. of Tyrus, 10. 29. Buckingham, *Mesopotamia*, 111"' (Kn. in Di.). פדן ארם is only found in P as the name of Mesopotamia; so 28, 2. 6 f. 31, 18. 33, 18. 35, 9. 26. 46, 15.

21. ויעתר לו יהוה, lit. '*And Y. suffered himself to be prayed to*,' i. e. '*hearkened to him*.' The Nif'al = 'to let or cause a thing to be done to one' (the so-called *Nif'al tolerativum*); cf. Is. 53, 7 והוא נענה; 65, 1 נדרשתי ... נמצאתי; Jer. 6, 8 הוסרי; Ez. 33, 4. 5. 6 נזהר; see Ges., § 51. 2; Cheyne, crit. note on Is. 53, 7.

22. ויתרצצו is imperf. Hithpoʿ. of רצץ; see Ges., § 55. 1; Stade, § 532 a. γ; cf. יתגדדי from גדד, יתהללו from הלל.

אם כן למה זה וגו״=‘*if thus, why am I?*’ i.e. ‘*if it be thus, why do I live?*’ cf. למה לי חיים in 27, 46; so Pesh. The LXX, εἰ οὕτως [μοι μέλλει γίνεσθαι], ἵνα τί μοι τοῦτο; and so Vulg.; hence it has been rendered, ‘*if it be so, why am I thus?*’ i.e. pregnant; but זֶה cannot be predicate, as the LXX have taken it; זה merely strengthens the למה, as in 18, 13; cf. note on 3, 13.

23. (α) ‘*Two nations are in thy womb,*
(β) *And two peoples shall separate themselves from thy lap:*
(α) *And one people shall overpower the other,*
(β) *And the elder shall serve the younger.*’

The answer given to Ribqah's prayer is poetical in form. רב and צעיר in prose would require the article; cf. Ewald, § 294 a.

לאם מלאם. On מן used in comparison, see Ges., § 133. 1; Dav., *S.*, § 33; M. R., § 49. 2, and cf. 19, 9. 29, 19. 30. 37, 4. 41, 40. 48, 19. לאם is only found once again in the Pentateuch, 27, 29.

24. וימלאו ימיה. ‘*And her days were full;*’ so 29, 21. 50, 3.

תומם is contracted from תְּאֹמִים; so שֵׁלָה from שְׁאֵלָה 1 Sam. 1, 17; רֵמִים from רְאֵמִים Ps. 22, 22; cf. Ges., § 23. 2 and 3; Stade, § 111; Barth, *N.B.*, p. 289.

25. אדמוני, probably referring to the colour of his skin, rather than the hair; so David in 1 Sam. 16, 12. 17, 42 (all); cf. 19, 13.

שֵׂעָר. Probably an allusion to שֵׂעִיר (cf. 27, 11. 23), where (36, 8) Esau's descendants dwelt.

עֵשָׂו. '*Esau*'='*hairy one.*'

26. יעקב the author takes from עָקֵב, a denom. of עָקֵב '*heel*'='*heel-holder;*' cf. Hos. 12, 4. Reuss, *Gesch. des A. T.*[2], p. 52, explains Jacob as='*successor;*' taking the root עקב as='*to be behind,*' '*to follow after.*' In 27, 36 another explanation is given; see the note there.

בלדת אתם; cf. on 24, 30.

27. ידע ציד. 'ציד is acc. after ידע, not gen., for then יְדַע would be necessary,' Wright: the form יְדַע, however, does not occur in the O. T. Cf. 2 Chron. 2, 11 יֹדֵעַ שֵׂכֶל ובינה; Ps. 44, 22 יֹדֵעַ תעלומות לב, which are parallel to this passage. The pl. cstr. is used in 1 Kings 9, 27. Amos 5, 16.

איש שׂדה='*a field man,*' one who spends his time in the fields hunting; but איש האדמה, 9, 20,='*an agriculturist.*'

איש תם. '*A quiet, domestic man.*' '*An upright man*' does not suit the context here, and hardly fits in with the later accounts of Jacob's dealings with his brother. Elsewhere תם always='*upright,*' except Ex. 26, 24. תם is here the German '*fromm,*' which also means *ruhig* (*quiet*), thus 'ein frommes Pferd,' *a quiet horse.*

אֹהָלִים for אֳהָלִים; see Ges., § 23. 3. Rem. 2; Stade, § 109.

28. כי ציד בפיו. '*For venison was in his mouth,*' i. e. was according to his taste; cf. 27, 5–7.

30. מן האדם האדם הזה. '*From the red* (*stuff*), *this*

red stuff;' the words האדם הזה being epexegetical; cf. M. R., § 72. 3.

31. מכרה כיום. *'Sell now first of all,'* etc.; see M. R., § 56. 2. Rem. a, who points out the different shades of meaning in כַּיּוֹם and כְּהַיּוֹם; and cf. Driver, *Sam.*, pp. 24, 55.

32. הנה אנכי הולך למות. *'Behold, I am going to die,'* i. e. Esau's life was a dangerous one, and he might meet his death at any moment. Tuch prefers the rendering, *'I am at the point of death,'* i. e. from hunger, which is not so natural (so A.V. and R.V.), and would be better expressed by הנני מת.

26.

3. את כל הארצת האל, i. e. Canaan and the adjoining districts, ארצת being used of the different portions of what was afterwards the land of Israel, only here and ver. 4; cf. 1 Chron. 13, 2. 2 Chron. 11, 23. האל, cf. note on 19, 8.

7. לאשתו = *'concerning his wife;'* cf. 32, 30 למה זה תשאל לשמי *'why dost thou then ask about my name?'* 43, 7 שאול שאל האיש לנו ולמולדתנו *'the man asked indeed about us and about our birth-place.'*

8. מצחק את רבקה. *'Sporting with R.'* צחק את = צחק עם, of mutual playing or caressing, and so distinct from צחק ב, where the action is not mutual; see 39, 14 (Luzz. cited by Del.[4]).

10. כמעט שכב אחד העם וגו״. *'One of the people might have lain with thy wife, and so thou hadst brought'* etc., lit. *'almost had one of the people;'* cf. Ps. 119, 87 כמעט כלוני בארץ; Prov. 5, 14 כמעט הייתי. והבאת is the perf. with waw conv., after כמעט; cf. Ges., § 112. 3 *a*, *γ*; Dav., *S.*, § 57.

R. 1; Driver, p. 133: the tone being thrown forward on to the last syllable. Del.[5], p. 361, explains the position of the tone on והבאת as due to the ע following, which would otherwise be scarcely audible, comparing Is. 11, 2 וְנָחָה (where, however, the tone on the last syllable may be due to the waw conv.; cf. Driver, § 110. 5). See also ver. 22 רבוֹ עליה, and cf. Ewald, §§ 63 c, 193 b; so 40, 15 שָׂמוּ, before א.

12. מֵאה שׁערים. *'A hundred measures,' 'a hundredfold.'* שׁער in Biblical Hebrew does not occur again in this sense. In Aramaic and the language of the Mishna, שָׁעֵר, Pa'el of שְׁעַר = *'to reckon, estimate'* (cf. Targ. Onq. here, עַל חַד מְאָה בִּדְשַׁעֲרוּהִי = *'the hundredfold of that which they had estimated it (the field);'* cf. Levy, *Chald. W. B.*, ii. p. 504), and שׁערא subst. = *'interest, price;'* see Levy, l.c., and cf. the Arabic سِعْرٌ *'pretium annonae,'* and *Genesis Rabba*, § 64 מאה שערים. מלמד שהאמידו אותה ועשׂתה מאה כמה שהאמידוה *'A hundred measures. This shews that they had estimated it, and it yielded a hundred times as much as they had estimated.'* LXX and Pesh. incorrectly read שְׂעֹרִים *'barley.'* 'A hundred measures' would imply that the harvest was very abundant. The neighbourhood of Gerâr was very fruitful, and at the present day the Arabs have grain magazines at Nuttâr Abu Sumâr, a little north-west of Elusa; Rob., *Pal.*, i. p. 562.

13. הלוך וגדל. Cf. the note on 8, 3. גדל, the participle, here takes the place of the more common inf. abs.; so Judg. 4, 24 ותלך יד בני ישראל הלוך וְקָשָׁה; 2 Sam. 16, 5. 18, 25 וילך הלוך וקרב; cf. Ewald, § 280 b; M. R., § 108; Ges., § 113. 3 b. Rem. 2; Dav., *S.*, § 86. R. 4.

14. עבדה only here and in Job 1, 3; ע״ is abstract for concrete, *servitium=servi;* cf. גבורה Is. 3, 25, and θεραπεία, Matt. 24, 45.

15. סתמום . . . וימלאום. Notice the masc. suffixes referring to feminine nouns; so ver. 18. 31, 9. 32, 16. 33, 13. 41, 23; see Ewald, § 249 b; Dav., *S.*, § 1. R. 3; Ges., § 135. 5. Rem. 1; cf. also, for the instances in this verse, § 60. Rem. 6.

וימלאום with double acc., according to Ges., § 117. 5 a; Dav., *S.*, § 75 b; M. R., § 45. 2.

18. בימי אברהם. LXX, *οἱ παῖδες*; so Sam. and Vulg., reading עבדי, possibly from עבדי יצחק in ver. 19.

ויסתמום is imperf. with waw conv. in continuation of חפרו.

19. מים חיים. '*Living*, i.e. *flowing water*,' as contrasted with still water; so Lev. 14, 5. Jer. 2, 13.

20. עֵשֶׂק = '*strife*;' the word only occurs here.

21. שִׂטְנָה = '*hostility*.'

22. רחבות = '*wide spaces*.' Probably the modern Ruḥaibe, about three hours south of Elusa, eight hours south of Beersheba, where remains of fountains are still to be found; cf. Robins., i. p. 289 ff.

כי, not = *ὅτι recitativum*, but as in 29, 32. 33. Ex. 3, 12, affirmative, '*surely*,' '*indeed*.'

ופרינו is perf. with waw conv. without a preceding imperf.; cf. 17, 4, and the note on 20, 11.

26. ואחזת מרעהו. אחזת is a pr. n. with the fem. ending ַת, like בָּשְׂמַת, גָּלְיַת, ver. 34; מָחֲלַת 28, 9; cf. Dr., p. 236: so LXX, Pesh., Vulg., Saad. Onq., who renders וְסִיעַת רַחֲמוֹהִי, Berl. (some texts מֵרַחֲמוֹהִי), seems to have taken אחזת as fem. cons. state of אחזה, in the sense of

'*a troop*,' '*crowd*,' a meaning אחזה never has: and מרעהו as compounded of מן and רע (if we follow the reading מֵרַחֲמוֹהִי, and not Berliner's רַחְמוֹהִי). מרעהו, only here in the Pentateuch, = '*friend*,' '*confidant*,' one who advised him, and rendered him other services; cf. 1 Kings 4, 5. 1 Chron. 27, 33. מֵרֵעֵהוּ has a firm unchangeable tsere in the first syllable. The LXX translate מרעהו by νυμφαγωγός; supposing that to be the capacity in which he acted as his 'friend;' cf. Judg. 14, 20, LXX (*Codex Alex.*). Translate, '*With Ahuzzath, his counsellor.*'

27. ואתם וגו׳. Render, '*Seeing that* (or *since*) *ye hated me, and sent me away from you.*'

28. רָאוֹ, inf. abs. Qal of ראה for רָאֹה; so שָׁתוֹ, Is. 22, 13; and see Ges., § 75. Rem. 2.

תהי נא אלה. The jussive is here used in making a request; cf. 9, 27. 13, 8. 18, 30. 19, 7. 30, 24. 31, 49. 44, 33. 45, 5, and see note on 18, 30.

אלה = here a compact ratified by a solemn oath; so Deut. 29, 11. Ez. 16, 59.

29. תעשה is pointed with tsere, instead of seghol, under the ה; so in three other places, Josh. 7, 9. 2 Sam. 13, 12. Jer. 40, 16 (Kri). In the last two instances and here, 'in order to avoid, by emphasizing the final sound of the first word, any confusion in sound with the initial sound of the next' (Del.). Cf. also Ges., § 75. Rem. 17; König, *Lehrg.*, p. 531; Stade, § 143 e. Rem. 3, who gives other instances, e.g. Josh. 9, 24 וַנַּעֲשֵׂה; Lev. 5, 9 יִמָּצֵה; Nah. 1, 3 יְנַקֵּה (but not Baer and Del. in their edition, who point יְנַקֶּה with seghol).

R

רק טוב. '*Only good*,' '*nothing but good*;' cf. 6, 5 רק רע; Deut. 28, 33 רק עשוק ורצוץ.

31. איש לאחיו. Cf. the note on 13, 11.

33. שבעה = '*oath*.' The author takes it as equivalent to שְׁבֻעָה. The word is a ἅπαξ λεγόμ. Two accounts of the origin of the name Beersheba are given in Genesis in this ver. (J), in the time of Isaac, and in 21, 31 (E) in the time of Abraham. These are probably merely different accounts of one and the same event.

34. Cf. 36, 2 foll.

35. וַתִּהְיֶיןָ scriptio defectiva, for וַתִּהְיֶינָה; cf. 19, 33 וַתַּשְׁקֶיןָ; 27, 1 וַתִּכְהֶיןָ.

מרת רוח, cf. Prov. 14, 10 מרת נפשו, = '*bitterness of spirit*.' LXX, ἦσαν ἐρίζουσαι, but incorrectly; so Onq. וַהֲוָאָה מְסָרְבָן וּמַרְגְּזָן = '*they were disobedient and provoking to anger*' etc.; connecting it with מָרָה = '*to rebel*.'

27.

1. מראת = lit. '*away from seeing*,' i.e. '*so that he could not see*;' cf. 23, 6, and the note on 16, 2.

3. תליך. תְּלִי, a ἅπαξ λεγόμ., is from תָּלָה '*to hang*;' just as כְּלִי is from כָּלָה, דְּלִי from דָּלָה. The LXX, Vulg., Targ. Ps.-Jon., Ibn Ezra, etc. render '*quiver*.' Onq., Pesh., Rashi, '*sword*.' The former rendering is preferable, being more in accordance with the context (bow and quiver are more naturally mentioned together than bow and sword); cf. Is. 7, 24. 2 Kings 13, 15: and the root תלה, '*to hang*,' suits the rendering '*quiver*' better than '*sword*;' as a sword would be girded on, while a quiver was hung on the

shoulders. תליך = the later word אשפה, which occurs first in Is. 22, 6.

צידה. The Ktb. is צֵידָה, feminine of צַיִד; being what is called by the Arab grammarians a *nomen unitatis*, meaning '*a single head of game;*' while ציד would be '*game*' in general; cf. Wright, *Arab. Gram.*, i. § 246; see also Ges., § 122. 4 d; Ewald, § 176 a; Dav., *S.*, § 14. 3. The Kri is צַיִד (ה יתיר, ה *is redundant*), which was probably chosen by the Massoretes, as צידה usually means '*provisions for a journey*,' e.g. 42, 25. 45, 21; or they might have pointed it צַיִד here, as this word stands again so pointed in vers. 5. 7. 33. צידה, '*a single head of game*,' is quite suitable here—as Isaac would not require more—and is in no wise against vers. 5. 7. 33.

4. והביאה לי ואכלה. '*And bring it to me, and let me eat*,' i.e. '*and bring it to me that I may eat;*' so ver. 21. 19, 20. 30, 25. 28. 42, 2. 20; see Driver, § 60; Dav., *S.*, § 65 a; Ges., § 108. 2 a; M. R., § 10.

5. להביא. LXX read לאביו, τῷ πατρὶ αὐτοῦ; but להביא is justified by vers. 4 and 7.

6. אל יעקב בנה. '*To Jacob her son*,' i.e. her favourite child, Esau being the father's favourite; cf. 25, 28. The LXX, however, have τὸν υἱὸν αὐτῆς τὸν ἐλάσσω, reading בנה הקטן, cf. vers. 15. 42, perhaps on account of Esau's being called בנו הגדול in ver. 1; cf. ver. 42.

8. לאשר אני מצוה אתך = '*in regard to that which I am charging thee;*' cf. note on 17, 20 ולישמעאל '*and with regard to Ishmael.*' אשר includes the demonstrative pronoun; cf. note on 7, 23.

9. גְּדָיֵי. So לְחָיֵי: the pretonic ָ in the construct state is unusual; cf. Stade, § 332 d. 2; Ewald, § 212 b.

ואעשה אתם מטעמים. '*That I may make them* [*into*] *dainty dishes*.' עשׂה with a double acc.; comp. the note on 6, 14.

12. '*Perchance my father will feel me, and I shall be as one that mocks in his sight*,' etc.; cf. Driver, § 115; Dav., *S.*, § 53 b.

מתעתע is part. Pilpel, from תעע; cf. Ges., § 55. 4; Stade, § 281. תעע, like the Arab. تَعْتَعَ, means '*to stammer*,' '*stutter*,' and then '*to mock*;' cf. לוץ and לעג.

13. קללתך. '*Thy curse*,' i. e. the curse that shall come upon thee; cf. the note on 9, 2. Render, '*On me be thy curse!*' For the omission of the verb in the optative sentence, see Ges., § 141, 3 (cf. § 116. 5. R. 2. note); M. R., § 147; Dav., *S.*, § 133; so ver. 29. 3, 14. 9, 26. 14, 19. 43, 23.

14. ויקח . . . ויבא. The object is omitted, cf. note on 9, 22, and add to references given there Dav., *S.*, § 73. R. 5; M. R., § 34. R. b; 2, 19. 12, 19. 18, 7. 38, 18 etc.

15. החמדת = lit. '*costlinesses*,' '*costly things*,' '*desiderabilia*,' so בגדי must be understood before it. Esau's best clothes are intended, which he wore on any festive occasions; cf. Judg. 14, 12 ff. See Rob. Smith, *Relig. of Sem.*, p. 452 f., and cf. 35, 2.

20. מה זה מהרת למצא. '*How then hast thou found it so quickly?*' lit. '*how then hast thou made haste to find it?*' cf. Ges., §§ 114. 2. Rem. 3. note, 120. 2 a; M. R., § 114; Dav., *S.*, § 82. מהרת corresponds to the adverb in English.

24. ויאמר is really in point of time before ויברכהו in

ver. 23. In ver. 23 the transaction is briefly described by the single word ויברכהו, the particulars of the blessing being added by ו conv.; cf. Driver, § 75 β; so in 37, 6. 42, 21 ff. 45, 21–24. 48, 17. Cf., however, Di., p. 329, who regards vers. 24–27[a] (J) as a doublet to 21–23 (according to Di. E).

אתה זה בני עשׂו. '*Thou art then my son Esau*,'='*art thou then my son Esau?*' An interrogative sentence without the interrogative particle ה; cf. 18, 12. 1 Sam. 21, 16. 2 Sam. 11, 11; Ewald, § 324 a; Ges., § 150. 1; Dav., *S.*, § 121; M. R., § 143. זֶה is added to give emphasis to the question.

26. וּשְׁקָה. Cf. on 2, 12.

27[b]–29 are the words of the blessing. The blessing is poetical in form: observe the parallelism in the verses, and the poetical words and forms, e. g. רְאֵה for הִנֵּה, שְׁמַנֵּי הָאָרֶץ, הֱוֵה for הֱיֵה, גְּבִיר (masc. only here, and ver. 37), לְאֻמִּים.

27[b]. '*Behold, the smell of my son is as the smell of a field*
which Yahweh has blessed:

28. (α) *And may God give thee of the dew of the heavens,*
and of the fatnesses of the earth,
(β) *And abundance of corn and wine.*

29. (α) *May nations serve thee, and peoples bow down to thee;*
Be a prince over thy brethren, and may thy mother's
sons bow down to thee:
(β) *Cursed be those that curse thee,*
And blessed be those that bless thee.'

28. משׁמני, the שׁ is undageshed (cf. מִשְׁתֵּים, Jon. 4, 11; מְגֻבּוּרָתָם, Ez. 32, 30), as it is pointed with shewa. The word is compounded of מן partitive, and שׁמני, corresponding to מטל just before. שְׁמַנֵּי is plural cstr. from שָׁמָן, like קְטַנִּים

from קָטָן, גְּמַלִּים from גָּמָל, not from שֶׁמֶן. The A.V. takes it as pl. of מִשְׁמָן, but the sense and the parallelism are against this. On מִן part., see on 4, 3, and cf. 28, 11. 30, 14. Cf. the rendering of the R.V. in these verses. On the great fertility of the land of Canaan, cf. Ex. 3, 8. The dew is here mentioned instead of the rain; as in summer, in Palestine, there is very little rain, and the dew takes its place; cf. 49, 25. Deut. 33, 13. Hos. 14, 6. Zech. 8, 12; Sh., *G.*, p. 65.

תירש from ירש '*to take possession;*' so called as taking possession of the head or mind; cf. Hos. 4, 11.

29. וישתחו Ktb.; Kri וְיִשְׁתַּחֲווּ. The Kri is preferable, as the plural precedes (יַעַבְדוּךָ). The Ktb. is possibly—as in 43, 28—an incorrect way of writing the word. The sing. might perhaps stand by Ewald, § 316 a; Ges., § 145. 7 a; Dav., *S.*, § 113 b.

הֱוֵה for הֱיֵה. The verb הָוָה for הָיָה is North Palestinian and late; cf. the Aramaic הֲוָה and ܗܘܐ. The imper. occurs again in Is. 16, 4 and Job 37, 6 (with א for ה).

לאחיך . . . בני אמך; cf. Ps. 50, 20, where they are again rhythmically interchanged.

ארור . . . ברוך. The singular for plural; cf. Ex. 31, 14 מחלליה מות יומת; Lev. 19, 8 ואכליו עונו ישא; Num. 24, 9 מברכיך ברוך וארריך ארור; see Ewald, § 319 a; Ges., § 145. 5; M. R., § 135. 4 b; Dav., *S.*, § 116. R. 1.

30. אך יצא יצא יעקב. '*Jacob having only just gone out,*' circ. clause prefixed, not appended, and preceded by the introductory formula ויהי. See Dr., § 165, and cf. 15, 17. 24, 15. 42, 35; Josh. 4, 18 נתקו כפות רגלי הכהנים '*the soles of the feet of the priest having been withdrawn;*' 2 Kings 12, 7[b] לא חזקו הכהנים את בדק הבית '*the priests not having*

repaired the breach in the house;' Ges., § 111. 2. R. 1, cf. § 164. 1 b. note; M. R., § 154; Ewald, § 341 c; Dav., *S.*, § 141.

31. ויאכל is imperf. with weak waw in a jussive sense; so וישתחו, ver. 29; see Driver, § 134.

33. "ויחרד . . . חרדה וגו", so ver. 34 "ויצעק צעקה וגו"; the verb being followed by a substantive derived from it in the acc.; cf. Matt. 2, 10, and see note on 1, 11.

מי אפוא הוא הצד = '*who then is he, the one that hunted?*' cf. Ps. 24, 10 מי הוא זה מלך הכבוד '*who then is this one—the king of glory?*' Zech. 1, 9 מה המה אלה '*what are they—these?*' מי אפוא הוא anticipating the subject; see Driver, § 201. 2, and note on 21, 29.

הצד ציד ויבא. '*Who hunted game and brought it;*' cf. 35, 3 העֹנה אתי . . . ויהי; 49, 17 הנשך . . . ויפל. The participle breaks off into the *imperf.* with *waw consec.;* a fact being stated, not a possibility, in which case we should find the *perf.* with *waw consec.;* cf. Driver, § 117; M. R., § 15; Ges., § 116. 5. Rem. 7; Dav., *S.*, §§ 50 a, 100 e.

34. כשמע . . . ויצעק is either to be explained as 19, 15 by Driver, § 127 b, the imperf. with waw conv. after a time-determination, or the word וַיְהִי must be supplied with the LXX, Sam.; so Tuch, Di. ויהי might easily have fallen out after יהיה at the end of ver. 33. Hitzig emends as follows (his emendation being accepted by Geiger, *Urschrift*, p. 377), ואברכהו גם בָּרוּךְ: וַיְהִי. Cf. also Dav., *S.*, § 51. R. 1.

ברכני גם אני. Cf. 4, 26 לשת גם הוא; Num. 14, 32 ופגריכם אתם; see Ges., § 135. 2 a, and the note on 4, 26.

36. '*Is it that they have called his name Jacob? for he hath supplanted me now twice,*' etc.; cf. 29, 15 הכי אחי אתה. LXX, Δικαίως ἐκλήθη; Vulg. '*juste vocatum est nomen ejus;*' cf. Ges.,

§ 150. 2. Rem. 1; Dav., *S.*, § 126. R. 3; M. R., § 143. Rem. b; Ewald, § 324 b, who remarks that הכי 'is used when the reason is unknown' = the Lat. *numquid*, Ger. *etwa*. In 25, 26 another explanation of the name is given.

זה פעמים; so 31, 38. 41. 43, 10. 45, 6. Deut. 8, 2; cf. Ges., § 136. Rem. 3; Dav., *S.*, § 6. R. 2; M. R., § 91.

37. סמכתיו, with a double acc.; see Ps. 51, 14 ורוח נדיבה תסמכני; so סעד, Judg. 19, 5 סעד לבך פת לחם; cf. Ewald, § 283 b (2); Ges., § 117. 5 b. β; Dav., *S.*, § 75 b.

לְכָה, *scriptio plena* for לְךָ, only occurs here in the Pentateuch; cf. איכה in 3, 9 for איך; Ps. 141, 8.

38. הַבְרָכָה, see on 34, 31; and cf. Ges., § 16. 2. 2.

39. משמני, not מ partitive as the A.V. margin, nor cstr. plural of מִשְׁמָן as A.V. and M. R., § 136. Rem. a; cf. ver. 28, because מטל in the second half of the verse is against this, but privative (so most modern scholars). '*Away from the fatnesses;*' cf. vers. 37. 40, and see Dav., *S.*, § 101. R. 2. Render,

> '*Far from the fatnesses of the earth be thy dwelling-place,*
> *And far from the dew of heaven from above.*'

Other instances of מִן privative are Num. 15, 24 מעיני העדה '*out of sight of the congregation;*' Prov. 20, 3 מריב '*away from strife;*' Job 11, 15 ממום '*without blemish.*'

The sterility of Edom is here contrasted with the fertility of Palestine; so ver. 40,

> '*And by thy sword shalt thou live, and thy brother shalt thou serve;*
> *And it will be, when thou rebellest, that thou wilt break his yoke from off thy neck.*'

40. עַל חַרְבְּךָ, i.e. the sword is conceived of as the means of procuring the necessities of life, or as the basis on which Esau's life will rest; cf. על in Deut. 8, 3 על הלחם לבדו; Is. 38, 16 עליהם יחיו.

תריד. The root רוד occurs four times in the Old Test., twice in Qal, Jer. 2, 31. Hos. 12, 1, and twice in Hif'., here and Ps. 55, 3. רוד is the Arab. راد, conj. I. '*to go to and fro;*' III. and IV. '*to desire, long for;*' '*to strive after, wish.*' In Hebrew the root means '*to wander about unrestrained,*' a meaning which suits Hos. and Jer., loc. cit.; Judah being described (Hos. 12, 1 עד רד) as still wandering about with regard to God, i.e. independently, of his own free will, withdrawing himself from God; so Jer. 2, 31 רדנו '*we have wandered about,*' i.e. abandoned God. In Ps. 55, 3 אריד בשיחי (where the Hif'il is used) the meaning is slightly different, '*I wander to and fro in my meditation,*' '*I am tossed about by anxiety and care.*' Del. and Kn. render here, '*when thou roamest about,*' but this is unsuitable, as a yoke would not be broken by roaming about, nor could a person under a yoke be well conceived of as roaming about at will. כאשר in this case would be like Num. 27, 14. Tuch renders, '*when thou rebellest*' (cf. Jer. and Hos., l.c.), to which Di. objects that, every one who is under a yoke rebels, but does not get free; but this is not conclusive against Tuch's rendering. Di. prefers the rendering, '*when thou makest efforts* or *strivest;*' cf. راد IV, the meaning being, 'when thou, though in bondage, strivest to become free, thou shalt break off the yoke from thy neck, and attain thy desire.' The A.V. renders, '*when thou shalt have dominion*' (so Kimchi; cf. Ges., *Thes.*, p. 1269 a), as though תריד were from רדה, but this is impossible. Other renderings are, '*when thou shalt wish;*' '*when thou shalt bewail,*' both extremely doubtful. The Versions seem to have misunderstood the word. Onq. renders it by כַּד יְעִיבְּרוּן בְּנוֹהִי וגו׳ '*when his sons transgress*' etc., probably a paraphrase. Pesh. has ܘܐܢ ܬܬܘܒ '*and if thou repentest;*' but how they get this out of תריד is not clear. LXX have ἡνίκα ἐὰν καθέλῃς, probably connecting it with ירד, Hif'. הוריד. The Vulg. has a free paraphrase, '*tempusque veniet cum excutias, et solvas jugum ejus,*' etc. The Heb.-Sam. has תאדר, Nif'. of אדר ('*when thou becomest great*'), for תריד, so the Book of Jubilees. (Di.). The best rendering seems to be either Tuch's or Dillmann's. The R.V. renders, '*break loose.*' For the fulfilment of the blessing, cf. 2 Kings 8, 20 ff. 16, 6.

41. יקרבו ימי אבל אבי. Render, '*The days of mourning for my father,*' etc., i.e. Isaac would soon die (cf. ver. 4 and ver. 7), and then Esau contemplated taking vengeance on Jacob; אָבִי being obj. genit. Others, e.g. Luther, Kalisch, render as genit. of the subject, '*days of grief for my father,*' i.e. Isaac would grieve when he heard of Jacob's death. But the genitive after אבל is always obj. genit. See on 9, 2.

42. '*And they told* (lit. *it was told*) *Ribqah the words of Esau;*' on the construction, cf. the note on 4, 18.

מתנחם. '*Will revenge himself upon thee,*' lit. '*procure for himself satisfaction,* or *ease* (viz. by taking revenge);' cf. the Nif'. נחם in Is. 1, 24.

44. ימים אחדים. '*A few days,*' lit. '*some days;*' cf. 29, 20 כימים אחדים; Dan. 11, 20 ובימים אחדים. 'Ribqah mentions a short time in order to persuade Jacob more easily,' Di. ימים אחדים is acc. of time in answer to the question '*how many?*' cf. 7, 4. 24. 14, 4. 15, 13. 21, 34, and see Dav., *S.*, § 68 b; Ges., § 118. 3 b; M. R., § 42 a.

45. עד שׁוב . . . ושׁכח. '*Until thy brother's anger turn . . . and he forget;*' cf. Dr., p. 134; 18, 25 להמית . . . והיה, and the note there. עד שׁוב . . . ממך may be a doublet to 44[b]. Cf. Di., p. 332. These words certainly seem superfluous.

גם שׁניכם; cf. Prov. 17, 15. They would both perish, as the murderer would (9, 6) be put to death.

28.

2. פַּדֶּנָה אֲרָם. The construct state with ה local; cf. on 20, 1. The syllable ־ָה is pointed with orthophonic Ga'ya (cf. Ges., § 16, 3), so that its sound may be kept distinct from that of the following א in ארם; cf. 44, 2 גְּבִיעַ הַכֶּסֶף; 11, 25 תְּשַׁע־עֶשְׂרֵה (Baer and Del. ed.); see also Stade, § 56. פַּדֶּנָה=פַּדֶּנָה; cf. סֶלָה=סֶלָה; and see Del., *Comm.*, Ps. 3; 5th ed., p. 78.

3. יברך אתך . . . והיית. The perf. with waw consecutive, after the imperf. as a jussive; cf. on 1, 14.

5. Cf. Hos. 12, 13 ויברח יעקב שׂדה ארם.

6. וְשִׁלַּח. We should expect here וישׁלח; no adequate reason can be given for the use of the perfect with waw here, where the imperf. with waw cons. would be expected: possibly the present reading has arisen through י having dropped out between ו and שׁ. See Driver, § 133. Di. explains it on account of its being dependent on כִּי, but this would require the waw conv. with the imperf. when another perfect had preceded, as already וישׁמע in ver. 7.

בברכו . . . ויצו. The imperf. with waw conv. continuing an inf. cstr., a fact being stated; cf. Driver, § 118 ad fin. So

39, 18 ואקרא . . . כהרימי; see also Ges., § 115. 3. Rem. 1; Dav., *S.*, § 96. R. 2; M.R., § 120.

9. מחלת. In 36, 3 בָּשְׂמַת (cf. the note there) is the name of the daughter of Ishmael whom Esau married.

על נשיו = '*in addition to his wives,*' i.e. the wives mentioned 26, 34; so 31, 50 נשים על בנותי.

Verse 9 forms the apodosis to ver. 6; וישמע, ver. 7, being dependent on כִּי . . . וירא, ver. 6, and וירא, ver. 8, resuming the וירא of ver. 6.

11. ויפגע במקום. מקום with the article = '*the place,*' i.e. the place that was suitable for passing the night. Di. renders, '*the sanctuary;*' cf. on 12, 6; but see Dav., *S.*, § 21. R. 2. Ges., § 126. 4, mentions both ways.

מאבני המקום. '*Some of the stones;*' מִן partitive as in 4, 3.

מראשתיו = '*at his head.*' מְרַאֲשֹׁתָיו for מַרְאֲשֹׁתָיו; cf. מְתַלְּעֹתָיו for מַלְתְּעֹתָיו. The plural is the plural used to mark *extension* of space (as here) or time; see Ges., § 124. 1 a; Dav., *S.*, § 16; Stade, § 313 b. The feminine plural being used, according to Stade, § 322 c ('single things in which a definite quality appears'), מראשות = '*that which is at the head,*' just as מרגלות = '*that which is at the feet;*' cf. מטעמות and מעדנות '*dainties;*' נפלאות '*wondrous deeds.*'

12. סֻלָּם from סלל, with the ending ־ָם, as in אוּלָם from אול, כְּנָם; cf. Stade, § 293; Ges., § 87. 1 d. This ending is more frequent in proper names, e.g. בִּלְעָם, עֶדְלָם, אֲחֻזָּם, מִרְיָם, עַמְרָם. Cf. Barth, *N. B.*, p. 353. סלם is a ἅπαξ λεγόμ. It may perhaps occur in Phoen., cf. *C.I.S.*, i. p. 103 (Inscrip. of Idalion 88). Barth, however, *N. B.*, p. 23 f., cps. the Arabic سُلَّم, and maintains the ם is a radical and not an afformative;

he also thinks that ם in כִּנָּם is radical, and that אוּלָם is a technical word of foreign origin; cf. p. 352.

וראשו . . . השמימה. '*With its top reaching heavenwards;*' cf. 11, 4, and see note on 18, 16.

13. נצב עליו. '*Standing on it*' (the ladder). LXX, ἐπ' αὐτῆς; so Vulg., Pesh. Tuch, Del. and Di. render, '*standing by him*' (Jacob), which perhaps is better (cf. 18, 2), as one does not see why it should be said that Yahweh stood on the ladder, while the thought, 'Yahweh stood by Jacob,' is more natural; and if עליו referred to סלם, we should expect לו, or ליעקב, after ויאמר.

14. וָקדמה . . . וָנגבה; cf. on 1, 2.

15. עד אשר אם וגו׳. '*Until that I shall have done,*' lit. '*until that when;*' cf. on 24, 19 and Num. 32, 17 עד אשר אם הביאנם; Is. 6, 11 עד אשר אם שאו ערים.

16. ואנכי לא ידעתי = '*without my knowing it,*' circ. cl.; cf. Driver, § 160; see on 24, 31.

17. מה נורא. '*How dreadful!*' cf. Ps. 8, 2 מה אדיר '*how glorious!*' Num. 24, 5 מה טבו אהליך '*how goodly are thy tents,*' etc.; see M. R., § 93. Rem. c; Dav., *S.*, § 7 b; Ges., § 148.

19. ביתאל is situated to the north of Jerusalem, in the Judean plateau, which continues about ten miles to the north of Jerusalem, before it breaks into the valleys and mountains of Samaria. It stands about three miles from the end of the plateau, where three roads concentrate: a highway from the west by Gophna, the great north road from Shechem, and a road from the Jordan Valley through the passes of Mount Ephraim. Sh., *G.*, p. 290. The statement that the former

name of Bethel was Luz (35, 6. 48, 3. Judg. 1, 23; cf. Jos. 18, 13), probably only implies that the more modern Bethel was situated near the ancient Luz; cf. Di., p. 337. See also Bäd., *Pal.*, p. 213, where it is suggested that Bethel may be identified with the modern Bêtîn.

20–22. The apodosis commences with והיה יהוה לי at the end of ver. 21. Render, '*If God be with me, and keep me on this journey which I am going, and give me bread to eat, and raiment to wear, and I return safe and sound to my father's house, then shall Yahweh be my God, and this stone,*' etc.; so LXX, Pesh., Vulg., Di., Del., Dav., *S.*, § 130 c; and this division is more natural than that proposed by Tuch, who commences the apodosis with ver. 22. Cf. Driver, p. 130, on the perfect with waw conv. after an imperf. with אִם.

29.

1. The LXX add after ארצה בני קדם, *πρὸς Λάβαν τὸν υἱὸν Βαθουὴλ τοῦ Σύρου, ἀδελφὸν δὲ 'Ρεβέκκας, μητρὸς 'Ιακὼβ καὶ 'Ησαύ*, probably a gloss to harmonise this passage with 28, 5; the expression ארצה בני קדם for Mesopotamia—which is only found here—being in itself more or less indefinite.

2. '*And he looked up, and behold a well in the field, and behold there, three flocks of sheep were lying by it; for out of that well they used to water the flocks,*' etc. 3. '*And all the flocks used to be gathered thither, and they used to roll away the stone from off the mouth of the well, and water the sheep, and bring back the stone upon the mouth of the well to its place.*'

Observe the tenses, which are instructive. The participle רבצים, '*were lying,*' describing the condition at the particular occasion, the frequentative imperfect ישקו, and this followed by four perfects with waw conversive, ונאספו, וגללו, והשקו, והשיבו, describing what used habitually to be done; cf. Driver, §§ 31; 113. 4 β; M. R., § 25; Ges., § 112. 3 a. *a*; Dav., *S.*, § 54 b, and note on 2, 6.

ישקו. The indefinite, unnamed subject expressed by the 3rd person pl. of the verb. See Ges., § 144. 3 b; Dav., *S.*, § 108 b; M. R., § 123, and cf. 26, 18. 35, 5. 41, 14. 49, 31.

והאבן גדולה. '*And the stone on the mouth of the well was great,*' lit. '*and the stone was great on the mouth of the well;*' גדולה without the article, and therefore predicate; so in ver. 7 הן עוד היום גדול; cf. Ges., § 126. 2 i; Dav., *S.*, §§ 19, 103; M. R., § 125.

והאבן גדולה על פי הבאר, i. e. 'the stone on the mouth of the well,' etc., which in the more common construction would be וגדולה האבן אשר על פי הבאר; cf. Mic. 6, 12 ולשונם רמיה בפיהם.

With these two verses cf. 24, 11 ff. Ex. 2, 15 ff. (where, however, the tenses are different, a *single* occasion only being described).

4. אחי = '*my friends!*' cf. 19, 7.

6. באה = '*is coming,*' participle not perfect; in ver. 9 באה is accented on the penult., and is therefore the perfect.

7. לא עת האסף המקנה. '*It is not time for the cattle to be gathered together,*' lit. '*it is not the time of the being gathered together of the cattle,*' i.e. for the cattle to be collected and put up for the night. On the construction of the inf. cstr. with a subj. following and a construct state preceding, cf. Ges., §§ 115. 2; 114. 1 b; M.R., §§ 111, 117, 118; Dav., *S.*, §§ 90 b, 91.

8. כל העדרים. The LXX have πάντας τοὺς ποιμένας, reading כָּל־הָרֹעִים, an easier reading than that of the text; so the Sam. here and ver. 3.

עד אשר יאספו . . . וגללו . . . והשקינו. The impf. continued by the pft. with waw conv., as in Ex. 23, 30 עד אשר תפרה ונחלת את הארץ; Hos. 5, 15 עד אשר יאשמו ובקשו פני, and often; cf. Driver, p. 135; Dav., *S.*, § 53 b; Ges., § 112. 3 c. *a*.

9. עודנו מדבר . . . ורחל באה. Cf. on 19, 23, and see also Ges., § 116. 5. Rem. 4.

אשר לאביה. אשר ל to express the genitive, as in 40, 5 המשקה והאפה אשר למלך מצרים; 47, 4 לצאן אשר לעבדיך; see Ges., § 129. 2; M. R., § 83; Dav., *S.*, § 28. R. 5.

11. וישק יעקב. נִשֵּׁק (ver. 13) Pi'el = '*to kiss fondly*,' or '*cover with kisses*,' as distinguished from the Qal נָשַׁק (here) '*to kiss*;' cf. φιλέω and καταφιλέω in Greek.

13. את שמע יעקב. LXX, τὸ ὄνομα Ἰακώβ; so LXX in Num. 14, 15. 1 Kings 10, 1, possibly confusing שמע with שם, which was very similar in sound.

14. חדש ימים. '*A month, days*,' i.e. a whole month; cf. 41, 1 שנתים ימים '*two years*;' Num. 11, 20 חדש ימים: ימים being in apposition to חדש; see Driver, § 192. 1; Ewald, § 287 h; Ges., § 131. 2 c; M. R., § 71. 4; Dav., *S.*, § 29 d.

15. הכי אחי וגו". Cf. 27, 36. '*Art thou, as a brother, to serve me for nothing?*' lit. '*is it the case that thou art my brother, and shouldest serve me for nothing?*' cf. the Vulg. '*num quia frater meus es, gratis servies mihi?*' On ועבדתני, perf. with waw conv. after כִּי, without an imperf. preceding, cf. Driver, § 123 γ; Ges., § 112. 4 c; Dav., *S.*, § 56; M. R., § 26.

17. ועיני לאה רכות. The predicate in the plural with the subject in the dual, as the dual in Hebrew only occurs in a few nouns, never in the verb or adj. (contrast the Arabic); see M. R., § 134; Ges., § 145. 6; Dav., *S.*, § 31.

רכות. '*Weak*,' lit. '*tender*,' neither bright nor clear. So LXX and Pesh. But Onq. and Saadiah take רכות as meaning '*beautiful*,' as though Leah had fine eyes, but otherwise was not so handsome as Rachel. Good eyes were considered by the Orientals one of the essentials of beauty; cf. 1 Sam. 16, 12. Song of Songs 4, 1.

18. שבע שנים. Jacob wished to purchase his wife by seven years' service without hire, the seven years' service taking the place of the ordinary price (מהר) paid the wife's relatives before marriage; cf. 24, 53. 34, 12. 1 Sam. 18, 23 ff. Hos. 3, 2.

19. טוב תתי וגו״. '*It is better for me to give her to thee, than for me to give her to another man*;' cf. Ex. 14, 12 כי טוב לנו עבד את מצרים ממתנו במדבר; Prov. 21, 9 טוב לשבת על פנת גג מאשת מדונים וגו״; see note on 25, 23, and for inf. cstr. as subj. in nominal sentence the note on 2, 18. So Judg. 18, 19. 1 Sam. 29, 6. Ps. 118, 9. etc.

לאיש אחר, i.e. a stranger; cf. Jer. 6, 12. 8, 10. At the present day in Arabia the cousin is preferred as a husband to a stranger; cf. Lane, *Manners and Customs*, vol. i. p. 167.

21. הבה את אשתי. הבה is accented on the last syllable, on account of the light consonant א in את, that both ה and א may have their full sound; cf. לָמָּה, 27, 45.

22. משתה, i.e. the wedding banquet; cf. Judg. 14, 12. Tobit 11, 19.

23. The bride was brought to her husband veiled (cf. 24,

65), and so the deception practised by Laban could easily be accomplished.

26. לֹא יעשׂה וגו׳ = '*it is not customary in our land,*' lit. '*it is not wont thus to be done;*' imperf. as in 10, 9; see note on that passage, and cf. 50, 3. Ex. 13, 15. 33, 11. Judg. 14, 10. 2 Sam. 13, 12.

27. שׁבע זאת. The wedding festivities usually lasted a week; cf. Judg. and Tobit, l.c.

ונתנה, i.e. Laban and his relatives; cf. 24, 50. The LXX and Sam. read ואתן.

30. גם אל רחל. גם = '*also;*' the second גם in גם את רחל may either emphasize Rachel only (see Ges., *Thes.*, p. 294), or may be taken with מן = '*etiam,*' '*still more than,*' which is perhaps a little forced. Di. condemns both ways as against the usage of the language, and following the LXX and Vulg., rejects the second גם. Knobel takes the second גם with ויאהב, i.e. did not only go in to her, but also loved her: but this would require ויאהב גם אהב; cf. 31, 15. 46, 4.

ויאהב . . . מלאה. On the comparative, see note on 25, 23.

31. שְׂנוּאָה, not absolutely '*hated,*' but relatively '*less loved;*' cf. Deut. 21, 15. Matt. 6, 24.

32. אמרה כי. כי as in 26, 22; cf. the note there; so ver. 33.

ראה . . . בעניי. ראה . . . ב = '*to look upon with compassion;*' so 1 Sam. 1, 11 אם ראה תראה בעני אמתך; Ps. 106, 44 וירא בצר להם.

יֶאֱהָבַנִי; cf. 19, 19 and the note there.

33. שׁמעון = '*hearing.*'

34. ילוה . . . אלי. *'Will become attached to me;'* cf. Num. 18, 2. 4. לֵוִי as though = *'attachment'* or *'dependent.'*

קרא. As the mother in the case of the other three sons, Simeon, Reuben, and Judah, gives them their names, so probably the reading of the LXX (Lagarde), ἐκάλεσε (but Swete reads ἐκλήθη), Pesh. ܩܪܬ = קראה, is correct. קרא would = *'one called him,' 'people called him.'*

35. יהודה = *'praise,' 'a subject of praise.'* A Hof'al derivative; cf. Pss. 28, 7. 45, 18. Neh. 11, 17, where the ה of the Hif'. of ידה (ודה) is irregularly retained.

For proposed explanations of the proper names at the end of this chapter and in the first part of chap. 30, cf. Di., p. 342 f.

30.

1. מתה; cf. on 29, 6.

2. התחת אלהים אנכי. *'Am I in God's stead?'* i. e. am I all powerful, so that I might give you children? so again 50, 19 (אני); cf. 2 Kings 5, 7 האלהים אני להמית ולהחיות.

3. על ברכי; so 50, 23 על ברכי יוסף; cf. Job 3, 12. Rachel follows Sarah's example (16, 2), and gives her maid Bilhah to Jacob, so that she might rear up her (Bilhah's) child as her own, and in some measure escape the reproach of childlessness; cf. Stade, *Z.A.T.W.*, vi. p. 143 ff.

6. דָּנַנִּי with the tone-syllable doubled; so תְּבַעֲתַנִּי, Job 7, 14; cf. Stade, § 71. 3.

דן = *'judge.'* God heard Rachel's prayer, and decided (דין) according to her wish.

8. נפתולי אלהים = lit. '*struggles of God,*' i.e. struggles or wrestlings for God's favour; cf. ver. 6. 29, 31. 30, 2. The R.V. renders, '*with mighty wrestlings,*' i.e. for the husband's love: but the sisters were never rivals for the husband's love (cf. 29, 33 and ver. 15 of this chapter), as Rachel was always the favourite wife of Jacob. נפתולי is a ἅπαξ λεγόμ. and the only noun of this form; see Stade, § 251; Barth, *N. B.*, p. 156. נפתלי = '*one obtained by struggling*' (?). Di. *Kampfmann* ('*man of combat*' or '*struggling*').

11. בָּגָד = the Kri בא גד '*good fortune comes;*' so Onq. and the Pesh. (ܐܬܐ ܓܕܝ '*my fortune cometh*'): but this reading of the Kri is unnecessary. The Ktb. בגד, pointed בְּגָד (LXX, ἐν τύχῃ; Vulg. '*feliciter*')—the pausal form of בְּגַד—yields a good sense, '*I am in luck;*' cf. באשרי, ver. 13. גד (cf. Is. 65, 11, where it is the Babylonian god of good fortune, identified with Bel, and later with the planet Jupiter) was the name of an old Phoenician and Canaanitish god. Traces of the name are still preserved in the proper name בעל גד, Josh. 11, 17, and the Phoenician proper names גדנעם, גדעת; see Euting, *Sechs Phönizische Inschriften aus Idalion*, p. 14 (1875); and cf. *C. I. S.*, i. p. 110, line 3, and Bloch, *Phoenisch. Glossar*, p. 25.

The A. V. (but not the R. V., see Driver's paper on the Revised Version in *The Expositor*, July, 1885) and Gr. Ven. (ἥκει στράτευμα) give גד the meaning of גדוד; cf. 49, 19. But גד never means '*a troop,*' and 49, 19 is not decisive on the meaning here.

13. באשרי = '*In my prosperity!*' i.e. I am in luck; cf. ver. 11.

כי אשרוני. '*For the daughters are sure to call me lucky;*'

cf. Is. 11, 9 כי מלאה הארץ דעה; Jer. 25, 14 כי עבדו בם. The perfect of certitude or prophetic perfect; cf. Dr., § 14 β; Ges., § 106. 3 b; Dav., *S.*, § 41 a; M. R., § 3. 1.

אשר = '*the happy one;*' cf. אשרה ? '*the goddess of good fortune.*'

14. דודאים is pl. of דּוּדַי, obsolete; cf. לֻלָאוֹת, from an obsolete singular לוּלִי, ◌ִי of the singular being softened into א in the plural; so חֲלִי, pl. חֲלָאִים; צְבִי, pl. צְבָאוֹת and צְבָאִים; פְּתִי, pl. פְּתָאִים[1]; cf. Stade, §§ 122, 301 a. דודאים = '*love apples,*' i. e. the fruit of the *Mandragora vernalis*, or mandrake, of a yellow colour, and similar in shape to an apple; found in Palestine, especially in Galilee. There seem to have been two kinds of דודאים, the *Mandragora vernalis* and *autumnalis* (Song of Songs 7, 14), unless we suppose with Tuch that in this passage the fruit is intended (at the time of the wheat harvest, i. e. May to June), while in Song of Songs the blossom is meant (cf. the LXX rendering in Song of Songs, οἱ μανδραγόραι, with their translation here, μῆλα μανδραγόρου). On the supposed efficacy of the דודאים as love potions, see Tuch, p. 385 f., and the authorities cited by him.

15. '*Is thy taking away my husband a little thing, and* (*art thou*) *for taking away the love apples of my son too?*' cf. Esth. 7, 8 הגם לכבוש את המלכה; 2 Chron. 19, 2 הלרשע לעזר. ולקחת is not perf., so Tuch, but inf. cstr. used as a periphrastic future; see Driver, § 204 end, and cf. Dav., *S.*, § 94. There is no reason to alter the וְלָקַחַת into the 2 sing. fem. perf. with waw consec. as is suggested in Ges., § 114. 2. Rem. 5. Di. remarks that 'the inf. ולקחת ("*and to take*" = "*and thou wilt take*"?) expresses the intention more forcibly

[1] But cf. Baer and Del., *Liber Psalmorum*, Lipsiae, 1880, p. 115.

than the more natural construction with the perfect וְלָקַחְתָּ; see 20, 16.'

16. שָׂכֹר שְׂכַרְתִּיךָ. These words evidently contain an allusion to the name יששכר.

בלילה הוא; cf. 19, 33 and the note there.

18. יששכר. The reading given in Baer and Del.'s edition is pointed יִשָּׂשכָר, with the Kri *perpetuum* יִשָּׂכָר, i.e. wherever יששכר occurs in the O.T. it is always pointed יִשָּׂכָר, as though there were no second ש: this is the reading of Ben Asher (the Tiberian or Occidental punctuation). Ben Naftali reads יִשְׂשָׂכָר (the Babylonian or Oriental punctuation); cf. Baer and Del., *Gen.*, p. 84. On the readings of Ben Asher and Ben Naftali, see Bleek-Wellhausen, *Einl.*, pp. 563, 614 f.; Bleek, *Introduction*, Eng. trans., ii. p. 463; Strack, *Proleg.*, p. 36 f., *De codicibus Orient. et Occident.* Ben Asher's reading יִשָּׂכָר is perhaps a derivative from the Nif'al of שׂכר = '*got for hire*' (Wright); so apparently the LXX, 'Ισσαχάρ; Vulg. *Issachar;* Pesh. ܐܝܣܟܪ; Saad. يِسَّاخَارُ; Josephus, ἐκ μίσθου γενόμενος. The reading of Ben Naftali, יִשְׂשָׂכָר, is the same as that of Ben Asher, but written differently. Some think that Ben Naftali read יִשָּׂשָׂכָר ('*affert proemium*')=יִשָּׂא שָׂכָר; see Baer and Del., loc. cit., '*At certe de Ben Naf. falluntur.*' Mose ben Mocha read יֶשׁ־שָׂכָר '*est proemium,*' after Jer. 31, 16. 2 Chron. 15, 7. So Di.

20. זבדני and יזבלני are both ἅπαξ λεγόμ.

זבלון (of the same form as ישורון) perhaps = '*habitation.*' In this verse two explanations of the name are given, probably derived from two different documents (*a*) from E, זבדני . . . זבד '*presented me with a goodly present,*' and (*b*) from J, יזבלני (זבל with the acc. like שׁכן and גור) '*will dwell with me.*'

The meaning '*dwell*,' however, generally assigned to זבל, seems to be very doubtful, cf. Cheyne, crit. note on Is. 63, 15. It is, therefore, perhaps better to render '*will exalt*' or '*honour me*' (cf. LXX, αἱρετιεῖ). זבל = Assyr. *zabâlu, to bear, lift up*. See Del., *Proleg.*, p. 62, Del.[5], ad loc. This meaning of זבל is, however, questioned by Halévy, *R. E. J.*, 1885, p. 299, and Nöld., *Z. D. M. G.*, xl. p. 729.

21. דינה = '*vindicatio*;' the daughter's name is here given, as necessary to explain chap. 34. Jacob's daughters are elsewhere presupposed (37, 35. 46, 7), but not mentioned by name.

24. יוסף explained from ver. 23^b^ (E) אסף אלהים את חרפתי, as though it were יאסף = '*taker away*,' i. e. of my reproach of childlessness. In 24^b^ (J) the name is explained differently, יוסף יי" לי בן אחר '*may Yahweh add to me another son*,' so = '*multiplier*;' see on ver. 20, and cf. 35, 18.

27. אם נא מצאתי וגו". '*If now I have found favour in thine eyes,—I have observed the omens, that* (lit. *and*) *Yahweh has blessed me for thy sake*.' Dav., *S.*, § 146. R. 4, takes these words, '*I have divined and Yahweh*, etc.' as a clause with *and* in the place of an object. sentence; cf. 47, 6; Driver, p. 207; Ges., § 120. 2. R. 2 (cf. § 111. 2. R. 2. foot-note, which apparently contradicts Ges., l. c.). The apodosis to אם נא מצאתי וגו" is suppressed; cf. 38, 17. 50, 15; Ges., § 159. Rem. 2; the apodosis would perhaps run אל נא תעבר מעלי, as in 18, 3. The words cannot be translated '*Would that I had found favour in thy eyes*' (Ges. in *Thes.*), as this would require the imperf., not the perfect; cf. Pss. 81, 9. 139, 19. נחשתי; see on 44, 15. The LXX have οἰωνισάμην ἄν, making נחשתי into the apodosis to אם מצאתי; the Vulgate '*experimento didici*.'

28. עלי = lit. '*upon me.*' על because it will be as a burden to him; cf. 34, 12.

29. '*Thou knowest how I have served thee, and what thy cattle has become with me.*' את אשר עבדתיך and ואת אשר היה וגו״ are both accusatives after ידעת; cf. Ges., § 157 c; Dav., *S.*, § 146; M. R., §§ 158. R. b, 161 b. אתה is emphatic, '*thou* with whom I have been in service shouldest know.' אתי '*with me,*' i. e. under my care.

30. ויפרץ. Waw conv., as in 22, 24, which compare.

לרגלי, lit. '*at my steps,*' i. e. wherever I went; cf. Is. 41, 2 צדק יקראהו לרגלו '*whom righteousness meeteth wherever he goeth;*' Job 18, 11 והפיצהו לרגליו.

גם אנכי. Emphatic, '*I too.*' You have been prosperous, when shall I begin prospering?

31. אשובה ארעה. '*I will again feed;*' so 26, 18 וישב יצחק ויחפר '*and Isaac dug again.*' Two verbs to express one idea (here without ו cop.) where in English an adverb is used; so Ps. 7, 13 ישוב . . . ילטש '*will again sharpen;*' see Ges., § 120. 2 b. Rem.; M. R., § 30 a; Dav., *S.*, § 83 c.

32–43. These twelve verses are very obscure, possibly corrupt. In ver. 31, Jacob, in answer to Laban's request to tell him what reward he desires, replies that Laban is to give him nothing if he will accede to a proposal he has to make. In ver. 32, Jacob proposes to go through Laban's flock, and separate the particoloured and black sheep, and all the particoloured goats. The normal colour of the goats is black, or at least dark-brown; that of the sheep, on the contrary, white; see Song of Songs 4, 1. 2. 6, 5. 6. Dan. 7, 9; cf. Song of Songs 1, 5. The greater number of the sheep and goats would naturally be of normal colour, white and black respectively. Jacob proposes that the abnormal cattle shall be his hire. Laban, vers. 34–36, consents to Jacob's proposal, and separates the normal and abnormal coloured sheep and goats, and sends the latter off, under the charge of his sons, three days' journey distant from the remainder of his flock of normal coloured animals, left in Jacob's charge. Jacob, in order that the animals left with him may bring forth a greater number of abnormal coloured offspring than they would usually produce, has recourse to the stratagem of the peeled rods in the drinking-troughs (37–39). Ver. 40 seems to contain a second contrivance on the part of Jacob to increase his flock, but the text is very obscure and almost certainly corrupt (see the note there). Vers. 41. 42 either contain a third stratagem, or refer to the previous two (the frequentative tenses perhaps supporting the latter view), 41. 42 being a more detailed account of the contrivance practised in vers. 38. 39.

32. הַיּוֹם seems to imply that the cattle separated *that day*, if of abnormal colour, were to belong to Jacob; but against this is firstly ver. 31, where Jacob declines any hire, and secondly vers. 35. 36[b], where Laban, not Jacob, separates and drives off the abnormal coloured cattle, which seem, according to ver. 32, to belong to Jacob, but here are apparently regarded as Laban's. To avoid this difficulty, some, e.g. Tuch, suppose that Jacob's hire is to be the abnormal coloured cattle that would be born, cf. ver. 37 ff.; but nothing is said of this in ver. 32, and it is questionable whether והיה שׂכרי would fit in with this view. Well., *Comp.*, p. 40 f., attempts to remove the difficulty by inserting, after ver. 34, a statement to the effect that Laban, after the abnormal coloured animals had been separated by Jacob, found the promised reward too liberal, and so proposed to Jacob another arrangement

(31, 7 f.). Di. rejects this on the ground that such a lacuna would be inconceivable, and the contradiction with לא־תתן־לי מאומה would be too marked. Di. proposes two solutions of the difficulty: (i) that before or after והיה שׂכרי several words have dropped out of the text, or (ii) to alter the accentuation of ver. 32, and point the first טלוא with *Athnach;* then the meaning would be '*every black sheep among the sheep, and spotted and patched among the goats, shall be my hire,*' i.e. you are to give me nothing now, but the abnormal coloured cattle born after the division, in ver. 32, has taken place will be mine; cf. מחר, ver. 33. This seems the simplest solution of the difficulties.

הסר is inf. abs.; cf. note on 21, 16. Others prefer taking הסר as imperative; addressed to לבן, which suits ver. 35, but not אעבר. נקד וטלוא '*spotted and patched.*' טלוא is not found again outside this chapter, except in Ez. 16, 16, pl. fem. טְלֻאוֹת. והיה שׂכרי '*and (these) shall be my hire,*' i.e. the sheep and goats of abnormal colour that shall be born after the division mentioned in this verse has been carried out; see above. שׂה is used here of both sheep and goats, being further defined by כשׂבים and עזים. Ver. 35 is a more minute description of this verse. The LXX have παρελθάτω, reading the easier reading יַעֲבֹר כָּל־; Vulg. '*gyra omnes greges tuos*' (עבר בכל), both regarding הסר as imper.

כשׂבים. A form peculiar to the Pent., for which we find elsewhere כבשׂים.

33. וענתה בי צדקתי. Mühlau and Volck (Ges., *H.W.B.*, 11th ed.) render here and 1 Sam. 12, 3, '*bear witness for me;*' but as ענה . . . ב always elsewhere means '*to bear witness against,*' and as this meaning is not unsuitable in 1 Sam. 12, 3, it is preferable to follow Del. and render '*my righteousness*

shall testify against me,' i.e. I shall be self-condemned (Wright).

ביום מחר = '*hereafter;*' cf. Ex. 13, 14. Deut. 6, 20. Josh. 4, 6.

כי תבא . . . לפניך. '*When thou comest about my hire, before thee,*' i.e. when thou comest to inspect the cattle (my hire) which will be before thee; or לפניך may be connected with וענתה בי צדקתי, in the sense '*my righteousness will testify against me . . . before thee;*' but the position of לפניך, at some distance from וענתה בי צדקתי, is against this.

וחום = ואיננו חום, as the black sheep, being Jacob's hire, could not be regarded as stolen.

35. יָסַר, imperf. Hif'., not Qal, although the shortened imperf. third pers. masc. sing. Qal and Hif'. are the same, the context alone deciding the conjugation intended. Laban is here the subject, as is clear from בניו at the end of the verse, and בינו ובין יעקב in the next verse. The cattle left with Jacob were of normal colour, white sheep and dark-coloured goats.

36. בינו '*between him.*' LXX and Sam. בינם (ביניהם) '*between them,*' i.e. his sons.

37. מקל doubtless collective, hence the fem. (as בהן shews); elsewhere it is masculine.

לבנה = '*Storax*' (*Styrax officinalis*). Arabic لُبْنَى; cf. Löw, *Aram. Pflanzenn.*, 153. The noun לבנה is of the same form as פִּשְׁתָּה, אִשָּׁה, ـָה = ـי (cf. the Arabic name ending in ىَ = ـי, and see Stade, § 301 b), from לבן, so called on account of the milk-like gum that flows from it when its bark is cut. Others, following the Vulg. here and the LXX in Hos. 4, 13, render '*poplar;*' so R.V. here.

לוז = '*almond.*' Arabic لَوْز, Aram. ܠܘܙܐ. Del. remarks that לח is the more Aramaic-Arabic word for שָׁקֵד; cf. Löw, l. c. 49, 69, 374.

ערמון = '*plane tree*' (*Platanus orientalis*), from ערם '*to strip*,' so called because the bark peels off from year to year, and the tree becomes as it were naked.

מחשׂף = חשׂף, inf. abs. '*exposing the white;*' one of the very few instances in Hebrew of an abstract form with the force of an infinitive; so מִקְרָא, מַסַּע (as inf. cstr.) from נָסַע, מצוה (Neh. 12, 45, with acc.); cf. Ryssel, *De Eloh. Pent. serm.*, p. 50; Ges., § 45, l. c.; Ewald, § 239 a. In Aramaic the inf. of the first conjugation (=Qal) is formed by prefixing מ.

38. רהטים, rare and Aramaising, here explained by שׁקתות מים.

שׁקתות is pl. of שֹׁקֶת, like אִמֲרוֹת, Ps. 12, 7, from אֹמֶר; cf. Ges., § 95. Rem. 1; Stade, § 187 b; Ewald, § 212 b, who cites סִבְכֵי from סֹבֶךְ.

לנכח '*over against.*'

תָּבֹאןָ in this verse, and יָשִׂים in verse 42 are used in a frequentative sense.

ויחמנה from חמם (cf. Deut. 19, 6), instead of וַתֵּחַמְנָה, so 1 Sam. 6, 12 וַיִּשַּׁרְנָה; Dan. 8, 22 יַעֲמֹדְנָה (all). In Arabic the third fem. pl. form is يَقْتُلْنَ, and in Aramaic יִקְטְלָן; cf. Wright, *Comp. Gram.*, p. 185; see Ges., § 47. 3. Rem. 3; Stade, § 534. 1. *H. W. B.*, 11th ed., gives the root as יחם, not חמם, ייחמנה=יחמנה; cf. יֵשֵׁב from יָשַׁב, but admits that it is possible to derive the form from חמם. If it is from חָמַם it follows the analogy of יֵמַר, יֵרַךְ.

39. וַיֶּחֱמוּ, = וַיֵּחַמּוּ, plural masc., because the male animals are included. יחמו is either imperf. from חמם = יֵחַמּוּ, Hos.

7, 7, or imperf. Qal of יֵחַם, for יֵחֲמוּ or יֵחַמּוּ; cf. Judg. 5, 28 אֶחֱרוּ for אֵחֲרוּ; Ps. 51, 7 יֶחֱמַתְנִי for יֵחֲמַתְנִי: see Ges., §§ 64. 3. Rem. 3; 67. 5. Rem.; 69. 1 b; cf. Stade, § 523 d, who regards יֶחֱמוּ as lightened from יֵחֲמוּ, for יֵחַמּוּ, after the analogy of verbs ל״ה; and König, *Lehrg.*, pp. 365, 417 ff., who derives both words from יחם; comparing the inf. Pi'el in ver. 41.

אל המקלות. Cf. 24, 11 אל באר המים '*at the well of water.*'

עקדים = '*striped.*'

40. והכשׂבים are the particoloured animals, goats and sheep; these Jacob separated from the normally coloured animals in Laban's flock. He then turns Laban's normal coloured animals in the direction of the כשׂבים, so that they might have these before their eyes. But these abnormal coloured animals belong to Jacob, according to his agreement with Laban, and so cannot be spoken of as עקד וכל חום בצאן לבן. If the text were emended as follows, the difficulty would disappear, ויתן פני צאן לבן אל עקד וכל חום בצאנו, i.e. '*he set the face of Laban's flock towards what was striped and* (*towards*) *everything dark in his own flock.*' לבן has fallen out of its place after צאן, which then received the article, and the waw of בצאנו disappeared before the waw of וַיָּשֶׁת. Otherwise we must assume with Del., Di., and others that ויתן . . . לבן are a later addition to the text. Knobel emends by reading כל עקד, with Onq., Ps.-Jon., and takes פני for לפני '*before,*' as Ex. 23, 15. Ps. 42, 3; but then Jacob's dark and particoloured cattle are described as Laban's. Wright adopts Knobel's emendation, but avoids the above-mentioned difficulty by deleting לבן and reading בצאן. לבן might certainly have crept in, from the צאן לבן in the next line.

41, 42. The old translators explain these verses by the

fact that the strong cattle bring forth their young in winter, and the weak cattle theirs in the spring: thus המקשרות would be the winter cattle, and העטפים the spring cattle.

41. והיה . . . ושׂם, perfs. with waw conv. in a frequentative sense; see Driver, § 120. לְיַחֲמֶנָּה is inf. Pi'el of יחם, with the third pl. fem. suffix ־ֶנָּה for ־ָן; cf. 41, 21 קִרְבֶּנָה, and see Ges., § 91. 1. Rem. 2; Stade, § 352 b. 2, who remarks that the dagesh should be struck out.

43. צאן רבות, the collective being construed with a plural adjective; cf. 1 Sam. 13, 15 את העם הנמצאים עמו, 1 Sam. 17, 28 מעט הצאן ההנה; see Ges., § 132. Rem. 5 b; M. R., § 85. Rem. b; Dav., *S.*, § 31.

31.

1. הכבד הזה = '*this wealth;*' cf. Is. 10, 3. Ps. 49, 17.

4. השׂדה is acc. of place; see note on 12, 15.

5. ראה . . . את־פני . . . כי איננו. The logical subject of the object sentence attracted as object into the governing clause; see note on 1, 4. and Ex. 2, 2. 2 Sam. 17, 8. 1 Kings 5, 17. איננו refers to פְּנֵי; cf. Lam. 4, 16, where פני is followed by a singular verb.

6. וְאַתֵּנָה for אַתֵּן, also pointed אַתֵּנָּה (cf. the Arabic أَنْتُنَّ), is only found again in Ez. 13, 11. 20. 34, 17; see Ges., § 32. Rem. 5; Stade, § 178 c; Wright, *Comp. Gram.*, p. 102.

7. הֵתֶל for הֵתֵל, with retrogression of the tone by Ges., § 29. 3 b; Stade, § 88. 2 b. התל is Hif'. of חלל; cf. the Lexic. and Ewald, § 127 d. The ה of the Hif'. is retained, as though it were a radical letter, in the forms תְּהַתֵּלּוּ (notice

the dag. in ל), Job 13, 9; יְהָתֵלּוּ, Jer. 9, 4; וַיְהַתֵּל, 1 Kings 18, 27: see Stade, § 145 e, and Wright, *Arab. Gram.*, i. p. 37.

החל... והחלף. I. Either like Num. 11, 8 שטו... ולקטו, 'the fact being stated summarily by the perfect, and this tense being followed by the perfect with waw conv.;' see Driver, § 114 a; Ges., § 112. 3 *a*, *γ*. II. Or like 1 Sam. 12, 2 זקנתי ושבתי; Is. 1, 2 etc.: והחליף not being *subordinate* to התל (the imperf. with waw conv. would be required then) but *co-ordinate;* see Driver, § 132; Dav., *S.*, § 58 a.

עשרת מונים. '*Ten times;*' LXX, δέκα ἀμνῶν, possibly corrupted out of a reading μνῶν. The translators, not understanding מונים, wrote the Hebrew word in Greek, and this passed over into ἀμνῶν; cf. Frankel, *Einf.*, p. 18, and ver. 41. The word מונים is peculiar to this chapter, elsewhere פעמים is used, e.g. Num. 14, 22, or רְגָלִים, Ex. 23, 14. Aq. has δέκα ἀριθμούς, Symm. δεκάκις ἀρίθμῳ.

8. The account of the agreement made between Jacob and Laban in this chapter differs from that in chap. 30, and is derived from a different source; 30, 25–31, 1 being mainly from J; 31, 2–18[a] mainly from E. Cf. Dr., *Introd.*, p. 15; Di., pp. 338 f. and 349 f.

נקדים יהיה. יהיה, the singular is perhaps due to the following שכרך; see Ges., § 145. 7. Rem. 3.

'*If he were to say thus, The spotted shall be thy hire; then all the flock used to bring forth spotted: and if he were to say thus, The striped shall be thy hire; then all the flock used to bring forth striped.*' Cf. Num. 9, 19–21. Ex. 40, 37 ואם לא יעלה הענן ולא יסעו (the apod. being in the imperf., as the waw is separated from the verb by לא); see Driver, § 136 δ. Obs., cf. § 123 β; Dav., *S.*, § 130 b; Ges., §§ 112. 5 *a*, β; 159. 3. 2 e.

9. אביכם for אביכן; cf. Ges., § 135. 5. Rem. 1.

10. ברדים = טלוא, in 30, 32; it is found twice again in Zech. 6, 3. 6 (of horses), and = '*speckled.*' ברדים probably = '*covered as it were with hailstones*' (בָּרָד), so '*white spots on a dark ground*' (Tuch).

13. האל ביתאל. '*I am the God at Bethel,*' i.e. the God who appeared to thee at Bethel. So Dr., § 191. Obs. 2, who compares 2 Kings 23, 17 המזבח ביתאל '*the altar in Bethel,*' also Num. 22, 5. 2 Sam. 17, 26. Others regard הָאֵל as construct state with the article, see Ewald, 290 d (3), who cites other instances, e.g. Jer. 48, 32, etc.; see also Is. 36, 8. 16; and cf. M. R., § 76. R. b; Dav., *S.*, § 20. R. 4; Ges., § 127. Rem. 4 a (= הָאֵל אֵל ב״).

14. ותען . . . ותאמרנה. On the first verb with a compound subject in the singular and the second in the plural, see references in note on 7, 7, and cf. 9, 23. 21, 32. 24, 50. 33, 7. 44, 14.

15. ויאכל גם אכול. '*And goes on to eat up;*' cf.—for force of imperf. with waw conv.—note on 19, 9. Here אָכֹל inf. abs. comes *after* the verb for emphasis, and the inf. abs. is further strengthened by adding גם as in 46, 4 (cf. note). Num. 16, 13. See also note on 29, 30.

16. כי. Not '*so that;*' Del. and Kn., neither here nor in Job 10, 6. Deut. 14, 24; but Di. '*rather,*' or '*nay, rather;*' cf. Pss. 37, 20. 49, 11. 130, 4.

19. הלך לגזז. In 38, 13 we find לגז, the shorter form; cf. לסבב, Num. 21, 4, and the short form סב, Deut. 2, 3; see Stade, § 619 e; Ges., § 67. Rem. 10. הלך is pluperfect, '*had gone.*'

התרפים = '*The Teraphim,*' Laban's household gods.

LXX here τὰ εἴδωλα, but the word is variously rendered by them in the other passages where it occurs. The Teraphim were of human form (1 Sam. 19, 13), and were worshipped as gods (ver. 30. Judg. 18, 24). Their worship was not recognised as legitimate (see 2 Kings 23, 24; cf. Gen. 35, 4 and Hos. 3, 4), yet they were at all times regarded as household oracles (Judg. 18, 5. Zech. 10, 2. Ez. 21, 26), and (possibly) as bringing prosperity; therefore Rachel takes them with her, to avoid bringing misfortune or ill luck on her household; cf. Judg. 18, 17, where the Danites take Micha's household gods. The pl. form may here only denote a single image, as in 1 Sam. 19, 13 (see Ges., § 124 c; Dav., *S.*, § 16 c); cf. אדונים and בעלים, both used as intensive plurals; the pl. suf. in ver. 34, and אלהי in ver. 30, not being decisive in favour of taking תרפים as a real plural; cf. Ewald, § 318 a. No certain etymology has yet been found. The one most commonly given is from the Arabic تَرِفَ '*commode vivere*,' which would agree with the idea that the תרפים were the gods who were supposed to bring good fortune to those who worshipped them; but it is not certain that تَرِفَ does not rather mean '*to be soft*;' cf. Tuch, p. 395; Del.[4], p. 555, who also suggests a comparison with the Sanskrit *tarp*, '*to be full*.' The word has also been connected with רְפָאִים (Neubauer, *Academy*, No. 756, p. 297), and Assyr. *tarpu*, =*dimma*, '*a shade*' (Sayce, *Z. A.*, ii. 95), the meaning being, '*shades of the dead*,' but this explanation is very improbable, and cannot be supported by the usage of תרפים in the O. T. The תרפים stood in no connection with the שׂרפים.

20. ויגנב . . . את לב = '*deceived*;' cf. 2 Sam. 15, 6 וַיְגַנֵּב אבשלום את לב, but in the sense '*to win over secretly*;' cf. κλέπτειν νόον and κλέπτειν τινά (Del.).

על בלי is only found here. בלי = לא with the finite verb, occurs in Job 41, 18. Hos. 8, 7. 9, 16 (Ktb.). Is. 14, 6; see Ewald, § 322 a. Render, '*In that he did not tell.*' On על, cf. Ges., § 158.

21. הנהר. '*The river*' *par excellence*, i.e. the Euphrates; see Ges., § 126. 2 d; Dav., *S.*, § 21 c. So often, e.g. Is. 27, 12. Ps. 72, 8.

23. את אחיו. '*His friends and fellow-tribesmen;*' cf. Lev. 10, 4. 2 Sam. 19, 13.

24. מטוב עד רע. '*Either good or bad,*' i.e. *anything at all:* cf. ver. 29. 24, 50. Num. 24, 13. 2 Sam. 13, 22.

25. בהר . . . בהר הגלעד. From a comparison of vers. 21 and 23 with this verse, Jacob and Laban apparently encamped in the same place (so Vulg.); yet the narrative evidently implies that Laban encamped in one place and Jacob in another. Probably something has been omitted after בהר. Di.'s explanation of the text is ingenious, if not convincing. He assumes that הר in J was followed by a proper name (Lag. suggests בהר מצפה, cf. ver. 49). R omitted this, as it did not suit the text of E. Or J did not mention the name of the hill, as he wished to reserve his account of its origin, until ver. 48 (then 25^b comes from R).

26. עשית ותגנב. The imperf. with waw conv. used to define or explain עשׂה; so in 1 Sam. 8, 8. 1 Kings 2, 5; see Driver, § 76 a; Dav., *S.*, § 47.

27. למה נחבאת לברח. '*Why didst thou fly in secret?*' see on 27, 20.

ואשלחך. '*And so I could have sent thee away;*' see on 12, 19. On the ֲ in וָאֲשַׁלֵּחֲךָ, see Ges., § 65. 2. note; also Stade, § 633 a.

28. הסכלת עשׂוֹ = '*thou hast acted foolishly.*' עֲשׂוֹ for עֲשׂוֹת; cf. רְאֹה, 48, 11: עֲשֹׂה, 50, 20; עֲשֹׂהוּ, Ex. 18, 18; and see Ges., § 75. Rem. 2; Stade, § 619 k. In הסכלת עשׂו the construction is the same as in 8, 10 ויסף שלח.

29. יש לאל ידי. Cf. Mic. 2, 1. Prov. 3, 27; the neg. is אין לאל ידך, Deut. 28, 32. Neh. 5, 5. Hitzig explains the phrase as meaning '*My hand is for God,*' which would be suitable if the meaning intended were, '*I am capable* or *able to do everything,*' but scarcely suitable when the meaning is, as here, '*I have the power;*' lit. '*it is according to the power of my hand.*' אֵל is a noun=*strength*, cf. Barth, *N. B.*, p. 79. R. Ges., Del., Tuch, Di. render, '*It is in the power of my hand.*'

אביכם. The plural suffix refers to Jacob and those who were with him.

30. '*And now (when) thou art going right away, for thou longest sore for thy father's house, why hast thou stolen my gods?*' הלך and נכסף are infs. abs., prefixed to the finite verb for emphasis; see the note on 2, 16; and cf. 16, 10. 18, 10. 2 Sam. 5, 19. נכסף, on the form, cf. Ges., § 51. Rem. 1. The word is only found here in the Pent.

31. כי יראתי. Cf. the note on 20, 11.

32. עם אשר '*with whomsoever,*' for אשר . . . עמו; the phrase is unusual, yet imitated here by the Pesh. ܠܘܬ ܡܢ ܕ; see Ewald, § 333 a; Ges., § 138. 1. foot-note 2; M. R., § 158. Rem. a; Dav., *S.*, § 10. R. 1. In 44, 9. 10 we have the regular construction אשר . . . אתו.

33. האמהת is pl. of אמה, with the insertion of a ה; see Stade, § 188; Ges., § 96; and cf. the Arabic أَمَةٌ, pl. أَمَوَاتٌ, with و instead of the Heb. ה. The Aram. ܐܡܬܐ, pl. ܐܡܗܬܐ,

and אָמָא, pl. אַמְהָתָא, have ה as in Hebrew. Cf. also Lag., *B. N.*, p. 82, and Barth, *N. B.*, p. 8.

34. כר is ἅπαξ λεγόμ. LXX, εἰς τὰ σάγματα = '*saddle*.' כַּר, so called from its round basket-shaped form (root כרר), was protected by a cover or tent, in which the women sat, something like a modern palanquin; see Di., p. 354.

35. לקום מפניך. Cf. Lev. 19, 32. Rachel's plan was ingenious, as any attempt to examine the camel's saddle would involve contact with an unclean thing.

36. דלקת אחרי. דלק אחרי = '*to burn after one*;' i.e. to hotly pursue one; so 1 Sam. 17, 53 מדלק אחרי פלשתים.

39. טרפה לא הבאתי. Cf. Ex. 22, 12.

אֲחַטֶּנָּה, for אֲחַטְּאֶנָּה, as though from a verb ל״ה; see Ges., § 74. Rem. 4; cf. § 75. Rem. 21 c; Stade, § 111. חִטֵּא here is synonymous with שִׁלֵּם, Ex. 22, 12.

גנבתי יום with the old binding vowel ִי—; cf. on 1, 24. It always has the tone with the exception of two places, Lam. 1, 1 and Hos. 10, 11, in the former of which the accent is on the penult., on account of a word of one syllable following; cf. Ges., § 90. 3 a; Stade, § 343 d; Wright, *Comp. Gram.*, p. 141 f. The two imperfs. אחטנה, תבקשנה are frequentative.

40. Cf. Jer. 36, 30. In the East the cold at night is quite as intense as the heat by day. Cf. Sh., *G.*, p. 69 f.; Bäd., *Pal.*, p. xlvii.

41. עשרת מנים. Cf. ver. 7. Ten here, and ver. 7, is a round number = '*often*.'

42. פחד. So ver. 53; cf. מורא, Is. 8, 12. פחד is abstract for concrete; so σέβας = σέβασμα. The Pesh. uses ܕܚܠܬܐ here and Is. 8, 12 in a similar way. In the Jer.-Targ. on Deut. 32, 15, and the Targ. on Hos. 8, 6, and often else-

where, we find דְחִלָא used, as פחד here, and מורא in Is., l. c.; compare also a similar use of יראה in the Talmud, *Sanh.*, 64 a הוציא יראתו מחיקו וגו׳ '*he takes his god* (i. e. *idol*) *out of his bosom*, etc.' Render, '*If the God of my father . . . had not been for me . . . for then*;' an aposiopesis: or כי עתה may be regarded as an apodosis and rendered, '*indeed then thou hadst*,' etc.; cf. 43, 10 כי לולא התמהמהנו כי עתה שבנו; Num. 22, 29 לו יש חרב . . . כי עתה; 2 Sam. 2, 27 (כי אז); and see Driver, § 141. Cf. Ewald, § 358 a; Ges., § 159. Rem. 3; Dav., *S.*, § 131. and R. 2.

43. מה אעשׂה לאלה. '*What am I going to do to these?*' i. e. how am I going to harm them? For עשׂה ל in a bad sense, see 22, 12. 27, 45. Ex. 14, 11.

44. נכרתה . . . והיה. Cf. on 1, 14. The subj. to היה cannot be ברית, as this is fem., and the action itself (the making a covenant) cannot be regarded as a witness, and so cannot be subject. Di. therefore deletes the ל before עֵד, which then becomes the subject, = '*and let there be a witness*;' otherwise we must suppose with Olshausen that something has fallen out of the text.

45. וירימה מצבה, lit. '*and he set it up* (*so that it became*) *a pillar*;' cf. 1 Kings 18, 32 בנה את האבנים מזבח; Gen. 28, 18 וישׂם אתה מצבה; see note on 6, 14.

47. יגר שׂהדותא = Heb. גלעד, the first occurrence of Aramaic words in the O.T. שׂהדותא, cf. Job 16, 19 ושׂהדי = '*my witness*,' after the form of the Aramaic participle. The naming of the place with an Aramaic and Hebrew name was probably occasioned by its position on the frontier, between Aramaic and Hebrew-speaking people; see Di., p. 356.

הַר הַגִּלְעָד or אֶרֶץ הַגִּלְעָד is in the O.T. the name of the stretch of territory (chiefly mountain and hill country) which extended from the edge of the plateau of Moab up to the Yarmuk, being cut into two parts by the Wady Jabbok. The northern portion between the Jabbok and Yarmuk (Deut. 3, 13. Josh. 12, 5. cf. 1 Kings 4, 19) coincides with the modern district of 'Ajlun; and the southern portion, with that part of the Belka', which stretches from Mount Heshbon to the Jabbok (Deut. 3, 12. Josh. 12, 2). At the present day the long ridge south of the Jabbok is still called Jebel Jela'ad. Cf. Sh., *G.*, p. 583 f.; Bäd., *Pal.*, p. 176. The identification of the sites of the various places in Gilead is very uncertain; cf. Di., p. 358, and Sh., *G.*, l.c. Mizpeh, the scene of Jacob's covenant with Laban, has been placed by Conder at Sûf, a place of dolmens and stone-circles between 'Ajlun and Jerash (cf. Sh., *G.*, p. 586). This identification, however, is uncertain, as several Mizpehs are mentioned in the O.T. in different localities, and we have no certainty that these were the same, and even if they were identical, one site, which would suit all of them, can hardly be discovered; cf. Sh., l. c.; Di., l. c.

49. As the text stands, ver. 49 must be closely connected with 48, '*and Mizpah* (*he called the place*) *because he said,*' etc.; so Kn., Keil; but והמצפה is strange, as nothing has been said about a מִצְפָּה '*a look-out,*' '*watch-tower.*' Ewald emends, והמצבה המצפה '*and the pillar* (*he called*) *Hammizpah*' (*Komp. der Gen.*, p. 64), which is supported by Saadiah. The Vss. vary, and do not give any clue to solve the difficulty. Di., p. 356, suggests that ver. 49 in its present form does not come from J, but has been revised and modified by R; as at his time a Mizpah in Gilead was better known than a Maṣṣeba, but expresses some doubt as to whether R freely inserted all from יִצֶף to מֵרֵעֵהוּ, and 50b, which belongs to this, or made use of information derived from J.

50. אם in an oath, as in 14, 23, which compare.

52. **אם** with a following ואם=*sive . . . sive;* so Del. and Dav., *S.*, § 152, who compare Ex. 19, 13 אם בהמה אם איש לא יחיה '*whether beast or man, he shall not live.*' Di. prefers to take them as the אם in ver. 50, and renders, '*surely not I, I will not pass;*' the אם and then לא expressing a strong negative; but this seems unnecessary.

53. **ישפטו**. Perhaps the plural is used as the gods of Nahor are mentioned, the narrator supposing that Nahor worshipped idols, as Laban did (cf. the תרפים); see Josh. 24, 2. The words אֱלֹהֵי אֲבִיהֶם may, however, be a gloss. They are wanting in the LXX, and some Hebrew codices. They are rejected by Kennic., Olsh., Welh., Geiger, *Urschrift*, p. 284, and Di. LXX, Pesh., Sam., Vulg. give the sing. ישפט.

54. Cf. 26, 30. Ex. 24, 11. 2 Sam. 3, 20.

32.

1. **אתהם** is rare; cf. Ex. 18, 20. Num. 21, 3. Ez. 34, 12. 1 Chron. 6, 50 (all), and once אוֹתֵהֶם, Ez. 23, 45. The usual form is אֹתָם. In the fem., on the contrary, the usual form is אֶתְהֶן (אֹתָן only in Ez. 16, 54).

3. **מחנים**='*two camps.*' LXX have παρεμβολαί, as though מ״ were a plural from מַחֲנֵי. The dual, however, suits vers. 8–11 better than a plural. The two camps were his own, and the angel host he had just met. On the proper names in Hebrew which are apparently duals see the note on 37, 17. מחנים was situated on the borders of the territory of Gad, Josh. 13, 26. 30. It lay probably to the north of the Jabbok, and was one of the most important towns in Gilead (cf. 2 Sam. 2, 8. 12. 29. 17, 24. 27. 1 Kings 4, 14). Its identification has not yet been determined. 'Conder places

Mahanaim near Buḳei'a to the east of Salt, a region not likely to contain so important a town, and hardly on the border of Gad (Josh. l. c.). Merrill suggests Khurbet Suleikhat, 300 feet above the Ghôr, in the Wady 'Ajlun,' Sh. *G.*, p. 586. Kiepert places it provisionally between the Jordan and the Jabbok, a little south of Amathus.

5. תאמרון. Cf. Ges., § 47. Rem. 4; Stade, § 520 a; see on 3, 4.

וָאֵחַר is imperf. Qal, by syncope, for וָאֶאֱחַר; so אֹהֵב for אֶאֱהַב, Prov. 8, 17: see Ges., § 68. 1. note; Stade, § 112 c.

6. ואשלחה. Cf. on 41, 11.

7. וגם הלך לקראתך. The participle without any subject expressed; so אף חבב, Deut. 33, 3; אם משלחים, 1 Sam. 6, 3; cf. Gen. 24, 30. 37, 15. 38, 24. 41, 1 (all with הנה): see Driver, § 135. 6. 2; Ewald, § 303 b; Ges., § 116. 5. Rem. 3; Dav., *S.*, § 100 a.

8. וַיֵּצֶר is imperf. Qal from צרר, Ewald, § 232 c; Stade, § 510 g. The ֶ in the last syllable is due to the tone being drawn back to the penult., as in Job 20, 22 יֵצֶר לוֹ.

9. אל המחנה האחת. מחנה, usually masc., is here fem., as in Ps. 27, 3; as the masc. immediately follows, the fem. is strange; the Heb.-Sam. reads הָאֶחָד, which is probably the correct reading.

אם יבוא . . . והכהו. Cf. 18, 26. 24, 8. 28, 20, and ver. 18 of this chapter, where כי takes the place of אם; see Driver, § 136 a, and cf. p. 130; M. R., § 24. 2 a; Dav., *S.*, § 130, and R. 1; Ges., § 112. 5 a, *a*.

פליטה is abstract, '*escape*,' and then concrete, '*escaped ones*.'

11. קטנתי מכל, render as a present, קטן being a *stative*

verb, '*I am unworthy*,' lit. '*too small;*' see Driver, § 11; M.R., § 2. 1; Ges., § 106. 2 a; Dav., *S.*, § 40.

מכל. On the (comparative) מן here = the positive with '*too*,' see M. R., § 49. 2. Rem. a; cf. notes on 18, 14 היפלא מיהוה דבר; 4, 13 גדול עוני מנשוא.

כִּי בְמַקְלִי. ב is pointed with dag. lene, although the preceding word ends in a vowel, and has a conjunctive accent, because the aspirate in the connected sounds במ is hardened (i.e. removed), just as in בְּב, כְּכ, בְּפ, כְּב, כְּפ; see Ges., § 21. 1. Rem. 2, and Del.[4], p. 416.

הייתי לשני מחנות. '*I have become* (*and still am*) *two camps;*' see Driver, § 8.

12. ירא . . . אתו. Cf. 22, 12 and note on 4, 14.

אם על בנים. The phrase occurs again in Hos. 10, 14 (cf. Deut. 22, 6), and is a proverbial expression. על depicts the mother hovering over her children, and vainly trying to defend them: or על may be taken as in Job 38, 32. Ex. 35, 22 האנשים על הנשים '*the men together with the women.*' The first explanation is perhaps preferable. The clause is a circumstantial clause, so ver. 31; cf. note on 12, 8.

14. מן הבא בידו = '*of what he had*,' lit. '*of that which had come into his hand;*' cf. 35, 4 אשר בידם. R.V. '*of that which he had with him.*'

15. ותישים עשׂרים. The numeral after the noun, in apposition, is rare in the earlier books of the O.T.; cf. ver. 16, and see Dav., *S.*, §§ 36 c, 37 b.

16. בניהם. The masc. suff. for the fem., as in 31, 9; cf. 26, 15 and the note there.

פרים = '*young bullocks*,' standing in the same relation to

פרות as עירים '*foals*' (here '*asses' foals*') to the אתונות. וְעִיָרִים is for וַעְיָרִים; cf. Ges., § 28. 2.

17. עדר עדר לבדו, lit. '*flock, flock alone*,' i.e. 'by herds or flocks,' so that each flock had one servant; cf. Ges., § 123 d. 2; M. R., § 72. 2; Dav., *S.*, § 29. R. 8.

18. יִפְגָשְׁךָ. So pointed in Baer and Del.'s edition, following Ben Asher's reading. Ben Naftali reads, however, יִפְגָּשְׁךָ. Ben Asher's reading was pronounced *yif-ghā-shăcha*, Ben Naftali's *yif-gosh-cha;* cf. Baer and Del., *Gen.*, p. 85. The imperf. יִפְגַּשׁ would be a by-form of יִפְגֹּשׁ; cf. 1 Sam. 25, 20. On the Ḥatef-pathach under שׁ, cf. on 2, 12 וּזֲהַב.

20. בְּמֹצַאֲכֶם, for בְּמָצְאֲכֶם; see Ewald, § 63. 1, and Ges., § 74. Rem. 2; and cf. הֹעֲלָה, for הָעֱלָה; and Stade, § 109. במצאכם = '*when you find*,' lit. '*in your finding*.'

23. בלילה הוא. Cf. 19, 33 and the note there.

יבק is the present Wady Zerkâ, which divides the districts of 'Ajlun and Belka', and falls into the Jordan in the latitude of Shechem, N. of the Dead Sea. The modern name Zerkâ, = '*blue flood*,' is derived from the clear blue colour of the water. Cf. Bäd., *Pal.*, p. 178; Sh., *G.*, p. 583 f. The name יבק is probably to be derived from בקק '*to pour out;*' here it is brought into connection with the root אבק, as though יַבֹּק = יַאֲבֹק = '*striver*,' '*wrestler;*' cf. Ges., *Thes.*, p. 233 a.

25. ויאבק = '*he wrestled*,' is found only here and ver. 26. אבק is possibly connected with חבק, or perhaps is only a dialectic variation of the same; the word is probably chosen on account of the pr. n. יבק. In Hos. 12, 4 ויאבק is explained by שָׂרָה. Tuch and *H. W. B.*, 11th ed., propose a derivation, as Niph. denom., from אָבָק '*dust*,' i.e. '*to scatter oneself with*

dust;' as κονίεσθαι, from κόνις, the powder with which wrestlers were sprinkled after being oiled. In C. P. Ges. the word is explained as a denominative, '*to wrestle*' = *get dusty;* cf. Strack, *Pirke Aboth*, i. 4, וֶהֱוֵי מִתְאַבֵּק בַּעֲפַר רַגְלֵיהֶם = *sit at their feet.*

26. ותקע, imperf. Qal from יקע.

27. כי אם ברכתני. '*Except thou bless me;*' cf. 2 Kings 4, 24. Ruth 3, 18; and see Driver, § 17; Dav., *S.*, § 154; Ges., § 163. 2; M. R., § 168 c.

29. ישׂראל = '*God's striver,*' '*he who strives with God,*' in this passage and Hos. 12, 4 (hence the choice of the rare verb שׂרה in both places), as though ישׂראל = אשר ישׂרה עם אל (Wright). The name perhaps really means—as distinct from the meaning given in the text—'*God strives, fights,*' יִשְׂרֶה אֵל; cf. יִשְׁמָעֵאל; so Robertson-Smith, *Proph. in Isr.*, p. 36, who compares יַהְוֶה צְבָאוֹת. Ges. in *Thes.*, p. 1338 b, Tuch, Reuss, and others explain it as meaning '*Soldier of God,*' i.e. he who fights for and with God's help. In 35, 10 (P) we have another account of the alteration of Jacob's name.

וַתּוּכַל, (I) an imperf. Hof'. of יכל, used as the imperf. Qal; so Ewald, § 127 b: (II) Stade, § 486, and Ges., § 69. 2. Rem. 3, regard it as an imperf. Qal יוּכַל = יוֹכַל = יִוְכַל = יוּכַל; cf. the Arabic imperf. يَوْجَلُ from وَجِلَ, and Wright, *Arab. Gram.*, i. pp. 89–90.

30. Cf. Judg. 13, 17.

לשׁמי. '*About my name;*' cf. 20, 2 and the note there.

31. ותנצל נפשׁי. Cf. Ex. 33, 20; also Judg. 13, 22. Deut. 4, 33; and the note on 16, 14. וְ = *and yet;* see Driver, § 74 β; Ges., § 111. 1. R. 4; cf. M. R., § 18. 2; another expl. Dav., *S.*, § 48. R. 1.

פניאל, or פנואל in ver. 32,=*'face of God;'* cf. on 4, 18 מתושאל. In פניאל the י is the old binding vowel; see on גנבתי, 31, 39. The position of פניאל cannot be ascertained. Kiepert provisionally locates it on the south of the Jabbok to the NW. of Ramoth Gilead. 'Merrill suggests the Tulul edh-Dhahab, round and between which the Jabbok forces its way into the Jordan; Conder puts Penuel on the ridge of the Jebel 'Osha,' Sh., *G.*, p. 586.

33. את גיד הנשה וגו׳ =*'the hip-sinew, which is on the hollow of the thigh.'* גיד הנשה = the Arabic نَسًا, the nerve or tendon which goes through the thigh and leg to the ancle, the *nervus ischiadicus;* see Ges., *Thes.*, p. 921 a. The law forbidding the children of Israel to eat the גיד הנשה is not mentioned in the O. T. It is to be found in the Talmud, *Tract. Chullin*, chap. 7.

33.

3. והוא is emphatic, *he*, Jacob, as opposed to the persons mentioned in ver. 2; see Driver, § 160. Obs.; Dav., *S.*, § 107.

4. וַיִּשָּׁקֵהוּ. Mas. note, וישקהו כלו נקוד=*'with points on every letter.'* The Mid. Bem., cited by Strack, *Prol. Crit.*, p. 89, has וישקהו נקוד עליו על שלא נשקו מכל לבו, i. e. 'וישקהו *with points over it, because he did not kiss him with all his heart;'* cf. the Ber. Rab. in Strack, l. c., where Rabbi Yanai, answering Rabbi Simeon ben Eleazar, explains the points on וישקהו thus: שלא בא לנשקו אלא לנשכו *'because he did not come to kiss him* (*Jacob*), *but to bite him,'* and goes on to say that Jacob's neck was turned into marble; an account hardly in keeping with what we are told of Esau, who is never depicted in the O. T. as an inhuman person. The points probably here, as in the other cases where they occur, mark the word

as suspicious; cf. Ewald, § 19 d. The Targ. Ps.-Jon. explains that Jacob wept because his neck was painful, and Esau because the effort gave him the toothache!! In 45, 14. 46, 29 '*falling on the neck*' is immediately followed by '*weeping*,' and in the several MSS. of the LXX (Lag., *Gen. Graece*, p. 134) the trans. of וישקהו is wanting. It, therefore, seems best to omit the word.

5. מי אלה לך. '*Who are these to thee?*' לך is dat. of reference; cf. Ex. 12, 26. Josh. 4, 6. 2 Sam. 16, 2.

חנן with double acc. So ברך 49, 25. 28; see Ges., § 117. 5 b, β; M. R., § 45. 3; Dav., *S.*, § 78. R. 1.

6, 7. ותגשן, agreeing with the subj. immediately following; so ותגש, ver. 7. On the gender and construction of the verbs in these verses, see M. R., § 138 and Rem.; Ges., § 146. 2 b; Ewald, § 339 c; Dav., *S.*, §§ 113, 114.

8. מי לך כל המחנה וגו״. '*What to thee is all this camp?*' i.e. the cattle (32, 14–22) which Esau had already met; cf. אשר פגשתי. מי by attraction = מה, so Judg. 13, 17 מי שמך; cf. 32, 28 מה שמך. Ewald, § 325 a, and Di. prefer the rendering, '*Who to thee is the camp?*' i.e. '*what dost thou wish to do with them?*' 'because he brings the people into the foreground.' Cf. Dav., *S.*, § 8. R. 1.

10. ולקחת = '*pray take;*' cf. 40, 14 ועשית '*pray shew mercy;*' Judg. 6, 17 ועשית לי אות '*pray give me a sign;*' see Driver, § 119 δ; and cf. Ges., § 112. 5 a, β.

כראת פני אלהים. '*As one sees the face of God,*' i.e. Jacob sees that Esau's face wears a friendly (lit. divine) aspect. 'It is a divine friendliness with which he came to meet him,' Di. ראת, the subject to the infinitive, is here indefinite, as Ex. 30, 12; see Dav., *S.*, § 91. R. 1.

11. הֻבָאת is third pers. fem. sing. Hof'. from בוא, with the old feminine ending ת (instead of ה), which is preserved as the usual ending of the third fem. perf. in Arabic, Aramaic, and Ethiopic, and appears in Hebrew before the suffixes, and sporadically elsewhere; cf. Wright, *Arab. Gram.*, i. p. 60; *Comp. Gram.*, p. 167 f.; Ges., § 74. Rem. 1; Stade, § 407 b; Dr., p. 236. Other instances of the fem. ending are קָרָאת, נִפְלָאת, שָׁבַת, אָזְלַת (the only case with the strong verb). LXX have here ἃς ἤνεγκά σοι,= הֵבֵאתִי, possibly not understanding the anomalous form.

ברכתי=*'present;'* so Josh. 15, 19. Judg. 1, 15. 1 Sam. 25, 27. 30, 26. 2 Kings 5, 15. ברכה=*'a present,'* i.e. as a proof of favour, and often accompanied with a blessing. Knobel compares the presents paid the clergy in the middle ages, called *Benedictiones*.

וכי יש לי כל. *'And because I have everything.'* וְכִי as in Judg. 6, 30. 1 Sam. 19, 4. Is. 65, 16; see Ewald, § 353 a. Esau has רב *'an abundance;'* Jacob, being under especial divine protection, can say he has כל *'everything.'*

13. עלות עלי=*'lactantes,'* i.e. *'with young;'* so Is. 40, 11. עלי=*'upon me;'* cf. 48, 7. 1 Sam. 21, 16; i.e. the cattle who were with young were a burden and responsibility to Jacob. The R.V. *'with me'* does not sufficiently express the על.

ודפקום . . . ומתו, lit.=*'and they over-drive them . . . and they die,'* i.e. *'if they over-drive them . . . they will die,'* the death of the cattle being conditional on their being over-driven; cf. 42, 38 וקראהו אסון . . . והורדתם=*'and if trouble befall him . . . ye will bring down;'* 44, 4. 22 ועזב את אביו ומת; cf. 29. See, on two perfs. with waw conv. forming a conditional sentence, Driver, § 149; also Ges., § 112. 5 a, ϵ; Ewald, § 357 a; M. R., § 28; Dav., *S.*, § 132.

ודפקום, the masc. suffix for the fem.; cf. on 26, 15; and on the third pers. pl. used indefinitely, see note on 29, 2.

14. לאטי, lit.=‘*according to my gentleness*,’ i.e. gently. ל is the ל of ‘norm’ or condition, cf. 2 Sam. 15, 11. Is. 11, 3. 32, 1; see Ew., § 217 d; Dav., *S.*, § 101. R. b: so לרגל.

לרגל המלאכה=‘*according to the pace of the cattle.*’ מלאכה=‘*property*’ (cf. מִקְנֶה), here, from the context, including cattle; cf. Ex. 22, 7 with vers. 9 and 10; 1 Sam. 15, 9.

17. בית=perhaps, as Del.[4] suggests, ‘*a house*,’ i.e. not a tent, אהל 27, 15, but ‘*a building*;’ here opposed to סכת ‘*booths*,’ ‘*tents*.’ Hence the name of the place, סכת.

סכות was probably on the *eastern* side of Jordan, in a valley, a little further west than Peniel; cf. Josh. 13, 27. Judg. 8, 5. 8. Ps. 60, 8. Its exact position is uncertain; but it must probably be sought for S. of the Jabbok, near the ford of Dâmie, on the road from es-Salṭ to Nablous (Köhler, *Geschichte*, i. p. 147, Keil, Del., Di.). Sh., *G.*, p. 585, however, thinks Succoth may be the present Tell Deir ‘Alla, a high mound in the Jordan valley, about 1 mile N. of the Jabbok. At the present day a Sâkût (سَاكُوت) exists, south of Bethshan, on the *western* side of Jordan, which is apparently distinct from the סכת of this verse; at any rate, it can hardly be the Succoth mentioned here, as it would be too far away from the line of Jacob's journey; see Di., p. 367; Del.[5], p. 409; also cf. Bäd., *Pal.*, p. 167.

18. שלם=בשלום, 28, 21, ‘*safe and sound*,’ after his late meeting with Esau, and the danger there might possibly have

been in encountering him. The LXX, Pesh., Hier. take שׁלם as a proper name. The Heb.-Sam. reads שׁלום here; cf. 43, 27.

שׁכם, cf. note on 12, 6, and see Sh., *G.*, pp. 332, 368 ff.; Bäd., *Pal.*, p. 216 f.

את פני='*before;*' cf. on 19, 13.

19. מיד בני חמור אבי שׁכם. '*From the sons of Ḥamor, the father of S.*,' i.e. the father of Shechem (34, 2), after whom the city was called Shechem; cf. 4, 17. The LXX omit בני, 'in order to agree with 34, 1 ff.,' Di.

קשׂיטה. LXX, Onq., Hier. render, '*lambs;*' cf. Ber. Rabba, c. 79; Targg. Ps.-Jon. and Jer. '*pearls.*' Rabbi Akiba, in the Talmud, *Tract. Rosh ha-shana*, 26 a, relates that in Africa he heard a coin (מָעָה) called קשׂיטה. Probably the word='*that which is weighed,*' from קשׂט=Arab. قَسَطَ= '*to divide,*' '*fix;*' cf. قِسْط '*a weight,*' '*pair of scales,*' then '*a fixed weight,*' equally used with the shekel by the patriarchs. From a comparison with 23, 15. 16 some have supposed the ק״ to be equivalent to four shekels, but this is quite uncertain. קשׂיטה occurs twice again, Josh. 24, 32. Job 42, 11, but neither passage throws any additional light on the word. Cf. also Madden, *Jewish Coinage*, p. 6.

34.

1. בת לאה אשׁר ילדה ליעקב (cf. 16, 15 f. 25, 12), an instance of P's circumstantial style.

2. וישׁכב אֹתָהּ. שׁכב with the acc., as in Lev. 15, 18. 24. Num. 5, 13. 19. 2 Sam. 13, 14. Deut. 28, 30. Kri; cf. שׁגל, which is construed with an acc. and always has a Kri,

שׁכב. The Mass. punctuation regards את in these passages as sign of acc., the analogy of שׁכב with עם, and אצל, favours the reading אִתָּהּ, cf. Geiger, *Urschrift*, p. 407 f.

3. הַנַּעֲרָ. Cf. the note on 24, 14.

וידבר על לב הנער = '*and he spake kindly to the damsel;*' cf. 50, 21 וידבר על לבם; Is. 40, 2. Hos. 2, 16.

5. '*Now Jacob had heard that he (Shechem) had defiled Dinah his daughter, while his sons were with his cattle in the field, and Jacob was silent until they came.*' והחרשׁ probably, as in 37, 3 ועשׂה לו כתנת, frequentative; cf. Driver, p. 162. foot-note 1; Ges., § 112. 6 b. β. Dav., *S.*, § 58 b, takes it as simple waw.

7. ויחר להם. Cf. on 4, 5.

כי נבלה עשׂה בישׂראל = '*for he had wrought folly in Israel.*' עשׂה נבלה is the constant expression for any carnal offence; cf. Deut. 22, 21. Judg. 20, 6. 10. 2 Sam. 13, 12.

לִשְׁכַּב. See Ges., § 45. 1 a; Stade, § 619 a. If the second radical of the inf. constr. Qal is one of the six letters ת ,פ ,כ ,ד ,ג ,ב, when ל is prefixed, it usually is pointed with *dag. lene* (but not when ב and כ are attached), e.g. שְׁכַב with לְ = (by Ges., § 28. 1; Dav., § 6. 2 d) לִשְׁכַב, and with the *dag. lene* לִשְׁכַּב; cf. Dav., § 6 end. foot-note (where a list of the so-called half-open syllables is given which is useful for reference), and Ges., § 45. 2. note.

וכן לא יעשׂה. Cf. 4, 7; and see note on 20, 9.

8. שׁכם בני חשׁקה נפשׁו. '*Shechem my son, his soul cleaves*' etc. שׁכם בני, a *casus pendens;* cf. Deut. 32, 4 הצור תמים פעלו, Is. 11, 10 שׁרשׁ ישׁי . . . אליו גוים ידרשׁו; see Driver, § 197. 2; Ges., § 140. 3; M. R., § 132; Dav., *S.*, § 106.

בבתכם. The pl. suffix includes the brothers with the father; cf. 17 בתנו; 24, 59 f.

9. התחתנו אתנו. So Deut. 7, 3. Josh. 23, 12 (both with ב) = *to intermarry*. אֹתָנוּ (cf. ver. 2) might possibly be pointed אִתָּנוּ; cf. the construction התחתן בְּ. התחתן את is found again in 1 Kings 3, 1, but whether את in this passage is a prep. or the sign of the acc. is uncertain; cf. Ewald, § 124 b.

10. וסחרוה. סחר is construed with an acc. like a verb = *going;* cf. 42, 34 ואת הארץ תסחרו = '*traffic in the land,*' i.e. go to and fro in the land for the purpose of trading.

האחזו בה = '*settle down therein,*' lit. '*hold yourselves fast therein.*' The word is peculiar to P; so again 47, 27.

12. מהר ומתן. מהר = the price paid to the parents for their daughter; cf. Ex. 22, 15. 1 Sam. 18, 25: מתן = the gifts given to the bride; cf. 24, 53, where a like distinction is made.

13. וידברו אשר טמא. LXX, καὶ ἐλάλησαν αὐτοῖς, ὅτι ἐμίαναν, which would mean, '*and spoke, because they had defiled,*' or, (?) '*and said, that they had defiled,*' which would be better expressed by ויאמרו כי טמא. The first meaning being very lame and the second doubtful, it has been conjectured that דבר here must = the Arabic دَبَّرَ, and mean, '*to act craftily behind one's back,*' '*lay snares for;*' cf. 2 Chron. 22, 10 (but see Bertheau); so Ges. in *Thes.*, p. 315 a, Kn. This, however, is not certain (see Di., p. 373); so perhaps it is simpler to read וידברו במרמה instead of במרמה וידברו; so Pesh. ܘܡܰܠܶܠܘ ܥܰܡܗܘܢ ܒܢܶܟܠܳܐ. Kuenen emends, אחותנו for אחותם, but then וידברו would have to mean ויאמרו איש אל אחיו.

15. בזאת = '*on this condition,*' ב being the ב of price; cf. ver. 22. 1 Sam. 11, 2.

נאות, imperf. Nif'. of אות; it occurs again in vers. 22. 23, and 2 Kings 12, 9, but nowhere else. In Rabb. the part. Nif'. נאות is found, = '*suitable.*' Hitzig and Stade, § 585 a, prefer to take it as imperf. Qal, like יֵבוֹשׁ; cf. on 23, 13, where Hitzig reads אם אתה as perf. Qal from אות.

להמל. The subject of the inf. cstr. is here in the nominative, see Ges., § 115. 2. Rem. 2; Dav., *S.*, § 91 a; M. R., § 117. המול לכם כל זכר is a phrase characteristic of P; so 17, 10. Ex. 12, 48.

16. ונתנו. '*Then we will give.*' The perf. with waw conv.; the apodosis to אם תהיו כמנו in ver. 15; cf. vers. 17. 18. 26, and often.

19. אחר = אִחֵר, cf. מֵאֵן, the vowel being lengthened by way of compensation for the non-doubling of ח; see Stade, § 386 d. 2; Ges., § 64. 3.

20. אל שער עירם. Cf. 23, 10. 18. Is. 29, 21. Am. 5, 10. שער העיר was the oriental Forum.

21. '*These men, they are peaceably disposed towards us.*' *Casus pendens;* cf. on ver. 8; see Driver, § 198; and Ges., § 143 a; Dav., *S.*, §§ 104 b, 106 a. Cf. also 40, 12. 18. 41, 25-27. 42, 11. 45, 20. 47, 6. 48, 5 (לי הם).

שלמים '*peaceable.*' Geiger, *Urschrift*, p. 76, proposes the curious rendering '*Salemites*,' also taking שלם, 33, 18, as the name of a city belonging to Shechem.

רחבת ידים. '*Wide on both sides;*' so Judg. 18, 10. Is. 22, 18; also Ps. 104, 25 (הים . . . רחב ידים).

וישבו. LXX, Sam., Pesh., Vulg. omit the ו and connect ישבו with אתנו.

24. כל יצאי שער. Cf. 23, 10. 18, and the note on ver. 10. On the verbs יצא and בא with the accusative, and

so capable of the genitive construction with the participle, see Ges., § 116. 3. Rem.; Dav., *S.*, § 98. R. 1.

25. בהיותם כאבים, i.e. when they were attacked with the fever that appears on the third day after circumcision in the case of adults. The third day was the most critical time for the circumcised person; cf. Tuch, p. 409.

שמעון ולוי, i.e. Simeon and Levi with their fellow-tribesmen.

איש חרבו. '*Each one his sword;*' see Ges., § 139. 1; M. R., § 72. 3. Rem. a; Dav., *S.*, § 11. R. d; and cf. 42, 25 איש אל שׂקו.

בטח, elsewhere usually לָבֶטַח,='*in security,*' a circumstantial accusative, as in 1 Sam. 12, 11 ותשבו בטח; Ez. 30, 9 להחריד את כוש בטח; cf. Ges., § 118. 5; Dav., *S.*, § 70 b.

26. לפי חרב, not '*with the edge,*' but '*according to the mouth of*' etc., i.e. according to its ability to devour; cf. 2 Sam. 2, 26. 11, 25 כי כזה וכזה תאכל החרב. Usually לפי חרב is connected with הִכָּה '*to smite,*' but it is also found with other verbs, though only here with הרג (Di.).

27. בני יעקב. LXX, Pesh., Saadiah, Sam., and two MSS. (Wright) read ובני, which is not so abrupt; possibly waw originally stood before בני, and dropped out on account of the final ו of ויצאו, ver. 26; or the Vss. might have added it, to remove the abrupt commencement of the verse. The בני are probably only Simeon and Levi, not the other sons of Jacob; cf. ver. 30, where only Simeon and Levi are blamed.

30. להבאישני, lit. '*by making me stink,*' i.e. bringing me into evil repute; so Ex. 5, 21. 1 Sam. 13, 4. 2 Sam. 10, 6. Cf. the English phrase, '*To be in bad odour with any one.*'

מתי מספר, lit. '*men of number*,' i.e. so few that they might easily be counted; cf. Ges., § 128. 2 g; M. R., § 79. 4. Rem. a: so Deut. 4, 27. Ps. 105, 12; cf. Is. 10, 19. For מְתֵי, see on 4, 18; cf. Barth, *N. B.*, p. 5. It is only found in the plural; see Ewald, § 178 d; Stade, § 183.

ונאספו . . . והכוני. Cf. on 33, 13 ודפקום . . . ומתו.

31. הַכְזוֹנָה, so Baer and Del., with כ aspirated; cf. 27, 38. Job 15, 8. 22, 13; and the metheg (Ga'ya) before the pathach, to distinguish the ה interrog. from the ה of the article (Del.). The ordinary text has ז *majusculum*.

יעשׂה. Cf. Lev. 16, 15 ועשׂה את דמו.

35.

1. עלה ביתאל. Bethel was situated on a hill; cf. ver. 8 מתחת לביתאל; 1 Sam. 10, 3.

2. את אלהי הנכר, especially the Teraphim (31, 19) which Rachel had taken with her. אלהי נכר='*strange gods*,' lit. '*gods of strangeness;*' cf. Josh. 24, 23. Judg. 10, 16. So בן נכר '*son of strangeness*'='*stranger*' (17, 12. Ex. 12, 43).

הִטַּהֲרוּ for הִתְטַהֲרוּ, by Ges., § 54. 2 b; Dav., § 26. 3.

3. הָעֹנֶה אתי . . . ויהי. The participle continued by an imperf. with waw conv., a fact being stated; so 49, 17. Num. 22, 11 היצא ממצרים ויכס את עין; cf. on 27, 33.

4. הנזמים, i.e. the earrings that were worn as talismans and amulets, and so belonging to the heathen practices, which Jacob required them to give up.

תחת האלה. '*Under the terebinth*,' i.e. the well-known terebinth, which would be familiar to the reader; hence the article; cf. 12, 6. Possibly, as Tuch suggests, the tree mentioned here is the same as the one in Judg. 9, 6, where Abimelech was made king. אלה always = a single tree, and usually has the article.

The LXX insert here, καὶ ἀπώλεσεν αὐτὰ ἕως τῆς σήμερον ἡμέρας; which Frankel, *Einf.*, p. 56, explains as a marginal gloss, added by a pious reader who objected to ויטמן.

5. חתת אלהים, not '*a mighty terror*,' but '*a terror of God*,' i.e. one caused or sent by Him; cf. פחד אלהים, 2 Chron. 20, 29; פחד יהוה, 2 Chron. 14, 13. חִתַּת is a ἅπαξ λεγόμ. The genitive is an objective genitive; cf. on 9, 2.

7. נגלו אליו האלהים plural, perhaps because האלהים here includes the angels; cf. 28, 12; see also 20, 13. Josh. 24, 19. Onq. here has מַלְאֲכַיָּא דַיְיָ '*angels of Y.*;' but Berliner in his edition gives אִיתְגְּלִי לֵיהּ יְיָ, i.e. '*Y. appeared to him*;' cf. note on 20, 13.

8. אלון בכות, probably identical with the palm tree of Deborah, Judg. 4, 5, and perhaps with the Terebinth of Tabor, mentioned in 1 Sam. 10, 3. Cf. Well., *Comp.*, p. 215 (connects בכים, Judg. 2, 1, with אלון בכות).

10. Cf. 32, 29.

11. מחלציך. In 46, 26 we have יצאי ירכו; מתנים is never used in this connexion.

14. מצבה . . . מצבת אבן. מצבת אבן is epexegetical; cf. 15, 18. 25, 30; and see M. R., § 72. 3.

ויסך עליה נסך. Cf. 28, 18 ויצק שמן. נסך was probably a libation of wine (Targ. Ps.-Jon., wine and water). Some (Kn., Well.) take ויצק . . . שמן as epexegetical to ויסך.

15. אשר דבר אתו שם. Contrast ver. 13 and ver. 14, where שם is omitted, as no confusion can arise in the sentence through its absence; see M.R., §§ 156 d, 157 c; Dav., *S.*, § 9 d.

ביתאל. The narrative in this ver. is from P. The other account in 28, 19 is probably from J.

16. כברת הארץ occurs again 48, 7 and 2 Kings 5, 19; but neither of these passages throws any light on the word כברת; however, from 2 Kings, l. c., it could not have been a very great distance. LXX have here Χαβραθά, but in 48, 7 τὸν ἱππόδρομον Χαβραθά (a double translation), i. e. either a stadium, or like the Arabic شوط الفرس (i.e. as far as a horse can run), a measure common among the Arabs; see *H. W. B.*, 11th ed., p. 373. Pesh. ܦܪܣܚܐ, a '*parasang*,'= eighteen thousand paces or three German miles; cf. Bernst., *Syr. Lex.*, p. 408 b. Onq. has כְּרוֹב אַרְעָא = '*about an acre*,' etc.; cf. Levy, *Chald. W. B.*, i. 384 a. Del. and Tuch take it as = '*about an hour's journey*.' Cf. Ges., *Thes.*, p. 658 b.

17. המילדת, '*the midwife*' who would naturally be present. The article by Dav., *S.*, § 21 d, cf. on 14, 13: and see 18, 7. 22, 6. 24, 20. 26, 8. 38, 28. Ex. 2, 15.

כי גם זה לך בן. Cf. 30, 24, where Rachel wishes that she may have another son.

18. בן אוני = '*son of my sorrow;*' inasmuch as giving birth to him cost her her life. His father, however, instead of this ill-omened name, called him בנימין '*son of the right hand*,' i.e. son of good luck, the right side being considered by the ancients as the lucky side; cf. Ges. in *Thes.*, p. 599, and δέξιος and ἀρίστερος in Greek. בִּן is pointed with ḥireq like the pr. n. בִּן יקה in Prov. 30, 1; בִּן נון, Num. 11, 28, etc.; cf. בִּן לילה, Jon. 4, 10. Del. gives two other explanations of the name '*son of good fortune*.' I. He might have been so named because he was born when Jacob was free, his other children having been born when he was in Laban's service. II. Because

he completed the lucky number (twelve) of his sons. In Ps. 89, 13 ימין = '*the south*,' so Rashi explains the name as meaning the '*south son*,' as opposed to the others, who were '*north sons*,' being born in Aramea; but Canaan is nowhere called '*the south land*.'

19. אפרתה הוא בית לחם. So 48, 7, i.e. Bethlehem, two hours south of Jerusalem; cf. Sh., *G.*, p. 318 f.; Mic. 5, 1 בית לחם אפרתה; 1 Chron. 4, 4. Matt. 2, 16–18. Di., Thenius, and others, from 1 Sam. 10, 2 ff. (cf. Jer. 31, 14), consider that Rachel's grave must be sought for much further north, in the territory of Benjamin, or on the boundary between Benjamin and Ephraim, on the way between Ramah of Samuel and Gibeah of Saul, not far from Bethel. Di. points out that this would be more natural, as Rachel was the mother of Joseph and Benjamin; and as ancestress of the great northern tribes, we should hardly expect to find the site of her grave in the territory of Judah; cf. Bäd., *Palest.*, p. 121. An Ephrath, however, on the frontier between Ephraim and Benjamin has not yet been discovered. The writer here clearly means Ephrath, i.e. Bethlehem, and we must assume with Nöld. and Del.[5], that side by side with the Ephraimitic tradition, there existed a Judaic, according to which the grave was situated near the Judaic Ephrath. Otherwise we must suppose that here and 48, 7 הוא בית לחם is a gloss.

21. מהלאה למגדל עדר. '*On the other side of Migdal 'Eder*;' so Amos 5, 27 מהלאה לדמשק '*on the other side of Damascus*,' beyond Damascus.

מגדל עדר = '*Herd's tower*;' cf. 2 Kings 17, 9. 18, 8. 2 Chron. 26, 10. The narrative fixes its position between Ephrath and Hebron. Knobel places it at Jerusalem (cf. Mic. 4, 8); so the LXX, who place ver. 21 after מביתאל

in ver. 16 and read instead of ויסעו ver. 16, ויסע יעקב, and omit ויסע ישראל from the beginning of ver. 21. Del. considers that it was near Bethlehem.

22. בשכן with כ with dag., an exception to the rule given in the note on 34, 7.

וישכב וגו״. Cf. 2 Sam. 16, 22. 1 Kings 2, 22.

The Massoretes here have a note, פִּסְקָא בְּאֶמְצַע פָּסוּק, i.e. '*a gap in the middle of the verse.*' There are three of these פִּסְקָאוֹת in the Pent., and twenty-eight in the books from Joshua to Ezekiel. They are not mentioned in the Talmud or Midrash (Del.). Verse 22 down to ישׂראל has a double accentuation, according as it is read as a complete verse or as a half-verse. Geiger, *Urschrift*, p. 373, points out that in the public reading of the text the two verses 22 and 23 were read as one, so that the passage might be passed over in reading as quickly as possible, and the attention of the audience diverted from the evil deed of Reuben. The correct accentuation makes ver. 22 end at ישׂראל, and ver. 23 begin at ויהיו, one section ending at ver. 22, and a fresh one beginning with ver. 23. The first way of accenting the verses here (viz. making 22 end at ישׂראל, and 23 begin with ויּהיו) is called טעם תחתון ('*lower accentuation*'); the second way (viz. making the two verses one), טעם עליון ('*upper accentuation*'). Cf. the double set of accents in the Decalogue in Exodus and Deut., and cf. Num. 25, 19 and Deut. 2, 8, where there is a gap in the middle of the verse. The LXX have the addition, καὶ πονηρὸν ἐφάνη ἐναντίον αὐτοῦ = וירע בעיניו, possibly added to avoid the abrupt ending, which is regarded by Di. as intentional, to draw attention to 49, 3 f.

26. יֻלַּד. Sam. and Heb. MSS. (Di.) יִלְּדוּ, as in 36, 5.

אשר, as the text stands, is acc. case, cf. note on 4, 18.

36.

The Toledoth Esau follow in this chapter, preceding those of Jacob, just as Ishmael's preceded Isaac's; the object of the chapter, and its position before the account of Jacob's family, being to dispose of Esau, and leave the course of the narrative entirely free for Jacob's history. The Edomites, Esau's descendants, first appear again in Num. 20, 14 ff. Such a detailed account of the history of Edom can be explained sufficiently from the fact that Edom always passed as Israel's brother (cf. Num., l.c.), and occupied an important position in the history of Israel. A partial list of the descendants of Esau is given in 1 Chron. 1, 35–54.

2. In 26, 34 (P) Esau married Yehudith the daughter of Beeri the Hittite, and Basemath the daughter of Elon the Hittite. In 28, 9 (P) he takes, in addition to his other wives (על נשיו)—i.e. those of 26, 34—Maḥalath, Ishmael's daughter. Thus, according to 26, 34. 28, 9 (P), Esau's three wives were, 1. Yehudith, Beeri the Hittite's daughter; 2. Basemath, Elon the Hittite's daughter; and 3. Maḥalath, Ishmael's daughter. Here Esau's wives are given, 1. Adah the daughter of Elon the Hittite; 2. Oholibamah[1] the daughter of Anah, the daughter of Tsibeon the Hivite; 3. Basemath the daughter of Ishmael, the sister of Nebayoth. There are three serious discrepancies in the two accounts: 1. The Basemath of 26, 34 is here called Adah; 2. the Oholibamah the daughter of Anah, the daughter of Tsibeon the Hivite (cf. below)=(apparently) Yehudith the daughter of Beeri the Hittite of 26, 34; and 3. Ishmael's daughter Maḥalath, 28, 9, is here called Basemath.

[1] Names compounded with אהל (cf. Ex. 31, 6. Ez. 23, 4. 5) are also found in Phoenician, cf. *C.I.S.*, i. p. 72 אהלמלך, p. 74 אהלבעל; Bloch, *Phoen. Glossar*, p. 11.

With regard to ver. 2 בת צבעון החוי we must read (i) for חוי, חֹרִי, as ver. 25 (cf. ver. 20) shews; and (ii) either render בת '*granddaughter*,' cf. ver. 39 (?) and 29, 5 (where בן must= '*grandson*'); or emend and read בן, so Sam., LXX, Pesh. In vers. 20. 25 Anah is described as the son of Seir the Horite, in this verse and ver. 24 he is the son of Tsibeon. The difficulty as regards Anah may be solved by assuming that there were two different persons of that name. In ver. 25^b Oholibamah is the daughter of Anah son of Seir, but in this verse and ver. 10 she is the daughter of Anah the son of Tsibeon. To remove this discrepancy, Del. has proposed to place 25^b (? a gloss) after 24^b. Its present position may be due to the fact, that only a single name follows the formula, ואלה בני ענה ver. 25. Various hypotheses have been adopted to reconcile the different accounts of Esau's wives. Some have held that Esau had five wives; others (Hengst., Ros.) that the wives had two names, or had their names changed. Kn. and Ewald suppose that the names have been corrupted by copyists. If this is the case, the corruption must have been, as Di. points out, very great. Others (Del., Tuch, Nöld.) explain the difference in the two accounts as arising from two different traditions. This seems the most natural solution. We must then, however, assume that R, either in this chapter, or in 26, 34 f. 28, 9, has inserted into the text of P, the names of Esau's wives, from some other source. The former view is perhaps more probable. Although c. 36 belongs to P in the main, there are evident traces of revision by R from other sources, in vers. 2–5. 9–28. Cf. Driver, *Introd.*, p. 10, Di. and Del. ad loc.

6. Esau takes his wives and children, and all his property, and leaves Canaan for the land of Seir, out of the way of his brother Jacob.

אל ארץ as it stands yields no suitable sense. The Targums and Vulg. read אל ארץ אחרת. Ges. renders the text, '*to a land east of* (lit. *before*) *Jacob;*' but מפני can hardly mean this. LXX and Sam. read מארץ כנען, possibly a correction. The Pesh. has لܐܪܥܐ ܕܣܥܝܪ, cf. vers. 8. 9, which is probably the correct reading, so Di., Tuch.

7. משׂבת. Cf. 4, 13 מנשׂוא.

8. שׂעיר, at a later date, included (cf. Deut. 2. Ez. 35, 15) the hill country of Edom, east of the Arabah, between the Dead Sea and the Ælanitic Gulf. The northern half = the modern Ǵebâl, and the southern half = the modern eš-Serâ. Originally (Judg. 5, 4. Deut. 33, 2, cf. Num. 20, 16. Josh. 11, 17. 12, 7. 15, 1), the name Mount Seir was applied to the hill country west of the Arabah; which rises to a considerable height to the south of the '*bald mountain*' (הָהָר הֶחָלָק), the southern limit of the hill country of Judah; a wild and desolate region now inhabited by the Arab tribe, the 'Azâzime.

11. The Canaanitish line.

תימן is the name of a district of Edom (Jer. 49, 20. Amos 1, 12. Hab. 3, 3) celebrated for its wise men (Jer. 49, 7. Bar. 3, 22 f.); the home of Eliphaz, Job 2, 11.

אומר, צפו, and געתם are quite unknown.

קנז. Cf. 15, 19, where the Kenizites are mentioned among other tribes dwelling in the south of Canaan.

12. עמלק, not identical with the great Amalekite people mentioned in 14, 7, who dwelt in the south of Canaan; but probably only a portion of those, who attached themselves to the families of Eliphaz, or were subject to them (Di.); cf. ver. 22.

13. The Ishmaelitish line.

The names are not further known.

14. The Horite line.

Nothing further is known about the names here given.

15–19. The tribal princes of Edom.

15. אלּוּף, a denom. from אֶלֶף '*a thousand*'=*chiliarch* or *phylarch*, mostly used of the tribal princes of Edom, more rarely of those of Judah, Zech. 9, 7. 12, 5. 6; see Driver, *The Expositor*, July, 1885.

16. אלּוּף קרח, mentioned in ver. 18 as the son of Esau by Oholibamah, is wanting in the Sam. Codex and Vs., and one Heb. MS. (Wright), and is rejected as spurious by Tuch, Knobel, Del. Di. considers that it either crept in here by the oversight of a copyist from ver. 18, or is a gloss assigning Korah, according to another theory, to the family of Eliphaz.

20–30. The tribes of the Horites.

The inhabitants of the land, as opposed to the descendants of Esau, who took possession of it (Deut. 2, 12).

20. החרי from חור '*a hole*,' so '*a dweller in a hole* or *cave*,' '*a troglodyte*.' 'The land of Edom abounds in holes or caves' (Di.). The identification of the names in the following verses is uncertain; cf. Di., p. 386 f.

24. ואיה. Most commentators read איה with 1 Chron. 1, 40, LXX, Pesh., and Vulg.; the text as it stands yields no suitable sense.

הימם. Targ. Jer., Saad., Kimchi, Luther, '*mules;*' so the A. V.; more probably '*hot water springs*' (R. V. '*the hot springs*'), which Del. identifies with the hot springs of Callirrhoë, beneath Zerka Ma'in, on the east side of the Dead

Sea, about two hours distant from it; cf. Hieron., *Quaest.* ed. Lag., p. 56; Bäd., *Pal.*, p. 190; Sh., *G.*, pp. 562, 571. Onq. and Ps.-Jon. seem either to have read האימים, 'the giant race' mentioned in Deut. 2, 10, or to have taken הימם as meaning this. Pesh. gives מים, and one Heb. MS. (Wright).

26. דִּישָׁן. LXX, Pesh., Vulg., 1 Chron. 1, 41, and most commentators read דִּישֹׁן.

30. לאלפיהם. '*According to their tribal princes.*' LXX, ἐν ταῖς ἡγεμονίαις, reading לְאַלֻּפֵיהֶם, possibly the correct reading, as this is the only place in this chapter where אלוף is written without the ו. It is worthy of notice that many of the names in this list, vers. 20–30, are names of animals, e.g. שובל = in Arabic '*young lion;*' דישן *pygarg*, a kind of antelope or gazelle, Deut. 14, 5; cf. Di. on Lev. 11, 2 f.; צבעון = in Arabic '*hyena*,' etc.; cf. עכבור = *mouse*, ver. 38. Di. remarks, 'that it is a natural thing for peoples amongst whom the arts and trades were not developed to be fond of choosing their family names from the names of animals.' Cf. Rob. Smith, *Journ. Phil.*, ix. 75 ff.

31–39. The names of the kings who ruled in the land of Edom. The names in this list are also doubtful; cf. Di., p. 388 ff.

33. מבצרה, now a little village in Ǵebâl, Buṣêra, four miles south of the south end of the Dead Sea; cf. Bäd., *Pal.*, p. 151.

37. מרחבות הנהר. Several places in the O. T. are called Reḥoboth. The one mentioned here has been identified with Raḥba, رَحْبَة, on the western bank of the Euphrates (הנהר elsewhere being the river *par excellence*, i.e. the Euphrates), south of the spot where the Chaboras enters the river. But this identification is not certain.

40–43. A brief review of the tribal princes of Esau. The list contains partly names of individuals, e.g. קנז, אהליבמה, and partly names of districts, e.g. פינן, אלה. Most of the names of places in this list are uncertain.

אלה, perhaps the seaport אילת; cf. on 14, 6.

פינן, also called in Num. 33, 42 פונן, in Idumea, between Petra and Zoar, well known through its mines.

37.

2. '*Joseph, being seventeen years old, was tending the flock with his brethren, while yet a lad, with the sons of Bilhah, and with the sons of Zilpah, his father's wives, and Joseph brought an evil report about them to their father.*'

היה רעה. Cf. the note on 4, 17.

והוא נער. LXX, ὢν νέος. A. V. renders incorrectly, '*and the lad was with the sons of Bilhah,*' for the clause is a circumstantial one; cf. note on 20, 3. Pesh. and Onq. seem to have misunderstood the words; the Pesh. has ܘܗܘ ܡܬܪܒܐ ܗܘܐ ܥܡ ܒܢܝ '*and he was growing up with*' etc.; and Onq. וְהוּא רָבֵי עִם בְּנֵי '*and he was growing up with the sons of*' etc. את בני has been rendered variously. Knobel and Del.[5] give the following meaning to the words. Joseph was feeding the flock with his brethren, as servant to the sons of Bilhah, etc.; i.e. he was handed over to their charge to learn, or to help them in their business; comparing, for this use of נַעַר, Judg. 7, 11. 9, 54. 19, 13, but this is giving the words of the text a very forced meaning, and it is questionable whether נער can be used in this way. The rendering of the LXX, '*being yet a lad, with the sons*'—

את in the same sense as the את in את אחיו בצאן, just before —is unobjectionable. והוא נער . . . אביו is perhaps a doublet to יוסף בן שבע עשׂרה שנה . . . בצאן.

דבתם רעה. '*An evil report about them;*' רעה is intentionally indefinite, דבתם הרעה would mean, '*their evil report;*' cf. Ges., § 126. 5. Rem. 1 b. Possibly the words should be rendered, '*the report of them* (*as*) *an evil one*,' a sort of tertiary predicate; cf. Num. 14, 37 דבת הארץ רעה; 1 Sam. 2, 23 את דבריכם רעים. See also Dav., *S.*, § 32. R. 2. דבה in the Pent. only occurs in P.

3. כי בן זקנים הוא לו. Cf. 21, 2. 44, 20.

ועשׂה לו. Either a case of the perf. with simple waw; or, possibly, with waw conv. in a freq. sense (29, 3); cf. 1 Sam. 2, 19.

כתנת פסים only in this chapter and 2 Sam. 13, 18 (of Tamar's garment as the clothing of a king's daughter). פס = '*an end*,' '*extremity*,' used of the hands and feet; so כתנת פסים = '*a coat of extremities*,' i.e. one reaching to the wrists and ancles; and, as is apparent from 2 Sam. l.c., worn by the upper classes. The ordinary כתנת only reached to the knees, and had no sleeves. Cf. פס in Aramaic (e.g. Dan. 5, 5. 24), of the extremities of the hand and foot, and ܦܣܐ used in a similar way. This meaning is supported by the Pesh. here, and the Vulg., LXX, and Aquila in 2 Sam. l. c. The LXX and Vulg. here, and the Pesh. in 2 Sam., and A.V. here and 2 Sam., '*a coat of* (*many*) *colours*,' margin ('*pieces*'), but this meaning of פס = '*a piece*' or '*patch*,' and so כ״ פ״ '*a variegated garment*,' is very doubtful. The R.V. retains the rendering, '*a coat of many colours*,' though it gives in the margin, '*a long garment with sleeves*.'

4. דברו לשלם. '*To speak peaceably to him,*' or '*to address him in greeting,*' i.e. to greet him and answer his inquiries after their health (Del.). There is only one other instance of דבר with the person addressed, in the acc. case, viz. Num. 26, 3; but the text in this passage seems to be corrupt. Cf. Di. ad loc. Deut. 18, 21 f. quoted by Di. does not seem to be parallel, the suffix in each verse not being personal.

5. ויוספו עוד שְׂנֹא. Cf. on 8, 10.

7. '*And behold we were binding sheaves* (partic.) *in the midst of the field, and behold my sheaf rose, and also stood up; and behold your sheaves were moving round* (imperf.), *and bowed down* (imperf. with waw conv., denoting a single action) *to my sheaf.*' מאלמים '*were binding,*' participle, as in 13, 7; cf. the note there, and Dav., *S.*, § 100 f. תסבינה = '*began to move round.*' 'Joseph represents the sheaves as being in motion' (Driver, § 27 γ).

ותשתחוין, ןָ *scriptio defectiva* for נָה, '*and they did bow down,*' i.e. once, and not more; the imperf. with waw conv. describing a fact that happened once only in the past: contrast תסבינה, where the action has begun, and is still going on to completion.

8. הֲמלך . . . אִם. The disjunctive or alternative question is put with ה in the first clause and אם or ואם in the second, see Dav., *S.*, § 124; Ges., § 150. 2 and R. b; M.R., § 145; and cf. Josh. 5, 13. Judg. 9, 2. 2 Sam. 24, 13. 1 Kings 22, 15.

10. הבוא נבוא. See note on 2, 16. and for the inf. abs. emphasizing the verb in a question, ver. 8. 24, 5. 43, 7. Num. 22, 30. Judg. 11, 25.

11. ואביו שמר את הדבר. Cf. Luke 2, 19. 51.

12. אֶת צאן. את with two dots over it, probably because it was regarded as a doubtful reading. The Bereshith Rabba, cited by Strack, p. 89, explains the points as follows, ונקוד על את לומר שלא הלכו אלא לרעות את עצמן, i.e. '*With points on the* את, *meaning that they only went to feed themselves* (*not the flocks*)!' So the Midr. Bem., cited by Strack at the same place.

14. שלום = '*well-being*,' applied to the flocks and to Joseph's brethren.

והשבני דבר. Note the phrase השיב דבר = '*bring back word*,' 2 accus., by Ges., § 117. 5. R. γ; Dav., *S.*, § 75 d; M. R., § 45. 4.

15. והנה תעה for הננו תעה = והנה הוא תעה; cf. on 32, 7.

17. שמעתי אמרים. Cf. 27, 6 שמעתי את אביך מדבר; Dav., *S.*, § 78; M. R., § 46. 2; Ew., § 284 b. The obj. of אמרים is omitted, cf. Ges., § 117. 1. R. 4. Sam. Ver. reads שְׁמַעְתִּים.

דתינה '*towards Dôthân*.' Dôthân or Dôthain, = '*two fountains* (?),' or perhaps '*cisterns*,' was about five hours north of Samaria. In Judith 3, 9 f. 4, 6. 7, 3. 8, 3, it is called Δωταία or Δωθαΐμ, and is described as on the south side of the plain of Jezreel, between Scythopolis and Geba, near the ancient Ginnaea (Ǵenîn). Ruins, which still exist at Tell Dôthân 1½ hrs. S.W. of Ǵenîn, mark the site of the place, cf. Bäd., *Pal.*, p. 226; Sh., *G.*, pp. 151, 356. Through the plain of Tell Dôthân, south of Ǵenîn, the road from Bethshan and Jezreel to Ramleh and Egypt passes (Di.); cf. ver. 25 and Ebers, *Egypten und die B. Mose's*, p. 288. The form דּוֹתַיִן is apparently the Aramaic dual, of which דּוֹתָן is a contraction; cf. קַרְתָּן and קִרְיָתַיִם, עֵינָם and עֵינַיִם, and see Ges.,

§ 88. 1. Rem. 1, and the forms found on the Moabite stone, e.g. קריתן = קריתים, line 10; מאתן = מאתים ('*two hundred*'), line 20; דבלתן = דבלתים, line 30; חורנן = חורנים, line 31. Cf. Wright, *Comp. Gram.*, p. 150. Others consider that all the proper names ending in ַיִן and ַיִם are not duals, but merely diphthongal pronunciations of the endings ָן and ָם. Cf. Well., *Comp.*, p. 45. Barth, *N.B.*, p. 319, regards the ַיִם in proper names in Hebrew not as a dual, but as an ancient termination found in proper names of places, which was afterwards replaced by the endings ָן, ֹן, and ָם. Thus he considers the dual ending ַיִם as older than the endings ָן, ֹן, and ָם.

18. ובטרם יקרב . . . ויתנכלו. Cf. the note on 2, 5; also Driver, § 127 β; Dav., *S.*, §§ 50 b, 145 c; Ges., §§ 107. 1. R. 1, 111. 2. R. 1.

ויתנַכלו אתו. '*They plotted against him.*' Hithpa'el with the acc. as in 1 Chron. 29, 17 התנדבתי כל אלה; see Ewald, § 124 b; Ges., § 54. 3 c, and § 117. 4. Rem. 2; Dav., *S.*, § 73. R. 4; cf. Ps. 105, 25, where התנכל takes the prep. ב.

19. בעל החלמות. Cf. on 14, 13. הלזה as in 24, 65; cf. the note there.

21. לא נכנו נפש = '*let us not smite him as to life,*' i.e. mortally; so Deut. 22, 26 ורצחו נפש; see the note on 3, 15.

23. ויפשיטו וגו'. Verbs of '*clothing with,*' and '*stripping off,*' take 2 accusatives, see Dav., *S.*, § 75 c; Ges., § 117. 5 a; M. R., § 45. 1.

24. הברה. Cf. Jer. 38, 6 (where Jeremiah is cast into a pit with no water in it, but mud); Lam. 3, 53.

25. לאכל לחם = '*to take their meal,*' lit. '*to eat bread,*' the meal being so called from the chief article of food; cf. 31, 54. 43, 25. Matt. 15, 2.

ארחת ישמעאלים. So Is. 21, 13 ארחות דדנים; Job 6, 19 ארחות תמא. ארחת is the part. Qal fem. of ארח, used in a collective sense. אֹרֵחַ = '*a single traveller,*' אֹרְחָה '*a company of travellers,*' '*a caravan.*' Other feminines used collectively are אַחֲוָה '*brotherhood,*' from אָח '*brother;*' עֲנָנָה '*a mass of clouds,*' from עָנָן '*a cloud;*' גּוֹלָה '*a band of exiles;*' see Ges., § 122. 4 c; Stade, § 312 b; Dav., *S.*, § 14. 2.

נכאת = '*tragacanth gum,*' the resinous gum of the *astragalus gummifer:* צרי = '*balsam*' (צְרִי for צֳרִי, like רְאִי for רֳאִי, Job 37, 18; דְּמִי for דֳּמִי, Is. 38, 10): not real balsam, but the gum of the *pistacia lentiscus*, the mastic-tree: לט = '*ladanum;*' the aromatic gum of the cistus rose, or *cistus creticus*, three articles which even at the present day form the chief trade of the Arab-Egyptian caravans. Ebers, *Egypten*, etc., p. 292, has found נכאת and צרי on the Egyptian inscriptions, but not לט; he also (p. 293) mentions that gum, balsam, and incense are the chief imports from the East to Egypt at the present day, and—with the exception of a short distance by rail—are brought by the same method, i. e. caravans, as in the days of the patriarchs. The caravan road from Damascus to Egypt is the same now as in the time of Joseph.

26. מה בצע = '*what gain, that we kill?*' on the construction, cf. M. R., § 93. Rem. b; Dav., *S.*, §§ 8. R. 2, 53 b; see also Ewald, § 326 a.

28. מדינים. Cf. on 25, 2.

In this chapter there are two distinct parallel accounts of the way in which Joseph was taken to Egypt. In 37, 19–21. 25–27. 28b (to *silver*). 31–35. 39, 1 etc. J, Joseph is sold by his brethren to the Ishmaelites, cf. 45, 4b. In 37, 22–24. 28. 29–30. 36 E, his brethren cast him into a pit, from which he is stolen by the Midianites, without their knowledge, cf. 40, 15. In J the leading part is taken by Judah, so 43, 4 f. 44, 16 ff.; in E by Reuben, so 42, 22. 37, cf. Driver, *Introd.*, p. 16. f.; Di. p. 392.

בעשׂרים כסף. שֶׁקֶל omitted; see note on 20, 16. The LXX have εἴκοσι χρυσῶν, so in 45, 22. The price of a slave between five and twenty years was twenty shekels; see Lev. 27, 5. On slavery in Egypt, see Ebers' note, *Egypten und die Bücher Mose's*, p. 293 ff., where he shews that the narrative in this chapter is quite in accordance with what used to take place at the time of the Pharaoh whose favourite Joseph became.

32. הֲכתֹנת בנך. As כתנת is in the cstr. state ה cannot be the article, but ה interrog. Cf. Ges., § 100. 4. Rem.; Dav., *S.*, § 49 end.

33. טרף טרף. Inf. abs. Qal, with perf. Pu'al; cf. Ges., § 113. 3. Rem. 4; Dav., *S.*, § 86. R. 2, and see Job 6, 2 שָׁקוֹל יִשָּׁקֵל, the inf. abs. Qal and imperf. Nif'., Gen. 46, 4 אַעַלְךָ גַם עָלֹה, inf. Qal and imperf. Hif'.

35. כי, either (1) introducing the words of the speaker, or (2) the Latin *imo*, '*no.*'

ארד...אבל '*I shall go down as one mourning*' etc. Circ. clause, so Driver, p. 203, who cps. Lev. 20, 20. Dt. 4, 27. 9, 3, etc. Cf. Driver, l. c. note 2, and note on 15, 2.

שׁאלה = '*to Sheol,*' '*the underworld;*' always without the article. The word probably = '*the hollow place,*' from שׁאל =

שׁעל. Another derivation, now almost obsolete, is from שׁאל '*to ask*,' with reference to the inexorable demand made by death on all mortals, and then transferred to the place of death, to which all mortals must come, '*the house of meeting for all living*,' Job 30, 23; cf. Is. 5, 14. Hab. 2, 5.

36. המדנים either abbreviated or corrupted from מדינים, which is the reading of all the versions here.

לפוטיפר. פוטיפר is the same as פוטי פרע, 41, 45. 46, 20, the former name being abbreviated from the latter. LXX have both Πετεφρῆς and Πεντεφρῆς, see Lagarde, *Gen. Graece*, pref., p. 20, but Swete reads neither, preferring τῷ Πετρεφῇ. The name is the Egyptian *Pĕtĕprē*, '*whom Ra or the sun god hath given*,' i. e. a gift of the sun; cf. Ebers, p. 296. *Ra* is the Egyptian sun god, the chief place of his worship being Heliopolis. Brugsch, *Gesch.*, p. 248, explains the name as = *puti-par*, '*Gift of him that has appeared*.'

סרים, either to be taken in its literal sense, cf. Ebers, p. 299, or merely equivalent to '*officer*,' '*official*;' see further, Ebers, pp. 297, 300, who renders סרים '*courtier*;' remarking that סרים, among the Orientals, had much the same meaning as '*Schranz*' in German ('*parasite*,' '*courtier*').

שׂר הטבחים = '*captain of the executioners*.' The captain of the executioners was also chief of the body-guard and superintendent of the state prison (40, 3 f.), see Ebers, p. 301, who describes Potiphar's office as that of chief minister of police. A similar office existed among the Babylonians, 2 Kings 25, 8 ff. Jer. 39, 9. 52, 12. Dan. 2, 14. See further, Ebers, p. 300 ff. The LXX have ἀρχιμάγειρος, which rendering is perhaps due to 39, 6.

38.

1. ויט '*turned aside*,' Keil renders, '*removed his dwelling*,' sc. אהלו; but ויט without אהלו is not found in this sense, and further, no pr. name of a place follows עד.

עדלמי. Adullam was in the plain (שפלה) of Judah (Josh. 15, 33. 35. Mic. 1, 15. Neh. 11, 30. 2 Chron. 11, 7, cf. 2 Macc. 12, 38), presumably north-west of Hebron. The identification with Deir Dubban, north of Eleutheropolis, is very uncertain. Sh., *G.*, p. 229 f., thinks that the most probable site is 'Aid-el-ma, about midway between Achzib and Ke'ilah, a little to the west of Rabbah. Bäd., *Pal.*, p. 161, identifies it with a spot one hour to the south of Shochoh; near the hill Shêkh Madkûr. On the etymology of the name, cf. Lagarde, *B. N.*, p. 54.

2. איש כנעני. Onq. renders גְּבַר תַּגָּרָא (cf. Is. 23, 8. Prov. 31, 24) '*a merchant*,' possibly finding Judah's marriage with a daughter of Canaan objectionable. Berliner, however, in his edition has גְּבַר כְּנַעֲנָי, but mentions the other reading in his notes, p. 14 of part ii. Cf. Levy, *Chald. W. B.*, ii. p. 528.

3. ויקרא. Sam., Targ. Ps.-Jon., Heb. Codd. (Di.) read (probably correctly) ותקרא, see 29, 34 and vers. 3. 4.

5. והיה, see Driver, § 133. LXX has αὕτη δὲ ἦν, i.e. והיא, this reading gives a suitable sense and is doubtless the correct form of the text; see Dav., *S.*, § 58 c; Ges., § 112. 6 γ; Dr. l. c.; and cf. 1 Sam. 23, 15. 24. 2 Chron. 10, 2; see also Geiger, *Urschrift*, p. 462. As the text stands it must be rendered, '*he* (*Judah*) *was*,' but the perf. with waw is very harsh, and a reference to Judah is not what we should expect.

בכזיב = the אכזיב of Josh. 15, 44. Mic. 1, 14; it was also in the low country (שְׁפֵלָה) of Judah. Sh., *G.*, Map iv, places it a short distance N.E. of Shochoh, giving as its modern name Ain-el-Kezbeh.

8. ויבם = to perform the duty of marrying the deceased brother's widow when he left no son; see Deut. 25, 5. The brother-in-law in this case was called יָבָם.

9. והיה . . . ושחת. The perfect with waw conv. in a frequentative sense, see Driver, §§ 120, 121; Dav., *S.*, § 57; Ges., § 112. 4 d. R.; also Ewald, §§ 342 b, 345 b. Other examples are Num. 21, 9 והיה אם נשך הנחש . . . והביט . . . וחי; Judg. 6, 3 והיה אם זרע . . . ועלה; Ex. 33, 9 והיה . . . ירד, with a simple impf. following. Other instances of אם in a temporal sense with the perf. are Is. 4, 4. Amos 7, 2. Ps. 41, 7; compare Ges., § 164. 2; Dav., *S.*, § 130 b; Ewald, § 355 b.

ושחת ארצה; a pregnant construction, cf. note on 14, 3; so 19, 27. 42, 28. 43, 33. זֶרַע must be understood after ושחת.

נתן. Cf. the note on נשׂא, 4, 13.

11. בית אביך is acc. of place, see note on 18, 1.

12. ויעל על גזזי וגו״, lit. '*he went up about the shearers of his flock,*' i.e. to see after them; cf. the use of על in 30, 33 על שׂכרי.

רֵעֵהוּ. '*His companion.*' LXX and Vulg. read the consonants as רֹעֵהוּ '*his shepherd;*' so Luther.

תמנתה is probably the Timnah mentioned with Gibeah in Josh. 15, 57, between Shochoh and Bethshemesh, the modern Tibneh, Bäd., *Pal.*, p. 161; and not identical with the Timnah belonging to the Danites (Josh. 19, 43), on account of עלה; Di. after Kn. and Del.[5] Tuch (cf. Merx's note however) considers that there was only one Timnah. The name is found on the inscriptions in the form *Tamnaa*, Schrader, *C.O.T.*, p. 159. Rob., *Pales.*, ii. 343, mentions three Timnahs, and considers the one occurring here to be in the hill country of Judah.

14. ותסר בגדי אלמנותה. Cf. Judith 10, 3.

ותכס, i.e. the face; cf. Deut. 22, 12. Jon. 3, 6, where the object of כסה is omitted.

ותתעלף. '*And veiled herself;*' cf. Prov. 7, 10. LXX, Pesh., Onq. render, '*adorned herself.*'

בפתח עינים = '*at the gate of Enaim.*' עֵינַיִם is the same as עֵינָם (cf. on 37, 17 דתינה), Josh. 15, 34 (with the article), and עֵינַיִם in ver. 21 a city of Judah, in the Shephelah. Its position is not known. So most modern commentators. The Vss. took the word as a *nom. appell.*, contrary to ver. 21, excepting the LXX who give Αἰνάν. The Pesh. has ܦܘܼܠܵܓ݂ ܐܘܼܪ̈ܚܵܬܵܐ '*dividing of roads,*' Onq. פְּרָשׁוּת עֵינַיִם, lit. '*division of eyes,*' i.e. cross-way; cf. Levy, *Chald. W.B.*, ii. pp. 212 d, 304. Targ. Ps.-Jon. פַּרְשַׁת אָרְחִין דְּכָל־עַיְינִין מְסַתַּכְּלִין, i.e. '*the cross-ways whither every one's eyes look!*' Vulg. '*in bivio itineris.*' Saad. مَنْظَرَة '*a watch tower.*' The A.V. has, '*in an open place,*' margin, '*The door of eyes;*' R.V. '*in the gate of Enaim.*'

והוא לא נתנה לו לאשה = '*without her being given him to wife;*' circ. cl.

15. ויחשבה לזונה. Cf. 1 Sam. 1, 13 ויחשבה עלי לשכורה; Dav., *S.*, § 78. R. 5.

כי כסתה פניה. LXX and Vulg. add ולא ידעה '*and he did not know her,*' to explain כי כ״ פ״, which gives the reason why Judah did not recognise her, and not why he took her for a harlot.

17. אם תתן...עד שלחך. The apodosis is suppressed, cf. on 30, 27.

18. חתמך. '*The signet ring*,' which was worn round the neck on a chain (פתיל). As these were always worn by their owners, they would be easily identified again by them; cf. Song of Songs 8, 6.

ומטך. '*And thy staff*.' מטה was a carved or ornamented staff, and so different from מקל, a stick in its natural condition. Among the Babylonians every man carried a stick with an ornamented top, and wore a signet ring; see Herod. i. 195. The Versions render פתיל differently. LXX have ὁρμίσκον, '*a necklet*.' Hieron. '*armillam*.' Onq. שׁוֹשִׁיפָךְ '*thy cloak*.' Pesh. ܡܥܦܪܟ '*thy cloak*.'

21. הקדשה הוא. Cf. the note on 19, 33. קדשה = '*a religious prostitute*,' lit. '*one dedicated*' (קָדֵשׁ '*to set apart*,' '*dedicate*') to the goddess Ashtoreth (עשתרת). Cf. Deut. 23, 18 for the law forbidding this dedication to Ashtoreth in Israel; and see Movers, *Phönizier*, i. 680.

24. ויהי כמשלש חדשים. '*And it happened after about three months*;' the double preposition is exceedingly rare, but cf. 1 Sam. 10, 27 LXX כמחדש; 1 Sam. 14, 14 כבחצי; Lev. 26, 37 כמפני חרב, also Is. 1, 26 כבראשנה, and see Driver, *Sam*., p. 82. חדש is here fem., but nowhere else; the Heb.-Sam. reads the more correct שלשת.

ותשרף. This punishment in the Levitical law was applicable only to the daughters of a priest; see Lev. 21, 9. In other cases the offender was stoned, Lev. 20, 10. Deut. 22, 23 ff. John 8, 5.

25. '*She was being brought out, and she sent to her father-in-law, saying, By a man to whom these belong am I with child;*' a more expressive way of saying, '*As she was being brought forth, she sent*' etc.; so Judg. 18, 3 המה עם בית . . . והמה הכירו; 1 Sam. 20, 36 הנער רץ והוא ירה; see Ewald, § 341 c, and the note on 19, 23. Cf. also Ges., § 142. 1. R. 2.

מוּצֵאת is fem. partic. Hof'. of יצא for מוּצֵאֶת; cf. לֵאמֹר for לֶאֱמֹר, לֵאלֹהִים for לֶאֱלֹהִים; see Stade, § 112 c; Ges., § 23. 2 b.

28. ויתן יד. '*And one stretched out a hand,*' i.e. a hand appeared; cf. יתן in Job 37, 10 מנשמת אל יתן קרח; Prov. 13, 10 רק בזדון יתן מצה. Di. prefers to render, '*then he* (sc. הַנֹּתֵן) *stretched out*' etc., i.e. there was stretched out; see Ges., § 144. 3 a and Rem.; Dav., *S.*, § 108; M. R., § 123. 3; and cf. Cheyne's crit. note on Is. 14, 30; and Dr., *Sam.*, p. 102 f. Del.[5] mentions both renderings as possible.

שני, i.e. '*a thread coloured with crimson.*' שָׁנִי is the crimson colour derived from the cochineal; called in Heb. either שני, or more fully תולעת שני.

29. ויהי כמשיב, hardly, '*and he was as one drawing back his hand,*' i.e. made an attempt to draw back (Del.[4]); but rather equivalent to כִּהְיוֹתוֹ מֵשִׁיב, or כַּהֲשִׁיבוֹ '*and it came to pass when he drew back;*' so Di., who compares 40, 10 (?). Jer. 2, 17; Ewald, § 337 c; Dav., *S.*, § 100. R. 6; Ges., § 164. 2. R. 3 (the emendation כְּהָשִׁיב is also mentioned). Driver, § 135. 6. Obs. 2, suggests the emendation כְּהָשִׁיב as more in accordance with Biblical analogy, but Di. questions this, as being not sufficiently definite.

מה פרצת עליך פרץ = '*Why hast thou made a rent for thyself?*' (20, 3) עליך '*for thyself,*' '*on thy account;*' so LXX,

Aquila, Luther, Di., Del. Others (Ges., Kn.) render, '*Why hast thou made a breach?*' '*Upon thee a breach!*' cf. 16, 5 חמסי עליך: i.e. either (Ges.) '*thou must bear the guilt of this breach;*' or Knobel, '*may a breach come upon thee;*' but this is not so natural, and would rather require הפרץ.

39.

1. הישמעאלים. '*Ishmaelites*,' cf. 37, 28b (J).

2. איש מצליח. '*A prosperous man;*' מצליח in the next verse is slightly different = '*to cause to prosper*.'

3. וכל אשר הוא עשה. '*All that he was doing*,' almost equivalent to וכל אשר הוא יעשה; so ver. 6 אכל, ver. 22 עשים; 1 Kings 3, 2 מזבחים; see Driver, § 135. 2. Obs., 'the participle denoting not a *continuous state*, but a fact liable to recur.'

The position Joseph held in Potiphar's household was that of steward, somewhat similar to the post Eliezer occupied in Abraham's family (15, 2 f.); cf. Ebers, p. 303, who speaks of the position of steward as 'a dignity which we meet with at the earliest times in every great Egyptian household.'

4. וכל יש לו for וכל אשר יש לו; cf. ver. 5. Ex. 9, 4. 18, 20. On the omission of the relative, see note on 15, 13 and cf. M. R., § 160; Ewald, § 333 b, who remarks that 'the omission of the relative in *prose* is almost entirely confined to the books of Chronicles.'

5. מאז הפקיד. מאז with the perfect, as in Ex. 5, 23 ומאז באתי אל פרעה; 9, 24 מאז היתה לגוי; cf. Ges., § 164. 2; Dav., *S.*, § 145 d; M. R., § 164 c. In Ex. 4, 10 the inf. follows מאז.

6 ff. On the history of Joseph and Potiphar's wife, cf. the Egyptian tale, contained in the Papyrus d'Orbiney, translated by Ebers, p. 311 ff., and Erman, *Aegypten*, p. 505 ff.

ולא ידע אתו. אִתּוֹ referring to Joseph; cf. ver. 8 אִתִּי; '*and he did not know anything with him* (*Joseph*)' = he did not trouble himself about anything that was with him, i.e. he left everything to Joseph's care, except his food, which could not be entrusted to him on account of the strictness of the Egyptian laws as to cleanness and uncleanness; see 43, 32. 46, 34; so Kn., Ebers. Del., however, explains differently. Potiphar left everything he could to Joseph's care, except eating his food, which naturally could not be done by deputy. אִתּוֹ may also be taken reflexively, and referred to Potiphar = '*with himself*,' i.e. in his own mind; cf. note on 3, 7. The A. V. offers a third rendering, also regarding אתו as reflexive, '*And he knew not aught he had.*'

8. מה בבית. '*What is in the house;*' or מה = '*anything*,' as in Prov. 9, 13. Job 13, 13. The Heb.-Sam. has מאומה.

9. איננו גדול בבית הזה ממני = '*he is not greater in this house than I am*,' i.e. I hold the same position in this house that he does. These words are taken differently by Maurer, '*There is nothing in this house too great for me;*' and by the R. V., '*There is none greater in this house than I*' (the more correct rendering, in the margin). But איננו cannot be translated indefinitely, as it would be in these two renderings.

10. יום יום = '*day by day*,' '*daily;*' so Ex. 16, 5. Prov. 8, 30; see Ges., § 123 d. 1; Dav., *S.*, § 29. R. 8; Ewald, § 313 a; M. R., § 72. 2.

11. ויהי כהיום הזה. '*And it came to pass, just about that time;*' cf. Deut. 6, 24 לחיתנו כהיום הזה; Neh. 5, 11

השיבו נא להם כהיום. In 50, 20 we find the more usual form כיום הזה. See note on 25, 31.

12. בבגדו. In the singular we should—from the analogy of other words of the same kind, e.g. מַלְכֵּי from מֶלֶךְ, דַּרְכֵּי from דֶּרֶךְ—expect בְּבִגְדוֹ; cf. יִקְבְּךָ from יֶקֶב, in Deut. 15, 14; בִּגְדִי, Ezr. 9, 3; עָמְדִי, Dan. 8, 17; and see Ges., § 93. Rem. 1 D; Stade, § 345 b. In the plural the aspirate has no dagesh.

14. הביא לנו איש עברי = '*he* (*Potiphar*) *hath brought unto us a Hebrew man;*' or impersonally, '*one has brought,*' i.e. '*there has been brought.*' איש עברי, i.e. one whom the Egyptians would regard with little favour; cf. 43, 32. 46, 34. On עברי, cf. on 14, 13; the name has been supposed to be found in the Egyptian inscriptions, in the form '*apuriu;*' see Ebers, p. 316, but the *p* for *b* is a difficulty, and this opinion is now generally given up. It is also doubtful whether the *Chabiri*, so often mentioned in the Tel-el-Amarna Letters, are to be identified with the Hebrews.

לְצַחֶק בָּנוּ. Retrogression of the tone, cf. on 4, 17. See also Ges., § 64. Rem. 2; Stade, § 88. 2 b; so in ver. 17. לצחק בנו, as in Prov. 1, 26 = '*to wanton with us,*' different from צחק את, 26, 8. The LXX have ἐμπαίζειν; cf. Ewald, § 217. f. 2 δ.

בנו. Potiphar's wife wishes to imply that the other females of the household had been similarly treated by Joseph.

15. אצלי. Sam. has בידי, but, as Del. points out, she would then betray herself.

18. כהרימי . . . ואקרא. So Lev. 16, 1 בקרבתם . . . וימתו; Josh. 8, 24 ככלות . . . ויפלו; 1 Kings 18, 18 בעזבכם . . . ותלך; see Driver, § 118; Ges., § 114. 3. R. 1; Dav., *S.*, § 96. The

inf. is continued by waw conv. and the imperf., because a fact is stated; cf. the note on 18, 25. Render, '*When I lifted up my voice and cried.*'

20. אדני יוסף. So 42, 30. 33. *Pluralis excellentiae*, see Ges., § 124. 1 c; M.R., § 135. 2; Dav., *S.*, § 16 c.

בית הסהר = perhaps '*the house of surrounding*,' or '*shutting in*,' i.e. a prison surrounded by a wall, if סהר be related to סחר, סגר; cf. the Syriac ܣܘܚܪܐ. Ebers, p. 317 f., compares the fortress at Memphis called '*White wall*' (a name found on many inscriptions), with which he identifies the בית הסהר of this chapter, and 40, 3. 5. The LXX have ὀχύρωμα. The name for prison better known to the Hebrews was either בית הבור, Ex. 12, 29; בית כלא, Is. 42, 7; or מסגר, Is. 42, 7.

מקום אשר. The sentence commencing with אשר is a genitive after the construct state מקום; see Ges., § 130. 3; M. R., § 82 c; Dav., *S.*, § 25; so 40, 3 מקום אשר יוסף אסור; 2 Sam. 15, 21 במקום אשר יהיה שׁם.

אסורי, Kri אֲסִירֵי, the Ktb. being the part. pass. Qal, the Kri the adj. of the form *qăṭîl*; cf. Ges., § 84. 8; Barth, *N. B.*, p. 186.

אסורים. שׁם is omitted after אסורים, as in 35, 13; contrast 40, 3, and see Ewald, § 331 c. 3; cf. ver. 22, where the ordinary editions have Ktb. האסורים, with the Kri האסירים, as here, while Baer and Del. have האסירים in their text.

21. ויתן חנו, lit. '*gave his* (*Joseph's*) *favour in the eyes of*,' i.e. and gave him favour in the eyes of, etc.; cf. Ex. 3, 21. 11, 3. 12, 36 (all).

שׂר בית הסהר. In this chapter, which is mainly from J, Joseph is apparently confined in the royal prison, the governor of which is not mentioned by name, but is merely described as שׂר בית הסהר. In 40, 2–4 E, the governor of the prison is Potiphar, and the prison is in his own house, cf. Di. p. 403. Ebers, however, regards the person mentioned in this verse as the special governor of the prison for state prisoners. Potiphar was, as police minister, in control over all the prisons; but not an actual prison governor, but cf. Di. l. c.

22. עֹשִׂים is intentionally indefinite in contrast to הוא היה עשׂה at the end of the verse, see Driver, p. 171, and cf. Ges., §§ 116. 5. R. 3, 144. 3 d; Dav., *S.*, § 108 c.

היה עשׂה: Cf. the note on 4, 17.

23. Render, '*There was no governor of the prison overlooking* (lit. *seeing*) *anything that he did* (lit. *anything in his hand*), *in that Yahweh was with him, and that which he was doing Yahweh made to prosper.*'

40.

1. ויהי . . . חטאו. So 14, 1. 2 ויהי בימי . . . עשׂו; Ex. 12, 41[b] ויהי בעצם היום הזה יצאו; where instead of the *perfect* in the second half of the clause, the *imperfect* with *waw conversive* might stand, and most frequently does stand; see Driver, § 78; Dav., *S.*, § 51. R. 1; Ges., § 111. 2.

משקה מלך מצרים והאפה = '*the cupbearer and baker of the king of Egypt.*' Notice the difference in the idiom in English and Hebrew. English says, '*the cupbearer and baker of the king;*' Hebrew, '*the cupbearer of the king and the baker,*' or more commonly with the third pers. suffix, '*his baker;*' cf. 41, 8, and see Ewald, § 339 b; M. R., § 75. 2. Rem. a; Ges., § 128. 1; Dav., *S.*, § 27 b. The אפה has been discovered on the Egyptian inscriptions, but not the משקה; see Ebers, p. 321.

2. סָרִיסָיו with firm qameç, as in בָּרִיחַ, though the more usual form with simple shewa under the ס is also found. The form with qameç is explained by Stade, § 209, either from a by-form qaṭṭil, i.e. for סֵרִּים, and as ר cannot be doubled, סָרִים, so בָּרִיחַ; or through the influence of the counter-tone on the first syllable; for this he compares שָׁלִישִׁים for שְׁלִישִׁים, from שָׁלִישׁ. Cf. also פָּרִיצֵי and פְּרִיצֵי, Ges. in the *Thes. s. v.*, and Barth, *N. B.*, p. 197.

3. מקום אשר. Cf. the note on 39, 20.

4. ויהיו ימים במשמר, lit. '*and they were days*' etc., i.e. some time; cf. 4, 3 מקץ ימים = '*after some time;*' so we find ימים used indefinitely in 1 Sam. 29, 3. Dan. 8, 27. Neh. 1, 4. Cf. Dav., *S.*, § 11. R. 1; Ges., § 139. 4; contrast 27, 44. 29, 20.

5. איש כפתרון חלמו. '*Each according to the interpretation of his dream,*' i.e. each one dreamt a dream that had its special reference to himself, and its own interpretation.

המשקה והאפה אשר למלך מצרים. Cf. the note on 29, 9. This construction is closer to the English idiom than the one noticed in ver. 1, and must be used if the two words that should be in the construct state are to stand together; the construction מַשְׁקֵה וְאֹפֵה מלך מ״ hardly occurs (two construct states and one genitive), so we must, if we wish to keep אפה and משקה together, use אשר ל or ל, as in 7, 11; otherwise the alternative construction followed in ver. 1 must be adopted.

6. זעפים = '*of a sad countenance,*' '*cast down;*' so Dan. 1, 10; cf. פנים נזעמים in Prov. 25, 23. Symm. has σκυθρωποί here. On the importance attached to dreams among the Egyptians, see Ebers, p. 321.

7. מדוע פניכם רעים. Cf. Neh. 2, 2 מדוע פניך רעים = '*why dost thou look so troubled?*'

8. ופתר אין אתו = '*and there is no one to interpret it;*' cf. 41, 8 ואין פותר אותם; on אין, see Ges., § 152. 1. c. 4; M. R., § 128. 2 b; Dav., *S.*, § 127 b.

9. בחלומי והנה וגו׳. '*In my dream, behold a vine was before me;*' the apodosis without a verb being introduced by waw; so ver. 16 (cf. 41, 17, where waw is omitted); 2 Sam. 15, 34. Prov. 10, 25[a]; see Driver, § 125. Obs.; M. R., § 132 b; Ges., § 143. R. 2. הנה is inserted to attract the attention of the reader to the nature of the dream; contrast 41, 22 וארא בחלמי, where no especial stress is laid.

10. והוא כפרחת עלתה וגו׳. I. The A. V., Knobel, Tuch, Driver render, '*And it was as though it budded, and its blossoms shot forth;*' cf. the analogous use of היה כ in 19, 14, in the sense '*to appear,*' '*to seem.*' II. Di. and apparently Del. prefer taking כ in a temporal sense, and render, '*And it, as it budded, its blossoms shot forth,*' comparing 38, 29 כמשיב; cf. the note there, and Driver, p. 172, who points out that this usage of the participle, though common in the Mishna (see Geiger, *Lehr- und Lesebuch zur Sp. der Mishna*, p. 52), is without analogy in Biblical Hebrew.

נִצָּהּ '*its blossom.*' נֵץ occurs nowhere else in the Bible in the sense '*blossom,*' but is common in the Mishna; the feminine נצה being used in Biblical Hebrew (as a *nomen unitatis*, see note on 27, 3). The masc. here may be explained as a collective, and so construed with the fem. עלתה (Wright). Others take נצה as abbreviated from נִצָּתָהּ; see Ewald, § 257 d; Stade, § 347 c. 2 (and Del. on Ps. 27, 5), who gives as other examples, מִדָּהּ, פִּנָּהּ, צֵידָהּ, גְּלָהּ. נצה may be taken, cf. Ewald, § 281 b, as accus. to עלתה = '*and it* (*the vine*) *went up into blossoms;*' cf. עלה in Is. 5, 6. 34, 13. Prov. 24, 31; so הבשילו in the second half of this verse. Possibly the text ought to be pointed נִצָּה, the fem. ending ָה being altered into ָהּ (the suffix), to conform with אשכלתיה in the second half of the verse. Prov. 7, 8 (פנה), Job 11, 9 (מדה), Zech. 4, 2 (גלה), cited by Stade above, are similar to נצה in this verse, and may possibly be mistakes for the fem. forms.

אשכלתיה = '*its clusters.*' ענב = '*the ripe grape.*' On the use of wine in Egypt, see Ebers, p. 322 f.

12. שלשת השרגים, *casus pendens.* '*The three branches, they are three days;*' cf. on 34, 21.

13. ישא . . . את ראשך. '*Shall lift up thy head,*' i.e. shall take thee from prison; cf. 2 Kings 25, 27.

כמשפט הראשון, lit. '*according to the former custom,*' i.e. as thou wert accustomed to do.

14. כי אם זכרתני. Di., following Ewald, § 356 b, cf. § 342 b. 2, renders, '*only that thou rememberest me, with thee* (i.e. *thyself*), *when it is well with thee, and wilt shew me kindness,*' comparing 2 Sam. 5, 6. 2 Kings 5, 20. 23, 9 (see also Ges., §§ 106. 3 b. note 2, 163. 2. R.), which are different from this passage, as the כי אם is dependent on a previous verb. Wellhausen emends to אך, cf. 23, 13; and see Driver, § 119 δ. foot-note 2, who points out that there is no justification for rendering the *bare* perf. either as an imperf. or modal future. This reading would remove any difficulty, אם זכרתני . . . ועשית being a conditional sentence, exactly like 43, 9. 47, 6; see Driver, § 138. 1 a; M.R., § 26; Dav., *S.*, § 130 b; Ges., § 159. 3 d.

אתך. Cf. Job 12, 3. 14, 5.

15. כי שמו אתי בבור. '*That they should have put me in prison;*' cf. Ruth 1, 12 כי אמרתי '*that I should have said;*' 1 Sam. 17, 26b כי חרף '*that he should have defied;*' see Driver, § 39. δ. Obs.; Dav., *S.*, §§ 39 c, 150; Ges., § 166. 2.

16. סלי חרי. '*Baskets of white bread.*' חרי from חור '*to be white,*' properly an adj. = '*what is white,*' and then applied to what is baked; so the Arab. حُوَّارَى (Del.). Vulg. has '*canistra farinae,*' LXX κανᾶ χονδριτῶν; cf. ver. 17 מאכל פרעה. The baker carried his wares on his head, an exceptional mode of carrying things among the Egyptians; see Ebers, p. 331 f.

17. מכל מאכל פרעה. '*Of all kinds of food for Pharaoh,*' cf. Dan. 1, 5 פת־בג המלך; Gen. 49, 20 מעדני מלך. מכל, מן partitive; cf. on 4, 3.

19. ישא . . . מעליך. '*Shall lift up thy head from off thee,*' i.e. shall behead thee. There is a play on the words here, the phrase being the same as in ver. 13. Wright compares John 12, 32. The punishment of the chief baker was one of the heaviest that could befall an Egyptian. The exposure of the body was intended to make the sentence more severe, and was especially repugnant to the superstitious Egyptians, who regarded the life after death as dependent on the body remaining unmutilated; see Ebers, p. 334.

20. יום הלדת את פרעה. The construction is the same as in 4, 18; see the note there. הֻלֶּדֶת is inf. Hof'. of ילד, for the ordinary form הוּלֶּדֶת; cf. Ez. 16, 4 הוּלֶּדֶת, and מוּסָּד, Is. 28, 16 (see Ges., § 69. 2. Rem. 7; Stade, §§ 29, 246), the ל being doubled to compensate for the shortened vowel.

21. על משקהו = '*to his butlership,*' or '*cupbearership.*'

41.

1. ימים. Cf. on 29, 14.

והנה עמד. Cf. note on 32, 7.

היאר. Always with י without the dagesh. היאר '*the river' par excellence*, the Nile, is the Hebrew form of the Egyptian *aur-âa*, i.e. '*the great stream*,' Ebers, p. 338, which became in the mouth of the people *iar-â*, *iaro*.

On the participle in this and the two following verses, cf. on 13, 7.

2. באחו. אחו, LXX ἄχει, '*Nile-grass*,' is the Hebrew form of the Egyptian *aχu* or *aχuu*, '*reeds*' or '*grass*' growing in marshy ground; see Ebers, p. 338; and Wiedemann, *Samml. altaegypt. Wörter*, p. 16; also notice Hieron. ad Jes. 19, 7, who describes it as 'omne quod in palude virens nascitur;' and Ecclus. 40, 16.

2–4. The number of the cows, seven (cf. the same number in the next dream), was a sacred number among the Egyptians, as among other Oriental nations (Ebers, p. 337); cf. 21, 28. 30. On the dreams Kn. remarks, 'Both dreams were suitably interpreted by Joseph. The Nile floods are what the fruitfulness of Egypt chiefly depends on, therefore the cows in the dream come up out of the Nile. The ox was the symbol of the Nile (Diod. i. 51), and especially sacred to Osiris, the discoverer of agriculture (Diod. i. 21). The cow was, in the Egyptian hieroglyphic writing, the sign for the earth (Macrob., *Sat.*, i. 19), agriculture, and food (Clem. Alex., *Strom.*, v. p. 567). At the same time Isis was the goddess of the earth, that nourishes everything (Macrob., *Sat.*, i. 20), and is rendered fruitful by the Nile (Plut., *de Is.*, 38); the cow was especially sacred to her

(Her. ii. 41; Aelian., *h. an.*, x. 27). She was also goddess of the moon (Diod. i. 11), and her picture serves in the hieroglyphics as a sign for the year (Horapollo, i. 3); therefore the seven fat cows mean seven fruitful, and the seven lean cows seven unfruitful years; the seven lean cows coming closely upon the seven fat ones, point to the close succession of the unfruitful years to the fruitful years. The meaning of the second dream (the ears of corn) is self-evident. That the ears grow on one stalk, indicates that the seven years are regarded as following one immediately after the other.'

6. שׁדופת קדים. '*Blasted by the east wind.*' The narrator here mentions the wind that was most destructive in Palestine; cf. Hos. 13, 15. Jon. 4, 8. Ez. 17, 10. The winds in Egypt that were most hurtful came usually from the N.W. or S.E.; see Ebers, p. 340. Del. understands קדים here as the destructive Chamsin, which blew, in the spring months, from the S.E. quarter; see Ebers, l.c.

7. Knobel remarks on the dreams, 'The order in which they come is well chosen. First the Nile, which causes the fruitfulness, then the cows representing fruitfulness, and lastly the ears, as an evidence of fruitfulness.'

8. חרטמי מצרים, only here and Ex. 7–9 P in Pent. The word is also found in Daniel, probably borrowed from the Pent. LXX ἐξηγητάς. '*The lettered men of Egypt.*' The חרטמים are the Egyptian ἱερογραμματεῖς, represented on the inscriptions with writing materials in their hands, and a pen on their temples (Ebers, p. 345). They belonged to the Egyptian priesthood, and employed themselves in the study of the hieroglyphic writing and astronomy, and were also noted as seers or foretellers of future events; see Ebers,

p. 344 f.; Di., p. 412. They also had a great reputation as magicians, as it is clear from Ex. 7, 11. 22. 8, 3, etc. The word חרטם is taken by Harkavy (*Journ. Asiatique*, 1870, p. 168 f.) as equivalent to the Egyptian '*Cher-tum*,' '*Revealer of secrets*.' It may, however, be equally well derived from חָרַט '*to grave*,' or חֶרֶט '*a stylus*,' with the formative ending ֹם, like דָּרוֹם from דָּר, עֵירוֹם, פִּדְיוֹם; see Ewald, § 163 g; Stade, § 295. Tuch gives another derivation (*Comm.*, p. 443 f.), according to which חרטם is a quadriliteral form from חרט '*to write with a stylus*,' and חרם '*to be sacred*;' cf. חרגל from חגל, and רגל; this, however, is doubtful; see Stade, §§ 149, 150, on the formation of quadriliterals.

חכמים = '*the wise men*,' identified by Ebers, p. 345, with the *reχχat-u* of the inscriptions, '*those who know things*' (die wissenden der Dinge), probably a wide term, embracing all the higher classes of priests, especially the ὡροσκόποι of Clement, who were astrologers, calendar makers, and interpreters of signs or omens.

חלמו . . . אותם. אותם, the plural suffix, may be used with reference to the double nature of the dream, or the reading may be a *scriptio defectiva*, חֲלוֹמֹו for חֲלוֹמָיו, which the Sam. gives; so Pesh. and Saadiah.

9. אני מזכיר, not '*I remember*,' A.V.—for הזכיר means '*to cause another to remember*'—but '*I make mention of*.' On the order of the words obj. subj. verb, see Dav., *S.*, § 111. R. 1; Ges., § 142. 2 d; Driver, § 208. 2; M.R., § 131. 2. R. b; and cf. 37, 16. Judg. 9, 36. 2 Kings 5, 13. 6, 22. Is. 5, 17. This order of words is the usual one in nominal sentences with a participial pred. In other cases it is very rare.

10. אֹתִי, so Sam. Ver. LXX, and Pesh., more correctly, אֹתָנוּ. The Heb.-Sam. reads אֹתָם.

11. ונחלמה. The first person imperf. with waw conv. and the ה cohortative is rare; there are two other instances in Gen., viz. 32, 6 ואשלחה, and 43, 21 ונפתחה; see other instances in Driver, § 69. Obs.; Ewald, § 232 g; Ges., § 49. 2; Dav., *S.*, § 51. R. 7.

12. איש כחלמו. See on 9, 5.

14. ויריצהו. '*And they brought him quickly*,' lit. '*made him run*;' cf. 1 Sam. 17, 17 והרץ המחנה לאחיך; 2 Chron. 35, 13 ויריצו לכל בני העם.

ויגלח ויחלף שמלתיו. No one was allowed to appear before the king of Egypt unless he was quite clean; see Ebers, p. 350. Del.[4] and Tuch explain the verse from the Egyptian custom of regarding a prisoner as a mourner. He would then wear his beard and hair; see Ebers, p. 350. foot-note, against this view.

15. ואני שמעתי וגו״. '*And I have heard about thee, saying thou canst understand a dream*,' or '*thou hearest a dream*,' i.e. hast only to hear it, and can interpret it.

עליך, as in 1 Kings 10, 6 על דבריך ועל חכמתך.

On the construction—*oratio indirecta* without כי to introduce it—see note on 12, 13.

16. בלעדי. '*Not I*,' as in 14, 24. The LXX have ἄνευ τοῦ Θεοῦ οὐκ ἀποκριθήσεται, which means really the same as the Mass. text, and does not of necessity suppose a reading בִּלְעֲדֵי אלהים, and the addition of לא. The Sam.Ver. renders, '*Without me God will not answer the welfare of P.*'

יענה את־שלום, lit. '*answer the welfare*,' i.e. give such an answer as will be most conducive to Pharaoh's welfare.

19. רקות, so vers. 20. 27, possibly a mistake for דקות, which occurs in ver. 3.

לא ראיתי כהנה וגו״ = '*such as I have not seen in all the land of Egypt for badness*,' lit. '*I have not seen like these*' etc.; see ver. 38, and cf. M.R., § 56.

21. קרבנה. Cf. the fuller forms in 21, 29 לבדנה; 31, 6 אתנה (both E); the ֵ, defective for ֵי, has arisen out of the diphthong ַי; see Stade, § 352 b; cf. § 99. 2; Ges., § 91. 1. Rem. 2.

ומראיהן. The form is singular, not plural, the ֶי being the ending ֶי, מַרְאֵי = מַרְאֶה; see Stade, § 353 a. 1 β; cf. § 99. 2; Ges., § 93. 3. Rem. 3.

23. אחריהם. Masc. suffix for fem.; cf. on 26, 15; in ver. 27 we find the fem. suffix used.

25. חלום פרעה אחד הוא. Cf. on 34, 21.

26. שבע פרת הטבת. See the notes on 21, 29. שבע פרת וגו״ is a *casus pendens*, as in ver. 25.

32. '*And with respect to the repetition of the dream unto Pharaoh twice*, (*it is*) *because the matter is resolved on by God, and God hastens to do it*.' ועל השנות; cf. Ruth 4, 7 על הגאלה ועל התמורה '*with respect to ransoming, and with respect to exchanging*.' השנות is the Nif'. inf. cstr. of שנה. The Nif'al of this verb is not found elsewhere.

33. יֵרֶא. So the ordinary editions; but Baer and Del. in the text have יֵרָא, and in the notes to their edition, p. 78, they refer to Ibn Ezra in favour of the reading with ֶ. On יֵרֶא—for יֵרָא—, cf. Zech. 9, 5 תֵּרֶא (Baer and Del. תֵּרָא in text and notes, p. 83), and see Ewald, § 63 d; cf. Stade, § 489 b. 1. On יֵרָא, as an abnormal form, see Stade, l.c., and Ges., § 75. Rem. 3 b; König, *Lehrg*., p. 561. The jussive is used in making a suggestion, see Driver, § 50 β (cf. Ex. 8, 25. 1 Kings 1, 2); M.R., § 8. 2; Dav., *S*., § 63 b.

34. יעשׂה פרעה ויפקד = '*let P. set up and appoint*' etc.; cf. the use of עשׂה in 1 Sam. 8, 16. 1 Kings 12, 31. Ges. in *Thes.*, p. 1077, renders, '*faciat* (hoc) *P.* (sequatur consilium meum) *et praeficiat.*'

חמשׁ, a denom. from חָמֵשׁ, is a ἅπαξ λεγόμ. = '*let him exact the fifth part;*' cf. the Arab. خَمَّسَ '*take a fifth part,*' עִשֵּׂר = '*to take the tenth part of anything.*'

35. תחת יד פרעה = '*under Pharaoh's control.*' יד used as in 2 Kings 13, 5. Is. 3, 6.

39. אחרי הודיע אלהים אותך את כל וגו׳. On the construction, see Ges., § 115. 1; M. R., § 116; Dav., *S.*, § 91 c.

40. על פיך ישק כל עמי. I. Gesenius and Knobel render, '*And all my people shall kiss thy mouth;*' cf. 1 Sam. 10, 1. 1 Kings 19, 18. Hos. 13, 2. But the kiss of homage was not given on the mouth; and that Joseph had to receive the kiss from all the people would be a very unnatural thought; further, נשׁק על is not used in the sense '*to kiss,*' for which we find the acc. or ל. II. The LXX, Sam. Ver., Vulg., and most moderns, e.g. Del., Tuch, Di., prefer taking על פיך, as in 45, 21. Ex. 17, 1. Num. 3, 16, etc. = '*according to thy mouth,*' i.e. '*command*' etc., and render נשׁק '*dispose themselves,*' taking it intransitively. Cf. the Arabic نسق '*ordinare et disponere rem.*' III. Siegfried and Stade (*Hebr. Wörterb.*, p. 446) regard it as Impf. of נָשַׁק '*to arm,*' a denom. from נֵשֶׁק '*armour,*' so '*at thy command all my people shall arm themselves.*'

רק הכסא אגדל ממך. '*Only with respect to the throne will I be greater than thou.*' הכסא, accus. of respect; see Ges., § 118. 2 c; and cf. note on 3, 15.

41. נתתי. See on 1, 29.

42. טבעתו. Cf. Esther 3, 10. 8, 2, where the Persian monarch gives his signet first to Haman, and then to Mordecai.

שֵׁשׁ = '*byssus*,' '*fine white cotton*;' here בגדי שֵׁשׁ = '*clothing made of byssus*;' cf. Del.[5], p. 468. The priests' clothing was of byssus; cf. Her. ii. 37. For שֵׁשׁ, at a later period of the language, בוץ was used, e.g. in the books of Chronicles and Esther. שֵׁשׁ probably = Egypt. *schenti*, *schens*, '*something woven*,' from root *shent*, *plectere*, *conserere*. The Hebrews seem to have connected it with יָשֵׁשׁ, *album esse*, see Di., on Ex. 25, 4.

43. מרכבת המשנה = '*a carriage of the second rank*;' cf. כהן המשנה '*a priest of the second rank*.' מֶרְכָּבָה is probably a *nomen unitatis*, cf. note on 27, 3.

אשר לו. Cf. on 40, 5.

אַבְרֵךְ. Most probably the Hebrew form of an Egyptian word, cf. Brugsch, *Geschichte*, p. 247, who renders '*bow the knee*.' De Rossi explains it as = *ape-rek*, '*bow the head*.' Harkavy (in the *Berlin Aegyptological Journal*, 1869, p. 132) as the Egyptian *ap-reχ-u*, '*head of the wise*.' Benfey (*Verhältniss der Ägypt. Sprache*, p. 302 f.) takes it as equivalent to *a*, the sign of the imper., *bor* = '*projicere*,' and *k* the sign of the second person; so '*prostrate thyself*.' Jablonski (*Opusc.*, i. p. 6) explains it as meaning *ouberek*, '*bow towards*' (Joseph); Cook, *Speaker's Comm.*, i. p. 482, as *ab-rek*, '*rejoice thou!*' and Lepage Renoulf (*Proc. Soc. Bib. Archæol.*, 1888, xi. 1, p. 5 ff.) as *ab*(*u*)*rek*, '*thy command is our desire*,' we are at thy service. The Versions give various renderings. The LXX have καὶ ἐκήρυξεν ἔμπροσθεν αὐτοῦ κῆρυξ, apparently taking

אברך as '*a herald;*' so Sam. Ver., which has ࠑࠓࠅࠆࠄ. The Targums of Onq. and Jer. give אַבָּא לְמַלְכָּא, as though אברך were compounded of אב '*father*,' and רַךְ = the Latin *rex!* (cf. 45, 8). The Pesh. paraphrases ܐܒܐ ܘܡܕܒܪܢܐ ܥܠ ܟܠܗ ܐܪܥܐ ܕܡܨܪܝܢ '*Father and ruler over all the land of Egypt;*' and the Vulgate, which has '*Ut omnes coram eo genu flecterent.*' A possible explanation from the Hebrew is to take אברך as inf. abs. Af'el for Hif'il, instead of the imperative; cf. ver. 51 נשׁני, Pa'el for Pi'el, and accordingly Jose b. Dormaskith, quoted by Del.[5], p. 468, explains it by לְבִרְכַּיִם; cf. the Vulg. rendering, and Aquila's rendering cited by Hieron. (*Quaest.*, ed. Lag., p. 60), 'et clamavit in conspectu ejus ad geniculationem.' Hieron. himself follows the Targ. Ps.-Jon., and renders, '*tender father;*' cf. רך, 18, 7. Fried. Del. (*Par.*, p. 225, *Proleg.*, p. 145) compares אברך with the Assyrian *abarraku*, a title = possibly '*grand vizier.*' Sayce, *Relig. Bab.* (Hibbert Lecture), p. 183, mentions Assyr. *Abrikku* = Akk. *abrik*, '*vizier*,' from an unpublished tablet. Against this view, cf. Schrader, *C. O. T.*, p. 139; Nöld., *Z.D.M.G.*, xl. p. 734.

וְנָתוֹן. The inf. abs. continuing the narrative instead of וַיִּתֵּן; cf. the inf. abs. again in Ex. 8, 11 והכבד את לבו; Judg. 7, 19 ונפוץ הכדים; and see Ges., § 113. 4 a; M. R., § 106. 2; Ewald, § 351 c; Dav., *S.*, § 88 and R. 1. Probably the inf. abs. is used instead of the ordinary construction of the imperf. with waw conv., to shew that the appointment of Joseph over the land of Egypt was contemporaneous with the announcement of the herald, and the setting him in the second chariot; not subsequent (as it would be with waw conv. and the impf.); we might therefore render ונתון '*thus setting him.*' To connect ונתון with אברך is against the accents, besides giving an improbable sense, as the people would not have the appointment of vizier in their hands; cf. the next verse.

45. צפנת פענח. LXX, Ψονθομφανήχ. This name, as given in LXX, is, according to the testimony of Hieron., to be explained as = *Salvator mundi*, in Coptic, *p-sot-om-ph-eneh*; i.e. from *sot*, *sôte*, *redemptio*, *salus*, and *eneh*, *saeculum*. The *n*, however, in *p-sont* for *p-sot*, in Ψονθομφανήχ, cannot be explained, cf. Ges., *Thes.*, p. 1181. It is better therefore to follow the rendering of Bunsen, Lepsius, and others *sustentatio*, or concrete, *sustentator vitae*, from the Aegypto-Coptic *sônt*, '*to support, maintain*,' and *anh*, '*life*,' צפנת in the Hebrew form being transposed for פצנת by Ewald, § 78 b. Brugsch, *Gesch.*, p. 248, explains the word as equivalent to *za-p-u-nt-p-a-ānkh*, i.e. '*guardian* (*Landpfleger*) *of the district of place of life*.' Cook, *Speaker's Comm.*, i. p. 481, renders it '*food of the living*;' Steindorff, *Z.A.S.A.*, xxvii. 41 f., '*God speaks and he lives*.' The Jewish interpreters, Onq., Pesh., Saad., make it mean '*revealer of secrets*,' taking פען as equivalent to φαίνω! Cf. Di., p. 414 f.

אסנת = '*she who belongs to Neith*' (Pallas). LXX, Ἀσεννέθ. Brugsch, *Gesch.*, p. 248, makes it = *Snat* or *Sant*, the name of a woman; Cook, *Speaker's Comm.*, i. p. 479, proposes *As-Neit*, '*favourite of Neith*,' or *Isis Neit*.

און. LXX, Ἡλιούπολις, situated on the eastern bank of the Nile, the modern *Matariye*, about seven miles east of the Nile from Cairo, and about eighteen from Memphis, see Ebers, *Durch Gosen zum Sinai*, pp. 75 and 507; Wiedemann, l. c., p. 46. In Coptic the name of און is *Un* or *On*, meaning '*light*' or '*sun* (?);' cf. the Hebrew בית שמש '*house of the sun*.' Hieroglyphically it was *Anu* or *An*, more closely *Anu-mhit* (Brugsch and Ebers). Heliopolis was the chief seat of the worship of the sun-god *Ra*; cf. its name in Is. 19, 18 עיר ההרס ('*city of destruction*'), a play on the words for עיר החרס; cf. Jer. 43, 13, where it is called 'בית שמש *in the land of Egypt*.'

48. שבע שנים, as the text stands, quite indefinite, seems hardly correct. Del. and Ols. read שֶׁבַע שְׁנֵי הַשָּׂבָע. Cf. ver. 53. The LXX and Sam. read for שנים—היו, הַשָּׁנִים אֲשֶׁר הָיָה הַשָּׂבָע.

51. מנשה כי נשני = '*Manasseh, for he hath made me forget.*' The form נַשַּׁנִי, for נִשַּׁנִי, is used on account of its similarity in sound with the name מנשה; cf. Ges., § 52. 2. Rem. 1; Stade, § 387 a. In Arabic and Aramaic the *a* sound is regular, e.g. Heb. קִטֵּל, Arab. قَتَّلَ, Aramaic ܩܰܛܶܠ, and קַטֵּל; and that *a* was once the original sound in Hebrew is proved from the imperf. and partic. of the Pi'el; cf. Wright, *Arab. Gram.*, i. pp. 32, 33. The Pi'el with a double acc. may possibly, as Tuch and Di. suggest, have been chosen instead of the commoner Hif'il on account of the name מנשה.

52. אפרים, meaning perhaps '*double fruitfulness;*' cf. Hos. 13, 15. Other dual names are דִּבְלַיִם, Hos. 1, 3; דִּבְלָתַיִם (in בית דבלתים, Jer. 48, 22; called on the Moabite stone, l. 30, בית דבלתן; cf. Gen. 37, 17 דֹּתָיְן); also קִרְיָתַיִם and חֹרֹנַיִם (*ibid.*, lines 10, 31 קריתן and חורנן); see Schlottmann's monograph, p. 48, and the proper names of places, as עֵינַיִם, מַחֲנַיִם, etc. All these names, however, may not be duals, cf. on 37, 17.

53. היה is neuter, '*which there was*' (Germ. *die es gab*); contrast ver. 48; or היה may be referred to השבע.

56. את כל אשר בהם. LXX, *πάντας τοὺς σιτοβολῶνας*, Pesh. ܐܘܨܪ̈ܐ, Vulg. '*universa horrea*,' Onq. יַת כָּל אוֹצְרַיָּא דִּבְהוֹן עִיבוּרָא = '*all the storehouses wherein was grain*,' which point to a reading אוצרות בר. The true reading here seems to have been lost.

וישבר is probably to be emended to וַיַּשְׁבֵּר, cf. 42, 6, as שׁבר, Qal, always means, when a denom. from שֶׁבֶר, '*to buy*,' not '*to sell*.'

57. **וכל הארץ באו**. The plural verb as הארץ = '*the inhabitants of the land;*' see Ges., § 145. 2 c; M. R., § 135. 2; Dav., *S.*, § 115; so 48, 6. 1 Sam. 14, 25. 2 Sam. 15, 23.

42.

1. **שבר**. In all the passages where שבר occurs it means '*grain*,' as an article of merchandise, hence its frequent use from this chapter onwards. It is usually derived from שָׁבַר '*to break*,' from the corn being crushed in the mill; see the Lexica.

תתראו. '*Look at one another*,' i.e. look helplessly, one to the other, expecting aid and advice. It is not found elsewhere in this sense.

4. **פן יקראנו אסון**. '*Lest harm befall him.*' קרא is here equivalent to קרה, as in ver. 38. 49, 1. Ex. 1, 10.

אסון is only found again in ver. 38. 44, 29. Ex. 21, 22. 23.

6. **ויוסף הוא השליט**. ויוסף is a *casus pendens;* so 9, 18 וחם הוא אבי; 15, 2 ובן משק ביתי הוא דמשק; see 44, 17, note on 3, 12, and cf. M. R., § 127.

השליט = המשל in 45, 8. שליט is a word common in Aramaic, and occasionally found in late Hebrew, e.g. Eccl. 7, 19 (pl.). 8, 8. 10, 5; and in the fem. sing. שלטת, Ez. 16, 30 (all). Di. suggests that it is a technical word here, that has come over with tradition, as it agrees remarkably with

Salatis, or *Silitis*, the name of the first ruler of the Hyksos in Egypt, Jos., *Contra Ap.*, i. 14; so Tuch and Del. in their commentaries; cf. the Assyrian *šalaṭ*, '*viceroy*.'

7. In this chap., vers. 7–13, 30–32 E, Joseph accuses his brethren of being spies, in reply they volunteer the information that they have a younger brother. In chap. 43 J there is no allusion to the charge preferred by Joseph, and it is expressly stated that Joseph *asked* them if they had a brother (vers. 6–7, cf. 44, 19 J). Cf. Driver, *Introd.*, p. 17.

וידבר אתם קשות. קָשׁוֹת, the fem. pl., is here used as neuter; so קָשָׁה, fem. sing. in Ps. 60, 5 הראית עמך קשה, and 1 Kings 12, 13 ויען המלך את העם קשה; other instances of the pl. fem. as neuter are Ps. 12, 4 גדולות; Ps. 16, 11 נעימות; Zech. 4, 10 קטנות; see Ewald, § 172 b; M. R., § 63; Ges., § 122. 4; Dav., *S.*, § 14.

8. והם is emphatic, *they*, as opposed to Joseph; see on 33, 3.

9. להם. '*About them;*' see on 17, 20.

את ערות הארץ. '*The bareness of the land;*' cf. a similar use of the Arabic عَوْرَةٌ, *Qor.* 33, 13. Knobel further compares γυμνοῦσθαι (Homer, *Iliad*, 12. 339) and *nudari* (Caesar, *Gallic War*, vii. 70), and points out that the Hyksos were in constant dread of attacks from the Assyrians, who were at that time very powerful, and therefore fortified the eastern portion of the land of Egypt (Jos., *Contra Ap.*, i. 14).

10. ועבדיך. ו is here used after the negative, after which כי usually stands; so 17, 5 והיה, for the more usual כי יהיה; see Ewald, § 354 a; Ges., § 163. 1; cf. Deut. 11, 10 f.; 2 Sam. 23, 7.

11. נחנו for the longer form אנחנו is only found here,

Ex. 16, 7. 8. Num. 32, 32. Lam. 3, 42[1]; see Ges., § 32. Rem. 2; Stade, § 179 b; Dav., § 12. Rem. a. נָחְנוּ is the pausal form.

כנים in the sense of '*upright*,' '*honest*' (masc.), is only found in this chapter; כֵּן occurs, Num. 27, 7. Is. 16, 6. Prov. 11, 19, and elsewhere, in the *neuter* sense of '*right*.'

היו is here a stative verb = 'thy servants have not been, nor are they now, spies;' so Is. 15, 6; see Driver, § 11.

מרגלים. '*Spies*.' Del. remarks that the term מרגלים ('*those who go about with the object of spying*') was a more insulting term than תרים ('*those who go about with the object of exploring*').

12. כי ערות הארץ באתם לראת. The obj. is intentionally emphasized by being placed first.

13. אנחנו seems superfluous; possibly, as Olshausen suggests, it is a gloss from ver. 32, and should be rejected. Del.[4] renders, against the accents, '*Twelve are thy servants, brothers are we, the sons of*' etc.

הקטן = '*the youngest*;' see on 9, 24, and cf. M.R., § 86; Dav., § 47. 2, and *S.*, § 34; Ges., § 133. 3.

איננו, as in 5, 24.

14. הוא is here neuter, as in 20, 16. Job 13, 16.

15. חי פרעה. The Mass. pointed חֵי with a created object, but חַי with God; so Lev. 25, 36 וְחֵי אָחִיךָ עִמָּךְ; see Ges., § 93. 1. Rem. 7 note; Dav., *S.*, § 119. Cf. 1 Sam. 17, 55 (Saul). 2 Sam. 11, 11 (David). Di. remarks 'that this oath is very suitable here, as the Egyptians honoured their kings, ὡς πρὸς ἀλήθειαν ὄντας θεούς (Diod. i. 90).'

---

[1] נחנו, 2 Sam. 17, 12, quoted by Ges. l.c., is perf. Qal of נוח. LXX and Pesh. take it as a verb; cf. Dr., *Sam.*, p. 250.

אם. On this use of אם, cf. on 14, 23.

Render, '*As sure as P. lives! ye shall not go hence, except your youngest brother come hither.*'

16. **כי** (introducing the oath) = '*surely;*' see Ewald, § 330 b, and cf. 1 Sam. 14, 44. 20, 3. 2 Kings 3, 14.

17. **ויאסף**. Cf. Josh. 2, 18. Is. 24, 22.

18. **זאת עשׂו וחיו**, lit. '*Do this and live,*' i.e. 'if ye do this ye shall live;' see Ges., § 110. 2 a; M.R., § 10; Driver, § 152 i; Dav., *S.*, § 132 b; cf. § 64; Amos 5, 4 דרשׁוני וחיו; Prov. 3, 3 f. כתבם ... ומצא.

19. In vers. 19–24. 34–37 E, the detention of Simeon is a necessary feature in the narrative, but in 42, 38–43, 10, and 44, 18–34 J, there is no allusion made to him at all; cf. Driver, *Introd.*, p. 17.

אחיכם אחד. Cf. ver. 33 אחיכם האחד. On the absence of the art. here, see Ges., § 126. 5. Rem. 1 b, and § 134. 1. Rem.; M. R., § 76. Rem. c; Ewald, § 290 f.; Dav., *S.*, § 32. R. 2; so in 43, 14 אחיכם אחר.

שׁבר רעבון בתיכם. Cf. Is. 30, 23 מטר זרעך.

21 ff. give 'the details of the compendious ויעשׂו כן ver. 20.' Dr., § 75 *β*.

23. **שׁמע**. Cf. on 13, 7.

כי המליץ, i.e. the interpreter that was usually present in such cases; hence the article.

בינתם. Cf. בינותינו in 26, 28.

25. This verse seems to be connected with ver. 35. Special provision having been given them for the journey, ver. 25, the brethren would naturally only have discovered the money in their sacks at the end of the journey, ver. 35.

On the other hand, ver. 27 f. agrees with 43, 19 f., where the discovery is made at the lodging-place. The former account is probably from E, the latter from J. Cf. Driver, *Introd.*, p. 17; Di., p. 421 f.

כספיהם here, and ver. 35, the plural is used, because the silver of more than one is intended, Ewald, § 176 c; Ges., § 124. 1. Rem. 1 a, explains the plural differently; cf. note on 6, 14. The dag. in the פּ is unusual, though it is found in the sing. and dual, the aspiration is generally preserved in the pl.; so רִשְׁפֵּי, טַרְפֵּי, צִמְדֵי, etc.; see Ges., § 93. Rem. 1 F; Stade, § 71. 2.

איש אל שקו, so ver. 35. Cf. the note on 9, 5.

ויעש. The sing. is harsh; after וימלאו a plural would be natural. The Pesh. and Vulg. read the pl., while the Sam. and Onq. have the sing.; the LXX have ἐγενήθη αὐτοῖς οὕτως. If ויעש (sing.) is read it must be rendered impersonally, '*one did*,' i.e. '*it was done;*' the implied subj. being הָעֹשֶׂה.

27. האחד, i.e. the one who, as it were, made a beginning, and opened his bag (the others naturally opening theirs afterwards), so = '*the first;*' cf. 2, 11. 4, 19.

אמתחתו. The word is only found in Gen., chaps. 42–44 in J. E uses the commoner word שַׂק, 42, 25. 35.

28. ויחרדו וגו״. A pregnant construction; see note on 14, 3, and cf. 43, 33 ויתמהו האנשים וגו״.

30. אדני הארץ. See on 39, 20.

כִּמְרַגְּלִים is Ben Asher's reading. Ben Naftali reads כַּמְרַגְּלִים (with the article), see Baer and Del., *Gen.*, p. 86 [where, in note 3, Judg. 21, 29 should be Judg. 21, 19].

35. ויהי הם מריקים וגו״. '*And it came to pass, as they*

were emptying their sacks, that they found' etc. A circumstantial clause; so 2 Kings 2, 11 ויהי המה הלכים . . . והנה; cf. note on 27, 30.

36. כלנה. See on 21, 29. כלנה occurs again, Prov. 31, 29.

37. תמית = '*thou mayest kill.*'

38. וקראהו . . . והורדתם. Cf. the note on 33, 13.

43.

2. כלו לאכל. כִּלָּה with ל frequently occurs in J, e.g. 18, 33. 24, 15. 19. 22. 45.

3. העד העד '*protested strongly.*' Cf. note on 2, 16 and add to references there M. R., § 37 a.

בלתי אחיכם. Cf. ver. 5, Ex. 22, 19 בלתי ליהוה לבדו (Del.), see Ewald, § 322 a; and cf. the note on 12, 8.

4. אם ישך משלח. Cf. the neg. in ver. 5 ואם אינך משלח, and the note on 24, 42; here a cohortative alone follows the participle with אם יש, in 24, 42 a perf. with waw conv.

6. למה, here pointed with two qameçs and no dag., and the tone on the last syllable, as the next word begins with a guttural; see Ges., § 102. 2 d.

7. '*The man asked particularly about us, and our kindred,* etc., ... *so we told him according to these words; how were we to know that he would say?'* etc. על פי, as in Ex. 34, 27. Lev. 27, 8, and often.

הידוע נדע. On the inf. abs. see above on ver. 3, and for this (potential) use of the imperf., cf. Driver, § 39 β;

Ewald, § 136 d; M. R., § 7. 2. Rem. c; Ges., § 107. 4 b. 2; Dav., *S.*, § 43 b; so ver. 25 כי שם יאכלו; 2 Sam. 3, 33 הכמות נבל ימות אבנר, etc.

9. אם לא הביאתיו . . . וחטאתי. Cf. 47, 6 ואם ידעת . . . ושמתם; 2 Sam. 15, 33 אם עברת . . . והית; and see Driver, § 138 i. (a); M. R., § 3. 1 c; Dav., *S.*, § 130 b; Ges., § 159. 3. A. d. וחטאתי לך. Cf. 1 Kings 1, 21 אני ובני שלמה חטאים.

10. '*For had we not tarried, surely now we had returned*' etc. כי עתה, as in 31, 42; cf. the note on that passage.

11. מזמרת הארץ is usually rendered, '*from the song of the land*,' i.e. of the products of the land of Canaan that are celebrated and praised in song; cf. Jer. 51, 41. But Kn. and Del. point out that such a highly poetical expression would be very strange in this passage, and further that זמר and its derivatives are only used of songs in divine service. Del. derives זמרה here from זמר (cf. מזמרה) in the sense '*to cut off*,' so זמרה would mean '*produce*' or '*portion*.' But, as Di. remarks, 'זמר is only used of cutting off what is useless, or in the way.' Di. renders '*fruits*.' LXX, καρποί. Better is the explanation of D. H. Müller, in *H. W. B.*[10], p. 983, '*choice products*,' from a root זמר of doubtful meaning; but cf. in Arabic ذِمَارٌ '*a thing to be protected, sacred, inviolate*,' Lane, p. 978; Sab. ד̄מר '*protect*,' Aram. ܕܡܰܪ '*to wonder at*,' and ܕܡܺܝܪܳܐ '*wonderful, admirable*,' so זְמִירֹת, *die Merkwürdigkeiten des Landes;* cf. C. P. Ges., *sub voce*, and on זמר III.

צרי, נכאת, לט, see on 37, 25.

דבש, here probably not the honey of bees, but a syrup prepared by boiling from the juice of the grape, Arab. *dibs*, which is at the present day brought to Egypt from the neighbourhood of Hebron.

בטנים. *'Pistachio nuts'* = *Pistacia terebinthus*, see C. P. Ges., *sub voce;* Löw, *Aram. Pflanzenn.*, No. 44, *Pistacia vera.*

ושקדים. *'And almonds,'* the fruit of the *Amygdalus communis.* Almonds are found in Egypt, but only very rarely.

12. **וכסף משנה**. משנה is here either an abverbial acc., or in apposition to כסף; cf. ver. 15 משנה כסף *'double in silver;'* Ex. 16, 22 לחם משנה; Deut. 15, 18 כי מִשְׁנֶה שְׂכַר שָׂכִיר; Jer. 17, 18 וּמִשְׁנֶה שִׁבָּרוֹן. See Ges., § 131. 2 d, and Rem. 5 a; also Driver, § 194; Dav., *S.*, § 38. R. 5; M. R., § 71. 4; Ewald, § 286 d.

14. **את אחיכם אחר**. See the note on 42, 19. LXX and Heb.-Sam. read האחד here.

ואני כאשר שָׁכֹלְתִּי שָׁכָלְתִּי. *'And I, if I am bereaved, I am bereaved;'* cf. Esther 4, 16 וכאשר אבדתי אבדתי; 2 Kings 7, 4 ואם ימיתנו ומתנו. In שָׁכָלְתִּי notice the ָ in pause for ֹ, and cf. 49, 3 עָז for עֹז; 49, 27 יִטְרָף for יִטְרֹף; see Ges., § 29. 4 c; Ewald, § 93. 3; Stade, § 459 c. 1 (who accounts for the use of the pausal form with ָ here, 'der Euphonie wegen,' for euphony).

16. **טְבֹחַ** is imperative for the usual form טְבַח, but only in this passage, possibly, as Böttcher suggests, on account of the following טֶבַח, to produce a change in the sound of the final syllable of the first word (טְבֹחַ).

18. **השב**, 'because how it came there was unknown to them and inconceivable,' Del.[4]

להתגלל, lit. *'to roll oneself upon any one;'* cf. Job 30, 14 תחת שאה התגלגלו. להתגלל is inf. cstr. Hithpo'al from גלל.

20. **בי** is a precative particle, always followed by אֲדֹנִי or אֲדֹנָי = *pray!* Some suppose that בִּי = בְּעִי from בָּעָה = *'to ask,'*

and so lit. '*a petition;*' cf. the precative particles בְּבָעוּ, and ܒܒܥܘ, in Aramaic, and for the contraction, בֵּל from בְּעֵל; also Wright, *Comp. Gram.*, p. 48. Nöld., however (Wright, l. c., p. 287), thinks this improbable. It is, perhaps, better to derive בִּי from a root בָּיִי, בִּי = '*to entreat*,' cf. Arab. بَى '*to come as a suppliant, entreat*:' so בי אדני would = '*a supplication of* (i.e. *to*) *my lord*.' Cf. C. P. Ges., *sub voce*.

23. שׁלום לכם. Cf. Judg. 6, 23. 1 Sam. 20, 21. 'שׁלום לכם in the O. T. is always a formula of encouragement or congratulation, later in Hebrew, as in Aramaic and Arabic, a formula of greeting,' Del.

25. כי שׁם יאכלו לחם. '*That they were to eat bread there*.' Imperf., as in ver. 7. 44, 8. 34. 47, 15. 48, 17; Dr., § 39 β and γ; Dav., *S.*, § 43 b; Ges., § 107. 3 b; M. R., § 7. 2 b.

26. ויביאֿו. א with mappiq, perhaps to mark that it is a consonant; cf. Lev. 23, 17 תביאֿו; Job 33, 21 ראֻו ('cum א dagessato teste Masora, vide Michlol, 63 b;' note in Baer and Del.'s ed. of *Job*, p. 52); Ezra 8, 18 ויביאֿו ('א dagessatum auctore Masora;' note in Baer and Del.'s ed. of *Daniel, Ezra, and Neh.*, p. 108). It appears (cf. Ginsburg, *Verhandl. des 5 intern. Orient. Congr.*, II. 1. 136 ff.) that the four examples of a mappiq in א *mobile* are only remains of a much wider system of pointing the א *mobile* with mappiq, which was once more consistently carried out in MSS. See further, Ewald, § 21 e; Ges., § 14. 1. R. 2; Stade, § 42 b; Strack, *Proleg. Critica*, p. 19.

27. השׁלום אביכם. שׁלום is here used as an adj.; cf. 1 Sam. 25, 6. 2 Sam. 20, 9.

28. ויקדו, impf. Qal of קדד; see Ges., § 67. 5 end; Dav.,

§ 42. 6. foot-note 2. קדד and השתחוה occur together again in 24, 26. 48.

29. יָחְנְךָ. So again Is. 30, 19 for יָחָנְךָ; cf. Ges., § 67. Rem. 2; Ewald, § 251. 2 d.

30. כי נכמרו רחמיו. Cf. 1 Kings 3, 26. Hos. 11, 8 (with נחמים for רחמים).

32. כי לא יוכלון. Cf. Num. 9, 6. Deut. 12, 17. 22, 19, of legal and moral incapability. Kn. remarks on this verse: 'The predilection of the Egyptians for their own people and land, and their exclusiveness towards strangers (Diod. i. 67; Strabo, xvii. 1. 6), is well known. The priests neither ate nor drank anything that came from a foreign land (Porph. iv. 7); the Egyptian would use no eating utensils belonging to a Greek (Her. ii. 41). In a similar way they conducted themselves towards the Hebrews, especially as they were a nomad people, "tenders of flocks and herds" (see 46, 34; and cf. also 39, 6).'

33. ויתמהו. Cf. on 42, 28.

34. וישא is impersonal, the implied subject being הַנֹּשֵׂא; cf. 42, 25; Deut. 22, 8 כי יפל הנפל; 2 Sam. 17, 9 ושמע השמע. The LXX and Syr. have the plural here.

חמש ידות. Knobel calls attention to the frequency of the number five in matters relating to Egypt, e. g. 41, 34. 45, 22. 47, 2. 24. Is. 19, 18. For יד in the sense of '*portion*,' cf. 47, 24. 2 Sam. 19, 44. 2 Kings 11, 7.

וישכרו 'to be understood according to Hagg. 1, 6,' Del.

44.

1. כסק איש. See Ges., § 139. 1; M. R., § 94 b.

3. הבקר אור והאנשים וגו״. '*The morning dawned,*

and the men were sent away.' The construction is the same as in 38, 25 הוא מוצאת והיא שלחה, so in the next verse, הם יצאו . . . ויוסף אמר. See note on 19, 23.

אור, intrans. perf. like בוש, טוב (all); see Ges., § 72. Rem. 1; Stade, § 385 f.

4. **לא הרחיקו**. '*Without having gone far;*' so Ex. 34, 28 לחם לא אכל ומים לא שתה '*without eating bread, or drinking water;*' Lev. 13, 23 לא פשׂתה '*without having spread.*' The perfect is here equivalent to our past part. act.; see Driver, § 162; Ges., § 156. 3 b; Dav., *S.*, § 41. R. 3; M. R., § 153. R. b.

5. The LXX (cf. the Pesh. and Vulg.) insert at the end of ver. 4, ἵνα τί ἐκλέψατέ μου τὸ κόνδυ τὸ ἀργυροῦν; perhaps an explanatory gloss.

'*Is not this that wherein my lord is wont to drink, and he* (emphatic)[1] *would surely practise divination therewith*' etc.? On בּוֹ, cf. Ges., § 119. 3 b. 4. and foot-note; and M. R., § 52. 1. Rem. a, who compares *πίνειν ἐν χρυσῷ*, *bibere in ossibus*, and *boire dans un verre*, with the use of the prep. here. שתה ב occurs again in Amos 6, 6 השתים במזרקי יין. Tuch takes the sentence slightly differently, supplying בידכם after הלא. But this seems unnecessary.

נחשׁ ינחשׁ בו. Cf. 30, 27. This species of divination with cups, called *κυλικομαντεία* or *ὑδρομαντεία*, was much practised in Egypt; cf. Jamblich., *Myst.*, 3. 14, and Varro in Augustine's *Civ. dei*, 7. 35, Kn. cited by Di., p. 427. Kn., l.c., says: 'Water was poured into a glass or some other vessel, or pieces of gold, silver, or precious stones were thrown into

[1] Joseph had probably been admitted to the priests' caste, and would consequently practise divination, cf. 41, 45.

the water, and the figures or rings that appeared, when this was done, were supposed to give information about the future, or what was obscure to the inquirer.' The LXX have here *αὐτὸς δὲ οἰωνισμῷ οἰωνίζεται ἐν αὐτῷ*. So the Pesh. and Vulg. Onq. has וְהוּא בְּדָקָא מְבַדֵּיק בֵּיהּ '*and he makes discoveries through it*,' sc. the cup. Saadiah, quoted by Wright (*Genesis*, p. 109), has وَهُوَ إِنَّمَا ٱمْتَحَنَكُمْ بِهِ '*and he only proved you by it*.' 'Wishing to screen Joseph from such practices.'

נִחֵשׁ = properly '*to whisper*,' viz. magic formulae or oracles.

7. למה ידבר. 'After למה, מדוע, איך, אי מזה, the imperfect, as more courteous and adapted to a tone of entreaty, is often preferred to the perfect,' Driver, § 39 γ; so ver. 34. Ex. 2, 13 למה תכה; 1 Sam. 21, 15 למה תביאו אתו; cf. the note on 16, 8, and contrast the perf. in 26, 9. 2 Sam. 1, 14.

חלילה . . . מעשׂות. Cf. on 18, 25.

9. אשׁר ימצא . . . ומת. The perf. with waw conv. to introduce the apodosis; contrast ver. 10, where the simple imperf. follows; cf. ver. 17 (where 'the subject is reinforced by the personal pronoun' הוא); Judg. 8, 7. 9; and see Driver, § 123 γ. Obs.; M. R., § 26; Ges., § 112. 5 a δ; Dav., *S.*, § 56.

12. בגדול החל ובקטן כלה, circ. clause; see on 21, 14. LXX, *ἀρξάμενος*; so 48, 14 שׂכל את ידיו. Render, '*Beginning with the eldest, and finishing with the youngest.*'

הגביע is a cup shaped like the bell or calix of a flower; cf. Ex. 25, 31, where the word is used of the cup of a flower used in the workmanship of the golden candlestick.

15. הלוא ידעתם וגו״. '*Did ye not know that a man like me would be certain to practise divination*,' and so at once

discover the thief? איש אשר כמני, i.e. one of the wise men of Egypt; cf. Is. 19, 11; Kn.

16. ומה = ובמה, as in Ps. 116, 12.

18. כמוך כפרעה, lit. '*like thee, like Pharaoh,*' i.e. '*for thou art as P.;*' cf. 18, 25. Is. 24, 2. Hos. 4, 9. Ps. 139, 12; and see M. R., § 56. 1. Rem. a; Ges., § 161. 2. Rem.; Dav., *S.*, § 151. R. 2.

21. ואשׂימה עיני עליו, i.e. take him under my protection; cf. Jer. 39, 12. 40, 4. Pss. 33, 18. 34, 16. LXX, καὶ ἐπιμελοῦμαι αὐτοῦ.

22. ועזב . . . ומת; and ver. 29 וקרהו . . . והורדתם. See the note on 33, 13; and cf. Ges., § 159. 2 e. וָמֵת; cf. the note on 3, 22.

31. והיה introduces the apodosis to ועתה כבאי in ver. 30; and ומת is apodosis to כראותו.

33. ישב . . . יעל. The jussive is here used in making a request, as often; cf. the note on 26, 28.

45.

1. לכל הנצבים עליו. '*Before all those that stood by him,*' lit. '*with regard to all those*' etc. ל as in 17, 20 לישמעאל; cf. the note on that passage.

בהתודע. '*When he made himself known.*' התודע, cf. Num. 12, 6 (all), is the inf. Hithpʿ. of ידע, a verb פ״י, really פ״ו; in the Nifʿ., Hifʿ., and Hofʿ. the waw reappears, נֹודַע = נֽוֹדַע, הוֹדִיעַ = הֽוֹדִיעַ, הוּדַע = הֽוּדַע; but in Hithpaʿel the י usually remains, as יצב, התיצב, יעץ, התיעץ, התילד (den.

from יָלַד), התיחש (den. from יַחַשׂ), etc. With התודע, cf. התודה and התוכחה, Wright, *Comp. Gram.*, p. 241; Ges., § 69. 2.

4. **אשר מכרתם אתי**. See Ges., § 138. 1. Rem. 1; M. R., § 156. Rem. c; Dav., *S.*, § 9 b.

5. **כי למחיה**. '*For for the preservation of life,*' i.e. for the preservation of your life and that of other people; cf. Ezra 9, 8. 9.

6. **זה שנתים**. On this use of זה, see note on 27, 36. Render, '*Now two years has the famine*' etc.

אשר אין חריש וגו׳. Render, '*When there shall be neither ploughing nor harvest.*' אשר after words of time without the prep. and suffix is virtually = '*when,*' so 6, 4. 40, 13; see Dav., *S.*, § 9 c, and cf. Ges., § 138. 1.

7. **וישלחני** is connected only in *thought*, and not *chronologically*, with ver. 6; so ותלד, 36, 14. 46, 18. 25. See Driver, § 76 a.

לשום לכם שארית. '*To give you a remnant*' etc., i.e. that your descendants may live and your family not be destroyed from off the earth; cf. 2 Sam. 14, 7. Jer. 44, 7. To take שארית as the residue of the corn which the earth has brought forth is unsuitable, as שארית is never used of things.

ולהחיות לכם לפליטה גדלה. Del. renders '*to prolong for you life* (להחיות = לתת מחיה, Ezra 9, 8 f.), *to a great* (numerous) *deliverance,*' i.e. that you may be preserved, and become a numerous body of people, the second ל being the dat. of the product. החיה everywhere else is construed with the acc., but, as Del. on Is. 53, 11 shews, verbs in Hif'. are sometimes construed with a dative. Others (Schumann, Wright) take לפ׳ ג׳ as in apposition to לכם, and render, '*to keep you alive, a great body of fugitives.*' LXX and Heb.-Sam. strike out the ל before לפליטה. On פליטה, cf. Lag., *B. N.*, p. 85; Barth, *N. B.*, p. 314, who denies that the form (as some assume) is a diminutive.

8. לאב לפרעה. Cf. 1 Macc. 11, 32. A title bestowed on the first minister in the kingdom; see Ges., *Thes.*, p. 7. Di., referring to Brugsch, *Gesch.*, 207, 248, 252, 592, says *ab en pirāo* was, in documents of the nineteenth dynasty, the official title of the first (domestic) minister, and that '*adon* of the whole land' occurs in a similar sense in a document of the eighteenth dynasty.

משל is either acc. after וישימני, or, possibly, the force of the prep. ל (before לאדון) extends to this word also; cf. Ges., § 119. 5; Dav., *S.*, § 101; M.R., § 59.

10. בארץ גשן, called in P ארץ רעמסס, 47, 11 (cf. Ex. 12, 37. Num. 33, 5); the LXX also, in 46, 28, render גשן by εἰς γῆν Ῥαμεσσῆ. גשן must, probably, be sought for on the eastern side of the Nile. From Ex. 2, 3 f. Num. 11, 5, the Israelites seem to have dwelt near the Nile, and there is no reason to suppose that they ever crossed that river, as neither when they enter, nor when they leave Egypt is any mention made of their crossing the Nile. The LXX render גשן here, and 46, 34 Γέσεμ Ἀραβίας. In the Grecian and Roman periods Arabia was one of the twenty-three νομοί into which the Delta land was at that time divided, the capital being Φακοῦσσα (Ptol., iv. 5. 23; cf. Strabo, xvii. 1. 26). At the time of the eighteen and nineteen dynasties, the number of νομοί appears to have been fifteen, and the later νομοί of Arabia and Bubastis were included in the large district of On (*Heliopolis*), which was bounded on the east by what was afterwards the νομός of Heroonpolis (*Pithom*). The district two or three hours east

of Bubastis was called by the Egyptians *Kesem* or *Kes*. It has been conjectured (Brugsch, Ebers, etc.) that *Kes*=*Pa Kes*, i. e. Phacusa, the capital of the νομός of Arabia, and the word has been brought into connection with גֹּשֶׁן, which possibly is a Hebraized form of *Kesem*. See Di., p. 431 f.; Naville, *Land of Goshen*, Lond. 1887, pp. 15 ff. and 26; but cf. Groff, *Journ. Asiat.*, xiv. 527. Naville has discovered that the religious capital of this district was *Sopt* (the present *Sopt el-Henneh*); and he identifies the land around *Sopt*, eastwards of the *Abu-l-Munagge* Canal, between Belbeis in the south, and Abbaseh in the east, with Kesem. גֹּשֶׁן of the O. T. may therefore be the district stretching eastwards from Bubastis (Zagazig) towards Tel-el-Kebir, and southwards beyond Belbeis. The Israelites, of course, in time may have spread out further eastwards. The '*land of Ramses*' (P) is practically equivalent to Goshen, but probably covered a wider area, including that part of the Delta, east of the Tanitic arm of the Nile, and corresponding to the present province of Sharkieh, one of the most fertile parts of Egypt; see Nav., l. c., p. 20.

11. וכלכלתי. The Pilpel of כול; see Ges., § 55. 4; Dav., § 26. 3. Rem. c; Stade, § 157 b. The pass. וְכָלְכְּלוּ occurs in 1 Kings 20, 27.

פן תורש. '*Lest thou be brought to poverty*,' Nif'. of ירשׁ=רושׁ; so most of the Vss. Another rendering, which is less natural, is '*lest thou be taken possession of*,' from ירשׁ *possidēre*, i. e. through poverty became the property of some one else; cf. 47, 19 f.

12. כי פי המדבר, lit. '*that my mouth is the one speaking*' etc., i. e. '*that it is I myself that speaketh.*' Cf. the note on 2, 11, and add 'on the participle as direct predicate with the

article becoming co-extensive with the subject,' Dav., *S.*, § 99. R. 3; and cf. 42, 6. Deut. 3, 21. 22. 1 Sam. 4, 16.

17. טענו '*load*,' a ἅπαξ λεγόμ.; cf. 44, 13 (J), where עמס occurs.

18. טוב וגו״. '*The best of the land of Egypt*,' i.e. its best products; cf. vers. 20. 23, also 24, 10. 2 Kings 8, 9, etc.; so LXX, Vulg., Tuch, Del., Di. Rashi and others take טוב as = '*the best portion*,' i.e. Goshen; but this is מיטב, 47, 6. 11.

19. ואתה צויתה וגו״ must mean, '*And thou* (Joseph) *art charged, do ye* (the brethren) *this*,' which is very harsh. Possibly the text is corrupt. The Pesh. inserts after צוית, אֱמֹר אֶל־אַחֶיךָ; while the LXX, σὺ δὲ ἔντειλαι, and the Vulg., '*praecipe etiam*' etc., read the text צַוֵּה אֹתָם.

20. Compare the note in 34, 21 for the *casus pendens*, כי טוב וגו״, taken up by the pronoun הוא.

22. חלפות שמלת, i.e. '*changes of raiment*,' costly robes, which would be worn on special occasions, cf. 27, 15; see Judg. 14, 12 f. 19. 2 Kings 5, 5. 22 f. The brothers received a complete outfit, while Benjamin has five times as much, and three hundred shekels besides.

23. כזאת '*as follows*.' Usually pointed כָּזֹאת, and only here with no pretonic ָ.

מזון occurs only once again in the O.T., 2 Chron. 11, 23. The word is frequent in Aramaic.

24. אל תרגזו, scarcely '*do not fear*,' for such a warning would be superfluous in the case of persons who had already made the journey more than once, but rather '*do not quarrel*,' i.e. do not dispute about your conduct to me; cf. 42, 22, also Prov. 29, 9. Is. 28, 21.

26. וכי = '*and that,*' introducing the *oratio obliqua*.

ויפג לבו. '*And his heart grew cold.*'

27. ויַרא . . . ותחי רוח יעקב, lit. '*and he saw . . . and the spirit of J. revived;*' almost = '*when he saw . . .*' etc. (46, 29. 1 Sam. 10, 14. 17, 51^{b}); cf. Driver, p. 187; Ges., § 111. 1. R. 3. ותחי רוח; cf. Pss. 22, 27 יחי לבבכם לעד; 69, 33 ויחי לבבכם.

28. רב. '*It is enough;*' so Num. 16, 3. 7. 2 Sam. 24, 16.

46.

3. מרדה. רְדָה for רֶדֶת, like דֵּעָה for דַּעַת, Ex. 2, 4; לֵדָה for לֶדֶת, Is. 37, 3; see Ges., § 69. Rem. 1; Stade, § 619 h.

4. ואנכי אעלך גם עלה. On the inf. Qal and imperf. Hif'., see the note on 37, 33. The emphatic inf. abs. usually *precedes* the finite verb; see Ges., § 113. 3 a and b; Dav., *S.*, § 86 c; M.R., § 37 a; Ewald, § 312 b, who remarks that Qal after Hif'. is very rare; cf. Is. 31, 5. The inf. abs. is here further emphasized by גם, as in 31, 15 ויאכל גם אכול.

6. ומקניהם, sing. not plural; see the note on 41, 21.

8–27. A list of the family of Jacob who went down into Egypt with him. The names in this list are found again, with several variations, in Num. 26. 1 Chron. 2–8 (cf. also Ex. 6, 14–16), the variations being most numerous in the case of the sons of Benjamin.

Jacob's sons are classified according to his wives, the list falling under four heads: Leah, Zilpah, Rachel, Bilhah. Under the first head, Leah, come Reuben, with four sons; Simeon, with six; Levi, with three; Judah, with five; Perez and Zerah being regarded as his sons, though they really were his grandsons; Perez has two sons, and as Er and Onan died in

Canaan, Judah's sons and grandsons amount to five; Issachar has four sons; Zebulun, three; Leah's daughter Dinah is also mentioned: thus Leah's children and grandchildren amount to 26; and these 26 + Reuben, Simeon, Levi, Judah, Issachar, and Zebulun = 32, and with Jacob himself, 33. Under the second head, Zilpah, come Gad, with seven sons; Asher, with four sons, a daughter (Seraḥ), and two grandsons (7): thus 7 + 7 + 2 (Gad and Asher) = 16. Under the third head, Rachel, come Joseph and Benjamin; Joseph has two sons, Ephraim and Manasseh; and Benjamin, ten: thus 2 + 2 + 10 = 14. Under the fourth head, Bilhah, come Dan, with one son; and Naphtali, with four sons: in all, 1 + 4 + 2 (Dan and Naphtali) = 7. Thus all the family of Jacob including himself, was (33 + 16 + 14 + 7) 70. The LXX here (ver. 27), cf. Acts 7, 14, make the total number 75, counting (ver. 20) three grandchildren and two great-grandchildren among Joseph's descendants, from 50, 23. Num. 26, 28 ff. 1 Chron. 7, 14 f. The number 70 is mentioned again in Ex. 1, 5. Deut. 10, 22 (LXX in Ex. 75, but in Deut. 70). On the variations in the lists given in this chapter, Num., l.c., and 1 Chron., l.c., cf. the larger commentaries, i.e. Del.[5], p. 492 f.; Di., p. 437 f.; also on the difficulty that arises in the case of Perez, who, being born after the sale of Joseph into Egypt, and before Jacob came to Egypt, had, according to our list, two sons. Thus, as the time between Joseph's sale into Egypt and the coming of Jacob is only twenty-two years, the birth of Perez and his sons must have occurred within twenty-two years, which, of course, is not impossible, but not very probable. Another difficulty is also discussed by Di. and Del., viz. that Benjamin, the youth (43, 8. 44, 20, J), is represented here (ver. 21 P) as the father of ten sons.

15. ואת דינה. If the את is not corrupt, we must render, '*and also Dinah*' (governed by ילדה).

20. אשׁר refers to the object that is implied in ויולד ליוסף, viz. בנים.

27. הבׄאה. See the note on 18, 21.

28. להורת וגו׳. '*To shew the way before him into Goshen.*' This can hardly mean that Judah should act as guide from Palestine to Egypt, but rather that he should in Egypt either acquire the necessary information about the way to Goshen, or make all preparations to facilitate Jacob's entry into that district with his flocks and herds. As we should expect to find Joseph doing this it seems simpler to make Joseph subject to להורת = '*that he* (Joseph) *should give him* (Judah) *instructions before his* (Jacob's) *arrival,*' so Ges., Kn., Di. Del.[5] regards Judah as the subj. to להורת, and explains that he was sent on before the others, to announce the impending arrival of Jacob. The Sam. Ver., LXX, Pesh. apparently read להורת, as inf. Nif'. = לְהֵרָאוֹת (which is found in the Heb.-Sam.), or had this word in their text, which reading was accepted by Di.[5], who considered it was confirmed by וירא אליו in ver. 29, and rendered, '*That he* (*Joseph*) *should appear before him* (i.e. *come to meet him*) *to Goshen.*'

לפניו, i.e. '*before his* (*Jacob's*) *arrival.*'

29. ויעל, i.e. from the Nile land to Goshen, which lay on higher ground, Di.

עוד = '*again and again;*' cf. Ruth 1, 14.

30. הפעם, as in 2, 23. 18, 32. 29, 34.

31. אעלה, possibly used with reference to the ideal, or real high position of Pharaoh's royal residence, Di.; cf. Ges., *Thes.*, 1022.

33. מעשיכם, singular; cf. on 41, 21.
34. כל רעה. Cf. on 4, 2. The Sam. has the pl. רעי.

47.

2. ומקצה אחיו. '*Out of the whole number of his brethren;*' so 1 Kings 12, 31 מקצות העם (not as A.V., '*of the lowest of the people*'); Ez. 33, 2 איש אחד מקציהם; 19, 4 is different, cf. the note on that passage.

3. רעה צאן. On the predicate in the sing., see M. R., § 133. Dav., *S.*, §§ 17, 116. R. 3, takes רעה as collective. Di., however, considers that רעה is miswritten for רעי, comparing 46, 32; Ges., § 145. 7 b; Ewald, § 16 b. The Sam. and several codices (Wright) read the plural.

5 and 6. In the LXX text the arrangement of these two verses is different; 5^{a} is followed by 6^{b}, with the insertion ἦλθον δὲ εἰς Αἴγυπτον πρὸς Ἰωσὴφ Ἰακὼβ καὶ οἱ υἱοὶ αὐτοῦ· καὶ ἤκουσεν Φαραὼ βασιλεὺς Αἰγύπτου, καὶ εἶπεν Φαραὼ πρὸς Ἰωσὴφ λέγων, then 5^{b} and 6^{a} follow. Di., p. 441, prefers LXX to Mass. text; cf. Driver, *Introd.*, p. 10.

6. ארץ מצרים לפניך הוא. *Casus pendens;* see on 34, 21.

ואם ידעת ויש בם אנשי חיל. '*And if thou knowest that there are capable men among them,*' lit. '*and if thou knowest; and there are*' etc. On this union of the subordinate clause by waw, see note on 30, 27, and cf. Job 23, 3 ('*knew so that I might find him*').

אנשי חיל. '*Able* or *worthy men;*' cf. Ex. 18, 21. 25, and 1 Kings 1, 52 (בן חיל).

ושמתם, the perf. with waw conv. used in making a suggestion; see on 24, 14.

שׂרי מקנה. Cf. 1 Sam. 21, 8, where Doeg the Edomite is called אביר הרעים אשר לשאול.

7. ויעמדהו. Cf. העמיד in P with הציג in ver. 2 in J.

ויברך, as in 2 Kings 4, 29, used of greeting any one; cf. 2 Sam. 16, 16.

11. רעמסס. Cf. on 45, 10. רעמסס (only here and LXX, 46, 28) is the name of the district, so called from the town רעמסס mentioned in Ex. 1, 11 (built by the children of Israel). 12, 37. Num. 33, 3. 5 (the starting-point of the Exodus). The position of the town is uncertain, possibly it was situated near Phacusa, not far from the modern Tel-el-Kebir. Cf. Naville, *Goshen*, p. 20; *Exodus*, p. 7.

12. ויכלכל . . . את אביו . . . לחם. On כלכל with a double acc., see Ewald, § 283 b, and note on 26, 15.

לפי הטף, lit. '*according to the little children*,' i.e. '*according to their number and wants*,' 'little children being mentioned because they would require much food, and also because people would be less willing to see them in want,' Del. לפי as in Lev. 25, 16. 27, 16.

13. ותלה, ἅπαξ λεγόμ. Imperf. apoc. Qal of להה for לאה; on the form of the imperf. apoc., see Ges., § 75. Rem. 3 b.

14. הנמצא. Cf. הנמצאת, 19, 15.

15. אפס occurs only in this and the next verse in the Pent.; it is also found in Is. 16, 4. 29, 20. Ps. 77, 9 (all).

16. After לכם insert לֶחֶם, with LXX, Sam., Vulg., as ואתנה requires an obj.

17. וינהלם. '*And he sustained them.*' נִהֵל is only used in this passage in the sense, '*sustain*,' '*nourish*;' cf. Ps. 23, 2, LXX (ἐκτρέφειν). Elsewhere it means '*to lead*' or '*guide*;' so Is. 40, 11. Ps. 23, 2, and Cheyne, crit. note.

18. לא נכחד מאדני וגו״. '*We will not hide it from my lord, that if the money is spent, and the cattle we own be my lord's, there is nothing left*' etc.; כי אם being taken separately, according to the accentuation. Del. prefers to render, '*We cannot conceal it from my lord, but* (*must say*), *the money and the cattle we own are all my lord's, there is left*' etc., taking כי אם together and comparing 2 Sam. 15, 21. 1 Kings 20, 6. 2 Kings 5, 20 (where כי אם is preceded by a protestation), which are not quite parallel to this passage. Others (Kn., Ges.) render כי אם '*but, since,*' or '*but, because,*' which renderings assign to אם a meaning it can hardly bear. Di., following Kn., renders the words from כי אם down to אדני slightly differently, '*that if our money, and the cattle we own, are entirely at an end,* (*and come*) *to my lord,*' comparing for the pregnant construction 14, 15. 42, 28. 43, 33, a rendering that seems somewhat harsh and unnatural. אדני is used here, as in Num. 32, 25. 27. 36, 2, where more than one person is speaking. Del. compares the French '*Monsieur*.'

גויתנו = '*our bodies,*' i.e. '*ourselves,*' גויה being used of living beings, as in Ez. 1, 11. 23. Dan. 10, 6. Neh. 9, 37; elsewhere it is only used of a corpse.

19. Notice that נמות is zeugmatically connected with אדמתנו, cf. 4, 20 ישב אהל ומקנה.

גם אנחנו גם אדמתנו. גם . . . גם = '*both . . . and,*' as in vers. 3 and 19. 24, 25. 44. 43, 8. 44, 16. 46, 34; Dav., *S.*, § 136; Ges., § 154. foot-note c; M. R., § 148. R. b.

תשם, impf. Qal (intrans.) from שָׁמֵם; cf. Ges., § 67. Rem. 3; Stade, § 509. 2; see on 16, 4 (וַתֵּקַל). With this use of שָׁמֵם, cf. Ez. 12, 19 למען תשם ארצה; 19, 7 ותשם ארץ ומלאה.

21. ואת העם העביר אתו וגו״, usually rendered, '*and the people, he removed them into the towns;*' but such a removal

of all the people into the towns would be scarcely possible, and it is very doubtful whether העביר can mean this. It is better, if the text is left unchanged, to render, '*and the people he caused to pass over to the towns*,' ואת העם being a *casus pendens;* cf. the notes on 13, 15. 21, 13. The meaning being, the people were brought to the towns so that they might be fed from the stores of grain that were there; cf. 41, 48. Tuch interprets the Mass. text as meaning, '*he moved the people from one city into another throughout the whole land;*' possibly to remove them from the districts in which the land they formerly owned lay. But this would require מעיר לעיר; cf. 2 Chron. 30, 10. The LXX, καὶ τὸν λαὸν κατεδουλώσατο αὐτῷ εἰς παῖδας, so the Sam. ࠅࠀࠕ . ࠄࠏࠌ . ࠄࠏࠁࠉࠃ . ࠀࠕࠅ . ࠋࠏࠁࠃࠉࠌ, and Vulg. '*Subjecitque eam* (*omnem terram*) *Pharaoni, et cunctos populos ejus*,' which point to a reading ואת העם העביד אתו לעבדים (cf. Jer. 17, 4) = '*the people he made serve him* (*the king*) *as slaves*.' Di. adopts this reading, following Knobel; so Del.[5] Onq. has וְיָת עַמָּא אַעֲבַר יָתֵיהּ מִקְּרֵי לִקְרֵי, and the Pesh. ܘܠܥܡܐ ܐܥܒܪ ܐܢܘܢ ܡܢ ܩܪܝܐ ܠܩܪܝܐ, both = '*and the people, he removed them from town to town*,' a meaning which (see above) the Heb. text cannot bear. Di. remarks, in favour of the rendering of the text adopted by him, that the purchase of the people, corresponding to the purchase of the land, is demanded by the emphatic position of ואת העם; cf. vers. 19 and 23.

22. כי חק. חק as in Ez. 16, 27. Prov. 30, 8. 31, 15.

ואכלו. The perf. with waw conv. is frequentative; see Driver, § 120; Ges., § 112. 3 a. ζ; Dav., *S.*, § 54. R. 1.

23. הא = הנה occurs only once again in Heb., Ez. 16, 43. It corresponds with the Arab. هَا, Syr. ܗܐ.

וזרעתם. Cf. on 24, 14.

24. וארבע הידת יהיה לכם. '*And four portions ye shall have.*' וארבע הידת must be regarded as object after יהיה לכם, which is nearly equivalent to '*ye have.*' Cf. Ex. 12, 49 תורה אחת יהיה לאזרח; Num. 9, 14 חקה אחת יהיה לכם; see Ewald, § 295 d; Ges., § 145. 7. Rem. 3, and cf. Dav., *S.*, § 116.

הידת. See 43, 34.

ולאכל לטפכם is omitted in LXX. These words are possibly a gloss, or they may, as Ols. suggests, originally have come after ולאכלכם.

26. לפרעה לחמש. '*For P. with regard to the fifth part.*' It would be less harsh if the text were read לפרעה חמש, with the Pesh., as an explanation of אחת. The LXX have τῷ Φαραῷ ἀποπεμπτοῦν, as though the text were לפ" לְחַמֵּשׁ.

27. ויאחזו. See on 34, 10.

29. שים נא ידך תחת ירכי. See the note on 24, 2.

31. וישתחו ישראל על ראש המטה. '*And Israel bowed down towards the head of the bed;*' so Di., Del. The aged patriarch sat upright while speaking with Joseph, and as he was too weak to rise, turned and inclined himself towards the upper end of the bed, and offered up thanks to God that his request was granted; cf. the Vulg., '*adoravit Israel Deum, conversus ad lectuli caput,*' and 1 Kings 1, 47. Tuch renders, '*leant back upon the head of the bed.*' The LXX, Pesh., and Itala read הַמִּטָּה as הַמַּטֶּה, the LXX being quoted thus in Heb. 11, 21 (ἐπὶ τὸ ἄκρον τῆς ῥάβδου αὐτοῦ), Jacob being represented as bowing over the top of his staff, or, as others suppose, over the staff of Joseph (which he

carried as a token of his authority) as a mark of homage to him; cf. 37, 7. But this reading is not so natural as הַמִּטָּה, and a suffix would be required (מַטֵּהוּ), which the Vss. express.

48.

1. ויאמר ליוסף. '*And one told Joseph*' (sc. הָאֹמֵר). The third pers. sing. being here used like the impersonal, '*man sagte*,' '*on dit*,' Ewald, § 294 b; cf. note on 11, 9. In 22, 20 we find וַיֻּגַּד used; but here the active is employed by the narrator, although the pass. וַיֵּאָמֵר occurs in Josh. 2, 2; and would perhaps be more natural here. Cf. ver. 2 וַיַּגֵּד and again וַיֹּאמֶר. See also Ges., § 144. 3. foot-note 3, where the editor suggests that the original reading may have been וַיֹּאמְרוּ, the final *ū* not being indicated by ו, as in the Moabite stone, and Siloam inscription, cf. Ges., § 7. 2 a. Rem. and foot-note 2.

4. הנני מפרך והרביתך. The perf. with waw conv. after a word pointing to the future, see Driver, § 113. 1; M. R., § 24. 2 a; Ges., § 112. 3 c. ε; Dav., *S.*, § 100 e; and cf. 6, 17. 7, 4. 17, 19. Is. 7, 14.

מפרך. On the part. as *futurum instans*, see on 6, 17.

5. ועתה שני בניך . . . לי הם. On the *casus pendens*, see on 34, 21.

6. ומולדתך. '*And thy offspring;*' מולדת, as in Lev. 18, 9. 11. For construction cf. note on 41, 57.

על שם אחיהם וגו״. '*According to the name of their brethren shall they be called in their inheritance*,' i.e. their descendants shall dwell among the posterity of Ephraim and Manasseh, and be reckoned as belonging to them, and not as separate tribes.

7. מפדן. Everywhere else P calls Mesopotamia פדן ארם; cf. on 25, 20. Possibly the omission of ארם is due to a copyist's mistake. The Sam. has פדן ארם.

מתה עלי. *'Died, to my sorrow.'* For this use of על, cf. Eccl. 2, 17 כי רע עלי המעשׂה. See also 33, 13 and the note on that passage.

כברת ארץ. Cf. the note on 35, 16.

9. בזה *'here;'* so 38, 21.

קחם נא. Ewald, § 253 a, and Stade, § 631 e, compare קָחֶם here with בְּצַ֫עַם (Amos 9, 1), the suffix being attached to the word ending in a guttural, the tone being placed on the penult. קחם, however, here has no accent at all, as it is connected with נא by Maqqef, and so deprived of its accent; and the ֶ of ֶם is consequently shortened into ִם: and in Amos l. c. the tone on בְּצַ֫עַם is drawn back on to the penult. to avoid two tone-syllables coming together, the next word being בְּרֹאשׁ.

ואברכֶם. For the pausal seghol, cf. 21, 9 מְצַחֵק and the note there; also the frequent לְעוֹלָם וָעֶד, Ges., § 58. 3. Rem. 1; König, *Lehrg.*, p. 232. In Num. 6, 27 we find אֲבָרְכֵם in pause, also in ordinary editions in this passage.

11. רְאֹה for רְאוֹת, like עֲשׂוֹ for עֲשׂוֹת in 31, 28 (see the note on that passage), and עֲשׂה for עֲשׂוֹת, 50, 20.

פִּלָּלְתִּי. According to Ben Asher in the *Dikduke Hat*ᵉ*amim*, ed. Baer and Strack, Leipzig, 1879, § 49, the ֵ in the first person perf. Pi'el is always preserved in pause, except in this word; הִלַּכְתִּי, Ps. 38, 7; יִחָלְתִּי, Ps. 119, 43, etc.; יִשָּׁרְתִּי, Ps. 119, 128.

12. לאפיו, as in Num. 22, 31. In 19, 1. 42, 6 we find אפים alone used after וישתחו and וישתחוו respectively.

14. שכל את ידיו. '*Crossing his hands;*' the construction is the same as in 44, 12; cf. the note on 21, 14. This rendering is the same as that of the LXX, Pesh., Vulg., and most moderns, and is suitable to the context; cf. ver. 13. Cf. the Arab. شَكَّلَ '*plexuit,*' '*ligavit.*' Onq. and Saadiah render, '*he made his hands wise,*' i.e. 'he placed them so intentionally,' which assigns a doubtful meaning to שִׂכֵּל (=הִשְׂכִּיל); moreover with this rendering בידיו would be more natural, as Di. points out. With this verse cf. Matt. 19, 13 f. Mark 10, 16, where Christ in blessing lays His hands on those whom He blessed.

15. מעודי עד היום הזה. This phrase is only found once again in the O.T., viz. Num. 22, 30 מעודך עד היום הזה.

16. ויקרא בהם שמי. Cf. 21, 12 and the note there. '*In them let my name be named,*' i.e. 'be made famous through their offspring.' Del.[4] renders, '*On them let my name be called.*' בהם = עליהם, i.e. 'let them be regarded as my children, and sharers of the promises made to me and mine.'

ידגו. דגה is only found in this passage in the O.T.

17. ישית. Notice the tense, '*was placing;*' Jacob had not *actually* placed his hands on the heads of Ephraim and Manasseh, but was in the act of placing them; cf. Driver, § 39 β, and note on 43, 25. The imperfects with waw conv. give details of Jacob's blessing which have been omitted, though the actual blessing is given in the preceding verses; cf. note on 27, 24.

19. מלא הגוים (cf. Is. 31, 4) = המון גוים in 17, 5.

22. ואני נתתי לך שכם אחד על אחיך. '*And I give thee one mountain slope above thy brethren.*' שכם = '*shoulder,*' then applied to the slope of a mountain, like כתף,

Num. 34, 11. Josh. 15, 8. 10. 18, 12. 13. Is. 11, 14; see Ges., *Thes.*, 1407. The word שְׁכֶם is chosen with an obvious allusion to the well-known town of Shechem (cf. on 12, 6) in the territory of Ephraim (Josh. 24, 1. 25. 32. Judg. 9, 1. 1 Kings 12, 1. 25). Cf. the LXX rendering σίκιμα ἐξαίρετον. This Shechem Jacob gives to Joseph, in preference to his other sons. Joseph would therefore take precedence of his brethren; as the possessor of a mountain tract, in addition to his other territory, he would, as it were, be a 'shoulder' above them. אַחַד is *status absolutus* with the vocalisation of the *status constructus*, the shorter pronunciation being sometimes chosen in the flow of speech; see note on 3, 22, and cf. Ewald, § 276 b; Ges., § 130. 6; and Is. 27, 12 לְאַחַד אֶחָד; Zech. 11, 7 לְאַחַד קָרָאתִי ... וּלְאַחַד קָרָאתִי. שכם is taken by Onq. and Pesh. in the sense '*portion*,' a translation that is too indefinite. Tuch and others consider that שכם אחד means that two portions of territory should be assigned to Ephraim and Manasseh (cf. ver. 5), as contrasted with the one portion that the other tribes were to receive. But שכם אחד can hardly mean '*one portion*,' as one portion of land would embrace more than one mountain slope, and שכם אחד cannot = a district in which Shechem was situated, Di., p. 452.

אשר לקחתי. Tuch, Kn., Keil, and Del. take לקחתי as prophetic perfect; but cf. Di., l. c., who points out that if a future capture of Shechem is referred to, there is no reason why this particular town should have been selected by Jacob, and that we would rather expect תִּקַּח or תִּקְחוּ. The account of the acquisition of Shechem in this chapter is probably from E. It varies from that given in chap. 34 P and J (Driver, *Introd.*, p. 15; Di., p. 452). In 33, 19 and Josh. 24, 32, both E, Jacob is reported to have *purchased* the plot of ground at Shechem.

בחרבי ובקשתי are curiously rendered in some Vss., cf. Onq. בִּצְלוֹתִי וּבְבָעוּתִי '*with my prayer and entreaty*' (Berliner's text follows the Mass. text, see the notes in his edition, part ii, p. 17). Another curious paraphrase is proposed by Hieron. (*Quaest.*, ed. Lagarde, p. 66), 'dabo tibi Sicimam, quam emi in fortitudine mea, hoc est in pecunia quam multo labore et sudore quaesivi.' In his translation, however, he follows the Heb. text.

49.

In this chapter is contained the so-called 'Blessing of Jacob,' a name which owes its origin to ver. 28^{b}, which however probably belongs, not to the 'Blessing,' but to the following narrative 28^{b}–33, which comes from P. This designation cannot be regarded as a suitable one, as in point of fact only two of the tribes are really blessed, viz. Judah and Joseph, the utterances of the patriarch in the case of Reuben, Simeon, and Levi being full of reproach, and a future predicted for them the reverse of prosperous. It would be better designated by the title Del. gives it, 'The prophetic sayings of Jacob concerning the Twelve.' The six sons of Leah are first mentioned, then Bilhah's eldest son, Zilpah's two sons (the eldest first), Bilhah's second son, and Rachel's two sons, Joseph the eldest first. The order in which they occur is partly that in which they were born, and partly that in which the territories represented by them geographically stand, starting from the south of Canaan and going northwards (Ewald, *Hist.*[3], ii. p. 435; Eng. trans., ii. p. 308). Thus the four elder sons come first, Reuben, Simeon, Levi, Judah; but then the order of birth is abandoned, and Leah's other two sons, Zebulun (Jacob's tenth son) and Issachar (Jacob's ninth son), are inserted, Zebulun being placed before Issachar, as the future that Jacob predicts for him is more prosperous and honourable than that of Issachar (Di.). Cf. Deut. 33, 18, where Zebulun and Issachar come together, but Zebulun first, as here. The four last sons are cited according to their geographical position; Benjamin, Joseph, Naphtali, Asher (from south to north), Joseph and Benjamin also being in the proper order of their birth. Dan is probably placed after Issachar, as being the first son of Jacob by his wives' handmaidens (in order of birth he follows Judah, but as the order of birth is abandoned to enumerate Leah's six sons, Dan, the fifth, is mentioned first, after the six sons of Leah). Gad would then be placed after Dan, and before Naphtali, who was born before him, so as not to disturb the geographical arrangement—Benjamin, Joseph, Naphtali, Asher—and possibly to keep Zilpah's two sons together. In Deut. 33, the 'Blessing of Moses,'—which has many points of contact with this chapter, both in the figures it employs and the language used,—the order is varied; viz. Reuben, Judah, Levi (whose blessing contrasts strangely with Jacob's words in ver. 5), Benjamin, Joseph (Ephraim and Manasseh are mentioned by name), Zebulun, Issachar, Gad, Dan, Naphtali, Asher, while Simeon in the text as we now have it is not mentioned at all.

The language of this chapter should be noticed. In its elevated tone, in vigour and force, and in the numerous figurative expressions employed, it surpasses the other poetical passages in Genesis (9, 25 ff. 14, 19 ff. 24, 60. 25, 23. 27, 27 ff. 39 f.). Many of the expressions employed are rare, and unusual in the later stages of the language, e.g. פַּחַז (*ἅπαξ λεγ.*) and הוֹתִיר, ver. 4; מכרה, ver. 5 (a *ἅπαξ λεγ.* of uncertain meaning); מחקק, ver. 10 (occurring again in the poetical fragment Num. 21, 18. Deut. 33, 21. Judg. 5, 14. Ps. 60, 9);

סות, ver. 11 (ἅπαξ λεγ.); חכלילי, ver. 12 (ἅπαξ λεγ.); מִשְׁפּתים, ver. 14 (only found once again, Judg. 5, 16); שְׁפִיפֹן, ver. 17 (ἅπαξ λεγ.); שְׁלוּחה (only used thus in this passage), and שֶׁפֶר (ἅπαξ λεγ.) ver. 21; פרת, ver. 22 (observe the archaic fem. ending), only in this passage for פֹּרָה; רבו, ver. 23 (רבב is perhaps found again in Ps. 18, 15 ברקים רב, see the note on ver. 23); ותשב . . . קשתו, ver. 24, etc.; also the archaic ending ִי (the old binding vowel) in אסרי לגפן, בני אתנו; the suffix הֹ for וֹ, in עִירֹה and סוּתֹה, and possibly in שִׁילֹה (cf. the note on this word); the poetical עֲלֵי for עַל; כבוד, poetical for נפש, with which it is here parallel, ver. 6; אמרי, ver. 21, poetical for דברי (but cf. note); the poetical זרעי ידיו, ver. 24, etc. Probably this chapter is the oldest portion of the book of Genesis, being incorporated into one of the original documents (possibly J), out of which the present book grew, from a still older source. On the special literature of this chapter, see Tuch, p. 479 f., and Di., p. 456.

1. יקרא אתכם. קרא = קרה, as in 42, 4; cf. the note on that passage.

באחרית הימים. '*In days to come*,' lit. '*in the end of days*.' אחרית is used here as in Num. 24, 14. Deut. 4, 30. Jer. 23, 20, etc., denoting the end of the period which the prophet sees, or which he has in view. The LXX have ἐπ' ἐσχάτων τῶν ἡμερῶν; cf. Heb. 1, 2 and 1 Pet. 1, 20 (ἐπ' ἐσχάτων τῶν χρόνων); Pesh. ܒܚܪܬܐ ܕܝܘܡܬܐ; Onq. בְּסוֹף יוֹמַיָא; Vulg. '*in diebus novissimis*.' The formula is also common in prophecy in a somewhat different sense, e.g. Hos. 3, 5. Mic. 4, 1. Ez. 38, 16.

2. '*Gather yourselves and hear, sons of Jacob;*
And hearken unto Israel your father.

3. *Reuben—my firstborn art thou, my strength and the firstfruits of my vigour.*

Excelling in dignity and excelling in might.
Boiling over like water, excel not thou;
For thou didst go up to thy father's bed:
There thou didst pollute it; he went up to my couch!'

Reuben, Jacob's firstborn, excels his brethren in dignity and power, but loses his privileges through his sin. In the post-Mosaic time the tribe of Reuben sinks into obscurity. With the exception of one successful campaign against the Hagarenes (1 Chron. 5, 8–10), nothing more is known of the doings of this tribe.

בכרי אתה might be rendered, '*my firstborn, thòu*,' regarding אתה as a vocative; the rendering given above is, however, better.

כחי = '*my manly strength*.' אוני, און, as in Deut. 21, 17. Pss. 78, 51. 105, 36, of genital power. LXX, σὺ ἰσχύς μου καὶ ἀρχὴ τέκνων μου; Vulg. '*et principium doloris mei*' (as though און were אָוֶן), following (as often) Aq. κεφάλαιον λύπης μου, and Symm. ἀρχὴ ὀδύνης μου.

יתר שאת ויתר עז, lit. '*excellence of dignity and excellence of power*,' יתר both times being abstract for concrete. שאת as in Hab. 1, 7. Ps. 62, 5. Job 13, 11. 31, 23. עָז not an adj. but pausal form of עֹז, see on 43, 14; so יִטְרָף in ver. 27 in pause for יִטְרֹף. The LXX render σκληρὸς φέρεσθαι, καὶ σκληρὸς αὐθάδης, while Onq. renders as follows: לָךְ הֲוָה חָזֵי לְמִיסַב תְּלָתָה חוּלָקִין בְּכוֹרוּתָא כְּהוּנְתָא וּמַלְכוּתָא '*for thee it was provided to receive three portions, the right of firstborn, priesthood, and the kingdom*,' in accordance with the Jewish tradition, which assigned these three privileges to Reuben as the firstborn.

4. פחז כמים, lit. '*a bubbling over like water*.' The root פחז in Arabic (فخز I, V) = '*to boast;*' in Aramaic the subs.

ܦܣܠܘܬܐ occurs in the Pesh. Vers., 2 Cor. 12, 21. Eph. 4, 19 = ἀσέλγεια. The root properly = '*to exceed bounds, be inordinate;*' LXX well, ἐξύβρισας. Only the comparison gives the idea of *boiling* or *bubbling*. פַּחַז, like יֶתֶר in the preceding verse, is abstract for concrete; cf. Ewald, § 296 b; Driver, § 189. Obs. The words may be taken as vocative, or (with Del.) as a descriptive apposition to the subject רְאוּבֵן. The Heb.-Sam. has פָּחַזְתָּ, and the other Vss. render as though פָּחַזְתָּ stood instead of פַּחַז; but it is not necessary to suppose that the text they translated from actually had the second pers. of the verb, their renderings are probably chosen to express פַּחַז with greater clearness. פֹּחֲזִים, part. of פָּחַז, occurs twice in the O. T., Judg. 9, 4. Zeph. 3, 4; in the sense of '*wanton*' in Judg. l.c., and '*boasting*' in Zeph. l.c., of false prophets. Other renderings are suggested in Ges., § 147. 3, '*a bubbling up like water wast thou,*' אַתָּה being understood as subject; or as an exclamation, '*a bubbling up like water!*' the predicate being suppressed.

אל תותר, i.e. with reference to the יתר mentioned in ver. 3. Render, '*Do not thou excel*' (the jussive, with a negative, expressing a desire or wish, Driver, § 50 γ), i.e. 'mayest thou lose the privileges that belong to thee as firstborn,' viz. those mentioned in ver. 3. LXX, μὴ ἐκζέσῃς (cf. Lagarde's *Genesis Graece*, p. 202, notes), which Geiger, *Urschrift*, p. 373, regards, not as indicating a different reading, but as a paraphrase on the part of the LXX, who refer תותר back to פחז, the paraphrase being due to a desire to mitigate the effects of Reuben's sin. The Pesh. has ܠܐ ܬܦܘܫ, reading the text as תִּוָּתֵר.

כי עלית משכבי אביך. עלה is here construed with the acc., as in Num. 13, 17 ועליתם את ההר. מִשְׁכְּבֵי, Di.

explains the plural as meaning a double bed; Del. explains it by Ges., § 124. 1 a (nouns denoting extension of *space* or *time*, used in the plural); Dav., *S.*, § 17. R. 2, as a poetical usage. With the plural here, יְצוּעֵי אָבִיו of 1 Chron. 5, 1 may be compared, Reuben also being referred to.

יצועי עלה. These words are addressed, in astonishment at Reuben's sin, by Jacob to his other sons; therefore the third pers.; cf. Is. 42, 20. 51, 18. 52, 14. The LXX, Pesh., Onq. render as though the text had עָלִיתָ, possibly an attempt to amend the Heb. text, which is not necessary, while the Vulg. leaves עלה untranslated, and makes יצועי the obj. of חללת. Geiger, *Urschrift*, p. 374, supposes that these words were not the real text, but that יְצוּעֵי בִלְהָה was written originally, which afterwards was changed into יצועי עלה, as being too clear. He objects to our present text because everywhere else יצוע is used in the plural, and only in this passage in the singular. Di. describes his emendation, which is very needless, as 'the purest prose.' Ewald, *History*[3], i. p. 535, Eng. trans., i. p. 373, foot-note, renders, '*my couch of highness*,' '*my lofty couch*,' pointing עָלָה as עָלָה = '*a step*,' a rendering that can scarcely be justified. In 1 Chron. l. c. the right of firstborn, which Reuben lost, is given to Joseph, while Judah received his (Reuben's) privilege of royalty. In Deut. 33, 6 Reuben's blessing is as follows: יחי ראובן ואל ימת ויהי מתיו מספר '*Let R. live and not die, so that his men become few.*'

5–7. '*Simeon and Levi, brethren;*
Weapons of violence are their shepherds' staves.
Into their council, let not my soul come;
With their assembly, let not my honour be united;
For in their anger they slew men,
And in their wantonness houghed oxen.

Cursed be their anger, for it was fierce;
And their wrath, for it was cruel:
I will divide them in Jacob,
And scatter them in Israel.'

5. אחים, Kn. and Del. take אחים as predicate, better as in apposition to שִׁמְעוֹן וּלֵוִי. Simeon and Levi are brothers, not only as sons of the same parents, but as being alike in their dispositions.

מכרתידהם. The meaning of this word, which only occurs in this passage, is very uncertain. (1) It is commonly rendered '*sword*,' a meaning which was first hinted at by the Jews, who compared מכרה fancifully with the Greek *μάχαιρα*; see Bereshith Rabba, c. 99 מכרותיהם. אמר רבי יוחנן לשון יוני הוא מכירין פי'' קורין לחרבות מכירין ויש אומרים מכרותיהן מגורותיהם כמה דאת אמר מְכוּרוֹתַיִךְ ומולדותיך׃ '*Rabbi Joḥanan says the word* מכרות *is a Greek word, as they* (*the Greeks*) *call swords* מכירין (*μάχαιραι*). *Others think that* מכרות = מגורות, *comparing Ez.* 16, 3.' Hieron. and Rashi also render '*sword*,' cf. Ges., *Thes.*, p. 672. But, as Del. points out, מְכֵרָה is no more *μάχαιρα*, than the Assyr. *pilakku* the Gk. *πέλεκυς*. He derives it (after the analogy of מְקֵרָה, מְגֵרָה, מְאֵרָה) from כרר = '*to dig*' and '*to be round;*' so a weapon which makes a round gaping wound. But it is very doubtful whether כרר can combine the two meanings that Del. assigns to it. Del., *Proleg.*, p. 121 f., thinks it comes from כור = Assyr. *kâru*, a synonym of כרת, Assyr. *karâtu* = '*to cut*,' so '*a sword*.' (2) Tuch explains the word as meaning '*plot*' or '*contrivance*,' lit. '*windings*,' from כרר = '*to wind*,' but, as Del. points out, כרר does not mean '*to wind*,' but '*to be round;*' while L. de Dieu and Maurer also render '*plots*,' but get this meaning from מכר = măkără in Ethiopic and مَكَرَ in

Arabic, '*to plan*,' '*contrive*.' We must then, however, point the form מִכְרֹתֵיהֶם, not מְכֵרֹתֵיהֶם; see Ewald, § 260 a. (3) Kn., Böttcher, § 791 (though he adheres to the Mass. pointing), and others render, '*marriage contracts*,' as though מכר = the Aramaic ܡܟܰܪ '*desponsavit*;' מכר in Heb., however, means '*to sell*,' and if מכר can = ܡܟܰܪ (which in Heb. would usually be rendered by מהר), the reference to Dinah's brethren would be hardly suitable—though the next verse certainly refers to the incident narrated in chap. 34—and 'marriage contracts' could scarcely be called כלים. Knobel alters the reading into מִכְרֹתֵיהֶם. (4) Di. derives the word from כרר '*to be round*,' and says it means a '*round curved instrument*,' perhaps a '*curved knife*' or '*sickle*.' Ewald, *Hist.*[3], ii. p. 493, Eng. trans., ii. p. 349, and Wellhausen, *History of Israel*, Eng. trans., p. 144, render (also from כרר), '*shepherds' staves*,' or as we should say in English, '*shepherds' crooks*.' The LXX have *συνετέλεσαν ἀδικίαν ἐξ αἱρέσεως αὐτῶν*, as though the text were כִּלּוּ חָמָס מְכֵרוֹתֵיהֶם '*they ended the violence of their nature*;' so Geiger translates, *Urschrift*, p. 374 f., regarding this translation of the LXX as intended to tone down the violence of Simeon and Levi's conduct. The Pesh. has ܡܳܐܢܰܝ̈ ܚܛܽܘܦܝܳܐ ܡܶܢ ܩܢܽܘܡܗܽܘܢ '*instruments of violence from their nature*;' possibly they connected מְכֵרָה with מְכוּרָה '*birth*,' '*descent*.' Onq. renders גֻּבְרִין גִּבָּרִין בְּאֲרַע תּוֹתָבוּתְהוֹן עֲבָדוּ גְּבוּרָא '*mighty men, in the land they dwelt in they did a mighty deed*,' as though מְגוּרֵיהֶם = מְכֵרֹתֵיהֶם; so Kimchi and the A. V., who supply '*in*,' which is wanting in the Heb. text. Onq.'s rendering seems an endeavour to transform Simeon and Levi's cruel deed into a noble one. The Vulg. gives '*vasa iniquitatis bellantia*.'

6. The first portion of this verse is rendered as follows in the A.V. and R.V.: '*O my soul, come not thou into their*

secret (R. V. "*council*," marg. "*secret*"); *unto their assembly, mine honour* (R. V. "*my glory*,"), *be not thou united*,' taking תבא and תחד as second pers. sing. masc. (though נפש is more commonly fem.), and נפשי and כבדי as vocatives. The rendering given above is that adopted by Di. and Del.

תֵּחַד is imperf. Qal of יָחַד. The Heb.-Sam. reads אל יחר.

כבדי, '*my honour*' or '*glory*,' is rhythmically interchanged with נפש here. In Ps. 7, 6 כבדי is parallel to נַפְשִׁי, and in Pss. 16, 9. 108, 2 to לבי; cf. also Pss. 30, 13. 57, 9, where it is used in the sense of נפש. כבוד is here fem. by Ewald, § 174 b (names of invisible active powers are fem.; so נפש is usually fem., and כבדי being parallel to it, is also regarded as fem.). The LXX render אל תחד כבדי with *μὴ ἐρίσαι τὰ ἥπατά μου*, as though the text were אַל־יִחַר כְּבֵדִי; see Geiger, *Urschrift*, p. 319, who regards the rendering of the LXX as intentional, to avoid the possibility of confounding the human כבד (Doxa) with the divine, the word כבד, when equivalent to נפש, having 'both the idea of divine majesty and the idea of the higher human nature.' Di. points out that in Assyr. *kabidtu* (כָּבֵד) is rhythmically interchanged with *napištu* (נפש), he thinks, therefore, that כְּבֵדִי, '*my liver*,' i.e. '*my heart* or *soul*,' is intended here, cf. Del., *Assyr. Gram.*, § 68 end.

איש may be either collective—cf. the rendering given above—or the sing. may be used poetically for the plural.

וברצנם. '*In their wanton wrath*.' רצון, here parallel to אף, means '*unrestrained passion*;' cf. Esther 9, 5 ויעשׂו בשׂנאיהם כרצונם.

עקרו שור. '*They houghed oxen*,' i.e. severed the sinews of the thigh and so rendered the animals useless: so LXX, ἐνευροκόπησαν ταῦρον; cf. Josh. 11, 6. 9. 2 Sam. 8, 4. Onq., Pesh., Aq., Symm., Hieron., Vulg., and A.V. (but not R.V.) take שׁוֹר as שׁוּר, and render, '*a wall*' (this reading, according to Wright, being found in three MSS.), pointing עִקְּרוּ, עָקְרוּ (cf. Zeph. 2, 4), and taking עָקְרוּ in the sense, '*they destroyed*,' a meaning of the root which is common in Aramaic. Kn. points out that in 34, 28 f. Jacob's sons carried off the cattle as spoil, and Di., p. 459, suggests that the rendering '*wall*' may have been adopted to avoid a discrepancy in the narrative here and in chap. 34. Schumann and others consider that שׁוֹר = '*hero*,' or '*prince*,' refers to שׁכם, the son of חמור, comparing Ps. 68, 31. Deut. 33, 17, also Ps. 22, 13. Is. 14, 9, but this reference to שׁכם is very doubtful, and seems hardly justified by the passages cited in its defence.

7. עָז is the pausal form of עַז; so חָי pausal form of חַי, 25, 7, and דָּק pausal form of דַּק, Ex. 32, 20.

כִּי עַז . . . כִּי קָשָׁתָה. Cf. a similar change in Song of Songs 8, 6 כי עזה כמות אהבה קשה כשאול קנאה.

אֲחַלְּקֵם . . . וַאֲפִיצֵם. The use of the imperf. followed by the same tense with simple waw is more vivid and forcible than the ordinary prose usage of waw conver. with perf. Cf. Dav., *S.*, § 59; Dr., § 134.

The Heb.-Sam. text has אַדִּיר for אָרוּר, and וְחֶבְרָתָם for וְעֶבְרָתָם, probably an intentional change, so that Jacob should not be represented as cursing them. The Sam.Version renders in the same way as the Heb.-Sam. text; cf. Targ. Ps.-Jon.

In Deut. 33, 8 f. Levi's blessing is entirely different in its tone from the severe language used by Jacob in this chapter; while Simeon is not mentioned in Deut. 33, at least in our present text.

The Simeonites received as their portion several cities in the נגב, i.e. the southern portion of Palestine, in the midst of the territory of Judah (cf. Josh. 15, 26–32. 42 with Josh. 19, 1–9. 1 Chron. 4, 28–32); while Levi, according to Num. 35. Josh. 21, receives no special portion of territory, but has forty-eight cities assigned to him to dwell in by the other tribes.

8–12. '*Judah, thou, may thy brethren praise thee:*
May thy hand be on the neck of thy foes;
May thy father's sons bow down to thee.
A lion's whelp is Judah;
From the prey, my son, art thou gone up:
He couched, he lay down like a lion,
And like a lioness; who can rouse him?
The marshall's staff shall not depart from Judah,
Nor the leader's staff from between his feet,
Until he come to Shiloh;
And may the obedience of the peoples be his.
Binding to the vine his foal,
And to the Sorek vine his ass's colt:
He washes in wine his garments;
And in the blood of grapes his raiment:
Dark are his eyes with wine,
And white his teeth with milk.'

8. The *name* here suggests the form of the blessing; cf. 29, 35, as though it were, '*Praise . . . thy brethren shall praise thee.*'

אתה. On the pronoun, as *casus pendens*, cf. note on אנכי in 24, 27; also Ewald, § 309 b.

ידך בערף וגו״. Cf. Job 16, 12 ואחז בערפי ויפצפצני.

בני אביך. Not אחיך or בני אמך, but בני אביך; for all

Jacob's sons—not only those Leah bore him—shall praise Judah.

9. גור אריה יהודה. The comparison with a lion is not uncommon; see Deut. 33, 20 (where Gad is compared with a lioness), and 22 (where Dan is spoken of as a lion's whelp); cf. also Num. 23, 24. 24, 9 (which bears a striking resemblance to this passage, כרע שכב כארי וכלביא מי יקימנו), Mic. 5, 7.

מטרף בני עלית. '*From the prey, my son, art thou gone up*,' i.e. Judah is like a lion reascending to the mountain (cf. Song of Songs 4, 8) after having devoured his prey. LXX render עלית with ἀνέβης, and מטרף with ἐκ βλαστοῦ, taking it as in Ez. 17, 9 כָּל־טַרְפֵּי צִמְחָהּ '*all its fresh springing leaves*.' עלה Hif'. is found in Ez. 19, 3, meaning '*to bring up* (of a lion);' but as עלה is generally only used of vegetation in the sense to '*grow up*,' the rendering, '*From the prey, my son, art thou gone up*,' is preferable. If Judah were compared to a lion growing up, the addition of כאריה וכלביא would be hardly necessary.

כלביא. The lioness, defending her young, is fiercer than the lion (Herod. iii. 108).

10. לא יסור . . . עמים. The rendering given above is that adopted by Di. and Del. The text as it stands can only have this meaning, but as will be shewn below it cannot be satisfactorily explained. The same may indeed be said of all the explanations that have been proposed. First of all let us examine the rendering of the A.V. and R.V., '*until Shiloh come*.' שִׁלֹה[1] is here taken as a personal name, possibly

[1] The word שִׁלֹה is pointed שִׁילוֹ, שִׁילֹה, שִׁלֹה, and שִׁלוֹ. The first punctuation with the *scriptio plena*, being of a later date than שִׁלֹה, שִׁלוֹ, is only found a few times. It is worthy of notice that the *scriptio plena* is not found on the Moabite stone, nor do the Versions have it in שלה.

meaning '*peaceful*,' or '*peace-bringer*.' But, as is generally admitted (see Driver, in the *Cambridge Journal of Philology*, xiv. 2, and in *The Expositor*, July, 1885), there are serious philological difficulties in the way of this view. As pointed in our present texts, the ending ה must either stand for the suffix of the third pers. masc. sing., or mark the word as a pr. n.; cf. שְׁלֹמֹה, דודו, עדו, יתרו, etc. From these examples the word might, as far as its form goes, be a personal pr. n. If it be a pr. n., it must obviously, in a passage like the present, have some special significance. שִׁילֹה apparently must be connected with שָׁלָה, which denotes '*to be at ease*,' or '*quiet*.' The only exact parallel is גִּלֹה, the name of a place. But neither גלה nor שילה can be derived from גלה and שלה respectively, after the analogy of קִיטוֹר, פִּישׁוֹר; for—as Tuch argues, and Del. allows—they would, if derived from ל״ה verbs, following analogy, be גִּילוֹי and שִׁילוֹי. But the Gentile names גִּילֹנִי and שִׁילֹנִי (2 Sam. 15, 12. 1 Kings 11, 29) shew that שִׁילֹה and גִּילֹה are really apocopated from שִׁילוֹן and גִּילוֹן (cf. Lag., *B. N.*, p. 187), and have to be regarded as coming from the roots שׁול* or שׁיל, and גול* or גיל; cf. however, Barth., *N.B.*, p. 363. Further, if שילה could possibly be derived from שׁלה, 'שׁלה is not a full and significant word like שׁלם (Zech. 9, 10); at the most it denotes *mere* rest (Ps. 122, 6. 7), and is often associated with the idea of careless worldly ease (e.g. Job 12, 6. Ez. 16, 49).' So the rendering, '*peaceful one*,' or '*peace-bringer*,' can hardly be got out of the root שׁלה. Further, there is no allusion in any other part of the O. T. to *Shiloh* as a personal name. Del. and Di. adopt the rendering given in the translation of vers. 8–12, above, arguing that the philological difficulty just mentioned, the absence of any allusion in subsequent parts of the O. T. to Shiloh as a personal name, and the fact that שׁילה everywhere else in the O. T. is the name of a place, favour the rendering, '*until he come to Shiloh;*' acc. loci; cf. 1 Sam. 4, 12 ויבא שׁלה '*he came to Shiloh.*' They then, following the course of history, suppose that the prophecy was fulfilled in Josh. 18, 1, where the settlement of the land is described, pointing out that at an early date pre-eminence was assigned to Judah,—e.g. Num. 10, 14, the tribe marched first in the wilderness; Judg. 1, 2, advanced first to battle (cf. Judg. 20, 18); Josh. 15, was the first to receive its share when the land was divided,—and urge that the arrival of the Israelites at Shiloh was really a turning-point in their history, —the period of wandering was ended, the period of rest began,—a turning-point of sufficient importance to be noticed in the blessing; cf. Josh. 21, 42. 22, 4. The position Judah had gained was in subsequent years confirmed; the 'obedience of the peoples' was realised in the victories of David (2 Sam. 8), while it also included the ideal relation of Israel to the heathen, which is more distinctly spoken of by the prophets. The Messianic idea is thus not excluded in this view, though it cannot be attached to the word Shiloh. This view is also adopted by Herder (*Vom Geist der Hebr. Poesie*, ii. 6); Ewald, *Jahrbücher*, ii. 51; *Hist.*, ii. 283 f. (Eng. trans.), and others. It is objected to by Schultz (*Alttest. Theologie*, 1878, pp. 668–672), Cheyne (*Isaiah*, vol. ii [eds. 1, 2], Essay iv), and Driver, who points out that Judah is represented as possessing not only supremacy, but royalty; for שׁבט standing in ver. 10 alone, without any qualification, suggests rather a *sceptre* than a '*commander's staff*' (in Judg. 5, 14 שׁבט ספר may = '*a commander's staff;*' cf. הספר in 2 Kings 25, 19, but here שׁבט has no such qualification). The מחקק מבין רגליו represents rather a king sitting on his throne than a commander on active service, and the view that Judah will have not only supremacy, but royalty, is confirmed by a comparison of 8^{b} with 37, 7 f. ('*Wilt thou be king over us, or wilt thou rule over us?*'). Judah clearly enjoyed no royal power till long after Josh. 18, the passages in Num. and Josh. attributing only supremacy, not royalty, to him; and if שׁבט can bear the meaning assigned to it by Di. and Del., the context contains indications that the picture is one of royalty, and not mere supremacy. Bearing these facts in mind, it appears that the rendering '*till he come to Shiloh,*' must be abandoned. 'Judah is designated as the royal tribe: and the sceptre is confirmed to it עד כי יבא שׁילה ולו יקהת עמים. The parallelism is so carefully observed throughout that there is a presumption that in clause *c.* some person is designated to which ולו in *d.* may be referred, that we must render, therefore, either "*until he*—Judah, comes to . . ." or "*until . . . comes,* having the submission of the nations." Now the יקהת עמים, in one form or another, is a constant feature of the ideal future as depicted by the prophets—the relation being sometimes one of force (as 22, 17. 27, 29. Ps. 18, 43 f. Amos 9, 11 f.), sometimes one of spontaneous homage to the spiritual pre-eminence of Israel (Is. 2, 2 f. Jer. 3, 17. Is. 45, 14, etc.).' Driver, l. c., p. 26 f.

As Driver has shewn in his two articles already referred to, the word שׁלה is first connected with the Messiah in a passage in the Talmud, *Sanh.* 98 b, where the pupils of Rabbi Shila compliment their master by connecting his name with a title of the Messiah, calling him 'Shiloh,' on the ground of the present passage. The versions, as will be seen, have not interpreted it in this way, and it is doubtful whether the rendering, '*until Shiloh come,*' appears at all before the sixteenth century. The LXX render the verse,

Οὐκ ἐκλείψει ἄρχων ἐξ Ἰούδα, καὶ ἡγούμενος ἐκ τῶν μηρῶν αὐτοῦ, ἕως ἂν ἔλθῃ τὰ ἀποκείμενα αὐτῷ· καὶ αὐτὸς προσδοκία ἐθνῶν. Variants are ᾧ ἀπόκειται; ὃ ἀπόκειται αὐτῷ and ὃ ἀπόκειται, see *Journ. Phil.*, l. c., p. 4. The last two variants are unimportant. τὰ ἀποκείμενα αὐτῷ is a paraphrastic rendering, which takes שלה as = שֶׁלֹּה = אֲשֶׁר לוֹ (see 2 Kings 6, 11. Song of Songs 1, 7; and cf. the note on 6, 3). ἐὰν ἔλθῃ · ᾧ ἀπόκειται, this rendering is not a faithful reproduction of the Heb., as it supplies the subject ('until he comes, whose [it is]'), which is wanting in the Hebrew. ἐκ τῶν μηρῶν αὐτοῦ = מבין רגליו; cf. Deut. 28, 57 מבין רגליה: LXX διὰ τῶν μηρῶν αὐτῆς. προσδοκία for יקהת seems to connect it with קִוָּה, תִּקְוָה. Pesh. has ܠܐ ܢܥܒܪ ܫܒܛܐ ܡܢ ܝܗܘܕܐ ܘܡܦܩܢܐ ܡܢ ܒܝܬ ܪ̈ܓܠܘܗܝ ܥܕܡܐ ܕܢܐܬܐ ܗܘ ܕܕܝܠܗ ܗܝ ܘܠܗ ܢܣܟܘܢ ܥܡ̈ܡܐ '*The sceptre* (שֵׁבֶט) *shall not depart from Judah, nor an interpreter from between his feet, until he come whose it is, and him the nations expect.*' ܡܦܩܢܐ = '*an interpreter*,' '*announcer*.' The Pesh. in Deut. 33, 21. Judg. 5, 14. Is. 33, 22 uses the same word again for מחקק. Possibly this is a free translation on the part of the Pesh. Vers.; in the two passages in the Psalms (60, 9. 108, 9) where מחקק occurs, the Pesh. gives ܡܠܟܝ '*my king*.' The מחקק in both the Psalms is Judah. ܡܢ ܕܕܝܠܗ ܗܝ, the Pesh. renders שלה, like the LXX, = שֶׁלֹּה. In the present text the Pesh. has nothing to explain the fem. ܗܝ. Possibly the original form of the text has been preserved by Aphraates (c. 330–350 A. D.), who gives ܡܠܟܘܬܐ, = '*kingdom*,' after ܗܝ. This version also connects יקהת with קִוָּה, תִּקְוָה in its rendering ܢܣܟܘܢ. Onq. has לָא יְעְדֵּי עָבֵיד שׁוּלְטָן מִדְּבֵית יְהוּדָה וְסָפְרָא מִבְּנֵי בְנוֹהִי עַד עָלְמָא עַד דְּיֵיתֵי מְשִׁיחָא דְּדִילֵיהּ הִיא מַלְכוּתָא וְלֵיהּ יִשְׁתַּמְעוּן עַמְמַיָּא '*A ruler* (lit. *one exercising authority*) *shall not depart from those of the house of Judah, nor a scribe from among his sons' sons for ever, until*

Messiah comes, whose is the kingdom, and him the peoples shall obey.' Onq. takes שבט as '*ruler*,' and מחקק as '*scribe*,' מבין רגליו is interpreted similarly to the LXX, '*from his descendants*,' '*for ever*,' and '*Messiah*' are insertions, and שלה is taken as שֶׁלֹּה, following the construction of ᾧ ἀπόκειται, '*kingdom*' being inserted after it. For traces of a various reading in Onq., see Berliner, *Targum Onk.*, ii. p. 18. The Targ. Jerus. is substantially the same as Onqelos; but the Targ. Ps.-Jon. takes שלה as מַלְכָּא מְשִׁיחָא זְעֵיר בְּנוֹהִי = '*King Messiah, his youngest son*,' שילה being connected with שִׁלְיָתָהּ, Deut. 28, 57, where Onq. has זְעֵיר בְּנָהָא '*her youngest son*,' and Rashi בָּנִים הַקְּטַנִּים. This interpretation afterwards found considerable favour, and is perhaps embodied in the Massoretic punctuation שִׁילֹה (='*his son*'). The Old Latin has '*donec veniant quae reposita sunt ei*,' with the variants '*donec veniat cui repositum est*' (or '*cui reposita sunt*'); cf. the LXX translations. The Vulgate has '*donec veniat qui mittendus est*,' reading שלה as though it were שָׁלוּחַ. The Sam. Vers. has [illegible] for רגליו '*his ranks*.' The Heb.-Sam. has מבין דגליו '*from between his banners*,' דֶּגֶל for רֶגֶל. It retains the word שילה, and renders מחקק '*leader*' with the LXX (ἡγούμενος) and Vulg. ('*dux*').

Thus it will be seen that most of the versions took שלה as שֶׁלֹּה, which would be a poetical equivalent of אֲשֶׁר לוֹ (see above, on the LXX translation); the sentence being then rendered, (1) '*until there come that which* (or *he that*) *is his*,' or (2) '*until there come he to whom* (or *he whose*) *is*.' In the second case the sentence is without a subject, and requires some word, e.g. הוא or יהיה, referring back to שבט, or some expression denoting '*dominion*;' cf. the renderings of Onq. and (possibly) the Pesh. The suffix ה for ו does not occur with ל elsewhere; but בֹּה is only found once (Jer. 17, 24), and we have סוּתֹה and עִירֹה in ver. 11. Possibly Ez. 21, 32 עד בא אשר לו המשפט may be a reference to this passage; if so, it favours the punctuation adopted by most of the Vss. As regards the reading implied by these versions, it may be noted that of all the conflicting views, this is the only one that is based on any definite evidence, and it may perhaps be provisionally accepted in lieu of a more probable interpretation. As may be seen from the extracts given by Driver, the rendering of the Targ. Ps.-Jon. ('*his son*') is adopted by Yepheth Ben Ali (c. 950–990), Abulwalid (11th cent.), David Kimchi (d. 1235), etc. If שִׁיל means '*son*' in this verse, it is the only passage in the O. T. where the word occurs. The verse was interpreted in ancient times, by both Christian and Jewish writers, as Messianic; but this Messianic idea was derived, not from the word שלה, but from the context of the verse, especially from the promise of supremacy and success which is held out to Judah.

Other renderings of the passage that have been proposed are: (1) '*Till peace* or *tranquillity cometh:*' Ges. (Lex.), Reuss, Knobel, reading שֶׁלָה or שֵׁלָה, as שִׁילֹה is always a proper name. But neither of these words exists, and there is nothing in clause *c.* to refer to ולו. (2) '*Until he comes to peacefulness*,' Kurtz, Oehler; cf. Halévy, *Rev. Crit.*, 1883, p. 290, who reads שָׁלוֹם, Is. 57, 2, and renders similarly. (3) '*So long as one comes* (*=people come*) *to Shiloh*,' i.e. as long as the worship at Shiloh is continued shall Judah retain his supremacy, i.e. for ever; so Tuch and others, comparing the use of עד שׁ in Song of Songs 1, 12 ='*as long as*.' (4) Lagarde conjectures שְׁאִילֹה '*his desired one*,' anticipated by Matthew Hiller (*Onom. Sacra*, 1706). (5) Reading עד כי יבא (יו)שׁ(ת) or (יו)שׁ(ם) לה. This is the reading suggested by Cheyne (*Isaiah*, ii. Essay iv), who thinks that the LXX rendering presupposes a fuller text than שלה. The rendering with this reading would be, '*for whom it* (*the dominion*) *is appointed*.' Cf. Judg. 5, 14 מני אפרים שרשם בעמלק '*out of Ephraim* [*came down*] *they whose root is in A.*' (6) '*Till he come to that which is his*,' or '*his own;*' cf. Deut. 33, 7, the rendering adopted by C. von Orelli, *O. T. Prophecy*, § 15; see further, Di., Del., and Tuch in their commentaries, Driver, l. c., and the various authorities cited by them[1].

שבט. In the rendering adopted by Del., Di., and others, שבט means '*the leader's*' or '*commander's staff*.' In Judg. 5, 14 it certainly has this meaning, but in that passage it is qualified by ספר. Di. remarks that the term שבט is not exclusively applied to a king, and points out that it is used here, as מחקק in Ps. 60, 9. Num. 21, 18, of the leader's or chief's staff. מחקק, Di. and Del. '*leader's staff;*' cf. מחקק in Num. 21, 18. Ps. 60, 9 (Del.). If the view be adopted, that the description is one of Judah's royal supremacy, cf. p. 377 f., as שבט must then mean '*sceptre*,' מחקק must in the parallel clause = '*ruler's staff*.' The Pesh. has ܡܦܫܩܢܐ, which perhaps favours the rendering '*law-giver*,' and which could be applied to a '*leader*' or '*ruler;*' LXX ἡγούμενος; Onq., Targ. Ps.-Jon. (of actual '*scribes*' [teachers of law]), Jer. Targ. '*scribe;*' Vulg. '*dux;*' Sam. Ver. ࠌࠃࠁࠓ = '*leader;*' all (excepting perhaps the Targums) renderings that could be used of a commander or a king. The meaning of מחקק must be similar to that assigned to שבט, whether שבט

[1] See also the two articles by the Dean of Peterborough in *The Churchman*, Oct. and Dec., 1886, who, after pointing out the difficulties of the rendering '*till Shiloh come*,' adopts the rendering (2) of Kurtz and Oehler, *Theology of the O. T.*, § 229, '*until he come to rest* or *tranquillity*.'

be rendered '*sceptre*' or '*leader's staff*,' as the two portions of the verse are parallel.

מבין רגליו. '*From between his feet*,' the picture representing the leader, standing or sitting with his staff of office between his feet (Di., who compares the figures on the old Persian and Assyrian monuments), or the king on his throne, with the sceptre between his feet. The meaning, '*from among his descendants*,' is favoured by the LXX, Onq., Targg. Ps.-Jon., Jer., Vulg. ('*de femore ejus*'), but depends on a comparison with Deut. 28, 57, and is unsuitable here. Tuch renders רַגְלָיו as the plural of רגלי a '*foot soldier*;' cf. the Heb.-Sam. text, and the Sam. Vers. referred to above, a meaning which would suit the word if the picture is that of a military commander. Di. condemns this rendering as devoid of taste and ungrammatical, as רַגְלָיו cannot stand for רַגְלָיָיו; cf. Böttcher, *Heb. Gram.*, § 827. Di. also rejects the Heb.-Sam. rendering, '*banners*,' as incompatible with the מחקק.

עד כי יבא. On עד־כי in a temporal sentence, cf. Dav., *S.*, § 145 f.; Ges., § 155. 2 c; 26, 13 עד כי גדל; 41, 49 עד כי חדל; 2 Sam. 23, 10 עד כי יגעה ידו; and עד אשר in 27, 44.

ולו יקהת עמים. יִקְּהַת with the *dag. forte dirimens*; see Ges., § 20. 2 b; Dav., § 7. 4. note; Stade, § 138 a; so עִקְּבֵי, ver. 17; עִנְּבֵי, Deut. 32, 32; קַשְּׁתֹתָיו, Is. 5, 28; חַלְּקֵי־נַחַל, Is. 57, 6.

יקהת. The meaning '*obedience*,' which is also adopted by Onq. (see above), agrees with Prov. 30, 17 (where it also has *dag. dirimens*), the only other passage where the word occurs, and is corroborated by the Arabic وَقَى '*to obey*.' The A.V. renders, '*gathering of the people*' (but R.V. '*obedience*'), following Aq. (σύστημα), Tanchuma (9th cent.), and Rashi (הָעַמִּים

אֲסִיפַת). The Sam. Vers., Heb.-Sam., and Saadiah render יקהת similarly, possibly connecting the word with מִקְוֶה, נִקְוָה.

11. אסרי לגפן עירה. אסרי, the construct state with the binding vowel ִי, so בְּנִי; cf. 31, 39 and the note on that passage. On the cstr. state before a prep., see note on 24, 21; so (with the archaic connecting vowel ִי) Is. 22, 16 חֹקְקִי בַסֶּלַע; Obad. 3 שֹׁכְנִי בְחַגְוֵי־סֶלַע; Mic. 7, 14 שֹׁכְנִי לְבָדָד; Ps. 123, 1 הַיֹּשְׁבִי בַּשָּׁמָיִם.

עירה. On the archaic orthography ה (for ו), see the note on 9, 21. עִירֹה is for עֵירֹה (the abs. state is עַיִר); cf. בֵּיתוֹ, בַּיִת, לַיִל, and לֵיל; so שַׁיִת in Is. 10, 17 makes שִׁיתוֹ, not שֵׁיתוֹ; see Stade, § 100; Ewald, § 255 b, who also cites דִּישׁוֹ, Deut. 25, 4, as though from דַּיִשׁ; but דִּישׁוֹ may be inf. cstr. of דִּישׁ. Onq. and the Sam. Vers. and Heb.-Sam. take עירו as = '*his city!*'

שרקה. '*The sorek vine,*' so called from the red colour (شُقْرَة) of the grapes. Both the grapes and the wine were of a specially choice kind. In the territory of Judah the vine flourished; cf. Joel 1, 7 ff. 4, 18. 2 Chron. 26, 10, and Num. 13, 23 f., where the vineyards near Hebron, and Song of Songs 1, 14, where those of En-gedi, are mentioned.

כבס. Cf. the use of רחץ in Job 29, 6. Di. considers this a continuation of the part. אסרי; cf. Ges., § 116. 5. Rem. 7; Driver, § 117. In this construction the second verb is usually connected with the part. by waw conv., or simple waw and the perfect, the perfect being separated from the waw by some word or words: cf. ver. 17 הנשך . . . ויפל. It seems more natural to disconnect כבס and אסרי, following the accents, and to render as above. For the perfect, cf. Driver, § 12; Dav., *S.*, § 40 c; M.R., § 2. 2; Ges., § 106. 2 c. (a perfect of experience, or gnomic aorist); so Pss. 9, 11. 10, 3, etc.

סותה. This word only occurs in this passage; on the suffix הֹ, see on עִירֹה. The Heb.-Sam. reads כסותו, which is possibly the correct reading. But as there seems to be no authority for the elision of the כ (תֵּן for נְתֵן is not parallel), it will be better to derive the word from a root סוה '*to envelop*,' '*wrap up*,' סוּת being contracted for סְוּוּת; cf. the noun מַסְוֶה, which comes from the same verb סוה. סוה may = the Arab. زَوَى (the ס in Heb. corresponding exceptionally to an Arabic ز) = *abdidit*, *celavit*, conj. VII, *abdidit se*.

12. חכלילי עינים. The י is not the binding vowel, as in בני, אסרי, but חכלילי is an adj. from חכל (see Ewald, § 164 a), with a repetition of the last letter of the root (see Stade, § 149; Barth, *N.B.*, p. 215). Del. compares שְׁעֲרוּרִי, but this word does not actually occur, though the fem. form שַׁעֲרוּרִיָּה, Hos. 6, 10, is found in the Ktb., and might presuppose a masc. שַׁעֲרוּרִי. The adjectival ending ִי is common, e.g. פְּלִילִי, נָכְרִי, פְּרָזִי, רַגְלִי. The root חכל (which, however, is not found) corresponds (apparently) with حَكَلَ IV, '*to be obscure and doubtful;*' cf. C. P. Ges., *sub voce*. Del. on Ps. 10, 8 compares also the Arab. حَلِكَ '*to be jet black.*'

חכלילי עינים. Cf. Prov. 23, 29 למי חכלילות עינים. The construction is the same as in יפת תאר, 29, 17; see on 12, 11.

וּלְבֶן־שִׁנַּיִם. לְבֶן־ cstr. state of לָבָן, from an abs. state לָבֵן; so חֲלֵב cstr. state of חָלָב, from an abs. state חָלֵב, which with Maqqef would be חֲלֶב; so אֲבֶל־, Ps. 35, 14, from אָבֵל; see Stade, § 202 a; Ges., § 93. 2. Rem. 1. With this verse, cf. Joel 4, 18. Amos 9, 13. The pasture lands of Judah were celebrated; see 1 Sam. 25, 2. Amos 1, 1. 2 Chron. 26, 10.

13. *'Zebulun—on the shore of the sea shall he dwell:*
And he himself shall be on a shore of ships,
With his border by Sidon.'

There is possibly an allusion here to the meaning of the name Zebulun (*'dweller'*) given in 30, 20; but cf. note on that passage.

לחוף ימים ישכן. In Judg. 5, 17 Asher is spoken of thus, יָשַׁב לְחוֹף יַמִּים, and in Deut. 33, 19 Zebulun and Issachar *'suck the abundance of the seas'* (שפע ימים יינקו). Zebulun's territory apparently did not lie on the seashore (cf. Josh. 19, 10–16), so perhaps we ought to render על צ״ with Del.[4] *'towards Sidon,'* i.e. his border lay in the direction of Sidon, but was not actually on the seashore, only towards the coast district. The Sam. Ver., Heb.-Sam., LXX, Pesh., Vulg., and apparently Onq. (מְטֵי עַד) read עד = *'up to S.,'* which would express the meaning *'in the direction of'* more clearly than על. According to Jos. (*Ant.*, v. 1. 22; *Bel. Jud.*, iii. 3. 1) Zebulun inhabited the district from the lake of Gennesareth to Mount Carmel on the Mediterranean, and in support of this Tuch compares Josh. 19, 11 with Matt. 4, 13. Di. also conjectures that as the boundary between Asher and Zebulun in Josh. 19, 14 f. is not very clearly defined, it is not impossible that Zebulun might have possessed a strip of land, bordering on the Mediterranean Sea.

והוא לחוף אנית. On the rendering *'he himself,'* see Ewald, § 314 b (והוא added in a new proposition, with special force, as the subject). Cf. 2 Sam. 17, 10, where further emphasis is produced by the addition of גם.

14, 15. *'Issachar is a strong ass,*
Lying down between the sheep-folds:
And he saw a resting-place, that it was good,

And the land, that it was pleasant;
So he bowed his back to bear,
And became a servant in bondage.'

14. חמר גרם, lit. '*an ass of bone*,' i.e. a strongly built, powerful ass; so Aq. ὄνος ὀστώδης, Vulg. '*asinus fortis*.' The Sam. Vers. has ࠇࠌࠓࠀࠂࠓࠉࠌ, reading גֵּרִים ('*sojourners*'), which Geiger defends as the correct reading (*Urschrift*, p. 360), Issachar being '*an ass of strangers*,' i.e. bearing the burdens of strangers, and subject to them. But Del.[4] points out that this rendering destroys the force of the figurative expression חמר, and some other word, such as זרים or נכרים, would be expected rather than גֵּרִים. The Heb.-Sam. has גרים, which Tuch punctuates גְּרִים,= the Arab. جَرِيمٌ '*bony*.' The LXX have τὸ καλὸν ἐπεθύμησεν, which presupposes some such reading as חָמַד גֶּרֶם (Geiger); see Ps. 119, 20, LXX.

המשפתים. This word is only found once again, Judg. 5, 16, though we find שְׁפַתַּיִם in Ps. 68, 14 = '*sheep-folds*.' משפתים is probably from שפת = '*to fix*.' Ewald, § 180 a, explains the word as = '*double pen*,' with reference to the cattle being usually separated into two portions in the pen; while Stade, § 340 b, classes the word with those that denote 'instruments or other things consisting of two parts belonging to one another, or standing in pairs, one opposite to the other; so חמתים;' see also Ges., *Thes.*, 1471 f. The word in this verse, and Judg. 5, 16, is used as a proverbial expression for the easy life of the agriculturist. Onq. renders בֵּין תְּחוּמַיָּא '*between the boundaries*,' so Vulg. '*inter terminos*,' while the LXX have ἀνὰ μέσον τῶν κλήρων (but in Judg. ἀνὰ μέσον τῆς διγομίας), and the Pesh. ܒܝܬ ܫܒܝ̈ܠܐ '*between the paths*.'

15. מנחה, either '*rest*' or '*a resting-place*,' as the word occurs with both meanings.

טוב must be taken as a neuter subs. = '*a good thing.*' The Heb.-Sam. has טוֹבָה (fem. adj.), which perhaps suits the parallelism better (נָעֵמָה).

ויהי למס עבד, lit. '*and was* (*reduced*) *to the forced service of a labourer.*' The phrase היה למס עבד recurs Josh. 16, 10; and היה למס (without עבד) is found in Deut. 20, 11. Judg. 1, 30. 33. Is. 31, 8, both expressions always meaning the compulsory service rendered by slaves, prisoners, or conquered nations. נתן ... למס is also found Josh. 17, 13; הֶעֱלָה למס, 1 Kings 9, 21; and שִׂים למס, Judg. 1, 28. The derivation of מס is uncertain. Fleischer, in Ges., *H. W.B.*[11], derives it from נסס, as a contraction out of מֶנֶס (cf. מֶמֶר from מרר and Olsh., *Gram.*, § 198 b) = *quod alicui impositum est.* The pl. מִסִּים perhaps favours this view. Del.[4] points out that Issachar is not a פֶּרֶא, i. e. '*a wild ass*' wandering about at will, but a חֲמוֹר, i.e. '*a beast of burden,*' and sees in the last clause of the verse an allusion to the meaning of the name יששכר (= ישׂא שׂכר or יש שׂכר; cf. 30, 16. 18). Issachar, though strong and active, prefers a life of ease and indolence, sinking even into the condition of a bond-slave. Cf. Judg. 5, 16, where Reuben is reproached in similar language for his inactivity and aversion from active exertion. The LXX render the words ויהי למס עבד καὶ ἐγενήθη ἀνὴρ γεωργός, an attempt to do away with the reproach contained in the verse, and Onq. completely changes the meaning of the last clause of the verse in his paraphrase, '*He will subdue the provinces of the peoples, destroy their inhabitants, and those who are left among them shall be servants unto him, and bringers of tribute;*' cf. Geiger, l. c., p. 360.

16, 17. '*Dan shall judge his people,*
As one of the tribes of Israel.

Let Dan be a serpent in the way,
A horned adder in the path:
That biteth the horse's heels,
So that his rider falleth backwards.'

16. Dan, though a tribe by no means powerful, and possessing only a small territory, will maintain the cause of Israel, in its conflicts with the heathen nations, as valiantly as the other tribes; cf. Judg. 13–16.

דן ידין. Notice the play upon the name דן in the choice of the verb ידין.

ידין = '*will judge*,' i.e. plead the cause of, render help to; דִּין always has this meaning, cf. 30, 6. Deut. 32, 36. Jer. 22, 16, and not the meaning '*rule*' or '*govern*.'

עמו = the people of Israel, as in Deut. 33, 7. Others (Vatablus, Rosenmüller, etc.) understand עמו as the people belonging to the tribe of Dan, and explain the verse as meaning the small tribe of Dan will have its own administration and its own jurisdiction; or Dan, though a small tribe, will maintain its own independence (Tuch, Wellh.). But both these views take ידין = '*will rule*' or '*govern*,' a meaning which, as above remarked, דן does not have.

17. עלי דרך, so עלי ארח, עֲלֵי being the poetical form for עַל; cf. אֱלֵי, poetical for אֶל (but only in the book of Job); עֲדֵי, poetical for עַד.

שְׁפִיפֹן, a ἅπαξ λεγόμ.; perhaps the ending ון- is diminutive in this word (see Ewald, § 167 a; Stade, § 296 c), the word being probably from the root שׁפף = '*to crawl*.' שְׁפִיפֹן is probably the *cerastes* or horned adder, a small and very dangerous species of snake, of a bluish yellow or sand colour. Hieronymus renders it by '*regulus*' in his *Quaest.*, ed. Lagarde, p. 69; the Pesh. ܚܶܡܢܳܐ = '*a basilisk*,' the Vulg. '*cerastes*,'

Onq. פִּיתְנָא = '*an adder.*' The LXX, not understanding the word שְׁפִיפֹן, render it, in harmony with the context, ἐγκαθήμενος. In Arabic سِيفٌ = '*a serpent with black and white spots.*' In Deut. 33, 22 Dan is compared with '*a lion's whelp that springeth out of Bashan.*'

הַנֹּשֵׁךְ . . . וַיִּפֹּל. Cf. the note on 27, 33.

The meaning of the verse is, Dan, like the serpent lurking in the path, attacks his foes, not in open fight, but with stratagem; cf. Judg. 18, 27, and the history of Samson.

18. '*For thy help I wait, O Yahweh.*'

This verse breaks the connection of the poem, hence it is regarded by some (Maurer, Olshausen, etc.) as an interpolation; but if this is the case it must have been added at a later date by the redactor of the book, as a protest against Dan's idolatrous devices. It is found in all the Vss. Tuch explains it as 'an exclamation from the patriarch Jacob, who is exhausted and nerving himself for another effort before his death.' Kn., whom Di. follows, says, 'The patriarch here speaks in prayer, in the name of his descendants, who must, in the wars with the nations, e.g. the Philistines, put their trust in Yahweh, and look for His assistance.' So the Targg. Ps.-Jon. and Jer., Wright, Del., and Driver.

19. '*Gad—a troop shall press upon him,*
Yet he shall press upon their heel.'

Gad, who was settled in Gilead, though exposed to the attacks of his foes (cf. Josh. 13, 25. Judg. 11, 15), and probably often engaged in border warfare with marauding bands (cf. 2 Kings 5, 2. 6, 23), successfully defends himself and puts his enemies to flight (cf. Judg. 10 f. 12. 1 Chron. 5, 18 ff. 12, 8 f.); cf. Deut. 33, 20. 21. The name גד is here connected by the writer with גוד '*to assail,*' and גדוד =

'*a marauding band*' (see 2 Kings, l.c.), in the sense '*assailer*' or '*attacker*.' In 30, 11 another explanation of the name is suggested.

גד גדוד יגודנו. Cf. Hab. 3, 16 לעלות לעם יגודנו.

עקב, the rendering given above, follows the reading עֲקֵבָם, which is adopted by Bleek, Knobel, Ols., Wright, and others, the ם of מאשר being taken away and appended to עקב. Other instances of incorrect division of words are given in Dr., *Sam.*, p. xxx. The LXX, Pesh., Vulg., and Saad. in a measure support this reading, as they do not translate the commencement of the next verse מאשר, but אשר. עקב by itself, as Di. remarks, is sufficient, but, as Del. points out, with the rendering '*their heel*' (R.V. margin), 19^b and 20^a alike gain in clearness. All the other 'blessings,' except Joseph's in ver. 22, begin with the name of the person blessed, without any preceding word or particle.

The rendering '*heel*' is more forcible than '*rearguard*.' Gad is depicted as pressing hotly on his foes, almost on the heels of the retreating enemy. עקב cannot = אחור '*backwards*' (Vulg. '*retrorsum*'), nor '*at the last*,' A.V. The R.V. renders correctly, '*upon their heel*.'

20. '*Asher—fat is his bread,*
And he shall yield kingly dainties.'

This rendering follows the reading אשר, the pr. name being a *casus pendens*, like גד in ver. 19; cf. Deut. 32, 4. Ps. 11, 4, etc.

If the reading מאשר be adopted (so the Sam. Ver.), the rendering will be either, '*From Asher* (*comes*) *fat—his bread*,' so Tuch; cf. שמנים, Is. 25, 6; or, '*For Asher—his bread is too fat*,' Ewald. With the first rendering, מאשר = מארץ א״, which is perhaps not quite suitable to the context, and שמנה

fem. is not found as a noun; with the second, לחמו must be taken as feminine; see Bött., § 657, who distinguishes between לֶחֶם = '*bread*,' masc., and לֶחֶם = '*abundance of bread*' (Brotfülle), fem. The Sam. Vers., according to one reading, has שמן masc.

מעדני מלך. '*Dainties fit for kings.*' Cf. לחם אבירים, Ps. 78, 25. It is not necessary to think of a king of Israel in the term מלך.

The fertility and productiveness of Asher are again alluded to in Deut. 33, 24 f. Di. suggests that as the Phoenicians procured all sorts of country produce from the Hebrews (Ez. 27, 17. Acts 12, 20; Jos., *Antiq.*, xiv. 10. 6), Asher, from his geographical position, would participate largely in this traffic.

21. '*Naphtali is a slender terebinth*
That puts forth beautiful branches.'

אילה שלחה = '*a hind let loose*,' so A.V., R.V.; Aq. ἔλαφος ἀπεσταλμένος, Vulg. '*cervus emissus*,' Del.[5] The Pesh. paraphrases, but with the same meaning, ܐܝܙܓܕܐ ܡܛܟܣܐ '*a swift messenger*;' cf. Job 39, 5 מי שלח פרא חפשי וגו׳. Tuch and others take שלחה in the sense '*stretched out*,' so '*graceful*,' but there seems to be no authority for this rendering in the case of living beings. Knobel, comparing Is. 16, 2 (קֵן מְשֻׁלָּח), renders, '*a scared hind*,' but this thought is very unsuitable, and quite out of harmony with the context. The allusion in this part of the verse (following the reading of the text) is probably to the swiftness of the heroes and men of the tribe of Naphtali (cf. for the expression, Ps. 18, 34. Hab. 3, 19. Is. 35, 6; also 2 Sam. 2, 18. Song of Songs 2, 9). The Pesh. seems to interpret the first half of the verse as meaning that Naphtali is specially adapted for the duties of a messenger, while Christian writers see an allusion in שלחה to the apostles (Aramaic ܫܠܝܚܐ)!

הנתן אמרי שפר. The allusion here is to the poets of the tribe, Barak, however, being the only one of whom we hear anything (Judg. 5, 1). הנתן naturally refers to נפתלי, and not to אילה, which is fem.

The verse is explained as above by those who follow the Massoretic text. It is probable that the LXX has preserved the original text. The reading in that Version is Νεφθαλεί, στέλεχος ἀνειμένον ἐπιδιδοὺς ἐν τῷ γενήματι κάλλος, which seems to be equivalent to נַפְתָּלִי אֵילָה שְׁלֻחָה הַנֹּתֵן אֲמִירֵי־שֶׁפֶר, i. e. אֵילָה = '*terebinth*,' for אַיָּלָה, and אֲמִירֵי (cf. Is. 17, 6. 9) = '*topmost branches*,' for the poetical אִמְרֵי. This reading is accepted by Ewald, Ols., Di., C. P. Ges., etc., endorsing the opinion of numerous earlier scholars; cf. Di., p. 468. For the epithet שלחה, cf. Jer. 17, 8. Ez. 17, 6. Ps. 80, 12, and the noun שֶׁלַח '*shoot*,' '*blossom*,' Song of Songs 4, 13, and for the figure, ver. 22; the אמירי are then the leaders produced by the tribe of Naphtali; cf. Judg. 4, 6. 5, 18. 6, 35. 7, 23. With this reading the rendering would be as adopted above. Onq. has נַפְתָּלִי בְּאַרַע טָבָא יִתְרְמֵי עַדְבֵיהּ וְאַחְסַנְתֵּיהּ תְּהֵי מְעַבְדָא פֵּירִין יְהוֹן מוֹדָן וּמְבָרְכִין עֲלֵיהוֹן '*Naphtali, in a goodly land shall his lot be cast, and his possession shall be yielding fruits, they shall praise and bless over them*,' which apparently supports this reading.

22–26. '*A son of a fruit tree is Joseph,*
A son of a fruit tree by a fountain;
His branches run over the wall.
The archers harassed him,
And shot at him, and lay in wait for him;
But his bow remains firm,

And the hands of his arms are strong:
From the hands of the mighty One of Jacob,
From thence, (from) the shepherd, the stone of Israel:
From the God of thy fathers—so may he keep thee,
And with the Almighty—so may he bless thee,
With blessings of heaven above,
Blessings of the deep, that lieth beneath,
Blessings of the breasts and womb.
The blessings of thy father have prevailed over the blessings of the ancient mountains,
The desire of the eternal hills:
May they be upon the head of Joseph,
On the crown of the prince among his brethren.'

22. בן פרת יוסף. '*Son of a fruit tree is J.*,' i.e. '*a young fruit tree;*' cf. בן, Ps. 80, 16. בֵּן—though elsewhere pointed בֶּן־ or בִּן־, with Maqqef—must be taken as construct state, cf. שֵׁם, cstr. state, 12, 8, and שֶׁם־, 16, 15, or we must read בֶּן with Di. The Massoretes may, as Del. suggests, have taken בֵּן as sing. abs. fem., pl. בנות, with the meaning '*branch*,' and פרת as an adj. qualifying it = '*a fruitful branch;*' cf. Ges., § 96. *sub voce* בֵּן.

פרת with the archaic ending ָת (see Stade, §§ 213 c, 308 d; Lag., *B.N.*, p. 81; Ges., § 80. Rem. 2 b; Ewald, § 173 d) is not equivalent to فُرَارٌ '*a lamb*' (Ilgen, etc.), with an allusion to Rachel; nor to פָּרָה '*a heifer*' (Schumann, Wright). It = the later פֹּרָה, meaning '*a fruit tree;*' cf. פֹּרִיָּה, Is. 17, 6 (of the olive tree); probably a vine, cf. גפן פריה in Is. 32, 12. Ez. 19, 10. Ps. 128, 3; so Onq., Tuch, Ewald, Di. Possibly there is an allusion here to the name אֶפְרַיִם (perhaps '*double fruitfulness*'), 41, 52.

עלי עין. The moisture would promote the growth of the vine; cf. Ps. 1, 3. Jer. 17, 8.

בָּנוֹת צָעֲדָה. The בנות are the branches of the vine that grow over the wall (שׁוּר *wall*, cf. Ps. 18, 30, not '*ambuscade*,' Wright: Ps. 92, 12 it = '*lier in wait*'), which also protects the vine. On the construction of the plural, where inanimate objects are spoken of, with the sing. fem. expressing (as in Arabic) the *collective*, see Ges., § 145. 4; Dav., *S.*, § 116; M.R., § 135. 1; Ewald, § 317 a; cf. Joel 1, 20 גם בהמות שׂדה תערוג; Zech. 6, 14 והעטרת תהיה לחלם, and the construction, common in Greek, of the neuter pl. with a sing. verb, as τὰ θηρία ἀναβλέπει. Ewald reads the text here בְּנוֹת צְעָדָה '*daughters of ascent*,' but this alteration is unnecessary. The verse appears to have been entirely misunderstood by the Vss., and by Peters (*Hebraica*, iii. 111 and v. 190), who proposes the extraordinary rendering '*daughters have marched in procession to a bull*'!

23. וימררהו, lit. = '*they treated him bitterly*,' i.e. acted in a hostile manner towards him.

וָרֹבּוּ with pretonic qameç, as in תהו ובהו, 1, 2; see the note there. On the perf. with weak waw, cf. Driver, p. 160. רֹבּוּ is from רבב, with the intransitive punctuation (see Stade, § 385 b. 2; Ges., § 67. Rem. 1), meaning '*to shoot*;' so Ps. 18, 15 וברקים רב ויהמם; related to רבה and רמה; cf. רַבָּיו, Job 16, 13. Jer. 50, 29 (all). The LXX, Sam., Onq., and Vulg. seem to have read ויריבו, but בעלי חצים does not suit this.

בעלי חצים. So בעל החלמות, 37, 19; בעלי ברית, 14, 13, and the note on that passage. Compare with this verse the narrative in Judg. 6 ff. 1 Chron. 5, 18 f., of the hostility shewn to Ephraim and Manasseh by the neighbouring Arab tribes; and Josh. 17, 16 f., where the children of Joseph are commanded to drive out the Canaanites from the territory Joshua assigns them.

24. ותשב באיתן קשתו. '*Yet his bow remains in firmness.*' On the adversative force of the waw conv., see Ewald, § 231 b, and note on 32, 31; and cf. Deut. 4, 33. 2 Sam. 19, 29. On the action of the imperf. continuing into the writer's present, see Driver, § 79, and cf. the note on 19, 9.

באיתן. Del. explains איתן as a subst. = בִּמְקוֹם אֵיתָן; Ewald, § 299 b (cf. § 172 b), considers that the adj. here must be taken as neuter, '*in* or *with firmness*,' and the ב conceived as forming the predicate, comparing Ex. 32, 22 ברע הוא. The form איתן, cf. אכזב, אכזר, in Hebrew corresponds to the Arabic formation for adjectives أَفْعَل, with the signification of our comparative and superlative, and so called '*the noun of pre-eminence*' or '*elative*.' In Hebrew the forms have lost their original significance and are used as simple adjectives; see Wright, *Arab. Gram.*, i. p. 159; Ewald, § 162 b. Cf. also Barth, *N.B.*, p. 221; Ges., § 133. 1. foot-note 3. איתן seems to have been an old Canaanitish word; cf. *C. I. S.*, i. p. 93. lin. 1 and 2.

The LXX have καὶ συνετρίβη μετὰ κράτους τὰ τόξα αὐτῶν, reading וַתִּשָּׁבֵר, and the Pesh. ܘܗܦܟܬ ܒܥܫܝܢܐ ܩܫܬܗ '*his bow turned in strength*,' reading וַתָּשָׁב; so apparently Onqelos.

ויפזו. פזז means '*to be nimble*,' '*pliant*;' cf. the Arabic فَزَّ '*to be nimble*.' The root only occurs once again, in the Pi'el in 2 Sam. 6, 16 מפזז ומכרכר '*skipping and dancing*' (cf. Ges. in *Thes. s.v.*). The LXX have καὶ ἐξελύθη, Pesh. ܐܬܦܫܪܘ, Vulg. '*dissoluta sunt* [*vincula*],' reading perhaps וַיָּפֻצוּ, from פוץ.

מידי אביר יעקב, i.e. Joseph's strength comes from the hands of the mighty One of Jacob, which support him. אביר יעקב, cf. Is. 1, 24 (אביר ישראל). 49, 26. 60, 16. Ps. 132,

2. 5, where the phrase is borrowed from this passage. אֲבִיר is only found in the cstr. state; Barth, *N.B.*, p. 51, regards it as cstr. state of אַבִּיר, comparing פָּרִיץ, cstr. state פְּרִיץ.

משם רעה וגו״. In the rendering given above, which seems relatively the best in this difficult clause, רעה is taken as explaining מִשָּׁם, which probably means *'from heaven,'* cf. Eccl. 3, 17 (?), and אבן יש״ is a second name for God, in apposition to רעה. For the term רעה applied to God, cf. 48, 15. Pss. 23, 1. 80, 2. אֶבֶן must be taken as equivalent to the common title of God צור (Deut. 32, 4. 1 Sam. 2, 2. Is. 30, 29. Ps. 18, 32); אבן, however, never has this meaning anywhere else. Another rendering which is possible is that adopted by Tuch (cf. Ewald, § 332 d), '*whence is the Shepherd the Stone of Israel:*' מִשָּׁם = '*inde ubi;*' cf. מאז = '*ex quo tempore,*' 39, 5. Ps. 76, 8; and the Vulgate, '*inde pastor egressus est lapis*' etc. Ewald renders similarly, but reads רֹעֵה אֶבֶן יִשְׂרָאֵל ('*Shepherd of the Stone of Israel*'), the allusion being to 28, 18 f. 22. 35, 14, the phrase practically = the God of Bethel, 31, 13. Di. approves of this reading as רעה without the art. or ישראל following is awkward, and God is never elsewhere called אבן. Rosenmüller renders, '*From that time he (Joseph) was the shepherd and stone of Israel;*' cf. מִשָּׁם in Hos. 2, 17 (Heb.); R. V. renders, '*From thence is the Shepherd, the Stone*' etc., which may be explained as meaning, '*From thence,*' i.e. from God, Joseph became a guardian and defence of his people, viz. in Egypt. The Pesh. and Onq. (apparently) read מִשֵּׁם, instead of מִשָּׁם; cf. Ps. 20, 2, but this, though removing the awkward expression מִשָּׁם, does not stand very appropriately in parallelism with מידי. In all probability the text, as it stands at present, is corrupt.

25. מאל אביך. The מן continues the thought con-

tained in ver. 24, connecting ver. 25 with the preceding verse; but in this verse two blessings are inserted. 'The same God, who has hitherto helped him, will also give him the following blessings,' Di. מאל אביך, cf. 31, 5. 42. 48, 15. Ex. 15, 2. 18, 4.

וְיַעְזְרֶךָּ = וְיַעְזְרֶנְךָּ, the suffix being strengthened by the energetic nun; cf. note on 3, 9. Render, '*So may He help thee;*' cf. Ex. 12, 3. Num. 16, 5. Is. 43, 4. Ps. 69, 33. The weak waw with the imperf. (voluntative) takes the place of the perf. with waw conv., after words standing alone, in language of an excited and impassioned character; see Ewald, § 347 a; Driver, § 125; so ויברכך in the next clause.

ואת שדי. '*And with the Almighty,*' i.e. with the help of the Almighty. The Pesh., Sam. Ver., and Heb.-Sam., and a few MSS. read ואל, a reading which is perhaps supported by the LXX[1], Vulg., Saadiah. Bleek, Hitzig, Tuch, and Ewald adopt this reading, as being more suitable, the shorter title שדי being as a rule (it occurs however twice, Num. 24, 4 and 16) used without אל at a later period of the language (it is very common in the book of Job). If this reading be preferred, the force of מן in מאל אביך extends to אל שדי; so Judg. 5, 9. Is. 15, 8. Hab. 3, 15; see Ewald, § 351 a.

ברכת שמים וגו״. ברכת is the acc. after ויברכך = '*may he bless the blessings of,*' i.e. with the blessings of. Cf. on 33, 5.

מעל. Cf. 27, 39 ומטל השמים מעל. The ברכת שמים are the dew, rain, sunshine; cf. 27, 28. 39. The ברכת תהום are the springs, rivers, brooks, which are regarded as springing

[1] The LXX render ὁ Θεὸς ὁ ἐμός, which corresponds with their rendering of אל שדי in 17, 1 ὁ Θεός σου (see the note on that passage). 28, 3 (μου). 35, 11 (σου). 43, 14 (μου). 48, 3 (μου). Ex. 6, 3 (Θεὸς ὢν αὐτῶν).

from the subterranean תהום, and fertilizing the ground. The ברכת שׁדים ורחם are every kind of animal fruitfulness; contrast Hos. 9, 14. Compare Joseph's blessing in Deut. 33, 13 ff. with this verse, where the similarity in thought and language is most striking.

26. The translation given above follows the reading הוֹרֵי עַד, or perhaps better הַרְרֵי עַד, as הור only occurs as a proper name, and gives to תאוה its ordinary meaning '*desire.*' This rendering suits the parallelism (גבעת עולם), and is supported by Deut. 33, 15 (הַרְרֵי־קֶדֶם). Hab. 3, 6 (הַרְרֵי־עַד), and the rendering of the LXX, ὀρέων μονίμων, and is adopted by Ges., Ewald, Tuch, Kn., Wright, Di., C. P. Ges., *sub voce*, and R. V. (margin). The Massoretic text is supported by the Pesh., Onq., Vulg., Saadiah, the Jewish commentators, A.V., and R. V. (text). The rendering then must be, '*The blessings of thy father have prevailed over the blessings of my parents, up to the boundary of the eternal hills.*' הוֹרַי must be separated from עַד, following the accents, and taken in the sense '*parents,*' while תאוה must be translated '*boundary,*' from תָּאָה = '*to mark,*' '*limit;*' cf. Num. 34, 7 f.; also תָּוָה in 1 Sam. 21, 14. Ez. 9, 4; see Ewald, § 186 b. The word הוֹרַי, however, = '*my parents,*' seems very doubtful. Neither the plural הוֹרִים, nor dual הוֹרַיִם occurs with this meaning, and though the fem. הוֹרָה = '*mother*' is found in Song of Songs 3, 4. Hos. 2, 7, the original meaning of the root, i.e. '*to conceive,*' is still present in this word in both of the passages where it occurs. The reading of the Sam. Vers. is uncertain, but the Sam. Codex (Heb.-Sam.) has הָרֵי עַד. The later Samaritans, however, pronounced the words הָרִי עַד '*my mountain, up to*' etc., and understood it of Mount Gerizim, which was situated in the territory of the tribe of Joseph; see Tuch, p. 501. The LXX and Sam. Vers. read in the

first clause of the verse ברכת אביך ואמך, while the Jer. Targ. exhibits traces of both the renderings discussed above, viz. '*my parents*,' and '*everlasting mountains;*' see Geiger, *Urschrift*, p. 250.

לראשׁ יוסף ולקדקד נזיר אחיו. Cf. Deut. 33, 16, where these words recur. נזיר אחיו = '*the prince of his brethren*.' The Vulg. and Saadiah take נזיר in the sense '*Nazirite*,' a meaning which is unsuitable here. Onqelos takes נזיר '*the separated one*,' in the sense of '*prince*' or '*leader*.' His rendering is גַּבְרָא פְּרִישָׁא דַאֲחוֹהִי '*the man* (*who is*) *separated among his brethren;*' so Saadiah. This is the view adopted by most moderns, who, however, generally (following the Pesh.) connect נָזִיר with the noun נֵזֶר '*diadem*,' cf. Lam. 4, 7, and לראשׁ, though with no allusion to a kingdom in the tribe of Joseph. The meaning cannot, however, be regarded as certain.

Del. remarks that לראשׁ is chosen intentionally, as בראשׁ is the usual expression for a curse coming upon any one, while לראשׁ is used for a blessing; cf. Deut. 33, 16. Prov. 10, 6. 11, 26.

Joseph receives not only the blessings of the eternal hills, i.e. the rich and fruitful hill country of Ephraim and Manasseh (cf. Jer. 50, 19. Deut. 32, 14), but the blessings that surpass these, viz. the promises made by God to his forefathers.

27. '*Benjamin is a ravening wolf:*
In the morning he devoureth the prey,
And at even divideth the spoil.'

That Benjamin was a most warlike tribe is shewn by the share it took in the struggle for freedom under Deborah (Judg. 5, 14), and by the war it carried on with the other tribes (Judg. 19 ff.) after the outrage committed at Gibeah. Ehud, Saul, and Jonathan were also Benjamites.

זאב יטרף, lit. '*a wolf that ravens*,' the relative pronoun being omitted. Cf. Is. 51, 12 אנוש ימות = '*mortal man*;' Hos. 4, 14 עם לא יבין '*a people without understanding*;' and see Ges., §§ 107. 2 b. and 155. 2 b; M. R., § 159 a; Ewald, § 332 a; Driver, § 34; Dav., *S.*, §§ 44. R. 3. and 142.

יִטְרָף, pausal for יִטְרֹף; see on ver. 3, עָז. Kn. remarks on the comparison of Benjamin with a wolf, 'The figure of the wolf occurs elsewhere in the O. T., only in a bad sense (Zeph. 3, 3. Hab. 1, 8. Jer. 5, 6. Ez. 22, 27); hence in this passage it does not signify a full measure of praise, though it recognises Benjamin's warlike capabilities.' Di. supplements this remark by pointing out, 'that the lion has already been used in ver. 9, and that only a comparison with some small beast of prey would be fitting in the case of Benjamin, the smallest of the tribes. The wolf was used in comparisons by non-Semitic peoples of antiquity in a good sense.'

יאכל עד. Cf. Num. 23, 24 עד יאכל טרף.

28. איש אשר כברכתו ברך אתם. '*Each one with that which was according to his blessing he blessed them*,' בֵּרֵךְ being construed with a double acc., as in Deut. 12, 7. 15, 14; cf. ver. 25. The LXX, Pesh., and Sam. omit אשר. As the text is very awkward, Del. emends to איש איש כב״; cf. 2 Sam. 23, 21, where the Kri directs that איש is to be read instead of אשר, and Num. 21, 30, where the Kri marks the ר of אשר with a point, as suspicious. With this emendation, the verse may be compared with Ex. 36, 4 איש איש ממלאכתו; Lev. 15, 2 איש איש כי יהיה; Lev. 24, 15 איש איש כי יקלל, and often. Perhaps, however, it is better simply to omit אשר.

30. אשר קנה . . . את השדה. '*Which A. purchased . . . with the field*,' so 50, 13, Del.[5] Kautzsch (see Ges.,

§ 138. 1. note 1) and Di. prefer to connect אשר here and 50, 13, with the acc. את־השׂדה = '*which field;*' but with this construction, a suffix would be sufficient. The former way seems simpler. Abraham's object was not so much to buy the field, as to get possession of the grave which happened to be in the field.

32. מקנה וגו״. This verse does not seem to have any connection with the rest of the narrative. Tuch regards it as a parenthesis, referring to ver. 30; cf. Ps. 72, 14. Del.[5] and Di. consider it a gloss on 30b.

50.

2. לחנט את אביו. '*To embalm his father.*' Embalming the dead was an Egyptian custom, which was due to the popular belief in a permanent union of the body and the soul. The art was practised by a special class named ταριχευταί; see Herod. ii. 86 ff.; Diod. i. 91; Ebers in Riehm's *H.W.B.*, 352 f. The ταριχευταί are here called הרפאים. Joseph probably had his own special body of physicians.

3. החנטים. The plural is used according to Ges., § 124. 1 a; Ewald, § 179 a ('to embrace the scattered units into a higher idea, thus to form the meaning of an abstract').

שׁבעים יום. For a king the Egyptians used to mourn seventy-two days (Diod. i. 72). Jacob's death was mourned for by the Egyptians out of respect to Joseph. On the mourning customs of the Egyptians, see Herod. ii. 85; Diod. i. 91; Wilkinson, *Manners and Customs* (1878 ed., iii. c. 16).

4. בכיתו. Object. gen.; see on 9, 2. בכית is formed like שׁבית, חנית, by adding the ending ת to the third radical י; see Ewald, § 186 b; Stade, § 192 b.

5. כריתי לי. LXX ὤρυξα, so the Vulg. and most moderns; cf. 26, 25. 2 Chron. 16, 14, a rendering which suits בקברי better than that adopted by Onq. and Pesh., '*I bought*,' with which Deut. 2, 6 וגם מים תכרו מאתם may be compared.

10. עד גרן האטד. '*To the threshing-floor of thorns*;' probably not '*the threshing-floor of Atad*.' The locality is not further known.

בעבר הירדן, i.e. on the eastern side of Jordan, the narrator being in Palestine.

שבעת ימים. Cf. 1 Sam. 31, 13. Judith 16, 24. Ecclus. 22, 12.

11. אָבֵל מצרים. אָבֵל may be taken either as a verb, '*Egypt mourns*,' or as a noun, '*the meadow of Egypt*,' cf. the proper names, אבל מחולה, אבל השטים, אבל מים, אבל בית מעכה, אבל כרמים; but this rendering '*meadow of Egypt*' merely expresses the views of the punctuators. Tuch and Kn. explain the name as a meadow, as fertile as Egypt; cf. 13, 10. Di. thinks this unnecessary, pointing out that plenty of historical reasons can be conjectured for the origin of such a name, from the fact that the Egyptians for a long period were the rulers of Palestine before the time of Moses; as we now know from the Tel-el-Amarna Letters. The narrator evidently means that the words should be read אֵבֶל מצרים '*mourning of the Egyptians*,' so the LXX have here Πένθος Αἰγύπτου, and the Vulg. '*Planctus Egypti*.' The position of אבל מצרים is not known. It has been identified by some (Knobel, Ritter, etc.) with בית חגלה, on the southern boundary of Benjamin, the modern *'Ain Ḥajla*, a little north of the Dead Sea (cf. Rob., *Bibl. Researches*, i. p. 544; Bäd., *Pal.*, p. 170), following Hieron., who in the Onom. identifies *Area Atad* with בית חגלה. But this identification is precarious,

as Hieron.'s account is not trustworthy; and בית חגלה is also on the western, and not the eastern side of Jordan; see further, Di., p. 476; Del.[5], p. 535.

13. את השדה. '*With the field;*' cf. 49, 30.

15. לו ישטמנו יוסף. '*If Joseph were to hate us!*' cf. Ez. 14, 15. Ex. 4, 1 והן לא יאמינו לי '*and if they will not believe me!*' LXX here, μή ποτε μνησικακήσῃ ἡμῖν Ἰωσήφ. The imperf. in the protasis, where no apodosis follows, denoting either a *wish* or (as here) a *fear;* see Driver, § 142; Ewald, § 358 a, who compares a similar aposiopesis in Ps. 27, 13; see also M. R., § 165; Ges., § 159. 3. C. 2; Dav., *S.*, § 131. R. 1.

16. ויצוו. '*And they sent a message.*' LXX καὶ παραγενόντο, Pesh. ܘܩܪܒܘ, possibly a free translation, the translators not understanding ויצוו.

17. אָנָּא is only found once again in the Pent., viz. Ex. 32, 31 אָנָּא. Ewald, § 262 a,—cf. Stade, § 373,—remarks that the Massora regards אנא always as consisting of two words (אָהּ־נָא); hence the double accents here and in Ex. l.c. The tone is on the penult.

שׂא נא פשע . . . שׂא נא לפשע. נשׂא = '*to forgive*' (cf. 18, 24) is here construed, for the sake of variety, with the acc. and dat.; so with dat. of offence in Ex. 23, 21. Josh. 24, 19 (all E); see Ewald, § 282 d.

19. כי התחת אלהים אני. '*For am I in God's place?*' so in 30, 2; see the note there. Del. proposes a slightly different meaning here as an alternative, 'Am I authorised to interfere in what God does, am I not obliged to submit myself to Him?' Aq. ὅτι μὴ Θεὸς ἐγώ; Symm. μὴ γὰρ ἀντὶ Θεοῦ ἐγώ εἰμι; Onq. renders אֲרֵי דַחֲלָא דַיְיָ אֲנָא '*for a fearer of Y. am I,*' possibly reading חִתַּת אל״ (from חִתָּה), or more probably rendering freely; so Saadiah, أَخَافُ ٱللّٰهَ '*I fear God.*'

20. עשׂה. See on 48, 11.

21. וידבר על לבם. See on 34, 3.

23. וירא יוסף לאפרים. The ל as in 44, 20 ויותר הוא לבדו לאמו.

בני שלשים = '*sons of the third degree*,' i.e. not great-grandchildren, but great-great-grandchildren. שלשים—cf. Ex. 20, 5. 34, 7. Num. 14, 18. Deut. 5, 9—are the children of the third generation, cf. Ex. 34, 7; the first ancestor not being counted; בני שׁ״ = great-great-grandchildren. Elsewhere בני שלשים are called רִבֵּעִים; so Di. and Ewald (*Antiq.*[3], p. 225; Eng. trans., p. 169). LXX, Vulg., Pesh., Targg., Tuch, and Del. understand '*great-grandchildren;*' but then either בנים must be read (so Sam.), or the cstr. בני be taken according to Ewald, § 287 e (the cstr. state used where there is really only an appositional relation between the two words, and = '*consisting of*').

על-ברכי יוסף. Cf. 30, 3. Sam. Ver. reads בימי for על-ברכי, possibly the correct reading.

26. ויישׂם. See on 24, 33. Render, '*they put him*,' 3rd pers. sing. imperf.

בארון = here '*in the coffin;*' so in Phoenician ארון, pl. ארנת, = *sarcophagus;* cf. Bloch, *Phoen. Glossar*, p. 15. For the article in בארון cf. the note on 35, 17. 'The Egyptians used to place the embalmed body in a wooden coffin, and carefully preserve it in the vault (Her. ii. 86),' Kn. in Di., p. 479. With these verses, cf. Ex. 13, 19. Josh. 24, 32.

APPENDIX.

אֵל and אֱלֹהִים, יהוה.

The first two names of God, אֵל and אֱלֹהִים, as may be seen from the Concordance, are of frequent occurrence in the Old Testament. The plural of אֵל and the sing. of אֱלֹהִים, on the contrary, are rare; the plural forms of אֵל occurring about five times, and the sing. of אֱלֹהִים about 57 times. אֵל (sing.), on the other hand, occurs (including proper names of people and of places compounded with אֵל) over 300 times, and אֱלֹהִים over 2500 times[1]. It will be found, on a closer examination of the various passages, that אֵל, though of common occurrence, is essentially a poetical word, being very common in the poetical part of Job (about a quarter of the passages where אֵל is found are in Job). It is also found in the Psalms (but not so frequently as אֱלֹהִים) and in other poetical passages, and is used by the prophets from Hosea to Deutero-Isaiah and his contemporaries. אֵל is found in the Pentateuch in certain special phrases, such as אֵל־שַׁדַּי, אֵל־קַנָּא, but otherwise the less poetical parts of the Pentateuch and Prophets avoid it. אֵל apparently formed no part of the ordinary spoken language, as it is never used in Judges, Samuel, or Kings, and even in Chronicles only occurs in poetical passages. In proper names of persons and of places it is found from the earliest times. Thus from the O.T. it may be inferred that אֵל was a very old name of God, which, however, at a tolerably early date ceased to be used, and was only preserved in poetry, elevated prose, and in a few special phrases. אלהים was the common name of God, the word being used for the sing. and plural. The singular אֱלוֹהַּ is most common in the book of Job, and it is found elsewhere in only a few poetical passages. In pure prose it occurs only in two very late passages (2 Chron. 32, 15 and Dan. 11, 37–39); and even in the prose parts of Job is replaced by אֱלֹהִים. אֱלוֹהַּ may thus be

[1] Cf. Nestle, *Th. S. W.*, 1882, p. 243 f.

regarded as an artificial sing. of אֱלֹהִים[1]. So in the Hebrew the ordinary word for God was אֱלֹהִים, without a real singular, אֵל and אֱלוֹהַּ being nearly entirely confined to poetry.

In the other Semitic dialects אֵל is common, being found in Assyrian, Phoenician, and Himyaritic, but whether it is found in Northern Arabic and Aramaic is a disputed point[2]. אֱלוֹהַּ is found, on the contrary, only in Aramaic and Arabic, the word both in Aramaic and Arabic being probably indigenous and not borrowed from the Hebrew[3]. In Sabean אל and אלה occur, both words being used in much the same way as in Hebrew[4].

Various explanations of these names אֵל and אֱלֹהִים have been offered by different scholars, but no certain derivation for either appears yet to have been obtained.

Fleischer[5], whom Delitzsch and others[6] follow, takes אֱלֹהִים as the plural of אֱלוֹהַּ (a noun of the form קָטוֹל = قِتَال), deriving אֱלוֹהַּ from an unused root אָלַהּ = the Arabic أَلِهَ (وَلِهَ), which has the notion of '*wandering about*,' '*going hither and thither*' in perplexity or fear, and followed by إلى '*to betake oneself*' to a person, by reason of fright or fear, seeking protection[7]. אֱלוֹהַּ would thus, it is argued, = '*fear*,' and then '*the object of fear*' (cf. σέβασμα in Greek, and the Heb. מוֹרָא, פַּחַד, see Gen. 31, 42. 53), and so '*God*.' This derivation would appear, however, to be questionable. For in the verb the idea of 'fear' is altogether subordinate, and though in a particular case it may express the idea of seeking protection *with* a person, in fear (of course) of *other* things, it is difficult to understand how a substantive derived from it could be used to denote God as the *direct* object of fear. It might, conceivably, denote Him as a *refuge*, but hardly as *fear*, or the object of fear. אֵל is regarded by these scholars as belonging to a root אוּל, with the primary meaning '*strength*[8].'

---

[1] Nöldeke, *S. B. A. W.*, 1882, p. 1177; cf. Nestle, l. c., p. 249.

[2] Lagarde, *Orientalia*, ii. p. 3 f. (cf. Nestle, l. c., p. 251), denies the existence of אֵל as a real Aramaic and Arabic word: Nöldeke disputes this, and appears to have shewn that Lagarde is in error. See *M. B. A. W.*, 1880, p. 768 f., and *S. B. A. W.*, 1882, p. 1182.

[3] See Nöldeke, *S. B. A. W.*, 1882, p. 1189; but cf. Nestle, l. c., p. 252.

[4] See *Über* אל *und* אלה *im Sabäischen*, by Prof. D. H. Müller, Leyden, 1884.

[5] Del., *Comm.*[5], p. 47 f.

[6] Oehler, Schultz, Mühlau, Volck.

[7] See Lane, *Arabic Lex.*, p. 82.

[8] Cf. Ges., *Thes.*, pp. 42, 48.

Ewald[1] connects אֵל and אֱלֹהַּ, regarding אֵל as abbreviated from אֱלֹהַּ, and holding אלה '*to be strong*' to be the root of both.

Lagarde[2] has proposed an entirely different derivation for אֵל (the origin of אֱלֹהַּ he does not discuss). He regards אלי (אלה) as the root of אֵל, and compares the form אֵל with גֵּו (from גוה), Is. 50, 6, שְׂטִים=סֵטִים (from שׂטה), and כֵּלִים (but cstr. state כְּלֵי). אלי (אלה) he conjectures had the meaning '*to stretch out to*,' and God he considers called אֵל, as '*one whom men strive after*.' The vowel in אֵל Lagarde regards as originally short, evading the analogy of words like גֵּר, זֵד, מֵת, by the remark that such a word as אֵל, '*God*,' can hardly be, what its vowel ֵ would indicate that it is, a neuter passive participle (see more fully *Mitteilungen* (1884), p. 103 f.).

Nöldeke[3] holds that אֵל is a noun with a long vowel like כֵּן, פֵּךְ, שֵׁד, etc., almost all of which belong to verbs ע״ו and ע״ע, and refers it to a root אול = *to be in front*, so אֵל = *the leader, Lord*. He expresses no decided opinion as to the connection between אֵל and אֱלֹהִים, but thinks a connection may be possible[4].

Dillmann[5] regards אֵל and אֱלֹהִים as inseparable. אֱלֹהִים he considers to be a plural formed from אֵל after the analogy of אֲמָהוֹת from אמה, and ܥܡ̈ܡܗܬܐ from ܥܡ̈ܡ, ܐܒ̈ܗܬܐ from ܐܒܐ, and אֲבָהָת from אָב, in Aramaic, and شِفَاهٌ from شَفَةٌ in Arabic: אֵל (with an original short i), however, probably comes from אלה, and = '*might*.' From אלהים he derives the sing. אֱלֹהַּ. In the 6th edition he suggests that it may be due to the development of a √ל״ו or ל״י into a √ל״ה, comparing in Arabic سَنِيَة and سَنَةٌ, دَلِهَ and دَلِيَ, and دَجْهَ and دُجْيَةٌ.

Nestle[6], lastly, has proposed another explanation of the relationship between אֵל and אֱלֹהִים. He infers from the usage of language that אֱלֹהִים is the real plural of אֵל, and that אֱלֹהַּ is a secondary derivation from אֱלֹהִים. אֱלֹהִים he thinks has arisen out of אֵל, just as אֲמָהוֹת out of אָמָה.

The above is a brief account of the various views that are held as to the origin of אֵל and אֱלֹהִים, but none appears to be entirely free from objection.

---

1 *Jahrbuch*, x. 11, and *Lehrbuch*, § 178 b.

2 *Orientalia*, ii. p. 3 ff.

3 *M. B. A. W.*, 1880, pp. 760–776.

4 Nöldeke's view, as far as the derivation of אֵל from אול is concerned, is the same as Gesenius' referred to in note 8, p. 408, differing only as to the meaning borne by אול.

5 *Genesis*[6], p. 18.

6 In his article in the *Th. S. W.*, 1882, Heft iv.

That אֱלוֹהַּ comes from a root אָלַהּ, as Fleischer and Delitzsch maintain, is, as has been already shewn, doubtful. In favour of Ewald's view may be urged the fact that it connects both אֵל and אֱלֹהִים, by deriving them from a root אָלָה, and the existence of proper names compounded with אֵל exhibiting traces of י, e.g. אֱלִיהוּא, אֱלִימֶלֶךְ, and others[1], though it is only fair to admit that the evidence from proper names ought not to be pressed, as the י may be the suffix of the first person and not the third radical. But it does not account for the presence of the ה in אֱלֹהִים, and if אֵל is abridged from אֱלֹהִים, it is not clear why אֵל is found chiefly in poetical passages where we should naturally expect antique forms.

Lagarde, in so far as he derives אֵל from a root אלה, agrees with Ewald, though he assigns to this root a different meaning, viz. '*to stretch out to.*' Apart from the fact that the meaning thus assigned to אלה is conjectural, he can hardly be said to have proved against Nöldeke that the e of אֵל is short, and that it does not belong to a root ע״ו. The evidence Nöldeke adduces from the occurrence of Semitic proper names in Greek inscriptions, in favour of a long e in אֵל[2], does not seem to have been met by Lagarde, and in failing to observe the Aramaic use of אֵל[3], he has exposed himself to Nöldeke's objection, supported by the Syriac, that formations like כֵּן, פֵּה, etc., point to ע״ע or ע״ו stems[4]. Nöldeke's own view of אֵל (which is in the main the same as Gesenius held[5]) does not appear adequately to account for the shortening of the e in אֵל in the proper names אֱלְקָנָה, אֱלִיהוּא, etc.[6], nor for the י in the latter name, which would seem to imply a root ל״ה[7]. It also does not take into account the Assyrian *ilu*, which has always a short i, and which never appears as *êlu* or *îlu*[8].

Nestle's view has been examined by Nöldeke[9], who points out that the usage of language is against it, that the explanation of אֱלֹהִים as an extended form of אֵל is precarious, for only one clear case of this occurs in Hebrew (viz. אֲמָהוֹת from אָמָה; cf. Barth, *N.B.*, p. 8), and the cases that are found in the other Semitic dialects always have, in the expanded

---

[1] This also applies to Dillmann's view.

[2] See *M. B. A. W.*, 1880, p. 760 f.

[3] See *M. B. A. W.*, p. 772.

[4] See *M. B. A. W.*, p. 773.

[5] Cf. note 4 on p. 409.

[6] Nöldeke accounts for this on the ground that an unusual shortening of vowels is often found in proper names.

[7] Though, as has been just said, this might be the pronom. affix.

[8] Del., *Par.*, pp. 163–165. Brown in *The Presbyterian Review* (New York), 1882, p. 407.

[9] In the *S. B. A. W.*, 1882, pp. 1175–1192.

form, the plural feminine ending, whether the word itself be masc. or fem.[1] Nöldeke also remarks that long o for long a is difficult (the long a in אֲמָהוֹת goes back to short a[2]), and that if the e of אֵל is long, the ֱ in אֱלֹהִים is difficult to explain.

The following points seem to require a satisfactory explanation before the derivation of אֵל and אֱלֹהִים can be definitely fixed. (i) Are the two words really connected one with the other, and derived from the same root? (ii) Does אֵל really come from אול, or from a root אלה (i.e. אלי)? (iii) How is the ה of אֱלֹהִים to be accounted for? (iv) Can the evidence which Nöldeke brings forward to prove that the ֵ in אֵל is long be accepted as conclusive in the face of the fact that the vowel in the corresponding word in Assyrian (*ilu*) is short? (v) If the ֵ is really long, is Nöldeke's explanation of the shortening of ֱ in אֱלְקָנָה, אֱלִיהוּא, and other similar proper names adequate[3]?

The above is a brief sketch of the views held by scholars as to the derivation of אֵל and אֱלֹהִים. Both אֵל and אֱלֹהִים (אֱלֹהַּ) are old words in Semitic, and, *prima facie*, would appear to be distinct: their original derivation, however, is at present obscure[4].

יְהֹוָה

It is well known that the vowels with which the Tetragrammaton is punctuated in the ordinary editions of the Massoretic text do not really belong to it, but have been supplied from the word אֲדֹנָי, with the composite shewa changed into a simple shewa, unless this word precedes יהוה, when the points of אֱלֹהִים are used, e.g. Is. 28, 16. 30, 15. 49, 22. Ez. 2, 4. 7, 2. Amos 5, 3, etc. This is clear from the following considerations: (1) With the prefixes ב, ל, מ, ו we find בַּיהוָֹה (e.g. Ps. 11, 1. 32, 10. 11. 64, 11); לַיהוָֹה (e.g. Ps. 7, 1. 16, 2. 24, 1); מֵיְהוָֹה (e.g. Ps. 33, 8. 37, 39. Is. 40, 27); וַיהוָֹה (Gen. 13, 14. 1 Sam. 12, 12. Is. 53, 10), i.e. בַּאדֹנָי, לַאדֹנָי, מֵאֲדֹנָי, and וַאדֹנָי (cf. Ges., § 23. 2). (2) If the word that follows יהוה begins with one of the letters ב, ג, ד, כ, פ, ת, the dagesh lene is inserted, e.g. Gen. 13, 10. Ex. 15, 6. Num. 11, 25.

---

[1] Cf. *S. B. A. W.*, p. 1180 f. The masc. forms that occur in Syriac are, as Nöldeke points out, late. Nöldeke's remarks on this point also apply to Dillmann's explanation.

[2] Nöldeke, *S. B. A. W.*, p. 1181.

[3] See note 6, p. 410.

[4] It may be noted that אל as the name of a god occurs four times in the Sendschirli inscriptions always with two other gods רכבאל and הדד; see inscript. of Pannamu, line 22, and inscript. of Hadad, lines 2, 11, 18. Cf. *Die altsemit. Inschriften von Sendschirli*, D. H. Müller, Wien, 1893.

Judg. 21, 15. 1 Sam. 28, 19. 2 Sam. 23, 2. (3) Ewald in his *Lehrbuch*, § 228 b, draws attention to the fact that in Num. 10, 35, cf. ver. 36, קוּמָה is accented on the last syllable, though the ה is ה cohortative, because the next following word יהוה begins with a guttural, e. g. א, אֲדֹנָי = יְהֹוָה, cf. Ps. 3, 8 קוּמָה; 6, 5 שׁוּבָה; 7, 7. 10, 12, etc. (4) The abbreviations יָהוּ, יָהּ, יְהוֹ cannot come from יְהֹוָה. The objection to using the real punctuation of יהוה arises from an old misconception of the two passages, Ex. 20, 7 (לא תשא את שם יהוה אלהיך לשוא) and Lev. 24, 16 (ונקב שם יהוה מות יומת), which were interpreted as meaning that the divine name was to be treated as a *nomen ineffabile*. This interpretation of these two verses is mentioned by Philo, *De vita Mosis*, iii. pp. 519, 529; Josephus, *Archaeol.*, ii. 12, § 4; Talmud, *Sanhedrin*, chap. 2, fol. 90; Maimonides, *Yadh Chasaka*, chap. 14, § 10; Theodoret, *Quaest.* 13 in Exod.; Eusebius, *Praep. Evang.*, ii. p. 305; the passages (excepting that from Eusebius) being quoted by Gesenius, *Thes.*, p. 575 f. The LXX render the Tetragrammaton always by ὁ Κύριος (their ordinary translation of אדני), and the Samaritans used שׁימא (‘*name*’), and the Jews הַשֵּׁם for יהוה, when they had to pronounce the word. The pronunciation *Jehovah* seems to have been first introduced by Galatinus in 1520; but was objected to by Le Mercier, J. Drusius, and L. Capellus, as being against grammar and historical propriety. Cf. Bött., *Heb. Gram.*, § 88, and C. P. Ges., *sub voce*.

There is every reason to assume that the punctuation adopted by modern scholars for יהוה is correct, viz. יַהְוֶה, the form being an imperfect Qal (according to another view Hif'il) of הוה, which is an archaic and North Palestinian form of the verb היה (cf. the note on 27, 29); compare the other proper names formed after the analogy of the imperf. of the verb, e.g. יִצְחָק, יָאִיר, יַעֲקֹב, etc. That this assumption is correct is proved by the fact that the abbreviations יָהוּ (out of יַהְוְ), יְהוֹ and יוֹ (out of יַהְוְ = יְהַו) in compound proper names, and יָהּ (יַהְוֶה = יָהּ = יָהוּ) can easily be derived from יַהְוֶה, and by the statement of Theodoret that the pronunciation of the Samaritans was IABE, while Epiphanius, *Adv. Haer.* 20 (40), cites IABE as one of the names of God, explaining it (from Ex. 3, 14) as *ὃς ἦν καὶ ἔστι καὶ ἀεὶ ὤν*, see Ges., l. c. If this punctuation be conceded it will next be necessary to explain the meaning of the name. The class of words to which יהוה belongs is not very wide in Heb., and is practically limited to a few proper names (see Stade, *Lehrbuch*, § 259). The form יַהְוֶה, as far as the punctuation is concerned, may be the imperf. Qal or Hif'il of הוה; and the meaning we must assign to the word will obviously depend on which of these two conjugations we consider the form to come from. If it be imperf. Qal, it may mean, '*he that is;*' if it be imperf. Hif'il, '*he that causes to be.*' If the former view be adopted, the word being taken as imperf. Qal, we must, in interpreting the meaning of the name, be guided by the passage in Exodus, viz. 3, 14; for though the name יהוה may have been known to the Hebrews prior to the time of Moses—cf. the name of Moses' mother, Ex. 6, 20 יוֹכֶבֶד, and the formula '*God of thy father,*' Ex. 3, 6[1]—it was through him that it received its first explanation. The name has been considered by various modern scholars[2], reviving the view held by Le Clerc, and thrown out as a suggestion by Gesenius, as a Hif'il derivative, although the interpretations differ; e.g. Kuenen interprets the name as '*the giver of existence,*' '*creator;*' Schrader and Schultz, as '*the giver of life and deliverance*' (cf. הַוָּה Gen. 3, 20); Lagarde and Nestle, who follow Le Clerc, as '*he who brings to pass,*' i.e. '*the performer of his promises;*' Land, as '*life giver,*' '*creator,*' so Ges. in *Thes.* The objection to the derivation of the word from the Hif'il stem is that though היה is used of the fulfilment of a promise or prediction (e.g. in 1 Kings 13, 32), it requires the object of the promise to be at least indicated in the context, and further, that scarcely any Semitic language uses the causative form of היה[3]. The latter part of the objection applies also to Robertson Smith's view[4], that the name originally was intended to have some other causative force, such as, '*he who causes to fall*' (rain or lightning). This apparently seems to have been the primitive meaning of the root (cf. the Arabic) before it was spiritualized as in Exodus, and it occurs once in this sense in Job 37, 6 כי לשלג יאמר הוא ארץ. But whether the causal form, used absolutely, without any definite object being expressed, would convey this special sense, is very questionable, cf. Well., *Skizzen*, iii. 175. If this derivation be regarded as too uncertain, the alternative one, in which the word יהוה is treated as a neuter (Qal), must be adopted.

In the passage in Exodus (3, 14) God, in His answer to Moses, says אֶהְיֶה אֲשֶׁר אֶהְיֶה, then calls Himself אֶהְיֶה, and finally יהוה. It is clear from this that הָוָה (see above) is presupposed to be equivalent to היה, and that אֶהְיֶה, the shorter expression, must be explained by אֶהְיֶה אֲשֶׁר אֶהְיֶה. Then אהיה אשר אהיה must not be taken as a refusal to answer Moses' question '*I am* just *who I am,*' i.e. it is a matter of indifference to you who I am, and you should not seek to know, Le Clerc, Lagarde (*Psalt. Hieron.*, p. 156); as the following אהיה cannot bear this sense, and

[1] See Nestle, *Eigennamen*, p. 80 ff.

[2] Comp. Driver, in *Studia Biblica*, i. Oxford, 1885.

[3] Comp. Driver, l. c., p. 14, foot-note.

[4] *Old Test. in the Jewish Church*, p. 423; cf. Driver, l. c., p. 14.

אהיה אשר אהיה more naturally gives an explanation of the name. An explanation of the name is certainly found in the rendering adopted by Wellhausen (*Comp.*, p. 72), following Ibn Ezra, '*I am, since I am*,' אהיה being regarded as the name, and אשר אהיה as its explanation; but אֲשֶׁר for כִּי in this context is hardly probable, and Moses did not ask '*What is thy name?*' but '*What shall I tell them?*' Therefore א״אהיה אשר must be taken as a simple sentence, which has been variously rendered. The LXX and Knobel translate, '*I am he who exists*,' i.e. '*he who is*;' but it is doubtful whether אשר אהיה can = ὁ ὤν. Rashi renders אהיה as future, '*I will be with them in this affliction, what I will be with them in the subjection of their future captivities.*' Ewald[1] explains similarly, '*I will be it*,' namely the performer of his promises; cf. ver. 12 אהיה עמך with ver. 14 אהיה אשר אהיה '*I will be it, I who will be it*,' i.e. what I have promised to be. Robertson Smith[2] renders, '*I will be what I will be*,' i.e. your God and Helper. Di., Ex., p. 35, takes it as = '*the existing*,' '*ever-living*,' '*self-consistent*,' and '*unchangeable*.' The objection to this view is that what Jehovah will prove Himself to be is not expressed, but must be understood (see Di. on Ex. 3, 14). But it may be (as Del.[3] and Oehler[4] suggest) that היה is to be understood in a pregnant sense, '*give evidence of being*.' The most probable view is that the passage means, '*I am that I am*,' not that which fate or caprice may determine, but what my own character determines. היה has the idea not of fixity, but of change; not a capricious change, but a conscious one. The verb means properly not '*to be*,' but '*to come into being*' (cf. Del., *Comm.*[4], pp. 26, 60); so יהוה is a living active God, not a God of the past only, but also of the future, who cannot be named or defined, but whose divine nature is ever expressing itself, and manifesting itself under fresh aspects; a God who enters into personal relations with His worshippers, who is consistent with Himself, true to His promises, and unchangeable in His purposes (comp. Del., l. c.; Oehler, l. c.; Driver, l. c., p. 17; Di. on Ex. 3, 14)[5].

---

[1] *Die Lehre der Bibel von Gott* (1873), ii. p. 337 f.

[2] *British and Foreign Evangelical Review*, 1876; *Proph.*, p. 385.

[3] *Comm.*[4], pp. 26, 60.

[4] *Theology of the Old Testament*, § 39.

[5] On the various views held by scholars concerning the origin of the Tetragrammaton, the reader may be referred for further particulars to the paper by Driver, and to König's *Hauptprobleme der altisrael. Religionsgeschichte*, 1884, pp. 29–33 (translated in *Hebraica*, April, 1885, pp. 255–257).

ADDENDA ET CORRIGENDA.

ADDENDA.

Page 29, last line, add, See also Bloch, *Phoen. Glossar*, p. 27.

,, 45, line 4 from bottom, add after (Di.). This explanation is preferable to that given by Wellhausen, *Proleg.*, 1886, p. 322; *Skizzen*, iii. p. 217, after Nöldeke, who suggests *serpent* as possible meaning, cf. Arab. حَيَّةٌ. Robertson Smith, *Kinship and Marriage*, pp. 36–40, renders '*mother of every ḥayy*;' חי = *kinsfolk*, Arab. حَيٌّ, a group of families united by vital ties; cf. Driver, *Sam.*, p. 119.

,, 122, line 9 from top, add after חֲצַרְמוֹת (cf. Osiander, *Z.D.M.G.*, 1865, p. 239 ff. 1; D. H. Müller, *Z.D.M.G.*, 1883, pp. 18 and 412).

,, 138, הָעַי, add following: העי Gen. 12, 8 etc. probably the same place as עיא Neh. 11, 31, עיה 1 Chron. 7, 28; cf. עית Is. 10, 28, and Josh. 18, 23. The position of העי was probably to the E. of Bethel (Gen. 12, 8), N. of Michmash, by the side of a deep valley. The name has not survived, but it ought perhaps to be located in the neighbourhood of the present Dêr-Diwân, forty-five minutes S.E. of Bêtîn (Bethel) in Tell-el-Ḥajar (cf. תל Josh. 8, 28), on the S. side of the deep Wâdy Matyâ, through which at the present day the road from Jericho to the hill country passes, cf. Bäd., *Pal.*, p. 119.

,, 149, add after *Astarte*, line 9, Bloch, *Phoen. Glossar*, p. 51.

,, 196, On '*daughter of my father*,' cf. Robertson Smith, *Kinship and Marriage*, etc., ch. vi.

,, 208, add after (cf. מַעֲשֵׂיָה). The word may be equivalent to מְרָאִי יָהּ '*chosen of God*,' or better מַרְאֵה = מְרְאֵי יָהּ = *appearance of Yahweh*, cf. Böttcher, *Gram.*, § 45.

,, 240, ver. 21, שִׁטְנָה identified by Palmer with Wâdy Šuṭnet er-Ruḥeibe, which is probably the same as Wâdy Šuṭein in Rob., *Pal.*, i. p. 332.

CORRIGENDA.

Page ix, line 10 from bottom, *for* 10, *read* 10.
,, xxxi, ,, 16 ,, ,, ,, אֵדַר ,, אֵחַר
,, xxxii, ,, 1 from top, ,, Hithpael ,, Hithpa'el
,, 70, ,, 7 from bottom, *read* יָרוֹן
,, 97, ,, 3 ,, ,, *for* Tablet *read* Tablets
,, 114, ,, 7 from top, ,, 170 † ,, 170 f.
,, 123, ,, 5 ,, ,, ,, *Melanges* ,, *Mélanges*
,, 128, ,, 8 from bottom, ,, § 82 † ,, § 82 f.
,, 151, ,, 2 ,, ,, ,, *consist* ,, *consists*
,, 152, ,, 5 from top, *read* חמר
,, 152, ,, 8 from bottom, ,, רכשׁ
,, 154, ,, 6 from top, ,, בַּעֲלֵי
,, 168, ,, 12 from bottom, ,, אֱלָהָא
,, 204, ,, 1 from top, *for* Pilel *read* Pil'el
,, 220, ,, 1 ,, ,, ,, affix ,, suffix
,, 227, ,, 6 from top, *read* לשׂוּח
,, 234, ,, 2 from bottom, *for* Glases *read* Glaser
,, 236, ,, 2 from top, ,, יתגדרי ,, יתגדרו
,, 255, ,, 6 ,, ,, ,, ישקוּ ,, ישקו
,, 267, last line on page, *omit* 'here.'
,, 279, line 12 from top, *for* Welh. *read* Well.
,, 280, ,, 1 ,, ,, ,, Mahanaim ,, Maḥanaim
,, 297, ,, 2 from bottom, ,, יִלְדוּ ,, יְלָדוּ
,, 350, ,, 13 from top, ,, Tel-el-Kebir ,, Tell-el-Kebir
,, 399, ,, 10 ,, ,, *read* קֶדֶם

www.ingramcontent.com/pod-product-compliance
Lightning Source LLC
LaVergne TN
LVHW010223110826
845148LV00022B/1261

9781597522977